CHRIST DYING,

AND

DRAWING SINNERS TO HIMSELF;

OR,

A SURVEY OF OUR SAVIOUR IN HIS SOUL-SUFFERING, HIS LOVELINESS IN HIS DEATH AND THE EFFICACY THEREOF.

IN WHICH

SOME CASES OF SOUL-TROUBLE IN WEAK BELIEVERS, GROUNDS OF SUBMISSION UNDER THE ABSENCE OF CHRIST, WITH THE FLOWINGS AND HEIGHTENINGS OF FREE GRACE, ARE OPENED.

DELIVERED IN SERMONS ON THE GOSPEL ACCORDING TO JOHN,

CHAP. xii. ver. 27, 28, 29, 30, 31, 32, 33.

Where are also interjected some necessary digressions, for the times, touching divers errors of Antinomians; and a short vindication of the doctrine of Protestants, from the Arminian pretended Universality of Christ's Dying for all and every one of mankind; the moral and feigned way of irresistible conversion of sinners; and what faith is required of all within the visible church, for the want whereof many are condemned.

By the late Reverend, Pious and Learned,
Mr. SAMUEL RUTHERFORD,

MINISTER OF THE GOSPEL, AND PROFESSOR OF DIVINITY
In the University of St. Andrew's.

PROV. XXX. 4. *What is his name, and what is his Son's name, if thou canst tell?*
Isa. liii. 8. *He was taken from prison and from judgment; and who shall declare his generation?*

◈ℛℭ℘ ◈

Copyright 2009
Reformed Church Publications
P.O Box 171
Zeeland, MI 49464
www.reformedchurchpublications.org
Email:support@reformedchurchpublications.org

CHRIST DYING,

AND

DRAWING SINNERS TO HIMSELF.

JOHN xii. 27. *Now is my soul troubled; and what shall I say? Father, save me from this hour: but for this cause came I unto this hour.*
28. *Father, glorify thy name.*

It is a question, whether these words of our Saviour's soul-trouble be nothing but the same words and prayer, which Matthew, chap. xxvi. and Luke xxii. relate, to wit, *O my Father, if it be possible, let this cup pass from me,* when his soul was troubled in the garden, in his agony: some think them the same, others not. It is like they are words of the same matter: for, *First,* When Christ uttered these words, he was near his sufferings, and on the brink of that hideous and dark sea of his most extreme pain, and drew up against hell, and the armies of darkness; as the story sheweth. But that the Lord uttered these same words in the garden, and not before, is not apparent;

because

because upon this prayer it is said, *Then came there a voice from heaven, etc.* A voice speaketh to him from heaven: now, Mat. xxvi. Luke xxii. no voice is like to have come from heaven; for when he prayed in his agony, there were no people with him, as here; because of the voice, the people being present, *Some said, it thundered: others said, an angel spake from heaven:* there being now with Christ in the garden, when he prayed, *O my Father,* etc. none save Peter, James, and John, the three famous witnesses of his extreme suffering, and of his young heaven, of his transfiguration on the mount, when he acted the *Preludium* and the image and representation of heaven before them; as is clear, Mat. xxvi. ver. 37. *And he was removed from them also*, Mat. xxvi. 39. Luke xxii. 41. and they were sleeping, in his agony, Mat. xxvi. 40, 43, 45. But now there is a waking people with Christ, who heard this voice. But I deny not but it is the same prayer in sense: even as suppose it were revealed to a godly man, that he were to suffer an extreme, violent, and painful death; and withal, some fearful soul-desertion, as an image of the second death; it should much affright him to remember this, and he might pray that the Lord would either save him from that sad hour, or then give him grace with faith and courage, in the Lord, to endure it: so here; Christ, God and man, knowing that he was to bear the terrors of the first and second death, doth act over afore-hand (the time being near) the sorrow and anguish of heart that he was to suffer in his extreme sufferings: as it were good, ere the cross come, to act it in our mind, and take an essay and a lift of Christ's cross, ere we bear it, to try how handsomely we would set back and shoulders under the Lord's cross. I do not intend that we are to imitate the martyr, who put his hand in the fire, the night before he suffered, to try how he could endure burning-quick; but that we are to lay the supposition, What if it so fall out? (as Christ, being persuaded his suffering was to come, acted sorrow, trouble of soul and prayer be-

fore-

forehand) and to resolve the saddest, and *antedate the cross*, and say with our own hearts, Let the worst come; or to suffer our fear to prophesy, as Job did, chap. iii. ver. 25. Yet, suppose the hardest befal me, I know what to do; as the *unjust steward* resolveth on a way, beforehand, how to swim through his necessities, Luke xvi. 4. The Lord acteth judgment, and what they shall pray in the time of their extremity, who now spit at all praying and religion; they shall be religious in their kind, when they shall cry, Rev. vi. 16. *Mountains and rocks, fall on us, and hide us from the face of him that sitteth on the throne, and from the wrath of the Lamb.* You cannot believe that a Lamb shall chase the kings of the earth, and *the great men, and the rich men, and every bond-man, and every free-man, into the dens and the rocks of the mountains, to hide themselves.* But the Lord acteth wrath and judgment before your eyes. Men will not suppose the real story of hell. Say but with thyself, *Oh! shall I weep and gnaw my tongue for pain, in a sea of fire and brimstone?* Do but fore-fancy, I pray you, how you shall look on it, what thoughts you will have, what you shall do, when you shall, 2 Thess. i. 9. *be punished with everlasting destruction, from the presence of the Lord, and from the glory of his power.* 1. Foreseen sorrows have not so sad an impression on the spirit. 2. Grace is a well-advised and resolute thing, and has the eyes of providence to say, in possible events, What if my scarlet embrace the dunghill, and providence turn the tables? 3. It is like wisdom (grace is wise to see afar off) to fore-act faith, and resolve to lie under God's feet, and intend humble yielding to God; as 2 Sam. xv. 25, 26.

In the complaint we have, 1. The subject matter of it, The Lord's troubled soul. 2. The time; *Now, is my soul troubled.* 3. Christ's anxiety, wrought on him by this trouble; *What shall I say?* or, which is the sense, *What shall I do?* 4. And a shore is seen at hand in the storm, a present rock in the raging sea: what shalt thou say? Lord Jesus, what shalt thou do? Pray: And he prayeth, *Father, save me from this hour:*

5. There

5. There is a sort of correction, or rather a limitation; *But for this cause came I to this hour.* The Lord, forgetting his pain, embraceth this evil hour. 6. Going on in his resolution to embrace this sad hour, he prayeth, ver. 28. *Father, glorify thy name.*

Touching the first, the soul-trouble of Christ, we are to consider, 1. How it can consist with peace. 2. How with the personal union. 3. What cause there was. 4. What love and mercy in Jesus, to be troubled for us. 5. What use we must make of this.

1. *Pos.* This holy soul, thus troubled, was like the earth before the fall, out of which grew roses, without thorns or thistles, before it was cursed. Christ's anger, his sorrow, were flowers that smelled of heaven, and not of sin: all his affections of fear, sorrow, sadness, hope, joy, love, desire, were like a fountain of liquid and melted silver; of which the banks, the head-spring, are all as clear from dross, as pure crystal: such a fountain can cast out no clay, no mud, no dirt. When his affections did rise and swell in their acts, every drop of the fountain was sinless, perfumed and adorned with grace; so as the more you stir or trouble a well of rose-water, or some precious liquor, the more sweet a smell it casts out: or, as when a summer soft wind bloweth on a field of sweet roses, it diffuseth precious and delicious smells through the air. There is such mud and dregs in the bottom and banks of our affections, that when our anger, sorrow, sadness, fear, do arise in their acts, our fountain casteth out sin. We cannot love, but we lust; nor fear, but we despair; nor rejoice, but we are wanton, and vain and gaudy; nor believe, but we presume: we rest up, we breathe out sin, we cast out a smell of hell, when the wind bloweth on our field of weeds and thistles; our soul is all but a plat of wild corn, the *imaginations of our heart being only evil from our youth.* O that Christ would plant some of his flowers in our soul, and bless the soil, that they might grow kindly there, being warmed and nourished with his grace! If grace be within, in sad pressures it comes out. A saint is a saint

in

in affliction; as an hypocrite is an hypocrite, and every man is himself, and casts a smell like himself, when he is in the furnace. Troubled Christ prays. Tempted Job believes, Job xix. 25. The scourged Apostles rejoice, Acts v. 41. Drowned Jonah looks to the holy temple, Jonah ii. 4.

2. Christ's affections were rational; reason starts up before fear: reason and affection did not outrun one another. John xi. 33. when Christ sees his friends weep, he weeps with them; and that which is expressed in our text by the passive verb . *My soul is troubled*, is there expressed by an active verb, He groaned in the spirit, , and *he troubled himself:* he called upon his affections, and grace and light was lord and master of his affections. There were in Christ three things, which are not in us; *First,* The Godhead personally united with a man, and a man's soul had an immediate influence on his affections. This was Christ's personal privilege; and to want this, is not our sin; to have it, was Christ's glory: but the nearer any is to God, the more heavenly are the affections. *Secondly,* When God frameth the human nature and human soul of Christ, he created a more noble and curious piece than was the first Adam: it is true, *He was like us in all things, except sin*, and essentially a man; but in his generation there was a cut of the art of heaven in Christ more than in the forming of Adam, or than in the generation of men, suppose man had never sinned; as Luke i. 35. *The power of the Most High shall overshadow thee:* never man was thus to be born. Whence give me leave to think, that there was more of God in the human nature of Christ, as nature is a vessel coming out of the potter's house, than ever was in Adam, or living man; though man had never sinned: and so, that he had a human soul of a more noble structure and fabric, in which the Holy Ghost, in the act of sanctification, had a higher hand, than when Adam was created, according to the image of God; tho' *he was a man like us in all things, sin excepted.*

3. Pos.

3. *Pos.* Undeniably, grace did so accompany nature, that he could not fear more than the object required. Had all the strength of men and angels been massed and contemperated in one, they should have been in a higher measure troubled, than Christ was: so how much trouble was in Christ's affections, as much there was of reason, perfumed and lustred with grace. He was not as man in his intellectuals, wise, or desirous to be wise, (as Adam and Eve, and men now are taken with the disease of curiosity) above what was fit: so neither were his affections above banks: he saw the blackest and darkest hour that ever any saw; suppose all the sufferings of the damned, for eternity, were before them in one sight, or came on them at once, it should annihilate all that are now, or shall be in hell. Christ now saw, or foresaw as great sufferings; and yet, 1. Believed, 2. Prayed, 3. Hoped, 4. Was encouraged under it, 5. Suffered them to the bottom with all patience, 6. *Rejoiced in hope*, Psal. xvi. 9. Now our affections rise and swell before reason: (1.) They are often imaginary, and are on horseback and in arms as the stirring of a straw. (2.) They want that clearness and serenity of grace that Christ had, through habitual grace following nature from the womb. (3.) We can raise our affections, but cannot allay them: as some magicians can raise the devil, but cannot conjure, or command him; or, some can make war, and cannot create peace. It is a calumny of Papists, that say, that Calvin did teach there was despair, or any distemper of reason in Christ; when as Calvin saith, *He still believed with full assurance*. And this extremity of soul-trouble was most rational, coming from the infallible apprehension of the most pressing cause of soul-trouble, that ever living man was under.

4. *Pos.* Christ had now and always moral peace, or the grace of peace, as peace is opposed to culpable raging of conscience. *First,* He never could want faith, which is a serenity, quietness, and silence of the soul, and assurance of the love of God. *Secondly,* He could have no doubting, or sinful disturbance of mind; be-

cause

cause he could have no conscience of guilt, which could overcloud the love and tenderest favour of his Father to him. But as peace is opposed to pain, and sense of wrath and punishment, for the guilt of our sins; so he wanted physical peace, and was now under penal disturbance and disquietness of soul. So we see some have peace, but not pardon; as the secure sinners, 1 Thess. v. 3. *2dly*, Some have pardon, but not peace; as David, Psal. xxxviii. 3. who had broken bones; and complaineth, ver. 8. *I am feeble and sore broken, I have roared by reason of the disquietness of my heart.* And the troubled church, Psal. lxxvii. 1, 2, 3, 4. Some have both peace and pardon; as some, like Stephen, that are so near to the crown, as they are above any challenges of conscience: it is like, Satan giveth over, and despaireth of these, whom he cannot overtake, being so near the end of the race. When the sun riseth first, the beams over-gild the tops of green mountains that look toward the east, and the world cannot hinder the sun to rise: some are so near heaven, that the everlasting Sun hath begun to make an everlasting day of glory on them; the rays that come from his face that sits on the throne, so over-goldeth the soul, that there is no possibility of clouding peace, or of hindering daylight in the souls of such. Some have neither peace nor pardon; as those in whose soul hell hath taken fire. Christ never needed pardon, he was able to pay all he was owing: he needed never the grace of forgiveness, nor grace to be spared; *God spared him not.* God could exact no less blood of him than he shed; but he received an acquittance of justification, never a pardon of grace, 1 Tim. iii. 16. *Justified in the Spirit.*

The second point is, *How a troubled soul can stand with a personal union.* Can God, can the soul of God be troubled? I shall shew, 1. How this must be. 2. How this can be. It must be, *First*, Because the loss of heaven is the greatest loss. To ransom a king requireth more millions, than pence to ransom slaves. When we were cast and forfeited, more than an hundred and forty four thousand kings (in the Lord's decree

they

they were kings) were cast out of heaven: where was there gold on earth to buy heaven, and so many kings? And yet justice must have payment: a God-troubled Saviour, and a soul-troubled God was little enough. Oh, saith love to infinite justice, What will you give for me? Will you buy me, my dear children, the heirs of eternal grace? A price below the worth of so many kings, justice cannot hear of; equal it must be, or more.

Secondly, Law cannot sleep satisfied with a man's soul-trouble: for as sin troubles an infinite God's soul, so far as our darts can fly up against the sun; so must the soul-trouble of him who is God, expiate sin.

Thirdly, Heaven is not only a transcendent jewel, dear in itself; but our Father would propine rebels with a sonship and a kingdom, which is dear in our legal esteem. *What standeth my crown to God?* Why, it could not possibly be dearer? The soul of God was weighed for it: that not only freedom, but the dearest of prices, might commend and cry up, above all heavens, Christ's love.

Fourthly, If my soul, or your souls, O redeemed of the Lord, could be valued every one of them worth ten thousand millions of souls, and as many heavens, they could not overweigh the soul of God, the soul that lodges in a glorious union with God: and the loss of heaven to the troubled soul of this noble, and high and lofty One, tho' but for a time, was more, and infinitely greater than my loss of heaven, and the loss of all the elect for eternity.

Fifthly, I love not to dispute here, but God, if we speak of his absolute power, without respect to his free decree, could have pardoned sin without a ransom, and gifted all mankind and fallen angels with heaven, without any satisfaction of either the sinner, or his surety; for he neither punisheth sin, nor tenders heaven to men or angels by necessity of nature, as the fire casteth out heat, and the sun light; but freely: only, supposing that frame of providence, and decrees of punishing, and redeeming sinners, that now is, the Lord could not but be steady in his decrees; yet this is but

necessity

necessity conditional, and at the second hand. But here was the business, God, in the depth of his eternal wisdom, did so frame and draw the design and plot of saving lost man, as salvation was to run in no other channel, but such an one, the bank whereof was the freest grace and tenderest love that can enter into the heart of men or angels; for he drew the lines of our heaven through grace, all the way.

Secondly, Grace hardly can work but by choice and voluntary arbitration: choice and election is suitable to grace. Hence grace casts lots on man, not fallen angels; and the eternal lot of transcendent mercy must fall on the bosom of Jacob and some others, not on Esau and others. And our Lord contrived this brave way, to out his grace on us.

Thirdly, And he would not have love to lodge for eternity within his own bowels, but must find out a way how to put boundless mercy to the exchange or bank, that he might traffic with love and mercy, for no gain to himself; and therefore freely our Lord came under bail, and lovely necessity, to strain himself to issue out love, in giving his one Son (he had not another) to die for man: he framed a supernatural providence of richest grace and love, to buy the refuse of creature, foul sinners, with an unparallel'd sampler of tender love, to give the blood-royal of heaven, the eternal Branch of the princely and kingly Godhead, a ransom to justice. *You sin* (saith the love of loves) *and I suffer; You did the wrong, I make the mends; You sin and sing in your carnal joys, I sigh, I weep for your joy.* The fairest face that ever was, was foul with weeping for your sinful rejoicing. It was fitting that free love, in the bowels of Christ, should contrive the way to heaven through *free love*: we should never in *heaven, cast down our crowns at the feet of him that sits on the throne*, with such sense and admiration, if we had come to the crown by law-doing, and not by gospel-confiding on a rich ransom-player. O that eternal banquet of the honey-comb of the love-debt of the Lamb, that redeemed us for nothing! All the shoulders

in

in heaven are for eternity on an act of lifting up, and heightening Christ's free love, who has redeemed them with so free a redemption; but they are not all able, tho' angels help them, to lift it up high enough: it is so weighty a crown that is upon the head of the Prince-Redeemer, that in a manner it wearies them, and they cannot over-extol it.

Now, this must be a mystery: for tho' the essence of God, and more of God than can be in a creature, were in Christ, and in the most noble manner of union, which is personal; yet, as our soul united to a vegetive body, which doth grow, sleep, eat, drink, doth not grow, sleep, or eat; and as fire is mix'd or united with an hot iron, in which is density and weight, and yet there's neither density nor weight in the fire; so here, tho' the Godhead, in its fulness, was united, in a most strict union, with a troubled and perplexed soul, and the suffering nature of man, yet is the Godhead still free of suffering, or any penal infirmities of the soul: the vigour and colour of a fair role may suffer by the extreme heat of the sun, when yet the sweet smell doth not suffer, but is rather enlarged by exhalation. Yet is there great halting in these comparisons; because, tho' the soul cannot be sick when the body is distempered, for there is nothing of the elementary nature, nor any contemperation of physical humours in it, because of a more sublime and pure constitution; yet there is such alliance and entire society between the soul and the body, that the soul, through concomitancy and sympathy, does suffer; as the indweller is put to the worse, if the house be rainy and dropping: the soul findeth smoke and leakings of pain, in that 'tis pinned in a lodging of sick clay, and so put to wish an hole in the wall, or to escape out at door or window; as often our spirits are overswayed so with distaste of life, because of the sour accidents that do convey it, that they think the gain of life not so sweet, as it can quit the cost. But the blessed Godhead, united to the manhood, cannot so much as for company's cause be sick, pained, or suffer; nor can the Godhead be

weary

weary of an union with a troubled soul: we conceive in the grave and death, that glorious fellowship was never dissolved.

Secondly, Many things may suffer by invasion of contraries; as, shoot an arrow against a wall of brass, some impression may remain in the wall, to witness the violence that has been there; and we know that, *They shall fight against thee, but they shall not prevail*: but the blessed Godhead in Christ is uncapable of an arrow, or of repercussion; there is no action against God; he is here not so much as a coast, a bank, or bulwark, capable of receiving one spitting or drop of a sea-wave: only the man Christ, the rose of heaven, had in his bosom, at his root, a fountain; O how deep and refreshing, that kept the flower green, under death and the grave! When it was plucked up, it was fair, vigorous, green before the sun; and thus plucked up, and above earth, blossomed fair!

Thirdly, Not only the influence and effects of the glorious Godhead did water the flower, and keep strength in Christ, (so, I think, God can keep a damned man in the doubled torments of everlasting wrath, with strength of grace, courage, faith, the love of Christ for ever, as he could not be overcome by hell and devils) but there was the fulness personal of the Godhead, that immediately sustained the man Christ: it was not a delegated comfort, nor sent help, nor a message of created love, nor a borrowed flowing of a sea of sweetness of consolation; but God in proper person, infinite subsistence, the personality of the Son of God bottomed all his sufferings: the manhood was imped and stocked in the subsistence of the tree of life. 'Tis true, God is a present help to his saints in trouble; but his helping is in his operation and working; but he is not personally united to the soul. 'Tis abominable that some Familists teach, that *as Christ was once made flesh, so he is now first made flesh in us, ere we be carried to perfection*: because, not any saint on earth can be so united to God, as the *Son of Man;* for he being *made of a woman, of the seed of David*, the

Son

Son of Man, and not any but he, is the eternal *Son of God, God blessed for ever*. The *Child born to us*, is *the mighty God, the Father of Age, the Prince of Peace*, Isa. ix. 6. Rom. ix. 5. Gal. iv. 4. There is a wide difference between him the second Adam, and all men, even the first Adam in his perfection, 1 Cor. xv. 47. If Christ suffered without dissolving of the union, God keeping the tent of clay, and taking it to heaven with him, in a personal union, then God can in the lowest desertion dwell in his saints. We complain, in our soul-trouble of Christ's departure from us; but he is not gone: our sense is not our bible, nor a good rule; there is an error in this compass.

The third was the particular cause. What cause was there? Papists say, There was no reason of Christ's soul-suffering, except for sympathy with the body. We believe, that Christ becoming surety for us, not his body only, but his soul especially, came under that necessity, that his soul was in our soul's stead; and so, what was due to our souls for ever, our surety of justice behoved to suffer the same. Isa. liii. 10. *He made his soul an offering for sin.* Sure for our sin. Nor must we restrict the soul to the body and temporary life, seeing he expresseth it in his own language, *And now is my soul troubled.*

Secondly, There was no reason of Christ's bodily sufferings, when, in the garden, he did sweat blood for us; nor had any man at that time laid hands on him; and all that agony he was in, came from his soul only.

Thirdly, Nor can it be more inconsistent with his blessed person, being God and man, and the Son of God, that he suffered in his soul the wrath of God for our sins, than that his *soul was troubled, and exceeding sorrowful, heavy to the death, in an agony*; and that he complained, *My God, my God, why hast thou forsaken me?* And the cause of this soul-trouble was for sinners; this was surety-suffering. The choicest and most stately piece that ever God created, and dearest to God, being the second to God-man, was the princely soul of Christ, it was a king's soul; yet death, by reason of sin, pass-

eth

eth upon it; and not a common death, but that which is the marrow of death, the first-born and the strongest of deaths, the wrath of God, the innocent pain of hell, void of despair and hatred of God. If I had any hell on me, I should choose an innocent hell, like Christ's: better suffer ill a thousand times, than sin; suffering is rather to be chosen, than sin. It was pain, and nothing but pain: damned men, and reprobate devils, are not capable of a godly and innocent hell, they cannot chuse to suffer hell, and not spit on fair and spotless justice; because Christ's blood was to wash away sin, he could not both fully pay, and contract debt also. But if it be so, that death finding so precious a surety, as Christ's princely and sinless soul, did make him obey the law of the land, ere he escaped out of that land; what wonder that we die, who are born in the land of death? No creature but it travelleth in pain, with death in its bosom, or an inclination to mother-nothing, whence it came. God only goeth between the mightiest angel in heaven, and nothing: all things under the moon must be sick of vanity and death, when the heir of all things, coming in amongst dying creatures, out of dispensation, by law must die. If the Lord's soul, and the soul of such a Lord die and suffer wrath, then let the fair face of the world, the heavens, look like the face of an old man, full of trembling, white hairs, and wrinkles, Psal. cii. 26. Then let man make for his long home; let time itself wax old and gray-haired. Why should I desire to stay here, when Christ could not but pass away?

And if this spotless soul that never sinned was troubled, what wonder then many troubles be to the sinner? Our Saviour, who promiseth soul-rest to others, cannot have soul-rest himself: his soul is now on a wheel sore tossed, and all the creatures are upon a wheel, and in motion; there is not a creature since Adam sinned, sleepeth sound. Weariness and motion is laid on moon and sun, and all creatures on this side of the moon. Seas ebb and flow, and that's trouble; winds blow, rivers move, heavens and stars these

five

five thousand years, except one time, have not had six minutes rest; living creatures walk apace toward death; kingdoms, cities, are on the wheel of changes, up and down; mankind run, and the disease of body-trouble, and soul-trouble on them, they are motion-sick, going on their feet, and kings cannot have beds to rest in. The six days' creation hath been travelling and shouting for pain, and the child is not born yet, Rom. viii. 22. This poor woman hath been groaning under the bondage of vanity, and shall not be brought to bed, till Jesus come the second time to be midwife to the birth. The great All of heaven and earth, since God laid the first stone of this wide hall, hath been groaning and weeping for the liberty of the sons of God, Rom. viii. 21. The figure of the passing-away world, 1 Cor. vii. 31. is like an old man's face, full of wrinkles, and foul with weeping: we are waiting when Jesus shall be revealed from heaven, and shall come and wipe the old man's face. Every creature here is on its feet, none of them can sit or lie. Christ's soul now is above trouble, and rests sweetly in the bosom of God. Troubled souls, rejoice in hope. Soft and childish saints take it not well that they are not every day feasted with Christ's love, that they lie not all the night between the Redeemer's breasts, and are not dandled on his knee; but when the daintiest piece of the man Jesus, his precious soul, was thus sick of soul-trouble, and the noble and celebrious head-heir of all, the first of his kingly house, was put to deep groans, that pierced skies and heaven, and rent the rocks, why but sinners should be submissive, when Christ is pleased to set children down to walk on foot, and hide himself from them? But they forget the difference between the inns of clay, and the home of glory. Our fields here are sown with tares, grief grows in every furrow of this low land. You shall lay soul and head down in the bosom, and between the breasts of Jesus Christ; that bed must be soft and delicious, it is perfumed with uncreated glory. The thoughts of all your now soul-troubles shall be as shad-

ows

ows that passed away ten thousand years ago, when Christ shall circle his glorious arm about your head, and you rest in an infinite compass of surpassing glory; or when glory, or ripened grace, shall be within you, and without you, above and below, when feet of clay shall walk upon pure surpassing glory. *The street of the city was pure gold*: there is no gold there, but glory only; gold is but a shadow to all that is there.

It were possibly no less edifying to speak a little of the fourth, *What love and tender mercy it was in Christ, to be so troubled in soul for us.*

1. *Pos.* Self if precious, when free of sin, and withal self-happy. Christ was both free of sin, and self-happy; What then could have made him stir his foot out of heaven, so excellent a land, and come under the pain of a troubled soul, except free, strong and vehement love, that was a bottomless river unpatient of banks? Infinite goodness maketh love to swell without itself, John xv. 13. Goodness is much moved with righteousness and innocency; but we had a bad cause, because sinners: but goodness (for every man that hath a good cause, is not a good man) is moved with goodness: we were neither righteous nor good; yet Christ, tho' neither righteousness was in us, nor goodness, *would dare to die for us*, Rom. v. 7, 8. Goodness and grace (which is goodness for no deserving) is bold, daring, and venturous. Love, which could not flow within its own channel, but that Christ's love might be out of measure love, and out of measure loving, would outrun wickedness in man.

2. *Pos.* Had Christ seen, when he was to engage his soul in the pains of the second death, that the expence in giving out should be great, and the income small, and no more than he had before, we might value his love more: but Christ had leisure from eternity, and wisdom enough to cast up his counts, and knew what he was to give out, and when to receive in; so he might have repented and given up the bargain. He knew that his blood, and his one noble soul, that dwelt in a personal union with God, was a greater sum, in-

comparably,

comparably, than all his redeemed ones. He should have in little, he should but gain lost sinners; he should empty out (in a manner) a fair Godhead, and kill the Lord of glory, and get in a black bride. But there's no lack in love; the love of Christ was not private, nor mercenary. Christ, the buyer, commended the wares ere he bargained, Cant. iv. 7. *Thou art all fair, my love, there's not a spot in thee.* Christ judged he had gotten a noble prize, and made an heaven's market, when he got his wife, that he served for, in his arms, Isa. liii. 11. *He saw the travel of his soul, and was satisfied*: he was filled with delight, as a full banqueter. If that ransom he gave had been little, he would have given more.

3. *Pos.* It is much that nothing without Christ moved him to this engagement. There was a sad and bloody war between divine justice and sinners: love, love pressed Christ to the war, to come and serve the great king, and the state of lost mankind, and to do it freely. This maketh it two favours. 'Tis a conquering notion to think, that the sinner's heaven bred first in Christ's heart from eternity; and that love, freest love, was the blossom, and the seed, and the only contriver of our eternal glory: that free grace drove on from the beginning of the age of God, from everlasting, the saving plot and sweet design of redemption of souls. This innocent and soul-rejoicing policy of Christ's taking on him the seed of Abraham, not of angels, and to come down in the shape of a servant, to the land of his enemies, without a pass, in regard of his sufferings, speaketh and crieth the deep wisdom of infinite love. Was not this the wit of free grace, to find out such a mysterious and profound dispensation, as that God and man personally should both do and suffer, so as justice should want nothing, mercy should be satisfied, peace should kiss righteousness, and war go on, in justice, against a sinless Redeemer? Angels bowing and stooping down to behold the bottom of this depth, 1 Pet. i. 12. cannot read the perfect sense of the infinite turnings and foldings of this mysterious love. O love

heaven, and fairest of beloveds, the flower of angels, why camest thou so low down, as to bespot and under-rate the spotless love of all loves, with coming nigh to black sinners? Who could have believed that lumps of hell and sin could be capable of the warmings and sparkles of so high and princely a love? Or that there could be place in the breast of the high and lofty One, for forlorn and guilty clay? But we may know in whose breast this bred; sure none but only the eternal love and delight of the Father could have outed so much love: had another done it, the wonder had been more. But of this more elsewhere.

Use 1. We may hence chide our soft nature: the Lord Jesus his soul was troubled in our business; we start at a troubled body, at a scratch in a penny broad of our hide. *First*, There is in nature a silent impatience if we be not carried in a chariot of love, in Christ's bosom, to heaven; and if we walk not upon scarlet, and purple under our feet, we flinch and murmur.

Secondly, We would either have a silent, a soft, a perfumed cross, sugared and honeyed with the consolations of Christ, or we faint; and providence must either brew a cup of gall and wormwood, mastered in the mixing with joy and songs, else we cannot be disciples. But Christ's cross did not smile on him, his cross was a cross, and his ship sailed in blood, and his blessed soul was sea-sick, and heavy even to death.

Thirdly, We love to sail in fresh waters, within a step to the shore; we consider not, that our Lord, tho' *he afflict not, and crush not, Millebbo, from his heart.* Lam. iii. 33. yet he afflicteth not in sport: punishing of sin is in God a serious, grave, and real work: no reason the cross should be a play; neither Stoicks nor Christians can laugh it over; the cross cast a sad gloom upon Christ.

Fourthly, We forget that bloody and sad mercies are good for us: the peace that the Lord bringeth out of the womb of war, is better than the rotten peace that

we

we had in the superstitious days of prelates. What a sweet life, what a heaven, what a salvation is it, we have in Christ? And we know the death, the grave, the soul-trouble of the Lord Jesus, travelled in pain to bring forth these to us. Heaven is the more heaven, that to Christ it was a purchase of blood. The cross to all the saints must have a bloody bit, and lion's teeth; it was like itself to Christ, gally and sour, it must be so to us. We cannot have a paper-cross, except we would take on us to make a golden providence, and put the creation in a new frame, and take the world, and make it a great leaden vessel, melt it in the fire, and cast a new mould of it.

Fifthly, The more of God in the cross, the sweeter: as that free grace doth bud out of the black rod of God, to the soul that seeth not, and yet believeth, and loveth; the cross of Christ drops honey, and the sweetest consolations. We sigh under strokes, and we believe. The first Adam killed us, and buried us in two deaths, and sealed our grave in one piece of an hour; he concluded all under wrath. Now how much of Christ is in this? Omnipotency, infinite wisdom, (when angels gave us over, and stood aloof at our misery, as changed lovers) free grace, boundless love, deepest and richest mercy in Jesus Christ opened our graves, and raised the dead. Christ died and rose again, and brought again from the dead all his buried brethren.

Sixthly, We can wrestle with the Almighty, as if we could discipline and govern ourselves, better than God can do; murmuring fleeth up against a dispensation of an infinite wisdom, because 'tis God's dispensation, not our own, as if God had done the fault, but the murmuring man only can make amends, and right the slips of infinite wisdom. *Why is it thus with me, Lord?* (saith the wrestler) *Why dost thou misjudge Christ?* He who findeth fault with what the Creator doth, let him be man or angel, undo it, and do better himself, and carry it with him.

Seventhly,

Seventhly, We judge God with sense, with the humour of reason, not with reason; the oar that God rolleth his vessel withal, is broken (say we) because the end of the oar is in the water: Providence halteth (say we) but what if sense and humour say, a straight line is a circle? The world judgeth God in person a Samaritan, one that had a devil; if we misjudge his person, we may misjudge his providence and ways. Suspend your sense of God's ways, while you see not his ends that are under ground, and instead of judging, wonder and adore; or then believe implicitly, that the way of God is equal; or do both, and submit, and be silent. Heart-dialogues and heart-speeches against God, that arise as smoke in the chimney, as challengings and summonings against our highest landlord, for his own house and land.

Use 2. If Christ gave a soul for us, he had no choicer thing: the Father had no nobler and dearer gift, than his only begotten Son; the Son had nothing dearer than himself, the man Christ had nothing of value comparable to his soul, and that must run a hazard for man. The Father, the Son, the man Christ, gave the excellentest that was theirs, for us. In this giving and taking world, we are hence obliged to give the best and choicest thing we have for Christ. Should we make a table of Christ's acts of love, and free grace to us, and of our sins and acts of unthankfulness to him, this would be more evident; as there was (1.) Before time in the breast of Christ an eternal coal of burning love to the sinner: this fire of heaven is everlasting, and the flames as hot to day as ever; our coal of love to him in time, hath scarce any fire or warmness, all fire is hot: Oh, we cannot warm Christ with our love; but his love to us is hotter than death, or as the flames of God: *We were enemies in our minds to him, by wicked works.* Col. i. 21. *Heirs of wrath by nature.* Christ began with love to us, we began with hatred to him.

2. The

2. The Father gave his only begotten Son for us: how many fathers and Elies will not let fall one rough word to all the sons and daughters they have for the Lord? *God spared not his own Son, but gave him to the death for us all.* Earthly fathers spare, clap their sons, servants, friends; magistrates, flattering pastors, their people in their blasphemies for him.

3. Christ gave his soul to trouble, and to the horror of the second death for you: consult with your heart, if you have quit one lust for him. Christ laid aside his heaven for you; his whole heaven, his whole glory for you, and his Father's house: are you willing to part with an acre of earth, or house, and inheritance for him?

4. In calling us out of the state of sin, to grace and glory: Oh! I must make this sad reckoning with Jesus Christ. Oh, Christ turneth his smiling face to me, in calling, inviting, obtesting, praying, that I would be reconciled to God: I turn my back to him; he openeth his breast and heart to us, and saith, friends, doves, come in and dwell in the holes of this rock; and we lift our heel against him. O what guilt is here, to scratch Christ's breast, when he willeth you to come, and lay head and heart on his breast? This unkindness to Christ's troubled soul, is more than sin; sin is but a transgression of the law. I grant it is an infinite *but*; but it is a transgression of both law and love, to spurn against the warm bowels of love, to spit on grace, on tenderness of infinite love. The white and ruddy, the fairest of heaven offereth to kiss black-moors on earth; they will not come near to him. It is a heart of flint, and adamant, that spitteth at evangelic love: law-love is love; evangelic love is more than love, it is the gold, the flour of Christ's wheat, and of his finest love. Cant. v. 6. *I rose up to open to my Beloved, but my Beloved had withdrawn himself, and was gone; my soul passed away when he spake.* There be two
words

words here considerable, to prove how wounding are sins against the love of Christ. 1. *My Beloved hath withdrawn himself;* the text is, *Vedodi hamak, and my Beloved hath turned about.* Ari. Mont. *Circumjerat, Pagnin.* in the margin, *verterat fe,* the old version, *declinaverat.* Christ being unwilling to remove, and wholly go away, he only turned aside, as Jer. xxxi. 22. *How long wilt thou go about,* Tithhammakin, *O thou backsliding daughter.* This intimateth so much, as Christ taketh not a direct journey to go away, and leave his own children; only he goeth a little aside from the door of the soul, to testify he would gladly, with his soul come in. Now what ingratitude is it, to shut him violently away? 2. *My soul was gone;* the old version is, *my soul melted at his speaking?* Gnabar, *my soul passed over,* or went away; to remember his ravishing words it broke my life and made me die: (so is the word elsewhere used) that I remembered a world of love in him, when he knocked, saying, *Open to me, my sister, my love, by dove;* to sin against so great a bond as grace, must be the sin of sins, and amongst highest sins, as is clear, in these that sin against the Holy Ghost; then it must be impossible to give grace any thing, we but pay our debts to grace; we cannot give the debt of grace to grace in the whole sum.

Use 3. It cannot then be a sin so intrinsically, and of itself to be troubled in soul, if Christ was under soul-trouble, for sins imputed to him.

Hence let me stay a little on these two; *First,* What a troubled conscience is: *Secondly,* What course the troubled in soul are to take in imitation of Christ. A soul troubled for sin must either be a soul seared and perplexed for the penal displeasure, wrath and indignation of God, or the eternal punishment of sin, as these come under the apprehension of the evil of punishment; or for sin as it saileth against the love of God, or for both. In any of these three respects, it is no sin to be soul-troubled for sin, upon these conditions: 1. That

That the soul be free of faithless doubting of God's love. Now Christ was free of this, he could not but have a fixed, entire, and never-broken confidence of his Father's eternal love. If we have any sin in our soul-trouble for sin, it is from unbelief, not from soul-trouble; if there be mud and clay in the streams, it is from the banks, not from the fountain. Or, 2. If the soul fear the ill of punishment, as the greatest ill, and as a greater than the ill of sin, there is more passion, than sound light in the fear; this could not be in Christ. The aversion of the Lord's heart, from the party in whom there is sin, either by real inherence, or by free imputation, and the indrawing of rays, and irradiations, and outflowings of divine love, is a high evil in a soul that hath any thing of the nature of a son in him: now there was much of a son in Christ, as a man's nature could be capable of; and the more of God that was in Christ, as the fulness, the boundless infinite sea of the Godhead, overflowed Christ all over the banks; then for Christ to be under a cloud, in regard of the outbreathings of eternal love, was, in a sort, most violent to Christ, as if he had been torn from himself: and therefore it behoved to be an extreme soul-trouble; Christ being deprived, in a manner, of himself, and of his only soul's substantial delight and paradise. And this could not be a sin, but an act of gracious soul-sorrow, that sin and hell intervened between the moon and the sun; the soul of Christ, and his Lord. The more of heaven in the soul, and the more of God, the want of God and of heaven is the greater hell. Suppose we, that the whole light in the body of the sun were utterly extinct, and that the sun were turned in a body as dark as the outside of a caldron, that should be a greater loss, than if an halfpenny candle were deprived of light. Christ had more to lose, than a world of millions of angels. Imagine a creature of as much angelic capacity, as ten thousand times ten thousand thousand of angels, all contemperated in one; if this glorious angel were filled, according to his capacity, with the highest and most pure and refined

glory

CHRIST DYING AND DRAWING SINNERS TO HIMSELF.   23

glory of heaven; and again were immediately stript naked of all this glory, and then plunged into the depth of and heart of hell, and of a lake of more than hell's ordinary temper, of fire and brimstone; or suppose God should add millions of degrees of more pure and unmixed wrath and curses, this angel's soul must be more troubled than we can easily apprehend; yet this is but a comparison below the thing: but the Lord Jesus, in whose person, heaven in the highest degree was carried about with him, being thrown down from the top of so high a glory, and to a sad and fearful condition, an agony, and sweating of blood, (God knows the cause) that shouting and tears of this low condition, drew out that saddest complaint, *My God, my God, why hast thou forsaken me?* His loss must be incomparably more than all we can say in these shadows.

This sheweth the cause, why there is not among troubles any so grievous, as the want of the presence of God, to a soul fattened and feasted with the continual marrow and fatness of the Lord's house. No such complaints read you, so bitter, so pathetic, and coming from deeper sense, than the want of the sense of Christ's love. It is broken bones, and a dried-up body to David; it is bitter weeping and crying, like the chattering of a crane to Hezekiah; it is more than strangling, and brings Job to pray, he had been buried in the womb of his mother, or that he had never been born, or his mother had been always great with him; it is swooning, and the soul's departure out of the body, sickness and death to the spouse, Cant. v. 5, 6, 8. It is hell and distraction to Heman, Psal. lxxxviii. 15. It is to Jeremiah the cursing of the messenger that brought tidings to his father, *That a man child was born,* and a wishing that he never had being nor life. It is death to part the lover from the beloved; and the stronger love be, the death is the more death.

But in all that we have yet said, Christ's greatest soul-trouble as a Son (for that he was essentially) was, in that his holy soul was sadded and made *heavy even*

to

to death, for sin, as sin, and as contrary to his Father's love. The elect sinned against the Lord, not looking to him, as either Lord or Father; but Christ paid full dear for sin; eyeing God as Lord, as Father. We look neither to Lord, to law, nor to love, when we sin; Christ looked to all three, when he satisfied for sin. Christ did more than pay our debts; it was a sum above price that he gave for us; it is a great question, yea out of all question, if all mankind redeemed came near to the worth, to the goodly price given for us.

So, according to the sense of any happiness, so must the soul-trouble for the loss of that happiness be, in due proportion. *First*, As we love, so is sorrow for the loss of what we love. Jacob would not have mourned so, for the loss of a servant, as of his son Joseph. Now, no man enjoying God could have a more quick and vigorous sense of the enjoyed godhead, than Christ; so his apprehension and vision of God must have been strong. 2. Because the union with the Godhead, and communion of fulness of grace from the womb, must add to his natural faculties, a great edge of sense; his soul, and the faculties thereof, were never blunted with sin; and the larger the vessel be, the fulness must be the greater: what, or who of the highest seraphims, or dominions, or principalities, among angels, had so large and capacious a spirit, to contain the fulness of God, as Christ had? When *Solomon's heart was larger than the sand on the sea-shore*, and he was but a shadow of such a soul as was to dwell personally with the fulness of the Godhead bodily; O how capacious and wide must the heart of the true Solomon be! It being to contain many seas and rivers of wisdom, love, joy, goodness, mercy, above millions of sands, in millions of sea-shores. What bowels of compassion and love, of meekness, gentleness, of free grace must be in him? Since all the thousands of elected souls sat in these bowels, and were in his heart, to die, and live with him; and withal, since in his heart was the love of God in the highest.

Love

Love must make a strong impression in the heart of Christ; and the stronger, purer, and more vigorous that Christ's intellectuals are, the deeper his holy thoughts and pure apprehensions were, and more steeled with fulness of grace; his fruition, sense, joy, and love of God, must be the more elevated above what angels and men are capable of. Hence it must follow, that Christ was plunged in an uncouth, and new world of extreme sorrow, even to the death, when this strong love was eclipsed. Imagine, that for one spring and summer-season, that all the light, heat, motion, vigour, influence of life, should retire into the body of the sun, and remain there; what darkness, deadness, withering should be upon flowers, herbs, trees, mountains, valleys, beasts, birds, and all things living and moving on the earth? Then, what wonder, that Christ's soul was extremely troubled? His blessed sun was now down, his spring and summer gone; his Father a forsaking God, was a new world to him. And I shall not believe, that this complaint came from any error of judgment, or mistakes or groundless jealousies of the love of God: as his Father could not at any time hate him; so neither could he at this time, *actu secundo*, let out the sweet fruits of his love: the cause of the former is the nature of God, as the ground of the latter is a dispensation above the capacity of the reason of men or angels. We may then conclude, that Jesus Christ's soul-trouble, as it was rational, and extremely penal, so also it was sinless, and innocent. Seldom have we soul-trouble sinless but it is by accident of the way; for our passions can hardly rise in their extremity, (except when God is their only object) but they go over score, yet soul-trouble intrinsically is not a sin.

Then to be troubled for sin, tho' the person be fully persuaded of pardon, is neither sin, nor inconsistent with the state of a justified person; nor is it any act of unbelief, as Antinomians falsely suppose. For, (1.) To be in soul-trouble for sin (which cannot, to the perfect knowledge of the person troubled, eternally condemn

demn) was in Jesus Christ; in whom there was no spot of sin. And Antinomians say, sin remaining sin essentially, must have a condemnatory power; so as 'tis impossible to separate the condemnatory power of the law, from the mandatory and commanding power of the law. (2.) Because, as to abstain from sin, as it offendeth against the love of God shewing mercy, rather than the law of God inflicting wrath, is spiritual obedience; so also to be troubled in soul for sin, committed by a justified person, against so many sweet bonds of free love and grace, is a sanctified and gracious sorrow and trouble of soul. (3.) To be troubled for sin, as offensive to our heavenly Father, and against the sweetness of free grace and tender love, includeth no act of unbelief, nor that the justified and pardoned sinner, thus troubled, is not pardoned, or that he feareth eternal wrath, (as Antinomians imagine) no more than a son's grief of mind for offending a tender-hearted father, can infer, that this grief doth conclude this son under a condition of doubting of his state of sonship or filiation, or a fearing he be disinherited. We may *fear the Lord and his goodness*, Hos. iii. 5. as well as we fear his eternal displeasure. (4.) Sanctified soul-trouble is a fouly commotion and agony of spirit, for trampling under feet tender love, spurning and kicking against the lovely warmness of the flowings of the blood of atonement; checks, and love-terrors, or love-fevers, that Christ's princely head was wet with the night-rain, while he was kept out of his own house, and suffered to lodge in the streets; and fear that the Beloved withdraw himself, and go seek his lodging elsewhere, as Cant. v. 4, 5. Psal. v. 9, 10. *and that the Lord cover himself with a cloud, and return to his place,* and the influence of the rays and beams of love be suspended; are sweet expressions of filial bowels, and tenderness of love to Christ.

Libertines imagine, if the hazard and fear of hell be removed, there is no more place for fear, soul-trouble, or confession: therefore they teach, *That*
there

there is no assurance true and right, unless it be without fear and doubting. 2. That to call in question whether God be my dear Father, after, or upon the commission of some heinous sins (as murder, incest, etc. doth prove a man to be under the covenant of works. (3.) That a man must be so far from being troubled for sin, that he must take no notice of his sin, nor of his repentance. Yea, Dr. Crisp. Vol. 3. serm. I. Page 20, 21, 22. saith, *There was no cause why Paul* (Rom. vii.) *should fear sin, or a body of death; because in that place Paul doth* (saith he) *porsonato a scrupulous spirit, and doth not speak out of his own present case, as it was at this time, when he speaks it; but speaks it in the person of another, yet a believer: and my reason is, Paul in respect of his own person, what became of his sin, was already resolved,* chap. viii. I. *There is now no condemnation,* etc. *He knew his sins were pardoned, and that they could not hurt him.*

Answ. Observe, that Arminius, as also of old, Pelagius, exponed, Rom. vii. *de semi regenito*, of a half renewed man, in whom sense, which inclines to venial sins, fights with reason; that so the full and perfectly renewed man might seem to be able to keep the law, and be free of all mortal sin. And Crisp doth here manifestly free the justified man of all sin: why? because he is pardoned. So then, there is no battle between the flesh and the spirit in the justified man, by the Antinominian way to heaven; which, on the flesh's part, that *lusteth against the spirit*, deserveth the name of sin, or a breach of the law. Only 'tis *Asinus meus qui peccat, non ego*; as the old Libertines in Calvin's time said, *The flesh does the sin, not the man; for the man is under no law, and so cannot sin.* But that Paul, Rom. vii. speaks in the person of a scrupulous and troubled conscience, not as 'tis the common case of all the regenerate, in whom sin dwells, is a soul and fleshly untruth. (1.) To be carnal in part, as verse 14. to do what we allow not, to do what we would not, and what we hate to do, is the common case, not peculiar to a troubled conscience only, but to all the saints, Gal. v. 17.

v. 17. (2.) Paul speaketh not of believing, as he must do, if he speaks only of a scrupulous and doubting conscience; but he speaketh of of *working*, verse 15. *doing*, 17, 18. *willing*, 15, 19. not of believing only, or doubting: now, it is not like the apostle does personate a scrupulous soul, of whom he insinuates no such thing. (3.) A scrupulous and troubled conscience will never yield, so long as he is in that condition, that he does any good, or that he belongs to God; as is clear, Psal. lxxxviii. Psal. xxxviii. Psal. lxxvii. 1, 2, 3, 4, etc. But Paul in this case yieldeth, *he does good, hates evil, delights in the law of the Lord in the inner man; hath a desire to do good; hath a law in his mind that resisteth the motions of the flesh.* (4.) Yea, the apostle then had no cause to fear the body of sin, or to judge himself wretched; this was his unbelief, and there was no ground of his fear, because he was pardoned; he *knew that he was freed from condemnation.* It was then Paul's sin, and is the sinful scrupulosity of unbelievers, to say, being once justified, "Sin dwells in me, and there is a law in my members, rebelling against the law of my mind, and bringing me into captivity unto the law of sin; and I am carnal, and sold under sin; and I do evil, even that which I hate;" for all these are lies, and speeches of unbelief: the justified man sinneth not, his heart is clean, he doth nothing against a law. But I well remember, that our divines, and particularly Chemnitius, Calvin, Beza, prove against Papists, that concupiscence is sin after baptism, even in the regenerate; and it is called eleven or twelve times with the name of sin, Rom. chapters vi. vii. viii. And they teach that of Augustine as a truth, *Inest non ut non sit, sed ut non imputetur.* So we may use all these arguments against Libertines, to prove we are, even being justified, such as can sin, and do transgress the law; and therefore ought to confess these sins, be troubled in conscience for them, complain and sigh in our fetters, tho' we know that we are justified and freed from the guilt of sin, and the obligation to eternal

wrath

CHRIST DYING AND DRAWING SINNERS TO HIMSELF.

wrath. But sin is one thing, and the obligation to eternal wrath is another thing: Antinomians confound them, and so mistake grossly the nature of sin, and of the law, and of justification. Some impudently go so far on, that they teach, "That believers are to be troubled in heart for nothing that befals them, either in sin, or in affliction." If their meaning were, that they should not doubtingly, and from the principle of unbelief, call in question their once sealed justification, we should not oppose such a tenet; but their reasons do conclude, "That we should no more be shaken in mind with sin, than with afflictions, and the punishment of sin;" and that, notwithstanding of the highest provocation we are guilty of, we are always to rejoice, to feast on the consolations of Christ, 1. "Because trouble for sin ariseth from ignorance or unbelief; that believers understand not the work of God for them, in the three persons; the Father's everlasting decree about them; the Son's union with them, and headship to them, his merits and intercession; the Holy Spirit's inhabitation in them, and his office toward them, to work all their works for them, till he make them meet for glory. 2. Because such trouble is troublesome to God's heart, as a friend's trouble is to his friends; but especially, because the spirit of bondage never returns again to the justified," Rom. viii. 15. But I crave leave to clear our doctrine, touching soul-trouble for sin in the justified person.

Asser. 1. No doubting, no perplexity of unbelief, *de jure*, ought to perplex the soul once justified and pardoned. 1. Because the patent and writs of unchangeable purpose to save the elect, and the subscribed and resolved-upon act of atonement and free redemption in Christ standeth uncancelled and firm, being once received by faith; the justified soul ought not so to be troubled for sin, as to misjudge the Lord's bypast work of saving grace. 1. Because the believer, once justified, is to believe remission of sins, and a paid ransom: if now he should believe the writs once signed, were cancelled again, he were obliged to believe

thing

things contradictory. 2. To believe that the Lord is changed and off and on, in his free love and eternal purposes, is a great slandering of the Almighty. 3. The church, Psal. lxxvii. acknowledgeth such misjudging of God to be the soul's infirmity, Psal. lxxvii. 10. "I said, this is my infirmity."

Asser. 2. Yet, *de facto*, David "a man according to God's heart," 1 Sam. xii. 12, 13. fell in an old fever, a fit of the disease of the *spirit of bondage*, Psal. xxxii. 3. "When I kept silence, my bones waxed old, thro' my roaring all the day long." Ver. 4. "For day and night thy hand was heavy upon me, my moisture is turned into the drought of summer." So the church in Asaph's words, Psal. lxxvii. 2. "My sore ran in the night, and ceased not:" either his hand was bedewed with tears in the night, as the Hebrew beareth: or a boil of unbelief broke upon me in the night, and slacked not. Vers. 7. "Will the Lord cast off for ever? will he be merciful no more?" Then faith and doubting both may as well be in the soul, with the life of God, as health and sickness in one body at sundry times; and it is no argument at all of no spiritual assurance, and of a soul under the law or covenant of works, to doubt: as sickness argueth life, no dead corpse is capable of sickness, or blindness; these are infirmities that neighbour with life: so doubting with sorrow, because the poor soul cannot, in that exigence, believe, is of kin to the life of God: the life of Jesus hath infirmities, kindly to it, as some diseases are hereditary to such a family. 2. The habit or state of unbelief is one thing, and doubting and love-jealousies is another thing. Our love to Christ is sickly, crazy, and full of jealousies and suspicions. Temptations make false reports of Christ, and we easily believe them. Jealousies argue love, and the strongest of loves, even marriage-love. 3. By this, all acts of unbelief in souls once justified, and sanctified, should be impossible. Why, then the Lord's disciples had no faith, when Christ said to them, "Why doubt ye, O ye of little faith?" It haply may be answered,

that

that the disciples, Mat. viii. doubted not of their sonship, but of the Lord's particular care in bringing them to shore in a great sea storm. To which I answer, its most true, they then feared bodily, not, directly, soul shipwreck; but if it was sinful doubting, of Christ's care of them, *Master, carest thou not for us?* the point is concluded, that doubting of Christ's care and love may well infer, a soul is not utterly void of faith, that is in a doubting condition. 4. The morning dawning of light, is light; the first springing of the child in the belly, is a motion of life; the least warnings of Christ's breathings is the heat of life: when the pulse of Christ new-framed in the soul moveth most weakly, the new birth is not dead; the very swooning of the love of Christ cannot be incident to a buried man. 5. When Christ rebuketh little faith and doubting, he supposeth faith: he who is but a sinking, and crieth to Christ, is not drowned as yet. 6. The disciples' prayer, *Lord, increase our faith*; Christ's praying that the faith of the saints, when they are winnowed, may not fail; the exhortation to *be strong in the Lord, and in the power of his might*, prove the saints' faith may be at a stand, and may stagger and slide. 7. The various conditions of the saints; now its full moon, again no moon-light at all, but a dark eclipse; evidenceth this truth. The believer hath flowings of strong acts of faith, joy, love; supernatural passions of grace arising to an high spring-tide, above the banks and ordinary coasts; and again, a low ground-ebb. The condition of ebbings and flowings, in full manifestations and divine raptures of another world, when the wind bloweth right from heaven, and the breach of Jesus Christ's mouth and of sad absence, runneth through the Song of Solomon, the book of Psalms, the book of Job, as threads through a web of silk, and veins that are the strings and spouts carrying blood through all the body, less or more.

Asser. 3. The justified soul once pardoned, receiveth never the spirit of bondage, Rom. viii. 15. *to fear again*, eternal wrath; that is, this spirit in the intension

sion of the habit, such as was at the first conversion, when there was not a grain of faith; doth never return, nor is it consistent with the spirit of adoption. Yet happily it may be a question, if a convert brought in with much sweetness, and quietness of spirit, shall fall in some heinous sin, like the adultery and murther of David, have not greater vexation of spirit, than at his first conversion, but more supernatural.

But yet this must stand as a condemned error, which *(a)* Libertines do hold, *That frequency or length of holy duties, or trouble of conscience for neglect thereof, are all signs of one under a covenant of works.* And that which another *(b)* of that way, saith in a dangerous medicine for wounded souls. *Where there is no law,* (as there is none in, or over the justified soul) *there is no transgression; and where there is no transgression, there is no trouble for sin, all trouble arising from the obligement of the law, which demandeth a satisfaction of the soul, for the breach of it, and such satisfaction as the soul knows it cannot give, and thereby remains unquiet; like a debtor that hath nothing to pay, and the law too, being naturally in the soul, as the apostle saith, the conscience accusing, or else excusing; it is no marvel, that such souls should be troubled for sin, and unpacified, the law having such a party, and engagement already within them; which holding an agreement with the law, in tables and letters of stone, must needs work strongly upon the spirits of such as are but faintly and weakly enlightened, and are not furnished with gospel enough to answer the indictments, the convictions, the terrors, the curses which the law brings.* And a third, *(c) And indeed, God's people* (saith he) *need more joys after sins, than after afflictions, because they are more cast down*

(a) Story of the Rise, Reign, Error, 70. page 13.
(b) Saltmarsh Free Grace, art. 6. page 44, 45.
(c) Mr. Archer, if he be the author, Serm. Comfort for Believers, page 19.

CHRIST DYING AND DRAWING SINNERS TO HIMSELF.

down by them; and therefore God useth sins, as means by which he leads in his joys into them in this world, and also in the world to come, their sins yield them great joys: indeed, in some respects, they shall joy most at the last day, who have sinned least; but in other respects, they have most joy, who have sinned most; (for sin they little or much they all shall enter into joy at last,) etc.

Now all this is but a turning of faith into wantonness; whereas faith, of all graces, moveth with lowest sails: for, faith is not a lofty, and crying, but a soft, moving, and humble grace; for then David being moved, and his heart smiting him at the renting of king Saul's garment, should be under a covenant of works, and so not a man according to God's own heart, for a smitten heart is a troubled soul. David, Abraham, Rom. iv. And all the fathers under the law, were justified by the imputed righteousness of Christ apprehended by faith, as we are, Rom. iv. 23. *Now it was not written for Abraham's sake only, that it was imputed to him;* verse 24. *but for us also,* etc. David ought not to have been troubled in soul for sin, for his sins were then pardoned; nor could the Spirit of the Lord so highly commend Josiah's heart-melting trouble at the reading and hearing of the law; nor Christ own the tears and soul-trouble of the woman, as coming from no other spring but much love to Christ, *because many sins were pardoned,* if this soul-trouble for sin had argued these to be under the law, and not in Christ; nor can it be said, that the saints of old were more under the law, than now under the gospel, in the sense we have now in hand; that is, that we are to be less troubled for sin than they, because our justification is more perfect, and the blood of Christ had less power to purge the conscience, and to satisfy the demands of the law before it was shed, than now when it is shed; or that more of the law was naturally in the hearts of David, Josiah, and the saints of old; and so, more naturally, unbelief must be in them, than in us, by nature, under gospel-manifestations of Christ.

Indeed,

Indeed, the law was a severer pedagogue to awe the saints, than, in regard of the outward dispensation of ceremonies, and legal strictness; keeping men as malefactors in close prison, till Christ should come. But imputation of Christ's righteousness, and blessedness in the pardon of sin, and so freedom from soul-trouble for eternal wrath; and the law's demanding the conscience to pay, what debts none were able to pay, but the surety only, was one and the same to them, and to us; as Psal. xxxii. 1, 2. compared with Rom. iv. 1, 2, 3, 4, 5, 6. and Psal. xiv. with Rom. iii. 9, 10,11, 12, 13, 14, 19, 20. and Gen. xvii. 9. Chap. xxii. 19. Deut. xxvii. 26. with Gal. iii. 10, 11, 12, 13, 14. Heb. vi. 13, 14, 15, 16, 17, 18,19, 20. Who dare say, that the believing Jews died under the curse of the law, Deut. xxvii. 26. For so they must perish eternally. Gal. iii. 10. *For as many as are of the works of the law, are under the curse:* Then there must be none redeemed under the Old Testament, nor any justified, contrary to express Scriptures, Psal. xxxii. 1, 2. Rom. iv. 1, 2, 3, 4, 5, 6. Gal. iii. 14. Acts xv. 11. Acts xi. 16, 17. Rom. x. 1, 2, 3. Now, Acts xv. 11. *We believe that through the grace of the Lord Jesus, we shall be saved as well as they. And as they were blessed, in that their transgression was forgiven, and their sin covered, and that the Lord imputed no iniquity to them,* Psal. xxxii. 1, 2. our blessedness is the same, Rom. iv. 6, 7, 8. and Christ, as he was made a curse for them, so for us; that, Gal. iii. 14. *the blessing of Abraham might come on us the Gentiles through Jesus Christ, that we might receive the promise of the Spirit, through faith: and God sent forth his Son, made of a woman, made under the law;* for the Jews, who as heirs were under tutors, as we are under the moral law by nature, that we might be redeemed by him, *That we, who are under the law, might receive the adoption of sons,* Gal. iv. 1, 2, 3, 4. And God gave the like gift to the Gentiles, that he gave to the Jews, even repentance unto life, Acts xi. 16, 17. Then the law could crave them no harder than us; and they were no more justified by works,

than

than we are: *Yea, following righteousness, they attained it not, because they sought it not by faith, but as it were by the works of the law; for they stumbled at the stumbling stone laid in Zion,* Rom. ix. 31, 32, 33. *And they being ignorant of God's righteousness, and going about to establish their own righteousness, have not submitted themselves to the righteousness of God,* Rom. x. 1, 2, 3. and so came short of justification by grace; so do we. If then, to the justified Jews, *There was no law, no transgression, and so no trouble for sin*; all trouble of conscience arising from the obligement of the law; as it must be, because they were freed from the curse of the law, and justified in Jesus Christ, by his grace, as we are: then were they under no smiting of heart, nor wounding of conscience, more than we are; which is manifestly false in David, and in Josiah, and many of the saints under the Old Testament. Hence what was sinful and unbelieving soul-trouble for sin to them, must be sinful soul-trouble to us in the same kind. The law did urge the Jews harder than us, in regard to the Mosaical burden of ceremonies and bloody sacrifices, that pointed out their guiltiness, except they should flee to Christ; 2. In regard of God's dispensation of the severer punishing of law-transgression, and that with temporary punishments, and rewarding obedience with external prosperity: 3. In urging this doctrine more hardly upon the people, to cause them not rest on the letter of the law, but seek to the promised Messiah, in whom only was their righteousness; as young heirs and minors are kept under tutors, while their nonage expire: But, (1.) Who dare say, that the saints under the Old Testament, who lived and died in the case of remission of sins, of salvation, and of peace with God, Gen. xlix. 18. Psal. xxxvii. 37. Psal. lxxiii. 25. Prov. xiv. 32. Isa. lvii. 1,2. Heb. xi. 13. Psal. xxxii. 1, 2. Micah vii. 18, 19. Isa. xliii. 25. Jer. l.20. Psal. xxxi.5. and were undoubtedly blessed in Christ, as we are, Psal. cxix. 1, 2. Psal. lxv. 4. Psal. i. 1,2, 3. Psal. cxliv. 14, 15. Psal. cxlvi. 5. Job. v. 17. Psal. lxxxiv. 4, 5. and died not under the curse of God, or were in capacity to be delivered

by

by Christ, after this life, from the wrath to come, and the curse of the law? (2.) That they were to trust to the merit of their own works, or seek righteousness in themselves, more than we? (3.) Or that they believed not, or that their faith was not *counted to them for righteousness*, as it is with us? Gen. xv. 5. 6. Rom. iv. 3, 4, 5, 6, 7, 8. Psal. xxxii. 1, 2. (4.) Yea, they believing in the Messiah to come, were no more under the law, and the dominion of sin, than we are, Rom. vi. 6, 7, 8, 9. Rom. vii. 1, 2, 3, 4, 5, 6, 7. Rom. viii. 1, 2. Micah vii. 18, 19. Isa. xliii. 25. Jer. l. 20. Psal. xxxii. 1, 2. but under grace, and pardoned, and saved by faith, as we are, Heb. xi. 1, 2, 3, 4, 5, 6, 8, 9, 10, 11, 12, 13. Gal. iii. 10, 13. Acts xi. 16, 17. Rom. ix. 31,32, 33. (5.) Yea, the law was no less a letter of condemnation to them, than to us, Rom. viii. 3. Rom. x. 3. Deut. xxvii. 26. Gal. iii. 10, 13. 2 Cor. iii. 7, 8, 13, 14, 15. (6.) *They drank of the same spiritual rock with us, and the rock was Christ*, 1 Cor. x. 1, 2, 3, 4. Heb. xiii. 8. *and were saved by grace, as well as we*, Acts xv. 11.

2. 'Tis true, Josiah's tenderness of heart, David's smiting of heart, the woman's weeping, even to the washing of Christ's feet with tears, Peter's weeping bitterly for the denying of his Lord, as they were woundings, and gospel-affections, and commotions of love issuing from the spirit of adoption, of love, grace, and nothing but the turtle's love-sorrow; so it is most false, that they were no soul-trouble for sin, as if these had been freed from all the law of God, and these soul-commotions were not from any sense of the curse, or the law, or *any demands of the law, to pay what justice may demand of the self-condemned sinner;* yet were they acts of soul-trouble for sin, as sin: and it shall never follow, that the *parties were under no transgression, and no law, because under no obligement to eternal wrath;* for such an obligation to eternal wrath, is no chain which can tie the sons of adoption, who are washed, justified, pardoned; and yet if the justified and pardoned say, *they have no sin*, and so no reason to complain under their fetters, and

sigh

sigh as captives in prison, as Paul doth, Rom. vii. 24. nor cause to mourn for indwelling of sin, they are liars and strangers to their own heart, and do sleep in deep security; as if sin were so fully removed, both in guilt and blot, as if tears for sin as sin should argue the mourning party to be in the condition of those who weep in hell, or that they were no more obliged to weep; yea, by the contrary, to exercise no such affection, but joy, comfort, and perpetuated acts of solace and rejoicing; as if Christ had, in the threshold of glory, with his own hand, *wiped all tears from their eyes* already.

3. Nor see I any reason why any should affirm, *That the law is naturally as a party in the soul*, of the either regenerate and justified, or of those who are out of Christ. (1.) For the law's indwelling, as a party engaging, by accusing and condemning, is not naturally in any son of Adam; because there is a sleeping conscience, both dumb and silent naturally in the soul: and if there be any challenging and accusing in the Gentile conscience, Rom. ii. as stirring is opposed to a silent and dumb conscience that speaketh nothing, so the law-accusing is not naturally in the soul; a spirit above nature (I do not mean the spirit of regeneration) must work with the law, else both the law and sin lie dead in the soul: the very law of nature lieth as a dead letter, and stirreth not, except some wind blow more or less on the soul, Rom. vii. 8, 9. (2.) That the law weakeneth any sinner, and maketh the drunken and mad sinner see himself in the sea, and sailing down the river *to the chambers of death*, that he may but be occasioned to cast an eye on shore, on Jesus Christ, and with a landing on Christ, is a mercy that no man can father on nature, or on himself. (3.) All sense of a sinful condition, to any purpose, is a work above nature; though it be not ever a fruit of regeneration. (4.) 'Tis true, *Christ teacheth a man's soul, through the shining of the gospel-light, to answer all the indictments of the law, in regard that Christ the ransomer stops the law's mouth with blood,* else the sinner can

make

make but a poor and faint advocation for himself; yet this cannot be made in the conscience without some soul-trouble for sin. (5.) 'Tis strange that God's people "need more joy after sin, than after affliction;" and that in "some respect, they have most joy, who have sinned most:" sure, this is accidental to sin, this joy is not for sin; but 'tis a joy of *loving much*, because *much is forgiven*. Forgiveness is an act of free grace, sin is no work of grace: sin grieves the heart of God, "as a friend's trouble is trouble to a friend:" the believer is made the friend of God, John xv. 15. and it must be a cursed joy that lay in the womb of that which is most against the heart of Christ; such as all sin is. Yea to be more troubled in soul for sins, than for afflictions, smelleth of a heart that keep correspondence with the heart and bowels of Christ, who wept more for Jerusalem's sins than for his own afflictions and cross. As some ounces of everlasting wrath in the law, with a talent-weight of free gospel-mercy would be contempered together to cure the sinner; so is there no rational way to raise and heighten the price and worth of the soul-redeemer of sinners, and the weight of infinite love so much, as to make the sinner know how deep a hell he was plunged in, when the bone acheth exceedingly: for that the gospel tongue of the physician Christ should lick the rotten blood of the soul's wound, speaketh more than imaginable free love. Nor do we say, that gospel-mourning is wrought by the law's threatenings, then it were servile sorrow; but 'tis wrought by the doctrine of the law, discovering the foulness and sinfulness of sin, and by the doctrine of the gospel; the spirit of the gospel shining on both: otherwise, sounds, breathings, letters of either law or gospel, except the breathings of heaven shine on them, and animate them, can do no good.

Asser. 4. Sins of youth already pardoned, as touching the obligation to eternal wrath, may so rise against the child of God, as he hath need to ask the forgiveness of them, as touching the removing of present wrath, sense of the want of God's presence, of the in-

fluence

fluence of his love, the cloud of sadness and deadness, through the want of the *joy of the Holy Ghost*, and ancient consolations of the days of old. Psal. xc. 7. "We are consumed in thy wrath, and by thy hot displeasure we are terrified." verse 8. "Thou hast set our iniquities before thee, and our secret sin in the light of thy face." This was not a motion of the flesh in Moses the man of God. Antinomians may so dream. "The fury of the Lord waxed hot against his people:" so saith the Spirit of God: nor is this conceit of theirs to be credited against the text that Moses speaketh in regard of the reprobate party: Moses, by immediate inspiration, doth not pray for the "beauty and glory of the Lord," in the sense of his love, to be manifested on a reprobate party. Antinomian preachers in our times confess sins in public, but 'tis the sins of the reprobate and carnal multitude, that are in the society mixed with the godly; they think it a work of the flesh to confess their own sins: this is to "steal the word of the Lord from his people." So David, Psal. xxv. 7. "Remember not the sins of my youth, nor my transgressions." The sins of his youth, as touching obligation to eternal wrath were pardoned, I question it not; but in regard, God was turned from him in the flamings of love, and his sins sealed up in a bag, in regard of innumerable evils that lay on him: he prayeth, ver. 16. *Turn thee unto me.* Heb. *Set thy countenance on me.* God's favour in the sense of it was turned away. And ver. 18. "Look upon mine affliction and pain, and forgive all my sins;" the word [*Nasa*] with a point in the left side of [*Shin*] is to carry away. *Ferome aufer, Take away all my sins*, Isa. liii. 4. he carried, "or did bear as a burden, our iniquities." *Vetablus, portavit. pagnin. parce, condona,* "Spare or pardon all my sins:" Then sin here is pardoned only according to the present pain and grief of body and soul that was on David, Psal. xxxix. 4. "For mine iniquities are gone over mine head: as a heavy burden, they are too heavy for me." We have no reason to believe that David thought himself already a condemned man, and now in hell, tho' some sparks

of

of hell's wrath and fire, not in any sort as satisfactory to divine justice, or as a fruit of God's hatred and enmity, can fall on the children of God; yet 'tis not imaginary, but real anger. God was really angry with "Moses at the waters of strife." The thing that David did against "Uriah displeased the Lord;" not in David's opinion only. And though the hell for a time in the soul of God's children, and the hell of the reprobate, differ in essence and nature, in that the hell of the reprobate is a satisfactory pain, 2. And that it floweth from the hatred of God; but the hell of the godly not so: yet, in this materially they are of the same size; that the one as well as the other, are coals and flames of the same furnace; and neither are imaginary. Then again, sins of youth long ago pardoned, though sometimes dearly beloved, are like the ghost of a dear friend some years ago dead and buried, that re-appeareth to a man, as dead Samuel did to Saul; look how loving and dear they were when alive, they are now as terrible and dreadful, when they appear to us living out from the land of death; so are sins of youth, when they rise from the dead, and were pardoned in Christ long ago; they appear again to David and Job, and the saints with the vail and mask or hue of hell, and sealed with temporary wrath. Psal. xcix. 8. "Thou wast a God that pardonest, or forgavest them, though thou tookest vengeance of their inventions." The same word [*Nakum*] is given to God, when he taketh vengeance on his enemies, Num. xxxi. 2. Isa. i. 24. "I will be avenged of mine enemies." 2 Kings ix. 7. "That I may avenge the blood of my servants the prophets. So is the word [*Nakum*] vengeance used Deut. xxxii. 43. *He will render vengeance to his adversaries.* And if one and the same temporary judgment in the two thieves that were crucified with Christ, be so differenced, that mercy is stamped on the same death to the one, and wrath to the other; we may well say, there is a temporary vengeance and wrath, that befalleth both the saints and the reprobate in this life; and the difference is in the mind and intention of God, in both.

And

And that God pardoneth sin, when he removeth temporary wrath; so 2 Sam. xii. 13. *Nathan saith to David, The Lord also hath caused thy sin to pass away; Why? Thou shalt not die.* This is meant of temporal death especially; as the context cleareth, v. 10. *The sword shall not depart from thine house*; and ver. 14. *The child born to thee shall surely die.* Then the Lord's putting away of David's sin, was in loosing him from the sword, in his own person, not in his house and children; for by proportion of divine justice, (tho' tempered with mercy) the sword was punished with the sword. I do not exclude relaxation from eternal punishment, but remission going for relaxation of punishment. Then, as there be two sorts of punishments, one temporary, and another the eternal wrath to come; so there are in scripture two sorts of remissions, one from the temporary, another from eternal punishment. Therefore sin is put for punishment, Gen. iv. 13. *Mine iniquity* (saith Cain) *is more than I can bear;* or, *My punishment is more than I can bear.* Lev. xxiv. 15. *He that curseth his God shall bear his sin,* Ezek. xxiii. 49. *And ye shall bear the sins of your idols.* Num. ix. 13. *The man that is clean---and forbiddeth to eat the passover---that man shall bear his sin.* So when God layeth sin to the charge of the sinner, in punishing it he is said to lay a burden on the sinner, 2 Kings ix. 25. And to remove this burden is to pardon the sin, 2 Chron. vii. 14. *If my people humble themselves, then will I hear from heaven, and will forgive their sin, and will heal their land*; by removing the *locusts and the pestilence.* See, the pardoning of their sin is exponed to be the *removing of the locusts and pestilence.* And to call sins to remembrance, is to punish sin: the Shunamite saith, 1 Kings xvii. 18. *Art thou come to me (O man of God) to call my sin to remembrance, and to slay my son?* Job complaineth, chap. xiii. 26. *Thou makest me to possess the iniquities of my youth.* Now, though out of unbelief he might apprehend, that he was cast off of God, and a man rejected of God, and that his sins were never pardoned, and he himself never de-

livered

livered from the wrath to come; these legal thoughts might keep Job in a distance from God, to his own sinful apprehension; yet it shall be impossible to prove, that Job in all these complaints had no other but a mere legal esteem of God's dispensation; and that, 2. God stamped not temporary wrath, and the pain of a hidden and overclouded God, the subtraction of the sense of divine manifestations of love, (the Lord standing behind the wall) in all these afflictions. Now 'tis known, that, as these are often trials of the faith of the saints, yet they are four fruits of our fleshly indulgence to our carnal delights, and of our *not opening to our beloved, when he knocketh*, Cant. v. 2, 3, 4, 5, 6. And though the godly do stedfastly believe their salvation is in a castle, above losing; yet in reason, sin bringing broken bones, Psal. li. 10. a sad cloud, the damming up of a spring of Christ's love spread abroad in the heart, a temporary hell in the soul, it must be sorrowed for, hated, mourned for, confessed; and yet in all these there is no necessity of such a law-spirit of bondage to work these, nor is faith in any sort diminished, but put to a farther exercise. And the same sad fruits follow from the sins of the saints under the New Testament, as may be cleared from Rev. ii. 5, 16, 22. Rev. iii. 3, 17, 18. 2 Cor. i. 8, 9, 10. 2 Cor. ii. 7. 2 Cor. vii. 5, 6, 7. Rev. iii. 20. John xiv. 1. Nor can we think, that the strictness of the law gave those under the law an indulgence not to be a whit troubled in soul for sin, as it overclouded the influence and flowings of divine love, suppose they had assurance and freedom from the wrath to come, as is evident in the spouse, Cant. v. 1, 2, 3, 4, 5, 6. and chap. ii. 16,17. chap. iv. 7. Nor is it true, that gospel-grace and liberty entitleth the saints now to such wantonness of peace, as that persons fully assured of deliverance from the curse of the law, are never to be troubled for sins committed in the state of free justification; nor are they any more to mourn, nor groan under sin's captivity, nor to confess sin, in regard that Christ's blood hath washed soul, and eyes, and faces from all

tears

tears; and the salvation of the saints in this life is not in hope only, as wheat in the blade, but actual, as in the life to come; and therefore, "Holy walking and good works can no more be means or the way to the kingdom, (as M. Towne and other Antinomians say.) than motion within the city, can be a way to the city, in regard the man is now in the city, before he walk at all."

Asser. 5. If Jesus Christ had soul-trouble, because of divine wrath, for our sin, and was put to a sweat of blood, God roasting Christ quick in a furnace of divine justice, tho' every blobe of sweat in the garden was a sea of free grace, not his eyes only, but his face and body did sweat out of free love from his soul, Luke xxii. 44. Heb. v. 7. What must soul-trouble be in a fired conscience? 'Tis no wonder that wicked men wrestling with everlasting vengeance, cannot endure it. The devil's predominant sin being blasphemous despair, he tempts most to his own predominant sin; the issue and final intent of all his temptations is despair: because devils are living and swimming in the sphere and element of justice, they cannot bear it; they cry to Christ, the whole company and family making the despiting of Christ a common cause, *Art thou come hither, to torment us before the time?* Mat. viii. 29. Prov. xviii. 14. *The spirit of a man will bear his infirmity*, the spirit is the finest metal in the man; *but a wounded spirit who can bear that?* So the Hebrew readeth. Any thing may be borne; but break the man's soul, and break the choicest piece in the soul, the conscience, who can then stand? As conscience is the sweetest bosom-friend of man, so it is the sorest enemy. David is persecuted by his prince, and he beareth it; Jeremiah is cast in the dungeon by the rulers, priests and prophets, and he overcometh it; Job is persecuted by his friends, and he standeth under it; Christ is betrayed and killed by his own servants and kinsmen, and he endureth it; the apostles are killed, scourged and imprisoned by the Jews, and they rejoice in it: but Judas is but once hunted by the fury of hell in his breast, and he leaps overboard, into a sea of in-

finite

finite wrath: Cain, Saul, Ahitophel, cannot endure it: Spira roareth as a bear, and crieth out, *O that I were above God;* tho' we may hope well of his eternal state. Nero, after, to his other bloods, he had killed his mother, Agrippina, he could not sleep, he did often leap out of the bed, and was terrified with the visions of hell. Eternity, the resurrection, and the judgment to come, are virtually in the conscience. 2. What is fear? A tormenting passion. To hang a living man by an untwisted thread, over a river of unmixed pure vengeance; and let the thread be wearing weaker and weaker, what horror and paleness of darkness must be on the soul? 3. What sorrow and sadness, when there is not a shadow of comfort? But 4. Positive despair, rancour, and malice against the holy majesty of God; when the soul shall wish, and die of burning desire, to be above and beyond the spotless essence of the infinite majesty of God; and shall burn in a fire of wrath against the very existence of God, and blaspheme *the Holy One of Israel,* without date. Job saith of such, (chap. xxvii. 20.) in this life, *terrors take hold of him as waters, and a tempest stealeth him away in the night.*

But consider what it is to the saints; Job complaineth, chap. xiv. 16. *Doest thou watch over my sin?* ver. 17. *My transgression is sealed up in a bag, and thou sewest up mine iniquity.* Vatabl. "Thou appearest to be a watchful observer of mine iniquity," and addest (as Ari. Monta.) "Punishment to punishment, sewing sin to sin, to make the bag greater than it is. Now, tho' there be a misjudging unbelief in the saints, yet it is certain, that God doth inflict penal desertions, as real pieces of hell, on the souls of his children, either for trial, as in Job; or punishment of sin, as in David; whose bones were broken for his adultery and murder, Psal. li. 10. and whose *moisture of body was turned into the drought of summer,* through the anger of God in his soul, till the Lord brought him to the acknowledgment of his sin, and pardoned him, Psal. xxxii. 3, 4, 5, 6. But some will say, can the Lord inflict spiritual punishment, or any of hell, or

the

the least coal of that black furnace upon the souls of his own children? to which I answer, it is but curiosity to dispute, whether the pains of hell, and the flames and sparkles of real wrath, which I can prove to be really inflicted on the souls of the saints in this life, be penalties spiritual, different in nature. Certain there be three characters sealed and engraven on the pains of the damned, which are not on the real soul-punishments of divine wrath on the souls of the saints; as, 1. What pieces of hell, or broken chips of wrath, are set upon the souls of deserted saints, are honied and dipped in heaven, and sugared with eternal love. God's heart is toward *Ephraim as his dear child, and his bowels turned within* for their misery, even when he speaks against them; Jer. xxxi. 20, 21. But the coals of the furnace cast upon reprobates, are dipt in the curse of God; yea, so as in a small affliction, even in the miscarrying of a basket of bread, and the loss of one poor ox, there is a great law-curse, and intolerable vengeance, Deut. xxvii. 26. chap. xxviii. 17, 31. And again, in the in-breaking of a sea and flood of hell in the soul of the child of God, a rich heaven of a divine presence, Psal. xxii. 1, 8, 9. Psal. xviii. 4, 5, 6. (2.) The hellish pains inflicted on reprobates, are law-demands of satisfactory vengeance, and payment to pure justice; but fire-flashes, or flamings of hell on the deserted saints, are medicinal, or exploratory corrections; tho' relative to justice and punishments of sin, yet is that justice mixed with mercy, and exacteth no law-payment in those afflictions. (3.) Despair, and blasphemous expostulating and quarrelling divine justice, are the inseparable attendants of the flames and lashings of wrath in reprobates; in the godly there is a clearing of justice, a submission to God, and a silent psalm of the praise of the glory of his justice, in this temporary hell, no less than there is a new song of the praise of free grace in the eternal glory of the saints, perfected with the Lamb.

Nor should this seem strange, that God punisheth the sins of his children with such spiritual plagues of
unbelief,

unbelief, and jealousies, and lying misjudgings of God in their sad desertions, more than that the Lord punish the lifted-up heart of Hezekiah, with leaving him to fall on his own weight; and David's idleness and security, with letting him fall in adultery; and Peter's self-confidence, with the soul denying of his Lord. But 'tis a sad dispensation, when God cleaveth a saint with a wedge of his own timber; and linketh one sinful misjudging of God, in his fever of soul-desertion, to another: and justice seweth (in a permissive Providence) one sin to another, to lengthen the chain, if free grace, a link of gold, did not put a period to the progress thereof. Now, we are not to look at this as an ordinary calamity; Job's expressions are very full, chap. vi. 4. *For the arrows of the Almighty are within me, the poison whereof drinketh up my spirit: the terrors of God do set themselves in array against me.* An arrow is a deadly weapon when it is shot by a man, or by an angel: but it is soft as oil in comparison of the *arrow of the Almighty.* 1. It is the arrow of [*Schaddai*] the almighty did frame and mould, and whet it in heaven. 2. The arrow was dipt in poison, and hath art from hell and divine justice. One devil is stronger than an host of men; but legions of devils are mighty strong, when such archers of hell are sent to shoot arrows that are poisoned with the curse and bloody indignation of heaven. 3. What a sad stroke must it be, when the arms of omnipotency draweth the bow? The arms of God can shog the mountains and make them tremble, and can move the foundation of the earth out of its place, and take the globe of heaven and earth, and can cast it out of its place, more easily than a man casts a slung-stone out of his hand. When he putteth forth the strength of omnipotency against the creature, what can the man do? 4. Every arrow is not a drinking arrow, the arrows of divine wrath drink blood: suppose a thousand horse-leeches were set on a poor naked man, to drink blood at every part of his body, and let them have power and art to

suck

suck out the marrow, the oil, and sap of life, out of bones and joints; say also, that one man had in his veins a little sea of blood, and that they were of more than ordinary thirst and power to drink the corpse of the living man, as dry as straws or flax: what a pain would this be? Yea, but it were tolerable. 5. Arrows can but drink blood; arrows are shot against the body, the worst they can do, is to drink life out of liver and heart, and to pierce the strongest bones; but the *arrows of the Almighty*, are shot against spirits and souls: the spirit is a fine, subtile, immortal thing. Isa. xxxi. 3. *The horses of Egypt, are flesh, and not spirit*: the spirit is a more godlike nature, than any thing created of God. The Almighty's arrows kill spirits, and souls: there's an arrow that can pierce flesh, joints, liver, heart, bones, yea, but through the soul also: Never an archer can shoot an arrow at the soul; but this the Almighty can do. Say, your arrow killed the man, yet the soul is saved. 6. Many *love not their life to death, as the witnesses of Jesus*: death, as death, is clothed with apprehensions of terror; no man is wretched, *actu secundo*, within and without, but he that believeth himself to be so; here are terrors, felt-terrors: Jeremiah could prophecy no harder thing against Pashur, *The Lord* (saith he) *hath not called thy name Pashur, but Magor-missabib*, Jer. xx. 3. *Thou shalt be a terror to thyself.* Compare this with other pains: Job would *rather chuse strangling*, or the dark grave; and the grave to nature, is a sad, a black and dreadful house; but a believer may get beyond the grave. What do the glorified spirits fear a grave now? Or are they afraid of a coffin, and a winding sheet, or of lodging with the worms and corruption? Or, is burning quick a terror to them? No, not any of these can run after, or overtake them, and they know that. But felt-terrors are a hell carried about with the man in his bosom, he cannot run from them. Oh! he lieth down, and hell beddeth with him; he sleepeth, and hell and he dream together; he riseth, and hell goeth to the fields with him, he goes to his garden, there

is

is hell. It is observable, a garden is a paradise by art; and Christ was as deep in agony and wrestlings of hell for our sin, in a garden, a place of pleasure, as on the cross, a place of torment. The man goes to his table, O he dare not eat! he hath no right to the creature; to eat is sin, and hell; so hell is in every dish: to live is sin; *he would fain chuse strangling;* every act of breathing is sin and hell. He goes to church; there is a dog as great as a mountain before his eye: here be terrors! but what, one or two terrors are not much, tho' too much to a soul spoiled of all comfort. 7. *The terrors of God* (God is always in this sad play) *do set themselves in battle array against me.* Or, chap. xvi. 13. *His archers compassed me about round.* Heb. *His great ones;* or, *his bow-men* (because they are many, or, because the great ones did fight afar off) *have besieged me.* So, 2 Chron. xvii. 9. 1 Sam. vii. 16. *Samuel went in a circuit to Bethel, and Gilgal, and Mizpeh.* And Josh. vi. 3. *Ye shall besiege Jericho.* The wrath of God, and an army of terrors, blocked up poor Job, and stormed him. Now, here be these sore pressures on the soul. 1. The poor man cannot look out to any creature-comfort, or creature-help. Say, that an angel from heaven would stand for him, or a good conscience would plead comfort to him, it should solace him; but the man cannot look out, nor can he look up, Psal. xl. 12. The enmity of God is a sad thing. 2. A battle array is not of one man, but of many enemies: say the man had one soul, it should be his enemy; and that he had a hundred souls, he should have a hundred enemies; but as many millions of thoughts, as in his wearisome nights escape him, he has as many enemies; yea, as many creatures, as many stones of the field, as many beasts, so many enemies, Job. v. 23. Hos. ii. 8. Christ gave to the Father propositions of peace, and to the poor soul under sense of wrath, they are nothing: the fear of hell is a part of real hell to the man who knows no other thing, but that he is not reconciled to God. Creatures behind him, and before him, heaven above, and earth below, and

crea-

CHRIST DYING AND DRAWING SINNERS TO HIMSELF. 49

creatures on every side, within and without, stand with the weapons of heaven, and of an angry God against him; friends, wife, servants, acquaintance have something of wrath and hell on them; the man in his own thought is an out-law to them all; and the leader of all these archers is God. God, God is the chief party. See Job xix. 12, 13, 14, 15, 16, 17. And there you see, brethren, acquaintance, kinsfolk, familiar friends, man-servant, maid-servant, wife, young children, bone, skin, flesh, are all to Job as coals of the fire of hell. And Isa. viii. 21, 22. Men in this *shall curse their king and their God.*

Asser. 6. These being materially the same soul-troubles of deserted and tempted saints, and of plagued and cursed reprobates, do differ formally and essentially according to God's heart, his dispensation and intentions, his mercy and his justice regulating them: so I shall speak of the difference between Christ's troubled soul, and the saint's trouble. 2. Of some ways of God's dispensation, in the soul-trouble of the saints. Touching the former; there was in Christ's soul-trouble, 1. No misjudging of God; but in a strong faith, in that he still named God his Father, and God. 2. In that as this trouble came to a height, and more fuel was added to the fire of divine wrath, Luke xxii. 44.

, *he prayed with more extension of body* and spirit; he extended himself in fervour of praying. And, Heb. v. 7. *He offered prayers*, and *humble supplications* of the poor, or oppressed, that make their address to one who can help them: he put into God an humble petition, and a bill to his Father, as an overwhelmed man, and he offered this bill,

with an hideous cry and tears. Rev. xiv. 18. *The angel cried with a loud voice.* To cry with a full and lifted up voice, or with a shout; so is the verb used, John xviii. 40. *When men cry, and cast away their clothes, and cast dust in the air.* 3. His soul-trouble and death was satisfactory to divine justice, for our sins; he being free of sin himself: which can agree to no soul-trouble of the holiest
saint

saint on earth. But touching the second: these positions may speak somewhat, to clear the way of the soul-trouble of saints.

1. *Position.* Conscience, being a mass of knowledge, and if there be any oil to give light, 'tis here; 'tis then likest itself, when it most bears witness of well and ill-doing. Now, we are more in sinning than obeying God; and because of the corruption of nature, the number of natural consciences that are awake to see sin, are but very few. And when the renewed conscience is on the work of feeling and discerning guiltiness in its best temper, the more life, the more sense: sick ones in a swoon, or dying persons that do neither hear, see, nor speak, are half-gate amongst the dead. The conscience sick of over-feeling, and so under over-sense of sin, is in so far in a fever: for often a fever is from the exsuperancy of too much blood, and rankness of humours, the vessels being too full; and therefore 'tis like a river that cannot chuse but go over banks, the channel being a vessel too narrow to contain it all.

2. Pos. Therefore often the time of some extreme desertion and soul-trouble is, when Christ hath been in the soul with a full high spring-tide of divine manifestations of himself. And if we consider the efficient cause of desertion, which is God's wise dispensation: when Paul hath been in the third heaven, on an hyperbole, a great excess of revelations, God thinketh then good to exercise him *with a messenger of Satan;* which by the weakness and spiritual infirmity he was under, wanted not a desertion, less or more, whatever the messenger was; as it seems to be fleshly lust, after a spiritual vision. Paul was ready to think himself an angel, not flesh and blood; and therefore, 2 Cor. xii. 7. he saith twice in one verse, This befell me,

That I should not be lifted up above ordinary comets, up among the stars. But if we consider the material cause, it may be, that extreme and high overflowing of Christ's love break our weak and narrow vessels: Cant. v. 1. there is a rich and

dainty

CHRIST DYING AND DRAWING SINNERS TO HIMSELF.

51

dainty feast of Christ, *I am come into my garden, my sister, my spouse, I have gathered my myrrh with my spices, I have eaten my honey-comb with my honey, I have drunk my wine with my milk: eat, O friends, drink, yea, drink abundantly, O Beloved.* Yet in that song, the Spirit of God speaketh of a sad desertion in the next words, *I sleep, but mine heart waketh: It is the voice of my Beloved that knocketh,* etc. There is not only impiety, but want of humanity, that the church had rather that wearied Jesus Christ should fall down and die in the streets, in a rainy and snowy night, when his locks were wet with rain, than that he should come in and lodge in the soul. And let us not think that the thread and tract of the scripture's coherence, one verse following on another, as the Spirit of God hath ordered them, is but a cast of chance or an human thing: when the spouse rideth on the high places of Jacob, and saith, Isa. xlix. 13. *Sing, O heavens, and be joyful, O earth, and break forth into singing, O mountains: for God hath comforted his people, and will have mercy on his afflicted.* Yet this was nothing to the afflicted people; verse 14. *But Sion said, the Lord hath forsaken me, and my Lord hath forgotten me.* When the Lord's disciples, Mat. xvii. are in the sweetest life that ever they were in, at the *transfiguration of Christ,* when *they saw his glory,* and Peter said, *Master, it is good for us to be here,* even then, they must appear to be weak men; and Christ must forbid and rebuke their faithless fear, ver. 6. *They fell on their faces, and were sore afraid.* I leave it to the experience of the godly, if Jeremiah his singing praise in one verse, chap. xx. 13. and his cursing the day that he was born on, in the next verse, ver. 14. the order of scripture being of divine inspiration, do not speak God's dispensation in this to be such, as to allay and temper the sweetness of the consolation of a feast of God's high manifestation, with a sad desertion. So John his glorious soul-ravishing comforts, in seeing the *seven golden candlesticks,* and the Son of Man in such glory and majesty, Rev. i. 12, 13, 14, 15. Yet it appears to be a desertion that he

is

CHRIST DYING AND DRAWING SINNERS TO HIMSELF.

is under, when Christ forbiddeth him to fear, and when he must have the hand of Christ laid on his head, and when *he falleth down at Christ's feet as dead.* Ver. 17, 18. And when Isaiah saw the glorious vision, chap. vi. *The Lord sitting on his throne high and lifted up;* it must be a throne higher than the *heaven of heavens, that he sitteth on, and his train filling the temple.* 'Tis a desertion that he falleth in, ver. 5. *Then said I, woe is me, for I am undone, because I am a man of unclean lips, and I dwell in the midst of a people of unclean lips: for mine eyes have seen the King, the Lord of hosts;* he was a pardoned man before. 'Tis so with us, while the body of sin dwelleth in us, that we cannot, being old bottles, bear new wine; and therefore the fulness of God, breaketh crazy lumps of sinful flesh and blood: as a full tide is preparatory to a low ebbing; and full vessels in the body, to a fever. Would Christ, in his fulness of the irradiations of glory, break in upon us; he should break the bodily organs, and over-master the soul's faculties, that all the banks of the soul should be like broken walls, hedges, or clay channels; which the inundation of a river has demolished, and carried away from the bottom. Flesh and blood is not in a capacity of over-joy, and can hold but little of heaven, no more than earth could bear such a glorious creature as the sun: we must be both more capacious, and wider, and stronger vessels, before we be made fit to contain glory; we are leaking and running out vessels, to contain grace. Manifestations, and rays of divine love are too strong wine that grew up in the higher Canaan, for our weak heads.

Asser. 3. Desertion cometh under these considerations: 1. As 'tis a cross, and a punishment of sin; 2. As a trial from mere divine dispensation: 3. As 'tis a sin on our part, full of sinful misrepresentations of Christ.

In the first consideration, we are to submit to any penal overclouding of Christ: 1. Because the eye cannot water to look on any cross of Christ, where faith's as-

pect

pect goeth before, and faith, *Though I sit in darkness, yet I shall see light.* 2. There is required a sort of patience under sin, as 'tis either a punishment of another sin, as David was submissive to the sinful railing of Shimei, and the wicked treasons, and incestuous pollutions of his concubines, by his son Absalom: or as sin dwelleth in us, and in divine dispensation must be our cross, as well as our sin; we are to be grieved at our sins, as they cross God's holy will: but as they are our own crosses, and thwart our own desires, and now are committed by us, or dwell in us, we are not to bite at, and utter heart-railings against divine providence, who might have prevented, and efficaciously hindered these sins; and yet did not hinder them. 6. This dispensation should be adored, as a part of divine wisdom; that broken souls are not wholly cured, till they be in heaven. Sin is a disunion from God: Jesus doth not so completely solder the soul to God, but the seam hath holes and gapings in it, by reason of the indwellings of sin, Rom. vii. 17, 18, 19, 22, 23. And since Libertines will confound justification with regeneration, we say, their justification we speak of, is never perfected in this life. And because sin, as sin, which remaineth in our flesh, must make God and the soul at a distance, there cannot be such perfect peace as excludeth all soul-trouble; the blue fear of the wound remaineth so, and the dregs of that domestic falling-ill, that we have of our first house of Adam, are so feared in us, that as some diseases recur, and some pain of the head, when an east wind bloweth; so the disease we have in our head, the first Adam, sticketh to us all our life; and when temptations blow, we find the relics of our disease working, and foaming out the smell of the lees, and scent that remaineth. Christ has need to perfume our ill odours, with his merits; for our begun sanctification is so imperfect, as that yet our water smells of the rotten vessel, the flesh; and we cannot but have our ill hours, and our sick days, and so a disposition to sinful desertions. 4. Unbelief naturally stocked in the body of sin, is humorous and ill-
minded

minded to Christ: there is a liar in our house, and a slanderer of Christ, that upon light occasions can raise an ill fame of Christ, *That he is a hard man, and gathers where he did not sow:* that Christ is nice and dainty of his love; that he is too fine, too excellent and majestic to condescend to love me: and take this as the mother-seed of all sinful desertions, to blame Christ's sweet inclination to love us, as well as his love. *I knew thou wast a hard man;* 'tis dangerous to have ill thoughts of Christ's nature, his constitution, *actu primo.* The next will be to censure his ways, his sowing, and his gathering; which I take to be the current objection of old Pelagians, and late Arminius. O! he must gather where he did never sow, if he command all to believe under the pain of damnation, and yet he judicially, in Adam, removed all power of believing: so he putteth out the poor man's eyes, and cutteth off his two legs, and commanded him to see with no eyes, and walk with no legs, under pain of damnation. Men believe not they hate Christ by nature; and hatred hath an eye to see no colour in Christ, but blackness; as the instance of the Pharisees doth clear; who saw but devilry in the fairest works of Christ, even in his casting out of devils.

Asser. 4. Desertions, on the Lord's part, are so often mere trials, as we may not think they are greatest sinners who are most deserted. Desertion smelleth more of heaven, and of Christ deserted for our sins, than of any other thing; 'tis the disease that follows the royal seed, and the king's blood; 'tis incident to the most heavenly spirits, Moses, David, Heman, Asaph, Hezekiah, Job, Jeremiah, the church, Psal. cii. Lam. chap. i. Chap. ii. 3, 4. it is ore that adhereth to the choicest gold. But how is it, say some, that you read of so little soul-desertion in the apostles, and believers under the New Testament, and so much of it under the Old Testament? Is it not, because it belongeth to the law and the covenant of works, and to the spirit of the Old Testament, and nothing to the gospel of grace? So Antinomians dream. I answer, We read indeed

indeed of heavier and stronger external pressures laid on men, to chace them to Christ under the law, than under the gospel: because the gospel speaketh of curses and judgment in the by; and the law more kindly, and more frequently, because of our disobedience; and of the preparing of an infant-church, under non-age, for Christ. But tho' the gospel speak less of God's severity in external judgments, as in killing so many thousands, for looking into the ark, for idolatry; yet the apostle saith, that these things were not merely pedagogical, and Jewish; so as, because the like are not written in the New Testament, it followeth not, they belong not to us: for (saith he) 1 Cor. x. 6. *Now these things were our examples.* Verse 11. *Now all these things happened unto them for examples, and they are written for our admonition, upon whom the ends of the world are come.* Ergo, The like for the like sins, do, and may befal men under the gospel. Moreover, never greater plagues were threatened than by Christ's own mouth; never wrath to the full came upon any, in such a measure, as upon the city of Jerusalem, and the people of the Jews, *for killing the Lord of Glory.* And tho' no such desertions be read of in the apostles, as of Job, (who was not a Jew, and yet more deserted than David, Heman, or any prophet) Hezekiah, the church, Lament. Chap. ii. and iii. yet we are not hence to believe, that there were never such desertions under the New Testament: for as external judgments, so internal soul-trials, are common to both the saints under the Old and New Testament; as is evident in Paul, 2 Cor. i. 8, 9. 2 Cor. v. 11. 2 Cor. vii. 4, 5, 6. 1 Pet. i. 6, 7. And as both were frequent under the Old Testament, so were *they written for our learning.* And if it were to the Jews merely pedagogical, to have *terrors without, and fears within,* and to be *pressed out of measure;* or to afflict their souls for sin, were a work of the law; then to be afflicted in conscience, were a denying that Christ is come in the flesh, and simply unlawful: whereas the Lord's absence is a punishment of the church's not opening to Christ, Cant. v. 4, 5, 6. and God's act

of

of withdrawing his lovely presence, is an act of mere free dispensation in God, not our sin. For this would be well considered, that the Lord's active desertion, in either not co-operating with us when we are tempted, or, 2. His not calling, or the suspending of his active pulsation and knocking at the door of our soul, or, 3. The not returning of a present comfortable answer, or, 4. The withdrawing of his shining manifestations, his comforts, and the sense of the presence of Jesus Christ, cannot be formally our sins: indeed, our unbelief, our sinning, which resulteth from the Lord's non-co-operating with us, when we are tempted, our misjudging of Christ, (as if it were a fault to him to stand behind the wall) which are in our desertions passive, are sins.

Asser. 5. Saddest desertions are more incident to the godly, than to the wicked and natural men; as some moth is most ordinary in excellent timber, and a worm rather in a fair rose than in a thorn or thistle. And sure, tho' unbelief, fears, doubtings, be more proper to natural men, than to the saints; yet unregenerate men are not capable of sinful jealousies of Christ's love, nor of this unbelief, which is incident to the desertion we now speak of; even as marriage jealously falleth not on the heart of a whore, but of a lawful spouse. 2. According to the measure and nature of love, so is the jealousy, and heart suspicions for the want of the love, whence the jealousy is occasioned: the soul which never felt the love of Christ, can never be troubled, nor jealousy displeased for the want of that love. And because Christ had the love of God in another measure, possibly of another nature, than any mortal man; his soul-trouble, for the want of the sense and actual influence of that love, must be more, and of a higher, and it may be of another nature, than can fall within the compass of our thoughts: never man in his imagination, except the man Christ, could weigh, or take a lift of the burden of Christ's soul-trouble; the lightest corner or bit of Christ's satisfactory cross, should be too heavy for the shoulders of angels or men. You may
then

then know how easy it is for many to stand on the shore, and censure David in the sea; and what an oven, and how hot a fire must cause *the moisture of his body turn the drought of summer.* The angels, John xx. have but a theory and the hearsay of a stander-by, when they say, *Woman, why weepest thou?* She had slept little that night, and was up by the first glimmering of the dawning, and sought her Saviour with tears, and an heavy heart, and found nothing but an empty grave; *O they have taken away my Lord, and I know not where they have laid him.* And the daughters of Jerusalem stood but at the sick spouse's bed-side, and not so near when she complains, *I am sick of love.* To one, whose wanton reason denied the fire to be hot, another said, put your finger in the fire, and try if it be hot. Some have said, all this soul-trouble is but melancholy and imagination: would you try whether the body of an healthy and vigorous man, turned as dry as chaff, or a withered half-burnt stick, through soul-pain, be a cold fire, or an imagination: and what physic one of the smallest beams of the irradiation of Christ's smiling countenance is to such a soul; you would not speak so.

Asser. 6. Why some of the saints are carried to Abraham's bosom, and to heaven in Christ's bosom, and for the most, feast upon sweet manifestations all the way, and others are oftener in the hell of soul-trouble, than in any other condition, is amongst the depths of holy sovereignty. (1.) Some feed on honey, and are carried in Christ's bosom to heaven; others are so quailed, and kept under water, in the floods of wrath, that their first smile of joy is when the one foot is on the shore, and when the morning of eternity's sun dawns in at the window of the soul. Some sing, and live on sense all the way; others sigh, and go in at heaven's gates weeping, and Christ's first kiss of glory dries the tears off their face. (2.) Christ walks in a path of unsearchable liberty, that some are in the suburbs of heaven, and feel the smell of the dainties of the king's higher

house,

house, ere they be in heaven; and others, children of the same Father, passengers in the same journey, wade through hell, darkness of fears, thorns of doubtings, have few love-tokens, till the marriage-day. (3.) There be not two sundry ways to heaven; but there are (I doubt not) in the latitude of sovereignty, hundreds of various dispensations of God, in the same way. Jerusalem is a great city, and hath twelve, and many ports, and angles and sides to enter at; but Christ is the only way: he keeps in all, and brings in all; he keeps in angels that never come out, he brings in his *many children to glory.* But some go to heaven, and till the twelfth hour know nothing of *sin, death, God, Christ, heaven and hell.* Grace took a short cut, and a compendious way with the repenting thief. Christ can not only run, but fly post with some in few hours to heaven: grace hath eagles' wings to some; and some wrestle with hell, fight with beasts, make war with lusts, and are dipt in and out, as the oars in the river, in floods of wrath from their youth, and a long time. Caleb and Joshua for two generations were in the journey to Canaan; many thousands not born when they entered the journey, yea, new generations arose, and entered into that good land with them, and were there as soon as they.

Asser. 7. In consideration of desertions, as actively they come from God, and passively they are received in us, and consecutively, or by abused resultance are our sins, they have sundry and divers causes.

1. Sorrow for the withdrawing sense and influence of Christ's love, as formally a desertion passive in us, is not sinful; except sorrow, which is a luxuriant and too indulgent passion, exceed measure. For, 1. 'Tis a mark of a soul that liveth and breatheth much on Christ's love: now, if love be the life of some, it must be continued in sense, or some fruition of love, less or more. Now, as the irradiation of the sun's beams and light in the air yesterday, or the last year, cannot enlighten the air and earth this day; and the meat I did eat a year ago, the sleep I slept the last month, cannot

feed

CHRIST DYING AND DRAWING SINNERS TO HIMSELF.

feed and refresh me now, but there must be a new application of new food, and new sleep: so the irradiation of the manifested love of Christ in the years of old, must go along with us; tho' as experiences of old favours, they may set faith on foot again, when it is fallen; yet the soul that liveth by fruition of divine love, must have a continuated influence of that love: and to live on divine love, of itself, can be no sin. O 'tis a life liable to many clouds, overcastings of sadness and jealousies, that lives on the manifestations of Christ's love: 'tis sweet and comfortable, but has mixtures of hardest trials; for such set on no duties comfortably, without hire in hand, as it were; when Christ's love-letter from heaven miscarries, and is intercepted, the soul swoons: 'tis surer to *live by faith*.

2. To murmur, and impatiently to sorrow, as if *God had forgotten to be merciful*, is sinful sorrow; 1. Because the object of it is materially blasphemous: *the strength of Israel cannot lie, nor repent; nor can any change fall on him.* 2. 'Tis most unjust to complain and quarrel with him, who hath *jus, , right, law, full and unconstrained liberty to do with his own what he pleaseth;* but the heavenly irradiations and outshinings of Christ's love, and the influence of his free grace, are all his own, and most free; for if the seaman have no just cause to quarrel with God, because the wind bloweth out of the east, when he desireth it may blow out of the west; and the husbandman cannot in reason plead mal-government in the Almighty, because he restrains the clouds, and bindeth up the womb of heaven, in extreme drought, when he crieth for rain and dew to his withered earth and meadows, and valleys; so neither is there any just pleading (a sinless desire of the contrary is a far other thing) with the Lord, because he bindeth up the bowels of Christ from outing his love, or restraineth the winds and breathings of the Spirit from blowing. 3. We may desire the wind of the Lord to blow, because it is an act of free grace in him so to do; but to contend with the Lord, because he will not act himself in works of

free

free grace, at our pleasure, is to complain that grace is grace; for if grace were obnoxious, in all its sweet spirations and motions, to my will, or to your desires, it should not be grace, but a work of my hiring and sweating. 4. This sorrowing must accuse the free, holy, and innocent love of Christ, as if his love were proud, nice, humorous, high, passionate; whereas infinite freedom, infinite majesty, and loveliness and meekness of tenderest love, do all three concur admirably in Jesus Christ. Love cannot be hired, Cant. viii. 7. *If a man would give all the substance of his house for love, it would utterly be contemned.* And for the strength of tenderness of love, the same place pleadeth; *Many waters cannot quench love, neither can the floods drown it.* And Paul asserteth, Eph. iii. 18. the *breadth, and length, and depth, and height of it.* 5. There is required a submission under such a divine dispensation; else we upbraid grace, and will be wicked, because God will not be (*actu secundo*) as gracious in his influence, as we are humorous in our sickly desires. 6. If we could understand the sense of divine dispensation, the Lord often intendeth grace, when he suspendeth grace; and his desertions are wrapped up in more invisible love and free grace, than we are aware of: and why should not we, in faith, believe his way of dispensation to be mercy?

Asser. 8. Sometimes (2) God's immediate lashes on the soul, is the occasion of our sinful misjudging of God; Psal. xxxviii. 2. *Thine arrows stick fast in me, and thine hand presseth me sore.* Hence cometh a sad reckoning, ver. 4. *Mine iniquities are gone over my head, as a heavy burden they are too heavy for me.* And Psal. lxxvii. 4. *Thou holdest mine eye waking: I am so troubled, that I cannot speak.* And what followeth from this? A great misjudging of God. Ver. 7. *Will the Lord cast off for ever? will he be favourable no more?* Verse 8. *Is his mercy clean gone for ever? doth his promise fail for evermore?* Verse 9. *Hath God forgotten to be gracious?* 'Tis but a poor ground of inferring that God hath forgotten to be merciful, and Christ is

changed,

CHRIST DYING AND DRAWING SINNERS TO HIMSELF. 61

changed, because there is night and winter on your soul: Is the God of nature changed, because 'tis not ever summer, and day-light? because a rose withereth, and a flower casteth its bloom, and the sun is over-clouded, therefore God hath forgotten himself? Dispensations of God are no rules to his good pleasure; but his good pleasure regulates all his dispensations. If the soldiers of Christ quarter in the dry wilderness, not in the suburbs of heaven, their leader is wise.

3. Darkness and night are blind judges of colours; in desertion, 'tis night on the soul; and imaginations are strongest and biggest in the darkness; the species of terrible things plough deep furrows of strong impressions on the fancy in the sleep, when the man *walketh in darkness, and hath no light*, either of sound judgment, or soul-comfort: 'tis night with the soul, and then a bush moved with the wind, is an armed man; every conviction of conscience is condemnation. 2 Cor. i. 8. *We are pressed out of measure, above strength, insomuch that we despaired even of our life:* Ver. 9. *But we had the sentence of death;* there were loads and weights laid on us above strength: darkened souls put on Christ deep representations of wrath, and blackness of indignation; and change him in their apprehensions into another Christ.

4. Satan can drink up at one draught, a grieving and sorrowing spirit, 2 Cor. ii. 7. and he hath access to the fancy, and out-works of the soul of the child of God, so he can enlarge the species to a double bigness; let it be considered, if the grammar of Heman, be not a little swelled in more than ordinary rhetoric, Psal. lxxxviii. 4. *I am counted as these that go down to the pit as a man that hath no strength.* Verse 5. *Free amongst the dead, like the wounded that lie in grave, whom thou rememberest no more, and they are cut off by thy hand.* Ver. 7. *Thy wrath lieth hard upon me, and thou hast afflicted me with all they waves.* If God forgot him as a buried man, and not a wave of God's wrath, but was gone over his soul, what could God do more? And Job's words are a little beyond the line, chap. xiii. 24.

Wherefore

Wherefore hidest thou thy face from me, and takest me for thine enemy? Words arise up to mountains. Job was not holden of God to be an enemy: Satan can make every pin in the cross an hell, and put a new sense on God's dealing, other than ever he meaned. When Christ opens a vein to blood a conscience, Satan, if he may have leave, shall shut in his lion-teeth to tear the vein, and make the hole of the wound as wide as heart and life may come out; and therefore he raiseth up apprehensions, and sows strife and pleas with Christ, and waters his own seed. *Can love kill thee? Were it Christ that doth all this, would he not once come to the bedside of a sick son? Can Christ's love throw a poor friend to hell, and leave him there? He hath forgotten thee.* Satan can argue from dispensation and trials to the state. Which is false logic. This thou sufferest: *Ergo*, thou art not in the state of adoption. It is not good that such a minion as Satan, have the ear of a deserted soul; he can carry tales between Christ and the soul, to separate between friends. Never believe ill of Christ; *Love thinks no ill.* If you love Christ, two hells may cast water on your fire of love, but cannot quench it. Christ will believe no ill of you, let Satan speak his will.

5. Even the love of a saint to Christ, under an hard dispensation, is sick with jealousy, and travelleth in birth with fancied suspicions of Christ's love. Our love is swayed with misgivings; 'tis full of cares, and fears, and doubtings; because 'tis not always edged with heavenly wisdom. It takes life from sense and felt embracings, from presence, and reciprocation of warmness from Christ's bowels: and when *face answereth not face*, and Christ's love doth not echo, and resound to our love, then it fainteth. We too often measure Christ's love by our foot; we calculate Christ's love by our own elevation, not by his: and Christ's mysterious dispensation, should not point the hour; nor is the full moon, nor the noon-day sun of Christ's love, the compass that our affections and love should sail by. Yea, *having not seen Christ,* 1 Pet. i. 8. nor felt him, *yet we love him,* and *believe* in him; and this is

most

most spiritual love, and has most love in it; the more jealously without ground, the less love of Christ, at least the less solid constancy of love.

6. Unbelief is a special cause of soul-trouble. 1. In bodily diseases, pain doth not create itself; but sinful passive desertion does create itself. Christ cannot own unbelief, as coming within the compass of his creation; though *by him all things were created.* Unbelief spinneth out new calumnies of Christ, addeth oil to the fire, and maketh desertion a thousand talent-weight heavier than it would be. This may be evidenced in all the complaints of the saints under desertion; in which more is laid on Christ's name, than is true. Unbelief is a querulous thing. Isa. xlix. 14. *But Sion said,* unbelieving Sion said, *The Lord hath forsaken me, and my Lord hath forgotten me;* this was an untruth, and is confuted in the next verses. Mary Magdalene thought they had taken away her Lord; and he was as near her, as the turning about of her body, and she within speaking to him face to face. And when unbelief doth raise such thoughts, as *Christ hath forgotten to be merciful; Christ is changed, he loveth not to the end*; what pain must be at the soul's bottom, where such misjudging of Christ, and his love, is in the brim? And yet there is a coal of the love of Christ, smoaking in the bottom of the soul? A loving opinion of Christ is hardly expelled; especially, one particular misreport should not make me receive a misunderstanding of Christ. I never heard ill of Christ before, but much of his excellency and sweetness; and why should I admit of an untried impression, that the sun that giveth light to all, is dark; that fire is cold? 'tis not true like, that Christ is an enemy, if once a friend. Had we a storehouse, and a high bended habit of honourable, sublime, and high thoughts of Jesus Christ, his excellency, the weight of his preciousness, eminency, we should the more hardly give way to the lies that our unbelieving heart raiseth against him.

2. Our second misgiving from unbelief, is in believing our state. Psal. xxxi. 22. *I said in my haste, I am*

cut

cut off from before thine eyes. I am none of Christ's, is a too ordinary mistake; as (*he is changed, and not mine*) often goeth before. We often find more fault, and first blame in Christ, if not only, ere we see our own provocations. Hence the complaints of Job, chap. vi. chap. xiii. chap. xvi. chap. xix. and of Jeremiah, chap. xx. chap. xv. of Hezekiah, Isa. xxxviii. of Asaph, Psal. xvii. of Heman, Psal. lxxxviii. of the church, Isa. xlix. 14, 15. Isa. lxiii. chap. lxiv. Psal. cii. Psal. vi. Psal. xlii. Psal. xxxi. run more on the strain of complaining of God, and his unkind dispensation, than of the plaintiff's sins and provocations; and where there is one mistake of ourselves under desertion, the reader may find out ten mistakes of Christ; and when the deserted soul misjudgeth his own state, it issueth from, and reflecteth on the midjudged apprehension of Christ.

3. From unbelief issueth the misjudging of our own actions: I do no good; or if I do, 'tis not *bene*, on the right motives, and for the right end, the good that I do. The antecedent is true, but not the consequence: there is a cloud in our fairest sun, and clay in our water; but because good works are not our Saviour's, 'tis no good ground to say, they have no influence in the way of our salvation; and they are not way-marks in our journey, because they are no part of the ransom that bought heaven. We have a grand opinion of our own righteousness, and when we miss it, we think we miss Christ himself; which is a great misjudging, and argueth a believing in ourselves, not in Christ. And often soul-trouble ariseth from defects, omissions, and sins in ourselves. If simple grief for sin as offensive to love arise, that's good soul-trouble; but such soul-trouble as shaketh the bottom of faith, and turneth the soul of Christ to seek righteousness in itself, is damnable: as 'tis hard for an unregenerate man to see sin in its dreadfullest colours, and not despair; so 'tis hard for a regenerate person to see sin, as sin, and not to fall on unbelief, and doubting of Christ's love. Antinomians think any anxiety for sin, which expelleth actual rejoicing in Christ, or turning off Christ, and our casting

off

off the conscience again under the spirit of bondage, and work of the law. Which is contrary to truth, and the command of James, to be *afflicted and mourn;* and Christ's saying, *Blessed are they that mourn, for they shall be comforted;* and Peter, who saith, there may be need, that the saints be *in heaviness for a season.*

'Tis a great point of wisdom, 1. To know how far forth our spiritual walking may be a seed of comfort; we may easily err on either hands. 2. The logic would be humble; *Lord, I am not haughty,* ergo, I am comforted in thee. Paul saith well, *I know nothing by myself, yet I am not hereby justified*; we would not build a tower on a mole-hill. 3. From our sinful walking we may draw grounds of godly sorrow, yet not grounds of unbelief; faith and godly sorrow are consistent together. 4. 'Tis not safe to argue that we are not in Christ, from the wants adhering to our sincere performances. While we slander ourselves, we may slander the Spirit of God. 5. The measure of our obedience, cannot be a warrant to counter-argue Christ, as want is no warrant to stand far off from Christ: no more than it is good logic to flee from the fire, because you are cold; or to be at odds with gold, because you are needy and poor; poverty may conclude a failing with low fails, and humility, but not unbelief; your want of all things, should not empty rich Jesus Christ.

7. Absence of Christ, misapprehended through unbelief, occasioneth soul-trouble. In which there is something which evidenceth saving grace in the troubled soul, as is aforesaid. For the want of the thing loved, cannot but here be a gracious torment to the lover. The spouse is sick, and dieth, when she wanteth him whom her soul loveth, Cant. ii. 5. chap. v. verse 6, 8. David so expresseth himself, Psal. lxxxiv. 2. *My soul longeth, yea, even fainteth, or dieth, or is at an end, for the courts of the Lord; my flesh and my heart crieth out for the living God.* The word [*Chalab*] is to desire, or to be consumed, or to make an end of any thing. David's desire of enjoying God, was such, as it was

his

his death to want God; it may hold forth, as Pagnine observeth, that David's soul, either extremely desired the Lord, or died upon the absence of God. But to be anxiously troubled in an unbelieving manner, is the sinful soul-trouble. Why doth the soul doubt of Christ's winter, more than of his summer? Absence and presence, his coming, and his departing, are both his own works. God hath liberty in the one as in the other; as it is God's liberty to make fair weather and storms, to make a fair day, and a cloudy day; to make David a king, and his brethren shepherds and common soldiers; so hath he his own freedom in the breathings of his own Spirit, and the blowing of his own wind, or of the drawing a curtain over his own face, and hiding himself: and neither in this, nor in any of his ways of freedom, can we challenge the Lord, or plead against him. And if we think we do well to be angry, even to the death, at the motions and breathings of Christ's free love, then we may compel Christ to be kind, and visit us, as we think good. Whatever ye be, Christ is Lord of his own presence and visits, and 'tis good the king's chamber of presence be a dainty, and Christ's wine be not so common as water: nor can we here force kindness, or acts of heavenly manifestations on him; he hides himself. Why, he is as reasonable, and wise, in his going as in his coming.

2. Should we take on us to steward and husband the kisses and embracements of Christ, better than he can do himself; and should quarrel because the Lord had not thought fit to make heirs and minors, that are yet under non-age. Masters and lords of their own young heaven; this were not a good world for us. *Christ's love is better than wine*, Cant. i. Neither our head, nor our heart could endure to drink, at our own will, of this new wine of the higher kingdom. Better for us it is that Christ bear the key of the well of life, than children have it; and if the government of the higher and lower family be upon the shoulders of Christ, the leading of this or that single person to heaven, is worthy Christ's care.

3. And

3. And consider, that Christ goeth not behind the mountain, or hideth himself upon mere hazard, but for weighty reasons, that love may be sharpened through absence; that the house may be adorned with new hangings, and *Christ's bed made green;* that care may be had, when *he resteth in his love, not to stir up, nor awake the Beloved, until he please;* that the high tides and rich feasts of Christ's love, after sad and heavy desertions, may heighten the worth and esteem of Christ; that faith and love may with more of the violence of heaven, lay hold on Christ, after long seeking, and not part with him on so easy terms, Cant. iii. 1, 2, 3, 4. that we may know, what weakness is in our clay-legs, under desertion, and how we are to walk on Christ's legs, which are *pillars of marble set on sockets of gold*; that absence and presence, the frownings and smilings of Christ, may be to the saints the little images of hell and heaven, and broken men may read their debts in Christ's count book of free grace, with tears in their eyes, and songs of praise in their mouth; that we may be in high love, and sick for absent Christ, and may be at the pains through thick and thin to seek him, and learn to live less by sense, and more by faith, and resolve to die believing; and be charitable of Christ absent, and kiss his vail, when we can see no more; and be upon our watch-tower, and know what of the night, and observe a soul-communion with God; which the spirit of the world cannot do.

4. Nothing doth more cry aloud the softness and baseness of our nature than our impatience under sad dispensations, when we are positively resolved upon this, that God loveth us; yet, because of a cloud over our sun, and one scruple of gall in our joy, to lodge a new opinion, that Christ is changed into another God, and that his love doth plot, and contrive our destruction, argueth a weak and soon shaken faith. It speaketh lightness of love to Christ, that it is loosed at the root, with the scratch of a pin; he hides himself, and you say, Oh 'tis not Christ, but some other like him; for Christ would not so go and come. Well rooted friend-

friendship can scarce suffer you to believe so much of a brother, or a companion. But when ye thus misjudge Christ, we may gather, if he should appear in the garments of vengeance, as he doth to the damned; 'tis to be feared, this would drink up our faith and love, if Christ were not more gracious, than we are constant: *Lord, lead us not into temptation.*

5. I deny not but seeming wrath, and Christ's intercepting of messengers of love, and flamings of hell's fury on the soul, are prodigious like comets, glimmering over a trembling conscience; and that 'tis much to keep orthodox, sound, and precious thoughts of Christ, when the christian is not himself; yet when the child mileth about in a round, to say, the earth runneth about in circle, or to think the shore or the rock saileth from the ship that carrieth you, when the ship moveth and the shore standeth still, are but signs of a weak-headed and green sailor: so, because you are deeply affected with a sad absence, to believe Christ's love runneth a circle, and that you stand still as a rock, and the change is in Christ, argueth a green, raw wit, and instability of faith; and that the sea-sands can no more easily drink up a gallon of water, than that temptation would swallow up the poor man's faith thus fainting, if the invisible strength of the advocate, who intercedeth for the saints, did not uphold him.

Now is my soul troubled.

2. The second circumstance in the text, is the time,   , *Now is my soul troubled.* There is an emphasis in this *Now*: Christ had a troubled soul before, and was sensible of afflictions; but *Now*, he saw more in this cross than in all afflictions; he saw the *curse of the law,* and the *wrath of God*, stamped on this cross. Christ had never any now, or juncture of time, before or after, comparable to this *Now*. Observe, that Christ and his followers, must look for growing and swelling crosses, Matth. xxvi. 37. *Jesus began to be sorrowful, and very heavy:* he had all his life, Isa. liii. sorrow; verse 3. he was a man of sor-

rows

rows; as every piece of Christ had been sorrow, and had acquaintance with grief: [*Vinduang holi*] *and was known* and noted to all, marked out to all, *by his griefs;* but now he wadeth deeper in troubles. Let all Christ's followers look for a growing cross, and a sadder and sadder *Now*. Psal. iii. 1. *Lord, how are they increased that trouble me?* Psal. xxv. 17. *The troubles of my heart are enlarged.* Heb. become most broad. Psal. xlii. 7. *Deep calleth unto deep, at the noise of thy water-spouts, all thy waves and thy floods are gone over me.* One cross calleth to another; God raineth them down, as one wave of the sea calleth another. So Job's afflictions came on him, in a growing way. David, Psal. lxix. 2. *I sink in the deep mire, where there is no standing.* I wade deeper and deeper, till I lose ground and bottom. *I am come into the deep waters, where the floods overflow me.* (2.) Christ's sufferings are called a cup; it behoved to be filled to the brim, and Christ weigheth out in ounces and drams, so much gall in the cup, and yet some more; and because that worketh not the cure, yet an ounce more. (3.) Christ can appoint clothes for us, as we have cold; and a burden answerable to the bones and strength of the back. It is a doubt if David's faith would reach so far, as that he should bear it well, that another should sacrifice a wicked son Absalom to God's justice: O! how did David mourn that he was killed? Yet the Lord measured out to Abraham a cup of deeper gall, to kill with his own hand, his only son, a believing son, an heir of the promise. (4.) What if twelve years bloody issue be little enough for to work a woman to necessity of seeking to Christ? yet another must be eighteen years; and a sick man thirty and eight years. Our physician knoweth us well. Let us study for a growing faith to growing crosses: and if a cross as broad and as large as all *Britain*, and a sword as public as three kingdoms, yea, as all the bounds of Christendom come; so that there be *no peace to him that goeth out, or cometh in,* we are to be armed for it. Nor, 2. Is it enough after pestilence

and

and the sword, to sit down, and say, *Now I'll die in my nest, and multiply my days as the sand.* Stay, in heaven only, there be neither widows, nor killed husbands, nor beggars, nor plundered houses; understand the sense of providence right; *We have not yet resisted unto blood*; we have yet seas and floods of blood to swim through, ere we come to shore. A private cross is too narrow a plaister to our sore; and therefore a public one, as broad as all Scotland, as all your mother-country and church, is little enough. It must be yet broader, and we must yet lose more blood.

What shall I say?

3. The third circumstance in Christ's soul-trouble, is his anxiety of mind, *What shall I say?* It is as much as, *What shall I do?* But, what meaneth this anxiety of Christ? It is like a doubting of the event; but there is neither doubting nor despairing in it. There is fear, exceeding great heaviness and sorrow in it: and as an anxious man, through extremity of suffering, is put to his wits-end, as destitute of counsel, to say, *I know neither what to do, nor say;* so Christ had a sinless anxiety. Learned divines acknowledge, there was an innocent and sinless oblivion in the sensitive memory, in regard it was intent only upon the extreme agony, and not obliged in all differences of time to remember every duty: and affirmative precepts oblige not in all, and every juncture of time.
2. Nor is faith actually, always, without exception, to believe: It is possible, that faith in the act, and extreme fear in the same act, be physically inconsistent. 3. Neither were Christ's sensitive affections, in their physical and natural operations, so awed and restrained by a divine law, as that they may not put forth themselves to the utmost and highest degree of intention, when the light of reason sheweth the object in the superlative degree of vehemency. Reason and light could never shew to any suffering man, at one time, such a great death of evil of loss, and positive evil of sense, as it did shew

to

to Christ, at this instant of time. To be suspended from an immediate, full, perfect, personal, intuitive fruition, and vision of God, is a greater eclipse, than if ten thousand suns were turned into pieces of sackcloth of hair, and the light totally extinguished; or, than if all the angels, all the glorified saints, that are, or shall be, in heaven, were utterly excluded from the comfortable vision of God's face. You cannot imagine what a sad suspension of the actual shining of the immediately enjoyed majesty of God this was; and what a positive curse and wrath was inflicted on Christ, so as his anxiety could not exceed.

4. Christ was to suffer in his natural affections, of joy, sorrow, confidence, fear, love, yet without sin; and tho' I could not shew how this anxiety and faith could consist, yet it cannot be denied; for grace doth not destroy nature, nor could the vision of personal union hinder the exercise of all human affections and infirmities in Christ, in the state of his humiliation, as clothes of gold cannot allay the pain of the head and stomach: grace is a garment of cloth of gold, and the union personal, the perfection of grace; yet it hindered not Christ from being plunged in extreme horror and anxiety.

5. There were in Christ, at this time, some acts of innocent and sinless darkness in the sensitive soul, that he actually thinking of the blackness and dreadful visage of the second death, was now like a man destitute of counsel. But, 1. This was merely penal, and out of dispensation; for Christ's soul-pain is an excellent screen and shadow, or a sconce between the soul-troubled believer and hell; and Christ's anxiety, and his, *What shall I say?* is a bank and a great high coast between a distressed conscience, who is at, *What shall I do? whither shall I go? where shall I have relief and help?* and the extremity of his forlorn condition.

2. Christ's anxiety was not opposite to any light of faith, or moral holiness; as the simple want of light is not night, an eclipse of the sun removeth no light, nay, not at all one beam of light from the body of the

sun;

sun; all is light that is on the other side of the covering, it removeth only light from us, who are on this side of the interposed covering, when causeth the eclipse. This anxiety was only opposed to the actual happiness and natural fruition of God enjoyed in the personal union, not to any light of a moral duty required in Jesus Christ. But, 2. We are not to conceive that Christ's anxiety, fear and sorrow, were only imaginary, and supposed upon a mistake, that had not any *fundamentum in re*, ground in the thing itself; as *Jacob mourned and would not be comforted*, at the supposed death of his son Joseph, thinking he was torn with wild beasts, when the child was alive, and safe; and as the believer will sorrow that God hath *forsaken him*, and hath *forgotten to be merciful*, and that he is turned of a friend an enemy, when it is not so, but a great mistake; God hath not forgotten to be merciful; *The strength of Israel cannot repent and change.* Christ's darkness in this negative, and natural negative, he looking wholly on real sadness, death, wrath, the curse of the law; but not privative, or moral and culpably privative; for Christ had never a wrong thought of God, he did never believe God to be changed; nor did he, upon a misjudging of God, conceive God had forsaken him, when as he had not forsaken him, as if Christ's spiritual sense were deceived, in taking up a misapprehension of God, or his dispensation. And therefore that complaint, *Why [lamah] hast thou forsaken me?* hath not this meaning, as it hath in many places of scripture, *There is no cause why thou shouldst forsake me:* for there were just causes, why the Lord, at this time, should forsake his Son Christ. And therefore the forsaking of Christ was real; because grounded upon justice. The elect had forsaken God; Christ stood in their place, *to bear their iniquities*, Isa. liii. that is, the punishment which the elect should have suffered eternally in hell for their own iniquities: and in justice, God did for a time forsake his Son Christ, not only in sense and apprehension, but really. 2. Satan doth so mist and delude the weak believers, that because they will not mourn

nor

nor be humbled, for real objects, sins, unbelief, misspending of time, which are true causes of sorrow and mourning, they waste sorrow needlessly and sinfully; the righteous dispensation of God intervening for false and supposed causes, as through ignorance, for these things that are not sins, yet are falsely conceived to be fins; or through misapprehension, imagining that the Lord is changed, and become their utter enemy, when he cannot forget them, Isa. xlix. 14, 15, or through misjudging their own estate, conceiving they are reprobates, when there is no such matter. So, when we will not duly object, place and time our affections, 'tis righteousness with God, that we lose our labour, and spill and seed away our affections prodigally, in a wood of thorns, for nothing; because we do not give them out for Christ; and so we must sow and never reap. But Christ could not thus lavish away this fear, sorrow, sadness. I know there is a forsaking in God, joined with hatred: God neither in this sense forsook Christ, nor did Christ complain of this forsaking: God's forsaking of him, was in regard of the influence of actual vision, 2. Of the actual joy and comfort of union, 3. Of the penal inflicting of the curse, wrath, sorrow, sadness, stripes, death, on the man Christ.

Use. If Christ was put to, *What shall I say? what shall I do?* What a sad and forlorn condition are sinners in? how shiftless are they? Isa. x. 3. When God asketh of them, *What will ye do in the day of visitation, and in the desolation that shall come upon you from far? to whom will ye flee for help? where will ye leave your glory?* Jer. v. 31. *What will ye do in the end?* guiltiness is a shiftless and a forlorn thing. Take a man pained and tormented with the stone, he cannot lie on this side, he turneth to the other; he cannot lie, his couch cannot ease him; he casteth himself out of the bed to the floor of the house, he cannot rest there; no place, not paradise, say a man were tortured up in heaven before the throne, the place of glory, simply considered, should not ease him. What a desperate

course

course do the damned take, to *seek dens and rocks of the earth to hide themselves in?* Canst thou lodge under the roof of the creature, when the Creator armed with red and fiery wrath pursueth thee? And when that faileth them, and they dare not pray to God, they petition hills and mountains to be graves above them, to bury such lumps of wrath quick, Rev. vi.

2. I defy any man, with all his art, to be an hypocrite, and to play the politician in hell, at the last judgment, in the hour of death, or when the conscience is wakened. A robber doth never mock the law and justice at the gallows, whatever he do in the woods and mountains. Men do cry, and weep, and confess sins right-down, and in sad earnest, when conscience speaketh out wrath; there is no mind then of fig-leave-coverings, or of colours, vails, masks, or excuses.

3. Conscience is a piece of eternity, a chip that fell from a deity, and the nearest shadow of God, and endeth as it begins. At first, even by its natural constitution, conscience warreth against *concupiscence*, and speaketh sadly out of Adam, while it is hot, and not cold dead; *I was afraid, hearing thy voice, I hid myself*; and this it doth, Rom. i. 19. chap. ii. 15. While lusts buy and bribe conscience out of office, then it co-operateth with sin, and becometh dead: in the end when God shaketh an eternal rod over conscience, then it gathereth warm blood again, as it had in Adam's days; and hath a resurrection from death, and speaketh gravely and terribly, without going about the bush. O how ponderous and heavy! How far from tergiversation, clokings, and shifting, are the words that dying atheists utter, of the deceitfulness of sin, the vanity of the world, the terrors of God? Was not Judas in sad earnest? Did Saul speak policy, when he weepeth on the witch, and saith, *I am sore distressed?* Did Spira dissemble and sport, when he roared like a bear against divine wrath?

What

CHRIST DYING AND DRAWING SINNERS TO HIMSELF.

What shall I say?

This saith, that Christ, answering for our sins, had nothing to say; the sufferer of satisfactory pain, has no words of apology for sin. The friend that was to be cast in utter darkness, for coming to the supper of the great king, *without his wedding garment,* , his mouth was muzzled, as the mouth of a mad dog; he was speechless, and could not bark. When divine justice speaketh out of God, Job, chap. xl. answereth, v. 4. *Behold, I am vile, what shall I answer thee? I will lay my hand on my mouth.* When the church findeth justice pleading against her; 'tis thus, Ezek. xvi. 63. *That thou mayst remember (thy sins) and be confounded, and there may be no more an opening of a mouth, because of thy shame, when I am pacified toward thee, for all that thou hast done, saith the Lord.* I grant, satisfactory justice doth not here put men to silence, but it proveth how little we can answer for sin. Even David, remembering that Shimei, and other instruments, had deservedly afflicted him, in relation to Divine justice, saith, Psal. xxxix. 9. *I was dumb, I opened not my mouth, because thou didst it.* There were three demands of justice given in against Christ, all which he answered: justice put it home upon Christ, 1. All the elect have sinned, and by the law are under eternal wrath: to this claim, our Advocate and Surety could say nothing on the contrary; 'Tis true Lord. Christ doth satisfy the law, but not contradict it. The very word of the gospel answereth all these. In this regard, Christ's silence was an answer; and to this, Christ said, *What shall say?* I have nothing to say.

2. Thou art the sinner in law. To this Christ answered, *A body thou hast given me. The Son of man came not to be served, but to serve, and to give himself a ransom for many.* Mat. xx. 28. The whole gospel saith, *Christ, who knew no sin, was made sin for us.*

3. Thou must die for sinners; this was the third demand. And Christ answereth it, Psal. xl. Heb. x.

Thou hast given me a body, here am I to do thy will. To all these three Christ answered with silence; and tho', in regard of his patience to men, it be said, Isa. liii. 7. *He was brought as a Lamb to the slaughter, and as a sheep before the shearer is dumb, so he opened not his mouth;* yet it was most true, in relation to Divine justice, and the Spirit of God hath a higher respect to Christ's silence (which was a wonder to Pilate) before the bar of God's justice. O! could we by faith see God giving in a black and sad claim, a bill written within, and without, in which are all the sins of all the elect, from Adam to the last man; and Christ with watry eyes receiving the claim, and saying, *Lord, 'tis just debt, crave me, what shall I say on the contrary?* We should be more bold, not barely to name our sins, and tell them over to God, but to confess them, and study more for the answer of a good conscience, by faith to substitute an advocate, to answer the demands of justice for our sins: and if men believed that Christ, as surety satisfying for their sins, could say nothing on the contrary, but granted all; they should not make excuses and shifts, either to wipe their *mouth with the whore, and say, I have not sinned,* nor be witty to make distinctions, and shifts, and excuses to cover, mince and extenuate their sins.

Father, save me from this hour.

The fourth part of this complaint, is an answer that faith maketh to Christ's question, *What shall I say? What shall I do?* Say praying-wise (saith faith) *Father, save me from this hour.* A word of the coherence; then of the words. We often dream, that in trouble, help is beyond sea, and far off, as far as heaven is from the earth; when help is at our elbow: and if the Spirit of adoption be within, the prisoner hath the key of his own jail within, in his own hand. God was in Christ's bosom, when he was in a stormy sea, and the light of faith saith, *Behold, the shore at hand.* Death taketh feet and power of motion from a man; but, Psal. xxiii.4. yet faith maketh a

sup-

supposition, that David may walk and live, breathe in the grave, in *the valley of the shadow of death*. 'Tis the work of faith to keep the heat of life in the warm blood, even among clods of clay, when the man is buried. This anxious condition Christ was in (as other straits are to the saints) is a strait and narrow pass; there was *no help for him on the right hand, nor on the left*; nor before, nor behind, nor below. Christ, as David his type, Psal. cxli. 4. *Looked round about, but refuge failed him, no man cared for his soul;* but there was a way of escape above him, it was a fair easy way to heaven. The church was in great danger and trouble of war and desolation, when she spake to God, Psal. xlvi. Yet their faith seeing him to be very near them; *God is our refuge and strength:* true, he can save (saith sense) but that is a fowl flying in the woods, and over-sea-hop, far off: not far off (saith faith) *A very present help in trouble;* or a help easily, or [*Meod*] exceedingly found in trouble. So Psal. xliv. 9. *Thou hast cast us off.* Heb. *Thou art far from us, thou hast put us to shame.* What lower could the people be? v. 19. We are in the dungeon, *in the place of dragons*, we are in the cold grave, beside the worms and corruption; and thou hast covered us with the *shadow of death*, a cold bed. Yet then see what faith saith, verse 20. *We have not forgotten the name of our God. Our God* is a word of great faith. And to come to Christ; his soul was troubled; he was at, *What shall I say?* in a great perplexity. Yet he hath a strong faith, both of his Father, and of his own condition. He believed God to be his Father, and calleth him Father. Yea, in this hell, he applieth the relation of a Father to himself, Mat. xxvi. 39. *O my Father;* this is the warmest love-thought of God: and when his comfort was ebbest, his confidence in the covenant strongest; *My God, my God,* etc. 'Tis much glory to our Lord, that faith sparkle fire and be hot, when comfort is cold and low. O what an honour to God! the man is slain, and cold dead, yet he believes strongly the salvation of God! Christ kills the poor man, and the

man's

man's faith killeth and hangeth about Christ's neck, and says, *If I must die, let Christ's bosom be my death-bed.* Then he must believe, if God was his Father, by good logick, he must be the Son of God; and if God was his God, then the heir of all must claim the privileges of all the sons of the house in covenant. God (I may say) was more than Christ's God, and more than in covenant with God; as he was more than a servant, so more than a son, than a common one: and Christ's faith is so rational, and so binding with strength of reason, that he will but use such a weapon, as we may use, even the light of faith, and he will claim but the common benefit of all the sons in covenant, when he saith, *My God, my God.* Whatever Papists say, if ever Christ was in hell, it is now; but see, he hath heaven present with him in hell. If God could be apprehended by faith, in hell, as a God in covenant, then should hell become heaven to that believing soul, Christ took God, and his God, and his Father, as Jonah, a type of him, down to the bowels of hell with him: and as we see some dying men, they lay hold on something dying, and die with that in their hand, which we call the dead-grip; so Christ died with his Father by faith, and his spouse in regard of love stronger than the grave, in his arms. This was Christ's death embracings, his death-kiss; and Job professeth so much. Lower he could not be, than he complaineth he is, chap. xix. in all respects, of body, which was a clod of bones and skin; in regard of wife, servants, dear friends, of the hand of God in his soul: Yet, verse 25. *I know that my Goel, my kinsman, Redeemer liveth, and that he shall stand at the last man on the earth.*

Use. This leadeth us, in our forlorn perplexities, to follow Christ's footsteps, both under evils of punishment and sin. The people in their captivity in Babylon, Ezek. xxxvii. were an host of dead, and (which is more)

dry

† Saltmarsh, Free Grace, C. 5. p. 91, 93.

dry bones; the churches in Germany, in Scotland, are dry bones, and in their graves; the churches in Scotland and England, in regard of the sinful divisions and blasphemous opinions in the worship of God, are in a worse captivity, and lower than dry bones; and our woes are not at an end: yet the faith of many seeth, that deliverance and union there must be, and that our graves must be opened, and that the wind of the Lord must breathe upon the dry bones, that they may live. God hath in former times opened our graves, when strange lords had dominion over us: I would we were freed of them now also, but our yoke is heavier than it was; but God shall deliver his people from those that oppress them.

Again, as you see in great perplexity Christ believed God to be his Father, and that he himself was a Son; so are we, under pressures of conscience, and doubtings because of sin, to keep precious, high, and excellent love-thoughts of Jesus Christ.

Objection 1. "But what if a soul be brought to doubt of its conversion; because he findeth no good he either doth, or can do? True faith, is a working faith."

Answer. Some so cure this, as they prove physicians of no value to poor souls, I mean, Antinomians: for, say they, This is the disease, that *you, in doubting of your faith, because you find not such and such qualifications in you, therefore seek a righteousness in your self, and not in Christ.* I should easily grant, that man's inherent righteousness is, in his carnal apprehension, his very Christ and Redeemer; but in the mean time, these are two carnal and fleshly extremities, and faith walketh in the middle between them. 1. 'Tis a fleshly way to say, that, because I find sin reigning in me, I have killed my brother, saith a Cain, I have betrayed the Lord of glory, saith a Judas; yet I am not (saith a Libertine) to question, whether I believe or no; for this putteth fleshly and profane men on a conceit, *Be not solicitous what you are; take you no fear of serving sin and divers lusts, but believe,*

and

and never doubt, whether your faith be a dead, or a living faith, tho' you go on to walk after the flesh; but believe, and doubt not whether you believe or no. The other extremity is of some weak Christians, who because they find *that in them,* that is, *in their flesh, dwelleth no good,* and they sin daily, find much untowardness and back-drawing in holy duties; therefore (say they) *I have no faith, I am none of Christ's:* This is a false conclusion, drawn from a true antecedent, and springeth from a root of self-seeking, and righteousness which we naturally seek in ourselves; for I am not, being once justified, to seek my justification in my sanctification; but being not justified, I may well seek my non-justification in my non-sanctification. As Libertines say, this is the fault of all, when it is the fault only of some weak misjudging souls; so do they take the saints off from all disquietness and grief of mind for neglect of spiritual duties, as if all godly sorrow and displeasure of our sinful omissions, were nothing but a legal sorrow for want of self-righteousness and a sinful unbelief: but 'tis formally not any such thing, but lawful and necessary to make the sinner go with a low sail, and esteem the more highly of Christ; and 'tis only sinful, when abused to such a legal inference, *I omit this and this, I sin in this and this;* ergo, *God is not my Father, nor am I his son.*

But I hold this position, as evidently deducible out of the text, In the roughest and most bloody dispensation of God toward saints, neither soul-trouble, or anxiety of spirit, can be a sufficient ground to any, why they should not believe, nor question their sonship and relation to God, as their Father. 'Tis clear that Christ in his saddest condition believed and stood to it, that God was his Father: the only question will be, if sinful and fleshly waking be a good warrant. To which I answer, if any be a servant of sin, and walk after the flesh, and be given up to a reprobate mind to commit sin with greediness, such a one hath good warrant to believe that God is not his Father, and that he is not in

Christ;

Christ; because, 2 Cor. v. 17. *If any man be in Christ, he is a new creature.* If any be risen with Christ, he seeketh the things that are above, where Christ is at the right-hand of God. He is dead, and his life is hid with Christ in God. And he mortifieth his members on earth, Col. iii. 1, 2, 3, 4. He is redeemed from this present evil world. Gal. i. 4. He is dead to sin, and liveth to righteousness. 1 Pet. ii. 24. He is redeemed from his vain conversation. 1 Pet. i. 18. He is the temple of the Holy Ghost; he is not his own, but bought with a price; and is, being washed in Christ's blood, a king over his lusts, a priest to offer himself to God, *an holy, living and acceptable sacrifice,* 1 Cor. vi. 16, 20. Rev. i. 5, 6. Rom. xii. 1. But he that remaineth the servant of sin, and walketh after the flesh, and is given up to a reprobate mind, etc. is no such man; *ergo,* such a man hath no claim to God as his Father: and upon good grounds may, and ought to question his being in Christ. Only let these cautions be observed. 1. It is not safe to argue from the quantity of holy walking; for many sound believers may find untowardness in well-doing, yet must not cast away themselves for that. A smoking flax is not quenched by Christ, for that It hath little heat, or little light; and therefore ought not by us. 2. Beware we lean not too much to the quality of walking holily, to infer, *I fast twice a week, I give tithes of all I have*; then, *God I thank* him, I am not an hypocrite, as the publican, and a wicked man. Sincerity is a sensible speaking grace; 'tis seldom in the soul without a witness. *Lord, thou knowest that I love thee* (saith Peter) he could answer for sincerity, but not for quantity; he durst not answer Christ, that he knew that he loved him more than these. Sincerity is humble, and walketh on positives, *Lord, I love thee*; but dare not adventure on comparatives, *Lord, I love thee more than others.* 3. There be certain hours, when the believer cannot make strong conclusions, to infer, I am holy, therefore I am justified; because in darkness we see neither black nor white, and God's light hides our case from us, that we may be hum-

bled,

CHRIST DYING AND DRAWING SINNERS TO HIMSELF.

bled, and believe. 4. Believing is surer than too frequent gathering warmness from our own hot skin.

Saltmarsh, and other Libertines make three doubts that persons have as sufficient grounds, to question their being in Christ: 1. Backsliding. 2. The man's finding no change in the whole man. 3. Unbelief. Give me leave therefore in all meekness to offer my thoughts, in sifting and scanning this doctrine.

"This is then (*saith he**) your first doubt, that you are not therefore beloved of God, or in Christ, because you fell back again into your sin, so as you did. Suppose I prove to you, that no sin can make one less beloved of God, or less in Christ.

Answer. "Then I shall conclude, that sin cannot hinder the love of God to my soul.

Question "This I prove, 1. The mercies of God are sure mercies, his love, his covenant everlasting: Paul was persuaded that neither life, nor death, etc. could separate him from the love of God. The Lord changeth not in loving sinners. 2. Whom the Lord loveth, he loveth in his Son, he accounts him as his son; for he is made to us, righteousness, sanctification, and redemption. But God loveth his Son always alike; for he is the same yesterday, and today, and for ever: *Ergo*, Nothing can make God love us less; because he loves us not for ourselves, or for any thing in ourselves, etc. 3. God is not as man, or the son of man. Who shall lay any thing to the charge of God's chosen? The foundation of God standeth sure. God's love is as himself, ever the same."

Answer 1. The thing in question to resolve the sinner, whether he be loved of God, from eternity, as one chosen to glory, is never proved, because no sin can make one less beloved from eternity; and sin cannot hinder the love of God, (*non concluditur negatum;*) for

'tis

---

*Saltmarsh, in his Free-grace, or flowings of Christ's blood, etc. c. 4. p. 79, 80.

CHRIST DYING AND DRAWING SINNERS TO HIMSELF. 83

'tis true, sin cannot hinder the flowings and emanation of the love of election, it being eternal; else not any of the race of mankind, God seeing them all as guilty sinners, could ever have been loved with an eternal love. But the consequence is nought, *Ergo*, backsliders in heart, and servants of sin, have no ground to question, *whether they be loved with the love of eternal election, or not.*

2. This physician lays down the conclusion in question, which is to be proved, to the resolving of the man's conscience, that he may be cured; the thing to be proved to the sick man, say, he were a Judas wakened in conscience, is, that notwithstanding his betraying of Christ, yet *God loved him with an everlasting love, and he is in Christ.* Now he cureth Judas thus, God's love is everlasting, his covenant everlasting, no sin can hinder God to love Judas, or separate a traitor to Christ, from the love of Christ. Separation supposeth an union; less loving, supposeth loving: So he healeth the man thus; no disease can overcome or hinder the art of such a skilled physician to cure a dying man. But what if this skilled physician will not undertake to cure the man, nor to move his tongue for advice, nor to stir one finger to feel the man's pulse; *ergo*, The man must be cured. For if the man be a backslider in heart, and a servant of sin, Christ never touched his pulse. He hath as yet sure grounds to question, whether he be loved of God, or be in Christ, or no; for, except you prove the man *to be loved with an everlasting love,* you can prove nothing: and your argument will not conclude any thing for the man's peace, except you prove him to be chosen of God; which is his only question. But say that he *is loved from everlasting, and that he is in Christ,* by faith, 'tis easy to prove, that his *sins cannot change everlasting love, nor make him less beloved of God, nor separate him from the love of God.* You must then either remove the man's doubting, from signs inherent in the man, (and if he be a backslider in heart, you fetch fire and water from beyond the moon to cure him;) or you must fetch war-
rants

rants to convince him, from the mind, eternal counsels of love and free grace within God; and that is all the question between the man and you. You cannot prove God hath loved him from everlasting, because he hath loved him from everlasting. If Libertines in this argument intend to prove, that a chosen covert in Christ hath no ground to question, that he is not beloved of God and not in Christ, 1. That is nothing to the thesis of Antinomians, maintained by all, that *sinners, as sinners, are to believe God's eternal love in Christ to them; and so all sinners, elect or reprobate, are to believe the same.* 2. 'Tis nothing to the universal commandment, that all and every one in the visible church, wearied and loaden with sin, or not wearied and loaden, are immediately to come to Christ, and rest on him, as made of God to them, *their righteousness, sanctification, and redemption,* without any inherent qualification in them. 3. 'Tis nothing to the point of freeing all, and building a golden bridge to deliver all who are obliged to believe, elect or reprobate, from doubting whether they be in Christ or not, that they may easily come to Christ, and believe his eternal love and redemption in him, though they will be in the gall of bitterness and bonds of iniquity, and that immediately. Which golden paradise to heaven and Christ, Antinomians liberally promise to all sinners as sinners. I cannot believe that' tis so easy a step to Christ.

For the second: 'Tis a dream that God *loveth sinners with the same love every way, wherewith he loveth his own Son, Christ.* And why? Because God loveth us only for his own Son, and for nothing in us: *ergo,* far more it must follow, 'tis a far other, an higher, fountain love, wherewith the Father loveth his own eternal and consubstantial Son, the mediator between God and man; and that derived love wherewith he loveth us sinners. As the one is, 1. Natural, the latter free. 2. The love of the Father to the Son, as his consubstantial Son, and so far as 'tis essentially included in his love to Jesus Christ mediator, is not a love founded on grace and free mercy, which might never have been in God; because

cause essentially, the Father must love his Son, Christ, as his Son; and being mediator, he cannot for that renounce his natural love to him, which is the fundamental cause, why he loveth us for Christ his Son as mediator; but the love wherewith the Father loveth us for his Son, Christ, is founded on free grace and mercy, and might possibly never have been in God. For, 1. As he could not but beget his Son, he could not but love him; nature, not election, can have place in either; but it was his free will to create a man, or not create him. 2. He cannot but love his Son, Christ, but God might either have loved neither man or angel, so as chuse them to salvation, and he might have chosen other men and angels, than these whom he hath chosen; God hath no such freedom in loving his own consubstantial Son. 3. 'Tis an untruth, that God loveth his chosen ones, as he doth love his Son; that is with the same degree of love wherewith he loves his Son; I think that not far from either gross ignorance, or blasphemy. It possibly may be the same lover by proportion, with which the Father tendereth the Mediator or Redeemer, and all his saved and ransomed ones; but in regard of willing good to the creature loved, he neither loveth his redeemed with the same love wherewith he loveth his Son; except blasphemously we say, God hath as highly exalted all the redeemed, and *given to them a name above every name,* as he hath done to his own Son; nor doth he so love all his chosen ones, as he conferreth equal grace and glory upon all alike; as if one star differed not from another star in glory, in the highest heavens. Our own good works cannot make our Lord love us less or more, with the love of eternal election; but they may make God love us more with the love of complacency, and a sweeter manifestation of God in the fruits and gracious effects of his love. According to that, John xiv. 23. *Jesus said, if a man love me, he will keep my words, and my Father will love him, and we will come unto him, and make our abode with him.*

The third reason is the same with the first, and proveth nothing but a major proposition, not denied by the

dis-

disquieted sinner, which is this: *Whoever is justified and chosen, cannot be condemned; whomever the Lord once loveth to salvation, he must always love to salvation*; for his love is like himself, and changeth not. But the disquieted sinner is *chosen and loved to salvation.* This assumption is all the question; and the truth of a major proposition can never prove the truth of the assumption.

Saltmarsh, Free Grace, chap. iv. p. 83, 84, 85.
"Because you feel not yourself sanctified, you fear you are not justified. If you suppose that God takes in any part of your faith, repentance, new obedience, or sanctification, as a ground upon which he justifieth or forgiveth; you are clear against the word: *For if it be of works, it is no more of grace.* 2. It must then be the only evidence you seek for; and you ask for sanctification to help your assurance of justification: but take it in the scripture's way.

1. "In the scriptures, Christ is revealed to be our sanctification. Christ is made unto us righteousness, sanctification. I live, yet not I, but Christ liveth in me. Ye are Christ's, but ye are sanctified, but ye are justified in the name of the Lord Jesus. He hath quickened us together with Christ. We are his workmanship, created in Christ Jesus unto good works. Jesus Christ himself being the chief corner-stone. That Christ may dwell in your hearts by faith. That new man, which after God was created in righteousness and true holiness. We are members of his body, of his flesh, and of his bones. And being found in him, not having mine own righteousness. I can do all things through Christ which strengtheneth me. But Christ is all in all. Your life is hid with Christ in God, Heb. xiii. 20, 21. All these set forth Christ as our sanctification, the fulness of his, the All in all. Christ hath believed perfectly for us, he hath sorrowed for sin perfectly, he hath obeyed perfectly, he hath mortified sin perfectly; and all is ours, and we are Christ's, and Christ is God's.

"The

"The second thing is faith about our own sanctification. We must believe more truth of our own graces than we can see or feel; the Lord in his dispensation hath so ordered, that here our life should be hid with Christ in God, that we should walk by faith, not by sight: so we are to believe our repentance true in him, who hath repented for us; our mortifying sin true in him, thro' whom we are more than conquerors; our new obedience true in him, who hath obeyed for us, and is the end of the law to every one that believeth; our change of the whole man true in him, who is righteousness and true holiness. And thus, without faith, 'tis impossible to please God. This is scripture assurance, to see every one in himself as nothing, and himself every thing in Christ. Faith is the ground of things hoped for, and the evidence of things not seen. All other assurances are rotten conclusions from the word, invented by legal teachers, not understanding the mystery of the kingdom of Christ. The scriptures bid you see nothing in yourself, or all as nothing: These teachers bid you see something in yourself; so as the leaving out Christ in sanctification, is the foundation of all doubts, fears, distractions. And he that looketh on his repentance, on his love, on his humility, on his obedience, and not in the tincture of the blood of Christ, must needs believe weakly and uncomfortably."

Answer. If a servant of sin, any Cain, wakened with the terrors of God, see his sins, feel hell in his soul for them, and have no warm thoughts of love, and far-off affiance, at least in *Christ Jesus*; but flee from Christ, and go to the enemies of Christ for comfort, as Judas did; he may strongly conclude, I feel I am not sanctified, I hate the physician Christ, and run from him; *Ergo,* I am not justified. And from a true real non-feeling of sanctification, 'tis a strong consequence, there's no justification. But from a misprizing of grace and sanctification in myself, I cannot conclude,

I am not justified. We know, Papists, in point of certainty of salvation, argue so; many deluded hypocrites believe, or imagine, they have oil in their lamps, yet they are deceived; therefore the saints can have no certainty they are in Christ. 'Tis just like the answer now in hand: a misjudging of sanctification, cannot argue no justification; *Ergo*, a true and real judgment of no sanctification in hypocrites, and slaves of sin, cannot argue the persons to be justified, who thus argue. It is as if I should argue thus; a frantick and a sleeping man cannot know that he is frantick, and sleeping; therefore a sober and waking man cannot know that he is sober, and waking. For a deserted child of God is in some spiritual phrensy and sleep, and does misprize Christ in himself, and sanctification; and therefore argueth often, that he is not in Christ, upon false principles. But a wakened conscience in Cain, and Judas, do strongly conclude, I am not a new creature, but a servant of sin; *Ergo*, I am not justified, and not in Christ: and Cain in this consequence is sober, and not asleep.

2. Not any protestant divine, whom the author calleth legal teachers, ignorant of the mystery of the gospel; did ever teach, that faith, new obedience, repentance, are grounds upon which God justifieth a sinner. Antinomians, who make repentance and mortification all one with faith; and, as Mr. Den saith, they are but a change of the mind, to seek righteousness and mortification in Christ, not in ourselves; (thus much   doth signify) must say, As we are justified by faith, so also by repentance and mortification; if repentance be nothing but faith, as they say.

3. We seek only the evidence of justification in our holy walking; as the scripture doth, 1 Pet. i. 24. Gal. i. 4. 1 Pet. i. 18. 1 John iii. 14. Infinite places say, these that live to Christ, and are new creatures, must be in Christ, and justified, 2 Cor. v. 17. 1 Cor. vi. 9, 10, 11, 12. Gal. ii. 20. Col. iii. 1, 2, 3, 4. Then the arguing from the effect to the cause can be no rotten conclusion, except by accident, in a fool distempered under desertion and weakness.

4. These

4. These places that make Christ our sanctification, and Christ to live in us, and believers to be the workmanship of *Jesus, created in him, unto good works,* etc. make not these to be acts of *Christ formally repenting perfectly in us, sorrowing for sin, mortifying sin perfectly in us;* as if we were mere patients, and were only obliged to repent, sorrow, mortify sin, when the Spirit breatheth on us, and not otherwise, as Libertines explain themselves; which I hope to refute hereafter. 2. Nor do these places make justification and regeneration all one; as Mr. Towne*, with other Antinomians do: for, we are not regenerated by faith, but that we may believe; but we are justified by faith. 2. Regeneration putteth in us a new birth, the image of the second Adam; justification formally is for the imputed righteousness of Christ, which is in Christ, not in us. And it seems to me, that they make justification and sanctification all one: for, the author saith, that *Christ not only repenteth in us, but for us; Christ obeyed for us, and is the end of the law to every one that believeth.* Now, what mysterious sense can be here, I cannot dream; sure, it is no gospel secret: if the meaning (that *Christ repenteth, and obeyed for us,*) be, that Christ, by his grace, worketh in us repentance, and new obedience, and mortification, and the change of the whole man; 'tis a good and sound sense. But then, how must all assurances from repentance and new obedience, *be the rotten conclusions of legal teachers?* To see all these wrought by Christ, as the efficient and meritorious cause, and to ascribe them to the Spirit of Jesus, and thence conclude, we are justified, as all Protestant divines teach, is no rotten conclusion of legal teachers. For sure, if we ascribe them to nature, to free will, to ourselves, and confide in them, as parts of our righteousness; and from them, in that notion, draw the assurance of our justification, as Papists and Arminians do, and as the saints out of fleshly presumption may do;

this

---

*Towne's Asser. of grace, p. 32.

this is no doctrine of Protestants. Is the sun obliged to me, because I borrow light from it? or the floods and rivers beholden to men, because they drink out of them? The new man is a creature of Christ's finding. Cursed be they that sacrifice to free will; it is a strange God. The kingdom of grace, is a hospital of free graces to sick men: all we do, the least good thought, or gracious motion in the soul, is a flower, and a rose of Christ's planting, and an apple that grew on the tree of life; a sinner is the stock, but free grace the sap, Christ's Father the husbandman; life and growing is from Jesus the vine-tree; we are but poor twigs that bring forth fruit in Christ. But I fear the sense of this, that *Christ repenteth for us, and obeyeth for us, he being the end of the law to every one that believeth;* be far otherwise, to wit, That Christ's obedience of the law, he being the end of the law, as also his passive obedience, is ours. If this be the intended sense, then all our sanctification is nothing, but the sanctification and holy active obedience of Christ. I yield this to be a broad, a fair and easy way to heaven. Christ doth all for us, Christ weeped for my sins, and that is all the repentance required in me; if I believe that Christ was mortified, and dead to the world for me, that is my mortification; and if I believe, that the change of the whole man was truly in Christ, this is my true holiness: then my walking in holiness cannot be rewarded with life eternal, nor have any influence, as a way, or means leadeth to the kingdom. 2. Christ's active obedience, imputed to the sinner, can be no evidence of justification, because it is in Christ, not in me; any evidence, or mark of justification, must be inherent in the believer, not in Christ. 3. And one and the same thing cannot be a mark and a sign of itself. Now, the active obedience of Christ, imputed to the sinner, is holden to be a part of justification.

    5. The scripture doth indeed bid you see nothing in yourself, that can buy the righteousness of Christ, or be an hire and wages to ransom imputed righteousness; and legal teachers, not any Protestant divines,

bid

bid you see something, a great something of merit, and self-righteousness in yourself. And Antinomians say, That (*a*) the new creature, or the new man mentioned in the gospel, is not meant of grace, but of Christ. The scripture maketh Christ and justification the cause, and sanctification and the new creature the effect, 2 Cor. v. 17. *If any man be in Christ, he is a new creature.* And this assertion maketh sanctification, as formally distinguished from Christ and justification, just nothing. And Antinomians say, (*b*) That in the regenerate and saints, *There is no inherent righteousness, no grace or graces in the souls of believers, but in Christ only.* And Mr. Saltmarsh saith the same, *That our sorrow, repentance, mortification, and change of the whole man, are nothing in us; but they are in Christ, and must be apprehended by faith as things unseen:* Whereas, the divine nature is in the saints, 2 Pet. i. 4. *Faith dwelleth in us.* 2 Tim. i. 5. The new creation and image of *Christ is in the mind,* Eph. iv. 23. *The seed of God abideth in us,* 1 John iii. 9. *The anointing that teacheth all things, remaineth in you.* 1 John ii. 27. and Ezek. xxxvi. 26. *I will give you an heart of flesh, and I will put my Spirit* [*Bekirbechem*] *in the inner part, or the midst of you.*

Antinomians teach, (*c*) "That true poverty of spirit doth kill and take away the sight of grace." And, (*d*) "Sanctification is so far from evidencing a good state, that it darkens it rather; and a man may more clearly see Christ, when he seeth no sanctification, than when he sees it; the darker my sanctification is, the brighter is my justification." So Saltmarsh, "The scriptures bid you see nothing in yourself, or all as nothing; these teachers bid you see something in yourself. And 'tis a walking by faith, and not by

sight;

(a) Rise, Reign, Error, 7. p. 2.
(b) Rise, Reign, Error, 15. p. 3.
(c) Rise, Reign, Error, 17 p. 4.
(d) Rise, Reign, Error, 77. p. 15.

"sight; and a life hid with Christ in God, to believe more truth in our own graces, than we see or feel." Now, 'tis true, the saints out of weakness, misprize the Spirit's working in them; and while they undervalue themselves, they under-rate the new creation in themselves, and tacitly upbraid and slander the grace of Christ, and lessen the heavenly treasure, because it is in an earthen vessel; but poverty of spirit and grace will see, and do see grace inherent in itself, tho' as the fruit of grace, Cant. i. 5. *I am black (O daughters of Jerusalem,) but comely, as the tents of Kedar.* v. 11. *While the king sitteth at his table, my spikenard sendeth forth the smell thereof.* The saints, as they make a judgment of Christ and his beauty, so also of themselves; *My heart waked. I am sick of love.* Psal. cxvi. 16. *O Lord, truly I am thy servant.* Psal. lxiii. 1. *My soul thirsteth for thee, my flesh longeth after thee.* Psal. lxxiii. 25. *Whom have I in heaven but thee? and there is none upon earth that I desire besides thee.* Psal. cxxx. 6. *My soul waiteth for the Lord, more than they that watch for the morning.* So Hezekiah, Isa. xxxviii. 3. Paul, 2 Cor. i. 12. 2 Tim. iv. 7, 8. 1 Cor. xv. 9, 10. and others have set out in its colours, the *image of Christ* in itself; but not as leaving out Christ, and taking in merit: Nor doth the *sense of sanctification darken justification*, or lessen it to nothing, except where we abuse it to merit, and self-confidence, as Peter did; who, in point of self-confidence ought to have forgotten the things that are behind. 2. Yea, to say, *We see justification more clearly, when we see no sanctification,* is to make the *water and the Spirit*, 1 John v. 8. dumb, or false witnesses, that either speak nothing, or tell us lies. 3. It is against the office of the Spirit, which is to *make us know the things that are freely given us of God*, such as faith, repentance, love, mortification, Acts v. 3. 2 Tim. ii. 25. Phil. i. 29. Eph. ii. 8. Rom. v. 5. Gal. ii. 20. I grant, by accident, when sin appeareth to a saint out of measure sinful, and he seeth how little good he hath, that *he is blind, naked, poor, and hath no money, nor*

price

CHRIST DYING AND DRAWING SINNERS TO HIMSELF.

price, that he is sold as a wretched man under a body of sin, Rom. vii. 14, 24. it heighteneth the excellency and worth of the ransom and blood holden forth in justification: and white righteousness, free and glorious, set beside black guiltiness, and no sanctification compearing as price or hire, maketh Christ appear to be choicer than gold or rubies. Yea, when I see no sanctification to buy Christ, then justification is more lovely, eye sweet, taking, and soul-ravishing; as the more light, the more darkness is discovered; and the more sin, the higher is Jesus Christ. And by all this, the saints professing their own integrity, and holy walking before God, should see something in themselves, not understanding the mystery of the gospel, and err miserably with legal teachers, and darken free justification by grace: and one grace of God should obscure and destroy another; for to see, feel, and profess sanctification, is an act of supernatural feeling, and of grace: how then can it darken the faith of the remission of sins in Christ?

But, it may be asked, when the saints cannot be assured that God is their Father, in regard of sin, unbelief, and present deadness, what reasons would you use to raise their spirits up to the assurance of their interest and relation to God, as to their Father?

Ans. There is no way of arguing saints out of their unbelief, except he that laboureth to strengthen them, being an *Interpreter, one of a thousand,* who can shew a man his righteousness, be so acquainted with the condition of the afflicted soul, that he see in him some inherent qualification, that may argue to the physician, there is some, less or more, of Christ in the soul of the man; else, if he know him to be a person yet utterly void of Christ, sure he must deal with him that is under the law, in a more legal and violent manner, than with him whom he conceiveth to be under the gospel; for one and the same physic cannot suit with contrary complexions. The author professeth he dealeth with *sinners as sinners*, and so with all sinners; as if physic for the gout were fit physic for the stone in the blad-
der.

der. I go not so high, but speak to a weak son, who hath God for his Father, but, under soul-trouble, doubteth whether God be his Father or not.

If he lay down a principle, that he was never in Christ, because of such and such sins; you are not, whoever intends to cure him, to yield so much, and to deal with him according to a false supposal, as if he were not in Christ; but must labour to prove he is in Christ; which to no purpose is done, by proving fair generals, as Saltmarsh, with other Libertines, doth; that is, you but till the sand, and beat the air, to prove, *That God's love is eternal*, and his covenant and decree of election to his chosen, so stable and unalterable, as no sin can hinder the flowings of eternal love; when you make not sure to the man, that he is loved with an everlasting love.

Hence these considerations, for easing the afflicted conscience of a weak child of God.

Asser. 1. The soul labouring under doubts, whether God be his Father, is to hold off two rocks, either confiding or resting on duties, or neglecting of duties: the former is to make a Christ of duties as if Christ himself were not more lovely and desirable, than the comfortable accidents of joy, comfort, and peace in doing duties. Yea, take the formal vision of God, in an immediate fruition in heaven, as a duty, and as in that notion contradistinguished from the objective vision of Christ; then Christ is to be enjoyed, loved, rested on, infinitely above the duties of vision, beatific love, eternal resting on him, yea, above imputed righteousness, assurance of pardon, reconciliation; as the king is more than his bracelets of gold, his myrrh, spikenard, perfumes, ointment, kisses; the tree more desirable than a fleece of apples that groweth on it for the fourth part of a year. 2. Sin, it must be to sue and woo the king's attendants and courtiers by himself, or to make duties Christ, and Christ but a man servant and mediator to duties, sense, comfort, assurance, or the like. 3. The whelps of the bear are taken from her by swift riding away with them, and by

casting

casting down one of them, that she may lose time in gaining the rest, while she returneth back again so many miles to bring that one to the den. And the smell of some delicious fields, they say, so taketh the dogs, that they forget the prey, and follow it no more. To smell so much in duties, and to be so sick and impotent in loving and resting on them, as to lie down in the way, and seek Christ no more, is doubtless a neglect of Christ. And thus high our doctrine never advanced sanctification, nor enthroned any acts, duties, or qualifications, under the notion of witnesses, or creators of peace or reconciliation; how our hearts may abuse them, is another thing.

Asser. 2. What, advise you then a deserted soul to go on in duties, and seek righteousness in himself? By no means; to seek righteousness in himself, that is highest pride: but will you call it pride, for a starving man to beg? Is it self-denial for such a one to be stark dumb, and to pray none in his famishing condition for food? Did the spouse seek herself in this duty? Cant. iii. *Watchman, saw ye him whom my soul loveth?* Was this a resolution of pride? chap. iii. 2. *I will rise now, and go about the city, in the streets, and in the broad ways, I will seek him whom my soul loveth.* And is it self-righteousness for the spouse to send her hearty respects of service to Christ, when she cannot have one word from him, nor one smile? Cant. v. 6. *Tell my Beloved, that I am sick of love.* Nor do I think Mary Magdalene was in a distemper of pharisaical righteousness, when she rose and prevented the morning-sky, and came weeping to the grave; *O angels, saw ye the Lord?* Gardener, whither have you carried him? May I not do these duties, when I miss him? May I not wake in the night? May I not do well to feed a love-fever for the want of him? May I not both pray, and say, *Daughters of Jerusalem, pray for me?* May I not make a din through all the streets and the broad ways, and trouble all the watchmen and shepherds, and pray them, Can you lead me to his tent, and tell me where he lieth? O but all these were to be

done

done in faith: true, but are they not duties of lovesickness I owe to Christ also? I know they cannot bring me to everlasting righteousness; but is not seeking and knocking, stairs to finding and opening?

Asser. 3. Another counsel is, force not a lawsuit, seek not, buy not a plea against Christ. Conscience, a tender piece under jealousies, saith, O he loveth not me, Christ hath forgotten me: join not in such a quarrel with conscience. Have not cold and low thoughts of Christ's love to you; because he is out of sight, he is not out of languor of love for you.

Asser. 4. Unbelief is a witch, an inchantress, and covers Christ's face with a vail of hatred, wrath, displeasure. Examine what grounds of reason you have to misbelieve or break with Christ; say he had broken with you, yet because you know it not for suspicion, lose not such a friend as Christ; if you get never more of him, you may swear and vow to take to hell with you (if so he deal with you) the pawns, and love-tokens you once received, that they may be witnesses what Christ is, and may be the remnants, seeds, and leavings, of the high esteem you once had of him.

Asser. 5. A time Christ must have to go and come, and therefore must be waited on. We give the sea hours to ebb and flow, and the moon days to decrease and grow full; and the winter-sun and summer-sun months to go away and return; and whether we will or no, God and nature take their time, and ask us no leave: why had God given to us eyes within and without, but that David may wear his eyes, while they be at the point of failing, in looking up, and *in waiting for God?* Psal. lxix.

Asser. 6. And though you were in hell, and he in heaven, he is worthy to be waited on; the first warm smile of a new return, is sufficient to recompense all sorrow in his absence, to say nothing of everlasting huggings and embracings.

Asser.

CHRIST DYING AND DRAWING SINNERS TO HIMSELF.

Asser. 7. Nor is this a good reason; || I find sin, rottenness, and so a deserved curse, in all my works of sanctification; therefore, why should I make them any bottom for assurance? But I must take in Christ here for sanctification: for if works of this kind be not done in faith, to the knowledge of the doer; they can witness nothing, but bear a false testimony of Christ: nor do we ever teach, that Christ is to be discourted from our works of sanctification; but even faith itself, which is a bottom of peace to Antinomians, by this reason, must be cashiered. For as the love of Christ, our prayers, humility, are not formally sins, but only concomitantly, in regard that sin adhereth to them; as muddy water is not formally clay and mud, but in mixture 'tis clayey and muddy; so our faith is concomitantly sinful; both because often it is weak, and so wanting many degrees, and mixed with sin, deserves a curse, as well as works of sanctification; but it apprehendeth Christ and righteousness in him, and so it bottometh our assurance: if by apprehending, you mean to bring to you certain knowledge, and assurance that Christ is made my righteousness; then you beg the question, if you deny this to works of sanctification. For, 1 John ii. 3. *Hereby we know that we know him, if we keep his commandments.* Ver. 5. *And whoso keepeth his word, in him verily the love of God is perfected:* Hereby, (that is, by keeping his word, called twice before, *ver.* 3, 4. *The keeping of his commandments;* and verse 6. *walking as he walked:*) *Hereby* (saith he,) *know we, that we are in him, in Christ* our propitiation and righteousness; and thus we are justified *by keeping the commandments of God*, because by this we apprehend, and know that we are justified. 2. But then all that are justified, must be fully persuaded of their justification, and that faith is essentially a persuasion and assurance of the love of God to me in Christ; 'tis more than I could ever learn to be the nature of faith, a consequent separable I believe it is. 3. If by apprehending Christ and

his

|| Saltmarsh, Free Grace,c. 4. p. 18.

his righteousness, be understood a relying, and fiducial acquiescing and recumbency on Christ for salvation: it is granted in this sense, that faith is a bottom to our assurance of our being in Christ; but that it breedeth assurance, in a reflect knowledge, always that a believer is in Christ, is not true: for, 1. I may believe, and be justified, and not know; yea positively doubt, that I believe, and am justified; as thousands have pardon, and have no peace nor assurance of their pardon, and have faith in Christ, and in his free love, and have no feeling of Christ, and of his free love. For we believe (a) more truth of our own graces (and so of our faith and assurance of our pardon) *than we can see or feel, which is God's dispensation, that our life should be hid with Christ in God;* Ergo, the life of faith, by which the just doth live, is hid; and above the reach of feeling at all times. 2. As faith, which is the direct act of knowing and relying on Christ for pardon, is a work of the Spirit above the reach of reason; so also the reflect act of my knowing and feeling, that I believe and am in Christ, which proceedeth sometimes from faith, and the immediate testimony of the Spirit; sometimes from our walking in Christ, 1 John ii. 3, 4. 1 John iii. 14. is a supernatural work, above the compass and reach of our free will, and is dispensed according to the spirations and stirrings of the free grace of God; and as the keeping of his commandments, *actu primo*, and in itself, giveth testimony that the soul is in Christ, and justified, even as the act of believing, in itself doth the same; yet that we, *actu secundo*, efficaciously know and feel that we are in Christ, from the irradiation and light of faith, and sincere walking with God, is not necessary, save only when the wind of the actual motion and flowing of the Spirit concur with these means; just as the gospel-promises of themselves are life and power, but they then only actually, *actu secundo*, animate and quicken withered souls, when

the

(a) Saltmarsh, ibid. 84.

CHRIST DYING AND DRAWING SINNERS TO HIMSELF.

the Lord is pleased to contribute his influence, in the shinings of his Spirit. Otherwise I may walk in darkness, yea, believe, pray, love, die for pain of love, and have no light of reflect knowledge and feeling that I am in Christ, Isa. l. 10. I may be sick of love for Christ, call, knock, pray, confer with the watchmen and daughters of Jerusalem, and be at a low ebb in my own sense; yea the Beloved may to my feeling and actual assurance have withdrawn himself, Cant. iii. 1, 2, 3, 4, 5. Cant. v. 5, 6, 7, 8. and all my inherent evidences cannot quicken me in my tolerable assurance. 'Tis true, sanctification may be darkened, yea, and faith also, when there is nothing to the faith-failing and outer dying but this only of Christ the head, all the life of a saint retiring not to his faint heart, but to his strong head, *I have prayed for you that your faith fail not:* but the dark evening of David's, both faith and sanctification, and of Peter in his denying of his Master, and his judaizing, Gal. ii. When he and others, ver. 14.

do crook and halt between grace and law, as the people did between Jehovah and Baal; their profession of Jehovah and Christ's grace being long, and their practice short, and inclining too much to Baal, and salvation by the law: as halting is a walking with a long and a short leg, the body unevenly inclining to both sides of the way: this darkening (I say) was in the second acts of faith and sanctification; but life and sap was at the root of the oak-tree, when it was lopt, hewed, and by winter storms spoiled of the beauty of its leaves. We do not say, that sanctification doth at all times, actually bear witness, or alike sensibly, and convincingly, that the soul is justified, is in Christ; and there be degrees, and intermission, and sick days, both of faith and sanctification. But we say, roses and flowers have been ever since the creation, and shall be to the end of the world, because though they vanish in winter, yet in their causes they are as eternal as the earth; so is faith and the bloomings, and green blossomings of

sanc-

sanctification, always; but there is a summer when they cast forth their leaves and beauty.

Asser. 8. To press duties out of a principle of faith, is to press Christ upon souls; nor can the seeing of beams, and light in the air, or of wine-grapes on the tree, be a denying of the sun to be in the firmament, or of life and sap to be in the vine-tree: to see and feel in ourselves grapes, and fruits of righteousness, except we make the grace of Christ a bastard, and mis-father it, is no darkening of Christ, and free grace, 1 Cor. xv. 9, 10.

Asser. 9. There is a great difficulty, yea, an impossibility, when the Lord hides himself, and goeth behind the mountain, to command the flowing and emanations of free-grace.

1. Because desertion were not desertion, if it were under the dominion of our free-will. For desertion, as a punishment of sin, cannot be in the free-will of him that is punished; every punishment, as such, is contrary to the will of the punished: and desertion, as an act of free dispensation for trial, must be a work of omnipotent dominion.

2. As in works of nature and art, so is it here, that God may be seen in both; do not men sweat, till, sow much, and the sun and summer, and clouds, warm dews and rains smile upon corns and meadows, yet God steppeth in between the mouth of the husbandman and the sickle, and blasteth all; and the Lord takes away the physme, stay and staff of corn and grass; and there is bread enough, and yet famine and starving for hunger? Do not some rise early, and go late to bed, eat the bread of sorrow; yet the armed soldier of God, extreme poverty, breaketh in upon the house? Do not watchmen wake all the night, yet the city is surprised and taken in the dawning, because the Lord keepeth not the city? The Lord doth all this, to shew that he is the supreme and absolute Lord of all second causes. Why, but he hath as eminent and independent a Lordship in the acts of his free departure and return, in the sense of his love. Hath not the King of saints

a withdrawing room, and an hiding-place? Is not his presence and manifestations his own? The deserted soul prayeth, crieth, weepeth; the pastor speaketh with the tongue of the learned; the christian friend argueth, exhorteth; experience and the days of old come to mind; the promises convince, and speak home to the soul; the poor *man remembereth God, and he is troubled;* the church, and many churches pray, christians weep and pray; yet Christ is still absent; the man cannot have, from all these, one half smile from Christ's face; the vision will not speak one word of joy: all these can no more command a raging sea and stormy winds to be still, and create calmness in the soul, than a child is able to wheel about the third heavens, in a course contrary to its natural motion. Omnipotency is in this departure, God himself is in the dispensation, and absolute freedom of an independent dominion acteth in the Lord's covering of himself with a cloud, and putteth an iron crossbar on the door of his pavilion; and can you stir omnipotency, and remove it? Think you, praying can charm and break independent dominion, working to shew itself as a dominion?

3. The sense of Christ which is wanting in desertion, cannot be enforced by persuasion, no more than you can, by words, persuade the deaf to hear. Oratory cannot make the taste feel the sweetness of honey. There is a light that cometh from heaven, above the sun and moon; yea, above the gospel; and is not extracted or educed out of the potency of either the soul, nay nor of the gospel; (I conceive,) that bringeth forth, in act, the *white stone, and the new name*: and as nature and instincts natural perform their natural duties without any oratory, so as persuasion cannot make the fire to burn, nor the sun to shine, nor the bird to build its nest, nor the lamb to know its mother; nature doth all these: so neither doth the persuasion of Paul, preaching the gospel, Acts xxvi. 28. Acts xvi. 14. the same thing, and every way the same work that the Lord doth, in persuading *Japhet to dwell*

in

in the tents of Shem, Gen. ix. 27. I could easily admit, that we are patients in receiving the predetermination active of the Holy Ghost in either believing, or in actual enlightening, and the actual witness-light by which Christ shineth in the heart for producing actual assurance; though in the same moment and order of time (not of nature) we be also agents.

Asser. 10. Though means must not be neglected, as praying and waiting on the watch-tower, for the breathings of renewed assurance; yet as touching the time, manner, way and measure of the *speaking of the vision,* God's absolute dominion is more to be respected here, than all the stirrings and motions of the under wheels of prayer, preaching, conference.

Asser. 11. The soul should be argued with, and convinced thus: why, will you not give Christ your good leave to tutor and guide you to heaven? he hath carried a world of saints over the same seas you are now in, and Christ paid the fare of the ship himself, not one of them are found dead on the shore; they were all as black and sun-burnt as you are, but they are now a fair and beautiful company, without spot before the throne, and clothed in white; they are now on the sunny side of the river, in the good land where glory groweth, far above sighing and jealousy. You are guilty of the breach of the privilege of Christ; 1. He is a free Prince, and his prerogative-royal is uncapable of failing against the fundamental laws of righteousness, in the measuring out either work or wages, grace, or glory. Matth. xx. 13. *Friend, I do thee no wrong: mine own is mine own.*

Object. O but he is sparing in his grace! his love-visits are thin sown, as strawberries in the rock.

Answ. I answer for him; 1. The quantity of grace is a branch of his freedom. 2. Why do you not complain of your sparing improving of two talents, rather than of his niggard giving of one only? He cannot sin against his liberty in his measuring out of grace; you cannot but sin in receiving. Never man, except the man Christ, durst, since the creation, (the holiest I will

not

not except) face an account with God, for evangelic receipts; Christ to this day is behind with Moses, David, Isaiah, Jeremiah, Job, Peter, John, Paul, and all the saints, in the using of grace; they were below grace, and Christ was necessitate to write in the close of their counts, with a pen of grace, and ink of his blood, *Friend, you owe me this, but I forgive you.* They flew all up to heaven with millions of arrears, more than ever they wrought for: as some godly rich man may say, this poor man was indebted to me thousands, now he is dead in my debt, I forgive him, his grave is his acquittance; I have done with it. Christ upbraids you not with old debts, that would sink you; why cast ye up in his teeth his free gifts? 3. Think it mercy he made you not a gray stone, but a believing saint: and there is no imaginable comparison, between his free gifts, and your bad deserving.

2. The way of his going and coming should not be quarrelled. The Lord walketh here in a liberty of dispensation; a summer-sun is heritage to no land. It was not a blood of a daily temper that Paul was in, when he said, Rom. viii. 38. *For I am persuaded, that neither death, nor life, etc. shall be able to separate us from the love of God in Christ.* It was a high and great feast, when Christ saith to his church, Cant. v. 1. *I am come into my garden, my sister, my spouse; I have gathered my myrrh with my spice, I have eaten my honey-comb with my honey: eat, O friends, drink, yea drink abundantly, O Beloved.* 'Tis true, he is always in his church, his garden, gathering lilies; but storms and showers often cover his garden.

3. Were assurance always full moon, as Christ's saith in his saddest soul-trouble was bank-full sea, and full moon; and were our joy over full, then should the saints heaven on earth, and their heaven above the visible heavens, differ in the accident of place, and happily, in some fewer degrees of glory; but there is a wisdom of God to be reverenced here. The saints in this life are narrow vessels; and such old bottles could not contain the *new wine that Christ drinketh with his*

in

in his Father's kingdom. Mat. xvii. When the disciples see the glory of Christ in the mount, Peter saith, v. 4. *Lord, it is good for us to be here:* but when that glory cometh nearer to them, and a cloud overshadows them, Luke ix. 34. and they hear the voice of God speak out of the cloud, Mark ix. 7. *They fell down on their face,* Mat. xvii. 6.
. *They were sore afraid:* Why afraid? because of the exceeding glory, which they testified was good, but knew not what they said. We know not that this joy is unspeakable. We rejoice, with joy that no man can relate: how then can a man contain it? I may speak of a thousand millions of things more excellent and glorious than I can feel. Should God pour in as much of Christ in us in this life, as we would in our private wisdom or folly desire, *the vessel would break, and the wine run out:* we must cry sometimes, *Lord, hold thy hand.* We are as unable to bear the joys of heaven in this life, as to endure the pains of hell. Every drop of Christ's honey-comb is a talent weight; and the fulness of it must be reserved, till we be enlarged vessels, fitted for glory.

Asser. 12. We do not consider, that Christ absent hath stronger impulsions of love, than when present in sense and full assurance; as is clear in that large song of the high praises of Christ, which is uttered by the church, Cant. v. when he had withdrawn himself, ver. 6. and *she was sick of love for him,* ver. 9, 10, 11, 12, 13, 14, 15, 16. (2.) There is a sort of heavenly antiperistasis, a desire of him kindled, through occasions of absence, as we are hottest in seeking after precious things, when they are absent, and farthest from our enjoying. Absence sets on fire love. The impression of his kissing, embracing, lovely and patient knocking, *Open to me, my sister, my love, my dove;* the print of his footsteps, the remnants of the smell of his precious ointments, his shadow when he goeth out at the doors, are coals to burn the soul, Psal. lxiii. 6. *When I remember thee upon my bed, and meditate on thee in the night watches.* I cannot sleep for the love of Christ, in the

night.

night. What follows? Ver. 8. *My soul follows hard, cleaveth strong after thee.* Psal. lxxvii. 3. *I remembered God, and was troubled;* rather, I remembered God, and rejoiced: but the memory of old love, and of absent and withdrawn consolations, breaks the heart. How do some weep, and cast aside their harps, when they remember the seven-year-old embracements of Christ, and Christ's virgin love, and Sion-sweet songs in the days of their youth? Cant. v. when the *church rose,* but after the time, to open to Christ, when he was gone, and had withdrawn himself, Ver. 5. *Mine hands* (saith the church) *dropped with myrrh, and my fingers with sweet smelling myrrh upon the handles of the bar.* Then her love to Christ was strongest, her bowels moved; the smell of his love, like sweet-smelling myrrh, was mighty rank, and piercing.

Asser. 13. Why, but then, when the wheels are on moving, and the longing after Christ awaked, and on foot, we should pray Christ home again, and love him into his own house, and sigh him out of his place from beyond the mountain into the soul again; as the spouse doth, Cant. iii. 1, 2, 3, 4. 5. If ever he be found, when he is sought, it will be now, though time and manner of returning be his own.

Asser. 14. Nor are we to believe that Christ's love is coy or humorous in absenting himself, or that he is lordly, high, difficil, inexorable, in letting out the sense, the assurance of his love, or his presence; as we dream a thousand false opinions of Christ under absence, nor do we consider that security and indulgence to our lusts loses Christ; and therefore 'tis just, that as we sin in roses, we should sorrow in thorns.

Asser. 15. If the Lord's hiding himself, be not formally an act of grace, yet intentionally on God's part, it is; as at his return again, he cometh with two heavens, and the gold chain sodered is strongest in that link which was broken; and the result of Christ's return to his garden, Cant. v. 1. is a feast of honey and milk, and refined wines: when he is returned, then

his

his spikenard, his perfume, his myrrh, aloes and cassia, casteth a smell even up to heaven. In the falls of the saints, this is seen; David after his fall hearing mercy, feeling God had healed his bones, that were broken, Psal. li. there is more of God's praises within him than he can vent, he prayeth God would broach the vessel, that the new wine may come out, ver. 15. *O Lord, open thou my lips, that my mouth may shew forth thy praise:* and after the meeting of the Lord and the forlorn son, beside the poor son's expression, full of sense: consider how much sense and joy is in the father; it is a parable, yet it saith much of God, Luke xv. 20. *And when he was yet a great way off, his father saw him.* Christ the Father of age or eternity [*Abi gnad*] Isa. ix. 6. knoweth a friend afar off, and his heart kindles and grows warm when he sees him. Were he thousands and millions of miles from God, yet aiming to come, he sees him, *and had compassion;* he sees with moved bowels, *and ran,* how swift is Christ's love! *And fell on his neck and kissed him.* O what expression of tenderness! and to all these, is added a new robe, and a ring for ornament, and a feast, the *fat calf is killed,* and the Lord sings, and dances, ver. 23, 24, 25, Peter's denial of Christ, brought him to weeping, flowing from the Spirit of grace poured on David's house, Zech. xii. 10. And Peter had the more grace, that he losed grace for a time. As after drawing blood and cutting a vein, more cometh in the place; and after a great fever and decay of strength, in a recovery, nature repaireth itself more copiously. And often in our sad troubles, we have that complaint of God, which he rebuketh his people for; Isa. xl. 27. *Why sayst thou, O Jacob, and speakest, O Israel, My way is hid from the Lord, and my judgment is passed over from God?* that is, the Lord takes no notice of my affliction, and he forgets to right me, as if I were hid out of his sight: and David, Psal. xxxi. 22. *I said in my haste, I am cut off from before thine eyes.* 'Tis not unlike a word which Cain spake, with a far other mind, Gen. iv. 14. *From thy face shall I be hid.* But this is, 1. To judge God to be faint and weak, as

if

if he could do no more, but were expiring, Isa. xl. ver. 28. He will be both weak and wearied, if he forget his own; and our darkness cannot rob the Lord of light, and infinite knowledge; he cannot forget his office as Redeemer. God is not like the stork, that leaves her eggs in the sand, and forgets that they may be crushed and broken. When Christ goes away, he leaves his heart and love behind in the soul till he return again himself; if the young creation be in the soul, he must come back to his nest, to warm with his wings the young tender birth.

Asser. 16. Nor is Christ so far departed at any time, but you may know the soul he hath been in, yea he stands at the side of the sick-bed, weeping for his pained child; yea your groans pierceth his bowels, Jer. xxxi. 20. *For since I spoke against him* (saith the Lord) *I do earnestly remember him;* 'tis not the less true, that the head of a swooning son, lieth in the bosom, and the two arms of Christ; that the weak man believeth, that he is utterly gone away.

Asser. 17. Nor will Christ reckon in a more legal way, for the slips, misjudgings, and love-rovings of a spiritual distemper, than a father can whip his child with a rod, because he misknoweth his father, and uttereth words of folly in the height of a fever. Christ must pardon the fancy, and sins of sick love; the errors of the love of Christ, are almost innocent crimes, though unbelief make love-lies of Jesus Christ. There be some over-lovings, as it were, that foams out rash and hasty jealousies of Christ, when acts of fiery and flaming desires do outrun acts of faith; as hunger hath no reason; so the inundations and swellings of the love of Christ, flow over their banks, that we so strongly desire the Lord to return, that we believe he will never return.

Asser. 18. Though hid jewels be no jewels, a losed Christ no Christ, to sense; yet is there an invisible, and an undiscerned instinct of heaven, that hindered the soul to give Christ over.

Shall

Shall we, upon all this, extend all these spiritual considerations to all men, whether they be in Christ, or not? Some* teach us this, as the great gospel-secret concerning faith; "That none ought to question, whether they believe God to be their Father, Christ their Redeemer, or no; but are to believe, till they be persuaded, that they do believe, and feel more and more of the truth of their faith, or belief; righteousness being revealed from faith to faith: the first ground of this is, Christ's command to believe; now commands of this nature are to be obeyed, not disputed."

But this is so far from being a gospel-secret, that it is not a gospel-truth; and sends poor souls to seek honey in a nest of wasps, the path-way to presumption. For tho' these who truly believe, ought not to doubt of their belief, yet these who have lamps of faith, and no oil, ought to question, whether there be oil in their lamps or no, and true faith with their profession; else the foolish virgins were not far out, who never questioned their faith, till it was out of time to buy oil; and that these virgins should believe, they had oil in their lamps, when they had none, till they should be persuaded, that empty lamps were full lamps, and a bastard faith true faith, were to oblige them to feed upon the east-wind, till there should be a faith produced in the imagination, that the east is the west. 2. All the scriptures that charge us to try ourselves, 1 Cor. xi. 28. *To examine ourselves whether we be in the faith, and to know ourselves, that Jesus Christ is in us, except we be reprobates,* 2 Cor. xiii. 5. *and to know the things that are freely given us of God,* 1 Cor. ii. 12. and so to know our faith, Phil. I. 29. do evince that we are to try, and so far to question, whether we believe or not; as multitudes are obliged to acknowledge their faith is but fancy, and that there is a thing like faith, which is nothing such; and that we are not to deceive

ourselves

---

* Saltmarsh in his Free Grace, c. 5. p. 92, 93.

ourselves with a vain presumption, which looketh like faith, and is no faith. And, James ii. many who believe there is a God, and imagine they have faith, being void of good works, and of love, in which the life and efficacy of faith is much seen, have no more faith than devils have, ver. 18, 19, 20. (2.) It is true, that we are to believe on the name of his Son Jesus Christ, without any disputing concerning the equity of the command of believing, or of our obligation to believe; for both are most just: and to dispute the holy and just will of God, is to oppose our carnal reason to the wisdom of God; but we are not, because we cannot dispute the holy command of God, nor to reason our duty, not to examine, whether that which we conceive, we do as a duty, be a bastard and false conception, or a true and genuine duty; nor, because I may not reason the precept of believing, given by Jesus Christ, am I therefore to believe, in any order that I please, and to come to Christ, whether I be weary and laden with sin, or not weary and laden. Christ commandeth me to believe; *ergo*, remaining in my wickedness, regarding iniquity in my heart, without despairing of salvation in myself, I am to believe: I shall deny this consequence. It is all one, as if Antinomians would argue thus; all within the visible church are obliged to believe and rest on Christ for salvation; whether they be the elect or reprobate; whether their whorish heart be broken with the sense of sin, or whole: *ergo*, they are obliged to presume, or to rest on Christ their righteousness, whether they distrust their own, or not.

†*Object.* 2. "We find not any, in the whole course of Christ's preaching, or the disciples, that asked the question, whether they believed or not; or whether their faith were true faith or no. It were a disparagement to the Lord of the feast, to ask, whether his dainties were real or delusions.---The way
to

† Saltmarsh, 16, 64.

"to be sure of the truth of good things, is tasting and feeling: *Eat, O friends, drink, yea drink abundantly, O Beloved.*"

Answ. This reason would infer, that there is not a saint on earth capable of such a sin, as to doubt whether they believe or not; because we read not of it in any of the hearers of Christ, or the apostles: this is a bad consequence, except you say, all the various conditions of troubled consciences are set down in particular examples, in the New Testament; which is contrary to all experiences of the saints. 2. It is one thing to doubt of the truth of the promises, and another thing to doubt whether my apprehension of the promise be true or false: the latter is not always sin; for it may be my apprehension of the truth of the promises be beside the line, and off the way; and then I question not Christ's dainties (which to do, were unbelief) but my own deluded fancy, which may appear to be faith, and is nothing else; the former is indeed unbelief, not the latter. 3. 'Tis true, tasting makes sure the truth of the Lord's good things, that are inclosed in the promises; but then, an unconverted sinner, who is void of spiritual senses, cannot be the beloved, nor the friend that Christ speaketh to, Cant. v. 1. We do not say, a believer ought to doubt, whether he hath true faith or no: but because the command of believing obligeth the non-converted, as well as the converted, shall the natural man eat as a friend, and a beloved, he remaining in nature, and not yet converted, and this man in nature ought not to doubt whether his fancy be faith or not, but he is obliged to believe, that is, to imagine that his fancy is faith? 4. I see not how, if the faith of the saints be tried as gold in the fire, they may not through the prevalency of temptation be shaken in their faith, as Peter was, when he denied his Saviour; and Paul, who 2 Cor. i. 8. *was pressed out of measure, above strength, despaired of life, had the sentence of death,* 2. Cor. vii. 5. *was troubled on every side, fightings without, and fears within;*

CHRIST DYING AND DRAWING SINNERS TO HIMSELF.

within: and the sons of God, who may fear that they have received the spirit of bondage to fear again, opposite to the spirit of adoption, Rom. viii. 15. but that they may *faint in their tribulations*, Eph. iii. 13. and may be surprised with fear, *which hath torment, and must be cast out,* 1 John iv. 18. *and may be ready to faint and die*, Rev. iii. 2. and turn lukewarm, be wretched, miserable, poor, blind, naked, and yet believe the contrary of themselves, Rev. iii. 16, 17. All these may come, and often do come to that low condition of spirit, after justification, as to say and think *that all men are liars;* their faith is no faith; that they are forsaken of God, to their own sense, and cast out of his sight, and question whether they ever did believe, or no: and why would the apostle say, *patience bringeth forth experience, and experience hope, and hope maketh not ashamed*, Rom. v. 4. if experience that ever God loved me, or that ever I believed, to my present sense, cannot be removed? But this is but the doctrine of (a) Familists, who teach, "That after the revelation of the Spirit, neither devil nor sin can make the soul to doubt. And, (b) to question whether God be my dear Father, after, or upon the committing of some heinous sins, (as murder, incest, etc.) doth prove a man to be in the covenant of works." Do not they then teach us a way of despairing, who say, "That (c) we find not in the whole course of Christ's preaching, or the disciples, that any asked the question, whether they believed, or no; whether their faith were true faith, or no?" What then shall thousands of smoking flaxes and weak reeds do, who often ask this question, and say and think, Ah, I have no faith; my faith is but counterfeit metal? And then, by this doctrine of despair, believers ought to conclude, I am not under grace, but under the law, and a covenant of works, and so not in Christ; yea, whatever

lustres

(a) Story Rise, Reign, Error 32.
(b) Error 20.
(c) Saltmarsh Free Grace, chap. 5. p. 93.

lustres, were in me before, I am in no condition of any we read of in the New Testament, who were hearers of Christ and the apostles; for Libertines, never true believers, doubted whether their faith was true, or not.

*Object. 3. 'For any to doubt whether they believed or no, is a question, that Christ only can satisfy, who is the author and finisher of our faith. Who can more properly shew one that he sees, than the light which enlightens him?'

Answ. Christ solves not questions that no man ever made: S. thinks that believers never doubt, whether their faith be true faith, or not; which is a strong way of believing: and those must be so strong in the faith, who doubt not of this, as they are above all temptations. But this will be found against the experience of all believers. It is most true, none can work faith, but the only Creator and author of faith; but will the author hence infer, no man, the most wicked, or any that ever heard Christ or his apostles preach, doubted of their faith? 2. The sun, with all its light, cannot persuade a blind man who seeth not, that he seeth; believers often think they see, when they see not; and think they are blind, when they see; as experience and scripture, Rev. iii. 16, 17. John ix. 38, 39. teach us.

†Object. 4. 'Faith is truly and simply this, a being persuaded more or less of Christ's love: and therefore it is called a believing with the heart. Now, what infallible sign is there to persuade any that they are persuaded, when themselves question the truth of their persuasion? God only shall persuade Japhet. Who can more principally, and with clearer satisfaction, persuade the spouse, of the good will of him she loves, but himself? Can all the love-tokens, or testimonial rights and bracelets? They may concur and help in the manifestation, but it is the voice of the beloved, that doth the

turn:

* Saltmarsh, ibid, p. 64.   † p. 95.

'turn: my beloved spake and said unto me, Rise, my love, my fair one; saith the spouse.'

Answ. 1. Faith may be a persuasion in some sense, but that it is a persuasion, that my faith or persuasion is true, not counterfeit, and so formally, is utterly denied. How many believe and love Christ with the heart, who are not persuaded that they do so, yea, much doubt, whether they believe with the heart, and would give a world to know (if it were possible) that they truly love God? No divine, who knoweth that a direct act of faith, and to believe, is, when there is no reflex act, can deny this. 2. Arguments or sight, inaccurate speech, are not called infallible, *actu secunda;* the word of God is in itself infallible, *actu primo:* but to Aristotle, this, *In the beginning God created the heaven and the earth,* is not infallible, *actu secundo;* nor are the promises, *He that believeth shall be saved; knock, and it shall be opened; he that overcometh, shall inherit all things; actu secundo;* to a believer, who, under a distemper, doth doubt of them, infallible. So, *The love of the brethren,* 1 John i. 14. *The keeping of the commandments, and the word of Jesus,* is infallible in itself. That I know Christ savingly, and that he dwelleth in me, 1 John ii. v. 3. 5. but that it infallibly concludeth so to me, *actu secundo,* is not sure, except the wind blow fair from heaven, and the Spirit act in me. So, the love-tokens and testimonial rings and bracelets of the husband, my love to the saints, my keeping of his word, my holy walking in Christ, being the works of the Spirit, which dwelt in Jesus Christ, are *actu primo,* in themselves, as infallible signs of the Bridegroom's love to me; as the Beloved's word, *who spake and said, arise, my love:* and if the spirations and breathings of the Spirit go not along, both the voice and the love-bracelets (for Christ is no more counterfeit in his love-tokens, than in his word, when he speaks as a husband) are alike ineffectual to persuade the soul. I see no reason to call the works of sanctification *inferior helps* in the manifestation, more than the voice of the Beloved; for both, without the Spirit,

are

are equally ineffectual; and if the Spirit breathe and move with them, both are effectual, and *actu primo*, and *secundo*, and they infallibly persuade. It is then a weak argument, none can simply persuade Japhet but God; *ergo*, the word of the Bridegroom can only infallibly persuade: or, therefore love-bracelets cannot infallibly persuade: for, the word not quickened by the *Spirit of Jesus*, cannot simply persuade; and the Lord's persuading of Japhet, is the Lord's work of converting Japhet, not his enlightening of Japhet, to know his faith to be true faith. Hence, for that which infallibly persuadeth us, I say,

1. Our act of believing doth no more persuade of itself that we do believe, except the Spirit breathe with the act of believing; for actual illumination and persuasion, than any other act of loving Christ, his saints, or universal intention, or sincerity of heart to obey, doth prove to us, that we believe; for many believe, who know now, yea doubt of their believing, because the Holy Ghost maketh not the light of faith effectual to persuade, that they truly believe.

2. *Asser.* The testimony of the Holy Spirit is the efficacious and actual illumination and irradiation of the Sun of Righteousness and his Spirit, assuring us, that we are the sons of God. This light cometh from inherent acts of grace in us, 1 John ii. 3, 4, 5. chap. iii. 14. (2.) From the testimony and rejoicing which resulteth from a good conscience, 2 Cor. i. 12. 2 Tim. iv. 6, 7, 8. 1 Tim. vi. 17, 18. Heb. xiii. 18. (3.) From the experience they have had of the Lord's dealing with their souls, and the love of God spread abroad in the heart by the Holy Ghost, Rom. v. 3, 4, 5. (4.) From a sincere aim, and respect to all the commandments of God, Psal. cxix. 6. Acts xxiv. 16. 1 John iii. 20, 21. 1 Thess. v. 23. Phil. iv. 12. Rev. xxii. 14. 15. (5.) From the positive marks that Christ putteth on his children, as marks of true blessedness, Matth. v. 3, 4, 5, 6, 7, 8, 9, 10, 11. Psal. cxix. 1, 2. Psal. xxxii. 1, 2. (6.) From the judgment that the saints make of themselves, and their own begun com-

munion

munion with God, Psal. lxxiii. 25. Psal. xviii. 20, 21, 22. Psal. xxvi. 3, 4, 8. Psal. xl. 9, 10. Psal. vii. 8. Job xxxi. Job xxix. Isa. xxxviii. 3. Psal. xlii. 1, 2. Psal. lxiii. 1, 2, 3, 4, 8. Psal. lxxxiv. 2, 3, 4, 5. Psal. cxix. 30, 31, 40, 46, 50, 57, 60, 62, 63, 81, 82, 97, 98, 99, 101, 102, 111, 112, 125, 127, 128, 136, 139, 145, 148, 162, 164. Cant. i. 5. chap. ii. 4,5,6, 16. chap. iii. 1, 2, 3, 4, 5. chap. v. 6, 7, 8, 9, 10, 11, 12. All which were needless flourishes, if they had neither peace, consolation, nor assurance from these, as from marks and signs, which do infallibly convince, (the light, breathings and irradiations of the Holy Ghost concurring with them) that they are in a saving condition, who have these qualifications in them. (7.) Because by holy walking, the saints make their calling and election sure and firm, not to God, but to themselves, 2 Pet. i. 10, 11, 12. v. 5, 6, 7.

Asser. 3. As there is in the eye, *lumen innatum;* in the ear, *aer internus;* a certain inbred light, to make the eye see lights, and colours without; and a sound and air in the ear within, to make it discern the sounds that are without: so is there a grace, a new nature, an habitual instinct of heaven, to discern the Lord's Spirit immediately testifying, that we are the sons of God, Rom. viii. 16. 1 Cor. i. 12. Grace within knoweth Christ speaking without, *The voice of my beloved.* As the Lamb knoweth, by an internal instinct, the mother; but for wakening and quickning of the instinct to apprehend this, there is need of opened eyes, and the presence of the mother to the eye, or of the bleating of the mother, to a waking ear; for instincts cannot work in the sleep: if the spirit speak, and the voice behind be heard, the soul knoweth what sound it heareth, but not otherways. It is but curiosity, so to compare the evidence by signs and marks of sanctification, with that evidence that cometh from the Spirit's immediate voice, or testimony, so as the former should be less sure, fallible, conjectural; and the latter infallible, sure and efficaciously convincing. For, the evidences are both supernatural, certain, divine, and strongly convincing, if there be any deception in either, it is because of the dullness of our apprehension, or our imagination, which fancieth, we see what we see not; or from our unbelief, who will not be convinced. For the Holy Ghost speaketh the same thing, by his operations of grace, in holy walking, that he speaketh by either the word preached, or by the word, and immediate voice of the Spirit, witnessing to our spirits; and there is the same authority revealing to us a thing hid, and the same thing revealed. It may be, there be a variation of the degrees of light, and divine irradiation; or, the one may carry into the soul a more deep impression of God than the other, and the radiation of light in the subject, may be more strong in the one, than in the other: but of themselves they are both infallible, supernatural, and convincing.

It is doubted which of these evidences be more free and partake more of the nature of grace. Antinomians conceive that an evidence by marks in ourself is more selfy, less free, and nearer to a seeking of assurance in ourself, than that evidence which resulteth from the immediate testimony of the Spirit. But the ground they build on is false, and the superstructure is less sure. If it were a matter of giving and receiving, or of wages and work, it were something; but tis a matter of mere knowledge, God revealing our condition to us one way, not another. Possibly the more external, the more immediate, and farer a thing be from a condition, even of grace, the more free; as the election to glory, the paying of the ransom of Christ's blood, or the act of atonement are most free, for they require not so much as the condition of faith wrought by the free grace of God: but justification (say our divines) requireth faith, as a condition. And here God may keep his hands free of any knot, or obligation of a condition; and it would seem that the immediate testimony of the Spirit, is more free than evidence from inherent marks: the wind seemeth to be freer in its motion, which hath not a restriction to fixed causes, rather at this hour, than at that; the sea again in its ebbing and flowing, and the sun in its rising and going down, are more fettered to set times, and condition of natural causes: yet all these detract nothing from the freedom of God the Creator, in his concurring with these causes; nor do conditions, that are wrought in us irresistibly by the grace of God, lay any tie on that independent, sovereign, and high freedom of grace, which doth no less justify, and save us freely, than chuse us to glory, and redeem us with the same freedom, without price and hire: only I will mind Libertines, who deny that justification, the covenant of grace and salvation, have any the most gracious conditions in us; for that should obscure the freedom of grace. They say, all within the visible church, without any preparations, are immediately to believe salvation and remission of sins to themselves in particular. But I hope, faith is a work of free grace, and must presuppose conversion and a new heart, as an essential condition; else, with Pelagians, they must say, that, out of the principles of nature, all are to believe; and this obscureth far more the freedom of the grace of God working faith in us, than all the conditions of grace, which we hold to be subservient, not contrary to the freedom of grace.

Object. 5. "We ought to believe, till we be persuaded that we believe. Eph. i. 13. In whom, after ye believed, ye were sealed. The way to be warm, is not only to ask for a fire, or whether there be a fire or no, or to hold out the hands a little toward it, and away, and wish for a greater, but to stand close to that fire, and gather heat."

Answ. 1. That believing bringeth persuasion, I doubt not; but not such a sealing with the broad and great seal of heaven, as excludeth all doubting, as Antinomians teach; nor doth the place prove it. For these who can flee with such strong wings, and are above all doubting, (1.) Need not Christ's intercession, that their

faith

---

* Page 95.

faith fail not, they are above, and beyond the sphere of all obligation to grace: Nor (2.) need they pray, *lead us not into temptation.* Nor (3.) need they bear in meekness, the overtaken weak ones, who trip and stumble unawares, considering, lest they also be tempted, Gal. vi. 1. (4.) The faith of the strongest is not full moon, or uncapable of growing, Phil. iii. 12. (5.) There is need of praising of grace, for the prevailing victory of a faith beyond doubting. (6.) Nor need such pray Christ to increase their faith. Judge then of Libertines, who talk of a broad seal, of perfect assurance, and say, *(a) There is no assurance true and right, unless it be without fear and doubting.*

2. The way to be warm at a painted fire, such as is the immediate revealing of Christ to an unconverted sinner, never humbled, nor despairing of himself, which is the Libertine's dead faith, is not the way to be warmed; nor are we to believe in Christ, but in Christ's own way and order: and it is safe to call in question, whether such a painted fire be fire; nor are we to go on in this believing, till we be persuaded that we believe. Truly this is no gospel-secret.

If Libertines say, It is impossible to believe, but we must despair in ourselves. I answer, So I believe; but then it must follow, that Libertines deceive, and are deceived, when they teach, *That sinners, as sinners, are to believe,* because sinners despairing of salvation in themselves, must be fewer in number, than *sinners as sinners;* for sinners, as sinners, comprehendeth Pharisees, and all secure and malicious slaves of hell, but self-despairing sinners include not any such, far less include they all sinners; they be only such sinners as are half-sick, looking afar off, with half an eye to Jesus Christ, not daring fully to make out to Jesus Christ: proud Pharisees despair not of salvation in themselves, for then they should not be proud Pharisees in so far. But Libertines teach us, that Pharisees, remaining Pha-

risees,

(a) Rise, Reign, Error, 42.

risees, without any preparations going before, are immediately to believe in Christ. If they say, *Self-despair is an essential part of faith, not a preparation going before faith;* they err: Judas, Cain, despair of salvation both in themselves and in Christ, yet have they not any essential part of saving faith, nor can any essential part of saving faith be in such; nor can any come to Christ, and believe in him, while first they know *sin by the law, and their mouth be stopped, that the law cannot justify nor save them,* Rom. iii. 19, 20, 21. And Mr. Eaten and the Antinomians that are not mere Familists and enthusiasts, rejecting all written scripture, do also grant this; then it must be impossible, that any can believe, but some preparation foregoing there must be; and because all sinners, as sinners, have not such preparation, all sinners, as sinners, are not at the first clap, to believe in the soul-physician Christ, but only such as in Christ's order are ploughed, ere Christ sow on them, and self-condemned ere they believe in Christ.

*Object. 6. "We are no more to question our faith, than we ought to question Christ the foundation of our faith; for salvation to the soul in particular, is destroyed by unbelief: they entered not in, because of unbelief; the word profited not, being not mix'd with faith."

Answ. 1. We cannot question Christ, more than we can question whether God be God; but we may examine Paul's doctrine, as the Bereans did; *we may try our own faith,* if it can hold water. If some would wash their false coin, and bring it to the touchstone, the false metal would be seen. 2. The unbelief in weak ones doubting of their faith, is not that which destroys salvation, and excludeth men out of the holy land: they are cruel to weak reeds, who exclude them out of heaven, because in their misjudging distempers they exclude themselves: were Christ as cruel to a

faint

---

* Saltmarsh. 65.

faint believer, who is sick of misgivings, as he is to himself, who would be saved? But a believer may appeal from himself, ill informed, and doubting groundlessly, to meek Jesus well-informed, and judging aright a weak reed, to be a reed; a sick believer, and a swooning faith to be a believer, and a faith, that will bear a soul to heaven. A weak hackney, if spirity, may accomplish a great journey.

*Object. 7. "Satan puts us clean back here; we are proving our faith by our works, when as no works can be proved solidly good, but by our faith; for without faith it is impossible to please God. We know that every piece of money is valued according to the image and superscription; if Caesar be not there, tho' it be silver, yet it is not coin, it is not so current: so there is not any thing of sanctification current, and of true practical use and comfort to a believer, if Christ be not there. Crispe (a) saith, sanctification and good works are litigious grounds of our faith." This bordereth with the language of Libertines. (b) It is a fundamental and soul-damning error, to make sanctification an evidence of justification. And (c) Christ's work of grace can no more distinguish between an hypocrite and a saint, than the rain that falls from heaven, between the just and the unjust. And (d) The Spirit gives such full evidence of my good estate spiritually, that I have no need to be tried by the fruits of sanctification; this were to light a candle to the sun.

Answ. 1. That which the Spirit of God calleth saving knowledge, 1 John iii. 14. *Hereby know we,* etc. 1 John ii. 3, 4, 5. that do Libertines affirm *to be a policy of Satan, leading us back again, and a soul-condemning error.* (2.) 1 John iii. 10. *In this are the children of God manifest, and the children of the devil: Whosoever doth not righteousness, is not of God, neither he*

that

---

* Ibid. 69.
(a) Crisp. Vol. 2, Ser. xv.
(b) Rise, Reign, Error, 72.
(c) Ibid. 73.
(d) Error, 75.

that loveth not his brother. This is some other difference than the *rain can make between the just and the unjust.* And, 1 John v. 8, *And there are three that bear witness on earth, the Spirit, and the water, and the blood; and these three agree in one.* And that we may know that the Spirit is in us, is evident, 1 John iv. 12, 13. *No man hath seen God at any time. If we love one another, God dwelleth in us, and his love is perfected in us. Hereby we know that we dwell in him, and he in us; because he hath given us of his Spirit.* Now, 1 John iii. 3. *Every man that hath this hope in him, purifieth himself, even as he is pure.* And, Rom. viii. 1. *There is therefore now no condemnation to them that are in Christ Jesus, which walk not after the flesh, but after the Spirit.* 2 Cor. vii. 1. *Having therefore these promises (dearly beloved) let us cleanse ourselves from all filthiness of the flesh and spirit, perfecting holiness in the fear of God.* Hence we argue, whoever *walketh after the Spirit,* must know his guide that leads *the sons of God,* Rom. viii. 14. And whoever purgeth himself, and loveth his brother, and perfecteth holiness in the fear of God, he must know that he so doth; but he that doth walk so, knoweth that he is in Christ, *freed from condemnation,* and that *God dwelleth in him;* for it is express scripture: he that is holy, may know he is chosen to be holy, Eph. i. 4. Now, *Who shall lay any thing to the charge of God's chosen? It is God that justifieth,* Rom. viii. 33. He that is conformed to the image of his Son, and called, may know that *he is predestinated* thereunto, Rom. viii. 29, 30. and *shall be glorified.* Now, Crispe (a) laboureth to prove, that these which commonly go for marks and infallible signs of our justification and interest in Christ, which are *universal obedience, sincerity, love to the brethren,* are either found in no man in their perfection, or they be such marks as agree to good and bad, to hypocrites and saints, and so are not infallible marks; just as the

falling

(a) Serm. xv. Vol. 2.

falling of rain, and the shining of the sun, doth not difference between just and unjust men, because both have a like portion and share in sun and rain. Now, for the former reason; faith and the light of it is imperfect, capable of accession, and so tainted with sin: and if this be a strong reason, it cannot give assurance; which Libertines do not all hold. The other is the saying of papists, teaching us to doubt of our salvation, because there be such shifts, wiles, circuits, lurking-places in a man's heart, that he can give no infallible judgment, with any divine certainty, of himself or his own spiritual state. But is there not so much darkness, so much night and blindness in our mind, as in admitting of the light of immediate witnessing of the Spirit, (which they call, the broad-seal of heaven) we may no less be deceived, than we are in the light that resulteth from our signs of sanctification? There is a like darkness, and no less delusions, from the white spirits, the day-light-ghosts and angels of enthusiasts, and dumb and scriptureless inspirations, than in black spirits. But sure we walk not in the ways of sanctification sleeping, nor doth the Spirit perfect holiness, in the saints, as in a night-dream; we being led with fancy as frantic men are. Shall the saints, when they attest the Lord of their sincere desire and unfeigned intentions, tho' mixed with great weakness, bring before God their integrity, and their rejoicing of a good conscience, as Paul, the apostles, Peter, John, James; *Lord, thou knowest that I love thee;* David, who desired God might try him; Job, Hezekiah, Jeremiah, Daniel, etc. hold forth to God their conjectures, fancies, and such moth-eaten and rotten signs of their justification, as Crispe and others say may be, and were in Pharisees, in Papists, hypocrites, and bloody oppressors, carnal Jews following the righteousness of the law, publicans, heathens, harlots, all the wicked sects? For Crispe saith, *All these have your marks (b) of sanctification, such as are*

(b) Vol. 2. Ser. 14. page 434-441, etc.

are universal obedience, sincerity, zeal for God, love to the brethren. *Zechariah and Elisabeth were righteous before God, walking in all the commandments and ordinances of the Lord, blameless,* Luke. i. 6. Was this such a righteousness, attested by the Holy Ghost, as is in Paul a persecutor, in heathens, Pharisees, in carnal Jews? I grant it was not that righteousness of God through faith, Phil. iii. yet it was a fruit and infallible sign of that righteousness, and such as did prove them to be in Christ. And, 2. All our acts of sanctification are no acts, no infallible marks of justification to my soul, except *they be done in faith;* yea, *without faith they are sin*, Rom. xiv. 23. but when I find they are done in faith, they add a further degree of evidence and certitude, that they argue me to have saving faith and interest in Christ, *as in the Lord my righteousness,* Jer. xxiii. 6. for that *is his name.* And this reason doth conclude, 'tis unlawful to seek any ground of assurance in sanctification, except we would with Papists argue in a circle; thus, 'How know ye that your works are signs of justification? Because they are stamped with faith. And how know you that your justification and faith are not counterfeit? by your works.'

But this is not the Papists' circle, because works, to my sense and spiritual discerning, may, and do add evidence and light to faith, and faith addeth evidence and lights to works; as we prove the cause from the effect, and the effect from the cause, especially under desertion, without the fault of circular arguing; but Papists believe the scripture to be the word of God, because the church saith so, else it should be no word of God, to them, more than the Turk's Alcoran; and they believe that the church saith, that the scripture is the word of God, because the scripture saith, that the church saith so.

This is no proof at all, and a vain consequence, *without faith, it is impossible to please God;* no work can be proved solidly God's, without faith; but how then followeth it; *ergo,* we cannot prove faith to be true from good works. Saltmarsh can make no logic out

of

of this; nothing followeth from the antecedent, but *ergo*, by hypocritical works done without faith, we cannot prove our faith to be true faith, *valeat totum*, the conclusion is not against us. We acknowledge, except good works carry the stamp and image of faith, they are not good works; but if they carry this stamp, as we presuppose they do, in this debate, because works are more sensible to us than faith, it followeth well, then we may know our faith by our works; and a believer doing works in faith, and out of warmness of love to Christ, and a sincere sense of his debt, he may be ignorant that he doth them in faith, but a coal of love to Christ, smoking in his soul, and a sincere sense of the debt that love layeth on him to do that, yea, and to swim through hell to pleasure Christ, are ordinarily more sensible than faith, and lead us to know, there must be faith where these are.

3. Nor are ours litigious and disputable marks, except when our darkness raiseth disputes, more than the gospel itself, is litigious; for men of corrupt minds, raise doubts against the gospel, and weak believers sometimes would argue themselves out of faith, Christ out of imputed righteousness, election of grace and effectual calling; yet are not these litigious points, and say, that the evidence of the Spirit be as light and evident as the sun-light in itself: so is the gospel; yet are we to seek evidences for our faith and peace, in such marks as the Holy Ghost has made way-marks to heaven; by this we know, etc. but we build our knowledge and sense on these marks, as on secondary pillars and helps, which a divine, and supernatural certitude furnisheth, tho' without the influence of the Spirit, they shine not evidently to us: but our faith resteth on the testimony of the Spirit, witnessing to our hearts; and this is not to *bring a candle to give light of the sun;* but to add the light of supernatural sense, to the light of divine faith; else they may as well say, that the confirming evidence, that comes to our sense from the sacraments, addeth something to the word, which is a light, and a sun-light to our eyes. If we did confide

in

in them, as causes of our justification, it were pharisaical: but divine motives, and secondary grounds, tho' they be mixed of themselves with sinful imperfections, may be, by divine institution, helps and confirmatory grounds of our faith and joy; and the scripture saith so, as we heard alledged.

The question proposed by F. Cornewell, I shall not father upon that learned and godly divine, Mr. Cotton: *Whether a man may evidence his justification by his sanctification?* He should have added, whether he may evidence to himself, or his own conscience, his justification; for that so he may evidence it in a conjectural way to others, no man doubts. 2. The question is misstated; as if sanctification did formally evidence justification, as justification, *in abstracto*, and faith in its actual working: it is enough against Antinomians, if it evidence to the sense of the person, that he is in the state of justification, and that he hath faith to lay hold on Christ's righteousness, when he esteems the saints precious, and placeth his delight in them. Sanctification does not, as Libertines would imagine, evidence justification, as faith doth evidence it, with such a sort of clearness, as light evidenceth colours, making them actually visible; no light is no sign or evident mark of colours. Love and works of sanctification do not so evidence justification, as if justification were the object of good works; that way faith doth evidence justification, but sanctification doth evidence justification to be in the soul, where sanctification is, tho' it doth not render justification actually visible to the soul, as light maketh colours to be actually visible; or as faith, by the light of the Spirit, rendereth justification visible: for, even as smoke evidenceth there is fire there, where smoke is, though smoke render no fire visible to the eye; and the moving of the pulse evidenceth that there is yet life, though the man be in a swoon, and no other acts of life do appear to the eye; and the morning star in the east, when it is dark, evidenceth that the sun shall shortly rise, yet it maketh not the sun visible to the eye; and the streams prove
there

there is a head spring, whence these streams issue, yet they shew not in what part of the earth the head spring is, so as to make it visible to the eye; so doth sanctification give evidence of justification, only as marks, signs, and gracious effects, give evidence of the cause: as when I find love in my soul, and care to please God, in all things; and this I may know to be in me, from the reflex light of the Spirit, and from these I know there is faith in me, and justification, though I feel not the operation of faith in the mean time, yet the effect and sign makes a report of the cause. As acts of life, eating and drinking, and walking in me, doth assure me, that I have the life of nature: so the vital acts of the life of faith do, as signs and effects, give evidences of the cause and fountain; yet there is no necessity that with the same light, by which I know the effect, I know the cause; because this is but a light of arguing, and of heavenly logic, by which we know (by the light of the Spirit's arguing) that we know God, by the light of faith; because we keep his commandments, and know, *arguitive*, by God's logic, that we *are translated from death to life, because we love the brethren:* in effect we know, rather the person must be justified, in whom these gracious evidences are, by hearsay, report, or consequence; than we know, or see justification itself, *in abstracto*, or faith itself; but the light of faith, the testimony of the Spirit, by the operation of free grace, will cause us, as it were, with our eyes, see justification and faith, not by report, but as we see sun-light. A third error there is in the state of the question, that never a protestant divine (Arminians and Socinians I disclaim, as no protestants) made either 'sanctification a cause of justification, but an effect; nor common sanctification that goeth before justification, and union with Christ, void of all feeling of our need of Christ; an evident sign of justification.' If Mr. Cornewell dream, that we thus heighten preparations before conversion, as he seems in his arguments, against *gracious conditions in the soul be-*

fore

before faith; he knows not our mind; and as other Antinomians do, refutes he knows not what. And, 4. We had never a question with Antinomians, touching the first assurance of justification, such as is proper to the light of faith. He might have spared all his arguments, to prove, *that we are first assured of our justification by faith, not by good works:* for we grant the arguments of one sort of assurance, which is proper to faith; and they prove nothing against another sort of assurance, by signs and effects, which is also divine. To Antinomians, 1. to be 'justified by faith; 2. and to 'come to the sense and knowledge of justification, which either was from eternity, as some say; or when Christ died on the cross, as others; or when we first take life in the womb, as a third sort dream:' and 3. to be *assured of our justification,* are all one. And so to be *justified by faith,* should be, to be *justified by works,* which they in their conscience know, we are as far against, as any men. But they should remember, that the peace and comfort that the saints extract out of their holy walking, is a far other peace, than that peace which is the natural issue of justification, of which Paul saith, Rom. v. 1. *Being therefore justified by faith, we have peace with God through Jesus Christ our Lord;* and the peace that issueth from our holy walking; or at least, if they be the same peace, it comes not one and the same way. For, 1. Peace, which is the fruit of justification, is a peace in the court of God, as the peace that a broken man hath in the court of justice, when he knoweth his surety hath paid the debts; he dare look justice in the face without any war, having assurance that war is removed, and enmity with God cried down, and all sins are freely pardoned: the peace that issues from our holy walking is in the court of conscience, and sense of sincerity, and straightness of walking; and is grounded on holy walking, as on a secondary help; and if there were not some confidence, that the sinfulness of these works, are freely pardoned, there should be little peace at all.

2. The

2. The former peace is immediately from pardon, that is the true cause of peace; the latter from signs, which dwell as neighbours with pardon; and is only peace, as it hath a necessary relation to pardon, and is resolved in some promise of God, and not as it is a work of our own: as hungering for Christ, as 'tis not the ground of pardon, so 'tis not the ground of peace that issueth from pardon; yet it is the ground of a comfortable word of promise, *Blessed are they that hunger and thirst for righteousness, for they shall be satisfied.* And the like, I say, of assurance, comfort, joy, that result from holy walking, and from justifying faith; we never placed good works in so eminent a place, as to ascribe these same effects to them, and to faith in Christ.

Then Mr. Cornewell loseth his labour to prove, that 'God doth not first declare and pronounce us righteous, upon sight and evidence of our sanctification, which is a righteousness of our own.' For to pronounce us righteous, is to justify us; and doth Mr. Cornewell know any protestant divines, who teach that God, either first or last, doth justify us for our inherent sanctification?

Then Mr. Cornewell does confound evidence and assurance of justification, as if they were both one. For many saints have assurance of justification, so far as they are assuredly justified; and doubt much of their estate, through want of evidence: as many believe, and many times doubt, whether they believe or no. Therefore the argument to prove Abraham's assurance of justification, Rom. iv. cannot conclude, that Abraham had not divine evidence and assurance, that he was justified, by his holy walking, as by signs and fruits of faith. The assurance of Christ's righteousness is a direct act of faith, apprehending imputed righteousness: the evidence of our justification we now speak of, is the reflect light, not by which we are justified, but by which we know that we are justified: and the argument that proves the one, cannot prove the other.

Object.

CHRIST DYING AND DRAWING SINNERS TO HIMSELF.

*Object. 3. *If the promise be made sure of God unto faith, of grace, then it is not first made sure of faith unto works:*

But the promise is made sure of God, to faith, out of grace, Rom. iv. 5. *To him that worketh not, but believeth: the opposition between grace and works,* Rom. xi. 6. Rom. iv. 4. *is not only between grace and the merits of works, but between grace and the debt due to works: now to him that worketh is the reward not reckoned of grace, but of debt,* Rom. iv. 4. *right of promise maketh work to be of a debt, not of grace.*

Answ. The promise is made of righteousness and free justification by the grace of Christ; *by the promise,* and that is by the promised seed, Rom. iv, but these places speak not one word of the reflect evidence that a man hath in his own soul, by which he knows in himself he is justified. The disputer knows not what he says: he proves we have no promise to be justified by works, nor any assurance thereof from working; that is not the question now; but he should prove that we cannot know and make evident to our own souls that we are assuredly justified, and that we believe, when we bring forth the fruits of faith: there is one cause why there is life in this tree, and another cause, why all that pass by, and the tree itself, (if we suppose it to be capable of reason, as man is) doth know it hath life and sweet sap: this latter is known to the tree and to others, by bringing forth good fruit. As if there may not be sundry causes, and of the being of a thing, and to know the being of a thing: bringing forth fruit is not the cause of the life of the tree, good works are not the cause of our justification; but we know well the tree hath life, when we see it brings forth fruit; as we know we are justified, and in Christ, when we *walk after the Spirit, and not after the flesh.* The whole argument is of a direct assurance,
called

* Cornewell, page 12.

called, *certitudo entis,* or of the object: The question is, touching reflect certainty, how persons may be sure in their own conscience, called *certitudo mentis;* and so it concludeth not the question.

2. 'Tis Antinomian doctrine, to make opposition between the gospel-promise, and the debt of the promise; the debt of works, Rom. iv. and Rom. xi. is law-debt due to the worker, as an hireling is worthy of his wages, because he hath done the work perfectly, according to a covenant made with his master: in which case, no man says the wages of the labourer is a free gift. But if whatever the Lord promise to us in the gospel, make God a debtor, and the thing promised to be debt, then let Antinomians speak out; for they say, (a) *The whole letter of scripture,* (and so of the whole gospel promises) *hold forth a covenant of works,* contrary to Gal. iv. where there be two covenants, one of works, another of grace; and contrary to the promises of grace in the gospel, John iii. 16. Heb. viii. 10, 11, 12. Matth. xi. 28. 1 Tim. i. 15. (2.) All the promises of the gospel must make salvation debt: was not Christ promised in the prophets to the lost world? Rom. i. 2. The inheritance is not by law, but by promise, Gal. iii. 17, 18. Rom. ix. 8, 9. Luke i. 45, 54, 55, 68, 69, 70. Is Christ come to save sinners by debt, or by grace? Is salvation debt? 'tis promised. Is not righteousness promised to him that believes, Rom. iv. 5. then righteousness must be debt, and so not of grace; for Cornewell telleth us, page 13. 'The right which a man hath by promise to a work, maketh the assurance of the promise but of debt unto him; and then the promise is not sure to him out of grace.' Then all the promises of an established kingdom to David and his seed, if they should keep God's commandments, all the blessings and salvation promised to believers in the Old and New Testament, so they bring forth the fruits of a lively faith, are mercies *of*

debt,

(a) Rise, Reign, and Ruin, Er. 9.

debt, not of free grace. I well remember that the Familists (b) say, "It is dangerous to close with Christ in a promise." And (c) "There can be no true closing with Christ in a promise, that hath a qualification or condition expressed." I rather believe the Holy Ghost, *Ho, every one that thirsteth, come to the water, come buy wine and milk without money and without price,* Isa. lv. 1. *And if any man thirst, let him come to me and drink,* John vii. 37. *And whosoever will, let him take of the water of life freely,* Rev. xxii. 16. Mark i. 15. If Cornewell can free willing, thirsting, desiring, from working, he hath much divinity: yet the water of life and salvation promised to such cannot be debt, but free grace; for they are promised to these freely, and to be bestowed *without money.* Of the same strain is the fourth argument of Cornewell.

*Object. 5. 'When sanctification is not evident, it cannot be an evidence of justification:

'But when justification is hidden and doubtful, sanctification is not evident;

'Therefore sanctification cannot be our first evidence of justification.

'The minor is proved, because when faith is hidden and doubtful, sanctification is not evident: but when justification is hidden and doubtful, faith is hidden and doubtful; therefore when justification is hidden and doubtful, sanctification is not evident.

'The proof of the major is, 1. Faith is the evidence of things not seen; and so makes all things evident: then, when faith is hidden, what can be clear?'

2. 'Because no sanctification can be pure and sincere, but when it is wrought in faith; and so it cannot be evident, but when it clearly appeareth to be wrought in faith.'

Answ. 1. There is in the conclusion (first) the *first* evidence of justification, that is not in the premises,

against

(b) Rise, Reign, Er. 62.
(c) Rise, Er. 38.
*   Cornewell, p. 15.

X

against all art. The proposition, 'When sanctification is not evident, it cannot be an evidence of justification,' is weak, and weakly proved: for there is a twofold evidence, one of sense and feeling spiritual, another of faith. When sanctification wants the evidence of faith, that I cannot believe salvation from mine own christian walking, yet may the soul have evidence of feeling and sense, that we trust we have a good conscience in all things, willing to live honestly, Heb. xiii. 18. and we dare say, *Lord, we delight to do thy will, and long for thee, O Lord, as the night-watch watcheth for the morning;* and, *Whom have we in heaven but thee?* etc. and can out of sense give a testimony of ourselves, yea, and can place all *our delight in the excellent ones,* Psal. xvi. 3. and cxix. 62. 1. John iii. 14. so as the heart warms, when we see the saints; and in this case sanctification is evident, when remission of sins may be under cloud; else this argument does conclude, if it have any feet, that sanctification ever and at all times is dark, when justification is dark; and so sanctification is never an evidence of justification, but when justification is evident: so the wisdom of God is taxed, as if he would never have us to *know that we are translated from death to life, because we love the brethren,* but when we evidently know, we are thus translated, though we had no love to the brethren: then the Lord hath provided a candle for his weak ones, by this argument, when it is day-light; but hath denied any candle-light, moon-light, or star-light, when it is dark night. 2. The major is not proved: faith is not the evidence of all things, as that it maketh all things evident to our spiritual sense; for Cornewell granteth, faith may be hidden; then it can evidence nothing when it is hidden. Love to the brethren, keeping of his commandments, yield sensible evidences that we are justified, even when faith is not evident; and how many are convinced they have undoubted marks of faith and justification, who doubt of their faith and justification? And so the minor and probation of it is false; for it is most false, that when faith is hidden and

doubt-

doubtful, sanctification is not evident: this is asserted gratis, not proved: as if ye would say, ever when the well-head is hidden, the streams are not seen; when the sap and life of the tree is not seen, but hidden, the apples, leaves and blossoms are not evident. This is a begging of the conclusion: for then should a man never, neither first nor last, 'know that he is translated from death to life, because he loves the brethren:' Why? Because when translation from death to life, or when faith and justification is hidden, the love to the brethren, and all the works of sanctification, are hidden, saith this author.

3. The second proof of the major is lame; 'sanctification is never pure and sincere, without faith,' (saith he;) Ergo, 'It cannot be evident, but when it appeareth to be wrought in faith.' The consequence is null; just like this, sweet streams cannot flow but from a sweet spring; *ergo*, It cannot be evident and clear to my taste that the streams are sweet, except I taste the water at the fountain-head, and see it with mine eyes; and my taste cannot discern the sweetness of the fruit, except my senses were within the trunk or body of the tree, to feel, see, and taste the sap of life, from whence the fruit cometh. Yea, the contrary consequence is true, because I smell sincerity, love, single intentions to please God in my works of sanctification; therefore I know they came from faith; so the Holy Ghost should delude us, when he saith, 'We know, we know, or believe in Christ, because we keep his commandments.' *Ergo*, We cannot know this, except it be evident, that our keeping his commandment come from faith, and the knowledge of God.

†*Object.* 6. "Such a faith as a practical syllogism can make, is not a faith wrought by the Lord's almighty power; for the conclusion followeth, but from the strength of reasonings, not from the power
"of

† Cornewell, page 16, 17, 18.

"of God, by which alone divine things are wrought, Eph. i. 19, 20. Col. ii. 20.

"But faith wrought by a word and a work, and the light of a renewed conscience, without the testimony of the Spirit, is such a faith as a practical syllogism can make: *Ergo*, such a faith, so wrought, is not wrought by the Lord's almighty power.

"The minor is proved, because all the three, the word, the work, and the light of conscience, are all created blessings and gifts, and therefore cannot produce of themselves a word of almighty power; and the word of itself is a dead letter, the work is less: for faith cometh by hearing a word, not by a work."

Answ. When Mr. Cornewell saith, *By the power of God alone, divine things* (such as faith that layeth hold on Christ's righteousness) are wrought, Eph. i. 19. Col. ii. 20. he excludeth the ministry of the gospel, and all the promises thereof, for they are created things, and so they have no hand nor influence in begetting faith. Antinomians will have us believe, that Paul, Ephes. i. 19, 20. Col. i. 20. thinks no ministry of the word, nor any hearing of the preached word, begetteth faith; contrary to Rom. i. 16. Rom. x. 17. but by the only immediate power of the Spirit we are converted without the word. Nor is here that which is in question concluded; never protestant divine taught, that without the actual influence of omnipotent grace, can faith or spiritual sense that we are justified, be produced by the word, work, or created light alone; nor can the corn grow alone by power in the earth, clouds, or rain; nor any creature move without the actual influence of the omnipotent Lord, in whom we move: therefore by this reason we could not know that the sun shall rise, by the rising of the morning star; nor can we have any supernatural sense, by our holy walking, contrary to scripture, 1 John ii. 3. John iii. 14. But we know by this, all faith is ascribed by Antinomians, to the immediate testimony and enthusiastical inspiration of the Spirit.

Spirit. As for the searching of scripture (say *they) "tis not a sure way of searching and finding out Christ, 'tis but a dead letter, †and holds forth a covenant of works in this letter;' and therefore, with the old Anabaptist, they'll have no teaching by scripture, but only teaching by the Spirit. We hold that conditional promises are made to duties of sanctification, therefore we may have comfort and assurance from them, in our drooping condition. Cornewell answereth, page 23, 24, 25. 'The promises are not made to us, as qualified with such duties of sanctification; for then they should belong to us of debt, not out of grace, Rom. iv. 4. But in respect of our union with Christ, in whom they are tendered to us, and fulfilled to us, satisfaction is made to the thirsty, not for any right his thirst might give him in the promise, but because it directeth to Christ, who fulfilleth the condition, and satisfieth the soul; and the soul must first have come to Christ, and gotten his first assurance from faith in Christ, not from these conditions and duties.'

Answ. 1. This is a yielding of the cause. We say, there be promises of the water made to thirsty souls, not as if the right, *Jus*, law, merit, debt, that we have to them, belonged to us, for the deed done, but for Jesus Christ only. 2. Not as if we upon our strength, and the sweating of free-will, did conquer both the condition and reward. 3. But yet we have comfort and assurance, when we by grace perform the duty, that our *faithful Lord, who cannot lie,* will fulfil his own promise. 4. He knoweth nothing of the gospel, who thinketh not God by his promise cometh under a sweet debt of free-grace are consistent. But Antinomians breath smell of fleshly liberty; for they tell us, (a) *conditional promises are legal, contrary to the gospel,* Rom. x. 9. John iii. 16. John v. 25. That (b) *'tis*

not

* Rise, Er. 39 † Er. 9.
(a) Rise, Reign, Err. 48. (b) Er. 38.

'not safe to close with Christ in a conditional promise; if (c) any thing be concluded from water and blood, 'tis rather damnation than salvation. That (d) 'tis a sandy foundation to prove that Christ is mine, from a gracious work done in me by Jesus Christ, were it even faith; for we are (e) completely united to Christ, without faith wrought by the Spirit. (f) 'Tis incompatible with the covenant of grace, to join faith with it. To be (g) justified by faith, is to be justified by works. That (h) to say there must be faith on man's part to receive the covenant, is to undermine Christ.' Neither Cornewell nor Saltmarsh oppose these blasphemies, but extol the patrons of them in New-England.

Father, save me from this hour.

Father is a word of faith. But, had Christ need of faith?

Answ. Not of faith of confiding in him that justifieth the sinner, except he had faith of the justifying of his cause, in God's acquitting him of suretiship, when he had paid all; but he had faith of dependency on God in his trouble, that God would deliver him; *and he was heard in that which he feared.*

And, *Quest.* 2. How could there be a faith of dependency in Christ, for he was the same independent God with the Father?

Answ. There were two relations in Christ; one as Viator, going toward glory, and *leading many children with him to glory;* another as Comprehensor, seeing and enjoying God. 2. There were two sights in Christ, one of vision, another of union; the sight of union of two natures, is the cause of the sight of vision. Christ being on his journey travelling toward glory, did with a faith of dependency rest on God as his Father, seeing and knowing that the union could not

be

(c) Er. 30. (d) Er. 69. (e) Er. 37
(f) Er. 27 (g) Er. 21 (h) Er. 38

be dissolved; but as a comprehensor, and one at the end of the race, enjoying God in habit, there was no necessity that Christ should always, and *in omni differentia temporis*, actually see and enjoy God, in an immediate vision of glory.

For, 1. This implieth no contradiction to the personal union, even as the seeing of God habitually, which is the most joyful sight intelligible, and by necessity of nature does produce joy and gladness, may, and did consist in Christ, with groanings and sadness of Spirit, even before his last sufferings: so the interruption for a time, of the actual vision of God, might stand with Christ's personal happiness, as God-man. 2. If we suppose there were just reasons, why God should command that angels and glorified spirits should not actually see God for a time, there were no repugnancy in this to their true blessedness, so it fell not out through their sins; no more than the sun should lose any of its nature, if we suppose God should command it to stand still, and to be covered with darkness many days, as in Joshua's time it stood still in the firmament some hours, and for a time was covered with darkness at the suffering of Christ. What an interposed cloud of covering it was, or what a skreen did interrupt the flux of the beams and rays of the Godhead from actual irradiation on the soul, and faculties and powers of the soul of the man Christ, is more than I can determine. Certain it is, God was with the manhood, and so near as to make one person, but there was no actual shining on the powers of the soul, no heat and warmness of joy, but as if his own infinite sea of comfort were dried up, he needed a drop of the borrowed comfort of an angel from heaven. Now, whether this angel, Luke xxii. 43. did wipe the sweat of blood off his holy body, and really serve him that way; or if the angel was sent with good words from the Father, to comfort him, and say to this sense, *O glorious Lord, courage, peace, and joy, and salvation, shall come; thy Father has not forsaken thee utterly;* it cannot be known: but Luke saith, *An angel appeared from heaven strengthening him.*

But

But it was admirable, that the Lord of all consolation should stand in need of consolation, and a good word from his own creature; or that the great Lord, the lawgiver, should need the comfort of prayer, or any ordinance. O what a providence! what a world is this! that God-man, sweet Jesus, is put to his knees, and his prayers with it! Come see the Lord of life at a weak pass; he is at, *God help me;* at tears and sighing, *God save me.* This is more than if the whole light of the sun were extinguished, and it behoved to borrow light from a candle on earth; and the whole sea and rivers dried up, and they behoved to beg some drops of dew from the clouds to supply their want.

2. Christ himself refused comfort to himself: there was a sea of joy in Christ, within him; but not one drop can issue out on the powers of his soul: joy is sad, fairness black, faith feareth and trembleth; the infinite all, lieth under the drop of the comfort of a creature nothing. Riches beggeth at poverty's door, the light is dark, greenness withereth and calleth the bloom, life maketh prayers against the death of deaths, the glory and flower of heaven standeth sad and heavy at the jaws and mouth of hell. Mat. iii. 26. He prayed to this sense, fallen on his face to the earth once, *O my Father, remove this cup;* but he is not answered: he knocketh the second time, *O my Father, if it be possible, remove this cup.* O but here is a hard world! the substantial Son of God knocking and lying on his face on the earth, and his Father's door of glory fast bolted, the Son cannot get in. The like of this providence, you never read nor heard of. The natural Son of God crieth, *with tears and strong cries,* with a sad, heavy and low spirit, to his Father; he cannot get one word from heaven, or half a glimpse of the wonted glory that was natural and due to him as God. O rare and sad dispensation! He must cry the third time, *O my Father, remove this cup.* We storm, if the Lord do not open his door at the first knock: O what hard thoughts have some of God, if a flood of love issue not from his face at the first word! But the Lord's saints are not to look for a providence of the honey-

drops

drops of the fattest consolations of heaven, in every ordinance of prayer and praises. O what a sad administration! Psal. xxii. 2. *O my God, I cry in the day-time, and thou hearest not; and in the night-season, and am not silent.* The church speaketh sadly to God. What can be worse than this? Lam. iii. 7. *He hath hedged me about, that I cannot get out; he hath made my chain heavy.* Yet to open a sad heart in the bosom of a friend, far more to God, is much ease; but here is worse, verse 8. *Also, when I cry and shout, he shooteth out my prayer.* Psal. lxix. 3. *I am weary of crying, my throat is dried; mine eyes fail, while I wait for my God.* It is grace to put a construction of love and faith on the Lord's not answering our desires. These experiences may silence us; 1. It may be good that the Lord answer, and not good that he answer now: the saints are often ripe for praying, when they are unripe for the mercy of a real answer and help from God. Two things necessitate prayer, (1.) Our duty to worship. (2.) Our necessity and straits. But on our part we are not ripe for an answer for any of these, being yet not humbled, and praying with slow desires, little fervour of faith. 2. 'Tis possible it be our duty to pray, as supposing a real necessity of what we need, and yet it is not our good that God hear us now. No doubt Abraham and Sarah both prayed for a son, many years before the one was an hundred, the other ninety and nine years old; but it was not good that God should hear them, till it be a miracle, and a new way, and more than ordinary providence they were answered. 3. God refuseth never to hear us, for favours that are non-fundamentals toward everlasting life, but when it is better be not heard, than heard: Moses might possibly not know a reason, but it was better for him that he saw afar off the good land, (more for faith and mortification, and heavenly-mindedness, which he saw not) than that he should enter with the people into that land, which he prayed for. 4. Not any of the saints, considering that *all things work together for good to them that love God;* but as they praise God that he

hath

hath heard their prayers, so they praise God in some things that their prayers lie at a fast bolted door, and take it well in other things that he was displeased with them, and so that they have cause to be humbled that God did grant their desire. Let it be that David prayed for a son, and God gave him Absalom; it is a question, if David had not cause to wish he had never been born. 5. God hath equally regulated and limited our desires to be heard, and our willingness, faith, submission and patience, and our praises according as we are heard or not heard; yet we are less in praises when we are heard, and our desires fulfilled, and in submission, when we are not heard, than we are forward to praise; because necessity and straits can more easily obtain of us to pray, and to set on moving the wheels of our affections, than grace can keep our spiritual affections in heat of motion, or limit and border our natural affections in praising, when they take them to their wings. David, Psal. xxi. Psal. lxix. *O my God, I cry night and day,* till my throat be dry in asking; but where doth he say, *O my God, I will praise night and day,* till my throat be pained in praising, and my heart and eyes are wasted and spent in submissive waiting for thee, and praising for not hearing me in some things? 6. God is equally gracious to his own, in not hearing and granting, as in fulfilling their desires. 7. No man should take it hard, not to be answered at the first, when the prime heir Christ was kept knocking at his Father's door. 8. Heard or not heard, the prayers of faith have a gracious issue, tho' the dross of them be cast away. 9. As praises have no issue, but to give to God, not to ourselves; so prayers in faith are to be offered to God, as God, tho' nothing return in our bosom, that God may be extolled. Christ knew deliverance from this hour cannot be granted, yet he prays. 10. Faith is required no less to believe the good that the Lord mindeth us in not hearing us, than the good he intendeth in hearing and fulfilling our desires: no condition of providence can fall wrong to faith, which can fly with any wings, and fail with every wind, so long as Christ liveth.

Fa-

Father, save me from this hour.

Christ bottometh his prayer on the sweetest relation of a Father and a Son; *Father, save me.* So, John xvii. *Father, glorify thy Son.* v. 5. *And now, Father, glorify me.* Six times in that prayer he useth this style. Mat. xi. 25. *I thank thee, O Father, Lord of heaven and earth,* Mat. xxvi. *O my Father, remove this cup.* His Father was great in his esteem; none like his Father. It is a strong argument to Christ, to persuade an hearing and a deliverance; and he was heard in that which he feared: he had no end in his coming into the world, but to do the will of his Father, John v. 30. (2.) Love is a sweet ingredient in prayer: the beloved disciple John, who only, of all the evangelists, setteth down Christ's love-prayer, chap. xvii. useth it more frequently than any of the other three evangelists. (3.) Propriety, interest, and covenant-relation is a sweet bottom, and a strong ground for prayer: so in praying, hath Christ taught us to say, *Our Father which art in heaven.* And, Psal. v. 2. *Hearken to my voice, my King, and my God.* 2 Kings xix. 19. *Now therefore, O Lord, our God, I beseech thee, save us out of his hand.* Ezra bottometh his prayer on this, chap. ix. 6. *O my God, I am ashamed and blush.* And Jehoshaphat, 2 Chron. xx. 12. *O our God, wilt thou not judge them?*

Use. In prayer, consider what claim and interest you have to God, if you be a Son, and he a Father: bastards cannot pray; strangers without the covenant, and heathen, having no right to God, as their God and Father, may petition God, as a subdued people do their conqueror, or as ravens cry to God for food, and as some *howl upon their beds for corn and wine,* Hos. vii. 14. but they cannot pray; for in praying aright to God, there is required not only gracious ingredients in the action, but also a new state of adoption and filiation: many speak words to God, who do not pray; many tell over their sins, who confess not their sins to God;

many

many speak good of God, who do not praise God; many sigh and groan in praying, and have no deep sense of God, or their own sinful condition. Trees growing together make not always a wood. Ah, our prayers, God knows, are often out of their right wits. Many cry, Father, to God, but lie; for they are not sons, and their words are equivocation. Thousands claim Fathership in God, where there is no Sonship, nor *fundamentum in re*, no ground in the thing itself. A new nature is that only best bottom of praying, that taketh it off from being a *taking of the name of God in vain*. All creatures speak of God, and, in their kind, to God; but only a son can speak to God in prayer, as to his Father: calling upon God, with a pouring out of the soul to him in Christ, is essential to sons.

Father, save me from this hour.

Christ had no means of refuge safer and surer in his trouble, when he knew not what to do, than prayer. Christ had never a greater business in hand, than now he was to transact with God, and divine justice, the law of God, in the weighty bargain of paying a ransom of dearest and preciousest blood, to open the new way to heaven; he had to do with *devils, principalities and powers, and hell:* to subdue devils, and death and hell, and to redeem his catholick church from the second death; and he was to offer himself a sacrifice to God, *through the eternal Spirit,* for the sins of the whole elect; and he must use prayer in all this great work. The greatest works have been thus effectuated. For the dividing of the Red-sea, Moses cried to the Lord, and it was done. Hezekiah obtaineth fifteen years lease of his house of clay from Jehovah his landlord: and how! 2 Kings xx. 2. *He turned his face to the wall, and prayed.* Jonah broke the prison of hell by prayer. Jeremiah had many against him, chap. xx. 12. *Unto thee* (saith he to the Lord) *I have opened my cause.* Daniel, in his captivity; Ezra, when the people were under wrath; Esther and her

maids,

maids, when the church's destruction is warped, and in weaving, by prayer loose the captive-bands, and break death's jaws. So low a man as Job, chap. vii. 26. was, *What shall I say to thee, O preserver of man?* David looketh back to his prayers, Psal. xxxiv. 6. and when he is overwhelmed, Psal. lxi. 2. *From the ends of the earth will I cry to thee, when my heart is overwhelmed.* To Elias, this is the key that openeth heaven. The last great work, the perfecting of mystical Christ, the judging of the world, the putting crowns on the heads of so many thousand kings, must have prayer to bring it to pass: *Even so come, Lord Jesus.* The putting and keeping on the crown on Christ's head, is by prayer: his sword, crown and sceptre, stand and prosper by this prayer, *Thy kingdom come.* 2. Tho' Christ knew of his own deliverance, and was sure of it, yet he will not have it but by prayer. Christ had Son-right to heaven, yet he will take a new gift of heaven by prayer-right: Christ maketh prayer his new charter, Joh. xvii. 5. *Father, glorify me, with the glory which I had with thee before the world was.* Christ will have his spouse, tho' his by conquest, and the law of buying and ransom, made over to him by a *de novo damus*, Psal. ii. 8. *Ask of me,* (pray to me) *and I will give thee the heathen.* His kingdom's pillar, is prayer, Psal. lxxii. 15. *Prayer also shall be made for him continually,* that his throne may stand, and he may bear the crown. What, must we pray for Christ, he prays for us? Yea, we pray for mystical Christ, and his crown. It is better to hold lands of Christ by prayer, than by conquest or industry, by right of redemption of heritage; even the rich, who have broad lands, when the bread is at their lip, and on the table before them, are to pray, *Give us this day, our daily bread.* Have you wisdom, honour, learning, parts, eloquence, godliness, grace, a good name, children, peace, ease, pleasure, wife, houses, lands, see how ye got them; if not by prayer, in so far they are unjustly purchased: the next best, is to

get

get a new charter of them by prayer. I grant, conversion is not obtained by my praying, because an unconverted man cannot pray, no more than the birth can pray itself out of the mother's womb; yet 'tis gotten by Christ's prayer. Some after sickness have health, as robbers have the traveller's purse, they have them by spoil, not through Christ, or any prayer-right: victories, and subdued cities, are better taken and enjoyed by prayer, than by bribes or money.

Use. They know not the use of prayer, who teach, that we are not to pray against that which cannot be avoided: so, Libertines (a) say, *That we are not to pray against all sin, because it cannot be avoided;* but the old man must be in us, so long as we live. The Lord hath so decreed the end, as that he hath ordained prayer to be a necessary way to accomplish his end, yea, Paul, 1 Thess. v. 23. prayeth, *That the very God of peace may sanctify the Thessalonians throughout* . And we know, that we cannot be free of temptations in this life; yet pray we, not to be led into temptation: which is not so much, that the body of sin may be fully rooted out in us, and inherent sanctification may be perfected in this life, as that we may be delivered from guilt and damnation, and from the power and dominion of sin, and that prayer may be stairs up to the laying of the last stone of the new building. Yea, tho' it was revealed to Peter, and the disciples, that they should deny Christ, and as sheep be scattered away, *when the sword should awake against the Shepherd;* and this was unavoidable, in regard of the decree of God, and *fulfilling of the scripture,* Zech. xiii. Yet were the disciples to pray, they might be so guarded against that temptation, as they might not leave, and forsake Christ in his sufferings.

Father, save me from this hour, .

That which Christ deprecateth, hath two things considerable, 1. That his sufferings were so timed, and
defined,

(a) Rise, Reign, Ruin, Error, 3, 4.

defined, as they should endure but for an hour, 2. But it was a sad hour; there is an emphasis put on it, *this hour.*

1. Christ's sufferings are but hour-sufferings, we behoved to suffer eternally.

Object. Ergo, Christ suffered not that same punishment, that we were to suffer for sin, if Christ had never died for us.

Answ. 1. He suffered not all, according to every accident and circumstance, that we were to suffer; it is true, we should have suffered sinful despair, and there could be no mixture of sin in his cup. 2. We should have suffered for ever; he exhausted all the pain, and the curse, in some few hours. But he suffered all that we were to suffer, according to the due equivalency, worth, and substance of the suffering. Christ paid (as we say) *as good*: a debtor oweth ten thousand millions to a prince, to be paid in silver, at so many several terms; the surety of this broken debtor paid the whole sum at one term, and in gold, the excellentest metal: it is the very same debt, and the same bond acquitted, as if the sum had been paid by the chief debtor. Christ, by paction, paid all *in cumulo,* at one term, and in excellent metal and coin, being the dear blood of God. A traitor is to die, and suffer hanging or heading for such a high point of treason; the prince's son will die the same death for him; only, by paction, he hath because of the eminency of his person, a privilege, which the principal man had not: what, if he be hanged in a chain of gold, and a crown on his head, or beheaded with a silver axe; it is the same satisfactory death for law and justice, as if the other had died like himself. There were some sparkles of the Majesty and crown of heaven, or some glistering rubies and diamonds did shine in Christ's death, which could not have been in ours, and it was convenient it should be so.

2. Christ's time-sufferings are more than our eternal sufferings, because of the dignity of his person. It is true, a poor man's life is as sweet and dear to him, *physically,* as the life of a prince, in the court of na-

ture;

ture, in curia naturae; it is alike taking to every man; but *in curia fornesi,* if we speak legally, and in relation to many. David a king is more, for his royal place, to save and judge many thousands, than ten thousands of the people. 2. A prince shamed and disgraced, shall lose more honour, than a man of a low, poor and base condition; the honour of a free, and just prince, is by a thousand degrees more than the loss of honour in a wicked and base slave. Sinners had little to lose in comparison of the *Prince of Life,* like us in all things, except sin.

3. The more noble privilege that life hath, as the more immediate communion with God, the loss of life is a greater loss. It is more for glorious angels to lose their happy and blessed life in the fruition of God, than for damned devils to lose their being, who are in chains of darkness. It is more for the spirits of just and perfect men, who are now before the throne, to be made miserable, to lose life, and such a life, glory, and such a glory; than for slaves of hell, living in wickedness, to be thrust down to hell with everlasting shame. It is more that the whole sea and all the rivers be dried up, than that one water-fountain be dried up. Christ had more to lose than all angels and men; even to be suspended of the vision of God, for a time, was more than all that angels and men could lose for ever.

4. It is true, the influence meritorious from Christ's person on his suffering is not real, but infinite in a moral estimation. But give me leave to think it disputable, whether or no, it dependeth not on the free decree and pleasure of God, that the punishment of sin be infinite in duration; or if it depend on the nature of sin, and of divine justice; so as essentially God be necessitated, not from any free decree (that is not properly necessity) but essentially from that spotless and holy justice, which is essentially in him, to punish those who equally sinned on earth, with equal torments in hell, and all with eternal punishment. Yet, notwithstanding all this, Christ, by his death, not only exhausted the infinite punishment due to us; as infinite mountains

of

of sands can drink up all the finite seas, rivers, brooks and fountains of the earth; but he purchased to us an infinite and eternal weight of glory, by the worth of his merit. Now, by this, there must be more in Christ's death, than we can easily conceive; as it is less to bring Israel out of Egypt only, and divide the Red-sea, and to present them living men on the shore, than to do that, and also to give them in peaceable possession, *that good land which floweth with milk and honey:* and it is much to deliver a slave from perpetual poverty, misery and bondage; and not only that, but positively to make him a rich, honourable, and glorious king; all which, Christ by his blood purchased to us: I leave it then to be disputed, whether Christ's sufferings had not only a moral, meritorious and legal worthiness, from the free act of God's acceptation, or also an intrinsical worth and weight, real, and intrinsically congruous, and proportionable to the pain and shame he delivered us from, and the glory that positively he conquested for us. It is more to pay a poor man's debts, than to make him rich.

Quest. 1. *If Christ's sufferings were limited, in regard of time, and hours, why then could he suffer infinite punishment? It involveth a contradiction, to limit that which is infinite; and if an angel was sent to comfort him, it is like, God did extend mercy, and not unmixed and satisfactory justice, to him.*

Answ. Moderation in suffering, as an angel to comfort him, that not a bone of him shall be broken; that he should not lie three full days in the grave; that his body *should not see corruption:* all these may well stand with sufferings that are *infinite, morally,* and from the worth of his noble and glorious person, who is *God blessed for ever.* And it proveth that all the exactest justice that the Lord followed, in the pursuing Christ to the second death for our sins, was not in inflicting punishment on Christ intensively, and intrinsically infinite, and which should be infinitely satisfactory, if we lay aside all supposition of the punishment of the person suffering, who was infinite, and of the free and voluntary acceptation of God.

Quest.

Quest. 2. *But then was not all the infiniteness of justice in punishing Christ, not in inflicting pain infinitely and intensively extreme on him, but in that the person was infinite, but the pain finite, both in time and otherwise.*

Answ. We hold that the suffering for the time, was so extreme, that he, and he only, could endure the infinite wrath of God; but whether all the infiniteness of pain flow from this, that the person was infinite, or that the pain was intrinsically infinite, we desire not too curiously to determine: sure, the infiniteness of his person confessed infiniteness of worth to his merit; so as he purchased *a church by the blood of God,* Acts xx. 28. *The Lord Jesus gave himself for his church,* Eph. v. 25, 26. *and a ransom for many.* Math. xx. 28. 1 Tim. ii. 6. But I see no reason why Christ's sufferings should be thought finite, because he suffered in some few days; then the Lord's acts of creating the world, of raising the dead, working of miracles, should be finite acts, because absolved in a short time.

Hence we cannot say, what an obligation is on us to Jesus Christ. Love for love is too little; because our drop of dew can bear no proportion to his infinite and vast sea of tender love to us. As Christ gave himself an infinite ransom, by law, for us; so he brought us under an infinite debt of love and service to him. Christ paid all our debts of law to infinite justice, but we shall never pay all our debt of love to him. O! how many thousand talents are we owing to Christ? And because glory is a love engagement to Christ, the longer we enjoy the glory of heaven, through millions of ages, the debt *to the Lamb, to him that sitteth on the throne,* will be the greater, and shall grow infinitely: praises for eternity shall take nothing down of the debt. Know, you are the sworn and over-engaged and drowned debtors of Jesus.

Use 2. The sufferings of *mystical Christ* are but for an hour; *for a night, and joy in the morning,* Psal. xxx. 5. *a little season,* Rev. vi. 11. *Three days,* Hos. vi. 1. *A short time, and the vision will speak, and will not*

not tarry, Hab. ii. 3. Heb. x. 37. It is but *tribulation ten days,* Rev. ii. 10. And, which is shorter than all, *a moment,* 2 Cor. iv. 17. and the shortest of all, Isa. liv. 7. *a little moment.* All the generations of the first-born, that were *in great tribulations,* and in the womb and belly of the Red-sea, are now come off safe, and landed on the shore, and are now up before the throne in white, triumphing *with the Lamb;* the hour is ended, some of them two thousand years ago are eased of burning quick, of the sword, of the *teeth of lions.* Job's face now is not *foul with weeping;* David's soul *droopeth away, and melteth no more with heaviness,* as Psal. cxix. The traces of tears on Christ's fair face, are fifteen hundred years ago washed off, and dried with his Father's hand, Paul is now beyond *fears without, terrors within, and the sentence of death.* All the martyrs now are above the fire, the faggots, the rack, the gibbet, the axe. What thoughts hath John Baptist now of beheading? or Stephen of stoning to death? The gashes and wounds of the stripes of the apostles, scourged for the name of Jesus, are over now: there is not one sigh, nor one tear, nor one cry, nor one death, now in heaven; *all the former things are gone.* Afflictions are but a short trance, for an hour; our short-living sufferings will be over quickly: we are near the shore. Our inch of winter shall wear out, there is but a little bit of sour death before us; the ceremonies of death is approaching, of the noise of its feet, of its awful and dreadful gloom, the train of little images of death, the aching of bones, the stitches of heart, the pain of the side, and such soft passing accidents, and the name, are more than death itself; and all these shall pass over quickly. We have not centuries, nor millions of years to suffer; he who limited a time to the head Christ's sufferings, hath set so many sand-glasses, and determined so many hours for all our sufferings. Yea, 2. The gall in our cup must be weighed by God's own hand: not a man killed more in the two kingdoms, nor a house burnt, nor a scratch in the body, nor one wound in the poor soldier of
Christ,

CHRIST DYING AND DRAWING SINNERS TO HIMSELF.

Christ, but all are numbered; all go by ounces, grains, and scruples in heaven: there is a pair of just and discreet balances before the throne. Crucify Christ, and pierce his side, but not one of his bones can be broken; there be broken bones of two, one at either side of him, within the breadth of five fingers to him. Cast Joseph in the dungeon, but he must not die there. Cast Moses in the river, when he is an infant, to die there, but Pharaoh's daughter must bring him up as a prince. Let Job's body be afflicted, but save his life. Imprison and scourge the apostles, but there is more to do by them, ere they be killed. Make the kingdom of Judah weeping captives in Babylon, but the dry bones must live again. Let David be sore afflicted, *but he cannot be delivered unto death*, Psal. cxviii. Let Daniel be a captive, and meat for the lions, but he must be saved and honoured. Appoint a day for the destruction of the Jews under Ahasuerus, let death be shaped, warped, but they shall not die. Love, even the loved Christ, whose seven spirits full of wisdom are before the throne, is a straight line, a just measure, and weigheth all to the tempted souls, that nothing shall go above their strength; no burden more than their back, no poison, no death in their cup, no gall more than their stomach can endure. You may, O redeemed ones, refer your hell to Christ's love, and make over all your sorrows to his will; see if he will destroy you. Let Christ be a moderator to brew your cup, and free grace be judge of your portion of Christ's cross; and the cross may bruise your shoulder, it shall not grind you to powder. Had I ten eternities of well or woe, I durst refer them to the bowels of Christ's boundless mercy and free love. Shall I be the first that Christ's warm love over-killed, and over-destroyed? Christ's love is infallible, and above error. Fatherly Providence determines all so equally, measureth all so straightly, tempereth all so sweetly, that black death is sugared with white heaven, the sad grave a palace-royal for a living and victorious king: apples of life grow on the saddest cross that the saints bear. The love of
Christ

Christ hath soft and silken fingers: love measureth out strokes, Rev. iii. 19. And can love kill and destroy a son of God's love?

Use 3. The sufferings of Christ and the saints, be measured by hours: God is the creator of time, and tempereth the horologe. *My times are in thy hands*, Psal. xxxi. *How long Ephraim a raw cake shall be in the oven*, is decreed from eternity. 2. Put away your scum, your froth, and the ill blood, and you have a diet-drink from Christ the shorter while. 3. You think long to have Britain's hour, or the ten days of pestilence and sword on Scotland, or the vastations of Ireland, the wars, divisions, and new blasphemies of England, gone and over; but tho' we lose much time, and have bidden farewel to yesterday, and shall never see it again, yet the Lord of time loseth not one moment: if through acquaintance and familiarity you may become good friends with the cross, and bear it patiently; do for Christ, what you will do for time; the former is an act of grace, the Lord will thank you for it; the latter is the work of a carnal man, and will yield you no thanks. 4. Life is a burden to you, when it hath such a sour and sad convoy as heavy afflictions; and the soul looks out at the windows of the clay-prison, O when will the jailor come with the keys, and enlarge a prisoner? But why should you fall out with a friend, for a foe's cause. Christ hath sewed them together for a time; *The vision will not tarry.* Christ is on his journey, wait on, let patience have its perfect work; it is a flower that lieth long under ground; it is a long quarter between sowing and earing, yet faith hath ay a good crop.

This hour.

Among all the hours that Christ had, this was the saddest. 1. Christ saw that his life in this hour would be taken from him; it was convenient that Christ, who was a man, *like us in all things except sin*, should not be a stock in dying, but have actual pain and sense in

the

the losing of his life; for Christ had as much nature, tho' no corruption, as any man: and life is a sweet inheritance, its nature's excellent freehold; and no man is willingly, and without one sigh or tear, cast out of this freehold; and Christ's nature was not brass or iron. Sorrow and sadness found a kindly lodging in him. 2. He had a clay tent of flesh and blood, as the children have, that, Heb. ii. 15. *he might deliver them, who through the fear of death, were all their lifetime subject to bondage.* He must in our nature put on actual fear, to deliver the saints from habitual fear. Nature cannot, without horrour, and a wrinkle on the brow, look straight out on the breadth of death's black face. The martyrs kissed death, because the joy of heaven took lodging in their soul, by anticipation before the term-day, to confirm the truth of God; but death has a sour bite, and sharp teeth, with all its kind kisses. Yea, but Christ must read in the face of death more millions of curses (a curse for every elect, single man, Deut. xxvii. 26. Gal. iii. 10.) than would have affrighted millions of angels. O but there was black and doleful paintrie, hell; and thousand thousands of deaths in one, all written on the visage of death, which was presented to Christ now; and when there was a sad, dark, and thick curtain drawn over Christ's heaven, it must be a sour kiss, to lay his holy mouth to such a black face as death now had. Christ was in sad earnest, when he said, Mat. xxvi. 38. *My soul is extremely out of measure, heavy, even to the death.* 3. Christ having well tempered affections, his soul never being out of joint with sin, was not in dying fool-hardy or bold-life-wasting; for casting away the soul for a straw, is forbidden in the sixth commandment. He saw sad and bloody bills given in against him. O how many thousand of sins, were all made his sins, by imputation? And justice was to sell all the elect over to Christ, and to deliver them all, by tale, to free grace, at no cheaper rate, than the rendering of the soul of Christ to harder than then thousand millions of ordinary deaths. Christ be-

hoved

hoved to earn heaven at the hardest cost, for all his own, with no less than the noble and eminent life and blood of God; such a sum was never told down in heaven, before or after. 4. There is much weight on this hour, in regard of Christ's opposites: three hosts came against Christ, *heaven, hell, earth*; any adversary but God; the enmity of men cannot make me, or any man formally miserable. There be great edges and emphasis in these words, *My God, my God, why hast thou forsaken me?* Not a point, not a letter of them can be wanting, they are all so full and emphatic. 1. *My God, my God*; the forsaking of angels is nothing; that men, all men, *friends, all my inward friends, forsake me*, is not much; they do more than forsake, *they abhor* Job their friend, Job xix. 19. that father and mother, and all my mother's sons forsake me, is hard, yet tolerable, Psal. xxvii. 10. Psal. xxxi. 11. Psal. lxxxviii. 18. Yea, that *mine own heart and flesh forsake me*, is an ordinary (*may be*) amongst men, Psal. lxxiii. 26. But God's forsaking of a man is sad. 2. If he be a God in covenant with me; both God, and then *my God*, that is a warm word, with a child of love; if he forsake me, it is hard: when our own leave us, we forgive all the world to leave us. 3. In forsaking there is a great emphasis; any thing but unkindness, and change of heart and love, is well taken; this speaketh against faith; tho' Christ could not apprehend this; the Lord cannot change, Christ could not believe such a blasphemy, yet the extremity of so sad a condition, offered so much to the humane and sinless and innocent sense of Christ, a change of dispensation. 4. Me, *why hast thou forsaken me*, the Son of thy love, thy only begotten Son, *the Lord of Glory*, who never offended thee? But the relation of Christ to God, was admirable; he was as the sinner, *made sin for us*; in this contest, the enmity of a lion and a leopard is nothing, Hos. xiii. 7, 8. the *renting of the caul*, of the web that goeth about the heart, is but a shadow of pain, to the Lord's running on a man as a giant, in fury and indignation. 2. Hell, and all the powers of darkness, came against Christ in this hour,

hour, Col. ii. 14, 15. (3.) All the earth, and his dearest friends, stood aloof from his calamity; there was no shore on earth to receive this ship-broken man.

In regard of that which was taken from Christ, it was a sad hour; which I desire to be considered thus. 1. The most spiritual life that ever was, the life of him, who saw and enjoyed God in a personal union, was vailed and covered. (1.) Possession in many degrees was lessened: but *in jure*, in right, and in the foundation, not removed. 2. The sense and actual fruition of God, in vision, was over-clouded, but life in the fountain stood safe in the blessed union. 3. The most direful effects, in breaking, bruising, and grinding the Son of God, between the millstones of divine wrath, were here; yet the infinite love and heart of God, remained the same to Christ, without any shadow of variation or change. God's hand was against Christ, his heart was for him. 4. Hence his saddest sufferings were by divine dispensation and economy. God could not hate the Son of his love; in a free dispensation, he pursued in wrath the surety, and loved the Son of God. 5. It cannot be determined, what that wall of separation, that covering and vail was, that went between the two united natures, the union personal still remaining entire, how the Godhead suspended its divine and soul-rejoicing influence, and the Man Christ suffered to the bottom of the highest and deepest pain, to the full satisfaction of divine justice. As it is easy to conceive how the body in death, falleth to dust, and ill-smelling clay, and yet the soul dieth not; but how the soul suffereth not, and is not sadned, is another thing. How a bird is not killed, and doth flee out, and escape, and sing, when a window is broken, with a great noise in the cage, is conceivable: but how the bird should not suffer, or be affected with no affrightment, is harder to our apprehension; and how ship-broken men may swim to the shore and live, when the ship is dashed in an hundred pieces, is nothing hard; but that they should be nothing affrighted, not touch the water, and yet come living to shore, is not so obvious to our con-

sideration,

sideration. Yea, that the soul should remain united with the body in death, and the ship sink, the passengers remaining in the ship, and not be drowned, is a strange thing. The Lord suffered, and died; the ship was broken and did sink, the soul and body separated, and yet the Godhead remained in a personal union, one with the manhood, as our soul and body remain together, while we live and subsist entire persons.

Use 1. Christ hath suffered much in these sad hours for us: he hath drunken hell dry to the bottom, and hath left no hell behind for us, Heb. xii. 2. *Jesus the author and finisher of our faith*: He hath not only suffered so much of the cross, but he hath suffered all the cross; he hath endured the cross, despised the shame. In the original, the words are without any article, . It is as much as he hath left no cross, no shame at all to be suffered by us: and, Phil. ii. 8. *He was obedient to the Father;* he saith not to the death, but *to death, even the death of the cross,* . It holdeth forth to us, that Christ suffered so much for us, as he hath taken up to heaven with him the great cross, and hath carried up with him, as it were, the great death; and hath left us nothing, or very little to suffer: and indeed Christ never denied, but affirmed, he himself behoved to die; but for the believer, he expressly denieth *he shall die,* and that with two negations, John xi. 26

He shall never, in any sort, die. And for our sufferings, Paul calleth them, Col. i. 24.

The remnants, the leavings, the dregs, and after-drops of the sufferings of Christ, the sips and dew-drops remaining in the bottom of the cup, when Christ hath drunken out the whole cup; so are our afflictions, and being compared with what Christ suffered, they are but bits, fragments, and small pieces of death, that we suffer; for the first death that the saints suffer, is but the half and the far least half of death, 'tis but the lips, the outer porch of death; the second death, which Christ

suf-

suffered for us, is only death, and the dominion, lordship and power of death is removed. Why do ye then murmur, fret, repine under afflictions, when you bear little wedges, pins, and chips of the cross? Your Lord Jesus did bear for you the great and only cross, that which is death, shame, and the cross, by way of excellency so called. It is true, the spouse of Christ, since the beginning of the world, and since Christ's time these 1600 years, hath been crying as a woman travailing in birth of a man-child, and the dragon near pursuing her, and is not yet brought to bed. *Lord Jesus, when will the man-child be born, and thy spouse be eased of the birth?* Yet is not this disease deadly; Zion, as soon as she *travailed, brought forth her child,* Isa. lxvi. 8. All her shadows of sufferings shall be quickly gone: the spouse cannot die of child-birth pain; Christ will save both the mother's life, and the babe.

Use 2. Sin is a dear and costly thing: in heaven, in the count-book of justice, it goeth for no less than the *blood of God, the shaming of the Lord of glory;* justice, for the request of all the world, and the prayers of Christ, could not abate one farthing. A man's soul is a dear thing: exchange of commodities, of silks, purple, fine linen, is much; exchange of sapphires, diamonds, rubies, and other precious stones, for baser commodities, is much more; and that ships-full of the gold of Ophir should be given for bread, and things obvious, is a rich trafficking: but the market and value of souls, as it hath not, since God made man on earth, fallen or risen; so it is ever above a world, Mat. xvi. 26. *What hath a man profited, if he lose this?* God will not take silks, nor purples, nor sapphires, nor rubies, nor navies loaden with fine gold, nor any corruptible thing, 1 Pet. i. 18. for souls. The price is one and the same: souls were never bought, nor sold, nor exchanged, nor ransomed, but once; and the price is one, and as high as the soul and blood of the Lord of life. Job xxvii. 8. *What is the hope of an hypocrite, though he hath gained, when God taketh his soul from*

him?

him? Let him cast up his accounts, and lay his charges, he stands a poor man, a man without a soul. What madmen are we, who sell souls daily for prices so far below the Lord's price? A man that would wadset a lordship of many thousands yearly, for a base sum, some pence, or for a night's sleep in a straw-bed, and bind himself not to redeem it, what a waster were he? how worthy to beg? Satan is going through the world, and he gives some pence in hand: O how sad a reckoning, when the devil the cozening creditor comes at night, with his back counts, pay me for your sweet lusts I gave you; answer my bill for your idle oaths, your lies, oppressions, cozening, covenant-breaking, your unjust judging, your starving, and murdering of the widow, and the fatherless, by detaining of the wages of the soldier, your slighting of Christ, and reformation, and the price is referred to God, and the market known! Satan can abate nothing, thy soul he must have, and within few days the body too: is this wisdom to earn hell? and to make away a noble soul for a straw?

3. What are we to give for Christ? what bonds of love hath he laid on us, who earned our heaven for us at so dear a price? I desire only these considerations to have place in our thoughts.

1. As God had but one Son, and one only begotten Son, and he gave him for sinners; so Christ had two loves, one as God, and another as man, he gave them both out for us; and two glories, one as God, one as man and mediator; the one was darkened for us,
he emptied a sea of glory for us, he poured it out for us; and for his other glory, he laid it down, as it were in hell, endured infinite wrath for us.

2. He went to death and the grave, made his testament, and left his love, grace, and peace in legacy to us.

3. *Greater love than this hath no man;* but he saith not, *greater love than this hath no God.* That God did let out so much love to men, is the wonder of the world, and of heaven. We may find words to paint

paint out creatures, and the garment may be wider than the thing; but should angels come and help us to find out expressions for Christ's love, words should be below and in this side of Christ.

4. Behold the man, saith an enemy of Christ; but behold him more than a man, behold the Lord in the garden, sweating out of his holy body, great blobs and floods of love, trickling down upon sinners of clay. Men and angels, come see, and wonder, and adore.

5. Love was Christ's cannon-royal, he battered down with it all the forts of hell, and *triumphed over principalities and powers:* Christ was judgment-proof; he endured the wrath of God, and was not destroyed: he was hell-proof, and grave-proof; he suffered, and rose again; but he was not love-proof, (to borrow that expression) he was not only love-sick for his church, but sick to death, and died for his friends. Cant. ii. 4. *His banner over his church, was love.* Saints, be sworn to his colours, die and live with Christ: and take Christ in the one arm, his cause, and the gospel in the other, and your life between both, and say to all enemies, take one, take all. *The midst of Christ chariot is paved with love, for the daughters of Jerusalem*, Cant. iii. 10. Christ's royal seat, both in the gospel, in which he is carried through the world as a conqueror, Rev. vi. 2. and in the souls of his children, is love. From the sense of this, it were our happiest life, to live and love with Christ; for he hath carried up to heaven with him, the love, and the heart, and the treasures of the sons of God; so as all ours are with him above time.

6. We are not to fear death extremely, nor hell at all. Christ feared both for our comfort: he hath taken away the worst of death; in that, 1. He hath subdued hell and sin, and there remained to us but the outer side of death. 2. The believer but half-dies, and swooneth, or rather sleepeth in the grave. 3. He dieth by will, because he chooseth to be with Christ, Phil. i. 23. rather than by nature or necessity. 4. As dying and sufferings are the cup that Christ drank;

so are we to love the cup the better, that Christ's lip touched it, and left the perfume of the breathings of the Holy Ghost in it. In common inns, by the wayside, princes, and common travellers, and thousands lie in one bed; the clothes may be changed, but the bed is the same. Christ tasted of death, Heb. ii. for us; but there was gall in his cup, that is not in ours: Christ's wormwood was bitter with wrath, ours sweetned with consolation.

7. All the saints are in Christ's debt of infinite love. When we grieve the Spirit purchased by Christ, we draw blood of his wounds afresh, and so testify, that we repent that Christ suffered so much for us. The Father hath sworn, and will not repent, that he is an eternal priest, and stands to it, that his blood is of eternal worth; and when the Father sweareth this, Christ is the same one God with him, and swears, that he thinketh all his blood well-bestowed, and will never give over the bargain: his bride is his bride, tho' dear bought; and his intercession in heaven speaketh his hearty *Amen*, and fullest consent of love to our redemption.

8. All this was done by Christ for nothing; grace fell from God, on the creature, by mere grace. Grace is the only hire of grace.

9. When ancient love looked first on sinners, how ugly and black did the Lord see and foresee us to be? But Christ loved us, not according to what we were, but to what grace and love was to make us; and that was fair and spotless. And this love was so free in the secret of eternal election, that it was not increased by Christ's merits and death; but the merits, death, and fruit of this love, had being and worth from Christ's eternal love; and Christ's love hath no fountain and cause, but love.

10. The law of gratitude tieth us to love Christ, for he hath loved us. If the love of Christ be in us; it worketh nothing in order to merit or hire; (Libertines need not weaken Christ's love from doing, upon this fear;) but love doth all in order to the debt of

love,

love, and obliged expressions to love, which excludeth not law, but the law's rigid cursing and imperious commanding. Christ's love is most imperious, but is no hireling, and looks not to the penny wages, but the free crown.

But for this cause came I to this hour.

Here is the fifth article in this prayer; a sort of correction, in which Christ doth resign his will, as man, to the will of God; as Mat. xxvi. 39. Luke xxii. 42. *Nevertheless, not my will, but thine be done.*

In this there is offered to us a question, whether or no there be in this prayer any repugnancy in the human will of Christ to the will of God? For, 1. A correction of the human will, seemeth to import a jarring and a discord. 2. Christ desired that, the contrary whereof, he knew, was from eternity decreed of God. 3. The law of God is so spiritual, straight and holy, that it requireth not only a conformity to it, in our will, actions, words and purposes; but also in all our affections, desires, first motions, and inclinations of our heart, that no unperfect and half-formed lustings arise in us, even before the compleat consent of the will, that may thwart or cross the known law and command of God; and by this, *Thou shalt not lust*, Rom. vii. and the duty of the highest love we owe to God, to *love him with all the heart, soul, mind, and whole strength*, Mat. xxii. 37. Mark xii. 33. Luke x. 27. Some Arians and Arminians, John Geysteranus at the synod of Dort, have said blasphemously, That there was concupiscence and a will repugnant to God's will in the second Adam, as in the first. But this they spoke against the consubstantiality and deity of the Son of God. To which we say,

Asser. 1. *Jesus Christ, that holy thing*, Luke i. 35. was a fit high priest, *holy, harmless, undefiled, separated from sinners*, Heb. vii. 26. *Which of you* (saith Christ to the Jews) *convinceth me of sin?* John viii. 46. There could not be a spot in this *Lamb sacrificed for*

the

the sins of the world, no prick in this rose, no cloud in this fair sun, no blemish in this beautiful well beloved.

Asser. 2. An absolute, resolved will or desire of heart, to lust after that which God forbiddeth in his law, must be a sinful jarring between the creature's and the Creator's will. Now Christ's will was conditional, and clearly submissive; it lay ever level with his Father's holy will.

Asser. 3. I shall not with some affirm, that which in the general is true, a will contrary to God's revealed command and will, called *Voluntas signi,* which is our moral rule to oblige us, is a sin; but a will contrary to God's decree, called *Voluntas bene placidi,* which is not our rule obliging, except the Lord be pleased to impose it on us, as a moral law, is not a sin. Peter and the apostles, after they heard that prophecy of their denying of Christ, and their being sinfully scandalized, and their forsaking of Christ, when the shepherd was smitten, were obliged to have a will contrary to that decree, and to pray that they might not be led into temptation, but might have grace to confess their Saviour before men, and not flee, nor be scattered: here is a resolute will of men lawfully contrary to the revealed decree of God; yet not sinful. But the Lord's will that Christ should die for man, as it was a decree of the wise and most gracious Lord, pitying lost man, so was it also a revealed commandment to Christ, that he should be willing to die, and be *obedient to the death, even the death of the cross*; Phil. ii. 8. Yea, a rule of such humble obedience, as we are obliged to follow; as is said, verse 5. *Let this mind be in you, which was also in Christ Jesus,* etc. If the Lord's will that Christ should die, be nothing but his mere decree, it could not oblige us in the like case to be willing, as John saith, *To lay down our life for the brethren.* Yea, John x. 18. Christ hath a commandment of God, and the revealed will of God, to die for us; *No man taketh it from me, but I lay it down of myself: I have power to lay it down, I have power to take it a-*
gain:

gain: *this commandment have I received of my Father.* Here is an express commandment given to Christ, to die for sinners; and the Father loveth Christ for obedience to this commandment.

Asser. 4. A conditional and a submissive desire, though not agreeable to a positive law and commandment of God, is no sin; nor doth the law require a conformity in all our inclinations, and the first notions of our desires, to every command of God, tho' most contrary to nature, and our natural and sinless inclinations.

1. If God command Abraham to kill his only begotten son, and offer him in a sacrifice to God, which was a mere positive commandment; for 'tis not a command of the law of nature (nor any other than positive) for the father to kill the son; if yet Abraham retain a natural inclination and love, commanded also in the law of nature, to save his son's life, and to desire that he may live: this desire and inclination, tho' contradictory to a positive command of God, is no sin; because the fifth command, grounded on the law of nature, doth command it. Nor did God's precept (Abraham, *kill now thy son, even Isaac thine only begotten son*) ever include this, Abraham, *root out of thine heart all desire and inclination natural in a father to preserve the life of the child.* So the positive command of the Father, that the Son of God should lay down his life for his sheep, did never root out of the sinless nature of the man Christ a natural desire to preserve his own being and life, especially he desiring it with special reservation of the will of God commanding that he should die.

2. A martyr, dying for the truth of Christ, may have a natural and conditional desire and inclination to live tho' his living be contrary to the Lord's revealed will, commanding him to seal the gospel with his blood, and to confess Christ before men.

If the brother, son, daughter, wife or friend, that is as a man's own soul, Deut. xiii. 6. *blaspheme God*; yea, if father or mother do it, Deut. xxxiii. 8, 9. yet is a

fa-

father obliged to stone the son or daughter; the son being a magistrate, or a Levite and priest, to judge according to law, (*the priests lips should preserve knowledge*, Mal. ii. 8.) that his father or mother ought to be stoned to death; yet ought not father or son to lay aside the natural desire of being and life to son, father, brother, which the law of nature in the fifth command doth require; especially the desire being conditional, with submission to God's will, as the desire of Christ is here: and the command to stone the blasphemer, that the father stone the son, the son the father, being positive, and tho' founded on the law of nature, that a man prefer his Lord Creator and God before son, or father and mother, yet are they not precepts of the law of nature, such as is the precept of nature, that a man desire his own life and being, the father the life and being of the son.

Asser. 5. The apparent opposition (for it is not real) is rather between Christ's sensitive and his sinless mere natural desire and affection, and his reasonable will, than his will, and the will of God: nor can any say there is a fight or jarring between the conditional desire of Christ, subjected, in the same act of praying, to the Lord's decree, and the resolute and immutable will of God. The law of God, because holy and spiritual, doth require a conformity between all the inclinations and motions of our soul, and the law of nature; but an absolute conformity between all our inclinations and every positive command of God, such as was the Lord's command that Christ should die for sinners, is not required in the law of God. If Adam submit his natural hunger or desire to eat of the forbidden tree, to God's law, and eat not, there is no sinful jarring between his will and God's positive law, *Thou shalt not eat of the tree of knowledge of good and evil.*

It becomes us, as Christ's example goeth before us, to submit in the hardest and most bloody providences, to the straight and holy will of God. 1. Christ professeth he hath no will divided from God's will; he

layeth

layeth down his glory, his heaven, his life, his fruition of the sweet influence of an highest vision, love, presence, feeling of God in a personal union, at the feet of God, that the Lord may carve and cut and dispose of him, and his blood, as he thought good. 2. All the difficulty in us, in whom dwelleth a body of sin, is to answer the objections that flesh and blood hath against a sad providence; which I will labour to do, and then give some rules for direction.

Ob. 1. *This is a bloody and rough way that the Lord leadeth his people, that they drink wormwood and gall of blood, and not tears only.*

Answ. Providence is full of mysteries; let the way be shame, the crown is glory; and the present condition be hell, the end is heaven: providence is a hand-writing of mercy, tho' we cannot ever read it, more than Belshazzar could read his bill of justice. We see a woman with child, but cannot tell whether it be a living or a dead birth she shall bring forth; or whether the child shall be base and poor, or honourable and renowned, ere he die. The births in the womb of providence are invisible to us; out of the ashes of a burnt and destroyed church, the Lord raiseth up a phenix, a *king's daughter, a princess that shall rule the nations with a rod of iron, a Zion that hath the strength of an unicorn; yea, Jacob's seed shall be in many waters, his king shall be higher than Agag, and his kingdom shall be exalted: God brought him out of Egypt,* Num. xxiv. 7, 8. Christ breweth the water of life, out of drink of gall, wormwood, and blood; if the head be gold, as Christ is, the body cannot without great incongruity be base clay.

Ob. 2. *But all go wrong, confusion and vastation lie on the people of God.*

Answ. To him who sitteth on the throne, and gives law and judgment to the most unconstant things imaginable, the waves of the sea, and orders them, and rules *a sea of glass*, a brittle and frail thing, and a sea of most unnatural confusions, a *sea mingled with fire*, nothing can be out of order; hell, the beast and dragon that *make war with the Lamb*, the laying waste

the

the holy city, the killing of the witnesses, are all orderly means, ranked by the Lord, whose armies cannot reel, not spill their march; when he draws them up to the execution of his wise decrees, the confusion is to our eye; but judgment, law and order there are, tho' not visible to us. Who can pull him out of his invisible and high throne of wisdom, counsel and power? It may be, he sits not always on his throne of justice.

Ob. 3. 'But what a providence is it, that those that open their mouth against heaven, are fat, and shine, and prosper; and those that fear God, are plagued every day, and killed all the day long, and counted as sheep for the slaughter?'

Answ. 1. *Offend not against the generation of the children of God*, as if it were lost labour, and as good to sow wheat in the sea, as *serve the Lord*, and walk *mournfully before him*: you see their work, but not their wages. 2. It is painful to trace providence in all its ways, circuits, bout-gates, lines, turnings. But, 3. Surely in the end God turneth the tables, he maketh all odds equal, the empty bucket goeth down, the full cometh up. 4. The Lord hath set the wicked in a chair of gold, but on the top of a house, and rolling stone above the mouth of a pit ten hundred fathom deep: this is a jogging and slippery condition. 5. They slip away to eternity and to hell *in a moment*. 6. Their happiness is a golden dream, Psalm lxxiii. 12, 13, etc.

Ob. 'Means fail, men change, creatures are weak.'

Answ. So long as Christ changeth not, and your head liveth, and steereth the helm of heaven and earth, all must be well. If all life, all health, and so much as eternal life be in the head, how can the heart ake or quake, except it first create, and then fancy fears, and do not really suffer.

Ob. 5. 'Our kingdom's strength is gone, we cannot subsist.'

Answ. Col. i. 17, 18. *In Christ all things subsist, he is the head of the body the church.* Faith is the substance; Budeus, the *boldness and fortitude;* Beza,
the

the *firm and constant expectation*; the *Syrian* and *Arabian*, the *confident gloriation* of, or in *things hoped for*, and a convincing light and *evidence of things not seen.* There is good reason to believe that God will lift up a fallen people, who desire to fear him, and wait for his help.

Ob. 6. *They plow upon Christ's back, and make long and deep furrows on Israel from her youth*, Psal. cxxix. 1.

Answ. True, plowing is a work of hope; but have you not seen enemies digging a grave for Christ, and preparing a coffin for him ere he be dead? and they have been fain to fill up the living man's grave; and they plow, but Christ cometh in and soweth joy in the hot furrow, and reaps the crop, and the quiet fruits of righteousness. The enemies plant, but the vintage is Christ's; *One sows, but another reaps.*

Ob. 7. 'But the souls under the altar do cry to God, and their blood is not avenged: their blood, and their graves in their kind, make supplications before the throne for justice, yet the enemies prosper.'

Answ. Hath not the Lord appointed a time for fighting and suffering, and a time for triumphing, when these that *have gotten the victory over the beast, and over his mark, and over the number of his name, stand on the sea of glass, having the harps of God, singing the song of Moses the servant of God, and the song of the Lamb*: There was a time when the Lamb did weep, and *in the days of his flesh, offered up prayers and supplications, with strong crying and tears, unto him that was able to save him from death.* Rev. xv. 23. Heb. v. 7. It is a sin to carve a date of our own for justice.

Ob. 8. 'But he delays his coming.'

Answ. 'But he is not slack, as some count slackness.' If general justice to a world must be measured by thousands of years, as but one day to God; particular judgments may have hundred of years: and when the saints are killed, Christ surviveth them, to redeem them from blood and disgrace; when they are dead, when their cause is judged, and they rotten into powder in

the

the grave, they are redeemed, even when the souls under the altar are avenged on their murderers.

Ob. 9. 'It stumbleth many, that wicked men are fat, and their faces shine, as if God were with them.'

Answ. If they be fat on common mercies, the more shame to the saints, if they be not fat, and *their bones green as an herb*, upon the same fare, and the same mercies, perfumed with Christ; and there is more fatness and marrow in the higher than in the lower house. Saints are lean through their own unbelief.

Now, for rules of submission to providence in order to the text, let these be considered;

Rule 1. Christ's patience, and so our submission must be bottomed on a looking above-hand to the will of God; every wheel in a great work, moves according to the motion of the highest and first wheel that moves all the rest. Every inferior court acts as ordered by the highest and supreme senate, the greatest in the kingdom. Every inferior orb in the heaven is moved in subordination to the *Primum mobile*, the highest that moveth all the rest; the motion of rivers regulate the flowings of lesser brooks. And things that move on earth, as the heavens move, so are they carried: the principle of motions and ways in all mortals, beginneth at the highest mover, the just and wise will of God; all are to say, *Not my will, but thy will be done.*

Rule 2. There is no ground of submission in a cross providence, but to look to the end that Christ looked to, the Lord's wise and holy will: *he curseth, because the Lord biddeth him*, saith David of Shimei; and there he fixeth his stake. The Lord hath taken away, saith Job; and upon the Lord's taking away, he saith, *Blessed be the name of the Lord*: any man can say, *Blessed be the name of the Lord, who giveth*; the greatest part of men break their teeth, in biting at the nearest link of the chain of second causes, but they arise never up to God, the first mover.

Rule 3. Christ not only submitteth to God's will, but he approveth that it may be done. So Hezekiah, Isa.

xxxix. 8. *He said, moreover, good is the word of the Lord; the thing was heard, that all in his house should be carried away to Babylon, and his sons should be captives.* Yet the will of the Lord was good and just, when the thing willed and decreed of God was evil to him.

Rule 4. Christ will not hinder God to do what he thinks good; *Thy will be done.* Murmuring is a stone in God's way; murmuring is an antiprovidence, a little god, setting itself against the true God, that steers all in wisdom; and the murmurer doth what he can to stop up God's way. Old Eli, when he heard sad news, says, 1 Sam. iii. 18. *It is the Lord,* [Vagnase] *Let him, I hinder him not to do, what is good in his eyes.* David saith, 2 Sam. xv. 26. *If the Lord say, I have no delight in thee, behold, here am I, let him do to me what seems good in his eyes. Here am I,* is as much as, I will not flee him, nor hinder him; I lay myself under him, to receive his strokes. So Christ, Heb. x. 5. Psal. xl. *Thou hast prepared my ears, or my body, here am I*; v. 7. *Here am I, to do thy will.*

Rule 5. Christ gave not away his natural will; but in the act of willing, he submitted it; it was a broken will that Christ reserved to himself, or a submitted will, *hic & nunc.* Christ seeketh not the resigning of natural faculties in hard providences, but that we quit contest with God; and that our will be not abolished, but broken; especially, that we do not quarrel with justice. Lament. iii. 28. *He sitteth alone, and keepeth silence, because he hath born it upon him.* v. 29. *He putteth his mouth in the dust, if so be there may be hope.* v. 30. *He giveth his cheeks to him that smiteth them; he is filled with reproach.* There be here many sweet signs of a broken will. 1. Solitary sadness. 2. Silence, the soul not daring to quarrel with God. 3. The stooping to the dust, and putting clay in the mouth, for fear that it speak against God's dispensation, as Job xl. 4, 5. 4. A willing accepting of buffets on the *cheeks, and reproaches*: so, Mic. vii. 9. *I will bear the indignation of the Lord, because I have*

sin-

sinned. When the soul is made like a broken and daunted heifer, or a silly *heartless dove,* so as the man, like a well-nurtured child, kisseth the rod of God. He is a bad soldier, who followeth his captain sighing and weeping; faith sings at tears, and rejoiceth under hope in the ill day.

Rule 6. It is the child's happiness, that the wise father's will be his rule, not his own; and for the orphan the tutor's wit is better than his own will. Our own will is our hell, Ezek. xviii. 31. *Why will ye die, O house of Israel?* Christ's will is heaven. Christ thinks it is best, that his Father's will stand, and his human will be repealed, Rom. xv. 3. *For even Christ pleased not himself;* to have no will of your own, is the pearl in the ring, a jewel in submission. (2.) That the Lord's end is good, he minds to have me home to heaven; then, as in his six days work of creation, he made nothing ill, so he hath been working these five thousand years, and all his works of providence are as good as his works of creation; he cannot chuse an ill mean for a good end: if God draw my way to heaven through fire, tortures, blood, poverty, though he should trail me through hell, he cannot err in leading, I may err in following.

Object. *But there is a better way beside, and he leads others through a rosy and green valley, and my way within few inches to it, is a wilderness of thorns.*

Answ. Gold absolutely is better than a draught of water: but comparatively, water is better to Samson, dying for thirst, than all the gold in the earth: so, cutting a vein, is in itself ill; but comparatively, letting blood through a cut vein, is good for a man in danger of an extreme fever; there is no better way out of heaven for thee, than the very way that the Lord leads thee. God not only chuses persons, but also things; and every cross that befals thee, is a chosen and selected cross, and it was shapen in length, and breadth, and measure, and weight, up before the throne, by God's own wise hand: heaven is the work-house of all befals thee, every evil is the birth that

lay

lay in the womb of an infinitely wise decree; so God is said to frame evil, *as a potter doth an earthen vessel,* (so [*Ratzai;*] *Jatsar*) signifieth, Jer. xviii. 11. *To frame a vessel of clay,* is a work of art and wisdom; so it is a work of deliberation and choice: God is said to *devise judgment against Babylon,* Jer. li. 12. *And the Lord hath done to his people the things which he devised.* [*Zamam*] is to think, meditate, study, devise, Deut. xix. 18. and Isa. xlv. 7. *He creates darkness and evil*: it is such a work of omnipotency and wisdom, as the making of a world of nothing. Then, if God follow infinite art in shaping vengeance against Babylon, far more must he wisely study to mould and shape afflictions for his own; for no afflictions befal the saints, but they be well framed, chosen, wisely studied, forged, and created crosses. A potter cannot frame by deeper art and judgment, a water-pot for such an end and use; a fashioner cannot frame clothes in proportion for a man's body, so fitly, as the wise Lord, in judgment and cunning, shapes and frames this affliction as a measure for thy foot only; poverty for this man, and it is shapen to his measure; wicked children and the sword on David's house, fitted for him; such a lothsome disease for this saint; want of friends and banishment for such a man; another more and heavier should be shapen too wide for thy soul, and another lighter should have been too strait, short, and narrow for thee. It is comfortable, when I believe the draught, portraiture, and lineaments of my affliction, were framed and carved in all the limbs, bones, parts, qualities of it, in the wise decree, and in the heart and breast of Christ. It were not good to bear a cross of the devil's shaping: were there as much wormwood and gall in the saint's cup, as the devil would have in it, then hell should be in every cup; and how many hells should I drink? and how often should the church drunk death? It is good I know Christ brewed the cup, then it will work the end; for, be it never so contrary and sour to my taste, and so unsavoury, Christ will not cast poison in it; he hath

pur-

purposed I should sail with no other wind to heaven, and I know it is better than any wind to me, for that port.

Rule 7. Christ prescribes no way to his Father, but in the general, *The Lord's will be done on me,* (saith he) be what it will; let hell, and death, and devils' malice and heaven's indignation, and enmity, and war, ill-will, and persecution from earth, hard measure from friends and lovers, if the will of my Father so be, welcome with my soul; welcome black cross, welcome pale death, welcome curses, and all the curses of God, that the just law could lay on all my children, (and they are a fair number) welcome wrath of God, welcome shame, and the cold grave. The submission of faith subscribeth a blank paper, let the Lord write in what he pleaseth; patience dares not contest and stand upon pennies or pounds, on hundreds or thousands with God: Moses and Paul dare refer their heaven, and their share in Christ, and the book of life, to Christ, so the Lord may be glorified: submissive faith putteth much upon Christ, *Let him slay me, yet will I trust in him,* said Job, xiii. 15. Heman alledgeth, it was not one single cross, Psal. lxxxviii. 7. *Thou hast afflicted me with all thy waves.* And David, Psal. xlii. 7. *All thy waves and all thy billows are gone over me.* One of God's waves could have drowned David; afflictions coming in armies, and in a battle-array, say, that one single soldier cannot subdue us. Lawful war is the most violent, and the last remedy against a state, and it argueth a great necessity of the sword. Job had an army sent against him, and from heaven too, chap. vi. 4. *The terrors of God do set themselves in array against me.* See what a catalogue of sufferings, Paul did refer to God, 2 Cor. xi. 23, 24, 25, etc. One good violent death would have made away a stronger man than Paul, yet he was willing for Christ to be in *deaths often, many deaths, many stripes, many prisons, five times nine and thirty stripes; this was near two hundred stripes,* every one of them was a little death: *thrice beaten with rods, once stoned, thrice in shipwreck,*

NUMB. II. C c

night and day sailing in the deep, in journeying often, in perils of waters, in perils of robbers, in perils of his own countrymen, in perils by the heathen, in perils in the city, in perils in the wilderness, in perils in the sea, in perils among false brethren, in weariness, and painfulness, in watching often, in hunger, in thirst, in fasting often, in cold, in nakedness, etc. Many of us would either have a cross of our own carving; as we love will-worship, and will-duties, so we love will-suffering, and desire nothing more, than if that we must suffer, Christ with his tongue would lick all the gall off our cross, and leave nothing but honey, and a cross of sugar and milk; we love to suffer with a reserve, and to die upon a condition. An indefinite and catholic resignation of ourselves without exception to Christ, and to undergo many furnaces, many hells, many deaths, as Christ will, is a rare grace of God, and not of ordinary capacity.

Rule 8. Christ, in submitting his will, maketh the prophecies, the revealed gospel his rule: and in the matter of duty, is willing to be ruled by God's revealed will; in the matter of suffering, he is willing that the Lord's will stand for a law, to which he doth willingly submit, and will in no sort quarrel with everlasting decrees. To be ruled by the one, is holiness; to submit to the other, is patience: for patience is higher than any ordinary grace, in regard 'tis willing to adore and reverence something more and higher than a commanding, promising, and threatening will of God. It was a grace in Christ most eminent, in the *Lamb of God*, dumb, meek and silent before his shearers, the meekest in earth and in heaven, that he did not only never resist the revealed will of God, but never thought, motion, nor any hint of a desire was in him, against the secret and eternal decree and counsel of God. Christ will not have us to make images of him, who is the invisible God; but when, in his works of justice, power, love, free-grace, he setteth before us the image of his glorious nature and attributes, he will have us to adore him in these. According to his decree of re-

probation,

probation, he raised up Pharaoh to be clay to all men; on whom as on a voluntary and rational vessel of wrath, they might read power, justice, truth, sovereignty; in these works we are to tremble before him, and adore the Lord. So in works of grace, that are the image of the invisible God, the Lord is to be loved. 1 Tim. i. 16. *In Paul the chief of sinners*, the Lord holds forth an image of the freest grace, no less than in the revealed will of God; for, 1. Christ made an example of mercy and free grace in him. 2. He made a speaking and crying spectacle to all ages, an
a printed copy of crying grace to all the world: and in this we are to adore and submit to him. Such a limb of hell hath received mercy, not I, who before men was holier. O submit to this work of grace, as to the copy of his eternal decree, and be silent.

Rule 9. Christ putteth nature and natural reason, that his natural will might seem to plead withall, under the Lord's feet: so it would seem strange. God hath many sons, but none like Christ: he was a son, his alone; he had never a brother by an eternal generation; he was the only heir of the house; but never a son so afflicted as he: this seems against all reason. But Christ brings in his Father's will with an
But, Mat. xxvi. 39. John xii. 27. Luke xxii. 42. Mark xiv. 36. *But thy will be done.* 'Tis against submission, to put absolute interrogatories upon the Lord: we love to have God make an account of his providence to us, and that the last and final appeal of the ways of the Lord should be to our reason, as to the great senate and supremest court in heaven and earth. 'Tis true, Christ putteth a *why* upon God, *My God, my God, why hast thou forsaken me?* But, 1. with the greatest faith that ever was, a doubled act of believing, *My God, my God.* 2. With the extremest love, that ever was in a man; 'tis also a two-fold cord of warmness of heart to his Father, *My God, my God.* 3. 'Tis a word relative to the covenant between the Father and the Son; for *my God* is a covenant-expression, that the Father will keep what he hath promised to his Son; and relateth to the

infinite

infinite faithfulness of the covenant-maker. 4. God relateth to the dominion, lordship and sovereignty that the Lord hath, and therefore that Christ will submit to him. 5. Christ's complaint of the Lord's forsaking, sheweth the tenderness of his soul, in prizing the favour of his Father, more than any thing in heaven and earth. And therefore Christ's *why* is a note of, 1. Admiration: 2. Of sinless sorrow; conjoined with love, tenderness and submission to God. Christ cannot speak to his Father, beside the truth; *but every man is a liar*; and we seldom put questions and queries upon sovereignty, but we prefer our reason to infinite wisdom. Job is out, and takes his marks by the clouds, and the moon, when he saith, Job xiii. 24. *Why holdest thou me for thine enemy?* Chap. iii. 11. *Why died I not from the womb? Why did I not give up the ghost, when I came out of the belly?* And Jeremiah xv. 18. *Why is my pain perpetual, and my wound uncurable, which refuseth to be healed?* Chap. xx. 18. *Wherefore came I out of the womb to see labour and sorrow, that my days should be consumed with shame?*

All the Lord's works are full, yea with child, of reason, wisdom, and grave, and weighty causes: and though we see not his acts to have a *why*, yet there is a cause, why he doth all he doth; reason is necessity to him, and an essential ingredient in all his actions.

Rule 10. In this administration of providence, with Christ, the Lord goeth many ways at once: in this very act he redeemeth the world, judgeth Satan, satisfieth the law and justice, glorifieth Christ, destroyeth sin, fulfilleth his own eternal will and counsel. In one war he can ripen Babylon for wrath, humble his church, deliver Jeremiah, punish idolatry. In the same war he can humble and correct Scotland, harden malignants, that they will not hearken to offers of peace; and blow up their haters, that they may be lofty through victories, and be ripened for wrath through unthankfulness to God. Providence hath many eyes, so also many feet and hands under the wings, to act and walk a thousand ways at once. There is a manifold

wis-

wisdom in providence, as in the work of redemption. In every work that God doth, he leaveth a wonder behind him; no man can come after the Almighty, and say, I could have done better than he. 'Tis natural to blame God in his working, but impossible to mend his work.

Rule 11. Nor is Christ made a loser, by losing his will for the Lord, but his will is fulfilled in that which he feared, Heb. v. 7. Providence submitted unto, rendereth an *hundred fold in this life*, Mat. xix. 29. God makes the income above hope, Gen. xlviii. 11. *And Israel said to Joseph, I had not thought to see thy face, and lo, God hath shewed me also thy seed.* One berry is not a cluster, that two men cannot bear, but 'tis a field, an earth of vine-trees in the seed, Eph. iii. 20. *He is able to do above all things, more than abundantly above that we can ask or think,* above the shaping or frame of my words or thoughts. But I can ask heaven, he can give more than heaven, and above heaven; yea, I can think of Christ, but he can give above the Christ that I can think on, because I cannot comprehend infinite Jesus Christ.

Rule 12. Christ is not so intent and heart bended on freedom from death and this black and sad hour, but he reverences a higher providence, that *God's will be done*; so are we to look to providence, and we are not to stumble at an external stroke in sad occurrences, when, Job. xix. 22. *God destroyeth the perfect and the wicked.* And he furbishes his sword, Ezek. xxi. 3. and saith, *I will draw out my sword out of its sheath, and will cut off from thee, the righteous and the wicked.*

Then, 1. *Arise, go down to the potter's house,* Jer. xviii. The earth is God's work-house; for clay, good and bad, are equally on the wheels; Christ as punishable for our sins, though a vessel of burning gold, is under art; sovereignty rolls about three in one wheel, the blaspheming, the repenting thief, and Christ who is virtue, grace, yea glory, in the midst. An elect and reprobate man may be both sewed in the same winding-sheet, they may touch others skins in the same grave,

grave, but they are not rolled in, in the same hell. Yea, *Ham* is saved in the ark, but as the unclean beasts are, he is preserved from drowning, but reserved to cursing.

2. There is a providence of grace, as there is in God a special love of free grace; the good and the bad figs are not in the same invisible basket; there is a pavilion, a cabinet of silk in God's privy chamber, seen to no eye, Psal. xxvii. 5. *And upon all the glory shall be a covering*, Isa. iv. 9. Christ's free and invisible love, is a fair white web of gold, that a saint is wrapped in, in the ill day. Where is he? he is hid, yet he goes thro' the sieve, and sifted he must be, but *not a grain of him falls to the earth*, Amos ix. 9.

3. There have been questions about the prerogative of kings, and the privilege of parliaments too; but undeniably in the market-road of providence, the Lord hath kept a prerogative-royal of justice to himself, to *cut off the innocent and righteous with the wicked*, in temporal judgments. 2. And of special grace of providence, when the godly man is blacked with a death-mark, and condemned to die; God's prerogative sends him a reprival of grace, above the law, and current of providence, Isa. xxxviii. 5. Hezekiah (saith the high landlord) is summoned to flit and remove, yet he shall dwell in his farm of clay, fifteen years. 3. This prerogative dispenseth with fire, not to burn; with the sea, not to ebb and flow, so long as the soles of the feet of Christ's bride are upon the new sound sands in the heart of the sea; yea, with hungry lions, not to eat their meat, when they have no food but the flesh of Daniel, beloved of the Lord. Christ here commits himself unto an unseen sovereignty. For Abraham to kill his own only begotten son of promise; to reason, 'tis a work of God, but 'tis a providence of nonsense. Neither law nor gospel, for ought that reason can see, shall warrant it; yet sovereignty commands it, and that's enough. Afflictions of trials, such as the prosperity of the wicked, and the trying sufferings of the godly, seem more to contradict God's promises, and revealed will in the

word,

word, than any other visitations of God; therefore, beside that they require patience, they must have faith in an eminent manner. To believe infinite wisdom can tie the murthering of Isaac by his own father, against the law of nature (as it seems) with the gospel, which cannot command unnatural bloods, must require much faith.

Rule 13. Christ declares, when matters are at the worst, there is good will for him, in the done will of God. 'Tis an objection to sense, and to sinless nature in *Christ-man*? O, dost thou not see sad and sour-faced death, is not thy soul, thy darling, in the power of dogs? Hath not hell long and bloody teeth? is not the furnace, the oven of the Lord's highest indignation, for the sins of all the chosen of God, very hot? when the flames of it makes thee a troubled soul, and cause thee to sweat out blood; what blood shall be left for scourging, for the iron nails of that sad cross? *True* (saith Christ) *I have* (God knows) *a heavy soul, my strength is dried up like a potsherd:* This cup casteth a savour of hell and fiery indignation, a sight of it would kill a man, yet I'll drink it; the good and just will of my Father be done, there I stand, further I go not. To be at a stand, and to lay silence on our tumultuous thoughts, who are compassed with a body of sin, and to be satisfied with the will of the Lord, is our safest; we should not be persuaded by the cross, or all that sense can say, far less what sin can say, from this, *The will of the Lord be done.* The friends of Paul, hearing what he must suffer, say, Acts xx. 14. *When he would not be persuaded, we ceased, saying, The will of the Lord be done.* It is grace to cease and say no more, when we see the Lord declare his mind to us; an holy heart will not go one hair's-breadth beyond the Lord's revealed will.

1. Because love, which thinketh not ill, does not black the spotless and fair will of God, when it is revealed to be from God, though hell were in that will.

2. Faith

2. Faith seeth, even in permitting of persecution from Pharoah and Egypt, the Lord's good-will in the burning bush, the very good-will by which he saveth his people redeemed in Christ, Mat. xi. 26. Phil. i. 13. *Who dwelleth in the bush*, Deut. xxxiii. 16. And 'tis considerable that the same good-will, which is the root of reprobation, and of permitting hell and devils, and devils persecuting instruments, to turn his church into ashes, and to a burnt bush; and devils and men to crucify Christ, is free grace, and the root of election to glory, and is extended to the saints, Rom. ix. 15, 16, 17. Eph. i. 11. Faith seeth and readeth free grace in a providence, which, of itself, is extended to devils and reprobate men, tho' not as extended to them; and it is an argument of true grace, if any can say Amen to hell and the saddest indignation coming from this will, tho' against a particular will of our own.

3. As we are obliged to adore God, so also his sovereignty and holy will, when 'tis revealed to us; and to murmur against it, because it crosseth our short-sighted, and narrow-witted will, is the highest contempt of God, and that which is the soul and formal of sin, and the determination of a wicked and ill-stated question; whether should my short and pur-blind will, stand for eternity; or the holy and infinitely wise will of God, which had eternity of duration, infiniteness of wisdom, and not seven, but millions of eyes, to advise what was decreed as fittest to be done.

4. Since there is not a *fatum*, nor an adamantine destiny and irrevocable decree but this; is it holy wisdom to knock hard heads with God? 'Tis true, pride grows green, and casteth out its golden branches in the fattest soil: but, Job ix. 4. *He is wise in heart, and mighty in strength; who hath hardened himself against him, and prospered?* There is infinite wisdom in God, and infinite power to bring to pass his decrees; will clay counterwork God's infinite counsel? The former of all things makes fire-works under the earth against sinners; can sinners make counter-mines to out-work the Almighty? Sure, if he be wise in heart,

who

who hath a most eminent, holy, and just providence in all that falleth out, when we hear that the gospel, and the church of Christ are oppressed in judgment, we are to look on that oppression, as on the sin of other men, and as our cross, and to mourn for it, in the former consideration; and in the latter, as it troubles us, to judge it good, necessary, and better than if it had been otherwise. The formal reason of goodness is the will of God, and your judgment is to esteem that good, which is ill to you, tho' it be sour and heavy; for it hath goodness from this, and goodness to you, that the Lord hath decreed it. To be sour and sweet, make up a middle taste most pleasant; Christ twisteth black and white in one web; the Jews sins, which he willeth not; and their sin is the redemption of man, which he loveth: and these two are pleasant to behold, and when they are mixed in one, and come from the most wise God, they have beauty to God; far be it from me, to judge them black, or unjust, which are fair, to him.

Rule 14. Christ submits his will to the will of God, in soul-desertions; so should we do. Christ's love to his Father, is no critic, no knotty questionist, to spin, and forge jealousies against the Lord's dispensation in the influence of heaven on his soul. He is willing to lay his soul-comforts in the bosom and free-will of his Father; and in this he judgeth the Lord's will, better than his own will. We have too many querulous love-motions against the reality of Christ's love, when he hides himself. O but we are covetous and soul-thirsty after our own will, in the matter of soul-manifestations! either I see little here, or we idol comforts, and would gladly have a Christ of created grace, rather than Christ, or his grace; and when we are thirsting for Christ, it is his comforts, the rings, jewels, bracelets of the bridegroom, we seek after, rather than himself; it is not an unmixed, not a pure marriage-love, to marry the riches and possessions, and not the person, Mat. xxii. 2. *The kingdom of heaven, is like unto a certain king, which made a marriage* [t⊥ hy⊥ autu] *for his son, not for his daugh-*

ter

ter in law. The glory of gospel-dainties, resembled to a marriage, are for the king's son, and the glory of Christ; not for our glory, but for our grace. Christ is the final end, for whom all the honey-combs, the myrrh, the spices, the wine, and the milk of the banquet are prepared, Cant. v. 1. We have need of Christ to cure, even our perfections; there be some wild oats, some grains of madness and will-wit in our best graces. 2. You cannot idolize Christ himself; love in pounds, in talent-weights, is too little for him; his sweet accidents, his delights, consolations, love-embracements are sweet, but swelling, and too fatening; and if Christ send these to a believer, in a box of gold, or in a case made of a piece of the heaven, or of a chip of the noon-day sun, and not come himself, they should not satisfy the soul. Cant. iii. 1. *I sought him whom my soul loved; watchmen, saw ye him?* O it is the beloved himself, that is a great man in the spouse's books; his wine, his spikenard, his myrrh, his ointments, his perfume, the savour of his garments, his apples of love, are all in that heavenly song set out for himself. Love tokens are nothing, duties nothing, inherent righteousness nothing, heaven nothing, if separated from Christ; but Christ himself is all in all.

Our 2d disease is, we forget that he that created the love of Christ in the heart, can only cure our love, when it is sick for Christ: as he that created the first world can rule it, so he that created the second new world, can guide it, and all the creatures in it, tho' our faith stagger, touching his special providence, in particulars of either, as we are deserted, and left to ourselves.

3. We often thirst after comforts, and sense, as the people did, and (Isa. lviii. 5.) were reproved for their fast: *Is it such a fast as I have chosen?* And Zech. vii. 5. *Did ye at all fast to me, even to me?* So may Christ blame us for the like sin, and say, *Have ye thirsted to me, and for me, and not rather for yourselves?* Let us examine delusions, and not father them upon Christ, except we know he will own them.

4. We

4. We desire a never-interrupted presence and sense of God; whereas Christ submitted to want it for a time, when he saw it was God's will so to do: and tho' we have not, nor can we have positively alway an edge of actual hunger, yet we negatively can be submissive to want, when we see it is his will we want; whereas he is the same Christ, with the same immanent, and eternal love of election, without variation of the degrees of the altitude and height thereof; the same infinite wisdom, when he frowns, and hides his face, and when he shines and smiles in his kingly manifestations. Clouds alter not the sun-light, coverings change not Christ, that he cannot love behind the curtain; except we take a cloud to be the sun, or created sweetness to be Christ. Were the beam separated from the sun, what should it be but as good as nothing? We dream that the curtains and robes of Christ's manifestations of love, add somewhat to his excellency; then he must be of more eminency, when he expresseth himself in love-embracements to us, than when he was from eternity the flower of his Father's delight. Christ's out-side in revealed sweetness, and in transient manifestations of his beauty, must then be more excellent than himself; this is too selfy a conception of Christ. The Lord Jesus is more within, than we can enjoy him, in his love-expressions; he loses none of that immanent sweetness, under his wise withdrawings; tho' you or I, or men, or angels, should never feed upon any time-enjoyments of sweetest love, and manifested glory from his revealed kindness.

5. 'Tis a great query, If it be expedient, that our motion to heaven, should be as the motion of the sun, that never rests, but moves as swiftly in the night as in the day? And if we should ever be on wings, I know 'tis our duty; but even the falling on our own weight, and the conscience of our clay-mould, our short breath, nature's weak legs in walking up the mount, are good for the adding wind and tide, and high sails to the praising of Christ, and free grace: *Utile est peccavisse, nocet peccare.* It is profit-
able

able that we have sinned, that grace may be extolled; it is ill to sin. Even to the nature of man, 'tis good that he hath died, and hath been in the grave; yet 'tis not good, but contrary to nature, to die and to lie in the grave.

6. 'Tis our forgetfulness, that we see not the dearest to Christ have been kept lowest, and most empty in their own eyes; hidden grace extolleth Christ. 2. That often the saints are kept in a condition of sailing with as much wind as blows, with praying, and believing. 3. That yet prayer and the sweating of faith cannot earn, nor promerit the renewed sense of Christ, so as Christ returneth to eat his honey-comb, and his wine, and milk, and banquet with the soul, rather at the presence of these acts, than for them; as some have said, (tho' with no strength of reason) that fire burneth not, the sun enlightneth not, the earth doth not send forth flowers, and herbs; but God, at the naked presence of these causes, doth produce all effects; yet in this case it hath a truth, that the sweating of all supernatural industry, cannot redeem the lest half glimpse of God's presence, in the sense of eternal love, when God is pleased for trial to hide himself.

7. Our great fault here is merit, that we tye the flowings and inundations of Christ's love to the beck of our desires; whereas we may know, 1. That the sun doth not shine, nor the rain water the earth, in order to merit. 2. We should know, that grace, and all the acts of grace, are alms, not debt; and that a rich Saviour giveth grace to us as beggars, and payeth it not to hirelings, as the due, or as wages we can crave for our work; but we love penny-worths better than free-gifts.

But for this cause came I to this hour.

Christ's work of redemption was a most rational work, and was full of causes [*dia tuto*]; this faith, that to redeem losed sinners, was not a rash and reasonless work.

1. There

CHRIST DYING AND DRAWING SINNERS TO HIMSELF.

1. There was no cause compelling. Love cannot be forced, John iii. 16. *God so loved the world, that he gave his only begotten Son*, etc. Grace worketh more from an intrinsical cause, and more spontaneously than nature. For nature often is provoked by contraries for self-defence to work, as fire worketh on water, as on a contrary; the wolf and the dog pursue one another as enemies. But grace, because grace, hath abundance of causality and power in itself, but hath no cause without it.

2. Any necessity of working from goodness in the agent, as from such a principle, is strong. 1 Tim. i. 15. *It is a true saying, and by all means worthy to be received, that Christ Jesus came into the world to save sinners.* If the thing be worthy [Gr. *papes apodoches*] of all receipt and embracing, then it must be good; an agent working from a principle of goodness doth in his kind work necessarily, though he may also work from another principle freely. John x. 11. *I am the good shepherd, the good shepherd giveth his life for his sheep.* Luke xix. 10. *For the Son of man is come to seek, and to save that which is lost.*

3. God will seek reasons or occasions without himself, to be gracious to sinners. When no reason or cause moveth a physician to cure, but only sickness and extreme misery; we know grace and compassion is the only cause; Ezek. xxxvi. 23. *I will sanctify my great name, Why? Which was prophaned among the heathen; and which ye have prophaned in the midst of them;* then the true cause must be expressed, verse 22. *Thus saith the Lord God, I do not this for your sakes, O house of Israel, but for mine holy name's sake.*

4. The Lord taketh a cause from the end of his coming, Mat. xx. 28. *The Son of man came not to be served, but to serve, and to give his life a ransom for many.* John xviii. 37. *To this end was I born, and for this cause came I into the world, that I should bear witness to the truth.* John x. 10. *I am come that they might have life, and have it in abundance.*

5. Some-

5. Something, yea very much of God, is in the creation; much of God in his common providence; but most of all, yea whole God, in the redemption of man. *God manifested in the flesh* is the matter and subject of it, grace the moving cause; most of all his attributes working for the manifestation of the glory of pardoning mercy, revenging justice, exact faithfulness and truth, freest grace, omnipotency over hell, devils, sin, the world; patience, longanimity to man, co-operate as the formal and final causes. It is a piece so rational and full of causes, that as he is happy (*Felix qui potuit rerum cognoscere causas*) who can know the causes of things; so angels delight to be scholars, to read and study this mysterious art of free-grace, Eph. iii. 10. 1 Pet. i. 12. Works without reasons and causes are foolish. The cause why we do not submit to God, is, Because we lie under blind and fatherless crosses: 'Tis true, *affliction springs not out of the dust*, and crosses, considered without God, are twice crosses. Three material circumstances in crosses are very considerable. *Quis, quare, quomodo.* 1. *Who, for what cause,* and *how doth God* afflict us? *Who* afflicts, is worthy to be known. Isa. xlii. 24. *Who gave Jacob for a spoil, and Israel to the robbers?* The highest cause of causes did it. *Did not the Lord, he against whom we have sinned?* 1 Sam. iii. 18. *It is the Lord, let him do what seemeth good to him.* 2. *For what end* God the Lord did this, is a circumstance of comfort; *Why led the Lord Israel through a great and terrible wilderness, wherein were fiery scorpions, and serpents, and drought?* Deut. viii. 16. *That he might prove thee, to do thee good at thy latter end.* 3. And how the Lord correcteth, is worthy to be known; *He correcteth Jacob in measure,* Jer. xlvi. 28. Mercy wrapped about the rod, and a cup of gall and wormwood honeyed and oiled with free love, and a piece of Christ's heart and his stirred bowels mixed in with the cup, is a merciful little hell. Psal. vi. 1. Jer. xxxi. 18, 19, 20. The law saith, *a bastard hath no father*, because his father is not known. The Philistines are plagued with Emerods; but whether that

CHRIST DYING AND DRAWING SINNERS TO HIMSELF.

ill was from the Lord, or from chance, they know not. The cross to many is a bastard. We suffer from prelates, because we suffered prelates to persecute the saints. Papists shed our blood; Why? Our forefathers burnt the witnesses of Christ, and we never repented. Christ and antichrist are at bloody blows in the camp: antichrist hath killed many thousands in the three kingdoms for religion; that is the quarrel: and when England had often before, and have now opportunity, they will not lift Christ up on his throne, nor put his crown-royal on his head, but do put it on their own head; but the judgment is not yet at an end. Scotland hath not walked worthy of the gospel, but have fallen from their first love. We take not a deliberate list of every limb, thigh, leg, and member of this national wrath; and we neither see wherefore we are afflicted, nor how.

For this cause came I to this hour.

There is some peculiar act of Christ's will here holden forth, and that is Christ's peculiar intention to die for his people; in which we are to consider the activeness of Christ's will in dying for man, which may be seen,

1. In his free offering of himself and his service to the Father, Psal. xl. 6. *Sacrifice and offering thou didst not desire, mine ears hast thou opened.* Heb. x. 5. *A body* (that is, the office-house, and instrumental subject of obedience to the death, as the ear is of hearing, and obeying the commandments of God) *thou hast prepared me.* Verse 7. *Then said I, Lo, I come (in the volume of thy book it is written of me) to do thy will, O God.* In these words, Christ is brought in as a servant, with three excellent qualities. 1. Physically, he is fitted with a body and a soul to offer to God for us; as in a servant there are required strong limbs and arms to endure drudgery, in this he was born of his mother, for this sad service: his master furnished him for this, even the seed of man's flesh and blood, for suffering.

2. There were moral habilities in him; promptitude of will. So the Lord is brought in, as a Lord and master

CHRIST DYING AND DRAWING SINNERS TO HIMSELF.

ter in justice crying, servant; *O Son and servant Jesus, I have a business for thee of great concernment.* At the first word, as all good servants do, Christ takes him to his feet, and compears before his God, his master and Lord, *Lo I come, here am I;* so servants of old answered their master: what service wilt thou command so hard, which I will not undergo? Master, here's a body for thy work, here be *cheeks for the nippers, a face for those that will pluck off the hair, a back for smiting,* a body for the cross and the grave. Christ as a servant uncovered, standing on feet, would say, Lord, send me thy servant to the garden, to work under the burden of thy wrath, till I sweat blood; bid me go to shame, to scourging, and spitting: is it thy will I go up on the cursed cross, and be made a curse for sinners, that I be crucified and die, that I go lower into the outer half of hell, the grave, which is a sad journey? Lo, here am I, willing to obey all.

3. There was in Christ, not only willingness, but delight, Psal. xl. 8. [*Heb.* Elohoi haphatzti] *My God, I delight to do thy will.* Every servant cannot say this to his master, *Thy law is in the midst of my heart.*

2. His willingness to die was a part of his testament and last-will; he died with good-will, and left in legacy his death, and the fruits of it, his blessing, his heart, his love, his peace, his life to his bride in testament, confirmed by law, to all his poor brethren and friends, Heb. ix. 17. and John xiv. 27. *Peace I leave (in testament) with you.* But the orphan and the poor friend gets not all that his dying father and friend leaves in testament, but Christ gives possession himself ere he die, *My peace I give to you.* But to the point: his latter-will, was willingness to die.

3. No external force could take his life from him, against his will, John x. 18. *No man taketh my life from me, but I lay it down of myself; I have power to lay it down, and I have power to take it again.* Yet, lest it should seem a will-action in Christ, and so not obedience, he addeth, *This commandment* (that is the will of a superior) *have I received of my Father.*

Com-

Compelled obedience is no obedience; exact willingness was a substantial and essential ingredient in Christ's obedience. Acts of grace cannot be extorted: can ye tear a shower of rain from God in an extreme drought: or bread from him in your hunger, against his will? Far less, since Christ's dying was an act of pure grace, can any compel him to die for man. Love arrested his holy will, and that made him run apace to die for us: O blessed be his good-will, who burned himself in the bush, in a fire of free-love!

4. Though dying be a passion; yet Christ's dying was both a passion and an action. Will added as much perfume and strength of obedience, as nature, and pain, hardship, shame, and abasement could do; his life was not so much plucked from him, as out of his own hand: as an agent, he offered his blood, and soul; *yea, himself to God, through the eternal Spirit*, Heb. ix. 14. Love was the cord, the chain that did bind Christ to the altar.

5. Christ [*dia tuto*] on this intention came to this hour; so is [*dia*] often in scripture. Not only his will, but the flower of his will, his intention was to die, for Christ's eye, and his heart, and his love was on his bride; the intention is the most eminent act that love can put forth. Christ's eye and his heart being upon his spouse, he made our salvation the end and measure of his love: to compass this end, the Lord laid many oars in the water; his rising early, his night-watching, his toiling, his sweating, his sore and hard soul-travel, as being heavy with child of this end, (O might I have a redeemed people) was all his care; and his soul was eased, when dying, bleeding, crying, he went through hell and death, and slept in death's black and cold prison, and his redeemed ones in his arms. When he came to the end of this sad journey, and found his ransomed ones, he said, *I have sought you with a heavy heart, fair and foul way, sad and weary;* and all is well bestowed, since I have gained you. Let us up together to the hill of spices, to our Father's house, to the highest *mountain of frankincense.* All that Christ did was

was for this end, *That he might deliver us from this present evil world,* Gal. i. 4. *That he might be a ransom for many,* Mat. xx. 28. *That we might have life, and have it more abundantly,* John x. 10. *That he might seek and save the lost.* Luke xix. 10. *That he might present his wife a glorious church to himself, not having spot or wrinkle, or any such thing: but that she should be holy and without blemish,* Ephes. v. 26, 27. *That we being dead to sin, should live to righteousness,* 1 Pet. ii. 24. Christ came to seek, and travelled ever till he found his desire, a redeemed and saved people, and then he rested; even as he journeyed through all the creation, but till he found man, a creature that he made according to his own image, he had no Sabbath, no rest. His willingness to die, respected his redeemed people, whom out of mere mercy he loved; and the worth of will and merit respected infinite justice, which he exactly satisfied.

Use 1. Hence we learn, 1. To imitate and follow our pattern Christ in voluntary obedience, delighting to do God's will, and to suffer God's will. 'Tis said of Christ, Heb. v. 8. *Though he were a son, yet learned he obedience through suffering.* He was the excellentest scholar among all his schoolfellows, and yet the rod of God was heaviest, and most frequent on him; he learned his lesson beyond them all. *He was quick in understanding, in the fear of the Lord,* Isa. xi. 3. He had in him an excellent spirit; *The spirit of wisdom, of counsel, of knowledge, and of the fear of the Lord;* and was holy and *obedient to the death, the death of the cross.* 'Tis much to learn to be active for God, but more to learn to be passive. That is a profound science. Phil. iv. xii. *I know how to be abased,------I am instructed to be hungry,------and to suffer need.* 'Tis the singular art of grace, to know how to love, fear and obey God, under death, pain, and hell. It is a high lesson to learn the mystery of that deep science, of hunger, want, sufferings, stripes, and torment and death for Christ. This is high, Heb. x. 34. *Ye took patiently the spoiling of your goods, knowing that in heaven ye have a better, and more enduring substance.*

They

They are but accidents we have here, and these very separable. Heaven is all substance. Our obedience passive is not willing, 'tis constrained. We might by grace turn clay into gold, hell into heaven: if we could look in faith and patience, on the persecution, and reproaches of men, as on the brutish and irrational motion of a staff, or an ax that beats and cuts us; suppose we knew no hand under God that wronged us, *He curseth, because the Lord hath bidden him.* For the freedom of Christ's kingdom, and the right government of his house, and for opposing blasphemies, and reproaching of Christ, his word, scripture, ordinances, *We are killed all the day long, and counted the off-scourings of men.* Could we overlook unthankfulness, malice, persecution from men, whom we with our lives and blood have redeemed from persecution, and behold the highest mover, and first wheel that moveth all under wheels, as if God only were our party, who humbles us that we may be humbled; then should we be silent, and our hearts should not rise at the exorbitances of men. There is too much of nature in our sufferings, too little submissive willingness. The more action of a sanctified will in our sufferings, 'tis the more acceptable, and cometh nearest to Christ, who did both run for the crown, and was active, and endured the cross, and was most passive in an heavenly manner, Heb. xii.

Use 2. Let us learn of Christ to intend obedience, to put a [*dia tuto*] to our obedience. Many hear the word, but they intend not to hear; many pray, and intend not to pray; many die in these wars for Christ, but intend not to spend their life for Christ; the holy and clean cause of God cometh through many dirty and foul fingers. This is the deep art of providence.

Quest. What is a right and straight intention in serving God?

Asser. 1. When the deliberation of a bended will concurs with the intention, 'tis right; as when there is an heart-conclusion for God. Psal. xxxix. 1. *I said, I will take heed to my ways, that I offend not with my tongue.*

tongue. Psal. xxxi. 14. *But I trusted in the Lord: I said, Thou art my God.* Psal. cii. 24. *I said, O my God, take me not away in the midst of my days.* This was an intended prayer. Psal. cxix. 57. *I have said that I would keep thy words.*

Asser. 2. The saints are not so perfect in their intentions, as God is their only end. 1. Because a piece of ourself is mixed with our end; there is some crook in our straightest line; an angle in our perfectest circle: when we run most swiftly, because of the indwelling of corruption, we halt a little. 2. Self-denial is not perfect in this life.

Asser. 3. 'Tis good, when God is so preconceived in the intention, as the principal actions and motions both have being and denomination from their predominant element. Honey is honey, though not pure from wax. A believer is not a simple element, nor all grace, and all sincerity. Now in bodies carried with a predominant element, the predominant is affirmed, the subordinate denied. 1 Cor. xv. 10. *Yet not I, but the grace of God with me.* 2 Cor. iv. 5. *For we preach not ourselves, but Christ Jesus the Lord, and ourselves your servants for Christ's sake.* Where Christ is the predominant element, he is of weight to sway the whole soul in its motion. And its right-down sincerity (whatever *Crisp* with Papists say on the contrary) though it require some grains of allowance to make it pass.

Asser. 4. Where self is the predominant, the intention is bastard and adulterate. Jehu saith, *Come see my zeal for the Lord*; but he only saith it. He could have said, *Come see my zeal for myself.* In the Jews zeal, Rom. x. 1. there is a pound of self-righteousness, for one half-grain of Christ, and of free-grace; therefore 'tis not the right *zeal of God.*

Asser. 5. There be two characters of an intended end, which are also here: 1. All that the agent doth, he referreth to his end; for his end is his god. The wretch doth all in reverence to gold, that is his end: and Joab did all for court and honour; for the chief end is the man's master, and useth a lordship over him.

Christ

Christ is so mighty through God, that he darkens the scribes and Pharisees light; because their end lieth in the fat womb of the world, and it is gain and glory; all they do is to make Christ out of the way. So, when the believer fails all winds, rolleth every stone, presseth all means for Christ, as his end, and his weight, then steers he to the right port. Christ's love hath a dominion over Lord-will; one adamant will cut another; the sinner is a rock, Christ's love an adamant. Christ's love setting on the will's intention, burns the soul to the bone. Mary Magdalene cannot sleep, (and it is a ticklesome game where the heart is at the stake) and Christ she must have; apostles, angels, Christ himself shall hear of it, ere she want him. And the rougher and harder the means be, when undertaken for Christ, Christ must be a stronger and more love-working end. When torment and burning quick are chosen for Christ, it is like he is the end; for love overcomes a rough and dangerous journey: a sweet and desireable home, is above a dirty and thorny way. Christ's love is stronger than hell. Our affections often take fire from difficulties; as absence of the beloved kindles a new fire; *stolen bread*, because stolen, *is sweeter*, and not our nature only; but longing after Christ, *nititur in vetitum*, inclineth to that which is forbidden. What if Christ be longed for, and loved more when absent, than present?

2. The other character is, that when the end is obtained, all operation for, or about the means, ceaseth, and the soul hath a complacency in the fruition of the end. When the wretch's chests are full, he hath an heart-quietness in gold, Luke xii. *Soul, take thine ease.* But if the soul have an aking and a disquieting motion after gold is obtained, it is not because gold was not his end, but because he hath not obtained it in such a large measure as he would; or because it is but a sick and lame end, and cannot satiate, but rather sharpen soul-thirst after such corruptible things. When Christ is obtained, the soul hath sweet peace; *He that drinketh of the water of life, thirsts no more; appetitu de-*

siderii,

siderii, as longing with anxiety for this, as we do for earthly things, which we want; tho' he have *appetitum complacentia*, a desire of complacency, and a sweet self-quietness, that his *heritage pleaseth him well, and his lines are fallen in pleasant parts*, and rests on his portion, and would not change it with ten thousand worlds. Men by this, who are fishing and hunting after some other thing than Christ, may know what is their end; when Christ and reformation come to their doors, they will have neither; but cast out their lines for another prey. Men now fish and angle for gain, in lieu of godliness.

Ver. 28. *Father, glorify thy name. Then came there a voice from heaven, saying, I have both glorified it, and will glorify it again.*

Here is the last article of Christ's prayer, *Father, glorify thy name.* 2. The return of Christ's prayer, by an audible answer from heaven.

This prayer, *Glorify thy name, Father*, is of an higher strain: *Father, I am willing to die, so thou be glorified in giving to me strength to suffer, and thou redeem lost man by me; and by so doing, glorify thy name.* Christ never in his hardest sufferings would be wanting to glorify God. Now, how far the glory of God, in doing and suffering, should be intended and desired by us, in these considerations I propose,

1. We are to prefer the Lord's glory to our own life and salvation: no point of self-denial, and renouncing of self-pleasing, can reach higher than this, when Christ is willing to be the passive object of the glory of God; *Put me, Father, to shame and suffering, so thou mayst be glorified.* Paul and Moses are not far out, but they are far out of themselves, when the one for the glory of the Lord, in saving the people of God, willeth his name may be razed out of the book of life; and the other, to be separated from Christ, for the salvation of his kinsmen, God's chosen people. When Abraham is willing, that *glory to the Lord* should be
writ-

siderii, as longing with anxiety for this, as we do for earthly things, which we want; tho' he have *appetitum complacentia*, a desire of complacency, and a sweet self-quietness, that his *heritage pleaseth him well, and his lines are fallen in pleasant parts*, and rests on his portion, and would not change it with ten thousand worlds. Men by this, who are fishing and hunting after some other thing than Christ, may know what is their end; when Christ and reformation come to their doors, they will have neither; but cast out their lines for another prey. Men now fish and angle for gain, in lieu of godliness.

Ver. 28. *Father, glorify thy name. Then came there a voice from heaven, saying, I have both glorified it, and will glorify it again.*

Here is the last article of Christ's prayer, *Father, glorify thy name.* 2. The return of Christ's prayer, by an audible answer from heaven.

This prayer, *Glorify thy name, Father*, is of an higher strain: *Father, I am willing to die, so thou be glorified in giving to me strength to suffer, and thou redeem lost man by me; and by so doing, glorify thy name.* Christ never in his hardest sufferings would be wanting to glorify God. Now, how far the glory of God, in doing and suffering, should be intended and desired by us, in these considerations I propose,

1. We are to prefer the Lord's glory to our own life and salvation: no point of self-denial, and renouncing of self-pleasing, can reach higher than this, when Christ is willing to be the passive object of the glory of God; *Put me, Father, to shame and suffering, so thou mayst be glorified.* Paul and Moses are not far out, but they are far out of themselves, when the one for the glory of the Lord, in saving the people of God, willeth his name may be razed out of the book of life; and the other, to be separated from Christ, for the salvation of his kinsmen, God's chosen people. When Abraham is willing, that *glory to the Lord* should be

writ-

written with the ink of his son Isaac's blood; and the martyrs, that their pain may praise God, they then level at the right end; for that must be the most perfect intention, that comes nearest to the most perfect. This is nearest to God's intention; for he created, and still worketh all for this end, that he may be glorified, Prov. xvi. 4. Rev. iv. 11. Rom. xi. 37. Now, if Christ put all to sea, and hazard all he hath, to guard the Lord's name from dishonour, and made his soul, his life, his heaven, his glory a bridge to keep dry and safe the glory of God, that it sink not; and if God would rather his dear Son should be crowned with the cross, and his blood squeezed out, with his precious life, than that any shame should come to his name; then are we to interpose ourselves, even to sufferings and shame, for the glory of God. Suppose a saint were divided in four, and every member with life in it, and torment of pain, fixed in the four corners of the heaven, East and West, and South and North, and the soul in the connexity of heaven, under the pain of the torment of the gnawing-worm that can never die, these five were obliged to cry with a loud voice in the hearing of heaven, of earth, of hell, of men, and angels, and all creatures, *Glory, glory* be to the spotless and pure justice of the Lord, for this our pain: And when the damned are too noted to speak against their sentence of condemnation, *When saw we thee hungry and fed thee not?* etc. Mat. xxv. It is clear they are obliged to acquiesce to this, that they are made clay-vessels, passively to be filled to the brim with the glory of revenging justice, and ought in hell to praise the glory of revenging wrath, as the saints in heaven are bottles and vessels of mercy, from bottom to brim, filled with the glory of mercy, to praise his grace in heaven, who redeemed them; the one psalm is as due and just as the other. What the damned do not, or do in the contrary, 'tis their sin. One prayed, his death, pain, torment, sad afflictions may out-run him, ere he escape into the grave; yea, that his hell might with his own good-will be a printed book, on which angels

and

and men may read the glory of inviolable justice.

2. We love that the holiness and grace of others were ours, that we might glorify God, but we glorify him not with that which he hath given us; yea, we have a sort of wicked emulation and envy if others glorify God, not we. Moses acquiesced to God's dispensation, the Lord might be glorified in the peoples' possessing of the holy land, tho' he himself should not be their leader; but not at the first. There is a cumbersome piece called, *I, Ego, Self*, that hath an itching soul for glory due to another.

3. O how unwilling are we, that the Lord's glory over-weigh our ease, and humour? Master, *forbid Eldad and Medad to prophesy*, saith Joshua. No, Moses will have God glorified, be the instruments who will.

4. There is a twofold glory here due to God, 1. *Active*; the glory of duties to be performed by us. 2. *Passive*; the glory of events, that results from the Lord's government of the world; we are to care for both, but we do it not orderly. We are more careful of God's passive glory, which belongs to himself, than we ought to be. Hence say we, What confusions be there in the world? Nation breaks covenant with nation; heresies and blasphemies prevail; Antichrist is yet on his throne; the churches over sea oppressed; the people of God led to the shambles, as slaughter-sheep, and destroyed, and killed; hundreds of thousands killed in Ireland, many thousands in England, and very many thousands about the space of one year taken away in Scotland, with the sword and the pestilence: and the Lord's justice is not yet glorified, nor his mercy in avenging the enemies: the cry of the souls under the altar is not heard, the church not delivered. We would here yield patience to divine providence; God hath more care of his own glory, than we can have. 2. What men take from God, he can repair infinitely another way. But we are less anxious for the Lord's active glory, to do what is our duty, and serve him, and glorify him in the sincere use of means. Some learn their school-fellows lesson better than their own. For

God's

CHRIST DYING AND DRAWING SINNERS TO HIMSELF.

God's glory of events, we are to be grieved, when he is dishonoured; but not to take the helm of heaven and earth out of his hand, but leave to God these, who would plunder Christ's crown off his head. We have nothing to do in the glory of events, but pray it flourish; but we take too much ado in it, and we do too little in the other.

5. There is a glory of God, twofold also; one of holiness and grace, another of bliss and happiness. This I consider, either as in the kingdom of grace or of glory. In grace's kingdom, the saints for their holiness, and Titus and the brethren, 2 Cor. viii. 23. *are the glory of Christ. I will place* (saith the Lord, Isa. xlvi. 13.) *Salvation in Zion, for Israel my glory.* Faithful pastors take in cities, and subdue crowns and kingdoms to Christ. Paul conquered many crowns to Christ, 1 Thess. ii. 19. *For what is our hope, or joy, or crown of rejoicing? are not even ye in the presence of our Lord Jesus Christ at his coming?* Christ wears the church on his head as a crown of glory, Isa. lxii. 3. How glorious is it to be for holiness, Christ's garland, his diadem, and crown? But in this there is a rent of the crown of heaven, a sovereign peculiar flower due to the king of ages, that no man must seek after; in this, the contexture and frame of the work of redemption is so contrived, that, 1 Cor. i. 29. *No flesh should glory in his presence.* No man can divide the glory of grace with Christ. In the higher kingdom, there is a glory ordained for saints. The gospel is a glorious piece, which, 1 Cor. ii. 7. *God hath ordained before the world was, unto our glory.* 1 Thess. ii. 12. *God hath called us unto his kingdom and glory.* 1 Pet. v. 4. *And when the chief Shepherd shall appear, ye shall receive a crown of glory that fadeth not away.* This is the reward of faithful elders, that *feed the flock of Christ.* The heaven of glory, is called the holy heaven, Psal. xx. 6. *The Lord will hear from his holy heaven;* and the new Jerusalem, the church, hath a brave crown on her head, Rev. xxi. 10. 11. *She comes down out of heaven from God*

having

having the glory of God. Grace, grace is a glorious thing.

6. O, but we come short in doing and suffering; when our doing, suffering, eating, drinking, dying, pain, abasement, shame, wants this end of the glorifying God; that adds an excellent lustre, beauty, and glory to all that we do. When Christ, the Father, heaven, are tied to the furthest end of all our actions, we are above ourselves. But we differ little in our aims from beasts, when the intention riseth no higher than this side of clay and time, Psal. xlix. 11. *That our houses may continue,* Isa. v. 8. *That we may be placed our alone on the earth.*

Verse 28. *And there came a voice from heaven, saying, I have both glorified it, and will glorify it again.*

In this answer, observe these, 1. The answer. 2. The airth it came from; *from heaven.* 3. The way and manner of its coming: by an audible *voice.* 4. The matter of the answer; *I have both glorified it, and will glorify it again.*

Christ is always answered of his Father; either in the thing he sueth, John xii. 42. Or, in that which he fears, Heb. v. 7. or by real comfort, Luke xxii. 42, 43. Or, in a full and perfect deliverance, Psal. xx. 20, 21. compared with Psal. xvi. 10, 11. Acts xxiv. 25. Acts v. 31. Or, in supply of strength for his suffering, Isa. l. 7, 8.

It is a proof of the worth of Christ's advocation and intercession. If I know myself to be in Christ's prayer-book, in his breast, among Christ's askings of the Father; 'tis comfortable. Psal. ii. 8. *Ask of me, and I will give thee the heathen for thine inheritance, and the uttermost parts of the earth for thy possession.* When Christ asketh souls of the Father, he gives him his asking: the Lord cannot withhold from this King *the desire of his heart,* Psal. xxi. 2. He asked a wife of his Father, and it was granted. Christ will have them

all

all in one house, to be co-partners of the crown of heaven with him: for, it is his prayer, John xvii. 24. The king and the queen in one palace. We cannot fall from grace, for we stand by Christ's prayers, Luke xxii. 31,32, Heb. ix.24.

We have many diseases, in the matter of the return of an answer, 1. We wait not on an answer; we speak words, we pray not, we breathe out natural desires for spiritual mercies; we have no spiritual feeling of our wants, and there is an end; Psal. xviii. 41. *The wicked cry, but there is none to save;* they do not pray, but cry. 2. We storm, and offend that our humour, rather than our faith, is not answered, either at our own time, or that the thing which we ask to spend on our lusts, (as James iv. 3.) is not granted. 3. We are more careful, and troubled, that we are not heard, than anxious to offer the rent, and pay the *calves of our lips*, in praying, which is God's due. Were we as serious in worshipping in prayer, as we are desirous of seeking wants, it were good; but there is more seeking in our prayer for ourselves, than there is adoring for God. 4. We employ not Christ as mediator and high priest in praying, and exercising faith so much, as we put forth pith and strength of words, that we may extort rather our needs, than obtain grace; as if praying, and the hearing of prayers, were work and wages, rather than begging, and giving of mere grace. 5. We consider not when we pray, and prayer is not returned in the same coin that we seek; that the Father hearing Christ's prayers, virtually and meritoriously answered all our prayers in substance, and for our good. For, 2. Christ can cull out, and chuse petitions more necessary and fundamental for my salvation, than I can do. 1. He is answered in all points; we are answered often in the general, and in as good only. 3. Christ could with more submission and sense pray, than we can do. Nature in Christ cannot boast and compel God to hear prayers: often our zeal is but natural boasting and quarrelling, as if we could force God to answer. Grace in Christ (and grace is the

most

most lowly and modest thing of the world) prays with all submission, *not my will, but thy will be done.* 4. All prayers are heard for Christ; *ergo,* his prayers are better heard than the prayers of the saints; except our prayers be folded in his prayers, they cannot be answered. The perfume, the sweet odours of Christ's prayers are so powerful and strong, as coming from God-man in one person, they must be both asking and giving, desiring and granting, praying and hearing, flowing from the same person, Christ. When our prayers go to heaven, Christ, ere they come to the Father, must cast them in a new mould, and leaveth to them his heart, his mouth: tho' the advocate taketh not the sense and meaning of the spirit from them; yet Christ presenting them with his perfume, he removeth our corrupt sense, so as they are Christ's prayers, rather than ours. Heb. xiii. 15. *Let us by him* (as our High Priest) *offer the sacrifice of praise* (then of prayers also) *to God continually.* The offering is the priest's as well as the people's, Rev. viii. 3. and far more here, because Christ, by his office, is the only immediate person who *maketh request to God for us,* Rom. viii. 34.

From heaven.

Hence, Christ troubled in soul, and afflicted believers on earth, keep correspondence and compliance with heaven.
1. Christ's prayers, in his saddest days, have their return from heaven. Posts and messengers fly with wings between God and a soul in a praying disposition; possible, ten posts in one night. Prayer hath an agent lying at the court of heaven, and an open ear there, Psal. xviii. 6. *He heard my voice out of his temple, and my cry came before him, even unto his ears.* Christ takes care that the messenger get presence, and be quickly dispatched with a return. Psal. cii. 19. *The Lord* (ere the messenger come) *looked down from the height of his sanctuary,* v. 20. *To hear the groaning of the prisoner, to loose those that are appointed to death.*

death. So, Lam. iii. Tears lie in heaven as solicitors with God, until he hear; *Mine eye trickleth down and ceaseth not,* v. 50. *Till the Lord look down, and behold from heaven.* 1 Kings viii. 30. *Hear thou in the heaven, thy dwelling place, and when thou hearest, forgive;* saith Solomon. Isa. lxiii. 15. *Look down from heaven, and behold from the habitation of thy holiness.* Our Saviour hath appointed the post-way in that prayer. *Our Father which art in heaven.* We have a friend there, who receives the packet; *An High Priest set at the right-hand of the throne of majesty,* Heb. viii. 1. *Who hath passed into the heavens,* Heb. iv. 14. *And is made higher than the heavens,* Heb. vii. 26. *And liveth for ever to make intercession for us,* v. 25.

2. In Christ's hardest straits, comfort came out of this airth. Luke xxii. 43. When he was in his saddest agony, *there appeared unto him an angel from heaven strengthening him.* In his lowest condition, when he was in the cold grave among the dead, heaven was his magazine of help and comforts. Mat. xxviii. 2. *An angel of the Lord came down from heaven, and rolled away the stone.* Heaven came to his bed-side, when he was sleeping in the clods.

3. The saints have daily trafficking with heaven: O my dear friend, my brother, my factor is in that land. Psal. lxxiii. 25. *Whom have I in heaven but thee?* What, are not angels, prophets, apostles, and saints there? Yea; but we have no acquaintance by way of mediation in that land, but Christ: he is the choice friend there, 1 Cor. xv. 47. *The second man* (both first, highest, second and all) *is the Lord from heaven.*

4. All our good, *every perfect gift comes from heaven,* Ja. I. 17. Manna came not from the clouds: how then? John vi. 32. *My Father giveth you the true bread from heaven.* We are ill lodged in bits of sick and groaning clay; our best house is in heaven, 2 Cor. v. 2. *We groaning, desire to be clothed with our house from heaven.*

5. The

5. The earth is but the believer's sentinel, or, at best, his watch-tower; but our hope is in heaven. 1 Thes. I. 10. *We wait for the Son of God from heaven.* Our life and treasure is there, Mat. vi. 20. *Lay up treasure for yourselves in heaven.* Our [Gr. politéuma] *our city-dwelling and our haunting, is in heaven,* Phil. i. 21.

What acquaintance have ye in heaven? what blood-friend have you in that land? The wicked man, [Heb. *Enosh minbaaretz*] is, *the man of the earth.* And Psal. xvii. 14. *Save me from men of time; men of this life.* Are you a burgess of time, or a citizen of the earth? or a man of the higher Jerusalem? Imagine there were a new-found land on earth, and in it there be twelve summers in one year, all the stones in the land are sapphires, rubies, diamonds; the clay of it, the choicest gold of Ophir; the trees do bear apples of life; the inhabitants can neither be sick nor die; the passage to it, by sea and land, is safe; all things there are to be had for nothing, without money, price, or change of commodities; and gold is there for the gathering: if there were such a land as this, what a huge navy would be lying in the harbours and ports of that land? how many travellers would repair thither? Heaven is a new land that the Mediator Christ hath found out, it is better than a land where there is a summer for every month of the year; there is neither winter, or night there: the land is very good, and the fruits of it delectable and precious; grace and peace, righteousness, *joy of the Holy Ghost, the fruits of that kingdom,* Rom. xiv. 17. are better than rubies, sapphires, or diamonds: Christ the tree of life is above all lands on earth, even his alone: and there's no need of price or money in this kingdom; grace is the cheapest thing of the world; *wine and milk are here without money, and without price,* Isaiah lv. 1. 'Tis a land that stands most by the one only commodity of grace and glory. Oh, there is little trafficking with heaven; when was you last there? It is an

easy

CHRIST DYING AND DRAWING SINNERS TO HIMSELF.

easy passage to heaven; David, who often prayed, even seven times a day, was often a day there. Prayer in faith is but one short post thither. Oh we have too much compliance with the earth.

A voice.

The third particular in this return, is the manner: in an audible voice the Lord answereth him. The multitude heard this voice, tho' they understood it not. We read not often of an audible voice from heaven to Christ; only at his baptism, there was a testimony given of him from heaven, Mat. iii. 16, 17. and at his transfiguration, Mat. xvii. Of which Peter speaketh, 2 Pet. i. 18. *And this voice we heard, when we were with him on the holy mount.* The Lord, in the hearing of men, gives a testimony of his Son Christ, and his good cause. He was accused because he made himself the Son of God; he prays to God, and calleth him Father openly; a voice from heaven openly answering, acknowledgeth him to be the Son of God; tho' they knew not the Lord's testimony from heaven. God maketh a good cause, tho' darkned, to shine as day-light, if men would open their eyes and see, Psal. xxxvii. 5. *Roll over thy way upon the Lord, and trust in him, and he shall bring it to pass.* But flesh and blood saith, innocency lieth in the dark, and weepeth in sackcloth in the dungeon, and is not seen. The Lord answereth, verse 6. *And he shall bring forth thy righteousness as the light, and thy judgment as the noon-day.* It is true, [Heb. *Vatza*] signifies to go from one place to another; 'tis here applied to the sun, and elsewhere to things that grow out of the earth, Judges xiii. 14. The sun in the night seems dead and lost, as if there were no such thing; yet the morning is a new life to the day and the sun. The grape of the wine-tree sown in the earth, is a dead thing; yet it springeth in some days, and cometh to be a fruitful tree. Christ was crucified, and buried; yet the wine-tree

grew

grew again; and, Rom. i. 4. *He was declared to be the Son of God with power, according to the Spirit of sanctification, by the resurrection from the dead.* The gospel and a good cause seems buried, and weeps in a dungeon, Joseph in the prison, and a sold stranger; yet in the eyes of his brethren he is exalted. The Lord cleared Daniel's cause, Psal. xcvii. 11. *Light is sown for the righteous, and joy for the upright in heart.* The light and joy of the saints, are often under the clods of the earth.

1. The reformation of religion goes vailed under the mask of rebellion, and of subverting fundamental laws; but God must give to this work, that is now on the wheels, in Britain, the right name, and call it, *The building of the old waste places, the rearing up of the tabernacle of David;* and cause it come above the earth.

2. The cross is that great stumbling-block, for which many are offended at Christ and the gospel. It is a sad and offensive providence, to see joy weep, glory shamed; this is the gall, the wormwood, the salt of the cross, that the Lord of life should suffer in his own person; yet here is heaven and the Father speaking, and returning a comfortable answer to Christ, in that which he most feared. The cross maketh an ill report of the gospel and Christ: for this the apostles are made a theatre, a gazing stock to men and angels, a world's wonder; and Paul would take this away, Eph. iii. 13. *Wherefore I desire that ye faint not at my tribulation.* Then saints may fall a-swooning at the very sight of the cross in others. And Peter, 1 Pet. iv. 12. saith, [Gr. mè xenìzesthe] *Be not stricken with wonder, or astonished as at new things and miracles,* Acts xvii. 20. when *ye are put to a fiery trial.* The comforts of the cross are the sweet of it, and the honey-combs of Christ, that drop upon that sour tree.

3. That the Father saith from heaven, There shall grow the fairest and most beautiful rose that ever higher or lower paradise yielded, out of this crabbed thorn,

was

was much consolation to Christ. Here grows out of the side and banks of the lake of that river of fire and wrath that Christ was plunged in, many sweet flowers: As, 1. A victorious Redeemer, who overcame hell, sin, devils, death, the world. 2. A fair and spotless righteousness. 3. A redeemed, a washed and sanctified spouse to the Lamb. 4. *A new heaven and a new earth;* behold, *He hath made all things new*, and hath cast heaven and earth in a new mould. 5. A new kingdom, a new crown to the saints, a choicer paradise than the first that Adam lost. 6. Riches of free-grace, unsearchable treasures of mercy and love: all these blossom out of the cross.

4. The cross is bought by, and in its nature much altered to the saints. 'Tis true, it is become a necessary inlet, and an inevitable passage, and a bridge to heaven; but the Lord Jesus, not Satan, keeps the pass, and commandeth the bridge; and letteth in, and letteth out passengers at his pleasure. But, 1. Christ hath strawed the way to heaven with blood and wars, and forbids us to censure his sad patrimony, in that the servants are no worse than the Lord, and flower of all the martyrs. Though blood hath been, and must be the rent and income of the crown of the noble King of kings, and the consecrated Captain of our salvation; yet it is short, and for a moment, and Christ hath a way of outgate, that none of his shall be buried under the cross, Rev. vii. 14. Psal. iv. 19. (2.) Christ hath broken the iron-chains of the cross, and the gates of brass: that the cross hath but a number of free prisoners, who have fair quarters, and must go out with flying colours, and be ransomed from the grave, John xvi. 33. Hos. xiii. 14. (3.) When you are in glory, and in a place above death; there shall be neither mark, nor print; no ceatrix of the sad cross, on back or shoulder, but the very furrow of tears wiped away, and perfectly washed off the face with the water of life, *For the former things shall be done away*, Revel. xxi. 4. Yea the saddest of crosses, the utmost and last blow that

that the cross can inflict, is death. I should think that Christ is the saint's factor in the land of death; he was there himself, and though he will not adjourn death, yet hath our factor made it cheap, and at an easy rate, all toll and custom is removed, and he hath put a negation upon death, John xi. 26. *He that believeth shall not die.* John xiv. 19. Much dependeth on our wise husbanding of the rod of God; yet if Christ did not manage, order, and oversee our furnace, it could not be well with us.

I have both glorified it, and will glorify it again.

This is the fourth considerable point, the matter of the answer.

Here is a lord-speaker from heaven, testifying that the Lord's name shall be, and was glorified: as, 1. In Christ's person and incarnation, John i. 14. *The Word was made flesh, and dwelt amongst us, and we beheld his glory.* So the angels did sing at his birth, Luke ii. 14. *Glory to God in the highest.* Christ's laying aside of his glory, and his emptying of himself for us, was the glory of rich mercy. 2. His miracles glorified God. John ii. 11. *This first miracle did Jesus to manifest his glory.* When he cured the paralytick man, Luke ii. 12. *they were amazed, and glorified God.* When he raised *Jairus his daughter,* Luke vii. 16. *There came a fear on all, and they glorified God.* 3. In all his life he went about doing good; and sought (John viii. 49.) to glorify his Father. 4. In his death, God was in a singular manner glorified. When the *centurion* (Luke xxiii. 49.) *saw what was done, he glorified God.* The repenting thief preached him on the cross to be a King: and this was a glorifying of Christ in his greatest abasement and shame. Yea, his glory was preached by the sun, when it was, contrary to the course of nature, darkned: and by the rocks when they were rent, and the temple cloven asunder, and the graves opened, when men weakly, or wickedly denied him, and would not only not preach his glory, but

blas-

blaspheme his name. 5. he was glorified in his resurrection, *being declared to be the Son of God, and obtained a name above all names, and was by the right-hand of God, exalted to be a Saviour, and a Prince, to give repentance to Israel, and forgiveness of sins*, Phil. ii. 9. Eph. i. 20. Acts v. 31. Acts iii. 13. (6.) He shall come again in his glory, Mat. xxv. 31. *And shall be glorified and admired in all his saints*, 2 Thess. i. 10. The fairest and most glorious sight, that ever the eye of man saw, shall be, when Christ shall come riding through the clouds, on his chariot of glory, accompanied with his mighty angels, and with one pull, or shake of his mighty arms, shall cause the stars to fall from heaven, *as figs fall from a fig-tree, shaken with a mighty wind*, and blow out all these candles of heaven with one blast of his ire; and *a fire shall go before him, and burn up the earth with the works that are therein*; when the higher house of heaven, and the lower of the earth shall meet together, and when mystical Christ shall be glorified.

Use 1. If there be so much glory in Jesus Christ and his sufferings, as he must bear the glory, Zech. vi. 13. And *all the glory of his Father's house be upon him*, Isa. xxii. 24. His crown of glory on his head, must be so weighty, and ponderous with rubies, sapphires, diamonds, that it will break the neck of any mortal man, king or parliament, to bear it. None on earth have a head or shoulders, for this so weighty a diadem; parliaments have no necks worthy to carry Christ's golden bracelets, nor a back to be honoured with his robe-royal; if they will but take his sceptre in their hand, it shall crush them as clay-vessels: this *stone hewn out of the mountain without hands*, shall crush the clay-legs of parliaments, and then how shall they stand?

Use 2. God properly glorifies himself; angels and men are but chamberlains and factors, to pay the rent of his glory; and because he will give himself, his Son, his Spirit to us, and his grace, and *yet will not give his glory to another*, let us beware to intercept the rents of the crown.

Object-

Object. *The Lord giveth grace and glory*, Psalm lxxxiv. *And he hath a crown of glory laid up for his saints, in the heavens.*

Answ. That glory is but matured and ripened grace, God's glory is the eminent, celebrious, and high esteem that men and angels have of God, as God, or the foundation of this; to meddle with this is to encroach upon the crown and prerogative-royal of God. Glory imparted to saints in heaven, is but a beam, a lustre, a shadow, or way of that transcendent and high glory that is in God; and is as far different from the incommunicable glory of God, as the shadow of the sun in a glass, or in the bottom of a fountain, and the sun in firmament. We may desire the chips and shadows, and rays of glory; but beware that we meddle not with that which devils and men always seek after, in a sacrilegious way.

Use 3. We are hence taught to admire the excellency of the unsearchable knowledge and skill of divine providence. Out of Christ's abasing himself to take on him our nature: 2. Out of his miracles, that were just nothing to blind natural men: 3. Out of his death and shame, the Lord extracteth the most eminent and high glory of his name. That omnipotency should triumph in the jaw-bone of an ass, in a straw, in a crucified man, commends the glory of God, and the art of his workmanship; to make gold out of clay and iron, diamonds and rubies out of the basest stones, would extol the art of man. A creation out of nothing, and flowers, roses, forests, woods, out of cold earth, is the praise of the wisdom and power of the Creator; the baser the matter be, the art of the author is the more glorious, if the work be curious and excellent.

God here, 1. Out of death, shame, sinful oppressing of the *Lord of glory*, raiseth the high work of man's redemption. 2. When we spill business, and mar all, through sinning and provoking God, then Israel must bring a spilt business to God, that he may right them, Judg. iii. 10, 11. God can find the right end of the thread, when matters are ravelled and disordered. We
see

see now, nations confounded, enemies rising against us: but blood, wars, confusions, oppression, and crushing down of Christ and his church, are good and congruous means, when they have the advantage of being handed by omnipotency. When we work the instruments must be as big as a mountain; and then our eye cannot see God, for the bigness of the instrument. God regardeth not the nothings, and the few that he worketh withal. Dead men can fight, when God putteth a sword in their hand; *men shall fall under wounded men.* Beware of robbing God of his glory. Did ever a decree or a counsel of God part with child? Or can omnipotency bring forth untimely births, or prove abortive? You see Christ now in the death-house of Adam's sons, and wrestling with hell; yet God, by Christ at the weakest, works his end: death is a low thing, sin is far more base; but when God acts at the end of either, they have a scope and end as high as God, to glorify God.

3. If God hath been, and must be glorified in all that is done, what do we do, to trouble ourselves to seek glory one of another? We are created for this end, and 'tis our glory to fetch in glory to God. What? can the airy applause of men be golden stilts for cripples to walk to heaven withal? Or, can the people's poor hosannas be silken sails to our ship, or golden wings, that by these you may sail and fly up to heaven? Where is Belshazzar who but built a house *for the glory of his own name?* Where is Herod, who did receive one word of a god, which the people did steal? Do not these fools take little room in print, and, at this day, as little in the clods of the earth? The *Roman state* would not permit Christ to be a God: what was their doom? Must not a kingdom cast its bloom, fall, and wither, that will not suffer Christ to be a king in his church?

Ver. 29. *The people therefore that stood by, and heard it, said, it thundered: others said, an angel spake to him.*

Another

Another effect of the prayer of Christ doth follow in the people. They had sundry judgments of this answer from heaven: some *said, it was thunder,* for they understood it not: others, nay, but it is above nature; *an angel hath spoken to him.*

It thundered.

Doth not any rude shepherd, or the most simple idiot know a thunder? 'Tis a place that holds forth to us, how ignorant we are of God, and of the gospel-way. Consider what was in this answer: 1. It was the gospel. In what language it was spoken, (belike not in a known language) cannot be determined out of the text. 2. It was a clear expression of that communion between Christ and his Father. 3. What God means, or what is his sense in his word or works, is unknown to us. 4. That they say the gospel is a thunder, and a word of nature, is a mere imagination and a dream. Yet these ways are among themselves all false, and they do not agree one with another.

Consid. 1. The gospel is the will of God from heaven; yet it is a riddle, a parable not understood, Mat. xiii. 14. *In the law it is written, with men of other tongues and other lips will I speak to this people,* 1 Cor. xiv. 21. And Isa. xxix. 11. *And the vision of all is become unto you as the words of a book that is sealed, which men deliver to one that is learned, saying, read this, I pray thee. And he saith, I cannot: for it is sealed.* Verse 12. *And the book is delivered to him that is not learned, saying, read this, I pray thee. And he saith, I cannot; I am not learned.* 1 Cor. i. 18. *For the preaching of the cross is to them that perish, foolishness.*

Consid. 2. God reasoneth not only with men's minds to convince them; but also with their will and affections. Acts ix. Christ from heaven proposeth a syllogism to Saul's fury, *'Tis hard for thee to kick against pricks.* God hath logick against anger, which hath neither ears nor reason; for if he could not out-argue

La-

CHRIST DYING AND DRAWING SINNERS TO HIMSELF.

Laban's hatred, and the haters of the saints, to whom he saith, *Touch not mine anointed, and do my prophets no harm*, Psal. cvii. He would not speak to their affections, nor would it be said, that in their affections they repute Christ and the gospel foolishness, if there were not a contrariety between the affections and the gospel.

Consid. 3. The understanding is a dark lantern that hath some light within, but casts none at all out, to apprehend things above hand: and as the will is irony and stiff to heaven, so it is waxy and apt to receive the impressions of the flesh, except Christ draw by the curtain of the flesh, to let you see the glory of the gospel. Otherwise, God speaks, and Samuel saith, *Eli, here am I, for thou calledst me*. To the woman of Samaria, Jacob is greater than Christ; and Jacob's well, as good as the water of life. Justice often puts one seal on the gospel, and another on the man's two eye-lids, that the vision is as dark as mid-night.

Consid. 4. The communion between Christ and the soul, as here between the Son Christ and the Father, is *quid pro quo*, a thunder, a work of nature, or any thing to the natural man; God speaking to the heart, is a mystery to him. John vi. 52. *The Jews say among themselves, How can this man give us his flesh to eat?* Very hardly, according to their papistical fancy of a bodily eating. 2. The high esteem of Christ above other beloveds, is a mystery to natural saints, in so far as they are natural. 'Tis a strange question for professors of the gospel to say, *What more is in Christ than other well-beloveds?* Yet they say it, Cant. v. 9. (3.) The natural understanding is the most whorish thing in the world; there is a variety of fancied gods there. *According to the number of thy cities, were thy gods, O Judah,* Jer. ii. 29. *They have made them molten images of their silver, and idols according to their own understanding,* Hos. xiii. 2. The understanding, even in the search of truth amongst the creatures is a rash, precipitate, and unquiet thing; and like a silk-worm, first makes a work of many threads and then

lies

lies fettered and entangled in that which came out of its own bowels. The mind spins and weaves out of itself fancies, dreams, lies, and then its work must be spent on these, and so creates its own chains and fetters. But in the matters of God it runs mad, plays the wanton; in the gospel knowledge it turns frantick, and when it comes to move and act within the sphere of supernatural truths, it but laughs and sports till it come out again, 1 Cor. i. 23. If Christ preached be foolishness, then Christ himself must be a fool to the Grecians, the excellentest wits in the world. 1 Cor. ii. 14. The gospel cannot come within the brain of a natural man, but as a notional *fancy*, a *chimera*. Yea, when the greatest wits came to the borders of divine truth, to look on the outside of divinity, called *Theologia naturalis*, to look on the Lord's back-parts, and contemplate and behold God in his works, they knew not what to make of God, Rom. i. 23. Some thought God to be a dainty *bird of paradise*; nay, said other great wits, he is a *four-footed beast*; nay, said another, but he is a *creeping thing*: and the most eminent of them, even head of wit among them, said he was *a corruptible man*, yea all of them, [Gr. *Emataiothesan en tois dialogismois auton.*] *They turned vain, soggie, reasonless, and stark-nought in their finer discourses and reasonings, in weighing and posing things.* Gen. vi. 5. *The frame of the heart of man is only evil.* [Heb. *Jetzer*] Gen. viii. 21. signifies, *a potter's vessel.* Isa. xxix. 16. *Your turning of things up-side down, shall be reputed as the clay* [Heb. *Hajjozer*] *of the potter: from the root* [Heb. *Jazer*] *to think, desire; to form a thing of clay as the potter doth.* From this is the potter named: [Heb. *Jozer*] Zech. xi. 13. Gen. ii. 7. Deut. xxxi. 21. *I know their imaginations*, or earthen pots, that be in the heart, mind, and head of men. Many vain frames are in our heads, as there be variety of pots, bottles, and earthen vessels in the potter's house. Many wind-mills, many pitchers and clay-frames are in the vain heart, but they are evil, wicked, and *only evil from the womb.* But especially, how many devices and

new

new moulds of religions, and sundry gods are in the heart of men? How many sundry opinions of Christ, are in men's brains? For concerning Christ, Mat. xvi. 14. *Some said he was John the Baptist, some Elias, and others Jeremiah.* 4. The love and affections are most whorish, light, and wanton; if Martha seek not one thing, she seeks many things: no one God is the natural man's God. It may be maintained, that an unrenewed man hath not one predominant, but indefinitely, sin is his king; and as many sins, as many kings. Rom. v. 14. 17. Rom. vi. 7, 8, 9. 'Tis true, pride, covetousness, or some particular sins may come to the throne by turns, as either complexion, strength of corrupt nature, or times bear sway; for as Satan is not divided against Satan, so not any natural man will be a martyr for a false god, or a predominant lust, in opposition to another known false god, tho' all may oppose the gospel. The Lord complains of a whorish heart, *that playeth the harlot with many lovers*, Jer. iii. 1. and heaven and saving grace stands on an indivisible point, like the number of seven; one added, one removed, varieth the nature: no man is half in heaven, half in hell; *almost a christian* is no christian. When Adam fell from one God, he fell *upon many inventions*; not upon one only, Eccles. vii. 29. Our wandering is infinite, and hath no home: either God is a thunder, or then he is an angel speaking from heaven.

Consid. 5. Men think the supernatural ways of God a thunder in the air, which is most natural work; the ebbing and flowing of the spirit, either natural joy or melancholy, naturally following the complexion of the body. 'Tis grace that puts a right sense on the works of God, as on the word: we are no les heterodox in mis-interpreting the ways and works of God, than in putting false and unsound senses on his word. Emerods plague the Philistines; they doubt if chance, or if the god of Israel have thus plagued them. Moses works miracles, the magicians work miracles, and the Egyptians doubt whether their false-god, or the living *God that made the heaven and the earth*, hath wrought

the

the miracles. When God and nature both work, natural men, or saints as natural, betake themselves to the nearest god. As sickness comes, the natural man saith, neglect of the body, health, the moon, humours, the air, cold weather did it; but he looks not to God. And the believer, guilty of a breach of the six command, in neglecting of second causes, and in needless hurting the body, seeth not this; but fathers all upon God, only in a spiritual dispensation, and considereth only dispensation in God, not sin in himself. 2. Mercies grow invisibly, and we see not; we are ready to sleep at mercies offered. When Christ knocks in love, we are in bed: Cant. v. (3.) Judgments speak in the dark, but we hear not: the Lord fatneth some slaughter-oxen for hell, and death is on some men's faces, even the second death on their person, but they see not. 'To hear the Lord's rod, and who hath appointed it,' is the man of wisdom's part, Mic. vi. 9. There is an orthodox wisdom and will, as there is an orthodox faith. Will, as well as the mind, can frame syllogisms; every unrenewed man hath a faith of his own in the bottom of his will. 2 Pet. iii. *Some are willingly ignorant;* some, Jer. ix. *through deceit refuse to know the Lord;* whereas lust puts out reason, and takes the chair. Lust hath stout logick against Christ; a fleshly mind vainly puffed up, is a badge of bastard-wit, out-reasoning all the gospel. O but grace is quick-eyed, sharp, and a witty thing, to see God vailed in, under the curtain of flesh; to see Christ and heaven through words, and the gospel with child of so great a salvation!

Consid. 6. What wonder that there be divisions about Christ. Some will have the Lord speaking from heaven, a thunder; others an angel. Christ is the most disputable thing in the world, Mat. xvi. 13, 14. there be five religions, and sundry opinions touching Christ; the Scribes and Pharisees had many sundry opinions, and one of them is the right way only, ten false. John vii. 40. Many say Christ is a prophet. Verse 41. *Others said this is the Christ;* others no, *shall Christ come out of Galilee, and there was a division among them.*

Luke

CHRIST DYING AND DRAWING SINNERS TO HIMSELF.

Luke ii. 34. *Christ is for a sign that shall be spoken against.* And amongst Christ's sufferings this is one, Heb. xii. 3. *He sustained* [Gr. antilogian] *contradiction of sinners.* Mat. xxiv. *Many false Christs shall arise.* There is but one heaven, and one way to heaven; and there is but one hell: but there be thousands of ways to hell: from one point to another, you can draw but one straight line; but you may draw ten thousand crooked, and circular lines. The truth is one, and very narrow, the lie is broad and very fertile and broody, error is infinite. 'Tis a blessed thing to find wisdom to hit upon Christ, and adhere to him; there be some dicers and cozeners, Ephes. iv. 14. *that lie in wait to deceive the simple; and they cast the dice for heaven*, and can cast you up any thing on the dice, either one, or seven. Do you then resign yourselves in this wood of false religions that now is, to Christ to be led to heaven. Many now teach, there be some few fundamentals; believe them, and live well, and you are saved. And many false teachers, that turn the gospel upside-down, say it is the same gospel, though the head be where the feet should be; and for errors, we wrong the truth, *so long as we hold nothing against fundamentals*: should a man remove the roof of your house, cut down the timber of it, and pick out all the fair stones in the wall, and say, friend, I wrong not your house, see the foundation-stones are safe, and the four corner-stones are sure; in the mean time, the house can fence off neither wind nor rain; would not this man both mock you and wrong you? He that keeps the foundation Christ, shall be saved, *though he build on it hay and stubble*, 1 Cor. iii. 'Tis true. But it was never the intent of the Holy Ghost, that a man believing some few fundamentals, though he hold, and spread lies and false doctrines, is in no hazard of damnation; or that he hath liberty of conscience, to add to the foundation *hay, and stubble, and untempered mortar*, and to daub dirt upon the foundation Christ, and not sin; the place speaks no such thing; but of this else-where.

Others

Others said, it was an angel.

These come nearer to the truth; for they conceive there is more in his voice, than a work of nature, such as a thunder is; they think an angel spoke to Christ; and they are convinced, that Christ keeps correspondence with heaven and angels.

Angels have been, and are in high estimation among men always; and there is reason for it.

1. There is more of heaven in angels, and more of God, than in any of their fellow-creatures. Sinful men have been stricken with fear at the sight of them; they are persons of a more excellent country than the earth. John the apostle did overvalue an angel, Revel. xix. Revel. xxi. *And fell down to worship him.*

2. Angels elect and chosen, never lost their birth-right of creation, as men and devils have done; they were created as the lilies and roses, which, no doubt, had more sweetness of beauty and smell, before the sin of man made them vanity-sick, Rom. viii. 20. but they have kept their robes of innocency, their cloth of gold, above 5000 years, without one spark of dirt, or change of colour, for they never sinned; innocency and freedom from sin, hath much of God. Adam (as many think) kept not his garments clean one day. Courtiers of heaven and saints would walk like angels, and keep good quarters with Christ. Grace is a pure, clean, innocent thing; teacheth saints to deny ungodliness; and so much the more have angels of God, that they are among devils and sinful men, and yet by grace are kept from falling; the more grace the more innocency. Grace as pardoning hath its result from sin, but is most contrary to sin. Grace payeth debt for sin, but taketh not on new arrears; 'tis abused grace that doth so.

1. But these, thus convinced that the Lord's voice is more than a thunder, go no further; they say here, *Others said, it was an angel.*

Hence

Hence, touching conviction,

Pos. 1. Conviction of conscience may be strong, and yet at a stand. *Never man spake like this man,* say the Jews, *yet they hate him.* John vii. 28. *Jesus cried in the temple, as he taught, saying, Ye both know me, and ye know whence I am; I am not come of myself, but he that sent me is true, whom ye know not.* Verse 29. *But I know him.* Then they knew Christ for conviction, and they knew him not; for, *They crucified the Lord of glory*; and if they had known him under the supernatural notion of the *Lord of glory, they would not have crucified him*, 1 Cor. ii. 8. Felix trembles, and is convinced, but imprisons Paul. The devils believe there is a God, and tremble, Jam. ii. But light is made a captive, and made a prisoner, Rom. i. 18. 'Tis a most troublesome prisoner, it holds the conqueror waking, and yet he cannot be avenged on it.

Pos. 2. Conviction, turned to malice, becomes a devil; the Pharisees convinced, go on against heaven, and the operation of the Holy Ghost. And the Jews saw the face of *Stephen, as it had been the face of an angel,* Acts vi. 15. Yet, Acts vii. 57, 58. *they run on him, and stone him to death.*

Pos. 3. Conviction maketh more judicial hardning than any sin; it revengeth itself upon heaven; hell near heaven is a double hell. John xii. 37, 38. *Though he had done so many miracles before them, yet they believed not.* A reason is, verse 40. *He hath blinded their eyes, and hardened their heart.*

Pos. 4. Omnipotency of grace can only convince the will. Preachers may convince the mind, and remove mind-heresy; but Christ only can give ears to love, fear, sorrow, and remove will-heresy, John vi. 45. There be reasonings and logick in the will, stronger than these in the mind: the will hath reason why it will not be taken with Christ, John v. 40. and a law, Rom. vii. 23. of sin, why it is sweet to perish, and death is to be chosen.

Pos. 5.

Pos. 5. It is the right conviction of the Spirit, to be convinced. 1. Of unbelief: 2. Of the excellency of Jesus Christ, that I must have Christ, cost me what it will; say it were all that the rich merchant hath, Mat. xiii. 45, 46. There is a white and red in his face, hath convinced the man's love, and hath bound his affection, hand and foot; that he takes pains on despised duties, that lie under the very drop of the shame of the cross, Acts v. 4.

Pos. 6. To be willing to do a duty that hath shame written on it, as to be scourged for Christ, as the apostles were; and for an honourable Lord of council as Joseph of Arimathea was, to petition to have the body of a crucified man to bury, it being a duty near of blood to the cross; both apparent loss, and present shame, is a strong demonstration, that the whole man, not the mind only, but the will and affections, are convinced. Some duties grow among thorns, as to 'be killed all the day long, and to take patiently the spoiling of our goods, for Christ.' Some duties grow among roses, and are honourable and glorious duties, as to kill and subdue, in a lawful war, the enemies of God. The former are no sign of wrath, nor the latter of being duly convinced of the excellency of Christ, except in so far as we use them, through the grace of Christ, as becometh saints, or abuse them; but it is more like Christ to suffer for him, than to do for him.

Pos. 7. God will have some half gate to heaven, tho' they should die by the way; some are more, some less convinced; the more conviction, if not received, the more damnation. The gospel is not such a messenger as the raven, that returneth not again: Isa. lv. 11. *My word that goeth forth out of my mouth, it shall not return to me void, it shall accomplish that which I please, and it shall prosper in the thing whereto I sent it.* The gospel, and opportunity of reformation, falleth not in the seabottom, when a nation receives it not, but it returns to God to speak tidings; we will not give an account of the gospel, but the gospel gives an ac-

count

CHRIST DYING AND DRAWING SINNERS TO HIMSELF. 217

count of us. 2. Even when the ordinances are rejected, *they prosper*, Isa. lv. 11. to harden men; they are seed sown, and rain fallen on the earth; they yield a crop of glory to God, even *a sweet savour to God, in those that perish, as in those that are saved*; 2 Cor. ii. 15, 16. The lake of fire and brimstone, as a just punishment of a despised gospel, smells like roses to God.

30. *Jesus answered and said, This voice came not because of me, but for your sake.*
31. *Now is the judgment of this world, now shall the prince of this world be judged.*

Now followeth the other effect of Christ's prayer, toward the world.
1. In general. The prayer is answered (saith Christ) not so much for my cause, to comfort me, (for he might otherwise be comforted) as for you, that ye may believe in me, hearing this testimony from heaven. 2. In particular: he sets down the fruit of his death, 1. On the unbelieving world; they shall be judged and condemned. 2. On the spiritual enemies, and by a Synecdoche, the head of them; Satan, the *god of this world, shall be cast out*, and sin, and death, and hell with him. 3. The prime fruit of all, v. 32. When I am crucified, by my Spirit of grace, the fruit of the merit of my death, *I will draw all men to me*.

This voice came not because of me.

Christ's well and woe, his joy, his sorrow, is relative, and for sinners. Christ, as Christ, is a very public person, and a giving-out Mediator. And it addeth much to the excellency of things, that they are public, and made out to many: as the sun, the stars, the rain, the seas, the earth, that are for many, are so much the more excellent: it is a broader and a larger goodness, that is public. Heaven is an excellent thing, because public, to receive so many crowned
kings,

count of us. 2. Even when the ordinances are rejected, *they prosper,* Isa. lv. 11. to harden men; they are seed sown, and rain fallen on the earth; they yield a crop of glory to God, even *a sweet savour to God, in those that perish, as in those that are saved*; 2 Cor. ii. 15, 16. The lake of fire and brimstone, as a just punishment of a despised gospel, smells like roses to God.

30. *Jesus answered and said, This voice came not because of me, but for your sake.*
31. *Now Is the judgment of this world, now shall the prince of this world be judged.*

Now followeth the other effect of Christ's prayer, toward the world.
1. In general. The prayer is answered (saith Christ) not so much for my cause, to comfort me, (for he might otherwise be comforted) as for you, that ye may believe in me, hearing this testimony from heaven. 2. In particular: he sets down the fruit of his death, 1. On the unbelieving world; they shall be judged and condemned. 2. On the spiritual enemies, and by a Synecdoche, the head of them; Satan, the *god of this world, shall be cast out*, and sin, and death, and hell with him. 3. The prime fruit of all, v. 32. When I am crucified, by my Spirit of grace, the fruit of the merit of my death, *I will draw all men to me.*

This voice came not because of me.

Christ's well and woe, his joy, his sorrow, is relative, and for sinners. Christ, as Christ, is a very public person, and a giving-out Mediator. And it addeth much to the excellency of things, that they are public, and made out to many: as the sun, the stars, the rain, the seas, the earth, that are for many, are so much the more excellent: it is a broader and a larger goodness, that is public. Heaven is an excellent thing, because public, to receive so many crowned

kings,

kings, and citizens, that are redeemed from the earth. The gospel is a public good for all sinners: eternity is not a particular duration, as time is, that hath a poor point to begin with, and end at; but the public good of angels and glorified spirits. Time indeed is a public thing; but because 'tis the heritage of perishing things, it is not public in comparison of eternity. And Christ, because a public spirit, for the whole family of elect angels and saints in heaven and earth, is a matchless excellent one. And 'tis observable, that there is nothing in heaven, that is the seat and element of happiness, and the only garden and paradise of the saints' felicity, but it is public and common to all: the inhabitants, the glorified saints and angels, all see the face of him that sitteth on the throne, (of degrees of fruition, I speak not;) they all drink of the water of life; all have access to eat of the apples of the tree of life, there is no forbidden fruit in heaven; all have the blessing of the immediate presence of the Lamb, and there is neither need of sun, or moon, or light of a candle to any; all equally enjoy eternity, there is one lease and term-day to the lowest inhabitant of glory, and that is eternity; there is common to them all one city, the streets whereof are transparent gold; that the poorest inhabitants of a town, walk on a street of gold of Ophir, is a great praise to the city: it is common to them all, that they shall never sigh, never be sad, never sicken, never be old, never die; and eternal life is common to them all; and then all feel the smell of the fairest rose that angels or men can think on, the flower, the only delight, the glory, the joy of heaven, the Lord Jesus; all walk in white and can sin no more. Then, a public spirit, who is for many, is the excellentest spirit. Men of private spirits, who carry a reciprocation of designs only to themselves, and die and live with their own private interests, are bad men. When ourself is the circle, both centre and circumference, we are so much like the devil, who is his own god, adores himself, and would have God to adore him, Mat. iv. 9.

Now,

Now, Christ is the most public, relative, and communicative Spirit and Lord that is. 1. All Christ's offices are for others than himself; he is not a Mediator of one: a Redeemer is for captives, a Saviour for sinners, a Priest for offenders and trespassers, a Prophet for the simple and ignorant, a King to vindicate from servitude all that are in bondage; the Physician for the sick; and this speaks for you, sinners. 2. Why did he empty himself, Luke xix. 10. 1 Tim. i. 15. and come into the world? For sinners. 3. Why was he a fitted sacrifice to die? John xvii. 19. *For their sake also sanctify I myself, that they also may be sanctified by the truth.* 4. His dying was a public and relative good, John x. 10. *For his sheep.* For, John xv. 13. *his friends.* For, Rom. v. 10. *his enemies. For his wife,* to present a bride without spot or wrinkle to God, Eph. v. 25, 26. 5. And he rose again for us, even *for our justification,* Rom. iv. 25. 6. And whose cause doth Christ advocate in heaven now? Ours. For *us, if we sin,* 1 John ii. 1. *he intercedes for us,* Heb. vii. 25. *That we may have boldness to enter into the holy of holiest,* Heb. x. 19. 7. Christ hath so public an heart, that he longs to return again, and to see us, John xiv. 3. *I will come again, and receive you to myself.* A surety is a very relative person, and for another: the head is for all the members, the meanest and lowest; and it is not enough to him to rent the heaven, and dig a hole in the skies once, when he was incarnate, but he makes a second journey, in coming down to rent the heaven, and fetch his bride up to himself. They are hence rebuked, that so improve Christ, as if he were a jewel locked up in a cabinet in heaven, to be touched and made use of by none: *Oh, I am a sinner, I am a wretched captive, what have I then to do with so precious a Lord, as Christ?* But, I pray, (1.) Wherefore is Christ a Saviour? is he not for sinners? Wherefore a Redeemer? Is it that he should lie by God, as useless? Was he not a Redeemer for captives? (2.) What if all the world should say so? Christ should be a Saviour, and
save

save none; a Redeemer, and ransom none at all; for all are sinners, all are captives. Christ's very office begets an interest in the sick to the physician: claim thine interest, O sick sinner.

Now, this voice was unknown to those that heard it, and yet it was for men that understood it not: Christ acteth for us, when we are sleeping. The people of God were to be seventy years in Babylon, and were going on in their obstinacy; yet then God saith, Jer. xxix. 11. *I know the thoughts I think toward you*, (you know them not; I love you, but ye know not) *even thoughts of peace, and not of evil, to give you an expected end.* Many glorious mercies are transacted in God's mind, without our knowledge: ere the corner-stone of the earth was laid, he had made sure work of our election to glory, Eph. i. 4. Rom. ix. 11. (2.) *The everlasting covenant between the Father and the Son,* that blessed bargain of free-redemption in Christ, was closed from eternity, Jer. xxxii. 39, 40. To do us good, when we are far off, and know no such thing, is a great and free expression of love. (3.) We should be narrow vessels, not able to contain our joy, without breaking, if we understood what an house not made with hands were prepared for us in the heavens; but *our life is hid with Christ in God*, it appears not now what we are. You never saw the bride, the Lamb's wife, broidered with heaven, free-grace, and riches of glory. Every saint is a mystery to another saint, and that is the cause that love to one another is so cold: every saint is a riddle, and a secret to himself. It was a privileged sight, even a privilege of the higher house, and of the peers of heaven, that John saw, Rev. xxi. 10. *And he carried me away in the Spirit to a great and high mountain, and shewed me the great city, the holy Jerusalem, descending out of heaven from God,* v. 11. *Having the glory of God: and the light was like a stone most precious, even like a jasper-stone, clear as crystal.* Here is a King's daughter, a beautiful princess, in the gold of heaven's glory, arrayed with Christ.

Christ. Who seeth this while we are here? Every one seeth not such a sight of glory.

Use 1. If there be such an active application on God's part, that Christ is fitted and dressed for sinners, there should be a passive application on our part: O what an incongruity and unsuitableness between Christ and us! He is a Saviour for sinners, we are not sinners for a Saviour: he is open and forward to give, we narrow and drawing to receive. A physician, that thrusteth his art and compassion to cure, is unfitting for a sick one, forward and unwilling to be cured. We should be for Christ, as for our only perfecting end; but it is not so. Oh, men are for their own gain from their quarter, Isa. lvi. 10. Their eyes and hearts are not but for covetousness, Jer. xxii. 17. *For the glory of their own name,* Dan. iv. 30. *For the continuance of their houses to many generations,* Psal. xlix. 11. *For the flesh, to fulfil the lusts thereof,* Rom. xiii. 14.

Use 2. If Christ be for the saints, then all other things are for them; all things are theirs; death is a water-man to carry them to the other side of time; the earth the saints inns; the creatures their servants; as sun, moon, stars, are candles in the house for them: providence for them, as the hedge of thorns, is to fence the wheat, the flowers, the roses, not the thistles; and all because Christ is their Saviour. v. 31. *Now is the judgment of this world, now shall the prince of this world be cast out.*

Two enemies are here judged, the world and Satan.

As touching the former enemy; we are to consider the time, Now: 2. The enemy, the world: 3. The restrictive pronoun, *This world*: 4. That which Christ acteth, *He judgeth the world.* But what is meant by the *judgment of the world?* Some understand, that now, by Christ's death, is the right constitution of the world, as if the world were put in a right frame, and delivered from vanity, and restored on its perfection by Jesus Christ's death. Others think, by the world, is meant the sin of the world, or the sinning world; in that *Christ condemned sin, in the flesh, by his death.*

But

But by the world is meant the reprobate, and wicked world, that are here ranked with Satan, for Christ in his death gives out a doom and sentence on the unbelieving world; because they receive not him; as John iii. 19. *This is the* [Gr. Krisis] *judgment of the world, that light is come into the world, and men loveth darkness*, etc.

Now, for the first of these: we see that hope helps the weak; before Christ yoke with devils, hell, and death, he seeth and believeth the victory: it was now a dark and a sad providence with Christ in his soul-trouble; but hope lying on the cold clay, prophesieth good; hope among the worms breathes life and resurrection, Psal. xvi. 10. 'Thou wilt not leave my soul in the grave.'---v. 11. 'Thou wilt shew me the path of life.' Psal. cxviii. 17. 'I shall not die, but live, and declare the works of the Lord.' He was at this time, in regard of danger, almost in death's cold bosom. Saw you never hope laugh out from under dead bones in a bed? Boily, rotten, and half-dead Job, chap. xix. 26. 'I know that my Redeemer liveth, and that he shall stand at the latter day on the earth: v. 26. And tho' after my skin, worms destroy this body, yet in my flesh I shall see God.' And 2 Cor. v. 1. Hope doth both die, and at the same time prophecy heaven and life: 'We know, if our earthly house of this tabernacle were dissolved, we have a building of God, a house not made with hands, eternal in the heaven.' Would any man say, Paul, how know ye that? The answer is, faith holdeth the candle to hope, and hope seeth the sun in the firmament at midnight. 'We know, if this house be destroyed, we have a better one.'

2. Hope is one of the good spies, that comes with good tidings, be not dismayed, God will give us the good land. When they were plucking the hair off Christ's face, and nipping his cheeks, hope speaks thus to him, and to all standers by, Isa. l. 7. *For the Lord God will help me, therefore I shall not be confounded: Therefore have I set my face as flint, and I know that I shall not be ashamed.* It is a long cable, and a sure

an-

anchor, Heb. vi. 19. 'Which hope we have as an anchor of the soul, both sure and stedfast, and which entereth into that which is within the vail.' Hope is sea-proof, and hell-proof, and Christ is anchor-fast in all storms: *Christ in you the hope of glory*, Col. i. 27.

3. A praying grace is such a prophesying grace, as both asketh when he prayeth, *Father, glorify thy name*, and taketh an answer; so doth Christ here take an answer. 'Now is the judgment of this world, now shall the prince of this world be cast out.' He was not yet cast out; but hope in Christ, with one breath, prayeth, *Father, save me from this hour*, and answereth, I shall be saved: the world, and the prince enemy, shall be cast out. It is a won battle, all shall be well. Faith and hope laugh and triumph for to-morrow, Psal. vi. *Rebuke me not, Lord, in thine anger*, v. 4. *Return, O Lord, deliver my soul*; v. 8. He takes an answer, *For the Lord hath heard the voice of my weeping:* v. 9. *The Lord hath heard my supplication.* Psal. xxxv. He prays, that the angel of the Lord would chase his enemies; and he answers himself in antedated praises, v. 9. *And my soul shall be joyful in the Lord.* v. 10. *All my bones shall say, Lord, who is like unto thee?* etc. He makes a bargain afore-hand; hope layeth a debt of praises upon every bone and joint of his body. Psal. xlii. Banished, forgotten, and withered David, complains to God, and in hope takes an answer, v. 8. *Yet the Lord will command his loving kindness in the daytime.* We have need of this now, when Scotland is so low. They cannot fall that are on the dust, and more thousands under the dust, with the pestilence, and the sword, and the heart-break of forsaking and cruel friends, that not only have proved broken cisterns to us in our thirst, but have rejoiced, as Edom did, at our fall, than ever stories at one time, in ancient records, can speak; and God grant, friends turn not as cruel enemies as ever the idolatrous and bloody Irish have been. 'Yet there is hope in Israel concerning this thing.' The Lord must arise, *and pity the dust of Zion: our bones are scattered at the grave's mouth, as when*

one

one heweth wood. Though we sit in darkness, we shall see light. Some say, There is no *help for them in God.* O say not so; they that are now highest, must be lowest: God must make the truth of this appear in Britain, Ezek. xvii. 24. *And all the trees of the field shall know, that I the Lord have brought down the high tree, and have exalted the low tree, and have dried up the green tree, and have made the dry tree to flourish; I the Lord have spoken it, and have done it.* Others say, We shall be delivered, when we are ripened by humiliation for mercy. No, 'tis not needful it be ever so. God sometime first delivereth, and then humbleth, and hath done it; the Lord delivered his low church, when they were in their graves, Ezek. xxxvii. but they were never prouder, than when they loaded the power, the faithfulness, and free grace of God with reproaches, and said, Ezek. xxxvii. 11. *Our bones are dried, and our hope is lost, we are cut off for our parts.*

This world.

This is the lost world, 1. Because it is the judged world, John iii. 19. (2.) It is that world of which Satan is prince; the world being the damned, is the worst of the creation; which I prove from the word, and withal shall give the signs and characters of the men of the world.

1. The world is the black company that lies in sin, all of them, 1 John v. 9. *The whole world lies in sin;* they are haters of Christ, and all his, John xv. 18. *If the world hate you, ye know* (saith Christ) *that it hated me before you.*

2. They are a number uncapable of grace, or reconciliation; which is terrible, and have no part in Christ's prayers, John xvii. 9. *I pray not for the world*: nor of sanctification; the Comforter that Christ was to send, is, John xiv. 17. *The Spirit that the world cannot receive.*

3. It is one of the professed enemies on Christ's contrary side, that he overcometh, and we in him. John xvi.

xvi. 33. *In the world, you shall have tribulation.* They are the only troublers of the saints. *But be of good cheer, I have overcome the world.* 1 John v. 4. *Whosoever is born of God overcometh the world.*

4. It is a dirty and defiling thing. *Pure religion* (saith James i. 27.) *keeps a man unspotted of the world.* It is the praise of the church of Sardis, Rev. iii. 4. that there was amongst *them a few names that had not defiled their garments*; but kept themselves from the *pollutions of the world*: it is a sooty pest-house; there be drops of soot that defiles men in it.

5. There can be no worst character, than to be a *child of the world*; it is a black mark, Luke xvi. 8. You know the Hebraism; *children of disobedience*; that is, much addicted to disobedience; as the son hath the nature of father and mother in him: *children of pride, of wrath*; much addicted, and far under the power of wrath, and pride; *so the sparks of fire* are called, Job v. [Heb. Benei resheph] *the daughters of the burning coal*: then a child of the world, is one that lay in the womb of the world, one of the world's breeding, opposed to a *pilgrim and a stranger on the earth*: for a stranger is one that is born in a strange land, Psal. cxix. 19. Psal. xxxix. 12. Heb. xi. 13. And contrary to *a child of light*; who hath the pilgrim's sigh, ordinarily night and day; Oh, *if I were in my own country.* Wrong him not; his mother is a woman of heaven, she is a mighty princess, and a King's daughter, Rev. xxi. 10. *The new Jerusalem, the church of God came down from heaven*: Father, mother, seed, principles, and all are from heaven. 2. There is a spirit called the *spirit of the world*, 1 Cor. ii. 12. This spirit is the genius, the nature and disposition of the world, 1 John ii. 16. and is all for the *lust of the flesh, the lust of the eyes, and the pride of life*; and these be the world's *all things.* Such a soul knoweth not the white stone, and the new name, nor can he smell the rose of the field and the lily of the valley; nor knows he the King's banqueting-house, nor the absence or presence of

Christ

Christ in the soul; the man's portion is in this world, Psal. xvii. 14. within the four angles of this clay globe.

This world.

The world, the Lord Jesus judgeth, is this world; a thing that cometh within the compass of time, and may be pointed with the finger.

1. It is near our senses, therefore called, Gal. i. 4. *The present evil world, the world that now is*, on the stage: So, 2 Tim. iv. 10 *Demas hath forsaken me, and hath loved* [Gr. tôn nyn aiona] *the world that is upon its present now.* The world that is on its post, and now, in its flux, motion and tendency to corruption, 1 Tim. vi. 17. *Charge them that are rich in this world, that they be not high-minded*; this world is opposed to eternity, and to life eternal, for the which the rich are to lay up a sure foundation, Luke xx. 34. *The sons of this world marry, and are given in marriage.* v. 35. *But these that shall be counted worthy of that world and resurrection from the dead, neither marry nor are given in marriage.* v. 30. *Neither can they do any more* [Gr. aeon ekìnos] *that world*; this puts a great note of excellency on the world to come.

2. This world is a thing that comes under our senses, and that [Gr. tô dè tì] a single one creature, that we may point with our finger. Satan from the top of a mountain shewed Christ, [Gr. pasas tàs basilèias kosmu] *All the kingdoms of the world, and the glory, or opinion of them,* Mat. iv. 8. And it is, Luke iv. 5. all the kingdoms, [Gr. tês ockoumènèsten stigmê chrònu] *he shewed him the fancy of the habitable earth in a point of time*; the life to come cannot come under your senses. Ye cannot point out the throne of God, and the Lamb, and the tree of life, and the pure river of water of life, that proceeds out of the throne of God, and of the Lamb, there be such various treasures of glory in the infinite Lord Jesus, so many dwelling-places in our Father's house, that ye cannot number them all. The kingdoms of this world, and the glory of

it

it comes within tale and reckoning; I grant this is meant of the structure and dwellings of the world, but they are the settled home of reprobate men.

It were good, if we could believe that the [Gr. sphèma] of the world, the figure and paintry of this house of lost men, 1 Cor. vii. 30. is in a trance, and passing away: ah! are ye conformed to the world? Your condition is woeful. The world swears, and so do you, the world serves the time in religion, and so do you; the world is vain in their apparel; the world cozens, lies, whores, and so do you; the world hates Christ and his friends, and so do you; the world lies in sin, it is the fashion of the world, and so do you. Oh! if you would be conformed to the new world, in righteousness and holiness. 1. The inn-dwellers are all the children of a king, and princes, and their mother a prince's daughter. 2. The lowest piece of the dwelling-house of that other world, the heavens, we see, are curious work; any one pearl, or candle of sun, or moon, or stars, is worth the whole earth, setting aside the souls of men. 3. *The foundation of the city is precious stones*, Rev. xxi. etc. What fools are we, who kill every one another for pieces and bits of the Lord's lowest footstool; for the earth, the seat of the worldly man, is but *the footstool of God.*

The Judgment of this world.

How did Christ condemn and pass sentence on the wicked world in his death.

1. He did it legally, in that his offering a sufficient ransom for sin, there is a seal put on the condemnation of all impenitent men, that they shall 'not see life, but the wrath of God (that they were by nature under, being the captives of the law) 'abideth on them,' John iii. 36. 'Because they believe not in the Son of God,' John xvi. 9. Christ's dying day was the unbelievers dooms-day.

2. He condemned the world declaratorily, in removing the curse from all the persecutions of the ill world; which was also more than a declaration, it being a

real

real overcoming of the world, John xiv. 33. He hath removed all offence from the enmity and deadly feud that the world beareth against the saints. Christ's good-will in dying, hath sanctified, sweetned, and perfumed the world's ill-will to the saints.

3. He judgeth the world in his death exemplarily; as it is said, Heb. xi. 7. *Noah condemned the world, in preparing an ark.* So Christ's example of obedience in dying for the world, at his Father's command, John x. 16. condemns the world's disobedience. Christ dying, and in his thirst, not master of a cup of water, is a judgment of the drunkard; his dying, his being stript of his garments, is a condemning of vain and strange apparel; his face spitted on, saith beauty, is vanity; his dying between two thieves saith, a high place among princes is not much, when the prince of the kings of the earth was marrowed with thieves; his being forsaken of lovers and friends, condemneth trusting in men, and confidence in princes, or the sons of men: all this is for our mortification, that we love not the world, for it is Christ's condemned malefactor.

Now is the prince of this world cast out.

Here two things are considerable, 1. Who is the prince of this world. 2. How he is by Christ cast out.

The prince of this world is Satan, so called, John xiv. 30. And the prince *that rules in the children of disobedience,* Eph. ii. 2. called with a higher name. 2 Cor. iv. 4. [Gr. hò theos tu aionos toutou.] *The god of this world.* What princedom, or what godhead can the devil have in the world? or, who gave to him a sceptre, a crown, and a throne? for Satan hath a throne, Rev. ii. 3.

The devil is not 1. A free prince. 2. Not an absolute monarch. 3. Not a lawful king; not free, because he is a captive prince, reserved in *everlasting chains of darkness, unto the judgment of the great day,* Jude 6. The Son of God is the only free prince in the world,

there

there be none independently free in heaven and earth but he, John viii. 36. The kingdom of grace is an ancient free estate; and never was, and never can be conquered, *not by the gates of hell,* Mat. xvi. 18. Zech. xii. 3. *and in that day will I make Jerusalem a burdensome stone, tho' all people of the earth be gathered together against it.* Sure, Christ is a free king, by all the reason, and lawful authority in heaven and earth, Psal. ii. 6, 7. Hell is no free princedom, all in it are slaves of sin, John viii. 34, 39, 40, 41, 42, 43, 44. The liberty of loving, enjoying, seeing, and praising God, and leisure, or thoughts, or cares to do no other thing, is the only true liberty, and liberty to be a king, and absolute over lusts, and wicked will, is the only liberty, Psal. cxix. 45. *I shall walk* [Hebr. Barehabah] in latitude, in breadth, in liberty; *for I seek thy precepts.* 2. He is not an absolute prince. 1. He is under bail, and in chains of irresistible providence; Satan's providence, in power, is narrower than his will and malice; or otherwise he had not left a church on earth. 2. He can do nothing without leave asked and given, against Job; nor could he winnow Peter, till he petitioned for it. (3.) He is not a lawful monarch, but usurpeth; and therefore is called the god of this world, 2 Cor. iv. 4. not that he hath any godhead, properly so called.

1. It is true, a black monarch weareth Christ's fair crown, and intrudes on his throne, in every false worship; Levit. xvii. *He that killeth ox, or goat, or lamb to the Lord, in the camp, and bringeth it not to the door of the tabernacle of the congregation, unto the priest,* v. 7. Offereth sacrifice to devils, 2 Chron. xi. 15. *Jeroboam ordained him priests for the high places, and for the devils, and for the calves that he had made.*

2. To fear the devil, the sorcerer, or him that can kill the body, (as Satan may bear the keys of prison-houses, and the sword, Rev. ii. 10.) more than the Lord, is to put a godhead on the devil.

3. Sa-

3. Satan usurpeth a godhead, over that which is the flower and most godlike and divine piece in man, the mind. 2 Cor. iv. 4. *In whom the god of this world hath blinded the minds of them that believe not*: and he makes a work-house of the souls of the children of disobedience, Eph. ii. 2. they are the devil's forge and shop, in whom he frames curious pieces for himself.

4. His crown stands in relations: fathers, tyrants by strong hand, and lords by free election were kings of old; so the devil is a father, hath children, and a seed, Acts xiii. 10. John iii. 10. the world his conquest, and his vassals, Acts x. 38. 2 Tim. ii. 26. 1 Pet. iv. 3. & 5. 8. are the world which he governs and rules, by the three fundamental principles of his catholic kingdom, which he hath holden these 5000 years, 'The lust of the flesh, the lust of the eyes, the pride of life, 1 John ii. 16. Sinners hold the crown on the devil's head; their loyalty to prince Satan acteth on them to die in wars against the Lamb and his followers.

A cause is not good, because followed by many. Isa. xvii. 7. in that day when the church is but 'three or four berries on the top of the olive-tree, a man, one single man, shall look to his Maker.' Men come to Sion, and follow Christ in ones and twos of a whole tribe, Jer. iii. 14. They go to hell in thousands; a whole earth, Rev. xiii. worship the western beast; and the eastern leopard hath the far greatest part of the habitable world; Indians and Americans worship Satan. Christ's are but a little flock; ah the way to heaven is over-grown with grass, there the traces of few feet are to be seen in the way: only you may see the print of our glorious fore-runner Christ's foot, and of the prophets, apostles, martyrs, and the handful 'that follow the Lamb.' Follow ye on, and miss not your lodging.

Shall be cast out.

There

CHRIST DYING AND DRAWING SINNERS TO HIMSELF.

There is a two-fold casting out of Satan; one for his first sin, 2 Pet. ii. 4. *God spared not the angels that sinned, but cast them down to hell,* Jude verse 6. This is a personal casting out, not spoken of here; but Satan must have two hells; for though the gospel was never intended to Satan, yet Satan is guilty of gospel rebellion, in that *the dragon fighteth with the Lamb,* and the weak woman *travelling in birth,* by the gospel, to *bring forth a man-child to God.* And (2.) as Satan is the mystical head and prince of that condemned body, he is *cast out;* and he hath a power in regard of the guilt and dominion of sin, both over the elect and the reprobate. Christ's death hath broken hell's bars, and condemned sin in the flesh, Rom. viii. 3. And *dissolved the works of the devil,* and taken his forts and castles; and, 1 John iii. 8. taken many of Satan's soldiers captives. Death was the devil's fort-royal; hell is his great prison-house, and principal jail: these he hath taken, 1 Cor. xv. 55, 56. Hos. xiii. 14. *I will ransom them from the power of the grave, I will redeem them from the power of death. O death, I will be thy plague: O grave, I will be thy destruction.* And these captives can never be ransomed out of Christ's hand again; for (saith he) *repentance shall be hid from mine eyes.* When Christ spoils, *he will never restore the prey again. He hath overcome the world,* John xvi. 33. And that was a strong fort; and he hath delivered the saints from the dominion of sin, because they are under a new husband, Rom. vi. 6, 7, 8, 9, 10. Rom. vii. 1, 2, 3, 4, 5, 6. All crosses have lost their salt and their sting; even as when a city is taken by storming, all the commanders and soldiers are disarmed: and when a court is cried down by law, all the members and officers of the court, judge and scribe, and advocates that can plead, pursevants, jails are cried down; they cannot sit nor lead a process, nor summon a subject: so when Christ cried down Satan's judicature, and *triumphed over principalities and powers,* and annulled all decrees, laws, handwritings of ordinances, that Satan could have against the saints, Col. ii. 14, 15. all the officers of hell

are

are laid aside; the devil is out of office by law, *jure*; the jails and pits are broken, Isa. xlix. 9. *That thou mayst say to the prisoners, go forth: to them that are in darkness, shew yourselves.* Zech. ix. 11. *When a righteous King cometh to the crown, he putteth down all unjust usurpers.*

If Satan be cast out, *we are not debtors to the flesh, to fulfil the lusts thereof,* Rom. viii. 12. Sin hath no law over us. There is a law of sin, a dictate of mad reason, by which the sinner thinks he is under the oath of allegiance to Satan, and his crown, sceptre, and honour he must defend; but there is no reason, no law in hell, and in the works of hell. And if he be once cast out, who is this usurping lawless lord, if you sweep the house to him, and take him in again to a new lodging, one devil will be eight devils; for Satan, *thus cast out, will return with seven devils worse than himself; remember Lot's wife*, if ye be escaped out of Sodom. Look not over your shoulder with a wanton and lustful eye to old forsaken lovers, let repentance and mortification be constant.

Now is the prince of this world cast out.

But yet to consider more particularly, Satan's princedom, and Satan's power: I add yet more of these two heads.

    1. *The power of Satan.*
    2. *The punishment of Satan.*

His power is held forth, in that he is a prince.

    1. *In his might and power natural.*
    2. *In his power acquired.*
    3. *In his power sinful, and judicially inflicted.*

The devil's power, he was created in, both in the mind and will, and executive faculty, by no scripture or reason can be imagined to be less before the fall of these miserable spirits, than the power of their fellow angels.

    1. The angels being all created holy, and according to God's image, they must have been created with their

face

face to God, and in their proper place and sphere: and so with power to stand in their place. Now what station can these immortal spirits be created in, rather than in a state of seeing God? 2. *Satan abode not in the truth*, (saith the Lord Jesus, John viii. 44.) and the bad *angels left*, (saith Jude verse 6.) [Gr. tò ídion oiketerion] *their proper dwelling.* These two places compared together, seemeth to hold forth that truth, and the first truth; God seen and known, though not immutably, was the first element, native country of the angels: they must then see God and his face.

'Tis a bold and groundless conjecture of some rotten schoolmen to say, that truth from which the angels are said to fall, was the gospel-truth; and that, *They envied that man was in Christ*, to be advanced above the angelic nature.

1. 'Tis a dream, that the gospel was revealed to the devils before their fall; for then their own fall and future misery, that they were to be kept eternally in chains of darkness, on the same ground, must be revealed to them. What horror and sadness must fill Adam's mind, and the angel's spirit, if hell and the necessity of God manifested in the flesh, was revealed to them in the state of happiness? 2. The mystery of the *riches of the glorious gospel was hid from the beginning of the world*; and the glorious elect angels come in time, Ephes. iii. 8, 9, 10. To learn that *manifest wisdom of God*; and delight in Peter's time, *to look into it*, as to a great secret of God, 1 Pet. i. 12. We have not then reason to think this secret was whispered in the ears of the devils, before they fell.

2. 'Tis true, Mat. xviii. *The elect angels.* [Gr. dià pantòs] *always now behold the face of Christ's Father*, for now they are confirmed, that they cannot look away, and turn their eyes off God's face; even when they come down as servants, *to the heirs of glory* on earth, they carry about with them their heaven, and the pleasures of the court they enjoy; no reason their posting among sinners should decourt them, or deprive them of

the

the actual vision of God: but it followeth not therefore the fallen *angels never saw the face of Christ's Father*; it follows only, they saw it not immutably, and in a confirmed way of grace and [Gr. dià pantòs,] always, as now the elect angels do.

2. 'Tis no princedom in Satan to know the thoughts of the heart; this is proper to God only, 1 Kings viii. 39. Jer. xvii. 10. Psal. xliv. 21. Nor hath he, or the good angels, any immediate princedom over the will, to know what are my thoughts, or to know one anothers thoughts, or to act immediately upon free will; not because the thoughts of the heart are objects of themselves so abstruse and high, that they are not intelligible; for a man's *own spirit knows the things in himself*, 1 Cor. ii. 11. Yea (2.) then they could not be known by revelation; for God cannot by revelation, cause a finite understanding comprehend an infinite object; because the object exceedeth the faculty in proportion infinitely. The thoughts of a man's heart, cannot so exceed the understanding faculty of a man, far less of an angel; therefore God, in the depth of his wisdom, by an act of his own free will, not from any mistiness or intrinsical darkness of the object, hath cast a covering over the thoughts of man's heart, that they are not seen clearly to any other men or angels. Nor could human societies, now in the state of sin, subsist, if but the father could read the heart of the son.

Nor have angels, good or bad, any immediate princedom over free will: nor would I say, Satan is the author, yea, or the immediate tempter to all sins: many sinful thoughts, and wicked acts are transacted in this dark chamber of presence, the heart of man, to which Satan can have no personal access, neither with his eyes to see, nor his hands of power to stir or move in them. The heart is the privy garden, weeds grow there without Satan's immediate industry; he may knock or cast fire-balls over the wall, or in at the windows, or send letters and messages in, but he cannot immediately talk with the heart, or act immediately on the will; we are to keep this virgin-love of the heart

to

to Christ; he can ravish it, and none but he. 'Tis the will that maketh the bargain in sinning: *with all keeping keep the heart.* We make away the created dominion over free will, that God gave us in our creation.

3. Satan hath a princedom, in, 1. *Knowledge natural*; 2. In *acquired knowledge.* In natural; because he is a piece of light, a lamp once shining in heaven; but now, for his sin, smoking and glimpsing in hell. The natural intellectuals of the devil are depraved, not removed. 'Tis a question, if he can remain a spirit, if that candle were extinct, by which he *believeth there is a God, but trembleth*, Jam. ii. *The acquired knowledge* of the devil is great, he being an advancing student, and still learning now above five thousand years; and he that teacheth others, becometh more learned himself: he is the great mint master and coiner of knowledge, in magicians, wise men, soothsayers, sorcerers, is a careful reader in turning over the pages of the book of nature, and the whole works of creation. But still Satan studieth man, better than man doth himself: he knoweth nature, in general, may sin: and that corrupt nature, must sin: he observeth second inclinations of humour, complexion, temper of body, disposition, ere he tempt; as no seaman sails, till he know how the wind bloweth: and he learned that by the prophets, and experience, which he saith, Luke iv. 34. *I know thee who thou art, the holy One of God.*

4. He hath a particular princedom of power, legally, over mankind, till Christ set them at liberty; as the executioner hath over the condemned man, from the judge. Heb. ii. 14. *Christ took part with the children of flesh and blood, that through death he might destroy him that had the power of death, that is the devil*; verse 15. *And deliver them, who through the fear of death, were all their lifetime subject to bondage.* Satan, from men's sins, hath a sort of conquered princedom, till the *Son of God make us free*, John viii. 36. And this princedom he keepeth over all the sons of disobedience, as their father, John viii. 44. as the king of the bottomless pit: and we have no ground to say

say that Satan at the day of judgment leaveth off to be king, because the damned and the devil and his angels are said to be tormented together in everlasting fire, Mat. xxv. For communion in pain, maketh not Satan to have no angels under him, or damned men, whom he torments.

Quest. But how keepeth Satan still power over Job, Peter, to winnow them and afflict them, in this life, if Christ hath cast him out of his princedom?

Answ. 1. 'Tis mere service for the trying of the saints and mortifying of their lusts, not dominion, not any legal power, such as he hath over the sons of disobedience, whom he keepeth captives at his will.

2. In relation to Satan it is a mere grant of permission; as a nobleman forfeited for treason, and kept some years in prison, before he die, hath the life-rent of his own lands, for his necessity, not by heritage as before, but by a grant or gift of grace, from the bounty of the prince and state; so hath Satan, not by grace to himself, but by a grant of mere permission, as it were his liferent to tempt, winnow, and try the saints, so long as Satan is in the way to his full doom in hell. Now, if Christ had not spoiled Satan, and dissolved his works; the use of his power had been, as it were, heritage, to Satan, in regard the law giveth him a sort of right over sinners, not made free in Christ. Yet I do not say, its his proper right, because Satan sinneth in tempting any to sin, yet the temptation, as it falleth passively on *the sons of disobedience*, is a work of divine justice, and as it falleth on the saints, an act of spotless and holy dispensation, for most just reasons known to God.

2. Satan is a prince in regard of magnificence, called a prince, a prince of the air, a god, for he hath a royal army under him, *the devil and his angels, are a great host,* Rev. xii. 9. *The devil, and Satan, and his angels, were cast out;* verse 7. *The dragon and his angels fought with Michael;* and he hath legions garrisoned in one poor man, he hath kept the fields above these five thousand years, with a huge and mighty ar-

my,

my, both by sea and land. Eph. vi. 12. *For we wrestle not against flesh and blood, but against principalities, and powers, against the rulers in the darkness of this world, against spiritual wickedness in high places.* Here be great persons in eminent places, and they can lead armies against us, and have in every single soldier, a strong garrison of concupiscence, and fleshly lusts, that war against the soul, 1 Pet. ii. 11. And the flesh is a strong fort-royal, a tower of imaginations, which exalt themselves against a strong King, the Lord Jesus, and cannot be his captives, but by the mighty power of God, 2 Cor. x. 5. The devil is not a despicable and poor enemy to be despised, it is not good war-wisdom to despise a mean enemy, far more should we not sleep, but watch and be sober; when the peers of hell, and princes and rulers in high places, who have the vantage of the mount above us, are against us.

3. Satan's princedom is especially seen in tempting to sin; which, that it may be better cleared, I shall shortly shew what a temptation in general is. 2. Open Satan's power in tempting. To tempt is to take a trial of any, to try what is in them; therefore the nearest end of tempting is knowledge; now the ways or manner of bringing out this knowledge, rendereth the temptation good or ill: for God tempteth, and Satan tempteth. "So temptation is a working upon the senses, reason, inclination, affections, by which any is, or may be moved under the colour of good, toward that which is offensive to God."

1. Temptation is a working, or an act of stirring in the tempter, not physical, but moral, and objective; no tempter, who is only a tempter, can by any real action fire the will. Satan doth but knock, by his logick, at the out-side of the door, but cannot open. Free-will is a tender, excellent piece of creation; and either the best or the worst of the whole creation of God. See well to it, 'tis a work of your whole lifetime to watch this door.

2. Temptation is an act of moving, or stirring the powers of man: as when wine is stirred, and wine

and

and dregs are jumbled through other; or a fountain troubled, and water and clay mixed in one; hence every tempted person is some way a sufferer, though he know not particularly it is so. As the fish tempted with the bait, the bird with the fowler's song, are sufferers, tho' they know not; there is a breaking in upon the fancy, sense, reason, will, and affections to strike a hole in the soul; so tempting is called piercing, *though the fool going to the chambers of death, knoweth not that it is for his life*, Prov. vii. 23. To be tempted is a matter of great concernment; illumination is most necessary here, and specially to know that God aimeth at the trial of our faith, and other glorious ends. And that, 1. Satan seeks some of his own work in us, as God seeketh to bring out some of his work in us. 2. That Satan aims to go between the believer and his strong hold. 3. That he aimeth at house-room in the soul.

3. The temptation works upon both the inward and outward man; on senses, fancy, mind, inclination, will and affection, but hath a special design at the soul.

4. By the temptation any is, or may be moved to sin; for all tempted, are not actually induced to sin. Christ was really tempted of the devil, but was never induced to sin. Satan shot his arrows at Job for nothing; he lost his labour in seeking the failing, and drinking up of Peter's faith. Therefore to be tempted of the devil, or the world, is not a sin.

5. The temptation worketh under the colour of good. The first printing-iron and master-sampler of tempting, hath this character of apparent good; Gen. iii. 6. *The woman saw that fruit was good.* 1. Because tempted persons are reasonable creatures, and as instinct taketh with birds, and beasts, and poor nature swayeth elements in their motion, so reason is a strong tying chain.

2. Every temptation hath a garment, or rather a shirt of truth in the understanding, and coming under the shadow and roof of the desiring faculty as good,

good, nothing hindereth it to take, but a marring of the understanding, in apprehending some black spot, in the fairness of it; when Satan saileth fair with favour of the wind, and cometh in his whites, and in cloth of gold, as an angel of light, we are as readily moved often (such is our childishness) with good-like as with good. Believe not therefore a white devil, because white. O because to yield your tongue to lick a honey-temptation, under the vail of sweetness. Receive things rather because lawful, than because good or pleasant. 2. Believe it, there can be no reason for sin, no reason can wash the devil to render him fair; neither thirst, nor company, can be a reason of drunkenness. An injury cannot justify every war and bloodshed; because injury is a sin, and to wash one sin with another, is as if you should wash a foul face with ink-water. 3. Believe sin to be folly and darkness, and light of reason can be neither father nor mother to folly and darkness; holiness is white and fair, within and without.

 6. The object of the temptation, in the definition; the *terminus ad quem*, is that which is offensive to the majesty of God. That we may understand this, remember four are said to tempt; 1. God, his tempting neither in the condition of the work, or intention of the worker, is sin, *But the Lord proveth you* (saith Moses to Israel) *that he might know, whether ye love the Lord your God.* 2. Our own lusts tempt and lead aside, Jam. xiv. And as fire cannot but make fire; so both in the intention of the work and the worker, the end of temptation is sin. Concupiscence is a mother that cannot bring forth a good daughter. 3. If men tempt to sin, as a magistrate, by good laws tempteth wicked men, the end is not necessarily sin in the intention of the doer; tho' no man can formally tempt another to sin, but he sinneth and tempteth to sin both ways. And when Satan tempts, he driveth ever at sin; both ways we are to fear God, to watch, to stand out, when he tempteth.

2. Now we are to consider, that tho' Satan be sentenced already, and as a malefactor under bail, and in chains, yet hath he leave to walk to and fro in the earth, and is not yet cast in prison, nor are we freed from his temptation, the personal persecution and malice of Satan; as we are from the persecution of the damned now in hell, who did persecute us here on earth, but cannot now. No doubt but as the good angels struck the men of Sodom with blindness, so the ill angels have the like power on the senses, a man possessed with the devil was both dumb and deaf, Job ii. 6. *Satan smote Job with sore boils, from the sole of his foot unto his crown*; and so devils have power over the senses, and bodily organs; and so of necessity over the blood, to cause rottenness in it, which must be in boils, and to alter and infect the humors. Psal. lxxviii. 49. Evil angels were ministers of the Lord's plagues on the Egyptians. But I shall not think it a good argument, to prove, that angels can jumble the humors, to make many things appear without that they are not; and that they can work on the internal senses, the fancy and imagination, because we ourselves, by an act of free-will can stir up the memory of things, and provoke our fancies to the apprehension of things: *Ergo*, angels either good, or evil, can do the like. This is but a sorry poor reason, for we ourselves can do many things within ourselves, which the angels cannot do; I know the thoughts of my own heart, when they come forth in act, 1 Cor. ii. 11. No angels good or ill can know them; I can with an obediential act of free-will, by grace, set my free-will on acts to command my memory, fancy, imagination, thoughts, to meditate on bypassed experiences of divine favours, and sweetly solace myself in God, with these thoughts; no angels in heaven or hell, can determine my free-will to those spiritual acts; yet, by the grace of God, I can do it. Nor is that true, whatever an inferior power can do, that a superior can much more do: if there be orders in angels, a superior angel cannot determine the

will

will of an inferior, as he himself can do. Sure, my knowledge and will are inferior powers, in comparison of angels, 1 Cor. xiii. 1. yet have I greater dominion over my own understanding and will, than the angels have over my understanding and will, and can know my own actual thoughts, and determine mine own will by grace, which no superior powers of angels, or any else, save the Almighty, can do.

I rather conceive, that the outward and inward senses, humours, imagination, fancy, memory, being natural agents; and scripture clearly shewing, that angels and devils can, and do work upon natural agents, have a power over all our dispositions, temperature, senses, fancy, imagination, memory; therefore what is natural in the acts of understanding and memory, not moral, angels do, and may know. What heart-secrets devils know from the disposition of body, paleness, redness, trembling, dejected countenance, are good conjectures, and surer it may be than we can apprehend, but no certain knowledge.

God only knows all the thoughts of man, and his secrets, 1 Kings viii. 39. *For thou* (even) *thou only knowest the hearts of all the children of men.* Prov. xv. 11. *Hell and destruction are before the Lord, how much more then the hearts of the children of men?* He that can read hell and destruction, and all the secrets of darkness, can also read, as a book opened at noon-day, the midnight thoughts of all the children of men. Psal. xliv. 21. Jer. xvii. Rom. viii. 27. 1 Thess. ii. 4. Rev. ii. 23. Acts i. 24. Pro. xvii. 3. Pro. xxi. 2. Job ii. 24, 25. Yea, to know the present thoughts, is proper to God, Mat. xix. 4. *And Jesus, knowing their thoughts, said, Wherefore think ye evil in your heart.* Nor can angels see the present thoughts come out in action; for otherwise, the man himself knoweth his own thoughts, when he actually thinketh them, 1 Cor. ii. 11. else he could not be convinced of the sinfulness of them, nor comforted in the spiritualness and preciousness of them.

It is a fond opinion of some, who say, angels can see the thoughts of the heart, when they are, but not
what

what they are, whether they be good or bad, love or hatred; for that is nonsense, to see moral acts, and not to be able to pass any judgment on them; or, that angels see our thoughts, but not whether they be intense and vehement, or cold and remiss; for it is proper to God, as the searcher of hearts, to know the secrets of the heart, and all the qualities of it, that he may accordingly judge them. And if angels see them as moral acts, they must know the vehemency, or slowness of them; the scripture placeth also the difficulty of knowing the thoughts, and the distance, and remoteness of them, from the understanding of men or angels, in the thoughts themselves, not in the vehemency or slowness of the thoughts; and it is but an evasion that some have, that angels may know the thoughts, and acts of the will in themselves, but not know to what end they are directed; and that the intention of the mind is the great secret that God hath reserved to himself. Because, 1. The scripture placeth the secrecy of the free acts of will and understanding in the acts themselves, and not in the intention; for so most of the actions of men and angels, their speaking this, not that; their walking in this city; their eating, sleeping, now, not another time; their praying, hearing, reading, shall be secrets known to God only, not to angels or men, just as the acts of understanding, the will, are; because the particular intention, whether we do these sincerely, for a good or bad end, yea, often for what end we do them, is amongst the secrets of the heart, as far distant from the understanding of men or angels, as any secret can be. 2. The intention of all our elicit acts, that issueth from will and understanding, are also acts of the heart and reins, that fall under the present question, and the greatest secrets in man, Heb. iv. 12.

Neither see I any reason, from the disproportion between the knowing faculty and the understanding of angels, why angels may not know the thoughts of my heart, as well as I know them myself: nor can the reason be, Suarez saith, because angels, tho' they have sufficient power in the faculty of understanding, to

know

know these things, yet have not in their understanding the species, the babies, images, and representations of heart-secrets. But with his good leave, this is *petite principii*; for the question is, How cometh it to pass, that angels, who have the species of higher and more profound things, as of the natural knowledge, that there is a God, that he is infinite, eternal, yet have not the species of an object far inferior, and yet intelligible, to wit, of the heart-actions of a man? 2. When I ask how cometh it, that an angel, or a man, knoweth not this? I ask indeed, how cometh it to pass, that an angel, or a man, wanteth such a species of such a thing? So Suarez saith in effect, 'angels know not heart secrets, because they know not heart secrets.' I conceive, God hath laid a covering over the hearts of man and angels, from his own free and wise will, and reserved that secret to himself: for God gave speech to men, and a way how angels should communicate their thoughts to angels and men, which is angel-speaking; and this gift had been useless, if angels and men could intuitively read and behold the thoughts of one anothers hearts: nor is it useful for the end of reasonable nature, for love and society, that we know the secrets of one anothers hearts; for the Author of nature giveth not that by nature, which with less impeachment of love, and not without danger of contention and hatred, may by industry be acquired. And we should take heed, what is written in the book of our heart, when such a searching eye readeth it, as God; and will one day read out to the hearing of men and angels, all these secrets, Eccles. xii. 14. Except we be pardoned in Christ, many state-secrets, many soul contrivances may come out, to our everlasting shame.

And for this cause, we are to bless the Lord, who hath reserved from Satan's princedom, and left out of his charter any power to compel our will. It is true, Satan hath a bordering, or (as it were) some out-land princedom over Saul's will, in that he can sit and ride on his melancholy; so as he is moved to throw a javelin at Jonathan, and to seek to kill David! yet so as

he,

he, that is so acted by an evil spirit, is blameworthy; and then it must be presumed, that he hath some dominion over his will, Acts v. 2. Peter saith to Ananias, *Why hath Satan filled thine heart, to lie to the Holy Ghost?* Here the Holy Ghost arraigneth not Satan, but Ananias for a lie, which yet came from the *father of lies*. Which is, 1. Because there was fewel and powder in the hearth before, and Satan did but blow the bellows, and brought forth the flame. 2. Because we willingly join, and love to have it so. 3. Because the act of sinning cometh formally from free-will, which cannot be forced, but may keep out the siege without violence, but yet basely rendereth.

If Satan be the *prince of the air*, and can raise mighty storms and winds, that can smite the four corners of an house, which is not like an ordinary wind, that bloweth from east or west, or north or south, but rather right down, Job i. 19. If he have power of floods, and seas, and be a roaring lion, and, by reason of his sagacity and skill in the secrets of nature, can do wonders, tho' no miracles, as to raise the dead, by applying actives and passives together; no question, the Lord letting loose some links of the chain he is fettered withal, he can work curiously and strongly on the walls of bodily organs, on the shop that the understanding soul lodgeth in, and on the necessary tools, organs, and powers of fancy, imagination, memory, humours, senses, spirits, blood, so nearly joined with the soul, as will, understanding, conscience, and affections sit in dangerous neighbourhood with such malignant spirits.

It is (no question) hard enough to give an exact delineation of the length and breadth of the borders of the princedom of Satan; nor is it necessary, for our edification, to know all the secrets and mysteries of the devil's power, how he assumeth a body, what he can do in the sphere of nature, how he acts upon men: sure, he hath some in his snare, as poor birds, *who are taken captives by him at his will*, 2 Tim. ii. 26. and that he sitteth at the helm, as it were of some, and

acts

acts and stirreth them so, the wind and tide of their lusts complying with him, that they cannot chuse but fail, and walk *according to the course of this world, according to the prince of the power of the air, the spirit that now worketh in the children of disobedience*, Eph. ii. 2. And that he can borrow tide and fair wind at his nod, and woo the soul by the shop and office-house, the body, the flesh, the senses; and reciprocally act, indirectly, by foreign embassies and missive letters, on the will and understanding, and the lusts, that are domestick friends within, to draw in the senses, and the fancies, and imagination, to join with him; as is clear in his first dealing with Eve. It is not his way, to deal with the senses only, or with reason only, or to keep such a method, as peremptorily to begin at one before another; but in Satan's first temptation of Eve, he acteth collaterally and reciprocally; he acteth on the ear, by speaking; and on the mind, by speaking reason, *Hath God said, Ye shall not eat of every tree?* Doth he so strictly tie you? Is that reason and justice, to put a law on an apple? Then you may not eat of every tree, which God hath made for eating. And Satan worketh on the sense by reason, Gen. iii. 5. *For God doth know, that in the day ye eat, then your eyes shall be opened, and ye shall be as gods knowing good and evil.* And this wrought upon the sense; for it is added, v. 6. *And the woman saw that the tree was good for food.* And again by the sense of feeling, Satan wrought on the will, to bring out the consent, verse 6. *And when the woman saw that the tree was good for food, and that it was pleasant to the eyes, and a tree to be desired to make one wise, she took of the fruit thereof, and did eat.* So Satan can make the body a tempter to the soul, and the soul and reason, a tempter to the body; as when the husband is leprous, and the wife infected with the pestilence, he rendereth her a leper, and she rendereth him sick with a running botch. When the body is pampered, and the vessels full, it draweth the soul's consent to fleshly lust; and the soul findeth reason, but corrupt rea-

son,

son, why the body should be a member of an harlot. And there is mutual help between concupiscence and conscience; the one tempting with strong acts of lusting, the other tempting with lustful reason, shew it should be so, and may be so; as in a water-work, drawing water from such a place, twenty empty buckets come down, twenty full buckets come up, and every one serveth another, for one common work. Nor is it a wonder that one devil doth kiss and embrace another.

Cast out.
The prince of this world's casting out, leadeth us to a further consideration of Satan's punishment: as there is a double sin in Satan, so a double punishing and casting out. The ill angels first sin I determine not; 'they abode not in the truth; they kept not their first and proper station.' God made all things good, and placed them all in due and fit houses and stations, and God was the station and house of the angels; the devils first left God, and left their own house; 'tis like they would have been higher, and affected a godhead: they would not sit contentedly, in the place God set them in. Shifting spirits, climbing men, that would be higher than God hath placed them, and would be without their own skin, and above their own element and proper sphere, have this, as a grain of the ill seed, that the old serpent spewed in Eve. The devil knew how to go out of his own house, and to climb above his own proper station, and he would lead Eve up the stairs, whither he did climb himself, to seek *to be like God, knowing good and evil*, Gen. iii. 5. The whole creation was like a well ordered army, at the beginning, all kept rank, and marched in order; the devils were the first soldiers in the army that spilt the comely rank, and marred the first order: the prince of darkness, that great lord of confusion, made the first jarring, and sampler and prime discord in the sweet musick, and song of the praises of the Creator, that all creatures did sing: Therefore God the Creator, in his justice, spared not him, and his fellow-mutineers, *but cast them down to hell, and delivered*
them

them unto chains of darkness, to be reserved unto judgment, 2 Pet. ii. 4. Christ, as Mediator, did not inflict this punishment on the fallen angels.

Now, there is a second sin of the devils, and that is not only the casting down of man, but the continuing without retreating in the first sin. 1 John iii. 8. *He that committeth sin, is of the devil; for the devil sinneth from the beginning.* John viii. 44. *Satan was a murderer from the beginning, and abode not in the truth; because there is no truth in him.* What, is not Satan's first sin a transient act gone and past; is Satan this day in the very act of murdering all mankind, and of murdering Adam and Eve, who many thousand years ago are dead? It is true, the act, physically considered, is gone; but morally, Satan is yet on that same sin, 1. Because he did, and doth spin out, in a long thread, the very first sin; and all Satan's life from that day to this, is one continued act of apostasy: in, 1. the not retreating, nor repenting his first sin, and his first murder; Satan's hands are wet and hot this very day with the blood of Adam and Eve's soul. 2. In the continuing in, and approving of the act of his first sinning, by still envying the glory of God, malicing his workmanship and image, so as the guilt of that sin goeth along with him. Hence, Christ addeth his seal, as Mediator, to the Lord's first sentence of justice, in casting him out of heaven; and in regard he continueth in that sin, and addeth new foul murderers, to his first transgression, in tempting, tormenting, hating, opposing the redemption of man, the gospel, the offices of Christ, the church of Christ; Christ cometh in by his office as his judge, to add to his chains. In which a word,

1. *Of the punishment of devils.*
2. *Of Christ, as he is the judge of devils.*

The punishment hath relation to his first sin; his first sin was against the Holy Ghost, in that being a lamp of light, shining up in the high palace, and standing before the throne, wanting not any wicked principle of concupiscence within, or any habitual aversion from God, looking God in the face, and beholding the first

truth,

truth, he sinned against God, and therefore was made an exemplary spectacle to angels and men, of pure and unmixed justice, without mercy, and cast down to hell, without hope of a Saviour, or redemption, Heb. ii. 16. *For verily he took not on him the nature of angels, but the seed of Abraham.*

The evils of punishment inflicted on Satan, are, 1. His being cast out of the presence of God, never to see his face again, nor enjoy his favour. 2 Pet. ii. 4. *For God spared not the angels that sinned, but cast them down to hell.* Hence, from this, schoolmen infer a second punishment, a perpetual sadness and dejection of mind, for the loss of that happy fruition of God. But I much doubt, whether sadness or the want of God's lovely presence, can consist with the extreme hatred of God and fiery averseness, implacable wrath, and burning envy, that Satan hath against the glory of God, or image of God, or any thing of God; especially against the *Lamb and his followers*, against whom he warreth continually; a sadness there may be in him, because he is a rational creature, in regard he is fallen from the good of happiness, not of holiness; but conjoined with wrath and hatred against God; and this is without question in all the damned.

2. The pain inflicted on the understanding, is the hurting of his natural speculative knowledge. Sure, if he see not God as the first truth, he seeth all deductions from the will, sovereignty, wisdom, justice of God, etc. more darkly than he did before, but, if his natural speculative knowledge was utterly lost, there should be no foundation remaining in him of wrath and envy against God, and his creatures and image. 2. His true and saving practical knowledge is lost, and in place thereof a crafty, versutious cunning, deceitfulness and subtility to deceive and tempt; such as is in the serpent to sting: such a bloody instinct as is in the dragon, in the lion to devour: but otherwise, the devil is the first fool of the creation of God, and hath played the fool above five thousand years; for in rational policy, the tempting of our first parents to sin,

sin, tho' it was a master-piece of wit, was the ruin of his kingdom; and the serpent, even in the crucifying of Christ, did buy a scratch in Christ's heel at a dear rate, with the bruising and grinding to powder the head and life of the serpent, and the full destruction of his kingdom. And by experience, Satan knoweth he is a loser, in tempting and persecuting the Lord Jesus and his members, yet malice having put on the light of prudence, he knowingly soweth sin, blood, wrath, in Christ's field; and in so doing, he sweateth in labouring the vineyard of the Lord, to make an harvest and vintage for Christ.

3. Infused grace Satan hath not at all; because grace supernatural is a stem and blossom of heaven: 'tis hard to think, that since Satan was thrust out of heaven, any of the fruits or blossoms of that paradise can grow in him. Acquired knowledge Satan may have. And,

4. From this Satan hath faith against his will, Jam. ii. 19. It is necessary in the specification rooted in a natural understanding; but in the exercise, as it were, forced and compelled; he would wish to want the constraining power of a natural knowledge; so as this is a wicked faith, and a tormenting virtue in the devil, as it is in many wicked men, who desire nothing more than to have conscience cut off from their soul: as some men are so pained with a gangrene in the foot, that they are willing their leg be sawn of: or like a man that hath a necessary servant, and most useful, and yet because he hath one intolerable gad, he must put him away. For light addeth fear and terror to some distracted persons, and maketh them out of measure furious; therefore ye must close door and window on them, and they are more sober when they have least light: so here, glancings of conscience serve but to make some see ghosts of hell, and terrifying sights.

3. Satan can have no hope of deliverance, but knoweth his prison-door is locked on him with a sad key, eternal despair; that so long as the Almighty liveth; and is *God blessed for ever*, so long shall he be miserable. Would sinners lend their thoughts and faith to e-

ternity,

ternity, that runneth out in so long a thread as *ever and ever*, and on pain, horrour, and torment *for ever and ever*, it might be they would not run and sweat so much in the way of sin.

6. Obstinacy, and invincible obduration and hardness, lieth on the mind, will, and affections of the devils; the cause of which, is his habitual continuance in, and love of the sin against the fair shining and convincing light of seen and enjoyed God, the justice of God, and the withdrawing of all grace and remedies against wilful hardning of the heart.

7. The breaking of Satan's hopes and counsels in all his ill attempts, his burning hatred of God, the Lamb's victories over the dragon, the chaining and bordering of his malicious power, etc. are great punishments.

8. I dare not, nor cannot determine, what the fire is that tormenteth him, nor the place of hell; 'tis more praise-worthy labour, to seek to be delivered, in Christ, from it, than to search curiously into it.

Satan's judge and caster out, is Christ; as may clearly be gathered from the words, *Now is the prince of this world cast out.* Hence,

Consid. 1. When Christ came to the office of Redeemer and Mediator of his church, to deliver his people out of the hands of Satan, he found Satan under old treason committed against God; for, before this, he kept mankind captive, and found him under a sentence for it, and cast down to hell: and because Christ was God, and the same God equal with the Father, therefore he made good his Father's deed, and putteth his seal and amen to that sentence; and for new treason against God, in man his image, whom God had made lord and little king of the earth, Christ gave out a new sentence against Satan, Gen. iii. 25. *I will put enmity between thee and the woman, and between thy seed and her seed: it shall bruise thy head, and thou shalt bruise his heel.*

Consid. 2. All punishment on Satan is now inflicted by the Mediator Christ; for since Satan came in the play,

to

to appear a Satan and adversary to man, he set up another kingdom of darkness, opposite to the kingdom of the Son of God, Col. i. 13. John xiv. 30. *he persecuteth the woman that brought forth the man child,* Revel. xii. 13. he goeth forth in his instruments to gather the kings of the earth, and the whole world, *to the great battle of that great day of God Almighty,* Revel. xvi. 14. *and maketh war with the Lamb,* Revel. xvii. 13, 14. he is *accuser of the brethren,* Revel. xii. 10. *The king of the bottomless pit, whose name in the Hebrew tongue is Abaddon, but in the Greek tongue hath his name Apollyon,* Revel. ix. 11. He is the arch-destroyer, and destroyeth all in relation to the man Christ and his church; therefore is Christ raised up a Redeemer, a Saviour, to revenge the cause of his brethren, and came in the flesh to destroy Satan, his kingdom and works, to enter in Satan's house to *bind the strong man, and spoil him of his goods,* Heb. ii. 14. 1 John iii. 8. John xiv. 30. Mat. xii. 29, 30. Gen. iii. 16. Col. ii. 15, 16. And when Christ, *by reconciling all things in heaven and earth to God,* Col. i. 20. became the head of angels and men, Col. ii. 9. Col. i. 18. Col. ii. 10. He was stated in a headship over all the tribes of men and angels, to confirm the good angels that they should not fall, and to redeem fallen men; and when all state-solemnities at the coronation of Jesus Christ are performed, and the Father had said, Psal. ii. 6. *Yet I have set my King on my holy hill of Zion;* Acts v. 31. he must, by his office and royal place, reign over the rebels, that are mixed with the willing subjects, and *bruise them with a rod of iron,* whether they will or no: and as when there is feud and wars between two houses, and blood on either side, there is an heir born of one of the houses to make peace between them, and take order with and subdue the rebellious, who refuse peace, and to revenge the injuries; so were there wars between the sovereign Majesty of the Lord our God, and both angel-nature and mankind. Angels and men had highly injured the Lord, and wounded his honour; Christ Jesus, a born heir of the seed of David,

and

and of the royal line of heaven, God equal with the Father, comes to the crown, and makes peace between the Lord and men, and so far reconcileth the good angels, that they cannot fall out with God, but stand by the grace of the new heir; and Christ revengeth upon the devils and the world the wrongs done to God, and subdueth both under God.

Consid. 3. It is considerable, that wisdom and counsel is here in war: Satan foiled man, and subdued him, as his vassal and slave, to the condemnation he himself was under; and man must be king, lord and judge over devils. Angels, who envied man's happiness, and destroyed mankind, must appear personally, be arraigned, sentenced, and condemned before the man Christ. Man was shut out of paradise by the envy of angels; now hath the man Christ the keys of paradise, of heaven and hell, and death and the grave. Christ's garments are wet and stained, not with Edom's blood, Isa. lxii. But (to borrow the expression) he goeth to heaven in triumph, and his apparel red with angel-blood, and so *leadeth captivity itself captive.* Other warriors take away the life of the living; but he taketh away the life of death itself. Others subdue captives; never one, save the man Christ, subdued captivity.

Consid. 4. Victory over devils, by the man Christ, is more glorious, than if God had interposed absolute sovereignty and power, because mercy, grace, truth, justice, are the sweet ingredients, going out with the blood of God in it; and omnipotency is much seen, in that one little despised man of clay, totally routeth and destroyeth Satan, and many legions, so that tho' devils keep the fields, and daily fight; yet they can never make head again against Christ, nor win one battle, or pull one captive out of Christ's hand.

Consid. 5. Heaven is not conquered again, nor hell and devils subdued by a sudden surprise, or a stratagem, but in fair wars, and in an open set battle, Col. ii. 15. *He on the cross made a shew openly, and triumphed over devils.*

Use 1. If God only know the heart, and its secrets,

and

and men and angels cannot; we should aim and study sincerity; one witness of integrity here, is more than millions of witnesses, this one witness? *the searcher of hearts*, will cast a man, though he had a jury of angels to absolve him, and all the men on earth were on the inquest and assize, to carry him up above the skies, and the heaven of heavens, as more innocent than all the angels; and if angels, all angels and men were on your jury to condemn you, to be as foul and guilty as the prince of devils, yet, Rom. viii. If ye be in Christ, verse 33. *Who shall lay any thing to the charge of God's elect? It is God that justifieth;* verse 34. *Who is he that condemneth?* Rest upon the testimony of no man; there be thousands fair and spotless standing before the throne, whom the world condemned to hell, as foul and black; we may instance in Jesus Christ, his apostles and the martyrs of Christ; and thousands the blind world have written in heaven amongst the stars, and gods above the clouds, in the quire of angels, as Augustus Cesar, and thousands of these whom Jesus Christ did never own, but as enemies. O what is the worth and price of a conscience *sprinkled in the blood of the Lamb?* And what a precious voice is the testimony of the spirit? And what a valid pass and a *Magna charta*, a noble testificate, is that in heaven and eternity, if Jesus Christ say, *Behold a true Israelite indeed, in whom is no guile.*

Use 2. What is light, and knowledge, though you had as much as the devils have, who are torches and lamps of hell for knowledge, if all your wisdom be against Christ? 'Tis a black condemnation, Jer. iv. 22. *My people are foolish, they have not known me, they are sottish children, and they have no understanding.* Yet they are wise as the devil is, *they are wise to do evil, but to do good they have no knowledge.* They go for heads of wit; and wise men, who are keep, politick, profound state-atheists, who can, with their contrivances, roll about the wheels of two kingdoms, and can stir the helm of Europe, and yet know nothing of God, but all their wit runneth in the devil's channel, to

plot,

plot, brew, and hatch wickedness, lies, subvert the cause of the just, crush the widow, murder and starve the fatherless, bear down religion, set up a human, earthly, civil structure of government in Christ's kingdom. Let them go for wise men, but they are wise for the devil; let the Lord speak to such, Jer. viii. 8. *How do ye say, we are wise, and the law of the Lord is with us.*----Verse 9. *Lo they have rejected the law of the Lord, and what wisdom is in them*? Can there be wise men and great state-wits, and not rather state-sots, who reject the wisdom of God? 'Tis now counted state-wisdom in Scotland, to patch up a false peace with Amalek, contrary to the covenant of God; tho' Saul give the Amalekites and their kings peace, God will give them no peace.

Use 3. If Satan be so understanding and subtile, so active a spirit; then the Famulists err, not knowing the scriptures; for they say, the devil is nothing, yea nor the creature any thing; but God, as (saith the bright star, Cap. viii. Pag. 68, 69.) "Nothing is but God and his will: pag. 77. There is nothing in the creature, which is not the creator himself; and therefore the sun is no sooner hid, but the beams cease to be; so if God hide himself, and withdraw his hand from the creatures, they suddenly return to their nothing. But as the beam and heat, tho' they contain nothing but sun and fire, yet lookt upon essentially as they are in themselves, they are not sun and fire, but only a certain dependent, or a spark of those: right so the creature, though all it consisteth of, is God; yet considered in the own proper nature, depends upon God; 'tis consequently somewhat." And that blasphemous piece, called *Theologia Germanisa*, written by a priest in high Dutch, and Englished by Giles Randal, printed at London 1646, by toleration, saith, "sin and the devil is nothing; but when the creature will challenge any good to itself, as to live, know, briefly to be able to do any thing that can be termed good, as tho' that good thing were appertaining to it, then the

crea-

"creature averteth itself from God, and that aversion is sin. And the devil's sin was, that he did arrogate this to himself, that he was something, and would be something, and that something was his, and in his right and power; this arrogancy, to be I, to myself to be me, and to be mine, was Satan's aversion and fall, and this is still in use." So this author. Hell and the devil cannot devise subtiller and vainer blasphemy; for so the creature is not the creature, the devil is not a creature, not a spirit, not a tempter, not the prince of the air, not a roaring lion, not a liar; and the Holy Ghost, in terming the devil an angel created in the truth, should sin. 'Tis true, nothing hath being of itself, and independently, and as the cause of all being, but only God, the cause of causes, and prime fountain of being, goodness and actions: but hence it cannot follow, that creatures are not true beings, by participation of, and dependence upon the first ocean, fountain, and cause of all being; and that goodness and actions may not be ascribed to them from their derived being they have from God.

2. Christ-man, in ascribing to himself that he is man, that he doth the will of his Father, that he loved his own to the death, should sin. Which is blasphemy.

3. It is false for men or devils, and sinful arrogancy, to say, they can subsist, or do keep their being, without a dependence on God, the only first essential being; but it is contrary to all truth, that they sin, when they say, they are the creatures of God, and the dependent rays and beams that flow from God and the good creatures of God (though by created and dependent goodness) they neither lie nor sin, nor commit any act of arrogancy; then should it be sin to say that there were any creatures in the world, which is to bely the scripture.

4. 'Tis the cursed self-denial of Familists, to say, when they do good or ill, righteousness or sin; *'Tis not I, but God in me that doth all.* And so that there is but one spirit of life that acteth, and working in all things in heaven, and in earth, and that is essentially

God,

God, and the will of God, which is all one with God.

5. That vain annihilation, and nothinging of ourselves, in being and working, yea to the annihilating of the man Christ, under pretence of extolling God, because God worketh immediately all good and evil in us (say they) and we but suffer God's will; and when we thus are mere patient, and suffer God to work his will in us, we are God himself, perfect as God, conform to his will, nothing in ourselves, we being no creatures, but the creator. 'That God manifested in the flesh, is God manifested in the flesh of all men; that the passion of Christ, in itself, is imaginary, but Christ crucified is our pains and tribulations, which we should welcome as Jesus Christ, and so cast all our afflictions into the furnace of Christ's torments; as it is said, let that mind be in you that was in Christ.' Bright star. Cap. 18. pag. 205. This (I say) is the dreadful blasphemy now printed and preached at London, without controulment, for the which the judgments of God, sad, and heavy, cannot be far from the land. I crave the reader's pardon, that I named such nonsenses and fooleries.

Use 4. By all means beware of sins against light, such as the devil's first sin was. 1. To sin with a witness in the breast, and a witness in heaven, is to laugh at Christ in his face. 2. 'Tis the devil's back fall; he, by such a sin, fell first from heaven, by staring God on the face, and out-daring light, God, conscience, and actual conviction; the devil, no question, by himself, was warned of his sin, and how dear it would cost him, before he sinned. Suppose we that there is a way in a mountain of ice, where thousands in former times have slidden and fallen, and bruised all their body and bones to powder, would we willingly climb the same rocks, and dream we should escape the same danger? Legions and millions of devils fell and bruised their souls to dust, on sins against light and knowledge; yet do we too daringly climb the same rocks, and sin daily against the sun-light of the gospel-grace of God, *teaching us to deny ungodliness, and worldly lusts*, and

the

the warnings of our own conscience; yea, too many go on against supernatural illumination, and we will but leap the damned devils unhappy leap; we know not that victory over one grain-weight of light, leaveth behind it pound weights of disposition and bentness to farther provoking of the Lord: a daring boldness to look God in the face, and sin turneth quickly in the very sin, as near in kin to the devil's sin, as can be; and rendereth it devilish to stoop, and fall down before the light of shining command, as the elect angels do, who receive God's commands with wings, and fly upon obedience as ministering spirits.

Use 4. Harden not your hearts, be not obstinate in evil, that is the plague of devils also. Men render themselves devils; with their own hands, they open hell, and go in, and lay the devil's chains and fetters on their own will and mind, when they resolutely, and deliberately, resist God, and God in a deep judgment in them bindeth them, and they cry not; he is deservedly a captive, who twists his own cords and chains about himself. Self-induration is a self-hell, and a self-bondage. How afraid should we be to keep loose watch over the heart, or to give the reins to our own will, to go on against God? For he, 1. Needs no more, but lose an army, and a strong armed garrison of sinful thoughts, are so many spirits of hell, that are within the town already, and they can destroy us. 2. The devil is near-by to put in our heart all wickedness; he hath the command of the out-works, the humours, fancy, disposition, the spies, and posts that go in and out, the senses; we have no need to lay the bands of a covenant on the eye, and if the devil be master of all the forts and sconses without the walls, we are in no small danger.

Use 5. From Satan's power and opposition against us, we want not both motives and encouragements to watch. For, 1. Satan is a great party; he is a prince, Ephes. ii. And 2. *A prince above us, the prince of the air.* 3. He hath large territories; the text saith, *he is the*

prince

prince of this world. 4. He is not a common prince, he is a prince of kings; many kings of the earth give their power and strength to him, and so he is a principality. 5. Not that only, but he has a great army, principalities, powers, rulers, potentates; we have a mighty army of lords and kings to fight against. 6. The more spiritual the enemy be, and the more subtile to come in at closed iron gates, and through strong walls, the more dangerous; Satan, for all your keys and locks, will be at the inner door of the heart, ere ever ye know of it: you watch, and he is at your elbow, and covenanting with your watches on the walls to corrupt them. 7. When the enemy is strong, if he be wicked, so much the worse. Now, Ephes. vi. 12. we fight against wickedness itself, against spiritual wickedness; the more wicked the enemy is, he hath a greater mind to fire, and destroy. 8. The more active, the worse is the enemy: Satan hath no office, but to be the butcherer and executioner of justice, and hath no distractions to withdraw him; he may attend upon bloods and soul-murthers, and walketh in a circle, compassing the earth to and fro, and goeth about like a roaring lion, seeking whom he may devour. 9. He hath friends within us, every saint is a divided party.

2. The quarrel is not money, civil liberties, laws, houses, lands, nor corruptible things, yet we run and strive for pence and pounds; but here peace of conscience, an incorruptible crown, 1 Cor. ix. 25. the Lord's glory is the garland at the stake.

3. We have noble witnesses. The Father, the Lord Jesus, the Spirit of glory, the glorious angels are beholding us.

4. The battle will not last for centuries, nor for many scores of years; the issue will be quickly, death will end the controversy.

5. We have Christ on our side, he hath spoiled principalities and powers; the Lord the master of the game, hath promised us his might, his strength, all his forces, grace, wisdom, power, his angels, that are

stronger

stronger than ill angels; here angels against angels, God engaged against hell.

6. We fight, but with a broken and overcomed devil, both spoiled, Col. ii. 15. and disarmed, Heb. ii. 14. 1 Cor. xv. 55, 56.

5. There is little required of us to victory, but a strong negative; consent not, render not, treat not with the enemy, though he fire, and kill.

8. The loss is the greatest of all, eternal misery; once fully end, close and make a covenant with the enemy, and ye can hardly be ever able to rebel, or make head against your conqueror; but once a slave, and eternally a slave.

9. The garland is fair and glorious, *the tree of life that is in the midst of the paradise of God*, Revel. ii. 7. *The hidden manna, the white stone, and the new name*, verse 17. *Power over the nations, and the morning star*, ver. 26, 27, 28. *To be clothed in white, and his name confessed before Christ's Father, and his holy angels*, Rev. iii. 5. *And he is made a pillar in the house of God, and on him is written the name of Christ's God, and the name of the city of Christ's God, Jerusalem that cometh down out of heaven, and Christ's new name*, verse 12. *And he sits with Christ on a throne, and with the Father of Christ*, verse 12.

10. The victory is certain, and ours by promise, all which should arm us with sobriety; a drunken warrior is seldom victorious, worldly pleasures and lusts are above our head and strength; and *to put on the whole armour of God, and watch and pray*, is wisdom.

Use 6. Let us thankfully acknowledge our obligation to Jesus Christ, who hath cast out *this prince of this world*. What service owe we to Jesus Christ who hath ransomed us from such an enemy? Sure we are his debtors for ever; the captive's whole service is little enough for his ransom-payer.

And, 1. We cannot be the servants of the world, if Christ have *ransomed us from this present evil world*, Gal. i. 4. and from the prince thereof. It is base to be

the

the vassal of the tyrant, from whose hands we are redeemed; the world is but Satan's vassal.

2. He is a spirit, who hath redeemed us from a cruel spirit. Christ-God is a Spirit, out-side-service cannot please him. When corruption, like poison, strikes into the heart, and the hands are pretty clean, 'tis most dangerous.

3. Redemption argueth not freedom from infirmities, but from such sins as are called the pollutions of the world. There is sin in all; but in the redeemed, sin defileth the actions, not the person, because he is washed; in the hypocrite, it blacketh both person and actions.

4. We cannot serve our ransom-payer in the strength of false principles, or natural gifts, but of his own grace.

5. Glorify God, by shewing forth his glory, for ye can add nothing really to him; and he will really glorify you, and put a weighty crown on your head, and also pay you home in your own coin, and declaratorily glorify you. *I will confess him* (saith Christ) *before my Father*, etc.

Verse 32. *And I, if I be lifted up from the earth, will draw all men to me.*

We have spoken of the power of Christ's death, and of his enemies, the world, and Satan. Now Christ speaks of the power of his death on the elect, in drawing sinners to himself.

The scope of the words is to hold forth the efficacy of Christ's death, in drawing sinners to him. In which we have these considerable points.
1. The *drawing itself.*
2. The *drawer, I will draw*, saith Christ. Christ is good, and of excellent dexterity at drawing of men to God.
3. The persons drawn, *All men.*
4. The persons to whom; the *terminus ad quem; To me*, saith Christ.
5. The

CHRIST DYING AND DRAWING SINNERS TO HIMSELF.

5. The condition; *if I be lifted up from the earth*: which is not a note of doubting, whether he would die for us, as we shall hear, but of a sure condition.
6. The way and manner of his lifting up from the earth is expounded, verse 33. To signify, to the hearers, what sort of death he would die, to wit, the death of the cross.

Of drawing itself; these are considerable.
1. The expression and metaphor of drawing.
2. The reasons moving Christ to draw; the fountain causes, and the disposition and qualifications going before drawing, in the party drawn.
3. The manner of drawing, or the way, and if it be some other thing than justification.
4. The power and efficacy of drawing.

[Gr. Elkyo] to draw; as the word [Heb. Maschach] Cant. i. 4. *Draw me, we will run after thee*, is first, a word of violence and strength. 1 Kings xxii. 34. *A certain man drew a bow* [Heb. Maschach] Job xiv. 1. *Wilt thou draw Leviathan with thy hook?* John xxi. 11. *Simon Peter* [Gr. Elkyse,] *drew a net to land.* Acts xvi. 19. *They caught Paul and Silas* [Gr. Elkysan,] *and drew them to the market-place to the rulers.* 2. Drawing is by wiles, and persuasion, or love; for (wiles is covered or pretended love) Judg. iv. 6. *Draw them* (by persuasion) *to mount Tabor to battle.* Hos. xi. 3. *I will draw them* [Heb. emschechem] *with cords of man, with bands of love.* It is such a drawing as is ascribed to the whore, (though another word) Prov. vii. 21. the whore, which made the young man to decline, with the softness of her lips, in fair words, *forced him.* Jam. i. 14. *Every man is tempted, when he is led, or drawn aside, by his own lust, and enticed.* This drawing is by wiles, to steal a man off his feet. So Psal. x. 9. *A bird is drawn in the net.* It is then a word borrowed from bodily strength, which draweth heavy bodies out of one place to another, by strong hand. The sinner is a heavy creature. Grace is a

strong

strong thing to pull the man out of his element. There be then in Christ's drawing, 1. Violence. 2. Persuasions of love, strong love runneth from the heart, thro' all the nerves and veins of Christ's right arm, to draw a sinner to God. 3. There is art and wiles, which is nothing but masked love: for wiles cannot work on the soul to draw it, but by the taking of reason with apprehension of good; hope is the painted net that draweth men to Christ, and the hope of the prey draweth the fox to the net, the hope of food, the bird to the snare. The violence that Christ useth, is not on the reason, will, or any vital principles of the soul; no principles of life can act as principles of life, from external drawings and stirrings, life is an internal thing; the line and first point of the line, in motions of life, is from within; all the violence is done to the corrupt accidents, and sinful qualities of the soul; as to darkness, and sinful ignorance, to unbelief, frowardness and sourness to Christ, hatred of God, eminty of the carnal mind to the law of God. Put the will once on moving, and set the wheels a stirring toward Christ, (which is all the difficulty) and the principles of life smile on Christ, and move apace; but the corruption of will must be removed first: as suppose, a millstone were kept fast in the air by a strong chain of iron, there is violence required to snap in pieces the iron chain, but none at all to draw the millstone down to the earth, its falls down of its own accord; this is but a comparison; for the will, in its motion to Christ, must not only be freed from the dominion of the clog of the body of sin, and these natural chains and fetters; but Christ must put new principles, and a new life, and new wings, and new wheels; and with them act, stir, and move the will; and then, *he drawing, we run*, Cant. i. 4.

He that is drawn to Christ, John vi. 44. is not altogether willing; as the fish hath no propension of nature to be haled out of its own element; all the propension cometh from that which setteth the will on work.

A

A child taketh medicine, but his propension is stirred from the sugar, that pleaseth his taste. He learneth, being hired; that which sets him on work, is not the good that he seeth in the book, nor the beauty that he conceiveth to be in virtue and learning; its the apples, the babies you give him as his hire, that acteth him; nor is the will here forced. A hireling carries a burden, not with a forced will, but there is nothing in the burden that doth take his heart; but the sweating under the burden, come all from money; he is hired, and therefore doth all from the stirrings of his will, that ariseth from his wages. Men's coming to Christ, comes not from their natural good-liking they bear to Christ, but from some higher principle within, and the discovered excellency, that the spirit lays open to the soul.

II.

Hence, 2. The reasons moving a soul to yield to Christ's drawing, come under a twofold consideration; as 1. Natural dispositions. 2. As lustred with some common grace, and so thought preparatory to conversion and drawing.

In the former consideration, divines, with good reasons, look at them as sins, and the greatest obstructions of conversion.

1. There is something that is taking with reason, why a man will not come to Christ; no man goes to hell without hire, and gratis. Hell is a death, but a golden death, and fair afar: ah! It is sweet to men to perish; hell is a most reasonable choice to the sinner, the chambers of death shine with fair paintry to the natural man's reason.

1. It is not single weakness, but wicked and wilful impotency, that keeps men from Christ: as a beggar would be a king, he hath no positive hatred of the honours, riches, pleasures of a king; but he hath not legs nor arms to climb so high, as to ascend to a throne. But the natural man neither will, not can chuse a king's life, and be a follower of Christ: nor is man any o-
ther

ther than a natural hater of Christ, tho' many think they bear Christ at good-will, John xv. 24. *But now they have seen, and hated both me and my Father.* The reason why men think they love Christ, is the lustre that education, and common literal report, from the womb, hath put upon Christ; our fathers and teachers said ever, Christ is the Saviour of man, and a merciful God, and therefore we have that common esteem of him; but were we born of Jewish parents, or among Jews, and taken from our parents, and heard nothing from the womb of Christ, but what the Jews say, and that is, that he is a false prophet, that he rose not from the dead, but that his disciples, by night, stole him away out of the grave, we should from the womb hate Christ, as well as the Jews. And the like we may see in Indians, who love and adore the devil from the womb, but with this difference, they love Satan truly, because both nature, now corrupt, and education carries them thereunto; but education can give no man a true love of Christ. (2.) Whence is it that the world hates the children of God? It is from instinct, and nature, rather than from any imperated acts, John xv. 19. *Because ye are not of the world, but I have chosen you out of the world, therefore the world hates you.* v. 21. *But all these things will they do unto you, for my name's sake.* To be chosen out of the world, to carry any thing of Christ and his image and nature, and to be born again, and of another seed than the world is born of, is no ground of arbitrary and elective hatred; but of such hatred as comes from divers natural instincts; such as is the hatred between the wolf and the lamb, the raven and the dove. If then the world hate the saints, as they do, Rom. i. 30. and hate Christ, and hate the saints upon this formal ground, because they have in them the nature of God, the image of Christ, some of the excellency of Christ, then they must hate Christ far more; for *propter quod unumquodque tale, id ipsum magis tale.* The world hated Christ for God; for there was more of God in the man Christ, than ever

was

was in any creature; then they hated God more, and with a higher hatred. So Christ is the sampler and copy to all the saints; therefore Christ must be more contrary to the wicked world, than the saints are. If you hate the servant for the master's sake, then you hate the master more: if you love the nurse for the child's sake, then you love the child more. So the *Jews killed the servants the prophets, they stoned them and beat them*, Mat. xxi. 35. but they did more to Christ, v. 39, *They caught him, slew him, and cast him out of the vineyard, and took the inheritance to themselves.* (3.) Men naturally hate the ways of God: if there be holiness in his ways, then it must be most eminently in God: if they esteem his yoke sour and heavy, and reformation a burden, then must they far more esteem so of himself.

2. Men have a sort of satisfaction in their natural condition: a whole man desires no physician. A dead man hath some negative content to lie in grave; he can have no acts of sorrow for want of life. (2.) We do not put forth any stirring of life or desire toward that which is naturally above us: a child in the belly hath no acts toward a crown or a kingdom in this life, because desires are bottomed and founded on nature; as an ape, or a horse, hath no desire to be a man. Pilate, as if he were burdened with Christ saith, Mat. xxvii. 22. *What shall I then do with Jesus that is called Christ? What availeth my birth-right to me*, saith Esau, *seeing I die for hunger?*

3. When beasts and birds are allured by the snare, and fishes by the bait, death cometh to them in the garments of life; for food is all their heaven: and instinct helpeth them to prosecute their ends; and there is a natural similitude and inclination between their nature and what they desire, bottomed on an instinct, even when the object of their inclination is but dyed with the hue and apparency of good. But there is no such instinct in the natural man, nor similitude between a cage of hell, and the beauty and excellency of Christ;

be-

between his sense and the hid manna, or the banqueting house of wine.

4. The natural man cannot come to Christ. In that place, John vi. 44. there be four things considerable.

1. The best of men is unapt to come to Christ; *no man*, whatever his parts and eminency be, and he a nature of gold, he cannot come to Christ.

2. He saith not, *no man cometh*, as denying the act, for so no man of himself is an excellent philosopher; but he denieth a power, [Gr. *Ou deis dunatai*,] *he cannot come*.

3. But help is much; haply if his eyes were open, the will is good, he would gladly come to Christ, if he were able: nay, saith Christ, he is unwilling and unable to both: he that cannot come, *except he be haled and drawn*, and some violence offered to his corruption, hath no good-liking of Christ. But,

4. It is but little drawing possibly that will do the business; some gentle blast, or air of golden words, some moral swasion, some breathings and spiration of fine reasonings, from men or angel, can do much. No, but it is not so; no less (saith Christ) can draw a sinner to me, than the *arm of the Father*, and a pull of his omnipotency, who is *greater than all*, John x. no man, whatever metal he be of, the finest of men, can come, or hath power to come to me, and to believe on the only begotten Son of God, *except the Father who sent me draw him.* We know, Christ was much to extol his Father, his Father was ever in his esteem an eminent One, as Mat. xi. 25, 26, 27. Mark xiv. 36. Luke xxiii. 46. John iii. 35. John vi. 21 & v. 27. Mat. x. 32. & xxiv. 37. John ii. 16 & v. 43. & x. 29. & xix. 2. Rev. ii. 27. John xv. 1.

So is there a power always denied to the natural man to close with Christ, Rom. viii. 7. 2 Cor. iii. 5.

A will to believe and to submit to Christ is denied to natural men, John v. 40. *Ye will not come unto me, that ye may be saved* [Gr. ou delete] Luke xix. 14. The enemies of Christ say, [Gr. ou theolomen tuton basileusai eph hèmas] *We will not have this man to reign over us.* v. 27. *But these mine enemies, that would not that I should*

reign

CHRIST DYING AND DRAWING SINNERS TO HIMSELF.

reign over them, bring hither, and slay them before me. [Gr. outìs mè thelèfanta mebasileusai ep' autòn]. These to me, seem to be allusions to Israel's wearying of the Lord of old, Isa. xliii. 23. *I have not wearied thee with incense.* Jer. ii. 5. *What iniquity have your fathers found in me?* Mic. vi. 3. *O my people, what have I done unto thee, and wherein have I wearied thee? testify against me.* It is strange that sinners can see a black spot on the Lord's fair face, or that their will, that is nearer of kin to reason, than the affections that are in beasts, should be averse to God: yet it is said of wicked men, that they are *haters of God,* Rom. i. 30. *His citizens hated him,* Luke xix. 14. John xv. 24. And especially, these speeches carry allusion to Psal. xviii. 12. *Israel would have none of me.* [Heb. *lo abahli*] Israel had no liking of me, *no will of me.* So that weakness simply, is not the nearest cause of our not coming to Christ, but wilful weakness, or rather weak wilfulness, 1. Because in agents that cannot work, their impotency, or lowness of nature, is the cause; as the reason why a horse cannot discourse as a man, it, because his nature is inferior to the reasonable nature of a man, and not because the horse will not, but because he cannot discourse. The cause why a lamp of clay casts not such light in the night, as a candle, or as a star in the firmament, is the baseness and opacity of the nature of clay to produce such an action, as to give light; there is not such a thing as will in the clay, which intervenes between its nature, and the no-giving light in the night. But men hearing the gospel, do not believe, not only because they cannot (for beasts cannot believe) but because as Christ saith, *They will not believe,* John v. 40. *They will have none of Christ,* Psal. xviii. 11. *They will not have Christ to reign over them,* Luke xix. 14. And will intervenes between the impotency of their will and their disobedience. 2. Because that hatred of God and Christ, ascribed to unregenerate men, Rom. i. 30. Luke xix. 14. John xv. 24. is the birth that lay in the womb of will, and comes from will as will, and not only from will as

weak;

weak; so men's delighting, and their loving to be estranged from Christ, and to satisfy themselves with other lovers, beside Christ, are high bended acts of the will; which argueth, that not only weakness, but wilfulness hath influence on men's unbelief. 3. The Lord chargeth men with this, Mat. xxiii. 37. *I would ye would not.* 4. Conscience taketh it on its will, and father's disobedience on the will. 1 Sam. viii. 19. *Nay, but we shall, or we will have a king.* Jer. xliv. 16. The people avow, their will and peremptory resolution is, *We will not hearken to thee.*

6. But for the ground, reason and cause on Christ's part of drawing, it is free-grace, and only free-grace; which are holden forth in these positions.

Pos. 1. As there is no merit, good deserving work, or hire in the miserable sinner dying in his blood, dead in sins, out of his wit, and *disobedient, deceived, and serving divers lusts,* Ezek. xvi. 4, 5, 6, 7, 8. Ephes. ii. 1, 2, 3, 4. Tit. iii. 4. So there is as much love, mankindness and free-grace in heaven, in the breast of Christ, as would save all in hell, or out of hell. I speak this, in regard, not of the Lord's intention, as if he did bear all and every one of mankind, a good-will, purposing to save them; but because there lies and flows such a sea and ocean of infinite love about the heart, and in the bowels of Jesus Christ, as would over-save, and out-love infinite world of sinners (so all could come and draw, and drink, and suck the breasts of over- flowings of Christ's free-grace) in regard of the intrinsical weight and magnitude of this love, that if you appoint banks to channel, or marches to bound this free-love, God should not be God, nor the Redeemer the Redeemer.

Pos. 2. Could any created eye of men or angels, reach or compass the thousand thousandth part of this love, with one look: such an act of adoration and admiration must follow thereupon, as should break the soul and breast of this creature, in a thousand pieces; but Christ in heaven, and out of heaven is hid. Infiniteness is a secret that angels or men never did, never

shall

shall comprehensively know; there is secret of love seen in heaven, but never seen: how little of the sea do our natural eyes behold? Only the superfice. We see but a little part of the skin or hide of the visible heavens with our bodily eyes; but so much as is seen, is of exceeding beauty. No eye bodily can see the bottom of the seas, or the large in fields in the visible heavens. If the infinite lump of the boundless love of Christ were seen at once, what a heaven's wonder, what a world's miracle would Christ appear to be? But as much of Christ is seen, as vessels of glory, tho' wide enough, can comprehend. But if angels and glorified saints, see much of Christ, and so accordingly as they see and know, do praise him, and yet cannot over-praise, and out-sing so much as they see: and if the inside of infiniteness of love, free-grace, mercy, majesty, dominion, be an everlasting mystery; angels and men are below merit, even in heaven, and angels and saints must be ashamed of, and blush at the imagination of merits; for an infinite lovely majesty seen and not praised, nor loved in any measure of equality or commensuration to his dignity and worth, must lay infinite, tho' sinless debt for eternity on all the citizens of glory, whether home-born or natives of that country, as elect angels; or adopted strangers, as glorified saints.

Pos. 3. The manner of grace's working on saints is gracious, and so essentially free; as is evident in our first drawing to Christ, when many sins are forgiven, and so the soul loves much; and the sweetest burden in heaven, or out of heaven, is a burden of the love of Christ: all debt must be a burden to an ingenuous spirit; but the debt of freer-grace, that lieth from eternity on angels and men, is a lovely and a desirable pain. That men, before they were men, and had being, and before all eternity, were in the bosom of Christ, the engaged debtors of the Lamb, in the purpose of free-grace, loved with an everlasting love, is a deep thought of love; and that being was a gracious being, before actual being, speaketh and crieth much love; and its the flower, the glory, the crown of free-grace, that God's

free-

free-love in Christ, calleth forth the morning rays and beams of the Redeemer's kind heart, on men, who are enemies, *darkness, haters of God, dead in sin,* dying in blood and pollution. And how broad, how warm, and how rankly must the fair and large skirts of Christ's love smell of admirable grace, when they are spread over the bleeding, the loathsome, the black, and unwashen sinner! Is not every word a heaven? Ezek. xvi. 8. *Now, when I passed by thee, and looked upon thee, behold thy time was the time of love, and I spread my skirt over thee, and covered thy nakedness: yea, I sware unto thee, and entered into a covenant with thee, saith the Lord God, and thou becamest mine,* etc. Christ's passing by, is as a traveller on his journey, who findeth a child without father or mother, in the open field dying, and naked, wallowing in blood, and then casting a covering of free-love (and love hath broad skirts) over his people; and 'tis an expression of much tenderness, and warmness of love. Many articles in that place extol free-grace.

1. Christ is brought in as a passing-by passenger, to whom this foundling was no blood-friend, but a meer stranger; so, if humanity and man-kindness had not wrought on his heart, he might have passed by us; we were to Christ nothing of kindred or blood, by our first birth, but strangers from the womb to God, going a-whoring so soon as we are born.

2. Christ looked on forlorn sinners, and there is love in his two eyes; it may be that bowels of iron, in which lodgeth nothing of a man, or of natural compassion, would move a traveller to see, and not see a young child dying in his blood: but (saith he) I saw thee, my heart, my bowels had eyes of love towards thee; there was tender compassion in my very look; my bowels within me turned and swooned at the cast of mine eye, when I saw thy misery.

3. Behold, and behold, he would own his own mercy and love; let angels and men wonder at it, that the great and infinite Majesty of God, should condescend to look on such base sinners, so far below the free-

love

love and majesty of God. There is a Behold, a sign put upon this door; come hither, angels and men, and wonder at the condescension. 2. Tenderness. 3. Strength of heat and warmness. 4. Freedom and unhired motions. 5. Riches and abundance. 6. Efficacy and virtue. 7. The bounty and reality of the free-love of Christ.

4. *Thy time was a time of loving.* What? of loving? it was a time of lothing: a time of love? When sinners were so base, so poor, wretched, so sinfully despicable, such enemies to God, in their mind, by wicked works, Col. i. 21. *dead in sins and trespasses, walking according to the course of this world,* (an ill compass to steer by) *according to the prince of the power of the air, the spirit that now worketh in the children of disobedience?* Was this a time of love? Yea, Christ's love cannot be bowed or budded with any thing without Christ: it is as strong as Christ himself, and sin and hell can neither break, nor counter-work the love of Christ; your hatred cannot countermand his imperious love.

5. It was not a time of single love, but it was a time of loves, *thy time*: Christ hath a time, and sinners have a time, when they are ripe for mercy; it was a time [*Heb.* dodim] *of loves*; of much loves, of much love. He loved us, *and shewed mercy on us,* Eph. ii. 4. [Gr. dia tèn polen agapèn] *for his great and manifold love,* Cant. vii. 12. *There I will give thee my loves.* Cant. vi. 2. *Thy loves are better than wine.* v. 4. *We will remember thy loves, more than wine.* It is a bundle, a wood of many loves that is in Christ. Then, v. 5. *I spread my skirt over thee.* He is a warm-hearted passenger, who, in a cold day, will take off his own garment to clothe a naked foundling, that he finds in the way: I (saith Christ) *laid on thee, a naked sinner, the skirt of that love, wherewith the Father loved me.* O what a strange word is that! John xvii. 26. *I have declared unto them thy name, and will declare it; that the love wherewith thou hast loved me, may be in them, and I in them.* It is true, Christ could not
be

be stript naked of the love, wherewith his Father loved him; and that love being essential to God, cannot be formally communicated to us, yet the fruit of it is ours; and the Lord Jesus spreads over his redeemed ones, a lap of the same love and bowels, in regard of the fruits of free-love, which the Father did from eternity spread over himself.

6. *I covered* (saith Christ) *thy nakedness.* O what a garment of glory is the imputed righteousness of Christ! *Bring forth the best robe, and put it on him.* This is the white raiment that clothed the *shame of our nakedness.*

7. *Yea, I sware unto thee, and entred in covenant with thee.* Equals do much, if they swear, and enter in covenant with equals: but, O humble majesty of an infinite God, who would enter in covenant with sinners, wretched sinners, at our worst condition, and would quiet our very unbelieving thoughts of sinful jealousy, with an oath of the most High, who hath no greater to swear by than himself!

8. *And thou becamest mine*, Heb. *thou wast for me*, set apart for me. Here stooping and low condescending love, to own sinners, and a claim and propriety on wretched and far-off strangers, to name dying, bleeding, sinning and God-hating dust, and guilty perishing clay, his own proper goods.

9. Verse 9. *Then washed I thee with water.* That Christ's so fair hands should stoop to wash such black-skinned and defiled sinners, in either free-justification, or in purging away the rotten blood and *filth of the daughter of Zion*, in regeneration, maketh *good* that, (*to the free-love of Christ, that which is black, is fair and beautiful.*)

10. *And I anointed thee with oil.* Free grace, and Christ dwelling by faith, Eph. iii. 17. in saints, that are the flower, gold, and marrow of the church, is a high expression of free-love. Sinners are worse than withered and dry clay, without saving-grace.

11. And to all these, Christ clothed his naked church

with

with broidered work, fine linen and silk; he putteth bracelets on her hands, a chain of gold (of grace) about her neck, a jewel on her forehead, ear-rings on her ears, and a beautiful crown on her head. The grace to profess Christ, and carry on the forehead the name of the Father, of the Lamb, of the new Jerusalem, the bride the Lamb's wife, before men and angels, is a fair ornament.

12. Beside, a name, and the perfume of a sweet and precious report in the world, addeth a lustre to the saints, *who are by nature the children of wrath, as well as others*, Ezek. xvi. 10, 11, 12, 13, 14. Eph. ii. 1, 2, 3, 4, 5.

Pos. 4. It is an abasement of Christ, that he who gives such a ransom to justice for free-grace, should wait for a penny from sinners; that sinners must bid and buy, and engage him to give, and Christ say, you must give me more, I must sell, not give grace for nothing. Your penny-worths cannot roll about that everlasting wheel of free-grace, the decree of election, or bow or break Christ's free heart to save you, rather than another. 2. There is more proportion between wages and saving-grace, than between wages and eternal glory. Now, there is much debt in heaven more than on earth, but no merit at all in either heaven or earth, except Christ for all. Merit cannot grow in a land of grace. 3. Grace is the sinner's gain, but no gain to Christ: is it gain to the sun, that all the earth borrows light and summer from it? Or to the clouds, that they give rain to the earth? Or to the fountains, that they yield water to men and beasts? Can ye make infinite Jesus Christ rich? Ye may add to the sea, tho' very little. The Creator could have made a fairer sun than that which shines in the firmament, tho' it be fair enough. But the Mediator Christ is a Saviour so moulded and contrived, that it is impossible to add to his beauty, excellency, loveliness; man or angels could not with a choicer Redeemer, than Christ; if your wages could add to him, he should be needy, as you are.

Pos.

Pos. 5. Free-grace is the loveliest piece in heaven or earth, it makes us *partakers of the divine nature*, 2 Pet. i. 4. And tho' the creature, graced of God, keep an infinite distance from God, and be not goded, nor christed, as some do blasphemously say; yet it is considerable, that there is a shadow (though but a shadow) of proportion between that expression of Paul, 1 Cor. xv. 10. [Gr. Charitì tu Theu eimi hò emi] *By the grace of God, I am that I am*; and that which the Lord saith of himself, Exod. ii. 14. speaking to *Moses*, [Heb. ebjeh asher ehjeh] *I am that I am.* Grace is but a borrowed accident of the creature; not heritage, not his essence; but Paul would say, all his excellency was from free-grace. Were any indifferent beholder up in the highest Jerusalem after the day of judgment, to see the company of the Lamb, and his court, so many thousand pieces of clay, then clothed with highest grace, smiling on the face of him that sits on the throne, made eternal kings; that, for glory and robes of grace, and the weighty crown, you cannot see a bit of clay, and yet originally, all these are but glistering bits of clay, and graced dust; it should tire the beholder with admiration. O but the second creation is a rare piece of workmanship! But, again, come and see that heaven of wonders, the Man-Christ, who as man hath, 1. Flesh and blood, and a man's soul, as we have; but O so incomparably wonderful, as the grace of God without merit hath made the Man-Christ! grace hath exalted this Man to an high throne; the Godhead, in person, dwelleth in this clay-tent of endless glory: and God speaks personally out of this man, and this Emmanuel is God; and the man is so weighted with glory, as all that are there, (and they be a fair and numerous company) are upon one continued act of admiring, enjoying, praising, loving Him, for no less date, than endless eternity; and they can never be able to pull their eyes off Him. And then grace seen, enjoyed as it groweth at the well-head, up in Emmanuel's highest and newest land, is of another strain, sweeter and more glorious than down here in the earth, which is not the

ele-

element of grace; they are but glimpses, borrowed shadows, chips, and drops of grace, that are here; that is a world of nothing but grace. All which I speak, to let us see, how far free-grace is from base hire, and that we may not dare to make Christ, who is an absolute free King, an hireling.

Pos. 6. Grace is not educed or extracted out of the potency of any created nature. Grace is born in heaven; and came from the inmost of the heart of Christ; it hath neither seed or parent on earth, therefore the Lord challengeth it as his own, 2 Cor. xii. 9. *The Lord said unto me, my grace is sufficient for thee.* 2 Tim. ii. 1. *The grace that is in Christ Jesus.* 1 Cor. xv. 10. *The grace of God.* 2 Cor. xiii. 14. *The grace of the Lord Jesus Christ.* Gal. i. 15. *He called me by his grace*: if we could engage the grace of God, or prevent it, then should grace be our birth; but grace is not essential to angels. It is a doubt if any creature can be capable by nature of any possibility natural, not to sin; it is much to know the just owner of grace, who begot it: it came out of the eternal womb and bowels of Jesus Christ.

Quest. But are there no preparations, either of nature, or at least of grace, going before saving-grace, and the soul's being drawn to Christ?

Answ. That we may come to consider preparations or previous qualifications to conversion; let us consider whether Christ, coming to the soul, hath need of an usher.

Asser. 1. Dispositions going before conversion, come under a four-fold consideration, 1. As efficient causes, so some imagine them to be. 2. As materially and subjectively they dispose the soul to receive grace. 3. Formally or morally, either as parts of conversion, or moral preparations having a promise of conversion annexed to them. 4. As means, in reference to the final cause, or to the Lord's end in sending these before; and what is said of these, may have some truth proportionally in a church's low condition or humiliation, before they be delivered. We may also speak here of

dis-

dispositions going before the Lord's renewed drawing of sinners already converted, after a fall, or under desertion, Cant. i. *Draw me, we will run.*

Asser. 2. No man but Pelagians, Arminians, and such, do teach, if any shall improve their natural habilities to the uttermost, and stir up themselves in good earnest to seek the grace of conversion, and Christ the wisdom of God, they shall certainly, and without miscarrying, find what they seek; 1. Because no man, not the finest and sweetest nature, can engage the grace of Christ, or with his penny or sweating, earn either the *kingdom of grace or glory,* whether by way of merit of condignity, or congruity. Rom. ix. 16. *So then, it is not in him that willeth, nor in him that runneth, but of God that sheweth mercy.* 1 Tim. i. 9. *Who hath saved us, and called us with an holy calling, not according to our works, but according to his own purpose and grace, which was given us in Christ Jesus, before the world began.* So, Eph. ii. 1, 2, 3, 4, 5. Tit. iii. 3, 4, 5. Ezek. xvi. 4, 5, 6, 7, 8, 9, 10. (2.) Because there is no shadow of any engagement of promise on God's part, or any word for it, *Do this by the strength of nature, and grace shall be given to you.* (3.) Nor are we ashamed to say with the scripture, it is as impossible to storm heaven, or make purchase of Christ, by the strength of nature, as for the dead man to take his grave in his two arms, and rise and lay death by him, and walk. Nor does this impossibly free the sinner from guiltiness and rebukes, 1. Because it is a sinfully contracted inability, except he would deny original sin. 2. It is voluntary in us, and the bondage that we love. 3. The scripture both calls it impossibility, and also rebukes it as sinful, John vi. 44. Rom. viii. 7, 8. Eph. ii. 1, 2, 3, 11, 12, 13. Chap. iv. 17, 18, 19. Chap. v. 8.

Asser. 3. All preparations, even wrought in us, by the common and general restraining grace of God, can have no effective influence to produce our conversion, from the scriptures alledged; for then should we be *called, saved, and quickned, when we are dead in sin,*

foolish,

foolish, disobedient, and enemies to God, [Gr. Katà tà erga hemòn, *and* ex ergòn tòn en diakaiosenè hòn epoiesamen hèmeis,] *According to our works of righteousness which we had done,* contrary to Eph. ii. 1, 2, 3, 4, 5, 11, 12, 14. 2 Tim. i. 9. Tit. iii. 3. (2.) Then common general gifts might also engage Christ's free-grace. 3. Men might prevent grace, and fore-stall Christ and his merits; which overturns the foundation of the gospel, and cries down Christ and free-grace.

Asser. 4. All these foregoing endeavours and sweatings, being void of faith, *cannot please God,* Heb. xi. 6. *These who act in the strength of them, are yet in the flesh, and not in the Spirit,* and so can do nothing acceptable to God, being yet out of Christ, Rom. viii. 8. John xv. 4, 5, 6. and the tree being corrupt, the fruit must be sour, and naught; humiliation, sorrow for sin, displeasure with ourselves, that go before conversion, can be no formal parts of conversion, nor any essential limbs, members or degrees of the new creature; nor so much as a stone or pin of the new building. Divines call them, *gradus ad rem, initium materiale conversionis; non gradus in re, nec initium formale:* for parts of the building remain in the building; when the house is come to some perfect frame, all those bastard pieces, coming not from the new principle, the new heart, Christ formed in the soul, are cast out as unprofitable. Paul, when he meets with Christ, casts off his silks and satins, that he was lordly of while he was a Pharisee, as old rags, *loss and dung,* and acts now with far other principles and tools. It is all new work after another sampler; heaven works in him now.

Asser. 5. Those are not moral preparations which we perform before conversion, nor have they any promise of Christ annexed to them; as, he that is humbled under sin, shall be drawn to Christ: he that wisheth the physician, shall be cured and called to repentance; we read of no such promise in the word. 2. A man, not in Christ, is without the sphere or element of Christ, at the wrong side of the door of the sheep-fold, he is

not

not in Emanuel's land; *and all the promises of God are in Christ, Yea and Amen*, 2 Cor. i. 20. The whole flock of gospel promises are put in Christ, as the first subject; and believers have them from Christ, at the second hand. Christ keeps, as the true ark, the book of the testament, the believer's Bible. It is true, the new heart is promised to the elect, even while they are not in Christ, but they cannot make claim to that promise till they be first in Christ; but those promises are made in a special manner to Christ, as to the head of the redeemed, to be dispensed by Christ, to those only whom the Father gave him before time. And as the promises are peculiar to Christ, so the persons and grace promised, both the one and the other, are due to Christ, and result from the head, to those who in God's decree only shall be members; as righteousness, life eternal, and perseverance, are made to those that are members. 3. *Many run and obtain not*, 1 Cor. ix. 24, 25, 26. *Many strive to inter in, and shall not be able*, Luke xiii. 24. Many lay a foundation, *and are not able to finish*, Luke xiv. 29. Many hunt, *and catch nothing*: many have storms of conscience, as Cain and Judas, who never go one step further. When therefore Antinomians impute to us, that we teach, *That to desire to believe, is faith; to desire to pray*, (a) *is prayer* (b); they foully mistake; for raw desires, and wishes after conversion, and Christ, are to us no more conversion, and the soul's being drawn to Christ, than Esau's weeping for the blessing, was the blessing; or Balaam's wish to die the death of the righteous, was the happy end of such as die in the Lord. But the sincere desires and good-will of justified persons, are accepted of the Lord for the deed: and when Christ pronounceth such blessed as hunger for righteousness, we say in that sense, a sincere desire to pray, and believe, is ma-

terially,

(a) Saltmarsh free-grace, Chap. 2. Pag. 17, 18. (b) M. Denne conference between the sick man and a pastor, pag. 2.

terially, and by concomitancy, a neighbour, and near of kin to believing, and praying. A virtual or seminal intention to pray, believe, love Christ, do his will, is, in the seed, praying, believing; when the intention is supernatural, and of the same kind with the act; as the seed is the tree: we say not so of natural intentions and desires. As Abraham's sincere intention to offer his son, was the offering of his son; the widow's casting in her mite, was, in her honest desire, the casting in of all that she had; certainly, not all simply, that had been against charity toward herself: but (2.) Single desires, unfeigned aims, weigh as much with Christ, as actions, in their reality. So we say many are, in affections, martyrs, who never die nor suffer loss for Christ; because nothing is wanting on the part of such saints, thus disposed, but that God call them to it. So Abraham offered his son Isaac to God; because Abraham did all on his part, and he was not the cause, why he was not offered and made an actual sacrifice to God; but God's countermand and his forbidding was to cause, and nothing else.

Asser. 6. The humiliation and sorrow for sin, and desire of the physician, by way of merit, or, 2. by way of a moral disposition, having the favour of a gospel-promise, do no more render a soul nearer to Christ and saving grace, than the want of these dispositions; for as a horse, or an ape, though they come nearer to some shadow of reason, and to man's nature, than the stork, or the ass, or than things void of life, as stones and the like; yet as there is required the like omnipotency to turn an ape into a man, as to make a stone a son of Abraham; so the like omnipotency of grace is required to turn an unhumbled soul into a saved and redeemed saint, as to turn a proud Pharisee into a saint: and merit is as far to seek in the one as in the other. So an unconverted sinner, tho' some way humbled, if the Lord of free grace should convert him, were no less obliged to free grace, and no less from laying any tie or bands of merits, or obligation, by way of promise, on Christ, for his conversion, than a

stone

stone, made a believing son of Abraham, should be in the same case of conversion. And, 3. The humbled soul, for ought he knows, (I speak of legal humiliation) hath no more any gospel-title or promise that saving grace shall be given to him, even of meer grace, upon condition of his humiliation, or external hearing, or desire of the physician, than the proud Pharisee. Yet as the body framed and organized is in a nearer disposition to be a house to receive the soul, than a stone or a block; so is an humbled and dejected soul, such as cast-down Saul, and the bowed-down jailor, and those that *were pricked in their hearts*, Acts ii. in the moment before their conversion were nearer to conversion, and in regard of passive and material dispositions made by the law-work, readier to receive the impression and new life of Christ formed in them, than the blaspheming Jews, Acts xiii. and the proud Pharisees, who *despised the counsel of God, and would not be baptized*, Luke vii. 30. There be some preparatory colours in dying of cloth, as blue, that dispose the cloth for other colours more easily; so is it here: and a fish that hath swallowed the bait, and is in the bosom of the net, is nearer being taken, than a fish free and swimming in the ocean; yet a fish may break the net, and cut the angle, and not be taken. A legally-fitted man may be *not far from the kingdom of God*. Mark xii. 34. and yet never enter in. And those same dispositions, in relation to God's end in saving the elect, are often means, and disposing occasions, fitting souls for conversion: though some be like a piece of gold lying in the dirt, yet it is both true metal, and hath the king's stamp on it, and is of equal worth with that which goeth current in the market. So, in regard of God's eternal election, many are in the way of sin, and not converted as yet, notwithstanding all the lustre of fore-going preparations, tho' they be as truly the elect of God, as either those that are converted, yea or glorified in heaven; yet their preparations do lead them, in regard of an higher power, (that they see not)

to

to saving grace. And for any thing revealed to us, God ordinarily prepares men by the law, and some previous dispositions, before they be drawn to Christ. I dare not peremptorily say, that God useth no prerogative-royal, or no privileges of sovereignty, in the conversion of some, who find mercy between the water and the bridge; yea, I think that *Christ comes to some like a roe, or a young hart, skipping and leaping over hills and mountains*, and passeth over his own set line, and snatcheth them out of hell, without these preparations; at least he works them suddenly: and I see no inconveniency, but as in God's way of nature, he can make dispensations to himself, so in the ways of grace, we cannot find him out. However, sure, of crabbed and knotty timber, he makes new buildings; and it is very base and untoward clay, that Christ, who maketh all things new, cannot frame a vessel of mercy of. To change one specie or kind of a creature into another, a lion into a lamb, and to cause the 'wolf and the lamb dwell together, and the leopard lie down with the kid, and the calf and the young lion and the fatling together, and a little child to lead them,' is the proper work of omnipotency, whatever be the preparations, or undisposition of sinners.

Asser. 7. Not any protestant divines, I know, make true repentance a work of the law going before faith in Christ. 1. The law speaks not one word of repentance; but saith, either do or die: repentance is an evangelic ingredient in a saint. 2. *Christ was made a prince, and exalted to give repentance*, Acts v. 31. and the law, as the law, hath not one word of Christ, tho' it cannot contradict Christ, except we say, that there be two contradictory wills in Christ, which were blasphemy; but some dispositions before conversion, I conceive, Antinomians yield to us. For one saith, (a) speaking of the manner of his conversion, 'One main thing, I am sure, was to get some soul-saving comfort,

that

(a) Saltmarsh free-grace, Chap. 2. page 10.

that moved me to reveal my troubled conscience to godly ministers, and not in general to allay my trouble.' Yet I can make good from scripture, that this desire can be in no unconverted soul; a physician that mistakes the cure doctrinally, will prove a conzening comforter. And another (b) saith, 'The persons capable of justification are such as truly feel what lost creatures they are in themselves, and in all their works: this is all the preparative condition that God requireth on our part, to this high and heavenly work; for hereby is a man truly humbled in himself, of whom God speaketh, saying, ---I dwell with him that is of an humble spirit,' etc. To make persons capable of justification, here is required 'a true feeling that they are lost in themselves, and in all their works.' But this can be no preparative condition of justification, as Eaton saith; because true feeling must follow faith, not go before it. And, 2. True feeling is proper to justified persons; nothing going before justification, and so, which is found in unjustified persons, can be proper to justified persons only. 3. Antinomians say, sinners as sinners, and consequently all sinners, are to believe justification in Christ, without any foregoing preparation. This man saith, 'prepared and feeling persons that are sensible of sin, are only capable of justification.' 4. To truly feel a lost condition, cannot be all the preparative condition; for the word hath annexed no promise of justification to the unjustified, who shall feel his lost condition. For the place, Isa. lvii. speaketh of a justified sinner, not of an unjustified, who is only prepared for justification. 1. Because God dwells in this humbled soul, then he must be justified and converted. Eph. iii. 17. *That Christ may dwell in your heart by faith.* 2. This is a liver by faith, and so justified; *The just shall live by faith*, Hab. ii. 4. Rom. i. 17. Gal. iii. 11. Heb. x. 38. And he *must live by faith*, whom *the high and lofty one* revives.

Ob-

(b) Eaton Honey-comb, chap. 2. page 7, 8.

Objections of Antinomians, especially of Saltmarsh, free-grace, chap. 2. pag. 19, 20. removed.

Object. 1. "But to bid a troubled soul be humbled for sin, and pray, and set upon duties, and speak nothing of Christ to them; whereas poor souls cannot pray in that condition, is to teach them to seek righteousness in themselves."

Answ. 1. Satan cannot say, that we teach any to set on duties, and to silence Christ's strength and grace, by which only duties may be done. 2. To bid them set on duties, as their righteousness before God, and as the way to find rest and peace for their souls, and that speaking nothing of Christ, we disclaim as antichristian and pharisaical. 3. It is no argument, but the Arminian objection against free-grace, not to bid a troubled soul pray, because he cannot pray without the Spirit; for Peter, Acts viii. bids Simon Magus, *who was in the gall of bitterness*, pray; yet without the Spirit he could not pray. Antinomians exhort troubled souls, tho' not converted, to believe in Christ; yet they are as unable to believe without the Spirit, as to pray without the Spirit. 4. To bid them set on evangelic duties, without trusting in them, that is, to feel their lost condition, to despair of salvation in themselves, to look afar off to Christ, to desire him, are the set way that Christ walks in, to fit us for saving-grace.

Object. 2. "Despair of salvation in myself, is a part of faith; so you exhort the troubled in mind at first to believe."

Answ. Not so: Judas and Cain both despaired of salvation in themselves, yet had they no part of saving faith. 'Tis impossible that any can rely on Christ, while they live resting on false bottoms; faith is a sailing and a swimming, ships cannot sail on mountains, it is unpossible to swim on dry land; as it is impossible to have a soul, and not to have a love; so we cannot have a love to ly by us, as useless; but a lover we must have: and Christ's work of conversion is orderly; as first to plow, and pluck up, so then to sow and plant; and first, to take the soul off old lovers. We are on a way of gad-

ding

ding to seek lovers, Jer. ii. 36. *On a high and lofty mountain to set our bed*, Isa. lvii. 7. God must straw thorns and briers in our love-bed, and take Ephraim off his idols, Hos. xiv. 6. and from riding on horses, and make the soul as white and clean paper, that Christ may print a new lover on it. Therefore 'tis young mortification in the blossom, to give half a refusal to all old lovers; this is Christ's aim, Cant. iv. 8. *Come from the lions dens, and the mountains of leopards with me.*

Object. 3. "Desires to pray and believe, being some times cold, sometimes none at all, cannot satisfy a troubled soul. I must have, besides desires, endeavours: desires to desire, and sorrow because I can sorrow for sin, are but legal works; not such as are required in a broken heart."

Answ. Desires going before conversion, are nothing less than satisfactory, nor are they such as can calm a storming conscience: he knows not Christ, who dreams that a wakened conscience can be calmed with any thing, less than the blood of Jesus Christ, that speaks better things than the blood of Abel. Never protestant divines promise soul-rest in preparations, that are wrought by the law. 2. If Antinomians can give soul-rest to troubled consciences, by all the promises of the gospel, and raise up the spirits of Judas or Cain to sound comfort, let them be doing: yea, or to weak afflicted souls: while the Spirit blows right down from the advocate of sinners, at the right hand of God, we much doubt. Sure there is a lock on a troubled conscience, that the gospel-letter, or the tongue of man or angel can be no key to open. Christ hath reserved a way of his own to give satisfaction to afflicted spirits. But the question is now, supposing ye deal with unconverted men, whether or no ye are not, first to convince them of the curses of the law to come on them, to humble them, and so chase them to Christ; and if to bid them be humbled, and know their dangerous condition, the state of damnation; and set to these preparatory duties, be to teach them to seek righteousness in themselves? We answer, No.

Crisp,

Crisp, vol. 3. Ser. 1. P. 130, 131, 132, 134, 135.

Object. 4. "If we preach wrath to believers, we must either make them believe they ly under that wrath, or no; if they be not under that wrath, we had as good hold our tongues. If we say, if they commit these and these sins, they are damned, and except they perform such and such duties, and except they walk thus and thus holily, and do these and these good works, they shall come under wrath, or at least, God will be angry with them; what do we in this, but abuse the scriptures? We undo all that Christ hath done, we bely God, and tell believers that they are under a covenant of works.-------I would have wrath preached to believers, that they may abstain from sin, because they are delivered from wrath, not that they may be delivered from wrath; for God hath sworn, Isa. liv. As the world shall be no more destroyed with waters, so he will be no more wroth with his people."

Answ. 1. We are to make believers know, if they believe not, and walk not worthy of Christ, in all holy duties; their faith is a fancy, and a dead faith, and the wrath of God abides on them, and they are not believers. 2. Tho' they be believers, wrath must be preached to them, and is preached to them every where in the New Testament; as death, Rom. vi. 21, 22. *Damnation*, Rom. xiv. 23. *the wrath of God*, Eph. v. 6. *Condemnation*, 2 Thes. i. 8. *Perdition, flaming fire, eternal fire,* 1 Cor. iii. 17. 1 Cor. xi. 32, 34. Jude 7, 8. 2 Tim. vi. 9. 1 Cor. xvi. 22. to the end they may make *sure their calling and election.* 3. What is this, but to make a mock of all the threatnings of the gospel? For, by this argument, the threatnings are not to be preached to the elect before their conversion, except we would make them believe a lie, that they are reprobates, and under wrath, when they are under no wrath at all, but from eternity were delivered from wrath; nor should the gospel-threatnings be preached to reprobates. Why; shew me one word where pastors are bidden tell men they are to believe, they are reprobates,

and

and under eternal wrath, peremptorily, except we know them to have sinned against the Holy Ghost. 4. Nor is deliverance from wrath to be believed as absolutely by us; whether we believe and walk worthy of Christ, or do no such thing, but walk after the flesh, as we are to believe the world shall never be destroyed with water; that is a comparison to strengthen the people's weak faith. Else I retort it thus, whether the world believe in Christ, or not, they shall never be drowned with water, and that we are to believe absolutely. Then, by this reason, whether men believe on Christ, or no, there is no condemnation, or wrath to be feared. The contrary is expresly, John iii. 18, 36. I take the mystery to be this: Antinomians would have no moral, no ceremonial law preached at all; and therefore one of them writeth expresly, 1. That there be no commandments under the gospel. 2. No threatnings or penalties at all. 3. That the whole law of Moses, moral, as well as ceremonial, is abrogated under the gospel. That is a merry life.

Saltmarsh.

Object. 5. "Other preachers bid the troubled soul be sorry for sin, lead a better life, and all shall be well."

Answ. Such as lead not men to Christ, with their sorrow for sin, or to any good life, that is not, or fits not for the life of faith, are none of ours, but the Antinomians.

Saltmarsh.

Object. 6. "But others bid the troubled soul believe, but he must first seek in himself qualifications, or conditions; but this is to will them to walk in the light of their own sparks."

Answ. If to bid men abstain from flagitious sins, and from seeking glory of men, that are both neck-breaks of faith, John v. 44. and bring men under external displeasure, both before and after we believe, be to walk in the light of our own sparks: then, when the Lord forbids these in his law, and commandeth both the believer and unbeliever the contrary virtues, he must counsel the same with us. To believe and not be humbled,

and

and despair of salvation in yourself, is to presume; he that believeth right, is cast on that broken board, like a ship-broken man, either must I cast myself on the rock Christ, or then drown eternally and perish: the unjust steward was at, what shall I do? Ere he came into a wise resolution; to go the road way that Christ leads believers, is not to walk in the light of our own sparks. 'Tis one thing to seek qualifications of ourselves, trusting in them; and another thing to seek qualifications in ourselves, as preparatory duties wrought by Christ's grace; the former we disclaim, not the latter.

Saltmarsh's own experience.

Object. 7. "I will relate mine own experience. First, when I was minded to make away myself, for my sin; the Lord sent into my mind this word, I have loved thee with an everlasting love. Ah, thought I then, hath God loved me with such an everlasting love, and shall I sin against such a God? 2. Many doubts and fears arose from the examination of myself, I was afraid of being deluded. 3. The promise, Isa. lv. 1. did sweetly stay my heart, Christ in his ordinances witnessed to me, that he was mine. 4. I went on for some time full of joy. 5. I was in fears again, that I could not pray; but I had a promise, I will fulfil the desires of them that fear me, etc."

Answ. The method of the conversion of a deluded Antinomian, is no rule to others. 2. Nor do I think that God keeps one way with all, especially, when this man's first step is from nature, and thoughts of self-murther, up to the Lamb's book of life, the secret of eternal election in the breast of God, I have loved thee with an eternal love. How knew the author this to be God's voice from a qualification in his soul? It kept him from self-murther. Ye see qualifications in ourself, which the author saith is the way of legal preachers, are required in any that believe. 2. It is utterly false, that the gospel-faith, commanded to all the elect and reprobate, is the apprehension of God's eternal love

to

to me in particular; the scripture saith no such thing. Experience contrary to scripture can be no leading rule. So the Antinomian way of conversion, is, that every soul troubled for sin, elect, or reprobate, is immediately, without any foregoing preparations, or humiliation, or work of the law, to believe that God loved him with an everlasting love. A manifest lie, for so reprobates are to believe a lie as the first gospel-truth. This is I confess a honey-way, and so evangelic, that all the damned are to believe, that God did bear to them the same everlasting good-will and love he had in heart to Jacob. 2. All reprobates may abstain from self-murther, out of this principle, of the Lord's everlasting love of election, revealed immediately, at first, without any previous signs or qualifications going before. 3. The gospel we teach, saith, eternal election is that secret in the heart of the Lamb, called his book; so as really God first loves and chooses the sinner to salvation, and we are blacked with hell, lying amongst the pots, till Christ take us up, and wash, and lick the leopard spots off us: but to our sense and apprehension, we first love and choose him as our only liking; and then, by our faith, and his love on us, we know he hath first loved us with an everlasting love: but there be many turnings, windings, ups and downs, ere it come to this. I have not heard of such an experience, that at the first, without any more ado, forthwith, the Lord saith, come up hither, I will cause thee read thy name in the Lamb's book of life. The same author saith, election is the secret of God, and belongeth the Lord, pag. 104. And shall the believing of the love of election to glory be the first medicine that you give to all troubled consciences, elect and reprobate? This is to quench the fire by casting in oil; but if Antinomians take two ways, one with the unconverted elect, troubled in conscience; another with unconverted reprobates so troubled; we should be glad to hear these two new ways. 4. In the second place, (he is so well acquainted with the way of the Spirit, as if through the casement of the cabinet counsel of

God

God, he had seen and reckoned on his fingers all the steps of the stairs;) he saith, *He had many doubts and fears to be deluded;* that is, he doubted if his faith was true and saving; for this is all the delusion to be feared upon self-examination: so, page 24. c. 2. You may read his words, chap. v. p. 93. *I find not any* (saith the same author) *in the whole course of Christ's preaching, or the disciples, when they preached to them to believe, asking the question, whether they believed, or no.* Then it is like, this experience finds no warrant or precedent in the saints, to whom Christ and the apostles preached. 5. The sweet witnessing of the Spirit, from Isa. lv. 1. *Ho, every one that thirsts, come to the waters,* is gospel-honey; but consider if there were no law-work preparing, no needle making a hole before, Christ should sew together the sides of the wound. 'Tis but a delusion; 1. Because, Isa. lxi. 1. no whole hearted sinners meet with Christ; none come at first laughing to Christ, all that come to Jesus for help, come with the tear in their eye. 2. To come dry and withered to the waters, Isa. lv. 1. is the required preparation. 3. The gold in a beggar's purse in great abundance is to be suspected for stolen gold, because he laboured not for it. This, I say not, because preparations, and sweatings, and runnings, that go before conversion, are merits, or such as deserve conversion, or that conversion is due to them. Antinomians impute this to us, but unjustly; I humbly conceive it not to be the doctrine of Luther, Calvin, or Protestants, which Libertines charge us with: That I may clear us in this, let these propositions speak for us.

Propos. 1. We cannot receive the Spirit, by the preaching of the law, and covenant of works; but by the *hearing of the promises of the gospel,* Gal. iii. The law its alone can chase men from Christ, but never make a new creature; nor can the letter of the gospel without the Spirit do it.

Propos. 2. When we look for any thing in ourselves, or think that an unrenewed man is a confiding person to purchase Christ, we bewilder ourselves, and vanish in

foolish-

foolishness: this wrong Libertines do us; from which we are as far, as the east from the west.

Propos. 3. It is not our doctrine, but the weakness of sinners, and of the flesh, that we should be shy to Christ, and stand aloof from the physician, because of the desperate condition of our disease. This is, as if one should say, It is not fit for the naked to go to him who offereth white linen to clothe him, nor that the poor should go to him, who would be glad you would take his fine gold off his hand, or to say, Set not a young plant, but let it lie above earth, till you see if it bear fruit. Unworthiness in the court of justice is a good plea, why Christ should cast us off; but unworthiness felt, tho' not savingly, is as good a ground to cast yourself on Christ, as poverty, want, and weakness, in place of a statute, and act of parliament to beg, tho' the letter of the law forbid any to beg.

Propos. 4. Acting and doing, tho' neither savingly, nor soundly, is not merit of grace, yet not contrary to grace; to obey the law of nature, to give alms, is not against grace. Libertines should not reject this, tho' it be not all, but a most poor all to engage Christ.

Propos. 5. Faith is a moral condition of life eternal, and wrought in us by the free grace of God. I never saw a contradiction between a condition wrought by irresistible grace, and the gift or free grace of life eternal; for life eternal given in the law, and Adam's doing and performing by the irresistible acting and assisting of God, are not contrary; yet the former was never merit, but grace; the latter was legal doing.

Propos. 6. We do receive the promise of willing and doing, wrought immediately in us, according to the good will and most free grace of Christ; and yet we are agents, and work under Christ.

Propos. 7. Luther (for I could fill a book with citations) Calvin, and all our Protestant Divines, are for qualifications void of merit, or promise, before con-

version,

CHRIST DYING AND DRAWING SINNERS TO HIMSELF.

version, and for gracious conditions after conversion under the gospel. Antinomians bely Luther.

Propos. 8. Antinomians yield the preaching of the law, and preparations before conversion, and conditions after, and peace from signs of sanctification, etc. yet they are to be reputed enemies to grace and holiness, and turn all sanctification in their imaginary faith and justification, of which they are utterly ignorant. Never Antinomian knew rightly what free justification is.

Propos. 9. Immediate resting on Christ for all we do, and drawing of comfort from the testimony of a good conscience, are not contrary.

Propos. 10. Holiness idolized, or trusted in, is to make Christ, the alone Saviour, no Saviour.

Propos. 11. God is not provoked to reprobate whom he elected from eternity, by new sins; yet is he displeased with David's adultery so far, as to correct him for it; and Solomon for his backsliding, with the rod of men.

Propos. 12. Works before justification please not God, but it follows not, that God keeps not such an order, as sense of sin, tho' not saving, should go before pardon and conversion; no more than, because Adam's sin pleased not God, therefore it should not go before the Son's taking on our flesh. If we are not to do, nor act any thing, before conversion; neither to hear, confer, know our sinful condition, nor be humbled for sin, despair of salvation in ourselves, because these are not merits before conversion, nor can they procure conversion to us; neither are we after conversion to believe, for believing cannot merit righteousness and life eternal; nor are we to hear, pray, be patient, rejoice in tribulation, for not any of these can procure life eternal to us: and why is not the doing of the one, as well as the other, a seeking righteousness in ourselves?

Propos. 13. The promise of Christ's coming in the flesh, (2.) and of giving a new heart, are absolute promises; the former requireth no order of providence, but that sin go before redemption; the latter requi-

reth

reth in order of providence, not of any gospel-promise, or merit, in any sort; there never was, never can be merit between a mere creature and God.

Propos. 14. There is no faith, no act of Christ's coin, or of the right stamp, before justification.

Propos. 15. We are justified in Christ virtually, as in the public head, when he rose again, and was justified in the Spirit. 2. In Christ, as his merits are the cause of our justification. 3. In Christ, apprehended by faith, formally, in the scripture's sense, in the Epistles to the Romans and Galatians; not that faith is the formal cause, or any merit in justification, but because it lays hold on imputed righteousness, which is the formal cause of our justification. 4. We are justified in our own sense and feeling, not by faith simply, (because we may believe, and neither know that we believe, nor be sensible of our justification) but as we know that we believe; whether this knowledge result from the light of faith, or from signs, as means of our knowledge. 5. Justification by way of declaration to others, is not so infallible, as that the scripture calls it justification, properly so named.

Object. 8. 'I was sixthly, in hearing the word, shined upon by a sweet witnessing of the Spirit; but O how I did strive against this work! I was called upon, but I put away all promises of mercy from me; I may justly say, the Lord saved me, whether I would or no. Sometimes I was dead, and could not pray; sometimes so quickned, that methought that I could have spent a whole night in prayer to God.'

Answ. 1. If the faith of the eternal love of free election was his first conversion, no wonder he was shined upon with light. But it was not scripture-light, but wild fire: for the method of Christ's drawing is not enthusiastical, up at secret election at first. There is no doubt we put Christ away from us after conversion, Cant. v. 1. and that so Christ saves us against our will. That the principle of saving is free-grace. 2. That free-will is neither free nor willing, till Christ

first

first draw us, till he renew and work upon the will: but I fear Antinomians will have free-will a block to do nothing at all: 'if Christ (a) will let me sin (say they) let him look to it, upon his honour be it.' And, (b) 'faith justifies an unbeliever; that is, that faith that is in Christ, justifieth me who have no faith in myself.' And, (c) 'it is legal to say we act in the strength of Christ.' And, (d) 'to take delight in the holy service of God, is to go a-whoring from God.' And, 'a man (e) may not be exhorted to any duty, because he hath no power to do it.' And, (f) 'the Spirit acts most in the saints, when they endeavour least.' And, (g) 'in the conversion of a sinner, the faculties of the soul and working thereof are destroyed, and made to cease.' Yea, saith the Bright Star, c. 3. p. 20. 'The naked influence of God annihilates all the acts of the soul.' c. 4. p. 28. 'Boiling desires after Christ, favour too much of action;-----hindereth the soul to be perfectly illuminated, and to arise to the rosy kisses and chaste embraces of her bridegroom.' See *Theolog. German*. C. 5. p. 9, 10. and (h) 'In place of them the Holy Ghost works.' And this (i) author saith, 'the spirit of adoption works not freely, when men are in bondage to some outward circumstances of worship, as time, place, or persons, that they cannot pray but at such hours, or in such places,' etc. Protestant divines teach no such thing. But his aim is to set on foot the Famulists' (k) doctrine, 'that we are not bound to keep a constant course of prayer in our families, or privately, unless the Spirit stir us up thereunto.' Saltmarsh saith, 'he thought he could have spent a whole night in prayer;' but, 1. Whether he did so or no, he expresseth not, lest he should contradict his brethren the Famulists of New-England, who teach, that to
take

(a) Rise, Reign, and ruin, unsavoury speech, Er. 4. pag. 19. (b) Er. 68. p. 13. (c) Er. 52. p. 10. (d) Er. 57. 11. (e) Er. 59. (f) Er. 43. (g) Er. 1. (h) Er. 2. (i) Saltmarsh, free-grace, chap. 49. p. 179. (k) Er. 49, p. 9.

take delight in the service of God, is to go a-whoring from God. 2. It would be asked, whether this fit was on him before, or after his conversion? To say before, would seem a delusion, or a preparation of eminency: if after conversion, 'tis to no purpose, except to be a mark of a converted man. And Antinomians have no stomach to marks: nor belongs it to the way of his conversion; which he relates. It is true, we cannot tie the Spirit to our hours; but then all the Lord's day-worship, all set hours at morn or at night, in private or in families, set times and hours for the church's praying, preaching, hearing, conference, reading, were unlawful; for we cannot stint the Spirit to a set time, nor are we tied to time, except to the christian-sabbath. Some may say, 'tis no charity to impute Famulists' errors of New-England to Antinomians. *Answ.* Seeing Saltmarsh and others here do openly own Antinomian doctrine as the way of free-grace, they are to be charged with all those, till they clear themselves, or refute those blasphemies; which they have never done to this day.

Object. 9. 'I seldom desired pardon of sin till I were fitted for mercies; but now I see we are pardoned freely. O rest not in your own duties.'

Answ. To desire pardon of sin before we be fitted for pardon, by no divinity is contrary to free pardon; tho' such desires be fruitless, as coming from no gracious principles.

Asser. 8. To believe and take Christ, because I am a needy sinner, is one thing; and to believe, because I am fitted for mercy and humbled, is another thing: this latter we disclaim. Preparations are no righteousness of ours; nor is it our doctrine, to desire any to rest on preparations, or to make them causes, foundations, or *formalia media*, formal means of faith; they hold forth the mere order and method of grace's working; not to desire pardon, but in God's way of foregoing humiliation, is nothing contrary, but sweetly subordinate to free pardon. And to cure too suddenly wounds, and to honey secure and proud sinners, and

sweeten

CHRIST DYING AND DRAWING SINNERS TO HIMSELF.

sweeten and oil a Pharisee, and to reach the Mediator's blood to an unhumbled soul, is but to turn the gospel unto a charm; and when by magic, you have drawn all the blood out of the sick man's veins, then to mix his blood with sweet poison, and cause him drink, and swell, and say, you have made him healthy and fat. Now Peter, Acts ii. poured vinegar and wine at first on the wounds of his hearers, when he said, *Ye murdered the Lord of glory; and they were pricked in their heart.* This is the law's work, Rom. iii. to condemn and stop the sinner's mouth. And you cannot say that Peter failed in curing too suddenly, because he preached first the law, to wound and prick them; for that they crucified the Lord of glory, before he preached the gospel of belief and baptism. And the Lord rebuking Saul from heaven, convincing him of persecution, casting him down to the ground, striking him blind, while he trembled, and the Lord's dealing with the jailor was sourer work, than proposing and pouring the gospel oil and honey of freely imputed righteousness in their wound at first; and a close unbottoming them of their own righteousness. And the Lord's way of justifying Jews and Gentiles, is a law-way, as touching the order, Rom. iii. *Having proved all to be under sin,* ver. 9, 10, 11, 12, 13, 14, 15, 16, 17, 18. he saith, v. 19. *Now we know that what things soever the law saith, it saith to them who are under the law, that every mouth may be stopped, and all the world become guilty before God.* Indeed, if they be convinced of sin by the Spirit, and so converted, and yet under trouble of mind, a pound of the gospel, for one ounce-weight of the law, is fit for them. But Antinomians err, not knowing the scriptures, in dreaming that converted souls are so from under the law, that they have no more to do with the law, no more than angels and glorified saints; so as the letter of the gospel doth not lead them, but some immediate acting of the Spirit. And that, 2. there is no commandment under the gospel, but to believe only. That, 3. Mortification and new
obedience,

obedience, as M. Town and others say, is but faith in Christ, and not abstinence from worldly lusts that war against the soul. 4. That the gospel commandeth nothing, but persuadeth rather, that we may be Libertines, and serve the flesh, and believe, and be saved. 5. That God hath made no covenant with us under the gospel; the gospel is all promise, that we shall be carried as mere patients to heaven, in a chariot of love. 6. That the way is not strait and narrow, but Christ hath done all to our hands. 7. That 'tis legal, not gospel-conversion, to keep the soul so long under the law for humiliation, contrition and confession, and then bring them to the gospel: whereas we teach, that the law purely and unmixed, without all gospel, is not to be used as a diet-portion, only to purge, never to let the unconverted hear one gospel-promise. It is true, Peter preached not law to Cornelius, nor Philip to the Eunuch, nor Ananias to Paul; but these were all converted afore-hand. We think, the unconverted man knows neither contrition nor confession aright. But I was more confirmed that the way of Antinomians is for the flesh, not for the gospel, when I read that M. Crispe (a) expounding confession, 1 John i. maketh it no humble acknowledging that the sinner in person hath sinned, and so is under wrath eternal, if God should judge him; but he maketh it a part of faith, by which a sinner believeth and confesseth, that Christ paid for his sin, and he is pardoned in him. Sure, confession in scripture, is no such thing; Ezra x. 1. Neh. ix. 2. In scripture, confession of sins is opposed to covering of sin, and not forsaking of it, Pro. xxviii. Joshua sought not such a confession of Achan. James commands not such a confession. Daniel's, Ezra's, Peter's confession were some other thing. John i. 20. Acts xix. 18. Heb. xi. 13. Prov. xxviii. 13. 1 John iv. 2. Mark iii. 6. Josh. vii. 16. Dan. ix. 4. Rom. x. 18. 1 Tim. vi. 13. Psal. xxxii. 5. Jam. v. 16. Lev. v. 5. Chap. xvi. 21. and xxvi.

(a) Vol. 3. Serm. 4. p. 160, 161, 162.

xxvi. 40. 2 Chr. vi. 24. In which places, faith and confession of sins cannot be one; nor are we justified by confession, as by faith. But these men have learned to pervert the scriptures.

Asser. 9. There be more vehement stirrings and wrestlings in a natural spirit under the law; as the bullock is most unruly at the first yoking, and green wood casts most smoke. Paul, Rom. vii. was slain by the law; but this makes more way for Christ; and tho' it do not morally soften, and facilitate the new birth; yet it ripeneth the out-breaking. Preparations are penal, to subdue; not moral, to deserve or merit; nor conditional to engage Christ to convert, but to facilitate conversion.

Asser. 10. There be no preparations at all required before redemption, 1 Tim. i. 15. Rom. v. 8. But there is a far other order in the working of conversion: those who (b) confound the one with the other, speak ignorantly of the ways of grace; for tho' both be of mere grace, without wages or merit, yet we are meer patients in the one, not in the other. Saltmarsh and Antinomians argue from the one to the other, most ignorantly.

Asser. 11. That the promises of the gospel are holden forth to sinners, as sinners, hath a two-fold sense: 1. As that they be sinners, and all in a sinful condition, to whom the promises are holden forth. This is most true and sound. The kingdom of grace is an hospital and guest-house of sick ones, fit for the art and mercy of the Physician, Christ. 2. So as they are all immediately to believe and apply Christ and the promises, who are sinners; and there be nothing required of sinners, but that they may all immediately challenge interest in Christ, after their own way and order, without humiliation, or any law work. In this sense, it is most false, that the promises are holden forth to sinners, as sinners: because then Christ should be holden forth to all sinners, Americans, Indians, and sinners who never,

by

(b) Saltmarsh, Free-grace, C. 5. P. 184, 185.

by the least rumour, heard one word of Christ. 2. Peter desires not Simon Magus to believe that God had loved him, in Christ Jesus, with an everlasting love; nor doth the gospel-promise offer immediately soul-rest to the hardened and proud sinner, wallowing in his lusts, as he is a hardened sinner; nor is the acceptable year of the Lord proclaimed, nor beauty and the oil of joy offered immediately to any, but those who *are weary and laden,* and who *mourn in Sion, and wallow in ashes,* Mat. xi. 28, 29, 30. Isa. xvi. 1, 2, 3. 'Tis true, to all within the visible church, Christ is offered without price or money; but to be received after Christ's fashion and order, not after our order; that is, after the soul is under self-despair of salvation, and in the sinner's month, when he hath been with child of hell. I grant, in regard of time, sinners cannot come too soon to Christ, nor too early to wisdom; but in regard of order, many come too soon, and unprepared. Simon Magus too soon believed. Saltmarsh saith, 'he misbelieved too soon; for he fastly believed: none can believe too soon.' *Answ.* To believe too soon, is to misbelieve; and Saltmarsh and Antinomians teach us the method of false-believing, when they teach us too soon to believe; that is, to believe that God hath loved you (be ye what ye will, Simon Magus, Judas, or others) with an everlasting love; for that is the Antinomian faith. Simon Magus, is, without any fore going humiliation, or sense of sin, or self-despair, to believe he was no less written in the Lamb's book of life from eternity, than Peter; and this he cannot believe soon enough. I say, neither soon or late ought a reprobate to believe any such thing. A covetous man, who had great possessions, had not yet bidden farewell to his old god Mammon, when he came to Christ; therefore he departed sad from Christ. Another came before he had buried his father: and some come, Luke xiv. 28, 29. before they advise with their strength, and what Christ will cost them. I desire I be not mistaken; none can be throughly fitted for Christ, before he come to Christ; but it is as true, some would buy the pearl before they

sell

sell all they have, which is not the wise merchant's part; and they err foully who argue thus, if I were not a sinner, or if my sins were less heinous, and so I were less unworthy, I would come to Christ and believe; but ah, I am so grievous an offender, and so unworthy, that I cannot go. Their antecedent is true, but the consequence is naught and wicked. It is true, I am sick, and good that I both say and feel that I am sick; but, *ergo*, I cannot, I will not go to the physician; that is wicked logick, and the contrary consequence is good: whereas the other consequence is a seeking of righteousness in ourselves. 2. Another false ground is here laid by Libertines, that we place worth and righteousness in preparations; or, (2.) That preparations make us less unworthy, and less sinners. But preparations are not in any sort to us money nor hire; we value them as dung, and sin; yet such sin, as sickness is in relation to physick. *2dly*, Preparations remove not one dram, or twentieth part of an ounce of guiltiness, or sin. Christ, in practice of free-grace, not by law, yea not by promise, gives grace to the thus prepared, and often he denies it also: yea, and there is a good hour appointed by God, when Christ comes. Other physicians take diseases so early as they can, lest the malice of the disease overcome art; but Christ lets sin of purpose ripen, to the eleventh hour, often to the twelfth hour: he knows his art can overtake and out-run seven devils, most easily. The omnipotency of grace knows no such thing, as more or less pardonable in sin; yea, of purpose to heighten grace, that sinfulness may contend with grace, and be overcome, the Gentiles must be like corn ripe, white and yellow, ere the sickle cut them down, and they be converted, John iv. 35. The boil must be ripe, ere it break; the sea full, ere it turn; therefore the Lord appoints a time, and sets a day for conversion. Tit. iii. 3. *We ourselves were sometime* [Gr. anoetoi] *mad;* but the Lord hath a gracious [Gr. hote de] *When; When the kindness and man-love of God appeared, he saved us.* And Jer.

I. 4.

I. 4. *In those days, and at that time, saith the Lord, the children of Israel shall come, they and the children of Judah, going and weeping, they shall seek the Lord.* Zech. xii. 11. *And in that day, there shall be a great morning in Jerusalem, as the mourning of Haddadrimmon in the valley of Megiddon.* 'Tis good to lie and wait at the door and posts of wisdom's house, and to lie and attend Christ's tide, it may come in an hour that you would never have believed. O what depth of mercy, when for natural, or no saving on waiting, or upon a poor venture, *What if I go to Christ, I can have no less than I have?* Beside any gracious intention the Lord saves; and the wind, not looked for, turns fair for a sea-voyage to heaven, in the Lord's time.

Asser. 12. The ground, moving Christ to renew his love in drawing a fallen saint out of the pit, is the same that from heaven shined on him at the beginning. Love is an undivided thing; there are not two loves, or three loves in Christ; that which begins the good work, promoves it, even the same love which Christ hath taken up to heaven with him, and there ye find it before you, when ye come thither. 2. Some love-sickness goes before his return, Cant. iii. *I was but a little passed, I found him whom my soul loves*: the sky divides and rents itself, and then the sun is on its way to rise; the birds begin to sing, then the summer is near; the voice of the turtle is heard, then the winter is gone; when the affections grow warm, the well beloved is upon a return. 3. You die for want of Christ; absence seems to be at the highest, when hunger for a renewed drawing in the way of comforting is great, and the sad soul lowest; he will come at night and sup, if he dine not. 4. Let Christ moderate his own pace; hope quietly waiteth; hope is not a shouting and a tumultuous grace. 5. Your disposition for Christ's return can speak much for a renewed drawing: as when the church finds her own pace slow, and prays, *Draw me, we will run;* then he sendeth ushers before, to tell that he will come. 6. Sick nights for the

Lord's

Lord's absence in not drawing, are most spiritual signs.

Antinomians believe, that all the promises in the gospel, made upon conditions to be performed by creatures, especially free-will casting in its share to the work, smell of some grains of the law, and of obedience for hire; and that bargaining of this kind, cannot consist with free-grace. And the doubt may seem to have strength, in that our divines argue against the Arminian decree of election to glory, upon condition of faith and perseverance, foreseen in the person so chosen; because then election to glory should not be of meer grace, but depend on something in the creature, as on a condition or motive at least, if not as on a cause, work, or hire. But Arminians reply, The condition being of grace, cannot make any thing against the freedom of the grace of election; because so justification and glorification should not be of meer grace; for sure, we are justified and saved upon condition of faith, freely given us of God. The question then must be, Whether there can be any conditional promises in the gospel of grace; or whether a condition performed by us, and free-grace, can consist together? Antinomians say, They are contrary, as fire and water.

Hence these positions, for the clearing of this considerable question.

Pos. 1. The condition that Arminians fancy to be in the gospel, can neither consist with the grace of election, justification, calling of grace, or crowning of believers with glory. This condition they say we hold, but they err; because it is a condition of hire, that they have borrowed from lawyers, such as is between man and man, *ex causa onerosa*, 'tis absolutely in the power of men to do, or not to do; and bows and determineth the Lord and his free-will, absolutely to this part of the contradiction, which the creature chooseth, tho' contrary to the inclination, and antecedent will and decree of God, wishing, desiring, and earnestly inclining to the obedience and salvation of the creature.

Now

Now, works of grace, and infinite grace, flow from the bowels, and inmost desire of God; nothing without laying bonds, chains, or determination on the Lord's grace, or his holy will. Could our well-doing milk out of the breasts of Christ's free-grace, or extrinsically determine the will or acts of free-bounty; grace should not be grace. But without money or hire, the Lord giveth his wine and milk, Isa. lv. 1. Eph. ii. 1, 2. Ezek. xvi. 5, 6, 7. 2 Tim. i. 9. Tit. iii. 3. (2.) Because such a condition is of works, not of grace; and so of no less law debt and bargaining, than can be between man and man. And the party that fulfilleth the condition, is, 1. Most free to forfeit his wages, by working, or not working, as the hireling, or labourer in a vineyard; yea, or any merchant engaged to another, to perform a condition, of which he is lord and master, to do or not do. 2. He is nowise necessitate nor determined any way, but as the hire or wages do determine his will; who so worketh; but the wages being absolutely in his power to gain them, or lose them, determine his will, which cannot fall in the Almighty. 3. Such a condition, performed by the creature, putteth the creature to glory, but not in the Lord, but in himself, Rom. iv. 2. For if Abraham were justified by works, he hath whereof to glory, but not before God. Yea, Adam, before the fall, and the elect angels, hold not life eternal by any such free condition of obedience, as is absolutely referred to their free-will, to do, or not to do; so our divines deny against Papists, with good warrant, the freehold of life eternal, by any title of merit. Sure, if God determine free-will in all good and gracious acts, as I prove undeniably from scripture. 2. From the dominion of providence. 3. The covenant between the Father and the Son Christ. 4. The intercession of Christ. 5. The promises of a new heart, and perseverance. 6. Our prayers to bow the heart to walk with God, and not to lead us into temptation. 7. The faith and confidence we have, that God will work in the saints to will, and to do to the end. 8. The praise and glory of all our good

works;

works; which are due to God only, etc. If God (I say) determine free-will to all good, even before, as after the entrance of sin into the world, and that of grace, (for this grace hath place in law-obedience, in men and angels) then such a condition cannot consist with grace. For such a condition puts the creature in a state above the creator, and all freedom in him.

Pos. 2. Evangelic conditions, wrought in the elect by the irresistible grace of God, and grace do well consist together. John v. 24. *Verily, verily, I say unto you, he that heareth my word, and believeth in him that sent me, hath everlasting life, and shall not come into condemnation; but is passed from death to life.* Chap. vii. 37. *If any man thirst, let him come to me, and drink.* Acts. xiii. 39. *And by him, all that believe, are justified from all things, from which ye could not be justified by the law of Moses.* Acts. xvi. 30. *The jailor saith to Paul and Silas, what must I do to be saved?* Verse 31. *And they said, Believe on the name of the Lord Jesus Christ, and thou shalt be saved, and thy houshold.* There is an express required of the jailor, which he must perform, if he would be saved. And Rom. x. look as a condition is required in the law v. 5. *For Moses describeth the righteousness of the law, that the man that doth these things, shall live by them;* so believing is required as a condition of the gospel, v. 6. *But the righteousness which is of faith,* etc. v. 9. saith, *That if thou confess with thy mouth, the Lord Jesus, and shalt believe in thine heart, that God hath raised him from the dead, thou shalt be saved.* Rom. iii. 27, 28, 29, 30. chap. iv. chap. v. Faith is the condition of the covenant of grace, and the only condition of justification, and of the title, right and claim, that the elect have, through Christ, to life eternal. Holy walking, as a witness of faith, is the way to the possession of the kingdom; as Rom. ii. 6. *Who will render to every man according to his deeds.* Verse 7. *To them who by patient continuance in well-doing, seek for glory,*

and

and honour, and immortality, eternal life. Verse 8. *To them that are contentious* -------------Verse 9. *Tribulation and anguish upon every soul of man that doth evil, of the Jew first, and also of the Gentile.* Mat. xxv. 34. *Then shall the King say to them on his right-hand, Come, ye blessed of my Father, inherit the kingdom prepared for you from the foundation of the world.* Verse 35. *For I was an hungred, and ye gave me meat: I was thirsty, and ye gave me drink*, etc. And let Antinomians say, we are freed from the law, as a rule of holy walking; sure the gospel and the apostles command the very same duties in the letter of the gospel, that Moses commanded in the letter of the law; as, that children obey their parents, servants their masters; that we abstain from murder, hatred of our brother, stealing, defrauding, lying, etc. that we keep ourselves from idols, swearing, strange gods. I do not say, that these duties, are commanded in the same way, in the gospel, as in the law: for, sure we are, out of a principle of evangelic love, to render obedience; and our obedience now is not legal, as commanded by Moses, in strict terms of law, but as perfumed, oiled, honyed, with the gospel-sense of remission of sins, the tender love of God in Christ. So that we justly challenge two extreme ways, both blasphemous, as we conceive.

1. Arminians object to us, that which the Antinomians truly teach, to wit, that we destroy all precepts, commands, exhortations, and active obedience in the gospel; and render men, under the gospel, meer blocks, and stones, which are immediately acted by the Spirit, in all obedience, and freed from the letter of both law and gospel, as from a legal bondage. This we utterly disclaim; and do obtest and beseech Antinomians, as they love Christ and his truth, to clear themselves of this, which to us is wild Libertinism. And by this, Arminians turn all the gospel, *in literalem gratiam*, in a law-gospel, in meer golden letters, and sweet honeyed commandments of law-precepts, and will have the law possible, justification by works, conversion by

the

the power of free-will, and moral swasion, really without the mighty power of the Spirit and gospel-grace, and receive the doctrine of merit, and set heaven and hell on new poles to be rolled about, as globes on these two poles, the nilling and willing of free-will; and they make grace to be sweet words of silk and gold. On the other hand, Antinomians do exclude works, letter-persuasions, our actions, conditions of grace, promises written or preached from the gospel; and make the Spirit, and celestial raps, immediate inspirations, the gospel itself, and turn men regenerate into blocks: and how M. Den can be both an Antinomian, and loose us from the law, and an Arminian, defending both universal atonement, and the resistible working of grace, and so subject us to the law, and to the doctrine of merit, and make us lords of our own faith, and conversion to God; let him and his followers see to it. We go a middle way here, and do judge the gospel to be an evangelic command, and a promising and commanding evangel, and that the Holy Ghost graceth us to do, and the letter of the gospel obligeth us to do.

3. The decree of election to glory, may be said to be more free and gracious in one respect, and justification, and glorification, and conversion, more free in another respect; and all the four, of meer free-grace. For election, as the cause and fountain-grace, is the great mother, the womb, the infinite spring, the bottomless ocean of all grace; and we say, effects are more copiously and eminently in the cause than in themselves; as water is more in the element and fountain, than in the streams; the tree more in the life, and sap of life, than in the branches: and conversion, and justification have more freedom, and more of grace, by way of extension, because good-will stayeth within the bowels and heart of God, in free election; but in conversion, and justification, infinite love comes out, and here the Lord giveth us the great gift, even himself, Christ, God, the darling, the delight, the only, only well-beloved of the Father; and he giveth faith to lay hold

on

on Christ, and the life of God, and all means of life in which there may be many divided acts of grace (to speak so) which were all one in the womb of the election of grace.

Pos. 4. Conversion, justification, are free for election; and therefore election is more free: but all these, as they are in God, are equally free, and are one simple good-will. Tho' Christ justify and crown none, but such as are qualified with the grace of believing, yet believing is a condition, that removeth nothing of the freedom of grace, 1. Because it worketh nothing in the bowels of mercy, and the free-grace of God; as a motive, cause, or moving condition, that doth extract acts of grace out of God. Only we may conceive this order, that grace of election to glory steers another wheel (to speak so) of free-love, to give faith, effectual calling, justification, and eternal glory. 2. It is no hire, nor work at all; nor doth it justify, as a work, but only lay hold on the Lord our righteousness.

Object. 'There is more of God in election to glory than in giving of faith, or at least of Christ's righteousness, and eternal glory; therefore there must be more grace in the one than in the other. The antecedent is thus proved; because God simply, and absolutely, may chuse to glory Moses, Peter, or not chuse them to glory; and here is liberty of contradiction, and freedom, in the highest degree: but having once chosen Moses and Peter to glory, if they believe, the Lord cannot but justify them, and crown them with glory; because his promise and decree doth remove this liberty of contradiction, so as God cannot chuse, but justify and glorify those that believe, both in regard of his immutable nature, who cannot repeal what he hath once decreed, and of his fidelity, in that he cannot but stand to his own word and promise in justifying and saving the ungodly that believe. Again, in election to glory, there is nothing of merit, but all is pure free-grace; no condition, no merit, no faith, no works required in the party chosen to glory; but in the justified there is more of man, ere he can be justified and saved, he must hear, consider, be

hum-

humbled, know the need he hath of a Saviour, and believe; and without these he cannot be justified.'

Answ. 1. I deny, that liberty of contradiction belongeth to the essence and nature of liberty. It is enough to make liberty, that, 1. It proceeds not from a principle determined by nature, to one kind of action; so the sun is not free to give light. 2. That the principle be free of all foreign force; the malefactor goeth not freely to the place of execution, when haled to it. 3. That it proceed from deliberation, reason, election, and wisdom, seeing no essential connexion, or necessary, or natural relation, between the action, and the end thereof, of themselves, but such as may be dispensed with; if these three be, tho' there be a necessity, in some respect, from a free decree, and a free promise, tho' there be not liberty of contradiction, simply to do, or not to do, yet is not any degree of the essence of liberty removed. I well remember Dr. Jackson denying all decrees in God, that setteth the Almighty to one side of the contradiction, resembleth God to the pope, whose wisdom he commendeth, in that the pope's decrees, grants, laws, promises, are fast and loose, and all made with a reserve of after-wit, so as if the morrow's illumination be better than the day's; while his life breatheth in, and out, he may change and retract his will; so saith he, *Papa nunquam fibi ligat manus*, the pope ties all the world to himself by oaths, laws, promises; but that lawless beast is tied to none. Now, the scripture teacheth us, that the decrees and counsels of God are surer than mountains of brass, and unchangeable, and that his promise cannot fail. But who dare say, when he executes his decrees, and fulfilleth his promise, that he forfeiteth or loseth one inch, degree, or part of his essential liberty? God should then be less free to create the world, than if we suppose he had never decreed to create it, and yet doth create it; as if the Lord's free decree lavished away, and should drink up, and waste any part of his natural freedom in his actions; or as if his faithfulness to make good what he promised, should render him lame, and dismember him of the

fulness

fulness and freedom of his grace; and so, the more faithful and true, the less gracious; and the more unchangeable in his counsels, the more fettered and chained, and the less free in all these actions, that he doth according to the counsel of his will. A gross misconception: and I deny, that God is less free in the justifying, and crowning the believer, than in electing, and chusing him both to glory, and to faith. It may be men's decrees, and promises that are rash, and may be at the second, or third edition, like their books, corrected by a new-born wit, or because they aim at under-board-dealing, diminish of their liberty; but it is not so in the Almighty. When the Lord by a promise to men, maketh himself debtor to his creature, and that of free-grace, with one and the same infinite freedom of grace, he contracteth the debt, and payeth the sum; for so the freedom of infinite grace should ebb and flow, as the seas, and ascend and descend as the sun, which I cannot conceive; the effects of free-grace I grant, being created and finite things in men are more or less according to the free dispensation of God.

Answ. 2. It is no marvel, that there be more of men in justification and glorification, that are transient acts passing out of the creature, than in election to glory, that is an immanent and eternal act; and so I grant justification to be more conditionate, than election; but if more gracious, that is the question: for the condition of grace, is a thing of free-grace. Indeed, we argue against the Arminian election, that hangeth upon a condition of free-will's carving, such as their faith is, and their perseverance; and from thence we conclude, from such a condition, their election to glory cannot be of free-grace, but in him that willeth and runneth; because man's will determining God's will to chuse this man to glory, not this man, is a running will, and a mad and a proud will, that will sit above grace.

Pos. 4. Tho' it be true, that grace is essentially in God, and in us by participation; yet it is false, that grace is not properly in us, but that faith, hope, repentance, and the like, that are in us, are gifts, not

graces,

graces. For grace in us may be called a gift, in that it is freely given us; as a fruit of the grace and favour of election, and free-redemption, which indeed is the only saving fountain-grace of God; but if grace be taken for a saving qualification, and a supernatural act, work, or quality, given freely of the Father through Christ, upon God's gracious intention, to cause us freely believe, repent, love Christ, rejoice in the hope of glory, work out our salvation in fear and trembling: so grace is not only in Christ, but in us properly; tho' Antinomians hold all saving-grace to be properly in Christ, and that there is nothing inherent in a believer, that differenceth him from hypocrites; all the difference must be in Christ (say they.) 1. The word saith, there was another spirit in Caleb and Joshua, than was in the rest of the spies; ergo, there was some distinguishing saving-grace in them. 2. John i. 16. *And of his fulness we have all received, and grace for grace.* When he ascended to heaven, he sent down the Holy Ghost, John xiv. 17. *He dwelleth in you, and shall abide in you.* John xvi. 13. *He will guide you in all truth------he will shew you things to come. So there is a Spirit of grace poured on the family of David.* Zech. xii. 10. *On the thirsty ground,* Isa. xliv. 3. *A new heart* put in the midst of the covenanted people, Ezek. xxxvi. 26. *Fear of God put in their hearts,* Jer. xxxii. 40. Jer. xxxi. 33. 1 John iii. 9. 3. There is grace in the saints, that denominates them gracious. 1 Cor. xv. 10. *By the grace of God I am that I am.* Gal. ii. 20. *I am crucified with Christ, nevertheless I live, yet not I, but Christ liveth in me,* etc.

There is a great deceitfulness in our heart, in the matter of performed conditions, so soon as we have performed a condition, tho' wrought in us by meer grace, we hold out our hand, and cry, Pay me, Lord, my wages, for I have done my work; so near of kin to our corrupt hearts, is the conceit of merit.

2. A second deceit is, when an obligation of obedience presseth us, we overlook the condition, and fix our eyes on the promise, when we should eye the precept;

cept; and when it cometh to the reward, when we should most look to the promise of free-grace, then we eye the precept, and challenge debt, and forget grace.

3. When we are pressed with the supernatural duty of believing, and should look only to free-grace, which only must enable us to that high work of believing, we look to ourselves, and complain, Oh, I am not weary and laden, and therefore not qualified for Christ; and so we turn wickedly and proudly wise, to shift ourselves of Christ; when we should look to ourselves, we look away from ourselves, to a promise of our wages; but our bad deservings, if looked to, would turn our eyes on our abominations, that we might eye free-grace; and when we should eye free-grace, we look to our sinful unfitness to believe, and come to Christ.

Use. Beware of false preparations, that ye take them not for preparations, or for grace: for, 1. Discretion, Mark xii. 34. is not grace, but wings and sails to carry you to hell. 2. Profession is a deceiving preparation, it blossoms and laughs, and deludes under forms. 3. Victorious strugglings against lusts, upon natural motives, look like mortification, and are but bastard dispositions. 4. Education, if civil and externally religions, and civil strained holiness from fear of eternal wrath, or worldly shame, are not to be rested upon. When the man is sick, and between the milstones of divine wrath, in heavy afflictions, his lusts may be sick, and not mortified. The strongest man living, under a fever, can make no use of his strength and bones, yet he hath not lost it. It may be a query, whether the Lord in-stamps something of Christ on preparations in the elect that are converted, which is not in all the legal dejections of Saul, Cain, and Judas. 2. It may be a query, whether this be any thing really inherent in these preparations; or only, which is more probable, an intentional relation in God, to raise these to the highest end purposed in the Lord's eternal election.

Use. If God bestow saving-grace freely on us, without hire and price, then temporal deliverances may be bestowed on the church, when they are not yet hum-

bled

bled: it is true, 1. The people of God are low, and their strength is gone, before the Lord delivereth, Deut. xxxii. 36. (2.) He delivereth his people when they are humbled, Levit. xxvi. 41, 42. But, 3. God keeps not always this method; nor is it like he will observe it with Scotland and England, first to humble, and then deliver; but contrarily, he first delivers, and then humbles. As, Ezek. xxix. 42. *And ye shall know that I am the Lord, when I shall bring you unto the land of Israel, unto the country, for the which I lifted up mine hand, to give it to your fathers.* v. 43. *And there is in that place,* [Heb. Scham] *when ye are delivered, ye shall remember your ways, and all your doings, wherein ye have been defiled, and ye shall lothe yourselves in your own sight, for all your evils, that ye have committed.* Ezek. xxxvi. 33. *And I will sanctify my great name, which was prophaned among the heathen, which ye have prophaned in the midst of the heathen.* (Then they were not humbled before they were delivered;) v. 24. *For I will take you from among the heathen, and gather you out of all countries, and bring you unto your own land.* So, when the Lord brought Israel out of Egypt, were they humbled? Nay, their murmuring against Moses and Aaron, Exod. v. 20, 21, 22. testifieth their pride: and in that miraculous deliverance, and greatest danger, when they were between Satan and the deep sea, they were not humbled; but Psal. cvi. 7. *They provoked him at the sea, even at the Red-sea,* Exod. xiv. 11, 12. The Lord must also now first deliver us, and shame and confound us in Scotland with mercy, and so humble us; for mercy hath more strength to melt hearts of iron and brass, than the furnace of fire hath, or a sea of blood, or a destroying pestilence.

Use. The third particular use is, we have no gracious disposition to Christ: every man hath a fore-stall'd opinion, and a prejudice against Christ; and our humiliation before conversion should humble us. The merit of decency, devised of late by Jesuits; of congruity, formed of old; or of condignity, to buy grace or glory, are all but counterfeit metal. Grace, the

only

only seed of our salvation, is the freest thing in the world, and least tied to causes without. 1. That of two equal matches in nature, two born brethren in one womb, the Lord chuseth one, and refuseth another. 2. Of two sinners, of which one hath one devil, another hath seven devils, he sheweth mercy upon one that hath seven devils, and forsaketh the other. 3. Of two equally disposed and fitted for conversion, tho' none be fitted aright, he calleth one of meer grace, and not the other. 4. Grace is so great, that, Rev. v. 11. *when ten thousand times ten thousand, and thousand of thousands*, are set on work to sing, v. 12. *Worthy is the Lamb that was slain, to receive power, riches and strength*: Yea, to help them, *every creature that is in heaven and earth, and under the earth, and such as are in the sea, cry, Blessing, and honour, and power, be to him that sits on the throne, and to the Lamb.* And they have been since the creation upon this song, and shall be for all eternity upon it; but all of them, for ever and ever, shall never out-sing these praises to the bottom; there is more yet, and more yet to be said of Christ, and ever shall be. What wonder then, that we have no leisure to praise grace, being of so little strength, and being clothed with time. Can you out-bottom the song of free-grace? Or can any soul say so much of Christ's love, but there is a world more, and another world yet more to be said? and when will ye end, or come to an height? I know not. O be in grace's debt, and take the debt to eternity with you.

III.

Of the third article. Touching the form and nature and manner of drawing, 1. It is a question, whether this drawing be justification, or sanctification? Antinomians say, it is both: but withal, both is one (say they.)

Answ.

Pos. 1. Drawing is relative to running and walking, Cant. i. 4. Now this is rather in acts of sanctification, and

and in running in the ways of God's commandments, Psal. cxix. 32. than in justification, though coming go for an act of believing and approaching to Christ, John vi. 44. and so excludes not faith.

Pos. 2. It is most unsound to affirm, that justification and regeneration are all one; for this must confound all acts flowing from justification, with those that flow from regeneration, or the infused habit of sanctification. 1. Justification is an indivisible act; the person is but once for all justified, by grace. But sanctification is a continued daily act. 2. Justification doth not grow; the sinner is either freed from the guilt of sin, and justified, or not freed; there is not a third. But in sanctification, we are said to grow in grace, 2 Pet. iii. 14. and advance in sanctification: nor is it ever consummate and perfect, so long as we bear about a body of sin.

Pos. 2. To repent, to mortify sin, is not to "condemn all our works, (as Mr. Towne saith) righteousness, and judgment, and our best things in us, and then by faith to fly to grace; nor is it to distrust our own righteousness, and embrace Christ's in the promise," 1. Because this is faith; and the scripture saith, we are justified by faith. 2. We receive Christ by faith, John i. 12. (3.) We receive and embrace the promise by faith, Heb. xi. 11. and are persuaded of them. 4. We are to believe without staggering, Rom. iv. 19. (5.) We have peace of conscience through faith, Rom. v. 1. (6.) *By faith we have access into this grace, wherein we stand,* Rom. v. 2. *And boldness to enter into the holy of holiest, and draw near to our High Priest, with full assurance of faith,* Heb. xix. 10, 20, 21, 22. Now, we are not justified by repentance and mortification; we neither receive Christ, nor embrace the promises by repentance. The apostle requireth in repentance, sorrow, carefulness to eschew sin, clearing, indignation, fear, zeal, desire, revenge, 2 Cor. vii. 10, 11. but no where doth the scripture require this as an ingredient of repentance,

that

that we have boldness and access, and full assurance: nor do Antinomians admit, that by repentance we have peace, or pardon; but this they ascribe to faith.

A second question is, how far the law can draw a sinner to Christ? Antinomians tell us of a legal drawing and conversion, and of an evangelic drawing; the legal drawing, they say, is ours; the latter theirs.

Asser. 1. The difference between the letter of the law, and the gospel, is not in the manner of working; for the letter of either law or gospel, is alike ineffectual and fruitless to draw any to Christ. Christ preached the gospel to hard-hearted Pharisees, it moved them not. Moses preached the law and the curses thereof to the stiff-necked Jews, and they were as little humbled. Sounds and syllables of ten hells, or twenty heavens and gospels, without the Spirit's working, are alike fruitless. And we grant the law is a sleepy keeper of a captive sinner; he may either steal away from his keeper, or if he be awed with his keeper, he is not kept from any spiritual, internal breach of the law, nor moved thereby to sincere and spiritual walking, but the difference between law and gospel, is not in the internal manner of working, but in two other things, 1. In the matter contained in the law and gospel; because nature is refractory to violence, and the law can do nothing but curse sinners, therefore it can draw no man to Christ. The gospel, again, contains sweet and glorious promises of giving a new heart to the elect; of admitting to the Prince of Peace, laden and broken-hearted mourners in Zion; and in conferring on them a free imputed righteousness; and this is in itself a taking way; but without the gospel-spirit utterly ineffectual. 2. To the gospel there is a spirit added, which worketh, as God doth, with an omnipotent pull: and this Spirit doth also use the law to prepare and humble; tho' this be by an higher power than goeth along with the law, as the law.

Asser. 2. The gospel-love of Christ freeth a captive from under the law, as a curser, and delivers him over to the law as to a pedagogue, to lead him to Christ, and

as

as an instructor to rule and lead him when he is come to Christ. Love is the immediate and nearest lord; law the mediate and remote lord. Love biddeth the man do all for Christ; the law now of itself, because of our sinfulness, is a bitter and sour thing; but now the law is dipped in Christ's gospel-love, and is sugared and honeyed and evangelised with free-grace, and receives a new form from Christ, and is become sweeter than the honey and the honey-comb, to draw and persuade; and all the law is made a new commandment of love, and a gospel-yoke, sweet and easy; but still the law obligeth justified men to obedience, not only for the matter of it, but for the supreme authority of the lawgiver; now Christ, who came to fulfil, not to dissolve the law, doth not remove this authority, but addeth a new bond of obligation, from the tie of redemption in Jesus Christ. And we are freed from the curse of the law. 2. The rigid exaction of obedience, every way perfect. 3. The seeking of life and justification by the law.

Asser. 3. There be two things in the law. 1. The authority and power to command, direct, and regulate the creature to an end, in acts of righteousness and holiness. 2. A secondary authority, to punish eternally the breakers of the law, and to reward those that obey. These are two different things. Suppose Adam had never sinned, the law had been the law; and suppose Adam had never obeyed, the law also should have been the law; and in the former case there should have been no punishment, in the latter no reward. Antinomians confound these two. Mr. Towne saith, 'it cannot be said, that my spirit doth that voluntarily, which the command of the law bindeth and forceth unto. It is one thing for a man at his own free liberty to keep the king's high-way of the law; and another to keep it by pales and ditches, that he cannot without danger go out of it.' It cannot be denied, but that the gospel both chargeth or aweth us to believe in Christ, and to bring forth good fruits, worthy of Christ, except we would be hewn down, and cast into the fire; and also that grace
worketh

worketh faith, and to will, and to do; and so voluntary obedience, and obligation of a command, may as well consist, as bearing Christ's yoke and soul rest; yea, and delight, and joy unspeakable and glorious, may be and are in one regenerate person. Crisp and his followers are far wide; for Christ died freely, out of extreme love, and yet he died out of a command laid on him, and laid down his life for his sheep, though no penal power was above Christ's head, to punish him if he should not die, John x. 18. Nor was there need of any power to force him *subpena*, or to awe him, if he should not obey; so do angels, with wings of most exact willingness, obey God, yet are they under the authority of a law, and command, but yet under no compelling punishment, Psal. ciii. 20, 21. Psal. civ. 4. So in the saints, love hath changed the chains, not the subjection. Love hath made the law silken cords. And whereas corrupt will was a wicked landlord, and lust a lawless tyrant, and the law had a dominion over the sinner, in regard of the curse; now the Spirit leads the will under the same commanding power of the law-giver, frees the sinner from the curse, and turns forcing and cursing power in fetters of love; so that the Spirit draws the will sweetly to obey the same Lord, the same law, only Christ hath taken the rod out of the law's hand, and the rod was broken and spent on his own back. The feud between the law and the sinner is not so irreconcilable, as the Antinomians conceive, so as it cannot be removed, except the law be destroyed, and the sinner's free-will loosed from law. It standeth in blessing and cursing, salvation and damnation, that are effects of the law, as observed, or violated. Now, Christ was made a curse, and condemned to die for the sinner; all the rest of the law remains. It is most false that Mr. Towne saith, To justify and condemn, are as proper and essential to the law, as to command. 2. It is false, that we are freed from active obedience to the moral law, because Christ came under active obedience to the moral

moral law; for the law required obedience out of love. Antinomians cannot say, that we are freed from obedience out of love; for it is clear, Antinomians will have us obliged by no law to love our brother; *to abstain from worldly lusts, that war against the soul*; but in so doing, we must seek to be justified by the works of the law. This consequence we deny. To keep one ceremony of Moses draws a bill on us of debt, to keep all the ceremonial law; because now 'tis unlawful in any sort. But to do the duties of the moral law, as by Christ we are enabled, lays no such debt on us, but testifies our thankfulness to Christ, as to our Husband and Redeemer.

The other considerable thing here, is, the way and manner of Christ's drawing.

Asser. 1. The particular exact knowledge of the Lord's manner of drawing sinners, may be unknown to many that are drawn. 1. In the very works of nature, the growing of bones in the womb, is a mystery; far more the way of the Spirit, Eccl. xi. 5. *Know ye the balancing of the clouds?* Job could not answer this. And who knows how the Lord patched together a piece of red clay, and made it a fit shape to receive an heavenly and immortal spirit? and at what window the soul came in? 2. How God with one key of omnipotency hath opened so many millions of doors since the creation, and hath drawn so many to him, must be a mystery. There be many sundry locks, and many various turnings and throwings of the same key, and but one key. 1. Some Christ draws by the heart, as Lydia, Matthew: love sweetly and softly bloweth up the door, and the king is within doors in the floor of the house before they be aware. Others Christ trails and draggeth by violence, rather by the hair of the head, than by the heart, as the jailor, Acts xvi. And Saul, Acts ix. Who are plunged over ears in hell, and pulled above water by the hair of the head: sure thousands do wear a crown of glory, before the throne, who were never at making of themselves away by killing themselves, as the jailor was. A third sort

know

know they are drawn, but how, or when, or the mathematical point of time, they know not: some are *full of the Holy Ghost from the womb*, as John Baptist. Ye must not cast off all, nor must saints say they are none of Christ's, because they cannot tell you histories and wonders of themselves, and of their own conversion: some are drawn by miracles, some without miracles; the word of God is the roadway. Arminians have no ground to deny that we are irresistibly converted, because we know not the particular way how omnipotency conspireth strongly, but sweetly, to win consent, without internal violence of our will, which so wills, as it may refuse. John ix. diverse times the Jews ask the blind man, *What did he to thee? how opened he thine eyes?* He gives them one sure and true answer, *One thing I know, once I was blind, now I see.* All can give this testimony, early or late, I know I am drawn. 'Tis good the soul can say, Christ is here, I find him and feel him; but whether he came in at the door, or the window, or digged a hole in the wall, I know not. All may know they were blind as well as others, and *by nature the children of wrath*; as ye know Adam hath had a building in you, (though now ye *be renewed in the spirit of the mind*) by the old stones and rubbish in the house, and by the stirrings of the old man: when ye see the bones of a half-dead man, and his grave, and find some warmness of life and heat, ye know there hath been life and strength in the man; so though ye cannot tell when Christ was first formed in you, yet ye find the bones and some warm blood, and some life-stirring of concupiscence in the old man, though Christ have made his grave, and he be well near completely buried, and his one foot in the grave. God hath appointed a time for the coming of the swallow; a season when flowers shall be on the earth, and when not; an hour when the sea shall be full tide; but there is no set day, not a determinate and set summer known to us, when the wind shall blow up doors and locks of the soul, and Christ shall come in. But yet they are not Christ's, who neither

know

know how they are drawn, nor can give any proofs that they are drawn. The apostle saith, 1 Cor. ii. 12. *Now we have received not the spirit of the world, but the Spirit which is of God, that we might know the things that are freely given to us of God.* The converted can say, I was such a man, 1 Tim. i. 13. [Gr. all eleèthen] *but I obtained mercy*; or, I was all be-mercied, filled with mercy. As Ezek. xvi. [Heb. gnittech gneth dodim] *Thy time was a time of loves.* As a constellation is not one single star, but many; so the converted soul observeth a confluence, a bundle, an army of free loves, all in one cluster, meeting and growing upon one stalk: as to be born where the voice of the turtle is heard in the land, 'tis free love; to hear such a sermon, free love; that the man spake such an excellent word, free love; that I was not sleeping when it was not spoken, free love; that the Holy Ghost drove that word into the soul, as a nail fastened by the master of the assemblies, it was free mercy: so that there's a meeting of shining favours of God, in obtaining mercy; and this would be observed.

Asser. 2. There be two ordinary ways of God, in drawing sinners: one moral, by words; another physical and real, by strong hand. Which may be cleared thus: fancy, led with some gilding of apparent or seeming good, as hope of food doth allure and draw the bird to the grin; and sometime pleasure, as a glass, and the singing of the fowler: so is fish drawn to nibble at the angle and lines cast out, hoping to get food. Now this is like moral drawing in men; and all this is but objective, working on the fancy. But when the foot and wing of the bird is entangled with the net, and the fish hath swallowed down the bait, and an instrument of death under it, now the fowler draweth the bird, and the fisher the fish, a far other way, even by real violence. The physician makes the sick child thirsty, then allures him to drink physick, under the notion of drink to quench his thirst: this is moral drawing of the child by wiles. But when the child hath drunk, the drink works

not

not by wiles, or morally, but naturally, without freedom, and whether the child will or no, it purgeth head and stomach.

That there is a moral working by the word, in the drawing of sinners to Christ, tho' most evident, yet must be proved against Antinomins and Enthusiasts, who (a) write, "That the whole letter of the scripture holds forth a covenant of works. And, (b) The due search and knowledge of the holy Scripture, is not a safe and sure way of searching and finding Christ. And, (c) There is a testimony of the Spirit, and voice unto the soul, meerly immediate, without any respect unto, or concurrence with the word. And, (d) Such a faith as is wrought by a practical syllogism, or the word of God, is but an human faith; because the conclusion followeth but from the strength of reasonings, or reason, not from the power of God, by which alone divine things are wrought;" Eph. i. 19, 20. Col. ii. 20. And that because such a faith wrought by the word, the works (of sanctification in the regenerate) and light of a renewed conscience, are all done by things that are created blessings and gifts; and these cannot produce that which is only produced by an Almighty Power. For the word of itself, without the Spirit, (yet the word is more than works of sanctification) is but a dead letter; but that God works faith by the word, his own Spirit concurring, is clear.

1. The prophets alledge this for their warrant, *Thus saith the Lord. Ergo*, You must believe it. And one more and greater than all the prophets, *But I say*; So Christ (God equal with the Father) speaketh.

2. Rom. x. 17. *Faith cometh by hearing, and hearing by the word of God.* verse 14. *How shall they believe in him of whom they have not heard?* 'Tis true, the word, the works of God, are not the principal object of faith, nor *objectum quod*; faith rests only on

God,

(a) Rise, Reign, etc. Er. 9. p. 2. (b) Er. 39. p. 8. (c) Er. 40. p. 8. (d) Francis Cornwell, a Conference of M. Cotton at Boston, with the Elders of New-England. P. 17, 18.

CHRIST DYING AND DRAWING SINNERS TO HIMSELF.

God, and the Lord Jesus, John xiv. 1. 1 Thess. i. 8. *Your faith toward God*, 1 Pet. i. 21. Deut. i. 32. John iii. 12. Gen. xv. 6. Dan. vi. 23. Rom. iv. 3. Gal. ii. 16. 2 Tim. i. 12. The word, promises, and prophets and apostles, are all creatures, and but *media fidei*, the means of saving faith; they are *objectum quo*, John v. 46. Psal. cvi. 12. Exod. iv. 8. Psal. lxxviii. 7. of themselves they are dead letters, and dead things, and cannot without the Spirit produce faith: yea, all habits of grace, of faith, of love in us, are like the streams of a fountain, that would dry up of themselves, if the spring did not, with a sort of eternity, furnish them new supply; so would habits of grace, being but created things, wither in us, if they were not supplied from the fountain Christ. And all beings created, in comparison of the first Being, are nothing; and *all nations to him are less than nothing, and vanity*, Isa. xl. 17. and so are the infused habits of grace nothing. If this were the meaning of Famulists and Antinomians, who say, that there is in us no inherent grace, but that grace is only in Christ, we should not contend with them. We teach no such thing, as that reasonings, syllogisms, or the scriptures, without the Spirit, can produce faith; yet it is vain arguing, to say, rain and dew, the summer-sun, good soil, cannot bring forth roses, flowers, vines, corns; because sure it is a work of omnipotency, that produceth all these; and so it is vain to say, that because faith is the work of the omnipotency of grace, therefore faith cometh not by hearing and reasoning from scripture: the contrary whereof is evident, in Christ's proving of the resurrection, by consequents from scripture, Mat. xxii. 31, 32. Luke xx. 37, 38. Nor can any say, Christ may make discourses from scripture, and his reasonings, because he is the King of the church, are valid, and may produce faith; but we cannot do the like, nor are our reasonings, scriptures; for Christ rebuketh the Sadducees, *Ye err, not knowing the scriptures*, etc. because they believed not the consequences of scripture as scripture, and made not the like discourse, for the building of themselves in the faith.

3. The

3. *The searching of the scriptures is life eternal,* the only way to find Christ, John v. 39. Acts x. 43. Rom. iii. 21. Isa. viii. 20.

4. Gen. ix. 27. *God shall persuade Japhet* (by the scriptures preached) *and he shall dwell in the tents of Shem,* Acts xvi. 14. *God's opening the heart, and Lydia's hearing and attending to the word that Paul spoke,* go together.

5. The way of enthusiasts, in rejecting both law and gospel, and all the written 'word of God is, because there is no light in them.' Some immediate sense of God, and working of the Holy Ghost, on the soul of the child of God, witnessing to me in particular, that I am the child of God, I deny not, and that my name expressly is not in scripture, is as true; but this testimony excludeth not the scripture, as if the *searching thereof, were no safe way of finding Christ,* as they blasphemously say, 1. Because this enthusiasm excludeth the only revealed rule, by which we try the spirits; and we are forbidden to presume *above that which is written,* 1 Cor. iv. 16. and enthusiasts have acted murders, and much wickedness, under this notion of the inspiration of the Spirit. 2. Because if the matter of that which is revealed, be not according to the written word, now, after the scripture is signed by Christ's own hand, Rev. xxii. 18. I see not what we are to believe of these inspirations. What extraordinary impulsions, and prophetical instincts, have been in holy men, and such as God hath raised to reform his churches, can be no rule to us. 3. If there be any mark of scriptural sanctification, that doth not agree to scripture, the rule of righteousness, though found in a person not mentioned in scripture, it is a delusion. 4. It is all the reason in the world, that a sinner be drawn to Christ; for Christ is the most rational object that is, he being the wisdom of God: and man is led and taken with reason. Christ is a convincing thing, and invincibly bindeth reason; so the forlorn son, before he return to his father, argueth, Luke xv. 17. *My father hath bread, he giveth it to*

servants,

servants, and I am a starving son; therefore, I'll return to my father. and the wise merchant must discourse, Matth. xiii. 45, 46. Christ is a precious pearl, all that I have in the world are but common stones and clay to him; therefore I cast my account thus, to sell all, and to buy him. So, Matth. ix. 21. the diseased woman hath heart-logic within herself, if a touch of the border of his garment may heal me, then I'll go to Christ: and the unjust steward cast syllogisms, thus, I cannot work, and a lodging in heaven I must have; and there is but one way to come by it, to make me a friend in heaven. Yea, a fool's paradise, a wedge of gold, is a strong reason, Prov. vii. 21. *The whore forced the young man* with gilded words and the outside of reason. Faith is the deepest and soundest understanding, the gold, the flower of reason. Christ can make me a king, therefore I'll be drawn to him. Poor Adam outwitted himself, turned distracted, he studied an apple; so, while he studied all his posterity out of their wits, and now we are born [Gr. *anontoie,*] made fools, Tit. iii. 3. What is the gospel? but a mass, a sea, a world of fair and precious truths, that says, come, born-idiots, to wisdom, and be made eternal kings: this is good reason. For the other way of drawing, we shall speak of it hereafter.

Asser. 3. In words and oratory, there is no power to make the blind see, and the dead live. Will ye preach heaven and Christ seven times, and let angels preach above a dead man's grave, ye do just nothing: but Christ's word is more than a word, John iv. 10. Jesus said, *If thou knewest that gift of God and who it is that saith unto thee, give me drink, thou wouldest have asked of him, and he would have given thee living water.* Psal. cxix. 33. *Teach me, O Lord, the way of thy statutes, and I shall keep it unto the end.* Psal. ix. 10. *Those that know thy name, will put their trust in thee.* Christ said but, *follow me,* to Matthew. *And I said unto thee, when thou wast in thy blood, live.* Ezek. xvi. 6. One word *live,* is with child of omnipotency; majesty, and heaven, and glory lie in the womb of one word; when

Christ

Christ speaks as Christ, he speaks pounds and talents-weights, Luke xxiv. 32. The disciples going to Emmaus say one to another, *Did not our hearts burn within us, while he talked with us by the way, and while he opened to us the scripture?* There be coals of fire, and fire-brands in Christ's words. Christ is quick of understanding, to know what word is the fittest key, to shoot the iron bar that keeps the heart closed; he opens seals on the heart with authority: violence may break up sealed letters, but it may be unjustly done; but authority can open kings' seals justly. Christ not only teacheth how to love, or *modum rei*, but he teacheth love itself, he draweth a lump of love out of his own heart, and casts it in the sinner's heart. The Spirit persuadeth God, Gal. i. 10. then he must persuade Christ, and persuade heaven; this is more than to speak persuasive words of God and Christ; it is to cast Christ in at the ear, and in the bottom of the heart, with words. Men open things, that they may be plain to the understanding: Christ opens the faculty itself to understand. The sun gives light, but cannot create eyes to see; Christ can heal the broken optic-nerves: he creates both the sun, and ties a knot upon the broken eye-strings, that the blind man sees bravely.

Asser. 4. One general is unseparable from Christ's drawing, that for the manner of drawing he doth it out of mere free-love. The principle of drawing on Christ's part, is great love. Eph. ii. 4. *God rich in mercy, for his great love,* [Gr. dìa tèn pollen agapèn.] *wherewith he loved us, even when we were dead in sin, quickened us in Christ.* Tit. iii. 4. *But when the bounty and man-love, or rather the man-kindness of God our Saviour appeared, he saved us.* Thanks to the birth of love, and of felt love. Col. i. 12, 13. *Giving thanks to the Father* [Gr. hos errusato hemàs] *who hath delivered, who hath snatched us with haste and violence, from the power of darkness, and hath translated us to the kingdom of the Son of his love.* 2. This love hath,

hath, in regard of its fervour, much haste, and loseth no time, but comes and draws, and pulls the sinner out of hell, before he be past recovery, and cold dead; as a father seeing his child fall into the water, and wrestling with the proud floods, he runs, ere he be dead out of hand, to pull him out. Luke xv. 10. *The father ran, and fell on his neck, and kissed him.* The father's running saith, that the love of Christ hath need of haste to prevent a sinner, and that he is eager and hot in his love; when Christ runs to save, he would gladly save; he draws with good-will, when he runs and sweats to come in the nick of due time to save: so Cant. ii. 8. when he cometh to save his church, or comfort her in her faintings, love's pace is swift, *like the running of a roe, or a young hart. Behold, he cometh leaping upon the mountains, skipping on the hills.* And it is an expression of the extreme desire that Christ hath of an union with us, and how fain he would have the company of sinners: so we difference between inviting or calling: yea, or leading and drawing: in calling and leading, Christ leaveth more to our will, whether we will come or refuse; but in drawing, there is more of violence, less of will.

3. In drawing, there is love-sickness, and lovely pain in Christ's ravishings, 1. When Christ cannot obtain and win the consent and good liking of the sinner to his love, he ravisheth, and with strong hand draws the sinner to himself; when invitations do not the business, and he knocks, and we will not open, then a more powerful work must follow, Cant. v. 4. *My Beloved put in his hand by the hole of the door, and my bowels were moved for him.* Christ drives such as will not be led. 2. And these who will not be invited, he must draw them, rather than want them: he draws with compassion, as being overcome with love; for *his bowels are moved for Ephraim.* Jer. xxxi. he draws while his arms bleed. 3. And does not only knock, but *he stands and knocks*, Rev. iii. 20. His standing, notes his importunity of mercy, how gladly he would be in; and he useth this as an argument to move his spouse, out of humanity, to

pity

pity him, and give him one night's lodging in the soul, Cant. v. 2. *Open to me, my sister, my love, my dove, my undefiled.* Why; I stand long, I wait on in patience, forcing my love on you; *For my head is filled with dew, and my locks with the drops of the night.* Every word is love, *Open, open, my sister,* I am a brother, not a stranger; *open, my love,* for I have interest in thee; every word is a talent-weight of free-grace.

4. Not only is drawing an expression of his love of union with sinners; for he bears the sinner, he translates the sinner [Gr. *metestese,*] he gives the sinner a lift to set him out of one country into another, into a far choicer land, out of a land of death, *into the kingdom of his dear Son,* Col. i. 13. And the little lambs that have no legs of their own, Christ shall be legs to them. Isa. xi. 12. *He shall gather the little lambs* (and so the Hebrew) *with his arm, and carry them in his bosom.* I wish no higher happiness out of heaven, than to be carried in the circle of Christ's arms, and to lie with the lambs in his bosom, and be warmed with the heart love that comes out of his breast. [Hebr. *Nasha*] is to carry on the shoulders: and Aaron is said in the same word, Exod. xxviii. *to carry the names of the children of Israel on his breast,* as a man is said to *carry his child in his arms* Deut. i. 31. And Christ, Luke xv. 5. *finding the lost sheep, layeth it on his shoulders, rejoicing.* Legs I have none (saith the sinner) and so cannot go to the new kingdom. What then (saith Christ) *I have legs and arms both for you, to serve you: I'll bear you if you can neither lead nor drive.* A sinner is as heavy as a mountain of iron, and cannot be drawn nor borne; but they be heavy lumps of hell that Christ cannot bear to heaven. Christ's love hath mighty arms, and great and strong bones; Christ now above five thousand years hath been carrying tired lambs up to heaven, in ones and twos, and is not yet wearied *of bringing up his many children to glory,* and will not rest till there be no one lamb of all the flock out of that great and capacious fold, and drawn they must be, whom Christ's love draweth.

Christ's

Christ's love is not so loose in gripping, as to miss any he intends to put in his bosom.

5. The particular way of love's drawing is lovely and sweetly, and with strong allurements.

1. Redemption is a sweet word to a captive, but redemption by law is not so sweet as redemption by love: for redemption is nothing comparable to redemption dipt and watered with free-love. I ought no more to be redeemed than damned devils: Christ is not my debtor, he owes me nothing, but eternal vengeance; nevertheless, he, out of only strong love, redeemed me. O this is two redemptions!

2. Drawing by free and strong love is an easy work, and so is it easy to be drawn; because all works of love are easy, as the act of marrying is no great pain, the solemnities and ceremonies of marriage are more toilsome than marriage itself. All the right marriages in the world are made by love; and there is no more but, *I consent, I say Amen, to have Christ for my husband*: and he saith, Hos. iii. 3. captive woman, *bought for fifteen pieces of silver, and for an homer of barley and an half, thou shalt be for me*, and not for another, *and I will also be for thee*; and there is an end. Christ's chariot runs on wheels of love, and the pace is soft and sweet.

3. The way of love's working through delight, is sweet to the drawn soul; when Christ hands the heart, and the love of Christ's soft fingers grasps about the soul, how alluring and captivating is Christ? when he comes in to the heart, *his fingers drop pure myrrh.* What honey, or what heaven-drops are these? Christ's honey-comb was gathered and made out of that flower, that incomparable rose, never planted with hands, out of Christ himself, from the bottom of eternity, from the head and root of infinite ages, which have neither head nor bottom; and out of Christ freely loving, freely chusing the creature to himself, Cant. i. 2. *Because of the favour of thy good ointments, thy name is as ointment poured forth; therefore do the virgins love*
thee.

thee. Cant. v. 11. *Christ's head is of most fine gold.* What think ye of the golden choice eminencies that are in Christ? of a clothing of uncreated glory that goes about Christ? Cant. ii. 3. *I sat down under his shadow with great delight, and his fruit was sweet to my taste.* Christ's love casteth so sweet a smell, that his love leads not, but draws; yet love's cords are softer than oil. The honey of Christ's love was gathered out of the flowers that grow in that highest mountain of roses, a larger field of flowers than ten millions of earths, and out of the fair blossoms, and sweet heavenly sap of the tree of life; *the glory of Lebanon, and excellency of Sharon*, is nothing to this. Bring all your senses, see, hear, feel, taste, and smell; what transcendent sweetness of heaven is in this love; a sea of love is nothing, it hath a bottom; a heaven of love is nothing, it hath a brim; but infinite love hath no bounds.

4. Love draws strongly and irresistibly: Christ never woo'd a soul with his free love, but he wins the love and heart. Death and the grave and hell are conquering things for strength, and have subdued huge multitudes since the creation; but the love of Christ is stronger and more constraining, Cant. viii. 6, 7. *The coals of love* burn more strongly than any other fire. *The flames and coals of God* are mighty hot: they burnt up hell and death to ashes: how much more will they take a sinner? Christ cast out coals of love with that word, *Matthew, follow me*: and there is no resisting, *he arose and followed him.* Christ's love draws till he bleed, and he loves till he die of love. His love must prevail, for omnipotency was in it. Had there been ten thousand worlds more of sinners, Christ hath love for them all. And had the elect world had ten thousand millions more of rebellions than they have, all these sins should have been infinitely below the conquering power of Christ's love. Never sinner went to hell victor, to say, *Love could not pardon me; I was in sin above Christ's omnipotency of love.* Never sinner went to heaven, but Christ's love had the better of him. Great heaven is but an
houseful

houseful of millions of vanquished captives, that Christ's love followed, and overtook, and subdued. O love's prisoners, praise, praise the Prince of love. Sense of this love so swells and so ascends, that the spouse, Cant. v. 10. is not master of words: every word is like a mountain, if you come to his person, nature, offices; none speak like Christ, none breathe like him; myrrh, aloes, and cinnamon, all the perfumes, all the trees of frankincense, all the powders of the merchants, that Assyria, or Egypt, or what countries else ever had, are but short and poor shadows to him: these are but hungry generals. 2. For beauty he hath no match amongst men; because *he is fairer than all the sons of men.* Christ hath a most goodly face. But of this hereafter. 3. For the sweetness and excellency of nature, he's God equal with the Father: when ye say God, ye say all things. God is a taking and a drawing excellency: the image of the invisible God; *he that is, he that was, and he which is to come, the Alpha and Omega, the beginning and the end, the first and the last,* of time, of creation, of what possible excellency we can conceive; for our conception can reach no higher than time, and created things. 4. For greatness of majesty. 5. For lowliness of tender love. 6. For freeness of grace. 7. For glory diffused through all his attributes. 8. For sovereignty and absoluteness of power, etc. who is like to our Lord Jesus? 9. For sweetness and loveliness of relations, the only begotten Son of God, no relation like this: 'the creator of the ends of the earth, the Saviour, the good Shepherd, the Redeemer, the great Bishop of our souls, the Angel of the covenant, the Head of the body the church, and of principalities and powers, the King of ages, the Prince of peace, of the kings of the earth;' the living ark of heaven, the song of angels and glorified saints, but they cannot out-sing him; the joy and glory of that land, the flower and crown of the Father's delights, the sweet rose of that garden of solace and joy. Compare other things with Christ, and they bear no weight: cast into the balance with him angels, and he

is

is wisdom, they but wise men; they are liars, and lighter than vanity, and Christ is the Amen, the faithful Witness, the express image of the Father's substantial glory: cast into the scales kings, all kings and all their glory, he is the King of all these kings: cast in millions of talents-weight of glory and gain, they are but bits of paper, and chaff; weight they have none to him: cast in two worlds, that is nothing; add to the weight millions of heavens of heavens, the balance cannot down, the scales are unequal; Christ is a huge over-weight.

To all these drawing powers in Christ, in the general, because Christ is the Master and King of the land, where his own created kings dwell; we may add a strong drawing argument, from the condition of the glorified in heaven; because Christ useth this as a strong argument to those that come to him, John vi. 37. Isa. lv. 3. John. v. 40. Mat. xi. 26. Rev. xxi. 6. and xxii. 17. we may use it after him. The earth is but a potter's house, that is full of earthen pots and venice-glasses, and withal taken by a conqueror, who can make no other use of these vessels, but break them all to sherds; it cannot be a drawing and alluring thing. Death hath conquered the earth, and these many hundred ages hath been breaking of the clay-pots, both men and other corruptible things, into broken chips and pieces of dust. But Christ draweth, by offering a more enduring city: that Christ can give, and promiseth heaven to his followers, is a strong argument, and draws powerfully. 1. Heaven is not one single palace, but 'tis a city; a metropolis, a mother-city, the first city of God's creation, for dignity and glory, Rev. xxi. chap. xxii. But a city is too little; therefore 'tis more, 'tis a kingdom, Luke xii. 32. and xxii. 23. Yea, but a kingdom may be too little; therefore 'tis a world, Luke xx. 35. It is a world, and for eminency, *a world to come;* Heb. vi. 5. the *world of ages.* 2. The lowest stones of it are not earth, as our cities here, but twelve manner of precious stones are the foundation of it. 3. In that city in the earth do men walk upon

gold?

gold? or dwell within walls of gold? But under the feet of the inhabitants there is gold, all the streets and fields of that kingdom and world are, Rev. xxi. 21. *Pure gold, as it were transparent glass.* 4. Then all the inhabitants are kings, Rev. xxii. 5. *And they shall reign for ever and ever.* Whole heaven entirely and fully enjoyed by one glorified saint, as if there were not one but this one person alone; all and every one hath the whole kingdom at his will, and is filled with God, as if there were no followers there to share with him. 5. O so broad and large as that land is, being the heaven of heavens! As the greater circle must contain the less, so all the dwellings here are but eaves under the earth, and holes of poor clay, in the bosom of this. But there are many dwelling places, Job. xiv. And there lodges so many thousand kings. O what fair fields, mountains of roses and spices! gardens, of length and breadth, above millions of miles, are nothing; and among these, trees of paradise; every bird in every bush sings, *Worthy is the Lamb*; every bottle is filled with the new wine of heaven: O the wines, the lilies, the roses, the precious trees that grow in Immanuel's land! and they sweat out balm of praises in those mountains. 6. If men knew what a drawing and alluring thing is the tree of life, that is in the midst of the street of the new land, the tree that beareth at once twelve manner of fruits, and yieldeth her fruit every month; an hundred harvests in one year are nothing here; and all are but shadows, there is nothing so low as gold, as twelve manner of precious stones; nothing so base in this high and glorious kingdom as gardens, trees, and the like: comparisons are created shadows, that come not up to express the glory of the thing. And for Christ himself, signified under this expression, he is the most, yea the only drawing glory in heaven and earth; 1. He is the high King of all the made and crowned kings in the land. 2. The only heaven and sum, yea, the all of all; the shadowed expressions of the kingdom, whatever is spoken of that glory comes home to this, to magnify Christ, to make

him

him as God, equal with the Father and the Spirit, all one, and all the only heaven of all heaven, and all in all, to the saints. Then created delights there, as divided from him, must be nothing in nothing, as he is All in All. 3. Nothing can take the eyes and hearts of the glorified, being now made so capacious and wide vessels to contain glory, as he can do. What can terminate, bound, and fill a glorified soul, but Christ enjoyed? Abraham, Moses, Elias, the prophets, the apostles, all the glorified martyrs and witnesses of Jesus Christ, especially now, being clothed with majesty and glory with Christ, must be more lovely objects than when they were on earth; and if Christ were not there, would appear more than they do: but the saints have neither leisure nor heart to feed themselves with beholding of creatures; but sure, all the eyes in heaven, which are a fair and numerous company, are upon the only, only Jesus Christ. The Father hath no leisure to look over his shoulder to the Son, nor the husband to the wife, in that city: Christ takes all eyes off created things there; it is enough for angels and men to study Christ for all eternity: it shall be their only labour to read Christ, to smell Christ, to hear and see and taste Christ: all the eyes of that numerous host of angels and men shall be on him; and he is worthy and above the admiration, the thoughts and apprehensions of all that heavenly army. 4. Then Christ shall appear a far other Christ in heaven, than we do apprehend him now on earth; not that he is not the same, but because neither we have eyes to see him in the kingdom of grace as he is, (narrow vessels cannot receive Christ, diffused in glory, as he now is) nor doth Christ make out himself in that latitude and greatness to us now, as he is to be seen and enjoyed in the heavens. 1 John iii. 2. *We shall then see him as he is.* What, do we not now see him as he is? No, we see him as he is in report, and shadowed out to us in the gospel; the gospel is the portraiture of the King, which he sent to another land to be seen by his bride, but the bride ne-

ver

ver seeth him as he is, in his best sabbath-robe-royal of immediate glory, till she be married unto him: so kings and queens on earth woo one another. And, 5. In heaven, Christ is (to speak so) in the element, prime fountain, and seat of God, as God, where he sheweth himself to be immediately seen and enjoyed; and it is as it were by the second hand, by messengers, words, mediation, that we enjoy Christ here; he sendeth to us, rather than cometh in person. An immediate touch of the apples of the tree of life, while they yet grow on the tree of life, is more than derived and borrowed communion. To see Christ himself, the red and the white in his own face, to hear himself speak, to see him as he is, and in his robes of majesty now at the right-hand of God, is in thousand thousand degrees, more than all the pictured (if I may so speak) and shadowed fruition we have here. The gospel is but the bridegroom's mirror and looking-glass, and our created prospect: but O his own immediate perfume, his myrrh, the ointments, and the smell that glory casteth in heaven, who can express? 6. We never see all the inside of Christ, and the mysteries of that glorious ark opened, till the light of glory discover him: thousands of excellencies of Christ shall then be revealed, that we see not now. 7. O what delights he casteth forth from himself! The river of life is more than a sea of milk, wine and honey. To suck the breasts of the consolations of Christ, and eat of the clusters that grow on that noble vine Jesus Christ, and take them off the tree with your own hand, is a desireable and excellent thing. The more excellent the soil is, the wines, the apples, the pomegranates, the roses, the lilies, must be the more delicious; and nearer the sun, the better; the more of summer, the more of day, the more excellent the fruits of the land are: believe it, the wines of that paradise grow in a brave land. O but Christ is a blessed soil! Roses and lilies, apples of love that are eternally summer-green are sweet, that grow out of him: the honey of that land, the honey of heaven, is more than honey; the honey of love, pure and unmixt,

must

must be incomparable. 8. The Mediator's hand wipes the foul face, and the tears off all the weeping strangers that come thither; he layeth the head of a friend under his chin, between his breasts, John xiv. 3. Rev. xxi. 4. Death is cried down; pain, sickness, crying, sadness, sorrow, are all acted and voted out of the house, and out from all the inhabitants of the land, for ever and ever. 9. It must be a delightsome city, that hath ever summer without winter; ever day, without night; ever day-light without sun or moon, or candle-light; *because the Lord God giveth them light*, Rev. xxii. 5. No danger of sun-burning, or summer-scorching, or winter-blasting: all morning, without twilight; all noon-day, without one cloud for eternity, is joyful; light, and day, and summer, flowing immediately from the Lamb, is admirable. 10. (1.) joy, (2.) full joy, (3.) fulness of joy, (4.) pleasures, (5.) pleasures that last for evermore, (6.) and that at God's right-hand; yea, (7.) in his face, is above our thoughts, Psal. xvi. 10, 11. 11. O the music of the sanctuary, the sinless and well-tuned psalms, the songs of the high temple, without a temple or ordinances as we have here, and these exalting him that sits on the throne for evermore! All which, with many other considerations, are strong drawing invitations to come to Christ.

Asser. 5. Christ draweth with three sorts of general arguments, in this moral way: the first is taken from pleasure; this is the beauty that is in God. 1. That is in a communion with God. 2. The delectation we have in God, as love-worthy to the understanding. For the drawing beauty of God, a word, (1.) Of God's beauty. (2.) Of God's beauty in Christ. (3.) Of the relative beauty of God in Christ to men and angels. *1st*, Beauty, as we take it, is the loveliness of face and person, arising from, 1. The natural well-contempered colour. 2. The due proportion of statute and members of body. 3. The integrity of parts; as that there is nothing wanting for bodily perfection. So, beauty formally is not in God, who hath not a body; nor speak we of Christ's bodily beauty, as man: then beauty,

by

by analogy, and eminently, must be in God. So as there be four things in the creature to make up beauty to the bodily eyes; and there be, by proportion, those same four things in God: for, if beauty be good, and a desirable perfection in the creature, it must be in an infinite and eminent way in God, as the perfection of the effect is in the cause. If the roses, lilies, meadows be fair, he must be fairer who created them; but in another kind. If the heavens, stars, and sun be beautiful, the lovely Lord who made them, must have their beauty in an high measure. Zech. ix. 17. *How great is the Lord's goodness? how great is his beauty?* What then is the beauty of God? I conceive it to be, 'The amenity and loveliness of his nature, and all infinite perfections, as this pleasantness offers itself to his own understanding and the understanding of men and angels:' and as bodily beauty satisfies the eyes, and so acts on the heart to win love to beauty; so the truth of the Lord's nature, and all his attributes, offered to the understanding and mind, and drawing from them admiration or wondering, and love, is the beauty of God: David maketh this his one thing, Psal. xxvii. 4. *That* (saith he) *I may dwell in the house of the Lord all the days of my life, to behold the beauty of the Lord, and inquire in his temple.* See then, as white and red, excellently contempered, maketh pleasure and delectation to the eyes, and through these windows to the mind and heart; so there ariseth from the nature of God and his attributes a sweet intelligibility; as David desires no other life, but to stand before God, and behold with his mind, and faith's eyes, God in his nature and attributes, as he reveals himself to the creature. The queen of Sheba came a far journey to see Solomon, because of his perfection; some common people desire to see the king. The Lord is a fair and pleasant object to the understanding.

2. There is in beauty a due proportion of members. 1. Quantity. 2. Situation. 3. Stature. Let a person have a most pleasant colour, yet if the ears and nose be as little as an ant, or as big as an ordinary man's leg,

he

he is not beautiful. 2. If members be not right seated, if the one eye be two inches lower in the face than the other, it mars the beauty; or if the head be in the breast, it is a monster. Or, 3. If the stature be not due, as if the person be the stature of ten men, and too big; or the stature of an infant, or a dove; had he all other things for colour and proportion, his beauty is no beauty, but an error of nature, he is not as he should be: now, the Lord is beautiful, because infiniteness, and sweetness of order is so spread over his nature and attributes; nothing can be added to him, nothing taken from him; and he is not all mercy only, but infinitely just. Were God infinitely true, yet not meek and gracious, he should not be beautiful; had he all perfections, but weak, mortal, not omnipotent, not eternal, his beauty should be marred; then one attribute does not overtop, out-border or limit another; were he infinite in power, but not infinite in mercy, the lustre and amenity of God were defaced.

3. There is integrity of parts in beauty. Were a person fairer than Absalom, and wanted a nose or an arm, the beauty should be lame. The Lord is complete and absolutely perfect in his blessed nature and attributes.

4. All these required in beauty, must be natural, and truly and really there. Borrowed colours, and painting, and fairding of the face, as Jezebel did, are not beauty. The Lord, in all his perfections, is truly that which he seems to be. Now, as there is in roses, gardens, creatures that are fair, something pleasant, that ravisheth the eye and heart; so there is in God so many fair and pleasant truths to take the mind, and God is so capacious, and so comprehensive a truth, and so lovely, such a bottomless sea of wonders, and to the understanding that beholds God's beauty, there is an amenity, goodliness, a splendour, an irradiation of brightness, a loveliness, and drawing sweetness of excellency, diffused through the Lord's nature. Hence, heaven is a seeing of God face to face. Rev. xxii. 4. Math. xviii. 10. Now, God hath not a face; but the face of a man

is

is the most heavenly visible part in man, there is a majesty and gravity in it, much of the art and goodliness of the creature is in his face. To see God's face, is to behold God's blessed essence, so far as the creature can see God. Now, as we may be said to see the sun's face, when we see the sun, as we are able to behold it; but there is beauty, and such vehemency of visibility in it, as it exceedeth our faculty of seeing; so do we see God's face, when we nearly behold him, not by hearsay, but immediately. Let us imagine, that millions of suns in the firmament, were all massed and framed in one sun, and that the sense of seeing that is in all men, that ever have been, or may be, yet this sun should far excel this faculty of seeing: so, suppose that the Lord should create an understanding faculty of man or angels, millions of degrees more vigorous and apprehensive, than if all the men and angels that are, or possibly may be created, were contempered in one, yet could not this understanding to see God's transcendent and superexcellent beauty, but there should remain unseen treasures of loveliness never seen; yea, it involves an eternal contradiction, that the creature can see to the bottom of the Creator.

All this beauty of God is holden forth to us in Christ, Psal. xlv. 2. *He is fairer than the sons of men.* [*Hebr.* Jophjaphith]. The word is of a double form, to note a double excellency. Cant. i. 16. *Behold thou art fair, my Beloved, yea pleasant;* [*Hebr.* Nagnam] signifieth lovely, amiable, acceptable. The seventy render it [Gr. hedenusthai.] Psal. cxlvi. *It is pleasant and sweet.* 2 Sam. i. 26. *Thou wast very pleasant to me.* Cant. v. 10. *He is white and ruddy.* v. 15. *His countenance is as Lebanon, excellent as the cedars.* Rev. i. 16. *His countenance is as when the sun shineth in his full strength.* All the beauty of God is put forth in Christ. Isa. xxxiii. 17. *Thine eyes shall see the King in his beauty.* Heb. i. 3. *Christ is the brightness of his Father's glory.* The light of the sun in the air is the accidental reflection of the sun's beams;

beams; Christ is the substantial reflection of the Father's light and glory; for he is God equal with the Father, and the same God.

3. This beauty to men and angels is an high beauty, *Angels have eyes within and without,* Rev. iv. 6, *to behold the beauty of the Lord*; and it takes up their eyes always to behold his face; and there is no *beauty of truth they desire more to behold.* [Gr. parakùpteìn] 1 Pet. i. 12. as to stoop down, and to look into a dark and vailed thing, with the bowing of the head, and the bending of the neck; the seventy use for [Heb. shazah,] Cant. ii. 9. where Christ is said to stand behind the wall, and look out at the casements, with great attention of mind: it is to look down over a window, bending the head. Exod. xxv. 18, 19, 20. John xx. 5. *They stooped down, and saw the linen clothes.* Luke xxiv. 12. Angels are not curious, but they must see exceeding great beauty, and wonder much at the excellency of Christ, when they cannot get their eyes pulled off Jesus Christ.

2. There is a beauty of Christ in a communion with God, which is a ravishing thing. When the soul comes to Christ, he seeth a beauty of holiness, and Christ is taken with this beauty, Psal. cx. 3. *So shall the King greatly desire thy beauty,* Psal. xlv. 11. *Thou hast ravished my heart* (saith Christ to the spouse) Cant. iv. 9. *My sister, my spouse,* ----v. 10. *How fair is thy love, my sister, my spouse? how much better is thy love than wine, and the smell of thine ointments than all spices,* v. 11. *Thy lips, O my spouse, drop as the honey-comb; honey and milk are under thy tongue, and the smell of thy garments is as the smell of Lebanon. Zion is the perfection of beauty,* Psal. l. 2. All this beauty and sweetness cometh from Christ; there is no such thing in the people of God, as they are sinful men, considered in their natural condition; and therefore it must be fountain beauty in him, as in the cause, and original of beauty.

Second. There is a delectation in a communion with God. This is one general, Prov. iii. 17. *All wisdom's*

ways

ways are ways of pleasure; to the spiritual soul, every step to heaven is a paradise.

1. What sweetness is in the sense of the love of Christ, to delight all the spiritual senses? 1. The smell of Christ's spikenard, his myrrh, aloes, and cassia; his ivory chambers smell of heaven; the ointment of his garments bring God to the sense. Psal. xlv. *All thy garments smell of myrrh, aloes, and cassia: out of the ivory palaces, there have they made thee glad:* Cant. i. 13. *A bundle of myrrh is my beloved to me, he shall lie all night between my breasts.*

2. To the sight, Christ is a delightful thing: to behold God in Christ, is a changing sight. 2 Cor. iii. 18. *But we all with open face beholding, as in a glass, the glory of the Lord, are changed into the same image, from glory to glory, even as by the Spirit of the Lord.* Eph. i. 17. Matth. xvi. 17. 1 John ii. 27. *To see the King in his beauty*, is a thing full of ravishing delight.

3. It taketh the third spiritual sense of hearing; the spouse, Cant. ii. 8. is so taken with the sweetness of Christ's tongue, that, for joy, she can but speak broken and imperfect words; *the voice of my Beloved:* it is not a perfect speech, but for joy she can speak no more. *It is the voice of joy and gladness*, that with the very sound can heal broken bones, Psal. li. 8. and which David desired to hear. O if you heard Christ speak! Cant. v. 13. *His lips are like lilies, dropping sweet smelling myrrh*: heaven's music, the honey of the new land is in his tongue; the church cheereth her soul with this, Cant. ii. 10. *My Beloved spake, and said unto me, Rise up, my love, my fair one, and come away.* Christ's piping in the joyful gospel-tiding, ver.—5. should make us dance, Matth. xi. 7. Christ harping and singing sinners, with joyful promises, out of hell to heaven, must have a drawing sweetness to move stones, if the sinner have ears to hear; and what heat and warmness of love must it bring, when Christ is heard say, Isa. liv. 11. *O thou afflicted, tossed with tempest and not comforted; behold I will lay thy stones*

with

with fair colours, and lay thy foundations with sapphires. He doubles his words, he desires Jerusalem's ears may own this cry, Isa. xl. 1. *Comfort ye, comfort ye my people, saith the Lord; speak to the heart of Jerusalem.*

4. Christ is sweet to the spiritual taste, Cant. ii. 3. *I sat down under his shadow with great delight, and his fruit was sweet in my mouth.* Psal. xxxiv. 8. *O taste and see that the Lord is good.* Christ is a curious banquet: the wine, the milk, the honey, and the fatted calf killed, are all but shadows to Christ's excellent gospel-dainties.

5. The sense of touching, which is the most spiritual, is the heavenly feelings, sense, and experience of God's consolations; and this sense is fed with the kisses of Christ's mouth, Cant. i. 3. *With the hid manna, the white stone, the new name.*

3. Joy is a drawing delight, Psal. xvi. 11. *In his face there is fulness of joy.* Look, how far God's face casts down from heaven sparkles of joy on us, as far goes our joy; and we are said, in believing, 1 Pet. i. 8. *to rejoice with joy unspeakable, and glorious.*

Fourthly, There is particularly delectation, Psal. xxxvi. 7. *They shall be abundantly satisfied with the fatness of thy house, and thou shalt make them drink the rivers of thy pleasures.* Should not this draw men to Christ? And there must be abundance of pleasures where there is a river of pleasures; as Psal. xlvi. 4. *There is a river, the streams whereof makes glad the city of God.* What a sea of seas must God himself be? His full and bright face, his white throne, his harpers and heavenly troops that surround the throne, the Lamb, the heaven of heavens itself, the tree of life, eternally green, eternally adorned both at once with soul-delighting blossoms, and loaden with twelve manner of fruit every month; peace of conscience from the sense of reconciliation, the first fruits of Emanuel's land, that lies beyond time and death; must all be above expression.

There is a second drawing motive in Christ, and this is from gain; which is eminently in Christ.

1. The

The drawn soul hath bread by the covenant of grace, his yearly rent is written in the New Testament, Christ is his rental-book and heritage. Isa. xxxiii. 16. *He shall dwell on high, his place of defence shall be the munition of rocks;* for his lodging, he shall not lie in the fields: *bread shall be given him, his waters shall be sure,* or faithful: bread and drink are unfaithful, uncertain, and winged to natural men. 1 Tim. vi. 17. *Riches hath* [Gr. adelotes,] *an uncertainty,* like ghosts or spirits that ye see, but they evanish out of your sight and disappear; or, like clouds, or fire-lightnings in the air, that come and go suddenly; but bread is faithful and sure to the soul drawn to Christ; when the covenanted people are so drawn, that they receive a new heart, then God saith, Ezek. xxxvi. 29. *I will also save you from all your uncleanness.* What then? *And I will call for the corn, and will increase it, and lay no famine upon you.* ver. 34. *And the land shall be tilled.* Does the New Testament provide for the plowing of your land? Yea, it doth. Yea, know wisdom's attendants and allacays, Prov. iii. 16. *On her right hand is length of days, and on her left hand riches and honour.* Eternity hath the honour, and the right-hand: riches is the left-hand blessing of wisdom.

2. It should draw us in its own kind to Christ, in regard Christ is more than gain, Prov. iii. 14. *Wisdom's merchandise is better than silver, and her gain than fine gold.* ver. 15. *She is more precious than rubies.* (2.) Job xxviii. 1. *Wisdom cannot be gotten for gold.* (3.) It there not some worth in gold? v. 16. *Wisdom cannot be valued with the gold of Ophir, with the precious onyx, with the sapphire,* verse 17. *The gold and the crystal cannot equal it.* (4.) May there not be bidding and buying, and words of a market here? Nay, the disproportion between Christ and gold is so great, that a rational merchant can never speak of such a bargain. v. 18. *No mention shall be made of coral, or of pearls, for the price of wisdom is above rubies.* Say, that heaven and earth, and all within the bosom and circumference

of

of heaven, and millions of more worlds were turned into gold, pearl, sapphires, rubies, and what else ye can imagine; ye undervalue Christ, if ye speak of buying him.

3. Being drawn to Christ, maketh all yours; when ye are hungry, all the bread of the earth is your Father's; when ye are in a ship, ye are in Christ's Father's waters; when ye travel in summer, ye see your Redeemer's fields, your Saviour's woods, trees, flowers, corns, cattle, birds; yea, and *all things are yours*, 1 Cor. iii. 21. Not in possession, but in a choicer free-holding, in free-heritage, Psal. xxxvii. 11. Ye have the broad rent, the fair income of *all things*. Your land is named, *All things*. Rev. xxi. 7. *He that overcometh, shall inherit all things.*

4. All you have, a morsel of green herbs, a bed of straw, want, hunger, wealth, are gilded and watered with Christ.

The third drawing thing in Christ, is honour. The *church is a Prince's daughter*, Cant. vii. 1. *A King's daughter*, Psal. xlv. 13. *A queen in gold of Ophir*, Psal. xlv. 9. *Kings and priests unto God*, Rev. i. 5. Not young kings only, but crowned kings. *And they had on their heads crowns of gold*, Rev. iv. 4. Every saint rules the nations with a rod of iron. Every believer is a catholic king, and sways the sceptre over all the kingdoms of the world. (1.) In regard that his head, Christ, guides all kings, courts, and kingdoms, all the world, and the weight of states, empires, not *indirectly*, and only *in ordine ad spiritualia*; but *directly*, and the weight of the church triumphing, and the church fighting, are upon the shoulders of our brother and Saviour. (2.) In that by faith he breaks and overcomes the world. (3.) And by prayer, which is more than the key of Europe, Africa, and Asia, he can bring in the nations to Christ, and shut and open heaven.

2dly, Consider what God makes them. To *him that lays hold on my covenant, saith the Lord*, Isa. lvi. 5. *I will give within my house, and my walls, a name*, but what is a name? a name is but a name: *a name*

better

better than the name of sons and daughters, even an everlasting name, that shall not be cut off. An everlasting name (I confess) is more than a name. Isa. xliii. 4. *Since thou wast precious in my sight,* [Heb. nichbadta] *thou hast been glorious, or honourable.* 1 Chron. iv. 9. *And Jabez was more honourable than his brethren;* the same word, and why? ver. 19. *And Jabez called on the God of Israel, saying, Oh that thou wouldst bless me indeed, and enlarge my coast.* It was said of Reuben, Gen. xlix. 4. *Reuben, thou shalt not excel,* [Heb. Jethar] nor be an overplus in praise: it is to remain or abound either in quantity or quality; for his incest deprived him of his excellency, Prov. xii. 26. *The righteous is more abundant* (the same word) *more honourable, glorious, or excellent than his neighbour.*

3. The Lord, who knows the weight of things, angels and men, esteems highly of them, Cant. v. 2. *My sister, my love, my dove.* The spouse must, in Christ's heart, have an high respect, when he saith, Cant. iv. 1. *Behold thou art fair, my love;* and that cannot content him, he addeth, *Behold thou art fair.* Cant. vi. 9. *My dove, my undefiled is but one, she is the only one of her mother, she is the choice one of her that bare her.* The saints in Christ's books are jewels, Mal. iii. 17. his only choice, the flower of the earth. All the world is Christ's refuse, and kings are but mortar to him; the saints are Christ's assessors, and the King's peers to judge the world with him, lords of the higher house; Christ divides the throne with them, Luke xxii. 30. 1 Cor. vi. 2. Rev. xxi. The Lord so far honoureth them, as to put them on all his secrets, Psal. xxv. 4. *The secrets of the Lord are with them that fear him.* John xiv. 21. *I will manifest myself unto him.* They are of his cabinet-council, Cant. ii. 4. *The King brought me into his house of wine;* his secrets of love and free-grace are there.

4. Christ so honoureth them, that he professeth, he desires a communion with them, Cant. iv. 8. *Come with me from Lebanon, my spouse.* John xiv. 12. *The Father*

and

and I will come unto him, and make our abode with him. Cant ii. 16. *He feedeth among the lilies, till the day-break:* the Lord familiarly converseth with them.

Use 1. All they who are taken with fair things, and are so soft, as pleasures they must have, and will not be drawn to Christ, the pleasantest and fairest one that ever heaven had, are much prejudged; ye warm yourselves, O children of men, at the outside of a painted fire. Your pleasures (and we may believe Solomon) are flowers worm-eaten, and as garments torn and thread-bare. Solomon's honey, and Samson's Delilah, are sweet drinks that swell them; when these work on their stomach, they are glad to vomit them out, and are pained with sickness at the remembrance of them; there is no drawing beauty to Christ. Behold him in all his excellencies, Cant. v. 10. *My beloved is white and ruddy, the chiefest among ten thousand.* Verse 11. *His head is as the most fine gold, his locks are bushy, and black as a raven.* Verse 12. *His eyes are as the eyes of doves by the rivers of water, washed with milk, and fitly set.* Verse 13. *His cheeks are as a bed of spices, as sweet flowers; his lips like lilies, dropping sweet smelling myrrh.* Verse 14. *His hands are as gold-rings set with beryl; his belly is as bright ivory, overlaid with sapphires.* Verse 15. *His legs are as pillars of marble, set upon sockets of fine gold; his countenance is as Lebanon, excellent as the cedars.* Verse 16. *His mouth is most sweet;* or in the abstract [Heb. Vecullo*] *sweetness, and he is all desires, all loves,* and all of him, or every piece of him is love; and when John sees him, Rev i. O what a *sight,* Verse 13. *He was clothed with a garment down to the feet, and girt about the paps with a golden girdle.* Verse 14. *His head and his hair were white like wool, as white as snow, and his eyes were as a flame of fire.* Verse 15. *and his feet like unto fine*

brass,

*Heb. *Ve cullo,* is in the Marg. And is emphatic, fig. *He all, or and all of him.*

brass, as if they burned into a furnace, and his voice as the sound of many waters. Verse 16. *And he had in his right hand seven stars.* He hath the churches, and all the elect in his right-hand, and out of his mouth went a sharp two-edged sword, and his countenance was as the sun shineth in his strength. When John saw him thus, he was so over-gloried with the beauty and brightness of his majesty, that whereas he wont to lean on his bosom in the days of his flesh, now he is not able to stand and endure one glance of his highest glory; but (saith he) verse 17. *And when I saw him, I fell down at his feet as dead.* And there was much lovely and tender affection lapped up in this glory; when poor John fell a swooning at his feet, Christ for all his glory, holds his head in his swoon. *And he laid his right hand on my head, saying unto me, Fear not, I am the First and the Last.* I am good for swooning and dying sinners. Why, *I am he that liveth, and was dead: and behold, I live for evermore.* Would sinners but draw near, and come and see this king Solomon in his chariot of love, behold his beauty, the uncreated white and red in his countenance, he would draw souls to him; there is omnipotency of love in his countenance, all that is said of him here, are but created shadows; ah! words are short to express his nature, person, office, loveliness, desirableness. What a broad and beautiful face must he have, who with one smile, and one turning of his countenance, looks upon all in heaven, and all in the earth, and casts a heaven of burning love, east and west, south and north, through heaven and earth, and fills them all? Suppose omnipotency would enlarge the globe of the world, and the heaven of heavens, and cause it to swell to the quantity and number of millions of millions of worlds, and make it so huge and capacious a vessel, and fill it with so many millions of elect men and angels, and then fill them, and all this wide circle, with love; it would no more come near to take in Christ's lovely beauty, than a spoon can contain all the seas; or than a child

can

can hide in his hand the globe of the world. Yea, suppose all the corns of sand in all the earth and shores, all the flowers, all the herbs, and all the leaves, all the twigs of trees in woods and forests since the creation, all the drops of dew and rain that ever the clouds sent down, all the stars in heaven, all the liths, joints, drops of blood, hairs, of all the elect on earth, that are, have been, or shall be, were all rational creatures, and had the wisdom and tongues of angels, to speak of the loveliness, beauty, virtues of Jesus Christ, they would in all their expressions stay, millions of miles, on this side of Christ, and his loveliness and beauty. It is the wicked fleshly disposition of Libertines, who turn all the beauty, excellency, freeness of grace in Christ, to a cloak of licentiousness, and a liberty of all religions; they highly undervalue free-grace, as any heretics that ever the church of Christ saw, who turn all sanctification, all the grace of Christ that should be expressed in strict, precise, accurate walking with God, (but as far from merit, as grace and debt, as Christ's free-grace, and the condemning law) into a notional speculative apprehension, or rather a presumptuous imagination, or Antinomian faith; that Christ hath obeyed, mortified the lusts of the flesh for the sinner; that no law, no commandment of God, no letter of the world, obligeth us to walk with God; only an immediate enthusiastical unwarrantable inspiration of a Spirit, without the word; or blasts of love when they come, and not but when they come, engageth believers to keep any commandment of God. Never Pelagian, Jesuite, Arminian, were such disgraceful enemies to Jesus Christ, to free justification, and the grace of the gospel, as Antinomians; for they make the law of God, and the love of God, in commanding holy walking, opposite. All the doctrine of the New Testament, that teacheth and commandeth to deny ungodliness; all the Old Testament, and particularly the cxix. Psalm, reconcileth the law, com-

manding

manding to keep the Lord's ways and testimonies, and the love of Christ, sweetning with delight and joy, holy walking, as one and the same way of God.

Use 2. Again, nothing more lesseneth Christ, than the heightening of the world in the hearts of men: Haman had the scum of the pleasures of 127 kingdoms, yet there was a bone wrong in his foot; anger and malice to see Mordecai, is a hell to him. 'Tis a sweeter burden to bear the fire and coals of the love of Christ in the heart, than the hell of envy in the soul: nay, say that all the damned in hell were brought up with their burning and fiery chains of eternal wrath to the outermost door of heaven, and strike up a window, and let them look in and behold the throne, and the Lamb, and the troops of glorified ones clothed in white, crowns of gold on their head, and palms in their hands, shewing their kingly and victorious condition; and let them, through a window in heaven, hear the music of the new song, the eternal praises of the conquering King and Redeemer, they should not only be sweetned in their pain, but convinced of their foolish choice, that they hunted with much sweating after carnal delights, and lost the fulness of joy and pleasures that last for evermore in the Lord's face.

Would we believe the spies that have been visiting the new land, that *Immanuel, God with us*, is Lord of; hear, for Moses he was in that land, and he saith, Deut. xxxiii. 29. *Happy art thou, O Israel: who is like unto thee, O people saved by the Lord, the shield of thy help, and who is the sword of thy excellency!* David was there a landed man, and what saith he of that new land that Christ hath found out? Psal. xvi. Canaan at its best is but a wilderness to it. Verse 6. *The lines are fallen to us in pleasant* (things, or) *places.* Then there must be multitudes of pleasures, not one only in God; *My heritage is pleasant above me*, above my thoughts, or I have a goodly heritage. Solomon was a messenger who saw both lands, and he saith, Eccl. ii. 13. *then I saw that wisdom excelled folly, as far as light exceedeth*

dark-

darkness. And the spouse saith, Cant. i. 12. *When the King sitteth at his table, my spikenard sendeth forth the smell thereof.* 13. *A bundle of myrrh is my beloved, he shall lie all night between my breasts.* Cant. ii. 4. *He brought me to the banqueting-house, and his banner over me was love.* All the song reporteth great things of the kingdom of grace. Ask of Isaiah, What saw ye there? he answereth, chap. xxv. 6. *It is a feast of fat things, a feast of wines on the lees, of fat things full of marrow.* And Ezekial saith, That there shall be a brave summer in that land, chap. xlvii. 12. *By the river upon the bank thereof, on this side, and on that side, shall grow all trees for meat, whose leaf shall not fade, neither shall the fruit thereof be consumed: it shall bring forth new fruit according to his month, because their waters issued out from the sanctury, and the fruit thereof shall be for meat, and the leaf thereof for medicine*: this hath real truth even in the kingdom of grace. And Jeremiah saw the fruits of the land, and a golden age there, chap. xxxii. 12. *Therefore they shall come and sing in the height of Sion, and shall flow together to the goodness of the Lord, for wheat, and for wine, and for oil, and for the young of the flock, and of the herd; and their soul shall be as a watered garden, and they shall not sorrow any more at all.* And Christ brings good news out of that country, Mat. xxii. that the life of all there, is the life of banqueters, called to the marriage-feast of a king's son, of which every one hath a wedding-garment. And if ye ask tidings of John, *what saw ye, and heard ye there?* He saith, I saw a prince's daughter with a crown on her head, Rev. xxi. 10. *He shewed me the great city, the holy Jerusalem descending out of heaven from God, having the glory of God.* Even an enemy, who saw the land afar off, and was not near the borders of it, saith, Numb. xxiv. 5. *How goodly are thy tents, O Jacob, and thy tabernacles, O Israel!* Surely, Prov. ii. 10. *Knowledge is pleasant to the soul.* O all ye pleasures of the flesh, blush, and be ashamed; all world-worshippers, be confounded, that ye toil yourselves

in

in the fire for such short follies; were there no other pleasure in godliness, but to behold the Lord Jesus, what a pleasant sight must he be! The temple that stately and kingly house, of fair carved stones, cedar-wood, almug trees, brass, silver, gold, scarlet, purple, silks, in the art of the curious fabric and structure, was a wonder to the beholders: what beauty must be in the samplar! O what happiness, to stand beside that dainty precious ark, weighted now with so huge a lump of majesty, as infinite glory! to see that King in his throne, the Lamb, the fair Tree of life, the branches, which cannot for the narrowness of the place have room to grow within the huge and capacious borders of the heaven of heavens! *for the heaven of heavens cannot contain him.* What pen, though dipt in the river of life that flows from under the sanctuary, can write? What tongue, though shapen out of all the angels of that high kingdom, and watered with the milk and wine of that good land, can sufficiently praise this heart-ravishing flower of angels, this heaven's wonder, the spotless and infinitely beautiful Prince, the Crown, the Garland, the Joy of heaven, the wonder of wonders for eternity to men and angels? What a life must it be, to stand under the shadow of this precious Tree of life, and to cast up your eyes and see a multitude without quantity of the apples of glory; and to put up your hand, and not only feel, but touch, smell, see love itself, and be warmed with the heat of immediate love that comes out from the precious heart and bowels of this princely and royal standard-bearer, and leader of the white and glorious troops and companies that are before the throne? If one said, but finding the far-off dew-drops that fall at so many millions of miles distance from that higher mountain of God, down to this low region, Psal. lxiii. 5. *My soul shall be satisfied as with marrow and fatness*; what must the glory itself be, that is in this dainty delightful one? We have but the droppings of the house here.

Use

Use 3. Natural men say, this kingdom is a sour, sad and weeping land; here is repentance, sorrow for sin, mortification. True; but tears that wash those lovely feet that were pierced for sinners, are tears of honey, and wine, and the joy of Christ's banqueting-house; and mortification, flowing from a lothing and a soul-surfeit of the creature, and a tasting of the new wine of Christ's Father's higher palace, is rather a piece of the margin and border of heaven, than a sour and sad life.

Object. 2. "But discipline, and the rod, and censures of Christ's house, makes the church terrible as an army with banners. Christ's yoke is easy; hath he not cords and bands to cut the necks of those that follow him?

Answ. 1. Yea, but this rod is a rod of love, only used that *the spirit may be saved in the day of the Lord Jesus,* 1 Cor. v. 5. *For the gaining of the soul,* Mat. xiii. 15. *For building of souls,* 2 Cor. x. 8. And Christ's cords are silken and soft, and bands of love, every thread, twisted out of the love of Christ, Hos. xi. 4. *I drew them with the cords of men, with the bands of love.* But consider, Psal. xlviii. *The Lord's mountain of holiness is glorious.* Verse 2. *Beautiful for situation, the joy of the whole earth, is mount Sion, the city of the great King.* But is it so to all? Verse 5. No: *But lo, the kings were assembled, they passed by together; they saw it, and so they marvelled; they were troubled and hasted away.* Verse 6. *Terror took hold on them, and pain, as a woman in travail.* What cause is there here that the kings should be afraid? They see a beautiful princess, the daughter of a glorious King, the joy of the whole earth; yet the Lord's people work on them, 1. a wondering; 2. more trouble of mind; 3. flying; they haste away, and cannot behold the beauty of God in a King's daughter: 4. Terror takes hold on them, and quaking of conscience: 5. When the powers of the world, princes, states, parliaments, see the convincing glory of another world in the church, they part with child for pain. It is known,

some

some have such antipathy with a rose, which is a pleasant creature of God, that the smell of it hath made them fall a swooning. *Jerusalem is the rebellious city*, Ezra iv. 12. therefore men are unwilling it should be built. Lusts in men's minds, either heresies, or any other fleshly affection, is against the building of the house of God.

Use 4. A believer is a rich man, and an honourable, say he were a beggar on the dunghill: Christ cannot be poor, and he is a fellow-heir with Christ, Rom. viii. 17. We must think the father of a rich heir hath bowels of iron, and sucked a tyger when he was young, who suffereth the heir, remaining an heir, to starve. As the natural man is but a fragment of clay, so he hath a life like an house let for money; and the rent and income that the house pays to the Lord of the land, is but hungring clay, a dead rent, and some new-born vanities of homage and service; but the promise, the *Magna Charta*, and the charter of food and raiment, that is an article of the covenant of grace, is a full assurance that the saints are noblemen, pensioners of the Prince of the kings of the earth: and Christ hath so broad a board, that he doth pay all his pensioners. And the saints are truly honourable, being come of the blood-royal, of the princely seed, John i. 13. 1 John iii. 1, 9. And the church is a spiritual monarchy: the plant of renown, their head, said of her, Isa. lxii. 3. *Thou shalt be a crown of glory in the hand of the Lord, and a royal diadem in the hand of thy God.*

Asser. 6. The other particular manner of drawing sinners to Christ, is real; in which we are to consider these two,

1. God's fit application of his drawing of the will.
2. His irresistible pull of omnipotency.

In the former way of working, I desire that notice be taken (for doctrine's cause, rather than for art of logical method) of these four ways.

1. God

1. God worketh by measure and proportion.
2. By condescension.
3. By fit internal application.
4. By external, providential accommodation of outward means.

1. In works of omnipotency without God, we see he keeps proportion with that which he works upon: when God waters the earth, he opens not all the windows of heaven, as he did in the deluge, to pour on mountains and valleys all his waters in one heap; for he should then not refresh, but drown the earth: therefore he makes the clouds like a sieve, and divides the rain in hosts and millions of drops of dew, that every single flower and inch of earth may receive moistening, according to its proportion. If the sun were as low down as the clouds, it should, with heat, burn up every green herb, tree, rose, flower, and our bodies; and if it were the highest of planets, all vegetables on earth should perish through extreme cold. It may be a question, tho' the omnipotent power of God move the will invincibly and irresistibly, whether omnipotency puts forth all its strength on the will; or, whether the will be able to bear the swing of omnipotency in its full strength? If the fowler should apply all his force and strength to catch the bird alive, he should strangle and kill it. Divines say, That Christ's dominion in turning the will, is, *Dominium forte, sed suave;* strong, but sweet and alluring: no wonder, if he *carry the lambs in his bosom,* Isa. xl. 11. the warmness and heat of his bosom must sweetly allure the will. Drive a chariot as swiftly as an eagle flieth, and ye fire and break the wheels: knock crystal-glasses with hammers, as if ye were cleaving wood, and ye can make no vessels of them. This is not to deny that God's omnipotent power must turn the will, but to show how sweetly he leadeth the inclinations.

2. The Lord by wiles and art works upon the will, Hos. ii. 16. *I will allure her, and bring her to the wilderness, and speak to her heart.* The word of alluring is [*Heb.* pathah] *seductus, deceptus suit;* to be beguil-

ed;

CHRIST DYING AND DRAWING   353
        SINNERS TO HIMSELF.

led; and the Hebrew is, I will beguile, or deceive her; as Deut. xi. 26. *Take heed to yourselves, that your heart be not deceived.* So Pethi is the simple man, that is facile and easily perswaded. Psal. cxvi. 6. *The Lord preserveth the simple.* Then he saith, he will speak to her heart, [Heb. gnal] *super, secundum,* he will speak friendly to her; not according to the renewed heart, for it was not yet renewed; not according to the corrupt and unrenewed heart, for nothing that the Lord speaketh according to sinners, is suitable, but contrary to the renewed heart, and to internal persuading; but he speaketh all reason, according to the temper and natural frame of the heart, to convince and perswade that there is more reason in turning to God, than that the wit or engine of man can speak against it. Grace is *pia fraus,* a holy deceit, that, ere the soul be aware, it is catched; and tho' that be spoken of Christ, Cant. vi. 12. *Ere ever I was aware, my soul made me like the chariots of Amminadib;* yet it hath truth in this, that, 1. No unconverted man intends to be converted, till God convert him; because spiritual intention is a vital act of the soul living to God: no living man can put forth a vital act of life, till the Lord be pleased to give him a new life. 2. That spiritual love, alluring the soul, worketh by such art as cannot be resisted: hence, conversion, and being drawn to Christ, is termed by the name of *Charming;* even as turning off Christ is a bewitching, or killing with an evil eye, as we say, Gal. iii. 1. and so being drawn to God, is called a charming. And the wicked are rebuked for this, Psal. lviii. 4, 5. that being strangers to God, *they are like the deaf adder, that stoppeth her ear, and will not hearken to the voice of charmers,* (or singers, who sing as witches and inchanters do) *charming wisely.* There be two words that signify inchanting; the former is to *mutter with

                                                                a

*[Heb. lahash] musitare, submissa voce loqui, quod occultum veils. 2 Sam. xii. 19. So Isa. iii. 3. *The prudent and wise man hath such a name, as to charm and bewitch, as eloquent orators do, or exorcists and conjurers of spirits.*

a low voice, as they do to serpents, to take and kill them: the other is to †conjoin and associate in one, as witches do, things most contrary. Conversion to God, is, to be allured, bewitched, overcome with the art of heaven, that changeth the heart. And the Lord made Peter and the apostles fishers of men. Christ layeth out hooks and lines in the gospel, Luke v. 10. to catch men with hope, as fishes are taken. Christ so condescendeth to work upon the will, as with art, and unawares, the will is taken, and made sick of love for Christ, and the man intended no such thing; as sickness cometh on men beside their knowledge or intention: so Christ maketh himself and heaven so lovely, and such a proportion and similitude between the soul and his beauty, as he appears most desirable, taking, and alluring. Gal. iv. 20. *I desire to be present among you* (saith Paul) *and to change my voice:* I desire not to speak roughly, and with asperity, as I have written; but as a mother speaketh to her children, to allure you. The word of God is an arrow that kills afar off, and ere ye see it. There is a great difficulty to persuade a man, who is in another element, and without the sphere of the gospel's activity; as Christ and the natural man are in two contrary elements: there is required art for a man on the earth, to take a bird flying in the air; or for a man in a ship, or on the bank of the river, to catch a fish swimming in the element of the water. Christ lays out the wit, the art, and the wiles of free-grace to charm the sinner; but the sinner stops his ear: there is need of the witchcraft of heaven to do this. The love of Christ, and his tongue is a great inchantress: Ezek. xvi. 8. *I said unto thee, when thou wast dying in thy blood, Live.*

3. Christ

†[Heb. habar] conjugere, sociare, by inchanting, Deut. xviii. 11. Isa. xlvii. 9. Septuaginta. [Gr. pharmakotai, pharmakeuomene parà sophû.

3. Christ knoweth how to apply himself internally to the will. Suppose one were to persuade a stiff and inexorable man, and knew what argument would win his heart, he would use that. The will is like a great curious engine of a water-work, consisting of an hundred wheels, of which one being moved, it moveth all the ninety-nine beside; because this is the master-wheel, that stirreth all the rest. Now, the Lord knoweth how to reach down his hand to the bottom of the elective faculty; and that wheel being moved, without more ado, it draws all the affections, as subordinate wheels. If the key be not so fitted in the work, wards and turnings of it, as to remove the cross bar, it cannot open the door. Omnipotency of grace is so framed and accommodated by infinite wisdom, as that it can shoot aside the dissenting power, without any violence, and get open the door. If free-will be the workmanship of God, as we must confess, it is a needless arguing of Arminians and Jesuits to say, That free-will is essentially a power absolutely loosed from pedeterminating providence; so as whatever God doth on the contrary, it may do, or not do; it may nill, will, chuse, refuse, or suspend its action; for such a creature, so absolute, so sovereign and independent, as he that made it, cannot without violence to nature, turn, move, bow, determine and master it, in all its elective power, for his own ends, and as seemeth good to the potter, for the manifestation of mercy and justice, is to say, he that made the free-will, cannot have mercy on it; he that framed the clay-vessel, cannot use it for honour to dishonour, as he pleaseth; he that moulded and created the horologe, and all the pins, pieces and parts, hath not power to turn the wheels as he pleaseth.

4. Christ in external means accommodates himself so in the revealing of himself, as he thinks good.

   1.   In accommodating his influence with his word.
   2.   With externals of providence.

The

CHRIST DYING AND DRAWING SINNERS TO HIMSELF.

356

The breathings of the Holy Ghost go so along with the word, as the word and the Spirit are united, as if they were one agent; as sweet smells are carried thro' the air to the nose. The word is the chariot, the vehiculum, the horse; the Spirit the rider. The word the arrow, the Spirit steeleth and sharpeneth the arrow. The word the sword; the Spirit the steel-mouth and edge, that cutteth and *divideth asunder the soul and the spirit, the marrow and the joints*, Heb. iv. 12. It is the same Christ, in all his loveliness and sweetness, that is preached in the word, and conveyed to the soul; not God or Christ as abstracted from the word, as enthusiasts dream. And though the preacher add a ministerial spirit to the word, to cause Felix tremble; yet he is not master of the saving and converting Spirit. Golden words, tho' all gospel, and honeyed with heaven and glory, planting and watering, without the Spirit, are nothing.

In externals of providence, God chuseth,
1. *Means.*
2. *Time.*
3. *Disposition.*
4. *Anticipation of the sinner's intention.*
5. *Fit words.*

1. In means. God appears to Moses, acquainted with mountains and woods, in a bush which burnt with fire; to the wise men skilled in the motion of the heaven, in a new star; to Peter a fisher, in a draught of fishes.

2. He setteth a time, and takes the sinner in his month, Jer. ii. 24. *In his time of love,* Ezek. xvi. 8. *When he is ripe,* like the *first ripe in the fig-tree,* Hos. ix. 10.

3. *Often he chuseth in the furnace,* Hos. v. last verse, *I will return to my place.* Hebrew, *till they make defection or be guilty;* for the most part, man is not guilty in his own eyes, while he be as Manasseh was in the briars. The fire melting the silver portrait of a horse,

causes

causes it lose the figure of head, feet, legs, and turns all in liquid white water; and then the metal is ready to receive a far other shape, of a man, or any other thing: the man is ductile and bowable, and impartial, when God seals and stamps the rod; he is not so wedded to himself as before; it may be also, that mercies, and great deliverances, and favours, melt the man, and bring him to some gracious capacity to be wrought on by Christ.

4. Christ anticipates the current of the heart and intention. When Saul is on a banquet of blood, Christ outruns him, and turns him; all men are converted, contrary to their intentions: thousands are in a channel and current of high provocations, and they are in the fury of swelling over the banks; and Christ gets before them, to turn the current to another channel. Christ is swift, and they are all chased men that are converted. Sure, Matthew, that morning he came to the receipt of custom, minded nothing but money, and his count book, and had not a foreset purpose of Christ; and because intentions, purposes, counsels, are, as it were, essential to rational men, as men, and the refined'st acts of reason, and their noblest, and most angel-like works; and Christ catcheth sinners contrary to their intentions; and, in this sense, saves the sinner, blesses him, and gives him Christ, and heaven against his will, whether he will nor not, that is, whether he spiritually will or no, or whether he savingly intend his own conversion, or not.

5. There is one golden word, (and God is in the word) one good word, that is fit and dexterous, *hic & nunc*, Prov. xxv. 11. *A word fitly spoken,* (Heb. A word fitly spoken on his wheels) *is like apples of gold in pictures of silver.* Sure, Christ's words, to a sinner ripe for conversion, move on wheels, that is, in such order, as two wheels in one cart, they answer most friendly one to another in their motion, because Christ observeth due circumstances, of time, place, person, congruency with the will and disposition; as, Hos. ii. 14. and Solomon's, Eccl. xii. 10. *The preacher sought to find*

out

out acceptable words, Heb. words of will, or of good will; Christ was greater than Solomon, and is a higher preacher than he, and seeks out words to the heart, that burn the heart, Luke xxiv. 32. Sure, there is more of heaven, more life and fire, in these words to Matthew, *Follow me*; and to dying Jerusalem, *live*; than in ordinary words, the Hebrews call vain words. Isa. xxvi. 5. *A word of life.* Prov. xiv. 23 [*Heb.* debar shephathaim] these be words of wind, that are empty, and have no fruit; the words of the Lord, fitted for converting, are words of the heart, and words of power which want not the effect. They are words fit for the heart, Isa. xl. 2. Hos. ii. 14. Such words as teach the heart, Isa. liv. 13. John vi. 45. There is an uncreated word suitable for the heart, that goes along with the word spoken, and that meets with all the biasses, turnings, and contradictions of the heart, and takes the man; and no word but that only can do the business, there is a word that is with child of love; a word cometh from God, and 'tis a coal from the altar, that is before the Lord's throne, and it fires up all iron locks in the soul, that the will must yield. *The woman of Samaria*, heareth but these words, *I am he that talketh with thee;* and her will is burnt with a strong necessity of love; she must leave her water-pot, and, for joy, go and tell tidings in the city, *Come and see, I have found the Messiah.* Christ maketh a short preaching to Magdalene, and in his own way saith, but, Mary; and Christ himself is in that word, her will is fettered with love. Peter makes a sermon, Acts ii. and there be such coals of paradise in his words, that three thousand hearts must be captives to Christ, and cry, *What shall we do to be saved?* Every key is not proportioned to every lock, nor every word fit to open the heart.

But though Christ speak to men in the grammar of their own heart and calling, I am far from defending the congruous vocation of Jesuits, once maintained by Arminus, and his disciples, at the conference at Hague; but now, for shame, forsaken by Arminians.

For

CHRIST DYING AND DRAWING SINNERS TO HIMSELF.

For the Jesuits take this way; asking the question, How cometh it to pass, that of the two men equally called, and drawn to Christ, and as they dream (but it is but a dream) affected and instructed with habitual and preventing grace of four degrees, the one man believes, and is converted; the other believes not, but resists the calling of God? They answer, Christ calleth, and draweth the one man, when he foresees he is better disposed, and shall obey; as his free-will being in good blood, after sleep, and a good banquet, and fitter to weigh reasons, and compare the way of godliness with the other way: and he calleth the other, though, both in regard of grace and nature, equal to him that is converted, when he foresees he is in that order of providence, and accidental indisposition of sadness, sleepiness, hunger, and extrinsical dispositions of mind, that he shall certainly resist; and both these callings are ordered and regulated by the two absolute decrees of election and reprobation from eternity.

The Arminians answer right-down, The one is converted, because he wills, and consents; whereas he might, if it pleased him, dissent and refuse the calling of God: and the other is not converted, because he will not be converted, but refuses; whereas he hath as much grace as the other, and may, if he will, draw the actual co-operation of grace (the habitual he hath equally, in as large a measure as the other) and be converted, and believe; nor is there any cause of this desparity in the man converted, and the man not converted, in God, in his decree, in his free-grace, but in the will of the one, and the not willing of the other.

Our divines say, 1. There never were two men equal in all degrees, as touching the measure and ounces of habitual saving internal grace; yea, that the never-converted man had never any such grace.

2. That the culpable and moral cause, why the one is not converted rather than the other, is his actual resistance, and corruption of nature, never cured

by

by having grace; but the adequate, physical, and only separating cause, is, 1. The decree of free election, drawing the one effectually, not the other. 2. Habitual saving grace, seconded with the Lord's efficacious actual working in the one, and the Lord's denying of habitual and actual grace to the other; not because the will of the creature casts the balance, but because the *Lord hath mercy on the one, because he will*, and leaves the other to his own hardness, *because he will*; and that the separating cause is not from the running, willing, and sweating of the one, and the not-running, and not-willing of the other; but from the free, unhired, independent, absolute grace of Christ.

But the Jesuits congruous calling we utterly reject, 1. Because this is the Pelagian way, sacrilegiously robbing the grace of God; for the Lord foreseeth, this man placed in such circumstances and course of providence will believe, the other will not, because he will do so, and the other will not do so; and both the placing of the one in such an opportunity, and his willing believing, and the other man's nilling not-believing, is in order before the fore-knowledge, and far more before the decree of God and his actual grace; and therefore free-will is the cause why the one is converted, not the other, for both had equal habitual grace; and the one is not to give thanks for his conversion comparatively, more than the non-converted, but to thank his own free-will. 2. The object of their fancy of their new middle science, is a foreseen providence, of the conversion of all that are willing to be converted, and voluntary perseverance in grace; and the non-conversion and final impenitency of all the wicked that are willing to refuse Christ; and these two go before the prescience, before the decrees of election and reprobation; so as God is necessitated to chuse these, and no other; and to pass by these, and no other. Whatever hath a future being before any decree of God, cannot by any decree be altered or otherwise disposed of than it is to be; so the Lord, in all things decreed, and that come to pass contingently, must have nothing

but

but an after-consent, and an after-will to approve them, when they were now all future before his decree: this is to spoil God of all free-will, free-decrees, liberty and sovereignty in his decrees, and that men's free-will may be free and independent, to lay God's freedom of election and reprobation under the creature's feet. 3. Jesuits dream, that Christ cannot conquer the will to a free consent, except he lie in wait to catch the man when he hath been at a fat banquet after cups, hath slept well, is merry; and when he sees the man is in a good blood, then he draws and invites, and so catches the man: and when he seeth the reprobate in a contrary ill blood, though he seriously will and intend their salvation, and gave his Son to die for them, yet then he draws, when he foresees they by the dominion of free-will shall refuse; and he draws neither after, nor before, but at the time when he knows free-will is under such an ill hour, as it freely came under, without any act of God's providence and free decree, and in the which the called and drawn man shall certainly spit on Christ, and resist the calling of God. But this resolves heaven and hell, salvation and damnation, into such good or ill humours, and orders of providence, as a banquet, no banquet, a crabbed disposition, or a merry; whereas grace, which by an omnipotent and insuperable power removes the stony heart, can more easily remove these humours, and win the consent, when the man is decreed for glory: and besides that, all men unconverted, and in their own element of corrupt nature, are ill to speak to, and in a sinful blood of resisting, except Christ tread upon their iron neck and subdue it; and *he spreads the skirts of his love over Jerusalem at the worst*, Ezekl. xvi. 6, 8. Scripture is silent of such a manner of drawing, and the grace of Christ and his decree lies under no such hazard or lottery, as such imaginary dispositions or good humours, thousands being brought in to Christ in chains, in saddest afflictions: nor is grace, being a plant of heaven, a flower that grows out of such clay-ground.

Asser. 7. Christ draws by such a power (and this is

the

the last point in the drawing) that it is not in the power of man to resist him.

1. He draws by the pull of that same arm and power by which he *commanded light to shine out of darkness,* 2 Cor. iv. 6. by which he *raised the dead out of the graves.* Eph. i. 18, 19. *by the exceeding greatness of his power, and the mighty power by which he raised Christ from the dead.* Arminians answer, This was *omnipotency of working miracles;* but what was it to the salvation of the *Ephesians, and to the hope of their glory, to know with opened eyes such a power as Judas knew?* and can the dead chuse but be quickned and come out of the grave, when God raiseth them? Job. v. 25. That *vaga necessitas*, the strong moral necessity talked of by Jesuits, when strong moral motives work, is a dream there, for it may come short: a man quickned in the grave, and put to his feet, as Lazarus was, of necessity must come out; he will not lie down in the grave again, and kill himself: a man starving for hunger, when meat is set before him on any terms he desires, if he be in his right wits, will necessarily eat and not kill himself: but the necessity of saving souls, in the tender and loving mind of God in Christ, is much stronger; and if we consider the corruption of will, this fancied vaging necessity cannot so bow the will, but it is necessary that corrupt will dissent, rather than consent to Christ.

2. God taketh away all resisting, and the vitious and wicked power of resisting, he removeth the stony-heart, openeth blind eyes, removeth the vail that is over the heart in hearing or reading the scriptures. Ezek. xxxvi. 26. 2 Cor. iii. 16, 17. Deut. xxx. 6. Col. ii. 11. takes the man's sword, and armour from him, cuts off his arms, so as he cannot fight or resist you. It is true, Christ taketh not from David, Abraham, prophet, apostle, or from any men or angels that are to be saved, the natural created power of nilling and willing, *purum* TO *posse nolle, Christo trahente,* but he taketh away the moral, wicked, and godless disposition of resisting.

3. God

3. God layeth bonds on himself by, 1. Promise, 2. Covenant, 3. Oath, *to circumcise the heart of the chosen ones,* Deut. xxx. 6. *To put his law in their inward parts.* Jer. xxxi. 32, 33. *To give them one heart to fear God for ever, not to depart from God.* Jer. xxxii. 39. 40. Heb. viii. 6, 7, etc. *To bless them,* Heb. vi. 16, 17. 18. Gen. xx. 16, 17. Psalm lxxxix. 33--37. Heb. i. 5, 6. We cannot imagine that God will keep covenant, promise and oath, upon a condition, and with a reserve, that we give him leave so to do; that is as much as the Creator will be faithful, if the creature will be faithful: and there is nothing glorious in the gospel and 2d covenant above the law and 1st covenant, if God promise not to remove the power of resisting: for, if God do not promise to work our obedience absolutely, without any condition depending on our free-will, then must free-will be so absolutely indifferent, as it can suspend God from fulfilling his oath. Now, the law had a promise of life, *if ye do this, ye live eternally*; but God neither did work, nor was tied by the tenor of that covenant, to work in us to do, to will, to continue, to abide in *all written in the law of God* to the end; and therefore it was a broken covenant. Nor can Arminians make the covenant, gospel promise, and oath of God, so conditional as the law of work, or as the promise of giving the holy land to the seed of Abraham, upon condition of faith, because many could not enter in, because of unbelief; except Arminians and Jesuits prove, 1. That all that entered into the holy land, young and old, did believe, and were elected to salvation, redeemed and saved, as Caleb and Joshua were, as all that enter into the true promised land are believers; otherwise they die, are condemned, and can never see God, John iii. 18, 36. v. 16. Joh. xi. 26 and v. 24. Mark xvi. 16. Acts xv. 11. Acts xi. 17, 18. But the former is most evidently false in the history of Joshua and Judges; multitudes entered in who never believed, as multitudes entered not in who believed, as Moses and many others. And therefore,

from

from this, that many entered not in, because of unbelief; the Arminians shall never prove, that as God makes a promise of life eternal, that believers infallibly and only shall be saved, and unbelievers excluded: so God made a covenant and promise, that all these of Abraham's seed infallibly, and all these only should enter into the holy land, who should believe, as did Caleb and Joshua. I put all Arminians and Papists, and patrons of universal atonement, to prove, any such covenant or promise. 2. Let Arminians prove that faith and a new heart was promised to all Abraham's seed who were to enter into the holy land, as it is promised to all the elect who are saved, and enter into the kingdom of heaven, Ezek. xxxvi. 26. Jer. xxxi. 32, 33. Jer. xxxii. 39, 40. 3. That the promise of eternal rest in heaven was typified by conversion to Christ, and conversion upon condition of faith, as they say, but without ground. The holy land was promised to all Abraham's seed upon condition of faith, the like we say to all conditional promises of God made in scripture, that are as the legs of the lame unequally paralleled with the covenant of grace. Because this is the only answer adversaries can give, tho' it be as a parable in fools' mouths; let it be considered, 1. The difference between the first covenant which was broken, Jer. xxxi. 32, 33, 34. and the better covenant which is everlasting, and cannot be broken, Jer. xxxi. 35, 36, 37. and xxxii. 39, 40. Isa. liv. 10, 11. Isa. lix. 19, 20. Heb. viii. 6, 7, etc. is expressly holden forth to make the new covenant better than the old; but its close removed, for both are broken covenants by this reasoning. 2. When God promiseth the removing of an old and *stony-heart, and to give a new heart*; he promiseth to take away resisting in us, for nothing can resist Christ's drawing, but the stony and old heart. 3. The apostle's reason, Heb. vi. 13, 14, 15, 16. of the Lord's two immutable things, his oath and promise, is, *That we might have strong consolation and hope.* Now, this makes undeniably the consolation, tho' never so strong, the hope never so sure, to depend on our free-will; if

the

the sinner brew well, he drinks well: if he resist not grace, as he may, or accept it as God's free-will thinks good, he is a tutor and lord of his own hope and consolation. Christ cannot help him to determine his will, if so be he be a bad husband of his own nilling and willing, let him see to it. 4. It must be in him that willeth, and runneth, and deserveth well, as on the separating cause, that saveth or damneth, not in God that sheweth mercy; by this vain arguing of loose and fast free-will, doing and undoing, all at its pleasure, let Christ do his best.

Arg. 4. Whom God predestinateth, them he also calleth and glorifieth, as all the predestinated are indeclinably called and glorified, Rom. viii. 30. Acts xiii. 48. 1 Pet. i. 2. Now, by this, multitudes should be predestinate, who are never called and glorified, if they have it in their free and independent choice to resist the drawing of Christ.

Arg. 5. *God* (as Augustine saith) *hath a greater dominion over our wills, than we have over them ourselves;* as he is more master of the beings, so of the operations, (that are created beings) than the creature is; and so he must use the creature's operations at his own pleasure, otherwise he hath made a creature free-will, which is without the sphere of his own power; whereas the freest will of a king, the most sovereign and independent on earth, must run in his channel, Prov. xxi. 1.

Arg. 6. Christ's Lordship and Princedom through his resurrection, is in turning of hearts. Acts v. 31. Rom. xi. 23. Grace is stronger than devils, sin, hell and death, Rom. xiv. 4. Eph. iii. 20. Jude 24. 1 John ii. 14. 1 John iv. 4.

Arg. 7. If it must lie at our door more than Christ's, to apply the purchased redemption, and actually to be saved; then we share more, if not large, equally with Christ, in the work of our salvation; nor can the church pray, *Draw me, we shall run*: why should we pray for that which is in our own power, saith Augustine, for we are drawn, and may not run. 2. Why should Peter give thanks, rather than Judas, or another Peter, both were equally drawn; free-will lost the day with the one, and wins it to the other. 3. Christ must but play an after-game, and can do nothing, tho' with his soul he would save; but as free-will hath first done, so must it be. 4. Nor am I to trust to omnipotency of grace for conversion; for if I husband well nature's hability, the crop is my own. 5. I may engage the influence of free-grace to follow me, and grace leads not, draws not my will, I draw free-grace.

Arg. 8. If free-will be lord-carver of the sinner's being drawn to Christ, then the making good of the articles of the bargain and covenant between the Father and the Son, must depend on man's free-will. Now, 1. I know the covenant between the Father and the Son is expressed first, by simple prophecy or promise: the Father passeth the word of a king, Christ shall be his first-born, the flower of the family, an ensign of the people; nothing can stand good, if the free-will of Gentiles refuse to come under this Prince-royal's standard. The Father prophesieth and promiseth, Psal. lxxii. 8. Christ shall have *dominion from sea to sea, and from the river to the ends of the earth.* Psal. lxxxix. 25. *The Lord shall set his hand on the sea, and his right-hand on the rivers: he shall call God his Father, his God, the rock of his salvation.* Now, there must be a condition in this royal-charter, in Christ's *Magna Charta*, nothing can be done, even when Christ goes up to a mountain, and lifts up his royal ensign, and standard of love, and cries, *All mine, come hither*: and when the people flock in about him, except free-will, as independent as God, say Amen; and yet it far rather may say, Nay, and refuse the bargain.

2. The Father bargaineth by asking and giving, Psal. ii. 8. *Ask of me, and I will give thee.* Christ must be an heir, by man's will, not by his Father's goodness: if Christ's suits, and demands, *Father, give me the ends of the earth, and Britain for my inheritance,* depends upon such an absolute *Ay,* and *No* of man's free-will, as may cast the bargain; whereas our consent was not

sought,

sought, nor were we called to council, when the Father bargained to make us over to his Son.

3. The Father bargains by way of work, and hire or wages, to *give his seed to his Son,* Isa . liii. 10. *When he shall make his soul an offering for sin, he shall see his seed*: this is not a bare sight of his seed, but it is an *enjoying of them; he shall see his seed, he shall prolong his days, the pleasure of the Lord shall prosper in his hand.* We cannot say, it depends on men, that Christ speed well in having a numerous seed, and that wages be paid to Christ for his sore work of laying down his life to save his people, except we be more play-maker than God in this covenant.

Arg. 9. The scripture right-down determineth this controversy, Rom. ix. *No man hath resisted his will; and it is not in him that willeth.* Augustine useth three adverbs in the Lord's manner of turning the heart; *emnipotenter, indecinabiliter, insuperabiliter;* omnipotently, inclinably, and without short-coming.

Use 1. O how sweet and strong is the grace of Christ; it is a conquering thing, Col. i. 11. *Strengthened with all might, according to his glorious power.* 2 Cor. x. 4. *The weapons of our warfare are not carnal, but mighty through God.* Were they mighty through angels and men, that were but one creature storming another: but when Christ besiegeth a soul, who can raise the siege? v. 6. *We bring down every height,* [Gr. păn psòma,] they go not to council of war, to advise upon quarters. 2. They cannot flee; *for every thought is brought captive to the obedience of Christ.* Christ riding on his horse of the gospel, and strength of free-grace, is swift and speedy, and hath excellent success. Rev. vi. *He went out* [Gr. kaì nil ŏn kaì hina nikese] *both conquering, and that he might conquer.* Christ shoots not at the rovers, to come short, or beside the mark; his arrows of love are sharp and conquering. The spouse is out of her own element, and sick, and pained with love, when she wants his presence, and cannot dissemble, nor hide it, nor command herself,

Cant.

Cant. iii. no more than a sick person can master death, or a swooning. Cant. v. 6. *My soul departed out of me:* drink once of this strong wine of his love. O death, the lion's teeth, burning-quick, all these torments are nothing to the love of Christ. O Christ, we cannot forsake. David's key is strong to open all hearts, to open hell, and bring in a new heaven of love to the soul. Natural habits and powers are strong, fire cannot but cast out heat, lions cannot but prey upon lambs, wicked habits are strong devils, and cannot chuse but be destroying devils. The coals of the fire of Christ's love burn not by election. 2 Cor. v. 14. *The love of Christ constraineth us;* there is a piece of eternity of heaven in the breasts of the martyrs of Jesus Christ. Abraham must go when he is called: Lydia cannot keep the door, when love removes the handle of the bar, and must be in. The Lord cast in fire-works of love, in at the windows of the apostles' souls: O, their nets and callings, and all their all became nothing, they must leave all and follow Christ.

We must be loggish and crabbed timber, that take so much of omnipotency, or else we cannot be drawn to the Son. Men think it but a step to Christ and heaven; ah! we have but a poor and timorous suspicion of heaven, by nature; it is no less than a creation, to be drawn to Christ. 2. We are needy sinners, and need as much mercy, as would save the devils; as may be gathered from Hebrews ii. 16. 3. We are, by nature, as good clay and metal to be vessels of revenging justice, and firewood that could burn, as kindly in hell, as devils, or any damned whatsoever. 4. Not only at our first conversion must we be drawn; but the spouse prays, Cant. i. to be drawn; there's need that Christ use violence to save us, while we be in heaven; for Christ hath said, Mat. vii. 14. *Strait is the gate, and narrow is the way that leadeth unto life.* I grant Antinomians *who loose us from all duties, and say *Christ*

hath

---

*Crispe, vol.1.Serm.4. page 110, 111. Antinomians reject the

hath done all to our hand, make little necessity of drawing at all. For Crispe saith, *The strictness of the way,* Mat. vii. 14. *is not the strictness of the conversation; but all a man's own righteousness must be cut out of the way, otherwise it is a broader way than Christ allows of.* I confess, if in this one point all the strictness of the way to heaven were; then the way, 1. should be strait and narrow only to those that trust in their own righteousness; but I hope, there is much more strictness than in that one point; as in mortifying idol-lusts, loving our enemy, feeding him when he is hungry, suffering for Christ, bearing his cross, denying ourselves, becoming humble as children, being lowly and meek, and following Christ's way in that.

2. Christ speaks of two ways, a wide and a broad way, and a narrow way. Now if the narrow way be all in a quitting our own righteousness only, as Crispe saith, perverting the text, then all the latitude and easiness of the broad way, must be, that all the world that run to hell, they follow no sins sweet and pleasant to the flesh; no delightful lusts, contrary to the duties of the first and second table; their only sin is to trust in their own righteousness, which is against both law and gospel.

3. Christ commandeth his hearers to enter in this strait way, which is clearly a way of holy walking, no less than of renouncing our own righteousness. For Christ, both in the foregoing, and in the following words, urgeth duties; as, not to judge rashly, verse 1. to eye our own faults, rather than our brother's, ver. 3, 4, 5. not to prophane holy ordinances, verse 6. to *pray assiduously,* ver. 7, 8, 9, 10. *to do to others, as we would they should do to us,* verse 12. *to be good trees, and bring forth good fruit*; not to content ourselves with an empty dead faith, as Dr. Crispe, and Libertines do; but to *do*

the narrow way that leads to life; their exposition of Mat. vii. 14. *rejected, as false and fleshly.*

do the will of our heavenly Father, to the end of the chapter.

But let the reader observe, as we do detest all confidence in our inherent holiness, and all merit, and deny that our strictest walking can in any sort justify us before God; so Libertines, in all their writings and conference, cast shame upon strict walking, as Popish, Pharisaical, and legal; and will have this our christian liberty, that holy walking is not so much as no part of our justification, which thing we grant; but (saith (a) Crispe) *All our sanctification of life is not a jot of the way of a justified person to heaven;* the flat contrary of which Paul saith, Eph. ii. 20. *For we are his workmanship, created in Christ Jesus unto good works, which God hath before ordained, that we should walk in them.* That which we should walk in, must be a jot and more of our way to heaven. And the same Crispe (b) saith, 'Believers are kept in holiness, sincerity, simplicity of heart; but all this hath nothing to do with the peace of their soul, and the salvation and justification thereof.' See, he confounds salvation and justification; as if sincere walking were no way to salvation, because it is no way to justification, and because 'tis not the meritorious cause of our peace and salvation; for Christ alone is so the cause: but therefore must it be no condition of salvation? It is a prophane and loose consequence. 'But do not Libertines teach, that no man is saved, but those that walk holily; and that sanctification is the unseparable fruit and effect of justification?

Answ. They say it in words, but fraudulently. 1. Because all sanctification to them, all repentance, all mortification, all new-obedience, is but an apprehension, that Christ hath done all these for them, and that is their righteousness; and so Christ repented for them, and mortified sin for them, and performed all active obedience for them. Now, this sanctification is faith,

not

(a) Vol. 1. ibid. page 89. (b) Serm. 1. page 22.

not the personal walking in newness of life that Christ requires.

2. This sanctification, by their way, is not commanded by God, nor are believers obliged to it, under danger of sinning against God; for though the imputation of Christ's righteousness (saith Crispe) (c) 'all our sins are so done away from us, that we stand as Christ's own person did, and doth stand in the sight of God, nor is there a body of sin in Christ.' I assume, but Christ is not obliged to our personal holiness, that were an impossible imagination.

(2) All acts of sanctification to the justified person are free; he may do them, yea, he may not do them, and can be charged with no sin for the omitting of them; for he is not under any moral law, and where 'there is no law, there is no sin,' (say, Libertines.)

(3) 'Men are kept in holiness, sincerity, simplicity of heart,' saith Crispe (d) What is that, *kept*? They are mere patients in all holy walking, and free-will does nothing, but the Spirit immediately works all these in us? If therefore we omit them, it must be the fault of the Spirit, as Crispe speaketh, not our fault; nor ought we to pray, but when the Spirit moves us, as before you heard: so that this sanctification is not any holiness opposite to the flesh, and to sin, forbidden in the law of God, but a sort of free, and arbitrary and immediate acting of the Spirit; in the omission of which acts, the justified person no more sins against God, than a tree, or a stone, which are creatures under no moral law of God, when these creatures do not pray, nor love Christ, nor out of sanctified principles abstain from these acts of adultery, murder, oppression†, which being commit-

ted,

NUMB. IV.   3 E

(c) Ser. 1. p. 18.   (d) vol. 1. Ser. 1. p. 22.

†It was the old error of the Libertines, of Antonious Pocquius priest, as Calvin saith, instruct, ad Libertinos, cap. 23. in opuscu. p. 450. Pocquius, existimabam me aliquid intelligere, nee quicquam

inteligo:

ted, would make rational men under guiltiness and sin before God.

(4) Town's assertion of grace, pag. 56, 57, and 58. p. 156. 'A believer is as well saved already, as justified by Christ, and in him. p. 159. Divines say, our life and salvation is inchoate; but they speak of life, as it is here, subjective, p. 160. Quantum ad nos spectat, or in respect of our sense and apprehension, here in grace, our faith, knowledge, and sanctification is imperfect; but in regard of imputation and donation, (p. 162.) our righteousness is perfect; and p. 160. He that believeth [Gr. echei] hath life, not he shall have it, or hath it in hope.'

Answ. If we have glory, really, actually, perfectly, but we want it only in sense; we have the resurrection from the dead also, actually and perfectly, and we are risen out of the grave already, and we want the resurrection only in sense: for sure, by merit, and Christ's death, we have as really the resurrection from the dead, as we have glory and life; and the one we have as really as the other; so we want nothing of the reality of heaven, but sense. But we are not yet before the throne, nor risen from the dead, nor locally above the visible heavens; except they say, as Famulists do, and as Hymeneus and Phyletus did, that the resurrection is a spiritual thing in the mind, and heaven is but a spiritual sense of Christ, and that Christ is heaven, and the life to come is within the precincts of this life: this were to deny a life to come, a heaven,

a

intelligo: Deus enim intellectus meus est, & virtus mea, & falus mea. Calvin answers excellently, Homo quidem fidelis, fe nihil ex fe ipso intelligere censet; sed an propteria debet occulos claudere, nec quid intueatur, ut vult iste insanus. ' A man (saith Calvin) in Christ, judgeth that he understandeth nothing of himself, (and so that he can neither pray nor believe, without the Spirit) but shall he therefore close his eyes, that he may understand nothing at all, as this frantic man imagines?'

a hell, a resurrection; which Antinomians will be found to do.

This is one special ground is much pressed by Mr. Town, and the generality of Libertines, to wit, That holy walking before God, is neither way to heaven, nor condition, nor means of salvation; in regard, we are not only in hope, but actually saved, when we are first justified; and as really saved and passed from death to life, when we believe, as we are said, Ephes. ii. 6. *To be raised up with Christ, to sit together with him in heavenly places.* And therefore holy walking can be no means, no way, no entrance, no condition of our possession of the heavenly kingdom; and therefore no wonder they reject all sanctification, as not necessary, and teach men to loose the reins to all fleshly walking.

But, 1. Rom. viii. 24. *We are saved by hope*, then we are not actually saved, but the *jus*, the right through Christ's merits to life eternal, is ours, and purchased to us. The born heir of a prince, is in hope a prince, but he comes not out of the womb with the crown on his head. Christ coming out of grave, which is the womb and loins of death, as the *first begotten of the dead*, is born a King, Acts v. 31. and all that are born of this Father of ages, Isa. ix. 6. his seed are heirs annexed with Christ the first heir, Rom. viii. 17. but heirs under non age, and minors, and waiting for the living and the crown, they have it not in hand. Rom. viii. 24. *Hope that is seen is not hope; for what a man seeth, why doth he yet hope for it?* Verse 25. *But if we hope for what we see not, then we do with patience wait for it.* Hence I argue, what we wait for, and see not, that we do not actually enjoy. But we hope for salvation, Rom. v. 2. 1 John iii. 1, 2, 3. The proposition is scripture; no man can hope for that which he enjoys already. 2. We can be no otherwise said to be saved, than the believer is said *to be passed from death to life,* and to be *risen again with Christ, and to sit with Christ in heavenly places.* For as we are saved and glorified in hope only

only, not actually; so we are passed from death to life, and sit with Christ in heavenly places, and are partakers of the resurrection, in hope only, or in our flesh, in regard our flesh is in heaven in Christ, who hath investment of heaven for us; as a man getteth a stone or a twig in his hand, and that is to get the land, but yet he may want real possession. Christ's presence in heaven is real in law, we are there with him. But it cannot infer our personal and bodily presence, and real resurrection, which we hope for, and want, not only in sense, but really. For we are not in this life immortal, beyond death and sickness, and burying and corruption actually; nor yet are we in glory, that which we shall be, when Christ our life and head shall appear: For, 1. We yet groan as sick creatures in tabernacles of clay, 2 Cor. v. 1, 2. and carry about with us sick and dying clay; and Christ promiseth, *That of all that the Father gives him, he will lose nothing, but raise them from the dead*, but that is, not in this life, but *at the last day*, John vi. 39.

3. Such as are really and actually saved, can *neither marry nor be given in marriage, neither can they die any more,* (marrying and dying are bloodfriends together) *but are as the angels in heaven*, Luke xxii. 36, 37, 38. *Their vile bodies are changed, and are fashioned and made like the glorious body of our Saviour the Lord Jesus Christ*, Phil. iii. 20, 21. and shall be heavenly bodies, spiritual, and as the stars of the heaven in glory, 1 Cor. xv. 40, 41, 42, 43. But we are not in that condition in this life; this *corruptible hath not put on incorruption, nor this mortal immortality.* Then, as we are saved in hope, and have *jus ad rem*, a full right to life eternal, and the resurrection of our bodies, in regard that the price is paid for us, a complete and perfect ransom, even the blood of the Son of God is given for us; and so we are saved in hope, 2. In law and *jure*. But sure we have not actual possession of the kingdom, in the full income, rent, and complete
harvest

harvest of glory, but only grapes, and the first fruits of Canaan.*

4. It is too evident to half an eye, that when Antinomians say we are actually saved, and perfectly freed from sin in this life, and as perfectly sinless as Christ himself; that their meaning is, that which the old Libertines in (a) Calvin's time said, 1. That our deliverance from sin in Christ is, *in infernali spiritualitate*, (as Calvin speaketh) in such a devilish and hellish

spirituality;

*Henry Nicholas of Low-Germany taught the same doctrine, a hundred years ago, chapter 1. Sent. 9. For behold in this present day is the glorious coming of the Lord Jesus Christ, with the many thousands of his saints; he cometh manifested, which hath set himself now upon the seat of his majesty, for to judge in this same day, which the Lord hath ordained, the whole world with equity. And chap. 35. Sent. 8. Behold, in this present day, is this scripture fulfilled, Isaiah xxvi. Dan. xii. 4. Esdras vii. 1 Thessalonians iv. Matthew xxiv. and xxv. Luke xvii. Acts i. Matthew xxiv. Revelations xiv. according to the testimony of the scripture, the raising up, and resurrection of the Lord's dead cometh also to pass presently in this same day, through the appearing of the coming of Christ in his majesty, etc. So this man denieth any life to come, or any resurrection; to which way Antinomians incline.

(a) Calvinus *in opusc. in instruc. advers. Libertinos.* cap. 23. p. 460, 461. and cap. 22. p. 458, 459. Pocquius in Libello, Scriptum est, non tendes ad malum, cavens ne adulteres in verbo, *(id est, in litera scriptura)* sicut multi *(non justificati)* saciunt. Talis ego fui, sed omnia remissa sunt. Nam scriptum est abstinete vos ab adulteratione, ut positis vas vestrum in sanctificatione et honore possidere, cum simus mortui legi per corpus Christi, ut alterius simus, qui suscitatus est ex mortuis, ut fructificemus Deo viventi, non igiturestis in carne. Quare relinquamas veterem Adamum, id est, animam nostram viventem, et veniamus ad rem majorem, id est, ad spiritum dictum enim suit. Adae quod moreretur, et revera mortuus est, nunc vivificati sumus cum secundo Adam, qui est Chrstus non cerendo amplius peccatum, quia est mortuum.

(b) Henry

spirituality; as that wicked priest *Anto Pocquius* said, was in judging neither murders, adulteries, perjury, lying, oppression, to be sins, when once the pardoned and justified person committed such villanies, because the Spirit of God was in him, and took sense from him. 2. Because the justified person is made one with Christ, one person; or, as Antinomians speak, we are christed, and made one with him, and he one with us, or incarnate and made flesh in us; (b) and (c) the new creature, or the new man, mentioned in the gospel, is not meant of grace, but of Christ; and (d) by love, 1 Cor. xiii. 13. *and by the armour mentioned* Eph. vi. *are meant Christ.* So said that vile man Pocquius, that we and Christ are made one, as Eve was formed out of a rib of Adam's side; he meaneth one person. 3. Man following his lusts, and committing of sin with greediness, is made spiritual and mortified by Christ's death: so also (e) Pocquius, who said, To sin without sense, is the spiritual life we are restored to in Christ: so that Antinomians aim at this, that whatever the regenerate do, they are as free of sin before God, as Christ or the elect angels; and this is the begun spiritual life. 4. Libertines in Calvin's time (f) said, That life eternal was in this life, and that the resurrection was past; as *Hymeneus and Phyletus, who made shipwreck of the faith, because a

man

(b) Henry Nicholas, chap. 34. Christ hath anointed me, with his godly being; he hath godded me. (c) Rise, Reign, Er. 11. (d) Er. 7. (e) Er. 8. Pocquius 16. apud Calvin, in opusc. 463. Obdormivit, (Christus) in cruce, & suit apertum latus ut costa reperiretur que est femina, ecclesia dicta, & unio (personalis) totius naturae humanae, and sieri omnes in uno membro cujus Christus est caput. (f) Pocquius 16. p. 461. Scriptum est omnia munda mundis, qui autem fide purificatus est, totuis gratus Deo. Calvinus ibid. Putidus iste hanc sententiam eo applicat ut latrocinia, scortationes, homicidia, pro mundis et santis rebus habeantur.

*Divers Antinomians deny the life to come, and the resurrection of the dead, as did Hymeneus and Phyletus.

man knows his soul is an immortal spirit living in the heavens, and because Christ hath taken away the opinion and sense of death, by his death, and so hath restored us to life. Mistress Hutchison and her disciples, the Famulists, of (g) New-England denying the immortality of the soul, and the resurrection of these our mortal bodies, affirmed, All the resurrection they knew, was the union of the soul with Christ in this life. I never could observe any considerable difference between the soul heresies of the Famulists of New-England, and of Old-England, either by the writings of, or conference with them, nor of either, from the damnable doctrine of Hymeneus and Phyletus, and the old Libertines, who said, The resurrection was past.

Use 3. The drawing of sinners to Christ, if he draw so sweetly and with such a loving condescension, cannot be a violence offered to free-will, by which the natural and concreated liberty of the creature is destroyed; for there remains a natural indifferency, by which reason and judgment proposeth to the elective faculty divers objects, that have no natural connexion with will; so as the will should be bowed to any of them, as the one fire casteth out heat, and the sun light, and the stone falleth downward. 'Tis true, in drawing of a sinner, Christ is carried into the heart with a greater weight of love, and a stronger sway of grace, than any other object whatsoever, and with so prevailing a sway, as masters the elective power, that it cannot will to refuse; yet it destroys not the elective power, because this *non posse repudiare*, impotency or unwillingness to reject Christ, (to speak so) is a most free, vital, kindly, voluntary, and delighting impotency, and comes from the bowels and innate power of will, and this is the virgin-liberty and power of will. But again, because
                                    Christ's

(g) Rise, Reign, Ruin, the body of the story, p. 59, 60, 62.

Christ's drawing is efficacious and strong, and carries the business with a heavenly and loving prevalency, the Arminian and Jesuitical indifferency that new Pelagians ascribe to free-will, as an essential property of it, by which when God, and the pull and nerves of the right arm of Jesus Christ in his free-grace, have done what they can to draw a free agent, nevertheless the man may refuse to be drawn, if so it please free-will, tho' it displease God, and cross his decree and most hearty and natural desire, is a wicked fancy.

1. Because, by this dream, God hath not a dominion and sovereign power over the created will of man, to determine it for his own ends, and to make use of it for the glory of his grace, tho' the Lord with his soul desire so to do; but the creature hath an absolute, free and independent power, to cross the desire of the Lord's soul, for its own destruction, and a far other end, which God intends but at the second hand, and contrary to his natural and essential desire (as they teach) to save his creature, to wit, that revenging justice may be declared in the eternal destruction of the most part of mankind; whereas it was his desire, that not only the most part, but that all and every single man and angel (the fallen devils not excepted) should be eternally saved.

2. We believe, that God the first cause, as he decrees to all things that were from eternity in a state of poor possibility: so as of themselves they might be, or might not be; a futurition, or *a shall be*, or a non-futurition, or *a shall never be*: so he is midwife to his own blessed decrees, and determines all created causes to bring forth these effects that were in the womb of his holy decrees; or all things that were to be, and do fall out in time, were births from eternity, that lay in the womb of the decree of God; evils of punishment, or sins as permitted, Acts xvii. 30. are not excepted. So Zephaniah, chap. ii. [Heb. *beterem ledeth hok*] willeth the people to flee to God, *before the decree, that is with child, bring*

forth

CHRIST DYING AND DRAWING SINNERS TO HIMSELF.

forth the birth: then God must in time open and unlock free-will for all its actions. Isa. xliv. 7. *And who, as I, shall call and set it in order for me, since I appointed or decreed the ancient people? and the things that are coming, or shall come? let them shew unto them.* So God taketh this to him as proper to appoint things to come; and no supposed god, nor power whatever, can share with him in it: and let any man answer and give a reason why of ten thousand possible worlds of infinite things, actions of men and angels, that from eternity of themselves were only possible, and might be, or not be; so many of them, not more, not fewer, received a futurition, that they shall come to pass, and so fall out in time; and others remained only possible, and came never further to being, and never fall out, but from the only free decree and will of God, who conceived in that infinite womb of his eternal counsel and wisdom, such things shall be, such things shall only remain possible, and shall never be, nor never come to pass? As it was decreed that wicked men should break the legs of the two thieves crucified with Christ, and that they should not break Christ's legs; yet the breaking of Christ's legs was in itself, and from eternity no less possible, than the breaking of the legs of the fellow-sufferers with him; but God's only decree gave a futurition and an actual being to the one, not to the other: so are all the actions, the chusings, refusings, nillings, willings of free-will determined to be, or not to be; and come to pass or not come to pass, according as they were births conceived in the mother-decree of God from eternity, Psal. cxxxix. 16. *In thy book were all my members written, which in continuance were fashioned, when as yet there were none of them.*

3. He *that works all things according to the counsel of his will,* as Eph. i. 11. He, *of whom, and through whom, and for whom are all things,* as Rom. xi. 36. *He that made all things for himself,* Prov. xvi. 4. *even the wicked for the ill day, and for whose pleasure all things are,* Rev. iv. 11. must be such an efficient and author,

such

such a final cause of all, as shapeth a particular being to things, actions, and every creature, as their determinate being must be from him*. If the being of the actions of free-will, rather than their not being, be from free-will, not from God, but in a general, universal, or disjunctive influence; that is, in such a way as, whatever God decreed from eternity, touching Peter's acts of willing or nilling, embracing or repudiating Christ, or what way soever the Lord shape and mould his influence and concurrence in time, either the one or the other may fall out, and Peter may embrace Christ or not embrace him, and so may Judas, and all men and angels; then shall I say, The king's heart, and his nilling and willing, is in the hand of his own heart; so the king turns his own heart whithersoever he determines his own will; and not, as Solomon saith, Prov. xxi. 1. *in the hands of the Lord*: and the creature is master of work; angels, men, free and contingent, necessary and natural causes, are mint-masters to coin what actions they will, this or this; election and reprobation, vessels of mercy and of wrath, believing or not believing, are in the hands of angels and men; the creature shall be both potter and clay: the great Lord and former of all things, and the vessel for God's conditional decree, his collateral and universal, his disjunctive and dependent influence, hath no force to cast the scale of free-will to willing, and so to salvation, election, inscription in the book of life; more than to nilling, damnation, and blotting out, or not inrolling in the book of life; but is indifferent to either, is determined and bowed by the free-will of man to which of the two shall seem good to lord will, and the Lord cannot turn the heart whithersoever he will. Which close sets up fortune, independent and absolute contingency, and a supremacy and principality of working every effect and event on both sides of the sun, and above the sun, in order of nature, by the creature, before and without the

efficiency

*Heb. [Col pagnal Jehovah lemagnancho.]

efficiency of the cause of causes, and the intention, or counsel of God, yea, it involves the Lord in a fatal chain; he must either concur, or the creature disposeth of the militia, laws, and affairs of heaven and earth, without the King of ages. 1. I cannot make prayers to the Lord, to determine my will to his obedience, not to lead me into temptation. 2. I cannot thank his free-grace for either. 3. I cannot intrust God with working in me to will and to do: nor, 4. Comfort myself in the Lord: 5. Nor be patiently submissive to God, under all my calamities that befal me, by the hand of men, devils, or creatures. Why? The Lord can do no more than he can; he had no more will nor counsel before time, nor hand and disposing of the business in time, for all these, than for the just contradicent of these; say the lord-patrons of indifferent and so absolute a free-will. 6. How doth Jacob pray that the Lord would give his sons favour with the governor of Egypt, whom he believed to be a heathen; and pray that God would change his brother Esau's heart; and Esther and her maids pray that God would grant her favour in the eyes of Ahasuerus, if God have not in his hand power to turn their hearts from hatred to favour, as pleaseth him? 7. The Lord takes on him to turn men's free-will in mercy or judgment, as pleaseth him: Pro. iii. *My son, forget not my law, so shalt thou find favour* (verse 4) *with God and man.* The Lord *gave Joseph favour in the eyes of Potiphar,* Gen. xxxix. 21. *God brought Daniel in favour and tender love with the prince of the eunuchs,* Dan. i. 9. *The Lord made his people to be pitied by all those that carried them captives,* Psal. cvi. 46. *The Lord turned the hearts of the Egyptians, to hate his people,* Psal. cv. 25. War and peace are from the free-wills of men, as second causes; yet the Lord saith, according to his absolute dominion, Isa. xlv. 7. *I form the light, and create darkness; I make peace and create evil.* And Isa. vii. 8. *The Lord shall hiss for the fly that is in the uttermost part of the river of Egypt, and for the bee that is in the land of*

Assyria,

Assyria, and they shall come, and shall rest all of them in the desolate valleys. Isa. x. 6. *I will send the Assyrian against an hypocritical nation.* So, Jer. i. 15, 16. Isa. xiii. 1, 2, 3. Chap. xv. 1, 2, 3. & xvii. 1, 2. 3. & xix. 1, 2, 3, 4. Now, God could not be the author of war and peace, as God and sovereign all disposer, if it were in the indifferent arbitriment and free election of men, that war should freely issue from man's free-will; so as God could neither decree, command, ordain it in his providence, threaten it in his justice, foresee it in his wisdom, and foretell it by his prophets, determine it by his free-grace, except the free-will of nations and men first pass an act in this poor low court of clay, in the heads and breasts of little lords, free-will-men, and make sure work on earth of its coming to pass; and so the Almighty Sovereign of all things should have the second conditional vote of an after-game in heaven, of all actions contingent and managed by free-will of angels and men, such as peace, war, honour, infamy, riches, poverty, health, sickness, life, or violent death, by sword, gibbet, poison, etc. hatred, favour, learning, ignorance, faith, unbelief, obedience to God, disobedience, salvation, damnation, long or short life, failing, selling, buying, eating, speaking, joying, weeping, building, planting, praying, praising, curing, Christ's coming of the seed of David, the use of prophets, prophesying, etc.

Object. 'Is it not contrary to the nature of freedom, to be determined by a foreign and external agent, and that by a power stronger than the free-will can resist or master? If ye with a stronger power tie a sword to my arm, and strongly and irresistibly throw my arm and sword both, to kill a man, can I be the murderer of this man?'

Answ. All the question here is, whether the Lord's freedom and dominion in these actions of clay-vessels, or men's, must stand? We had rather contend for the Lord and grace, than for the creature and free-will.

2. It is contrary to the nature of freedom, to be determined with one sort of determination, not with another. 1. With a such determination natural, as is

in

in the stone to fall down, the sun to give light; 'tis true; but now the assumption is false. 2. Should we suppose, that he who ties the sword to your arm, so as he carries along with him in that motion your reason, judgment, elective power, so as you join in your arbitrary and free election, yea and with delight and joy, (which is somewhat more than free-will) to strike with the sword, and he that lifts both arm and sword did not thwart or cross your internal vital, and elective power, as the Lord moves the will in natural acts, as acts, and all sinful deviations from a law, he should not free you from the guilt of murder: and so yet the assumption is false; for Christ so moves and determines the will to believe as all the in-works and vital wheels of will, reason, judgment, freedom, are so moved with such an accommodation and fit and congruous attemperation to free-will, as it goes along sweetly, gladly, freely with the grace of Christ in conversion; and too gladly, and willingly in acts to which wickedness and murder are annexed; as there can be no other straining or compulsion here dreamed of, but such as when a virgin is said to be ravished, who freely and deliberately appointeth time, place, persons, opportunities, and gladly comes to the place in which she is carried away; which neither law nor reason can make a rape. Now, I grant, neither man nor angel can so work upon the will; it is proper to the Lord, and communicable to no creature, to know what congruous ways can efficaciously draw the will. And, 2. 'Tis God only who can attemper irresistible strength, and sweetness and delectation of consent together.

Use 4. 'Tis not a good, nor a comfortable way; nor would I love a heaven that is referred to a may-be or a may-not-be: 'tis not a good heaven that referred to a venture. 2. Weakness, left of God, turneth wickedness: it is kindly to our corruption to be uncouth, strange, froward to Christ, and undiscreet to strong love. 4. Free-will is now like a bankrupt merchant, or a young and loose heir, who hath lost all credit: Christ dare not venture a stock in our hand. 4. Christ is a Shepherd,
who

who in feeding his flock *stands on his feet*, Isa. xl. 11. and sits not down, to ly and sleep: the first Adam sat down; all his sons ly down: never man on his own bottom can come to heaven. Let us chuse this sure way, that broken men may be tutored by Jesus Christ.

Use 5. If he be a drawing Christ, 'tis a terrible thing to be at holding and drawing with Christ. 1. God's soul lothes withdrawers; Heb. x. 38. *If any man draw back, my soul shall not be pleased with him.* The Greek word *hypostello*, is a word from soldiers, that leave their standing out of fear; the feared soldier sends himself away out of the army. But Habak. ii. 4. from whence this is cited, seems a far contrary word, *The soul that is lifted up* [Heb. gnaphal] *towered up or lifted up as a high tower, is not upright in him*, Isa. xxxi. 14. Fear makes men low and base, and pride makes them high and lofty: how then is withdrawing from God, so base and low a word in the apostle's style, expressed by the prophet Habakkuk in so high a word, as the towering up of the soul? There is a reciprocation of things in the word signified; for unbelief, resisting of Christ, and the sinner's withdrawing, is an act of the highest pride: he that will not be converted, and refuseth Christ, thinks he can fend without Christ, he hath a stronger castle to run to than Christ, and imagines that his sins and lusts shall shelter him in the ill day: and unbelief is a base, timorous, and cowardly thing, when men, for fear of a less evil and a poorer loss, steal away from Christ: and both is base or poor pride, and high or lofty beggarliness, in stealing away from Christ's colours; which the Lord abhors. 2. Withdrawing looks hell-like: he that is not saved in the nick of conversion, is eternally lost. Heb. x. 38. *But we are not of the withdrawing to perdition.* Withdrawing hath no home but hell. 3. 'Tis a sign of an obdurate heart, Zech. vii. 11. *But they have refused to hearken, and pulled away the shoulder, and stopped their ear lest they should hear.* And so judgment-like is withdrawing, and smells so of vengeance, that God plagues withdrawing with with-

draw-

drawing; Hos. v. 4. *They will not frame their doings to turn unto their God.* And what is the issue of that? *They shall go with their flocks and herds to seek the Lord, but they shall not find him; for he hath withdrawn himself from them.* Prov. i. 24. *I called, and ye refused;* verse 26. then this must follow, verse 28. (as also, John viii. 21. the like is) *they call upon me, but I will not answer.*

Use 6. 'Tis a terrible plague of God, which we would eschew as hell, to wit, provoking of God by such sins as may procure that God should in his judgment marr the lock of the heart, the will, that the door should neither shut nor open, and cast poison into the soul, so as angels and men, heaven and earth, cannot help or cure it: Christ is good at opening hearts, and drawing sinners; and he is as good at judicial closing of hearts: if he put his finger in the eye; and snap in pieces the optick nerves, all the world cannot restore sight, or open the heart. He that is nearest to be drawn to Christ, and yet never drawn, is deepest in hell; an evangelic-fire of God's fury is worse than a Sinai-fire, though it burn up to mid heaven. 1. Sinning against the light of nature, and the known will of God, as idolatry and the principles of your own religion, true and known to be so, brings delivering up to judicial blindness, Rom. i. 21. (2.) If ye put your finger in nature's eye, and blow out that candle, *God will give you up to vile affections*, Rom. i. 24. and *a reprobate mind*, ver. 26, 27, 28. Some blow out the candle of nature, and God blows out the sun of the gospel, that it is to them like sack-cloth of hair, and a moon like blood. 3. Resisting the call of God, brings on the plague of hardness of heart; Prov. i. 24, 25, 26, 27. Acts xxviii. 23, 24, 25, 26, 27. John viii. 21.

Use 7. We are hence taught, to put our heart in Christ's hand; he, and he only, who makes all things new, hath a singular faculty in making old hearts new hearts. Now there is no such way as to ly at the tide, and wait on a full sea and fair wind, and ship

in

in with Christ; attend the ordinances, watch at the posts of the door of wisdom.

Object. I have been a hearer, thirty, forty years; I am as far from being drawn this day, as the first day.

Answ. Such a soul would not be oiled at the first with the persuaded assurance of an everlasting love of election, as Libertines cure poor souls; but would be brought to see sin, and be humbled and plowed, that Christ may sow.

2. They would be taken off their own bottom, and discharged to confide and rest on humiliation, or any thing in themselves.

3. The manner, motives, and grounds of their complaining would be examined. Seldom or never is it seen that a reprobate man can be in sad earnest heavy in heart, touching his hardness of heart, and fruitless hearing of the word of God thirty or forty years: and withal, if there be a drachm of sincerity, the least grain of Christ, as if the soul do but look afar off, with half an eye, yet greedily after the Lord Jesus, it is a sweet beginning. 'Tis true, a talent-weight of iron or sand is as weighty as a talent-weight of gold, but in a saint an ounce-weight of grace hath more weight than a pound of corruption. It is no gospel-truth that Antinomians teach, That God loves no man less for sin, or no man more for inherent holiness. It is true of the love of election and reconciliation, in the work of justification; but most false of the love of divine manifestation in the work of sanctification; as is clear, John xiv. 21, 23. Nor are men by this taught to seek righteousness in themselves; because they are commanded to try and examine themselves, as 1 Cor. xi. 28. 2 Cor. xiii. 5.

4. Such souls would upon any terms be brought to reason and debate the question with Christ, that as the law may stop their mouth before God, so mercy may stop the mouth of the law and sin; and it may convincingly be cleared, that though scarlet or crimson can by no art be made white, yet Christ, who is a-

bove

CHRIST DYING AND DRAWING SINNERS TO HIMSELF.

above art, can make them white (Isa. i. 18.) as wool and snow. And therefore such would be brought in an high esteem and deep judgment of Christ's fairness, beauty, excellency, incomparable and transcendent worth: and tho' a soul have a too high esteem of his sins, yet say that he dies with an high esteem of Jesus Christ, he is in no danger; for faith is but a swelled, an high and broad opinion and thought of the incomparable excellency and sweetness of Jesus Christ.

Use 8. This powerful drawing teacheth humble thankfulness. (1.) The most harmless and innocent sinner must be in Christ's book for the debt of ten thousand talents. (2.) The sense of drawing grace is mighty engaging; every act of thankful obedience should come out of this womb, as the birth and child of the felt love of God. Christ did bid such a man battle. 2. He was Christ's enemy when he took him. (3.) It cost Christ blood, he died to conquer an enemy, Rom. v. 10. (4.) He kept the taken enemy alive, he might have killed him, he gave him more than quarters, he made a captive a king, Rev. i. 6. Suppose we, Christ should in his own person come locally down to hell, and look upon so many thousands scorching and flaming in that unsufferable lake of fire and brimstone, if he should pull out by the head and name so many thousands of them, even while they were spitting on Christ, blaspheming his name, and scratching his face, and should loose off the fetters of everlasting vengeance, and draw them from amongst millions of damned spirits, lay them in his bosom, carry them to heaven, set them on thrones of glory, crown them as kings to reign with him for evermore; would they not be shamed, and overcome with this love, kiss and adore so free a Redeemer? And thus really hath Christ dealt with sinners. Look on your debts written in Christ's grace book, would not such a redeemed one praise his Ransomer, and say, O if every finger, every inch of a bone, every lith, every drop of blood of my body, every hair of my head, were in an angel's perfection to praise Jesus Christ! O the

weight

weight of the debt of love! O the gold mines and the depths of Christ's free love!

3. Consider what expressions vessels of grace have used of free-grace; how far below grace Paul sees himself, lo here, Eph. ii. 8. *To me who am*, 1. *Less than a saint.* 2. Not that only, but *less than the least.* 3. *Less than the least of saints.* But, 4. Yet a little lower, *less than the least of all saints, is this grace given, that I should preach the unsearchable riches of Christ.* Gospel-riches is grace and mercy, but there is great abundance of it; 'tis a speech from quick-scented hounds, who have neither footstep, nor trace, nor scent left them of the game they pursue. Christ defies men and angels to trace him in the ways of grace. So Paul, 1 Tim. i. 13. *I was a blasphemer, and a persecutor, and an injurious person* [Gr. all' elèethan] *but I was be-mercied,* as if dipt in a river, in a sea of mercy. Verse 14. *And the grace of the Lord Jesus to me was abundant.* No, that is too low a word, [Gr. huperpleonase de hè charis] *his grace was more, or over-abundant.* One Paul obtained as much grace, even so whole and complete a ransom, without diminishing, as would have saved a world, Rom. v. 15. *If through the offence of one many be dead, much more the grace of God, and the gift by grace, which is by one man Jesus Christ, hath abounded unto many.* [Gr. eperissèuse] The word is exceedingly to abound, and borrowed from fountains and rivers, which have flowed with waters since the creation; but there is a higher word, verse 12. *Where sin abounded, grace far more, or exceedingly over-abounded, or more than over-abounded,* [Gr. huperisseusen hù charis] And verse 21. *Sin reigned unto death, that grace might reign unto life,* [Gr. basileúsè,] *that Christ's grace might play the king.* The saving knowledge of God, under the kingdom of the Messiah, Isa. xi. 9. *fills the earth, as the sea is covered with waters.* A sea of faith, and an earthful of the grace of saving-light, and a sun seven-fold, as the light of seven days, Isa. xxx. 26. hold forth to us a large measure of grace, and righteousness and

peace

peace *like a river, and the waves of the sea,* Isa. xlviii. 18. All these say, Christ is no niggard of grace.

And 4. Can they not wear and out-spend their harps, who fall down *before the Lamb,* Rev. xiv. and Rev. v. 8. who with a loud voice, praise the grace of God, verse 12. *for ever and ever?* Consider if it must not be a loud voice, when *ten thousand times ten thousand, and thousand thousands,* all join in one song, to extol grace; if we be not in word and deed obliged to express the virtues and praises of him, *who hath called us from darkness unto his marvellous light.*

Verse 32. *And I, if I be lifted up from the earth, will draw all men to me.*

Article II.

The next thing we consider, is the person that draws. *I* (says Christ) *will draw all men to me.*

There is a peculiar aptitude in Jesus Christ to draw sinners to himself.

1. As concerning his person, he is fit; for neither is the Father, nor the Holy Ghost, in person, Lord Redeemer, but Christ; as, in the deep of God's wisdom, the Son was thought fittest to make sons, Gal. iv. 4. the heir to communicate the right of heirship to the nearest of the blood, to his brethren, to make them joint-heirs with him; so is Christ a fit person, as Lord Saviour, to rescue captives and to draw them to the state of sonship: which I speak not to exclude the other two persons; for, John vi. 44. *The Father draws to the Son;* and the Spirit of grace, in the work of conversion, must be a special agent; but Christ is made, in a personal consideration, a drawer of sinners; God works and carries on all his state-designs of heaven by Christ, Heb. ii. 10. *He brings, or drives many sons to glory.*

2. Christ by office is a congregating and uniting Mediator, Col. i. 20. He makes heaven and earth one; *He is our peace, and made of twain one,* Eph. ii. 14. The

Shepherd

peace *like a river, and the waves of the sea,* Isa. xlviii. 18. All these say, Christ is no niggard of grace.

And 4. Can they not wear and out-spend their harps, who fall down *before the Lamb,* Rev. xiv. and Rev. v. 8. who with a loud voice, praise the grace of God, verse 12. *for ever and ever?* Consider if it must not be a loud voice, when *ten thousand times ten thousand, and thousand thousands,* all join in one song, to extol grace; if we be not in word and deed obliged to express the virtues and praises of him, *who hath called us from darkness unto his marvellous light.*

Verse 32. *And I, if I be lifted up from the earth, will draw all men to me.*

Article II.

The next thing we consider, is the person that draws. *I* (says Christ) *will draw all men to me.*

There is a peculiar aptitude in Jesus Christ to draw sinners to himself.

1. As concerning his person, he is fit; for neither is the Father, nor the Holy Ghost, in person, Lord Redeemer, but Christ; as, in the deep of God's wisdom, the Son was thought fittest to make sons, Gal. iv. 4. the heir to communicate the right of heirship to the nearest of the blood, to his brethren, to make them joint-heirs with him; so is Christ a fit person, as Lord Saviour, to rescue captives and to draw them to the state of sonship: which I speak not to exclude the other two persons; for, John vi. 44. *The Father draws to the Son;* and the Spirit of grace, in the work of conversion, must be a special agent; but Christ is made, in a personal consideration, a drawer of sinners; God works and carries on all his state-designs of heaven by Christ, Heb. ii. 10. *He brings, or drives many sons to glory.*

2. Christ by office is a congregating and uniting Mediator, Col. i. 20. He makes heaven and earth one; *He is our peace, and made of twain one,* Eph. ii. 14. The

Shepherd

Shepherd that gathers the sons of God in one. John xi. 52. And, he by the merit of his blood, maketh sinners legally one with God; he is Immanuel, God with us, fit to draw us in a law-union to God. We were banished out of paradise; the Son by office, was sent out to bring in the out-law sons.

3. God hath laid down, (in a manner) his compassion, mercy, gentleness, to sinners in Christ; and Christ hath taken off infinite wrath, and satisfied justice in his nature and office. God is nowhere (to speak so) so much mercy, graciousness, kindness, tender compassion to sinners, such a sea of love, as in the Lord Jesus. O but he is a most lovely, desirable, compassionate God in Christ? The sinner findeth all that God can have in him, or do for saving, in the Mediator Christ; there can nothing come out of God to the sinner, but through Christ. There is no golden pipe, no channel, but this; all God, and whole God, is in Christ, and all God as communicable to the creature; and were God seen in his loveliness, his beauty would be strong cords and chains to draw hell up to heaven. Love, grace, mercy, are sodering and uniting attributes in God: now, tho' these same essential attributes that are in one, be in all the three Persons; yet the mediatory manifestation of love, grace, and free mercy, is only in the Son; so as Christ is the treasure, storehouse, and magazine of the free goodness and mercy of the Godhead. As the sea is a congregation of waters, so is Christ a confluence of these lovely and drawing attributes that are in the Godhead. Christ is the face of God, 2 Cor. iv. 6. The beauty and loveliness of the person, much of the majesty and glory of the man is in the face; now the beauty, and majesty and glory of God is manifested in Christ; so, Heb. i. 3. *He is the brightness of his glory.* The Father is as it were all sun, and all pearl; the Son Christ is the substantial rays, light-shining, the eternal, and essential irradiation of this Sun of glory; the sun's glory is manifested to the world, in the light and beams that it sends out to the world; and if the sun should keep its beams and light

within

within its body, we should see nothing of the sun's beauty and glory. No man, no angel, could see any thing of God, if God had not a consubstantial Son begotten of himself by an eternal generation; but Christ is the beams, and splendor, and the shining, but the consubstantial shining of the infinite pearl, and outs God, as the seal doth the stamp; and, as God incarnate, he reveals the excellency, glory, and beauty of God. The pearl is a drawing and an alluring creature, from its shining beauty; so Christ is the drawing loveliness of God. Ye cannot see the creature's beauty, or the man's face, but ye see the creature and the man; so says Christ to Philip, John xiv. 9. *He that hath seen me, hath seen the Father.* I am as like the Father, as God is like himself: there is a perfect, indivisible, essential unity between the Father and me; *I and the Father are one*, one very God; he the begetter, I the begotten. So God hath laid down and empawned all his beauty, his loveliness, and his drawing virtue, in Christ the load-stone of heaven; he is the substantial rose that grew out of the Father from eternity. A man's wisdom makes his face to shine. Wisdom is a fair, lovely, and alluring beauty. Now, Christ is the essential wisdom of God; were your eyes once fastned upon that dainty lovely thing Christ, that uncreated golden ark, the eternal, that infinite flower and lily, that sprang out of the essence and beautiful nature of God, with eternal infinite greenness, fairness, smell, vigour, life, never to fade, that essential wisdom, and substantial word, the intellectual birth of the Lord's infinite understanding; if your eyes were once on him in a vision of glory, it should be impossible to get your eyes off him again; there would come such drawing rays, and visual lines of lovely beauty and glory from his face to your eyes, and should dart in through these created windows, to the understanding, heart, and affection, such arrows and darts of love, as ye shall be a captive of glory for ever and ever. Psal. xvi. 11. *In thy presence is fulness of joy.* Rev. xxii. 4. *They shall see his face,-*

'tis

'tis a King's face, and a kingly glory, to see it.---v. 5. *And they shall reign for ever and ever.*

4. Then there is so much warmness of heart, and such a fire of love, such a stock of free-grace, so wide, so tender, so large bowels of mercy and compassion towards sinners, as he would put himself into a posture of mercy, and in such a station of clay, as he might conveniently get a strong pull of sinners to draw them, a large and wide handful, or his arms full of sinners, as he would be a man for us, to get all the organs of lovely drawing of sinners to him: a man's heart to love man, a man's bowels to compassionate man, a man's hand to touch the foul leper's skin, a man's mouth and tongue to pray for man, to preach to men, and in our nature to publish the everlasting gospel; a man's legs to be the good shepherd, to go over mountain and wilderness, to seek or to save lost sheep; a man's soul to sigh and groan for man; a man's eyes to weep for sinners; his nature, to lay down his life for his poor friends: he would be a created clay-tent of free-grace, a shop, and an office-house of compassion towards us; he would borrow the womb of a sinner to be born, suck the breasts of a woman that needed a Saviour, *eat and drink with sinners and publicans*, came to seek and to save lost sinners, was numbred with sinners, died between two sinners, made his grave with sinners, (saith Isaiah, Isa. liii. 9.) borrowed a sinner's tomb to be buried in: and now he keeps the old relation with sinners, when he is in heaven; honour hath not changed him, nor hath he forgotten his old friends, Heb. iv. 15. *For we have not an High Priest that cannot be touched with the feeling of our infirmities, but was in all points tempted like as we are, yet without sin.* Christ cannot now sigh, but he can feel sighing; he cannot weep, he hath a man's heart to compassionate our weeping, in such a way as is suitable to his glorified condition. The head is in heaven, but he hath left his heart in earth with sinners: there can be nothing dearer to Christ, than the Holy Spirit; he hath sent us down that Comforter, the Spirit, to abide with us.

Use 1.

CHRIST DYING AND DRAWING SINNERS TO HIMSELF.

Use 1. O that men would come and look into this ark, and that Christ would draw the curtain! Do but hear himself crying to the cities of Judah, Isa. xl. 9. *Behold your God.* Isa. lxv. 1. *I said to a nation that was not called by my name, Behold me, Behold me*: the doubling of the word saith, Christ desires to out his beauty. Shall your farm and your five yoke of oxen keep you from him? Men will not be drawn to him to satisfy their love.

Use 2. Christ is a drawing and an uniting Spirit; then all that are in Christ should be united. Certainly the divisions now in Britain cannot be of God. The wolf and the good Shepherd are contrary in this; the good Shepherd loves to have the flock gathered in one, and to save them, that they may find pasture, and the flock may be saved: the wolf scatters the flock; or if the wolf would have the flock gathered together, it is that they may be destroyed. Then it would be considered, if a bloody intention of war between two protestant kingdoms, for carnal ends, and upon forced and groundless jealousies, be from an uniting Spirit, and not rather from him, who was a murderer from the beginning.

Use 3. Jews and Turks, and civil men, that are but moral Pagans, are not in Christ, nor can they have any communion with God, nor be drawn to Christ; because no man can be in love with God, except he see God as opened and made lovely to the soul in Christ: moral civility and pharisaical holiness is one of the most heaven-like, and whitest ways to hell that Satan can devise; many moral men go, by theft, to hell: Satan by open violence pulleth the prophane and openly wicked men to perdition; but he stealeth millions of civil saints, honest moral men, that have whereon to live in the world plentifully, to hell in their whites, as if they were saints, because civil and clean in the morals of the second table, yet not being born again, they cannot see the kingdom of God. And most men deceive themselves with country religion and moralities; but such be but civil honest antichrists, and deny there is any need that Christ should come in the flesh to die for

sinners;

sinners; for they can live honestly, and save themselves, and not be beholden to Christ for heaven, or mortification, or faith.

Verse 32. *And I, if I be lifted up from the earth, will draw all men.*
This drawing of sinners to Christ, is bottomed on Christ's dying on the cross; and his dying on the cross is an act of extreme and highest love, John iii. 16. John xv. 13. 1 John iv. 9, 10. Hence let us consider a little further what drawing and alluring power is in the love of God, and what way we may come to the sweet fruit of the strongest pull of Christ; which may be considered in.
1. *The revelation of the dying loveliness of Christ's dying.*
2. *The fulness of this loveliness.*
For the former, Christ openeth himself to us, we cannot discover him first; and there be two acts of this,
1. Christ opens the understanding, Luke xxiv. 25. and the heart, Acts xvi. 14. *He taketh away the thick vail, that is over the heart,* 2 Cor. iii. 15, 16. and rendreth the medium, the air (as it were) thin, clear, visible; as when the sun expelleth nightshadows, and thick clouds: so David's key, *that openeth, and no man shutteth,* Rev. iii. 7. removeth the door, and the seal that the first Adam's sin putteth on the heart, John xiv. 21. *He that loveth me, shall be loved of my Father, and I will love him, and will manifest myself to him.* And Christ can show the Father, the Lord Jesus cometh out of his depth and ocean of glory, and ivory chamber, as it were; and the Son of God revealeth the Son of God, as Gal. i. v. 12. compared with v. 15, 16. sheweth. He would not say, *Behold me, behold me,* Isa. lxv. 1. and then get into a thick cloud, and hide himself, if he had not a mind to reveal his glory, and to show himself, *The King in his beauty,* Isa. xxxiii. 17. all his loveliness, the mysteries of his love, the rosiness, whiteness, redness, comeliness of his face, Cant. v. 10. Nor would the spouse pray for a noon-day sight of Christ, Cant. i.

i. 7. if he could not offer himself to be seen in his loveliness of beauty. Thus *Christ doth make manifest the favour of his knowledge, in the ministry of the gospel,* 2 Cor. ii. 14. when he letteth out to the soul the smell of myrrh, aloes, of all the sweet ointments of his death, and wounds; that the soul seeth, smelleth, tasteth the apples of love, in the believed mercy, free grace, satisfied justice, peace reconciled with righteousness, purchased redemption in his blood; and he standeth behind the wall of our flesh, and so is called, our wall, Cant. ii. 9. *Behold he standeth behind our wall,* Or, *Behold that is he standing behind our wall; he looketh forth at the window, shewing himself,* [Heb. mezijz] *bewraying himself through the lattess;* yet this is not a perfect vision of God attainable in this life, as the author of the Bright Star* dreameth. I see a man more distinctly in the field and before the sun, than when he looks out at the grates or lattess of a window, and a window behind a wall; for so we but see Christ in this life.

The compleatness of the loveliness is, 1. In that there is no spot in Christ crucified, when he is seen spiritually, no blemish, no lameness, no defect. For an eternal and infinite redemption, and an absolute righteousness, more cannot be required, nay, not by God. 2. Nothing that the desiring faculty and appetite can stumble at; Paul's determination, the last resolved judgment of his mind, and his ripest resolution and purpose, was to know *nothing save Jesus Christ and him crucified,* 1 Cor. ii. 2. Christ's beauty can fill all the corners and emptiness of the wide desires of the soul. 3. There is no actual fulness of God spoken of, Eph. iii. Paul praying that the Ephesians may comprehend the great love of God, verse 19. saith, *That ye may know the love of God that passeth knowledge, that ye may be filled with all the fulness of God.* This is a satisfying fulness, and is an admirable expression. To be filled with God,

must

*Bright Star; c. 5. p. 58.

must be a soul-delighting fill. But, 2. To be filled with the fulness of God, is more; for there is unspeakable fulness in God. 3. The expression is yet higher, *That ye may be filled with all the fulness of God.*

Of this fulness, 1. A word of the measure of it. 2. Of the means of it. 3. Of the sufficiency of it in the kind and nature. Randall, in his epistle before the treatise called, †*The Bright Star,* "I have therefore observed the ever to be bewailed non-proficiency of many ingenious spirits, who through the policy of others, and the too too much modesty and temerity of themselves, have precluded the way of progress to the top and pitch of rest and perfection against themselves, as being altogether unattainable, and have shortned the cut with a *non datur ultra,* and are become such who are ever learning and never come to the knowledge of the truth." But for the measure, sure it is not, as Antinomians and Famulists dream, compleat and full in this life;

1. Because, according to the manner and measure of the manifestation of Christ and knowledge; so is love and the perfection of believers. This is a truth in itself undeniable, and granted by the author of the Bright Star, c. 5. p. 52. For Christ's excellency and drawing beauty in love goeth into the soul by the port and eye of knowledge. But, 1 Cor. xiii. 9. *We know in part, and we prophesy in part.*

2. Paul disclaimeth perfection, as being but in the way and journeying toward it, Phil. iii. 12. *Not as though I had already attained, either were already perfect; but I follow after, if that I may apprehend that for whioh also I am apprehended of Jesus Christ.* Now this perfection, which Paul professeth he wanteth, is opposed, v. 13, 14. to his pressing toward the garland, *for the prize of the high calling of God in Jesus Christ,* Heb. xi. 40.

3. Per.

†Bright Star, c. 4. p. 30. Town's assertion of grace, p. 76, 77, 78. Theolog. Germ. c. 8. p. 16.

CHRIST DYING AND DRAWING SINNERS TO HIMSELF.

3. Perfection, such as we expect in heaven, is in no capacity to receive any farther addition, or accession of grace or glory; nor is there a *growing in grace, and in the knowledge of our Lord and Saviour Jesus Christ,* enjoined us there, as is expressly here in the way of our country, 2 Pet. iii. 14. *and to run our race to the end,* Heb. xii. 1. and *be carried on to perfection,* Heb. vi. 1. 'Tis true, our good works are washed in the fountain opened for David's house, in which our persons are washed; but that washing removeth the sinful guilt and law-obligation from them, but not the inherent blot and sinful imperfection of our works, to make them perfect; for then might we be justified by our good works, if Christ's blood make them to leave off to be sins; but that blood hindereth them to be imputed to us only, but removeth not their sinful imperfections, as Antinomians say, that so they make us perfect in this life; nor doth that blood (as Papists say) add a meriting dignity and virtue to them, by which we are justified by works made white and meritorious in Christ's blood and merits. God hath so pourtrayed and chalked the way to heaven, that all the most supernatural acts, even those that have immediate bordering with the vision of glory, should need a pass of pardoning grace; and to believe that Christ's grace shall work in us acts void of sin, is not faith: therefore we are to believe the pardon of such ere they have being, and not sanctifying grace to eschew them. It seemeth to me unbelieving murmuring, to be cast down at these sins, in such a way as to imagine we can eschew them, or that grace sanctifying is wanting to us in these; for grace is not due to sinless acts. Nor doth the growing in grace, which lieth on us by an obligation of a command, stop the way to the journeying toward perfection and heaven, nor shorten the cut to heaven, because heaven is not attainable in this life; but by the contrary, if perfection were attainable in this life, the man that attaineth it might sit down, rest there, and go not one step further; for except he should go beyond the crown, and to the other side of heaven, and over-journey

Christ

Christ at the right-hand of God, whither should he go? And those *that are ever learning, and never come to the knowledge of the truth,* are, 2 Tim. iii. 5. *Lovers of pleasures more than lovers of God; such as we are to turn away from; as have a form of godliness, and have denied the power thereof, and are led away with divers lusts;* and are never entred into one only degree or step of the way of the saving knowledge of the truth, (of which Paul speaketh) and not the truly regenerate, who believe, with Paul and the scriptures, that our greatest perfection is to sweat and contend for the highest pitch of perfection, even that which is beyond time.

4. Those that are perfected, as we hope we shall be in heaven, feed not with the beloved *among the lilies, till the day break, and the shadows fly away*; but the perfectest, the spouse of Christ, so feedeth on church-ordinances, Cant. ii. 17. The perfect ones have the fullest pitch of the noon-day sun of glory; it shall never be afternoon, nor the evening of twilight-sky with them; nor shall any night-shadow nor cloud go over their sun.

5. In the kingdom of perfection there shall be no indwelling of a body of sin, no sin, no uncleanness of heart, no turning of the love and liking of the soul off God; but the perfectest in this life sin, and carry an indwelling body of sin with them, Prov. xx. 9. Eccl. vii. 20. Job saith, chap. xiv. 4. The perfectest that beget children are unclean. Rom. vi. 17, 18, 19, 20, 21, 22, 23. 1 John i. 8, 9, 10. 1 John ii. 1. All that have need of an high priest at the right-hand of God to intercede for them, have sin, and in so far are imperfect, as all the saints are, Heb. vii. 25. and iv. 15. and i. 17, 18, and viii. 1, 2, 3. and ix. 23—26. and 1 Cor. xiii. 8. Love never faileth: there the soul drinketh abundantly, and is filled to satisfaction, that the vessel can contain no more of God; and is transformed into the sea of transcendant light, and highest love, as it were lost in the deep fountain of universal and immensurable love, and light; and the creature's soul and love liveth and

breatheth, resteth in the bosom, in the heart, in the bowels of him who is an infinite mass of love: is wrapped in the sugared floods, in the honey-brooks, and overflowing waves and rivers of pure and unmixed joy; sleepeth and solaceth itself in the innocent embracings of the glory that shineth, rayeth, and darteth, world without end, out of Christ, exalted far above all heavens, all principalities, and powers: the souls there are sweetned, more than sweetned, over-solaced with the noon-day-light of the Bridegroom's glory, having in it the sweetest perfections of the morning-sun; they flee with doves' wings of beauty after the Lamb, they never want the actual breathings of the Spirit of glory, they can never have enough of the chaste fruition of the glorious Prince Emmanuel, and they never want his inmost presence to the full; they suck the honey, the floods of milk of eternal consolations, and fill all empty desires; and, as if the soul were without bottom, afresh they suck again, in acts for eternity continued. There be no such thing here in this life; yet hath Christ crucified, in his bosom, the promise and full purchase of this life on the cross, and holds it out to sinners to draw them.

5. We have not yet attained to the resurrection of our bodies, but carry about such clods of death, as the worms must sweetly feed on, and have a seed and subject of distempers in our clay tabernacles; all which we are uncapable of in the state of perfection, when the body shall be more naturally clothed with immortality, then the greenest and most delicious rose, or flower, which we could suppose were growing fresh, green, and beautiful for ever, in such a happy soil, as the fields that ly on the banks, and within the drawings of sap from the river of life.

6. We are not masters of the invasion, at least, of temptations of devils, of men here.

7. Perfection maketh the general assembly of all the sons of Zion: the heavenly family is never convened, but in place, country, condition separated, some born, some not born, some walking, some sleeping in the dust,

some

some in their country, some in the way to their country.

8. There is no temple, no ordinances in our country of perfection, Rev. xxi. 2. 1 Cor. xiii. 8.

9. There is no angel-life here, without marriage, eating, drinking, begetting children, Luke xxii. 26, 30. Mark xii. 25. Clay cannot live, remaining earthly, up above the clouds, and visible heavens, *till this corruptible shall put on incorruption*, 1 Cor. xv.

Now, for the means of attaining this fulness, we have no other known and revealed to us in this life, but the scriptures, and faith; the one without, and external, and the other within. Under these, I comprehend all the ordinances of God. Famulists rejecting scripture, terming it an human device of ink and letters, as antichrist did before them; they call their perfect ones, from all acting, praying, hearing the word; yea, from knowing, apprehending, willing; to a resting on God, as meer patients; God as their form and Spirit immediately acting on them. "The active annihilation (saith the *Bright Star*, chap. 11. pag. 106.) is a ceasing from all acts, vanishing of images, a doing of nothing, and a resting of all motion, or from doing the exterior will of God, expressed in the law and gospel in their letter. Pag. 107. Passive annihilation is, when the man himself, and all other things (meditation, knowing, desiring of God, praying, and the practice of a holy life) are cast asleep, and are made nothing. The active annihilation is, when the man himself, and all other things, are annihilated, not only sufferingly, as in the passive; but doingly, I mean by light in the understanding, as well natural, as supernatural; wherein he sees, and most infallibly knows, that all those things are nothing, and rests upon this knowledge in despite of feeling. Page 140. It is not best to forsake the passive annihilation, and the fruitive love, (the loving of God, as our last enjoyed end) depending thereupon, to take in hand by acts to practise the active annihilation; provided that by simple remembrance, she

stand

"stand to her part. For there it is, (pag. 141.) that the soul is so transported, inlarged, inlightened and united to God. There she tastes the chaste embraces, sweet intercourses, and divine kisses; there she seeth herself sublimed, ennobled, and glorified with angels at the celestial table; there she relisheth the fruits of her mortification, the treasures of her repentance, and the comforts of all her self-denials. Pag. 144, 145. To forsake such an experimental union with God, and that men should leap back to themselves, and re-betake themselves to their own acts, refuse to endure this emptiness, poverty of spirit, this will of God, and all spiritly intercourse, super-celestial, or essential illumination, though indeed the true and divine wisdom and naked seeing of God. -----So that by their flying back and returning to themselves, (that is, leaving the contemplative life of monks, and return to a practical walking with God) they do no other but far estrange themselves from all pure and imperial knowledge, and from all union and transformation into God, and so bide always straitned within themselves, and their own bowels, and in the fetters of the old-man. Now, if you ask what it is to put off the old-man, the *Theologia Germanica* saith, chap. 5. pag. 9, 10. It is to ascribe neither being, action, knowledge, nor goodness to yourself, but to God the eternal wisdom;----and thus man, and the creature evanisheth.----Thus ought man to become void of all things; that is, not to arrogate them to himself; and the less knowledge the creature doth arrogate to itself, it becometh the more perfect: the like we must conceive of love, will, desire, and all such things; for the less that men doth arrogate these things to himself, the nobler, the excellenter, and the diviner he becometh: and the more he doth assume these things to himself, so much is he made the more blockish, base and imperfect. *Theologia Germanica*, chap. 14. pag. 32. That a man die to himself, it is as much as if you would say as himself, or egoity should die. St. Paul saith,
"Put

"Put off the old-man with his works, pag. 34. If it could come to pass, that any man might wholly and absolutely cast off himself, so as that he lived without all things in true obedience, as the humanity of Christ was, then he should be void of himself, and one with Christ, and should be the same by grace, that Christ was by nature.----Pag. 35. This also is written, the more self-ends and egoity, the more there is of sin and unrighteousness; and the lesser there is of the one, the greater want there is of the other. This is also written, the more that myself doth decrease (that is, egoity or selfiness) the more doth God in me increase.----------Hence God is a Spirit acting, and all in all men; and for men to ascribe the good to God, and the Ill to themselves, is obedience; and to arrogate being, or good to themselves, is sin. So, *Theologia Germanica* taketh away the incarnation of Christ thus, chap. 22. pag. 52, 53. Yet are there ways to the life of Christ, as we have already said: when, and wherein God and man are joined together; so that it may be truly said, and truth itself may acknowledge it, that the true and perfect God, and the true and perfect man are one; and man doth so yield, and give place to God, that where God himself is, there is man, and that God also be there present, and work alone, and do, and leave any thing undone, without any I, to me, mine, or the like; where these things are, and exist, there is true Christ, and nowhere else.----It is the property of God to consist, and be without this, or that, without selfness, egoity, or the like; but it is the property of the creature to seek and will (in all things which it doth, or leaveth undone) itself; and those things which are its own, and this, or that, here or there. *Theologia Germanica*, chap. 39. pag. 109, 110. He who is illuminated with the eternal and divine love, is a divine and deified man. *Theologia Germanica*, chap. 28. pag. 71. Those who are led by the Spirit of God, are the sons of God, and not subject to the law: the sense of which words is, they are not to be

"taught

"taught what they should do, or leave undone, seeing the Spirit of God, which is their instructor, will teach them sufficiently; neither is any thing to be commanded, or enjoined them.---For he that teacheth them, commandeth them. They need no law, by means thereof to get profit to themselves, for they have obtained all already: and thus, page 70. Christ needed no law, but was above law, and removes ordinances, etc. *Theologia Germanica*, chap. xi. page 23. The soul of Christ was to descend to hell, before it could ascend to heaven: and the same must befall the soul of man; and this cometh to pass, when he knoweth, and beholdeth, and findeth himself so evil, that he supposeth it to be just, he should suffer all, even be damned for ever; and when he neither will, nor can desire deliverance and comfort, but doth bear damnation neither waywardly, nor unwillingly, but loveth damnation and pain, because it is just and agreeable to God's will. And (page 25.) When man desireth, in this hell, nothing but the eternal good, and understandeth the eternal good, to be above measure good, and this is his peace, joy, rest, satisfaction to him;-------this good becometh man's, and so man is in the kingdom of heaven,------this hell hath an end, this heaven shall never end;------man in this hell cannot think that ever he shall be comforted again, or delivered; and when he is in this heaven, nothing can hurt him;------neither can he believe, that he can be hurt or discomforted; and yet, after this hell, he is comforted, and delivered; and after this heaven, he is troubled and deprived of comfort.------Man can do or omit nothing, by his own means, whereby this heaven should come to him, or this hell depart from him:------For the wind bloweth where it listeth, etc. and when man is in either of these, he is in good case, and he may be as safe in hell as in heaven; and so long as man is in this life, he may often pass from the one to the other."

In opposition to these wicked foolries, and for further clearing of the truths formerly proposed, let these

positions

positions for the unfolding of the drawing loveliness of Christ be considered.

Pos. 1. The *scriptures are given by divine inspiration, able to make the man of God perfect, throughly furnished unto all good works,* 2 Tim. iii. 16, 17. The only mean to find Christ, for they bear witness of him, John v. 39. *And are written that we might believe, and in believing have life eternal,* John xx. 31. And all that *Christ Jesus heard of his Father, he made known to his apostles,* John xv. 15. And of these, one apostle Paul, who also *received the gospel, not from flesh and blood, but by revelation from Jesus Christ,* Gal. i. 12. 2 Pet. iii. 15, 16. Acts ix. 1, 2. etc. did declare to the *Ephesians, the whole counsel of God,* Acts xx. 27. and yet believed and preached no other things than these that are written in the law, or in Moses and the Prophets, Acts xxiv. 14. Acts xxvi. 22. And the majesty, divinity, power, harmony, doctrine, above the reach of flesh and blood; the end, which is not in this side of time and death, but beyond both, (as the places in the margin witness) do demonstrate that the one book of the Old and New Testament can be fathered upon none, but on God only.

Pos. 2. The scripture and all the ordinances are but created things, and not the ultimate object of our faith, and highest and compleatest love; that is reserved to God in Jesus Christ: yea, the most perfect we read of, Paul, a chosen vessel, stood in need of comfort from Titus, 2 Cor. vii. 5, 6. and the saints at Rome, Rom. i. 11, 12. and Peter of a rebuke, Gal. ii. and the beloved disciple *John, of the joy and comfort of the walking of the children of Gaius in the truth.* Eph. iii. 4, 5. And of a commandment of the law, which forbiddeth idolatry, and angel-worship, Rev. xix. 10. Rev. xxii. 8, 9. and of an evangelic precept to believe, and not to fear, Rev. i. 17. And the excellentest and perfectest member of the body hath need of counsel, exhortations from the lowest member. Rom. xii. 3, 4, 5, 6, 7, 8. Gal. vi. 2. 1 Cor. xii. 14, etc. and all the saints, to whom Paul, Peter,

James,

CHRIST DYING AND DRAWING SINNERS TO HIMSELF.

James, John wrote, amongst whom there were that had the anointing, that teacheth them all things, must hear and obey many exhortations, precepts and commandments out of the law, as evangelised: then the most perfect are not above the law, the gospel and ordinances, as Famulists say; else all the New Testament and canonical epistles were written to the saints for no purpose. But that we may understand this the better, we are to remember, that, 1. There is a twofold happiness of the saints, one formal, and another objective. 2. That there is a mediate seeing of God, one by ordinances and means, another immediate. 3. That there is a twofold will of God; one that is revealed in scripture, or the law of nature, and that is the moral good that God approveth and injoineth to us, rather than the will of God; this the Famulists call, *The exterior or accidental will of God,* because God's will, as his essence, should have been entire and self-sufficient, though God had never revealed any such will to men or angels; yea, though he had never made the world, or men, or angels. There is another will essential in God, which is not the thing willed, but the essential faculty of desiring or willing in God. Now to come nearer the point, the formal blessedness of the saints is in the act of seeing, knowing, loving, enjoying God, which on our part are created things, and so empty nothings, and are not essentially the happiness of man, but means by the which we enjoy God our happiness; so the using of all the means and ordinances are not our happiness. 'Tis true, our Saviour saith, *'Tis life eternal to know God, and his Son Christ,* John xvii. But he meaneth, it is the way and necessary means to happiness, and life eternal. God in Christ, and in the in-comings and out-flowings of the Spirit of glory, or the blessed one God, in three persons, is the object and happiness of the saints; and therefore we are to prefer Christ himself, to all the kisses, visions, out-flowings of glory, and all our acts of seeing, loving, and enjoying of God: we may love ordinances, and prize highly the

vision

vision of God; but God himself, and Jesus Christ, we must not only prize, but be ravished, overcharged with himself; as the bridegroom is far more excellent than his bracelets, chains, rings. In this sense, I would in my heart, and esteem, make away all ordinances, yea, all the honey-combs, all the apples, all the created roses that grow on Christ, all the sweet results, and out-flowings of glory; yea, whole created heaven, for Christ: Christ God himself, the bulk, the body, the stalk of the tree of life, is infinitely to be valued above an apple, yea, all the created apples and sweet blossoms, and soul delighting flowers that grow on the tree. Now here on earth we are happy as heirs, not as lords and possessors, and in an union with the exterior and revealed will of God, in believing, fearing, serving God, in Christ, in a practical union with God: but all this is but the way to the well, not to the well itself; and the union with, or vision of God, is mediate, far off, in a mirror, in the image, form, characters, elements, or looking-glass, of word, sacraments, ministry, ordinances, of hearing, praying, praising; but in heaven, we see God face to face, that is, without means, or the intervention of messengers, or ordinances. I cannot determine whether, when we shall know, and see the Lord, in an immediate vision of glory, our understanding shall receive created forms, intellectual species, images, characters of the lovely essence, the white, ruddy, pleasant, lovely countenance, of that desirable Prince, the Lord Jesus; 'tis a nicety not for our edification: sure, Christ shall infuse and pour in into every vessel of glory, so much of himself, his presence, loveliness, image, beauty, as from bottom to brim, the soul shall be full. And who knoweth what the eternal milkings, the everlasting intellectual suckings of the glorified ones are, by which they draw in, and drink from the honey-comb of uncreated glory, and the deep, deep fountain and river of endless life; the streams of joy, consolation, love, fruition of Jehovah, the soul being the channel, whose banks are eternally green with glory?

What

What are the emanations, the out-flowings of blessedness, from the pure essence, and bright *face of him that sitteth on the throne?* And what can these incomings, and the eternal flowings of the tide of that sea of matchless felicity be? Who knoweth? *Come up and see,* can best resolve; come up and drink, be drunk and giddy, and satiated with glory, and move no curious question of that fruition of God. Christ will solve all these doubts, to the quieting of your mind, when ye come up thither. Nor is it needful to say, that there is a vision of God in this life, which is heaven, and all the heaven we shall ever have; and this vision is without receiving any images, forms, characters of God, because it is purely spiritual, and abstracted from all acts of imagination; and in it we are mere patients, not agents, God pouring the immediate brightness of his own essence in us; truly, this is to be wise above what is written, and I crave leave to doubt, if Famulists have the images and species of this opinion from the Spirit of God; for that Spirit is a Spirit of sobriety; and the most spiritual and extatical visions, that the prophets, the men of God were taken up with: in them all, to me, there seems to be visions of forms, images, characters, a throne, angels with six wings, smoke, a woman clothed with the sun, etc. a pot toward the north, a cloud and a fire infolding itself,------a colour of amber, out of the midst of the fire; but a vision of God immediate in this life, and that ordinary, without forms, images, without word, sacraments, ordinances, I know not, I understand it not.

Pos. 3. The monkish conceit of the excellency of a contemplative life separated from all obligation to duties of the second table, above the practical life, hath been the first seed of wicked Famulism; the authors of both these books called, *Theologia Germanica,* and *The Bright Star,* being professed papists, though Mr. Randal extol both as pieces of rare price, and doctrines suiting only for the perfect (as if the scripture were not such a piece) yet professed gross idolatry,

and

and the adoring of the wood of the cross, is in *the Bright Star*, chap. 19. and divers other popish principles are in both.

Pos. 4. There is a twofold fulness of loveliness in Christ; one attainable in this life, the other reserved for the life to come. The full and highest pitch of the drawing loveliness of Christ, I think, excludeth all ordinances, scripture, sacraments, and means we now use. Because old monks and late Famulists make no heaven, but in this life only (as if a monk's coul were the very crown of eternal glory) and say, the resurrection is past; as their fathers Hymeneus and Phyletus said, and doubt of the immortality of the soul; therefore they, that they may be true to their own principles, must say, that there be a number of perfect men, that are above and higher than law, duties, ordinances, teaching of men, ministry, because these are for unperfect and unregenerate, (and the monks and Famulists are not such, but do already enjoy God, in a fruition of glory) but the scripture saith, that means, ordinances, are ever in use in this life, and only excluded from the life to come, 1 Cor. xiii. 8. *Charity never faileth: but whether there be prophecies, they shall fail: whether there be tongues, they shall cease; whether there be knowledge, it shall vanish away.* Verse 9. *For we know in part, and prophesy in part.* Ver. 10. *But when that which is perfect is come, then that which is in part shall be done away.* Ver. 12. *For now* (in this life) *we see through a glass darkly; but then (in the life to come) face to face: now I know in part, but then I shall know, even as also I am known.* And that this is a parallel between this life and the life to come, is clear from 1 John iii. 2. *Behold now we are the sons of God, and it doth not yet appear what we shall be; but we know, when he shall appear, we shall be like him, for we shall see him as he is.* 2. The life to come is holden forth, Rev. xxi. 22. to want all ordinances. *And I saw no temple therein* (saith John, when he saw the New Jerusalem) *for the Lord God Almighty, and the Lamb*

are

are the temple of it. Nor is there any ignorance there, Rev. xxii. 5. *And there shall be no night there, and they need no candle, neither light of the sun, for the Lord God giveth them light, and they shall reign for ever and ever.* Whatever any say of a personal reign of Christ on earth, the words prove, that while that life come, all the regenerate here have need of a temple, and ordinances, so long as there is night and darkness, and use for sun and moon; so the date of church-ordinances is holden for, Cant ii. 16. *My well-beloved is mine, and I am his; he feedeth among the lilies,*, v. 17. *Until the day break, and the shadows flee away.* Then there is a night on the church, and need of the moon-light of ordinances, so long as Christ by his ministry remains in the Shepherd's tents, feeding his flock in the strength of the Lord, and holding forth his presence to his justified ones, spotless and fair through the imputed righteousness of Christ; as lilies, while the fairest and most desirable day of that illustrious and glorious appearance of Christ dawn. And Paul clearly expoundeth these words, Eph. iv. shewing the term day of Christ's reign, in his saints, by the ministry of the gospel; and that the saints and body of Christ are but in the way to be perfected and edified by pastors and teachers, verse 13. *Till we all come to the unity of the faith, and of the knowledge of the Son of God, unto a perfect man, unto the measure of the stature of the fulness of Christ.* Hence saints are not perfected till that day. 2. The body of Christ is low of stature, capable of growing; the bride's hair groweth, she is not a perfect tall stature, but like a young girl, not yet fit for marriage to the Lamb, *till we meet all in the unity of faith*; so I know no active annihilation, no evanishing of, and ceasing from, all acts of the will of God revealed in the law and gospel; that is, from praying, hearing, meditating, loving, desiring, longing after Christ, *till the day that the shadows flee away;* then, I confess, I shall have no leisure to read on the book of the Old and New Testament, or to attend preaching, sa-

craments,

craments, or other ordinances, because I need no mirror, no portrait of Christ, no message of ministers, when I see and enjoy himself. 3. All who have God for their Father, and need daily bread, and are clothed with a body of clay, are to pray for remission of sins, not *to be led into temptation, or sinful omitting of duties*; all for whom the blood of Jesus is shed, are to *declare the Lord's death, till he come again.* What ceasing then from duties of law, love, the Spirit, and Christ, is this? Where is this fancied annihilation to be dreamed of? Scripture knoweth it not.

Pos. 5. There is a fulness of loveliness in Christ, that is begun in us by possession and title in this life, but never perfect till the life to come; in which there be these, 1. Union. 2. Fruition. 3. Rest. 4. Satisfaction. 5. Sense. 6. Living and acting in Christ. 7. Loving and solacing of the soul. Of which, to hold forth more of the drawing of Christ, we say,

Pos. 6. Christ's inviting us to come to him, and that before we can invite him, speaketh union. 1. Such an union as faith can make, which ariseth not to the pitch of sight, and immediate fruition; for it is the union of those, that are absent one from another, in regard of fulness of presence. 2 Cor. v. 6. *Knowing that whilst we are at home in the body, we are absent from the Lord.* John xvi. 7. *Nevertheless I tell you the truth, it is expedient that I go away.* Luke xix . 12. *He said therefore, A certain nobleman went into a far country, to receive for himself a kingdom, and to return.* Yet it is the union of those that are so near as the house and the guest, or as two friends that table together, Ephes. iii. 17. John xix. 23. Rev. iii. 21. 2. 'Tis an union of fruition, for Christ in some measure is enjoyed in this life, yet so as the fruition is in part, not compleat and full in degrees, as it shall be in the life to come; it is here for both a fruition of rest and of motion; of rest, in regard of the present fruition; of motion, in regard of advancing in the way to a compleat fruition, so as is in a journey, in regard of practical love, and at its home, in regard of love and union of

fruition;

CHRIST DYING AND DRAWING SINNERS TO HIMSELF. 411

fruition; so the soul is both satisfied with bread, and hungers no more, Isa. lv. 2. *but delighteth itself in fatness, and thirsteth no more,* having a present sense of complacency and content in the water of life, John iv. 14. and also, the soul is so far forth not satisfied, and its thirst not quenched, but that it hungereth and thirsteth for a fuller union and an immediate fruition; in which regard, the soul is both abroad in its way and motion to have more of Christ, and at home, and at rest, in regard it is fully satisfied exclusively, not inclusively; because this satisfaction excludeth and annihilateth all choice of another lover than Christ, and denies all deliberate comparing of Christ with any other lover, as holding and prizing him *the chief of ten thousand,* and resolving never to fix the desire on another husband or lover but Christ, as Cant. iii. 4. *It was but a little, that I passed from the watchmen, but I found him whom my soul loveth; I held him, and would not let him go, until I had brought him to my mother's house, and the chamber of her that conceived me.* Finding and holding of Christ, is as much as there is satisfaction and rest in the fruition of him; and yet the spouse's aim to go hand in hand on a journey to the house of the high *Jerusalem the mother of us all;* which, with submission I conceive, the spouse calleth her mother's house, doth clearly prove, that she is not perfect, but in a motion; not yet at her journey's end, till she come with Christ to the *palace of the prince's daughter, the bride the Lamb's wife,* Rev. xxi. 10, 11, 12. Hence we see how true that is, that the desires are swallowed up into the bosom of infinite Jesus Christ, as a little brook is swallowed up when it comes into the ocean, and yet the desires remain: they are swallowed up in Christ, in that the soul is at home, being quieted and perfected in Christ, and are no more restless and pained in the journey toward Christ; but as heaven is begun on earth, so hath David quietness of mind, and breaketh forth in praises, that the Lord gave him counsel to chuse God himself for his portion, Psal. xvi. 5, 6, 7. *So goodly and pleasant is the*
heritage;

heritage; and now there is no more desire for Christ as a thing absent, and the thirst is swallowed up in Christ, the soul thirsteth no more, John iv. 14. And yet the desire remaineth both in the sweet complacency and liking of the saints, delighting in present fruition, and also in an act of longing for the highest pitch of degrees of union; just as in the act of drinking, thirst is half swallowed up in begun satisfaction, and thirst remaineth in a liking, and a farther desire of a perfect cooling and refreshing overcoming of a full quenching of the appetite.

Pos. 7. Yet can it not be said, but here is a begun satisfaction; for, John iv. 14. Christ enjoyed, is a draught of the *water of life free given*, Rev. xxii. 17. *That whosoever will, may drink of the water of life freely.* John vii. 37. *In the last, and great day of the feast Jesus stood, and cried, saying, If any man thirst, let him come to me and drink.* 2. Not a drink only is offered, but a well, a fountain. Psal. xxxvi. 9. *For with thee is the fountain of life;* a fountain is more than a drink, because the whole is more than the part. But, 3. Every thirsty man cannot have a fountain within him, but yet it is so here, John iv. 14. *But the water that I shall give him, shall be in him a well of water springing up to life eternal.* And, 4. The scripture riseth higher, even to a river, and abundance of fatness. Psal. xxxvi. 8. *They shall be abundantly satisfied with the fatness of thy house,* [Heb. jirvin] *they shall be drunk with the fatness of thy house.* 'Tis a river of sweet oil and fatness that overjoyeth the soul; *Thou wilt give them to drink of the river of thy pleasures:* a river of which every drop is joy, and a whole well of pleasures must be sea of delights. But grace must make the soul a capacious vessel, when not a fountain, but a whole river, yea rivers of life, are within the soul: so Christ, John vii. 38. *He that believeth on me, as the scripture hath said, Out of his belly shall flow rivers of living waters.* Yea, 5. That no expression might be wanting, *The peace and righteousness of believers, is as the waves of the sea;* the sea is more

than

than a river, it is the lodging that receives all fountains and rivers in it, Isa. xlviii. 18.

Pos. 8. There must be much sense of God, in the fruition of Christ; because believing, tho' we see him not, (as we hope to see him) causeth *joy unspeakable and full of glory*, 1 Pet. i. 8. Thus, a high tide, a flood of joy and glory, a rich portion of an antedated heaven, cometh down on the heirs of heaven before-hand. Psal. lxiii. 5. *My soul shall be satisfied as with marrow and fatness*; a rich feast of only marrow and fatness, and a satisfying table, holdeth forth a great banquet, abundant and glorious; such as is made at the marriage of a great king's son.

Pos. 9. And this is not a ceasing from all actings of the soul, because there is an acting and living in Christ, 2 Cor. iii. 18. *But we all with open face, beholding as in a glass, the glory of the Lord, are changed into the same image from glory to glory, as it were by the Spirit of the Lord.* 1. The vail, that by the law's ministry, which can darken, but not enlighten, in the gospel is removed; and we with uncovered face see God revealed in Christ, in the brightness of the gospel-day. 2. We see, behold and enjoy glory: heaven darteth in the rays, and beams of God in Christ at our soul. 3. This is a changing glory: precious stones in the night-darkness cast out light, but bring them before the sun, and the beams and light of the sun changeth them into a greater measure of resplendency, and shining irradiation; we seeing the unspeakable resplendency, and heavenly glancing of divine majesty, in the Mediator Christ, are transformed and changed into the Lord Jesus his beauty of holiness; the gospel-light maketh us holy, as he is holy: as there is beauty in the feathers of a dove; but when the sun illuminateth, and shineth on them, they carry the glancing of silver and golden feathers, yet it is but a show: and so red and white roses, of themselves have excellent beauty; but set them between you and the sun, and they are far more beautiful: and the eastern sky, of itself, is but a dark, thin, formless

air,

air, that ye can scarcely behold and see; but when the sun riseth, and shineth upon that sky, it doth create and beget the fairest and most beautiful colour of red and azure, that is possible; for no bodily creature casteth a fairer and sweeter resplendency and colour, than the morning-red and purple sky: so when the glorious Sun of righteousness, Christ, shineth on saints in the morning day-light of the gospel, he createth the image of the glory of God in the soul, and changeth them into a lustre and beauty fairer to Christ's eye, than the sun, or the red morning-sky. Now, the sun, by beholding any creature, cannot change that creature into another sun; but Christ beholding his bride, and the bride beholding with the eye of knowledge, and faith, in the rays and beams of the gospel-light, *is changed into the glorious image of Christ.* Cant. vi. 10. *Who is she that looketh forth as the morning, as Aurora, the first birth of the young day*, when the sun casteth golden beams, *fair as the moon, clear as the sun?* 4. We live and act in Christ, and are changed from glory to glory; it is but a growing change by degrees. Then the kingdom of heaven and glory is not in this life, nor hell in this life, as these dreamers say; the conditions of happiness and misery, that follow Lazarus, and the rich glutton, after they die, and are buried, Luke xvi. 22, 23, 24, 25. say the contrary. 2. There is such a gulf between heaven and hell, that there is no passage, no failing, nor posting between the one and the other, Luke xvi. 26. as Famulists imagine. 3. That saints *should believe they can never be delivered, nor comforted,* in the hell they are pained withal in this life, when yet God hath promised to them in their saddest nights, deliverance and comfort; is against the faith and lively hope of the saints, and a sinful unbelief; and the man in sin cannot be as safe in a hell of sin, as if he were in heaven. 4. Hell is a condition of sinning and blaspheming of God; but to desire nothing but the eternal good, and to understand the eternal good to be above measure good, is not a condition of sinning, but of

hap-

happiness and holiness, and so cannot be hell. 5. These two conditions, sort not with the everlasting fire *prepared for the devil and his angels;* and life eternal *prepared for the blessed of the Father*, Mat. xxv. But to return, if life be the greatest perfection of being, the believer in Christ must enjoy an intellectual life in Christ, and live, see, know, enjoy God; and though the enjoying of Christ, be the highest degree of self-denial, and the man lose himself in Christ, that is, his sinful and fleshly, I, egoity, and selfiness in Christ, yet he loseth not, but findeth in Christ his sinless created self, his self perfected, with that high and supernatural ornament of Christ living in him. It is also most true, *Self*, as all created beings, are but mere dependencies on God: as the beams of the sun are but fluxes, results and issues, that have no being but in the sun; sure creatures depend more on their being and working on God, than accidents depend on their subject: but it is nothing less than blasphemy, against all reason and common sense, and subverteth all the scriptures of God, to say, that 'God is formally all things, that God is man, that God is the Spirit and form that acteth in all, that a holy man is God incarnate, and Christ God-man, and that Christ the Mediator is nothing, but God humanized, and man godded and deified;' and that Christ dwelling in a believer by faith, and the inhabitation of the Holy Ghost, is but God manifested in the flesh of every man. This destroyeth many articles of faith (as Famulists care not boldly to subvert all scriptures) for Christ then is not true man, born of the seed of David, and he is not God blessed for ever, in one person. 2. All creatures and created beings, compared with God, the first being of himself subsisting, and the infinite God, may be denied to be beings comparatively; and so our created self is nothing, to wit, nothing in dignity or excellency beside God, or nothing in the kind of a being that essentially is of itself; as God is *in genere intis par essentiam*, yet man is a being in the

kind

kind of being, by participation, *in genere entis per participationem.* Man, compared with God, is a poor, worthless, sorry, little nothing, a weeping, melting, evanishing cypher. Yea, sweetest ordinances, because it is but created sweetness that is in them, are near of blood to nothing, and, in comparison of God, mere shadows, that cannot bottom the immortal soul; and nothing, and partake of vanity common to all creatures. So the scripture saith, *man at his best state is altogether vanity.* Psal. xxxix. 5. *Behold, thou hast made my days as a hand-breadth, and mine age is nothing before thee: verily every man at his best state is altogether vanity.* Isa. xl. 17. *All nations before him are nothing, and less than nothing, and vanity.* Yet a heathen may say and think and demonstrate by reason, that self, and man, and all the world, are less, in comparison of the infinite God, than nothing to all things, a drop of water of the sea, the shadow to the body, a penny-torch to the light of ten thousand millions of suns in one; and yet be as far from self-denial, from putting off the old man, and mortifying the lusts of the flesh, as light is from darkness. 'Tis most vain to say, as it is the property of the creature to seek and will itself, and its own, and this or that, here or there; so it is the property of God to be without this or that, without selfiness, egoity or the like. Because every thing created, even worms, frogs, trees, elements, such creatures as beget creatures like themselves; they have such a sweet and natural interest in being, that without sin or deviation from law or rule, or any leading or directing principle of nature, they desire themselves, their own being; and when they cannot keep being in themselves, they desire to keep it in the kind, by propagation, and will fight it out against all contraries and enemies, to preserve their own being, though but borrowed from God; and I know no sin they are guilty of, in so doing: nor was Christ's conditional desire of life, and deprecating death, any whit contrary to innocent self-denial. 2. The Lord seeketh himself and his own glory, and made all things for himself, even the

wicked

CHRIST DYING AND DRAWING SINNERS TO HIMSELF.

wicked for the evil day, Pro. xvi. 4. And that is a most holy and pure act, which God ascribeth to himself, Isa. xliii. 21. *This people have I formed for myself, they shall shew forth my praise.*

Now, in all dwelling in Christ, there is a continual acting of life, by believing, joying, resting in God; as Philip saith, John xiv. 8. *Lord, shew us the Father, and it sufficeth us.* Here life seeks a soul-satisfying union with life, for life is only a satisfactory object to life. Living things seek no dead things as such to be their happiness, if reason do rightly act them; and God as revealed in Jesus Christ, is that in which the saints find a soul-sufficiency for themselves: and the act of seeing God in Christ, whether in this life, or in the life to come, is an act of life; for the soul liveth in the ocean, sea, and bosom of a fair eternal truth. But doth it act there? Yea, it doth, and the scripture expresseth its acting, by seeing God, drinking the fountain of life. Then the soul thus in Christ drinketh in love, and milketh and sucketh in the soul-rejoicing irradiations of Christ, and Christ letteth out the breathings of the sweetness of his excellency on the face of the soul, draweth and sucketh in reciprocally acts of admiration and wondering, Cant. ii. 8. *The voice of my beloved! behold he cometh leaping upon the mountains, and skipping on the hills;* behold is a word of wonder, John iii. i. *Behold what manner of love the Father hath bestowed on us!* not love, only, but the manner and the kind of the Father's love in Christ, is a world's wonder; and, Thess. i. 10. Christ, when he cometh, shall be wondred in them that believe. 2. Then again, when we see and enjoy the drawing loveliness of Christ, he, as the fountain and well of life, poureth in, in our intellectual love, and in the glancings and rays of our understanding, acts of divine light; lumps of fresh love from the spring of heaven's love, and the soul openeth its mouth wide, and taketh in the streams of Christ's nectar, honey, and milk, his consolations, and love-breathings; and in his light we seeing light, and in his love feeling love, he maketh our light

and

and love (as it were) co-eternal with borrowed eternity; and we go along with the out-shinings of Christ's bright countenance, to shine in borrowed light, to flame in borrowed coals of love. And as Christ is said, to *feed his flock among the lilies*, the garden of Christ his church being the common pasture for the lambs of the flock; so he feeds the souls of the saints that enjoy him, with the marrow, fatness, and dainties of his light, and love that shine in his face, even as the oil feeds the lamp; but with this difference, Christ's dainties are not lessened, because we feed upon them, as the oil is consumed with the burning.

Pos. 10. There is a living and solacing of the soul in Christ, even to satiety, in this enjoying of Christ.

Hence, 1. Love giveth strong legs and swift wings to the soul, to pursue an union with Christ. Love putteth the hand to the bottom of the desire, and draweth with strong cords, the lover to it. We have heard of Christ's invitation, *come to me*: but, suppose Christ had never outed his love in such a love-expression, *come to me*, Christ himself is such a drawing object, that beauty, the smell of his garments, his mountain of myrrh, and hill of frankincense, the sea and rivers of salvation, that capacious and wide heaven of redemption, are intrinsically, and of themselves, crying, drawing and ravishing objects; as gold is dumb and cannot speak, yet the beauty and gain of it crieth, *come hither, poor, and be made rich*.

2. Love's wings move swiftly, *Open, my sister*, etc. *My head is full of dew, and my locks, with the drops of the night;* there is no dumb and silent violence so strong, so piercing as Christ's love.

3. When the soul in any measure comprehendeth this love, the soul is *filled with all the fulness of God*, Eph. iii. 19. Hence must follow a stretching out of the soul to its widest capacity and circumference, being filled with God, and the fulness of Christ, that all created objects, because of their littleness and lowness, and the soul's stretched out and wide capacity, loses proportion with the soul: as if a man were in the top of a castle higher

CHRIST DYING AND DRAWING SINNERS TO HIMSELF.

higher than the third region of the air, or near the sphere of the moon, should he look down to the fairest and sweetest meadows, and to a garden rich with roses and flowers, or all sweet colours, delicious smells, he should not see any sweetness in them all; yea, the pleasantness, colour, and smell of all these, could never reach his senses, because he is so far above them: so the soul filled with the love of Christ is high above all created lovers, and they so far below the soul's eye, that their loveliness cannot reach or ascend to the high and large capacity of a spiritualized soul; as the light of a penny-candle put in a house of some miles in length, in breadth, and height, in a dark night, should not be able to illuminate all the house, and render the air of a mile in quantity, lightsome and transparent, as the day-light sun would do.

4. Because the glory of Christ's beauty, seen and loved, changeth the soul into a globe or mass of divine love and glory, *as it were by the Spirit of the Lord*, 2 Cor. iii. 18. Therefore the soul seeth Christ so near in his love-embracements, and close inchaining of Christ's left arm under the soul's head, and the right hand embracing it, that it cannot see itself, it cannot see another lover; it can see nothing but Christ's fairness, hear nothing but the beloved's voice, taste nothing but his apples of love, his flagons of wine, can small nothing but his spikenard and precious ointments; so that the soul is clothed with Christ, and his love, and can but breathe out love to him again; and Christ infuseth himself in his sweetness and excellency, so as the believer is apprehended by Jesus Christ, Phil. iii. 12. violently, but sweetly and strongly drawn in, and *holden in the king's house of wine*, Cant. ii. 4. sickned and overcome with love, Cant. ii. 5. Cant. v. 8. chained and compelled, 2 Cor. v. 14. wounded with the arrows of love; so as death, the grave, hell, angels, things present, or to come, cannot lick these wounds, nor embalm, or bind them up, or cure them, Psal. xlv. 5. Rev. vi. 1, 2. Cant. viii. 6, 7. Rom. viii. 38, 39. Yea, the soul must yield over its self, as a spouse under the power of her husband, and

lose

lose herself, and her father's house, in such a deep ocean of delights of *loves stronger than wine*, Psal. xlv. 10. Cant. v. 1. Cant. i. 2. as melted, dissolved, and fallen aswoon in Christ, Cant. v. 6. and therefore needeth, in that swoon, to be recovered with the flagons of the wine and apples of his consolations, Cant. ii. 4.

5. Nor can Jesus Christ but tenderly, lovingly, and compassionately deal with his beloved; for Christ must draw them, John vi. 44. sweetly allure them, Hos. ii. 14. Isa. xl. 1. *Take them by the two arms*, and teach them to walk, as the mother doth the young child, who hath not yet legs to walk alone, Hos. xi. 3. *Beareth them in his arms*, and dandleth them on his knee, Isa. xlvi. 3, 4. Exod. xix. 4. They are carried on Christ's warm wings, as the young eagles by the mother, Deut. xxxii. 11. they are laid in Christ's bosom, and nourished with the warmness and the heat of life that cometh from Christ's heart, Isa. xl. 11. carried on the shoulders of Christ, the good Shepherd, Luke xv. 5. and yet nearer Christ, as a bracelet about Christ's arms; so he wears his church as a favour and a love-token, Jer. xxii. 24. Cant. viii. 6. and engraven in letters of blood upon Christ's flesh, stamped and printed on the palms of his hands, Isa. xlix. 16. and yet nearer him, *set as a seal upon the heart of Christ*, so precious to him, as to lodge in his bowels and heart, Cant. viii. 6. and they *dwell in Christ*, 1 John iv. 13. and *dwell in God, and God is love,* and so they dwell in the love of Christ, 1 John iv. 16. are kissed with the kisses of Christ's mouth, Cant. i. 2. and lie between the right and left arm of Christ, Cant. ii. 6. Yet all these taketh not the soul off, but inflameth it to duties, for Christ's sake, who is so highly loved; nor are these raptures inconsistent with sinful infirmities.

6. As love moveth swiftly to the soul, as a roe, or a young hart, (for that is Christ's pace to his church, Cant. ii.) so it acts upon the soul co-naturally, as being a price to itself, apprehending the dignity and excellency of Christ the beloved. Love is not irrational, as a fury, and a fit of madness, that hath no reason,

but

but its own fire. Therefore the secrets of Christ, the deep and hidden things of his treasures of love and wisdom, must be opened up to the soul. The soul seeth now gold mines, new found-out jewels, never known to be in the world before, opened and unfolded in Christ. Here are the in-comings of the beams of light inaccessible, the veins of the unsearchable riches of Christ, as if ye saw every moment a new heaven, a new treasure of love, the deep bottomless bottoms of an ocean of delights, and rivers of pleasures; the bosom of Christ is opened, new breathings and spirations of love *that passeth knowledge*, Eph. iii. 19. are manifested; *nor hath the eye seen, nor the ear heard, nor hath it entred into the heart of man to conceive the things that God hath prepared for them that love him*, 1 Cor. ii. 9. yet are they revealed, in some measure, in this life.

7. And it is most considerable, how the soul in loving Christ is not her own; and in regard of loving, Christ is not his own, but every one makes over itself to another, and propriety or interest to itself in both sides (as it were) ceaseth, Hos. iii. 3. *And I said unto her, Thou shalt abide for me many days, thou shalt not play the harlot, and thou shalt not be for another man, so will I also be for thee;* so the marriage-covenant of grace saith, *I will be your God, and ye shall be my people.* And the spouse, Cant. ii. 16. *My well-beloved is mine, and I am his.* It is true, Christ leaveth not off to be his own, or to be a free God, when he becomes ours; but he demeaneth himself, as if he were not his own, and putteth on relations, and assumeth offices of engagement; *a Saviour, an Anointed, a Redeemer, a King, a Priest, a Prophet, a Shepherd, a Husband, a Ransomer, a Friend, a Head, a Guide,* and *Leader of the People*, all which are for us: and the soul enjoying Christ, posseseth Christ, and not itself; loveth Christ, not itself; liveth in Christ, not in itself; enjoyeth Christ, not itself; solaceth itself in Christ, not in itself; beholdeth Christ and his beauty, not itself, nor his own beauty; so that mind, will, love, desire,

hope,

hope, joy, sight, wondring, delighting, are all over in Christ, not in itself. And all this further confirmeth the point in hand, that Christ crucified, and laid hold on by faith, is a desirable and a drawing lover.

PART III. *All men.*

I will draw all men. The parties drawn to Christ, is the third article in the doctrine of Christ's drawing; and they are here called [Gr. pántes,] *all men.* It is a great question between us, and such as are for universal atonement, and grace universal, as many Anabaptists in England now are; what is meant by *all men*: in which these are to be observed,
1. *The state of the question.*
2. *The mind of the adversaries.*
3. *Our mind.*
4. *The clearing of places alledged by the adversaries.*
5. *The answering of that principal doubt, what faith is required of all within the visible church.*
6. *The uses of the doctrine.*
Of all these shortly.
The state of the question.
The question toucheth, 1. God's intention and purpose to save man. 2. In chusing some to salvation, not others. 3. God's purpose in sending Christ to die for some, not for others.

The first article is called universal grace; the second conditional, or, which to me is all one, universal election to glory, and so no election; the third is, the question touching the universality of Christ's death, or a fancied universal atonement made by Christ for all. I cannot particularly handle all the three.

For the first: God engageth all men as Christ's debtors thus far, that it is mercy that they live, or have any opportunity of seeking God, whatever be the means natural or supernatural; whereas, for the sin of

Adam,

Adam, God might by a like justice have destroyed the world and all mankind, vanity is penally inflicted on all the servants, for treason of the master against the King of heaven and earth: but in Christ there be two mitigations; 1. One is, that the servants are not destroyed for the sin of the master. 2. That as the forfeited Lord is restored, so the sick servants groaning under vanity shall be delivered from that bondage they come under for the sin of man, Rom. viii. 20, 21, 22. Hence it is, tho' we be out-laws by nature, that now, by a privilege of grace from the Mediator, the tenants receive and lodge the master, because Christ hath taken off the statute and act of forfeiture. 2. No man living on earth, but he is beholding to Christ (tho' many know him not) for common helps of providence; and experiences do teach him some more of God by nature. 3. The sound of Christ, God revealed in the gospel, in the apostles' ministry is declared, and is gone to the ends of the earth, and to the nations, Psal. xix. 4. Rom. x. 18. But some say, "These words, *have they not heard*, have relation to v. 14. the hearing of the gospel, or the publishing of the glad tidings of the gospel to all and every one of mankind; and must be meant of that same hearing."

Answ. It relates to hearing of God revealing himself in the means of salvation, say the adversaries. But then the question is, whether these means be the preaching of the gospel, or of the same God revealed as Creator, by the sun, moon, and stars, who is revealed in the gospel, and salvation by him? Now, the *sun, and stars, and heaven declare the glory of God,* and sound forth his praises and salvation through Christ, by this sense, to all and every nation, and to every single person without exception; not only when Paul wrote this to the Romans, but when David penned the xix. Psalm. What difference then between the Jews, to whom God revealed his testimonies, and the Gentiles, to whom God made no such revelation? Psal. cxlvii. 19, 20. Deut. iv. 33, 34, etc. Deut. v. 25, 26. Psal.lxxviii. 1, 2, etc. Psal. lxxxi. 4, 5. and this sound,

if

if it be the gospel preached to as many as see the sun, and ever when they see the sun; then at that time, and to this day, the sun and moon must be sent apostles and preachers, by whose words and ministry, all and every man that seeth the sun, then and now, and to Christ's second coming, are obliged to pray to God in Christ, and to believe, and *faith comes by hearing:* the sun, stars, night and day, preach Christ; for sure the same hearing of the gospel, v. 18. must be understood, which is spoken, v. 14, 15. for if the one be an hearing of the gospel by the apostles, which produceth faith and salvation, and the other a hearing of the sun and stars in the book of the creation, this produceth not faith and salvation by the confession of adversaries. 2. The apostle shall not answer his own objection. v. 18. *If all both Jew and Gentile have not heard the gospel, it is impossible they can believe; for faith cometh by hearing the gospel, from their mouth who are sent of God;* and if they hear not, they must be excused, because they believe not in Christ, *of whom they never heard.* The apostle must answer, yea, but they have heard the gospel. Why? They heard the sun, and the stars preach Christ, and salvation by him, to the farthest ends of the earth: for, sure, David, in the literal and native sense of that xix Psalm, speaketh of such dumb preachers. Now, this is no answer at all, for sun and stars are not sent of God to preach salvation by Christ. 2. Faith comes not by hearing the creatures preach Christ. 3. The prophets and apostles, not the dumb and lifeless creatures, have pleasant feet on the mountains to preach peace, as it is v. 14, 15, 16. cited from Isa. lii. 7. Nah. i. 15. But the native sense of the words, v. 18. is but a mere allusion, in scripture-phrase, to David's words, Psal. xix. It is neither citation nor exposition of them, but an using of scripture-language in comparing the gospel to the sun, the sound of the gospel preached, to the sound of the glory of the Creator in the works of heaven and earth, to show how ample the preaching of the gospel under the New Testament is: to wit, that it is not preached to one nation

tion of the Jews only, as of old; but to all nations, to the Jews, *and to the foolish people, by whom the Lord provokes the Jews to jealousy*, as is clear, v. 19, 20. and that voice [Gr. ho phthongos autòn] *their voice is gone to the ends of the earth*, is the voice of the *twelve apostles of the Lamb*, who preached the gospel to nations of all kinds, to Jews and Gentiles: 'tis not the voice of the creatures, the heaven and earth, but a mere allusion to that voice, Psal. xix. for the words have no sense otherwise; for the apostle avoucheth the gospel is preached, the promise of salvation published to all that call on the Lord's name, v. 12. *be they Jews or Grecians*, that is, Gentiles; and believe they must, or else they cannot pray; and needs they must hear, or then they cannot believe; and hear they cannot, except God send preachers. But God hath sent preachers with pleasant feet, to both Jews and Gentiles, as the prophets Isaiah and Nahum foretold, v. 13, 14, 15. and they have not obeyed, v. 16,17,18. But it may be said, *they have not all heard the gospel preached:* This must certainly excuse the Gentiles, if they believe not; having never heard of Christ, how can they believe? as it is, v. 14. It is a rational excuse, I cannot sin in not believing the gospel, saith the Gentile; yea, and Christ frees them from the sin of unbelief also, John xv. 22. *If I had not come, and spoken unto them* (and so, if they had not had a Lord-speaker from heaven) *they had not had sin*, that is, they should have been free of the gospel-sin of unbelief; *but now they have no cloke for their sin.* Now, they cannot say, *Lord, we cannot believe a gospel, never spoken to us by any, nor heard of by us.* But sure, the Jews heard these creatures and works of God, that preached his glory, Psal. xix. 6. And, if they preach Christ objectively, as Amyrald, and other Arminians fancy; then the not hearing, and not obeying the gospel thus preached, had been their sin, tho' Christ or his apostles had never spoken the gospel; which is contrary to Christ's word, John xv. 22. and contrary to Paul, *how shall they believe in him of whom they have not heard*, by the preach-

ing

ing of a sent minister, who subjectively and vocally must preach the gospel.

But to return to the state of the question. 4. So much of God is revealed to all, even to those who never heard of Christ, as serves to make all unexcusable, for that knowing willingly, and knowingly, they glorify not God as God, Rom. i. 19, 20, 21. 5. All within the visible church have means sufficient in their kind, *in genere mediorum externorum*, to save them.

6. As none can be saved by the light of nature, nor ever any used, or could use it so far forth, as to improve it for their sufficient preparation, to receive the tidings of the gospel, either from men, or angels sent to preach to them; or by any inspiration, bringing the sense, or things signified in the gospel: so saved they cannot be, *by any name under heaven, but by the name of Christ;* that is, Christ named, preached, and revealed in the gospel, Acts iv. 10, 11, 12. John xiv. 6. Heb. xi. 6. John v. 40. and 1 John v. 12. *He that hath the Son, hath life: and he that hath not the Son, hath not life.*

7. The question is, whether or no God so far forth willeth, desireth, intendeth, that all and every one, within, and without the visible church. Tartarians, and Indians (who never, by any rumour, heard of Christ) not excepted, that he giveth them sufficient means and helps of a common and universal grace; which if they would use well, the Lord should so reward, promove, or increase, whether out of decency, or a congruous disposition of goodness, or of equity, or of free promise, or any obligation, so far as to send the gospel to them, and bestow on them a larger measure of saving and internal grace; by which they should, if they so would, be converted to the faith of Christ, and saved? We deny, Arminians affirm.

2. Whether the Lord from eternity (late Arminians are for time election) hath absolutely, without any provision in, or prescience, or foreknowledge of good works, faith, perseverance in both, or of condition, reason, cause, merit, qualification in some certain and definite persons, rather than others, predestinated and
chosen

chosen them to glory and life eternal, and all the means conducing to this end, and that of meer free-grace, because he so willeth; or if the Lord pass no definite, complete, peremptory, and irrevocable decree, to save some certain persons, while he foresees them expiring, and dying in faith and holy conversation? Arminians hold, That the Lord's decree of election of men to glory, is general, conditional, incomplete, changeable, while he foresees they have ended their course in the faith; and then peremptorily, and irrevocably, he passeth a fixed decree to save such, and not others: we deny any such loose decrees in the Almighty, and believe that of free-grace. He chuseth some absolutely, without conditions in them, or respect to any good foreseen to be in them, rather than in others, because *He hath mercy on whom he will, and hardens whom he will,* Rom. ix. 17, 18.

3. Upon this general, indefinite, revocable, and conditional good-will and intention of God, to save all, and every one; whether or no did the Father give his Son, and the Son die for all, and every one, intending absolutely to impetrate and obtain to all, and every one of mankind, remission of sins, and especially, expiation of sin original, and all sins against the covenant of works; and salvation to them all, both within and without the visible church, and the opening of the gates of heaven; so as God hath laid aside his anger for all these sins, hath made all saveable, reconcileable, that notwithstanding of Divine justice's plea against men, all and every one may, according to the intention of God, be saved in his blood, so they would, as they may, and can believe in Christ? We deny, Arminians here affirm.

2. The mind of Arminians. Arminians run upon six universalities.

1. They say, God beareth to all, and every man, of what kind soever, an equal, universal, and catholic good-will; yea, to Esau, Pharaoh, Judas, as to Jacob, Moses, and Peter, to save them all; so as this love is not stinted to any certain persons, precisely, and absolutely, loved and chosen to salvation.

2.

2. That there is a catholic price, an universal ransom, given by Christ dying on the cross, for all, and every one; an atonement made, and a redemption purchased in Christ's blood; by which, all and every one, Pharaoh, Judas, Cain, all the Heathens, Tartarians, Americans, Virginians, that never herd of Christ, are made saveable, and reconcileable, and God made placable and exorable to them; so as tho' they be most in the first Adam, yet have they a new venture of heaven; and in Christ's death, the Lord hath a general, antecedent, and primary intention to save all without exception; yet no more to save Moses and Peter, than Judas and Pharaoh: yea, that the fruit of Christ's death, and the effect of it, may stand, tho' all, and every one of mankind, were eternally lost, and not one person saved.

3. As there was a catholic forfeiture of all, so there is a second covenant of free-grace made with all, and every one of Adam's sons, with promises of free-grace, a new heart, righteousness, and eternal life, to all and every one, upon fair conditions, if their free-will play the game of salvation and damnation handsomely; as if Christ were not free-will's choicest tutor.

4. All, and every man, are received into this covenant, in the new state of reconciliation, grace, and favour, and justification from any breach of the law, or the first covenant; all are once fairly delivered, both young and old, from damnation and wrath: all the heathen are reconciled and justified by Christ, in his blood; and all sins, now, are against the first covenant of grace; Christ and all mankind, now, begin to reckon on a new score. 2. Tho' the ship be broken, and all mankind sent to sea to die there, yet so are they cast overboard, as Christ, the surety of a better covenant, is made the great vessel, the ship-broken men may, if it seem good to lord free-will, swim unto, and so come safe the second time to land. 3. So as there be two redemptions in Christ, two justifications by grace. 4. Yet neither the tidings of this new covenant made with all men, nor this state of reconciliation, or justification, are ever revealed to the thousandth part of mankind and

tho'

tho' all and every one be under this law of faith, and covenant of grace; yet is this obliging and supernatural law never promulgate to millions of mankind, whom it obligeth to obedience, so far forth as by the good industry, and improving of common gifts of nature, or rather the hire and merit of men out of Christ, to make a conquest of the preached gospel and Christ, free-will doing its best.

5. All and every mother's son, and children of Adam, are called and invited; yea, and Christ, by our text, draweth all and every man, tho' they will not be drawn; say they, the sole cause of election, reprobation, of salvation, damnation, lying on man's free-will.

6. All and every one are furnished with all external means of salvation, with sufficient grace, and absolute indifferency and power of free-will to say ay, or no, to the drawing of Christ; and purchase, by industrious improvement, and careful husbanding of the common gifts or relicts of nature, and their new sufficient grace, (if they could give it a name to us) a farther degree of grace, while they conquess the preaching of the gospel, and the grace of conversion. Yet so are they, (let Christ do his best) as all may be converted, or not any one at all, but all lost; and all may persevere in grace, and be saved, as not one man shall be damned; and all may so totally finally fall away from grace, as not one man may persevere, but all be eternally lost, if free-will use his own liberty, notwithstanding of the Lord's eternal decrees of election or reprobation, or of Christ's death, the strength of free-grace, the intercession of Christ at the right hand of God, the unchangeable love of God; for all these can do nothing to marr the absolute and independent free-will of men, to work as it listeth, for either ways.

Propos. 1. Election is the decree of free-grace, setting apart certain, definite, individual, and particular men to glory.

1. The men chosen and drawn, are by head designed. Jacob, not Esau, before the children had done good or evil; tho' Esau be elder, Jacob must be the son of the

promise:

promise: father and mother were free-grace, rather than the seed of Abraham and Sarah, now passed nature's date; not Ishmael: Peter and John, not Judas the son of perdition: Abraham, and his house, worshipping idols beyond the river, is singled out, not any other: the Lord sets his love on the Jews, *because he loved them*, Deut.vii. 7. when their Father was an Amorite, and their mother an Hittite, and *they dying in their blood*, Ezek. xvi. 3, 4, 5, 6, 7. not any one of the rest of the Cananites. The tribe of Judah is the kingly tribe, not any of the rest of the families: low Jephthah's family, not any of the rest of the sons of that family: none of the seven sons, but the despised shepherd, the ruddy boy singing after the ewes, David forgotten by all, as none of the number.

2. They are pointed out with the finger, with pronouns, Psal. lxxxvii. 5. *And of Zion it is said, This man,* [Heb. isch veisch] *man and man shall be born in Zion,* Isa. xlix. 1. *The Lord hath called me from the womb, from the bowels of my mother hath he made mention of my name.* Thou art (head, or member, or of which the prophet spake, it is all one) in the mouth of God, by name from eternity, John, Anna, etc. Isa. xliii. 1. *O Israel, fear not, for I have redeemed thee, I have called thee by thy name, thou art mine.* So, the Lord points them out with the finger, Isa. xlix. 12. [Heb. hinnehelleh] *Behold these shall come from far, and behold these from the north,* (North-land men) *and from the sea,* (Islanders) or from the west, (West-land men) so it may be read, *and these from the land of Shimin,* Ezek. xxxvi. 20. These are the people of the Lord. Heb. xi. 13. *All these* [Gr. ôutoì pántes] *died in the faith;* they are named and told by the head, Rev. xiv. 4. [Gr. ôutoi] *These* are thrice in one verse. *These are they that are not defiled with women,-----These are they that follow the Lamb, whithersoever he goeth; these were redeemed from amongst men.*

3. They are defined by their country, Isa. xix. 18. *Five cities of the land of Egypt shall speak the language of Canaan.* Verse 24. *In that day Israel shall*

shall be the third part with Egypt and Assyria, even a blessing in the midst of the land; verse 25. *Whom the Lord of hosts shall bless, saying, blessed be Egypt my people, and Assyria the work of my hand.* Zephan. iii. 10. *From beyond the river of Ethiopia, my suppliants, even the daughters of my dispersed shall come.*

4. Their names are particularly inrolled *in the Lamb's book of life,* Luke x. 20. Rev. xiii. 8. Rev. xx. 15. As citizens of some famous incorporation, or senators that govern a city, are written in the book of records of the king or city; so these that are to follow the Lamb, clothed in white, are booked in the public register of heaven, in the mind of God, to be members of the heavenly society.

5. It was no blind bargain that Christ made; he knew what he gave, he knew what he got. Christ told down a definite and certain ransom, as a told sum of money, every penny reckoned and laid; and he knew who was his own, and whom, and how many, by the head and name, he bought: there is no hazard that one come in, in the lieu and room of another. John x. 14. *I am the good Shepherd.* How is that made good? He hath particular care of all the flock; by the head he knows how many, and who are his; if any be not his, if any be sick, or lost or wandred away, that proves a good Shepherd, *I know my sheep, and I am known of mine.* I know them, and they know me. Sure it is relative to that, 2 Tim. ii. 19. *Nevertheless, the foundation of God stands sure, having this seal, the Lord knoweth them that are his.* Sure, the sheep that Christ dieth for, John x. are the sheep that he giveth his life for, v. 12. and dies for; and these, (1.) v. 10. That have life in abundance. 2. The sheep known in the Lord's eternal predestination, and known by Christ in time. (3.) Such as he minds to call in, that there may *be one Shepherd, and one sheep-fold,* v. 16. (4.) *Such as are his own sheep, as he goeth before, and they follow him, and know his voice,* v. 4. and not fol-

low

low a stranger, v. 5. (5.) *Such as hear not a stranger,* v. 5. *but,* v. 2. *hear and know the voice of Christ, are known of him, and follow Christ.* (6.) Such sheep as are *gifted with life eternal, shall never perish*; and cannot fall away, no more than *there can be a greater than the Father, that can pluck them out of the hands of Christ*; for, ver. 28, 29. the standing of these that shall not be plucked out of the Father's hand, depends on the greatness and power of Christ's Father. *None can pluck them out of my hand,* (saith Christ) Why? *The Father that gave them me is greater than all.* Then he must be greater than Christ's Father, who plucks one of the sheep of Christ out of his hand; and where dwells he who is greater than the Father? Neither in heaven, nor hell. And for such Christ died.

6. He died for such sheep, as infallibly believe; because he saith, v. 26. *Ye believe not.* Why? *Because ye are not of my sheep;* then certainly they should believe, if they were of such sheep as Christ died for. I shall never believe that this reply can stand. David saith, and Job saith, *Thou, Lord, formedst me in the womb*; and the church, Isa. lxiv. *Thou art the potter, and we the clay*: but It will never follow, therefore God hath created none but David, Job, and his chosen church; so it follows not here. Christ died for his sheep therefore he died for no other but his sheep.

1. Because dying for sinners is a work of mere grace, bestowed only on some; as all the texts that ever Papists, Jesuits, Arminians, alledge, restrict ever these that Christ died for, to some certain persons, to believers, the sheep of Christ, these for whom Christ is an advocate at the right hand of God, etc. And there is not a text in scripture, in Old or New Testament, in which we may not limit the persons, on whom grace universal, and redemption in Christ's blood, are pretended to be bestowed, to the elect and believers

only;

only; these places I except, in which some are said to be redeemed in possession only, as may be demonstrated; and therefore this answer of Arminians is *petitio principii*, and a begging of what they cannot prove. And v. 2. upon the same reason, because God created man on the earth, and died for men, and for the world (as the scripture saith) they might infer, as God created not men only, but angels, beasts, birds, fishes, trees, sun, moon, so Christ died not for men only, but for angels, devils, beasts, birds, fishes, trees; yea, for worms, creeping things, and all, and every creature: for if we regard the free decree of God, devils are as capable of redemption by Christ as men, if so God had proposed from eternity; and in regard of the same decree, the reprobate can no more be saved, and believe of their own strength, than stones of themselves can be sons of Abraham, except God elevate them above their nature, and omnipotency effectuate the same.

2. There be some certain men oppignorated, and laid in pledge in Christ's hand, 2 Tim. ii. 12. Now all are not so, but certain definite persons only.

3. These whom the Lord hath chosen to life, *are given of the Father to Christ*, John x. 26. John vi. 37. John xvii. 2, 6, 8, 9, 12, 24. *And also such are raised up at the last day and saved*, John vi. 37, 39. and Christ cannot lose one of them, John xvii. 9. yea, he can lose nothing of them, neither soul nor body, neither a leg not a piece of an ear of his sheep, as he speaks, Amos iii. so Christ speaketh, John vi. 39. 1 Cor. xv. 23. *Every man shall be raised in his own order.* Verse 24. *Then cometh the end, when he shall have delivered up the kingdom to the Father:* he presents his conquessed ones; not one lad, or the most despised girl, fall by, or are miscounted in the telling. We have often groundless jealousies touching Christ. *O he hath forgotten me;* but that is to say, Christ is not faithful in his charge, and the Father gave so many thousands to his keeping, but he losed the largest half of them. Now, to be

given

given of the Father to Christ, must note Christ's accepting of the receipt of them, by dying for those so given of the Father to him; for another way of giving, but either in election from eternity, or of fitting them in time for actual believing, no man knows: but either ways all given, *are raised up at the last day*, John vi. 39. and so all redeemed must either be chosen from eternity, or then in time believe, and so be raised at the last day; then there can be none redeemed, but such as are chosen and saved. Mr. Moor's Universal Atonement, pag. 4, 5. tells us of a twofold reconciliation or redemption; one which Christ effected in his own body with God for men. This is perfect and accomplished fully, so as the Father is well pleased with his Son, Mat. iii. 17. and this is done by shedding of blood. There is a reconciliation, redemption, and salvation, which Christ effecteth, by the Spirit, in men to God; and this is by washing and blood-sprinkling. His proofs after shall be heard. Thus the Belgick Arminians explain the matter. They say, *"The former redemption, and reconciliation, is the pacifying of the offended party; or such an action, or passion, by which satisfaction, so far forth is made to the of-

"fended

*Remonst. Script. Synod. Art. 2. Redemptio seu reconciliatic, aihil aliud est quam partis offenseae placatio, sive actio five passio talis, qua offenso alicui satisfit hactenus, ut in gratiam cum eo qui offendit, redire velit.

Reconciliationes hujus effectus est divinae gratiae impetratio, id est restitutio in talem statum, in quo Deus nobis, non obstante amplius justitia vindicatrice, secundum misericordiae fuae effectum, de novo sua beneficia communicare, & potest, & vult, ea lege & modo, quo ipsi videtur per eam enim, salvandi affectus, qui fuit in Deo ex misericordiae instinctu (naturali) ablato impedimento in plenarium voluntatis propofitum qualfi exiit.

Remonst. Necessitas distinctionis inter impetrationem & applicationem apparet, quod impetratio ex natura rei ipsius (etiam si aliter futurum esse certo Deus noverit) posset sarta tecta manere, etiam si nulli essent, quibus applicaretur, aut qui fructum mortis Christi, sua culpa, perciperent.

"fended party, that he is willing to return in favour, and grace, with the offender; and the effect of this reconciliation, is the obtaining of the favour of God, that is, the restoring of men to such a state, in which God, without impeachment of revenging justice, according to the tender affection of his mercy, of new, may, and will bestow his benefits; and transact with man touching his salvation, and the conditions thereof, after the way and manner, seemeth good to God (whether by a covenant of works, or of grace, or of commanding faith in God, or faith in an angel, if so it seem good to him.) And by his law, the affection of saving man, which is in God from a natural instinct of mercy, doth break forth, as it were, in a full and compleat purpose of God's will to save: now, when the impediment is removed, by satisfaction given to justice;" And when Christ hath compleatly performed the former redemption, and by his death hath obtained this redemption; yet it may fall out, that not one man be saved. But as we deny not this distinction of salvation purchased, or the purchased redemption, and the applied redemption, as our divines acknowledge Christ to be a Saviour by merit and efficacy; so that the members of the distinction are different, but that they are separated, we deny: yea, the distinction, in the Arminian sense, we deny,

1. Because Christ Redeemer, is a relative person; there is a full redemption in Christ, but not for Christ: but that he might make over that redemption to his poor brethren, there is a purchased salvation in Christ, not to lie by him like a treasure of silver, rousted through not using; but they were so many heavens and salvations, and so much grace and gracious redemptions to be made away, as now purchased, and all these Christ disbursed; he was not a treasurer who kept from sinners the pensions of grace and glory, that the Father and King of the church allowed on his people. What Christ bought with his blood, that he gave out; and so much the places alledged by Mr. Moor the

Arminian,

Arminian, proveth just contrary to himself, John iv. 42. He is the Saviour, not of himself, to save God and justice, and the law; but the Saviour of the world, of poor sinners, not of the Jews only, but of the Samaritans and Gentiles, as Isa. xlix. 6. *I will also give thee for a light to the Gentiles, that thou mayst be my salvation to the ends of the earth.* This is the mystery hidden from the beginning of the world, *That Christ should be preached among the Gentiles*, Eph. iii. 8, 9. Now this is not a magazine and treasure of redemption to remain within the corners of Christ's heart and his bowels, but it is the mystery of the new covenant to be made out to the world of Gentiles, heirs of the same promise. This heritage Christ never purchased to keep to himself. And whereas Mr. Moor will have Christ to be, 1 John ii. *A propitiation for the sins of the whole world, by obtaining reconciliation of God to men*; he is far wide, for that place clearly speaketh of reconciliation of this whole world; the New Testament world, if I may so speak; or Christ's new conquest of the world of Gentiles; so is Christ the Saviour and Redeemer of the world of Gentiles, in opposition to Moses, the judges, who were saviours and redeemers of the people of Israel, who were but a spot, and a poor fragment of the world, in comparison of Christ's large world: God redeemed Israel by the hand of Moses, but never the world. So is Christ a propitiation for the sins of the whole world, in opposition to the propitiatory sacrifices of Aaron and the Levitical priests, (for to these he alludeth) which were propitiations only for the sins of a bit of the world; but sure, as the Levitical sacrifices were offered only in faith for the true Israel of God, otherwise they were no better than the cutting off a dog's neck, in a sacrifice, which was abomination; so were they types of that sacrifice, which was to be offered for the elect world, which is a whole world of Jews and Gentiles, in comparison of little Judea. And by what scripture is a propitiation for the sins of the world, which is only an acquiring of a new power to Christ to transact with

men

men, on what terms he thinketh best to pardon sins; this or that way, for faith or good works, a redemption of men? Or, how is it a taking away the sins of the world, an everlasting redemption, a suffering all that men should have suffered, a bearing of our sins on the tree, an answering as surety for the debts of broken men?

Object. "But if Christ purchased no salvation for me, how can I sin in not resting on Christ for a shadow? For a salvation, not purchased to me, is no salvation at all, but a very nothing."

Ans. If you were to believe first a salvation purchased to you by name, this objection were strong; but you are at first and immediately to believe no such thing, but only that Christ is able to save to the utmost all that come, that is, that believe, and you, if ye believe. 2. A salvation purchased by Christ, without an efficacious intention in God to apply it to all, and every one, is no less a shadow, and a very nothing, than the salvation purchased to all and every one; and this maketh as much against Arminians, as against us. Now, sure salvation is purchased with an efficacious intention in God, to apply it to those only who shall be saved, and the smallest part of mankind. 3. This way sendeth me at first to believe God's secret and efficacious good-will to save me by name, before ever I believe the gospel, That Jesus Christ came to save all believers, which is no gospel-order of believing; and raiseth in my mind jealousies against Christ, that he out of his love died for me, but putteth me on a ground of doubting, if he will apply his death to me, except I begin first to love him, and with free-will apply Christ: so Christ first extendeth raw wishes to save me, but I must extend to him real deeds of applying by faith, his wishing and half love to me; and the most real kindness begins at me, not at Christ.

But say I, by what scripture is a naked power to justify, pardon, wash, sprinkle sinners; and such a power, which may consist with the eternal perishing of

all

all men (saith Moor, p. 5. with the Arminians) an eternal perfect redemption, a perfect satisfaction of justice and the law of God? Are not so the sins of the world taken away, and yet they remain? Doth not Christ bear the sins of all the world; yet it may fall out, that all the world bear their own sins, and not one man be saved; yea, as it is, the greatest part of mankind bear their own iniquities, die in these same sins that were imputed to Christ, suffer the curses of the law, which Christ suffered for them?

Yea, Mr. Moor saith, *God's reconciling of the world, and his not imputing their sins to them, is the reconciling of all Adam's sons in Christ's body before God*; yet Paul and David both say, Blessed are they to whom the Lord imputes no sin. Moor saith, A whole world, to whom the Lord imputeth no sin, may be under the curse of the second death. 2. To put reconciling of the world to God, as Paul doth, 2 Cor. v. *for the reconciling of Christ in his own body with God*, as Mr. Moor doth, is strange divinity; for it is reconciling of God to man, instead of a reconciling of man to God, Heb. ix. 14. and cannot be meant of any reconciling of God in Christ's body, or of obtaining only of redemption without application. 1. Because the blood of Christ is compared with the blood of bulls and goats, which was offered for the reconciling of men to God, not of God to men. 2. Because that blood is said to sanctify and purge the conscience from dead works, to serve the living God; which cannot be said of God, but clearly holdeth forth, that Christ having offered himself without spot to God, through the eternal Spirit, those for whom he offereth himself, cannot eternally perish, as Mr. Moor saith, p. 5. but that their consciences, by his blood, are purged from dead works, to serve the living God.

And the place, 1 Pet. ii. 24. doth not prove that Christ *bare the sins of many, on the tree*, who are not actually saved by his death. 1. The place saith the contrary, and no such thing, as that *the Lord laid on Christ the iniquities of all*, and every one of mankind. 1. Peter

restrains

restrains it to believers, *elect according to the foreknowledge of God the Father, through the sanctification of the Spirit------begotten again unto a lively hope------who are kept through the power of God by faith unto salvation,* 1 Pet. i. 2, 3,4, 5. And there is no colour that Peter speaketh of all Adam's sons, of all the heathen, because he saith, *Christ bare our sins.* Which be these? The sins of these that be called to patient *suffering for well-doing, who are to follow Christ, who left us an example of patient suffering;* who when he was, verse 23. *reviled, reviled not again.* Now, what? Is this the Indians and Tartarians patient suffering, after Christ's example; to whose ears the name of Christ and his suffering, never came, by a dream, or imagination? 2. The sins of these, which Christ bare on his own body, on the tree, are these that are healed with Christ's stripes, and these that are returned to the *Shepherd and Bishop of their souls; and are to live to righteousness, being dead to sin by the death of Christ, who bare their sins,* v. 24, 25. Now these are the all that Isaiah speaketh of, chap. liii. when he saith, liii. 6. *The Lord laid on him the iniquities of us all.* That is, (if we believe Arminians) of all Moab, Ammon, Egypt, Philistines, Caldeans, Ethiopians, and all Adam's children, who never heard of Christ: for the thousandth part of Adam's sons never heard of Christ: then are they not *obliged to believe in him of whom they never heard,* nor is it their sin, that they believe not, Rom. x. 14. John xv. 22. Ergo, they are not obliged to live to righteousness, being dead to sin through Christ's death; because they never heard of Christ's death. Far less are all Adam's sons healed with Christ's stripes, and returned to the Shepherd and Bishop of souls: nor was the chastisement of all the heathen's peace upon Christ. And Isaiah expoundeth who be these all [Heb. col] whose iniquities were laid upon Christ. v. 8. *For the transgressions of my people was he stricken.* And v. 12. *He bare the sins of many,* as Mat. xx. 28. and xxvi. 28. *The blood which is shed for many, and he made intercession for sinners.* What? Doth he bear stripes for all the heathen? And is he entred as High Priest for all Adam's

sons

sons into the holy of holiest, and plead and advocate for such, as Cicero, Regulus, Scipio, Cato, such as Pharaoh, Cain, Judas, Julian? If he bare their iniquities, he must bear their apostasy, and final infidelity. Or, doth he intercede, for all and every one of mankind? 1 John i. 2. compared with 1 John i. 6, 7, 8, 9, 10. and Heb. ix. *He appeareth for us*, v. 24. for those that are sprinkled, v. 13, 14, 15, 16, 17. *and look for him the second time*, v. 28. *He maketh intercession for them that come to God through him*, Heb. vii. 25. *Who have a High Priest over the house of God*, Heb. x. 20, 21, 22. All these and many other places shew the contrary. And the *redemption that is in Jesus Christ*, Rom. iii. 24. is not a redemption which might have been confined within Christ to reconcile God to himself, and which might consist with the final, total and utter perishing of all mankind. 1. We are justified through this redemption, and not by the works of the law. 2. v. 25. God set forth Christ this Redeemer to be a *propitiation through faith in his blood.* 3. That Christ might appear *the justifier of the ungodly*, v. 26. and exclude boasting, by the law of faith, v. 27. and be the God of Jews and Gentiles, ver. 30, 31. so that it was never God's mind to imprison a reconciliation within the Father and the Son, and leave our heaven at such a dead and cold venture, as the discretion of indifferent free-will; so as it might fall out, if men pleased, that the surety Christ should die, and all his poor broken friends die eternally, and suffer the second death also. Arminians turn the gospel in the saddest and bloodiest bargain that ever was, and yet the new English Arminians, worse than their fathers, say, they preach not the gospel of grace, nor Christ, who preach not their universal atonement, in a grosser way than ever Arminians did: for, 1. Arminians durst not say, Christ died *vice, & loco omnium & singulorum, sed tantum in bonum eorum;* he died not in the person, place, and room of all mankind, but only for their good, as Socinus taught them; but master Moor saith this right-down, pag. 3. 2. Arminians durst not say, Christ died and rose again, and

pleadeth

CHRIST DYING AND DRAWING SINNERS TO HIMSELF. 441

pleadeth as High Priest and advocate for all, but only for believers. Master Moor saith, that for all he rose and acquitteth us of all our sins, p. 4.

The place, 2 Cor. v. 14, 15. doth not prove a reconciliation of all, within God, as master Moor dreameth.

1. The all that Christ died for, (if one died for all, then were all dead) by no reason must be in number equivalent to all that died in the first Adam. Nor is there any reason in the text, to make all those that are actually made alive in Christ, and live not to themselves, but to Christ, equal in number to all that died in Adam. 1. God gave not Christ to die for heathens, who were never to hear of Christ, that they might live to Christ. 2. These words, *Henceforth know we no man*, not Christ after the flesh, nor for the outward priviledge of Jewish dignity, circumcision, or a temporal kingdom; which fleshly dignity, the apostles sometime knew Christ for, and expected in him: but now this is taken away, and Christ hath died for all, that is, for Jews and Gentiles, without respect of any such differency; for Christ gave his life for the Gentiles, as well as for the Jews. 3. The Greek word, *huper*, for all, is a word of efficacy, and holds forth the Lord's effectual intention; but if master Moor's gloss stand, there is no effectual intention in Christ to save all and every one.

Nor doth the place, 1 Tim. ii. 4. 6. signify any reconciliation, not applied to persons; for *his being given a ransom for all*, noteth clearly an interest and propriety in these, for whom he gave himself a ransom, as Luke xxii. 20. *for many*, Mat. xx. 28. Mat. xxvi. 28. So [Gr. hupèr perì antì] doth in all Greek authors insinuate, John vi. 51. John x. 11. Rom. v. 8. such an interest.

Mr Moor's objections removed.

Object. 1. "But the reason were frivolous; we are to pray for all, except we know that God willeth salvation to all: how can we with the certainty of faith pray for all? It must be a doubting faith, and so no faith at all.".

Answ.

Answ. But seeing God will not have Nero, persecutors, apostates, rebellious unbelievers, men obstinate against the gospel, such as Paul was before his conversion, to be excluded out of our prayers; what certainty of faith have Arminians to pray for all? Or for the twentieth or hundredth part of all mankind? This therefore be denied; 'Christ gave himself for as many, as we are to pray for, but we are to pray for all without exception.' The proposition and the assumption both are false, nor doth our prayers for men, depend on the certitude of God's decree of election of men to glory, which is God's secret will, not known to us, to whom the Lamb's book of life is not opened; but on the revealed will of God, commanding us to pray for all, that sin not to death; but conditionally, and with a special reserve of the Lord's decrees of election and reprobation: and this, in effect, is to pray for the elect only; nor am I warranted, by the word of God, the rule of my prayers, to pray for any others. Nor is there promise, precept, or practice in scripture, to pray for all, and every one of mankind: therefore I retort the argument thus; we are to think God willeth so many to be saved, and his Son to give himself a ransom for so many, as we are warranted to pray for, that they may be saved; but we are not warranted to pray for all, and every one that they may be saved, but only for the elect. Ergo, God will have them only to be saved, and his Son to give himself a ransom for them only.

Object. 2. "Judgment of charity is no ground of our prayers. We have no charity to believe all and every one shall be saved, nor have we any faith or certainty in these prayers."

Answ. I may have judgment of charity touching this or that man, to pray for him; but this judgment is a motive to my affection, not a foundation to my faith. My faith is bottomed on a word of precept, to pray for the salvation of all, conditionally, but not for the salvation of any, but for my own only, absolutely.

Object.

Object. 3. "God will have as many to be saved, as he will have to come to the knowledge of the truth; but he will have all to come to the knowledge of the truth."

Answ. The argument is strong for us; the apostle speaketh of the gospel-truth, but he will not have the gospel preached to Samaritans, Mat. x. to Bithynians, and thousands others. 2. He will not open the hearts of thousands that hear the gospel, because he will, Mat. xi. 28. Rom. ix. 17. and many he blindeth, and judicially hardneth, Mat. xiii. 14. John xii. 37, 38. Isa. vi. 9, 10. Acts xxviii. 24, 25, 26, 27.

Object. 4. "It is uncertain whether ye pray for magistrates as such, or for vulgar men as such, and uncertain whether ye pray for this or that rank."

Answ. It is certain we are to pray for kings, subjects, men, women, Jews, Gentiles, reserving the Lord's decrees to his own sovereign liberty.

Object. "If we are to pray but for some, because God willeth the salvation of some, he should have said, we are to pray for no man, for the far largest part of the world are lost."

Answ. This is to censure the Holy Ghost's speaking, not us. Upon the same ground, a physician in a city cannot be called the healer of all diseased; nor a professor, a teacher of philosophy to all in the city, because many of the city die of the pest, and the twentieth person remain ignorant of philosophy; if God will have all to be saved, that he predestinates to life, he is rightly said to will all men to be saved, and in that sense we are to pray that all may be saved. 2. God, by his consequent will, desireth the far greatest part of the world to be damned. *Ergo*, By the Arminian way, he should say, "God willeth not any man to be saved, nor any to come to the knowledge of the truth, but that all may be damned." And because they say, there is in the Almighty an antecedent natural affection and desire, that justice may be satisfied in men and angels; which affection is in order of nature prior, and before God's full, peremptory, and deliberate will of damning all,

all, that are finally obstinate; as there is a natural antecedent will in God, to call, invite to repentance, offer Christ to all, and will the salvation of all and every one, which is afore and precedent to his peremptory, compleat, and irrevocable decree of electing to glory, all that God foreseeth shall die in the faith of Christ. Upon the same ground, it may well be said, God willeth the damnation of all, and every one of mankind, and the salvation and repentance of none at all; and that Christ died upon no intention natural to redeem or save any, but upon a conditional and natural desire, that justice might be declared in the just destruction of all; for sure, all God's natural affections and desires of justice, are as natural and essential to him, and so as universally extended toward the creature, as his desires and antecedent natural affections of mercy.

Mr. Moor's Universal atonement, c. xi. p. 55, 56.

Object. 5. "The sense of the word *all*, appears to be of Adam, and all that come by propagation of him. 1. The word *men* is used for Adam, and all his sons, Heb. ix. 27. (2.) Often in the fullest sense; not regenerated, or wholly reprobated, are called *men*, Job xi. 11, 12. Psal. xll. 1. & lv. 2. & llll. 2. (3.) Believers are called *men*, Acts i. 11. 1 Cor. iii. 21, 22. In regard of passions, Acts xiv. 15. Of carnal walking, 1 Cor. iii. 3. Yet they are called something more, *sons of God*, John i. 12. 1 John iii. 1. *Saints*, 1 Cor. i. 1. *Brethren, faithful*, Eph. i. 1. *Christians*, Acts xi. 26. Some, who have hardned their heart, are called *men*, but something more, *reprobate*, Jer. vi. 28, 30. *Seed of the serpent*, Gen. iii. 15. *Children of Belial*, Deut. i. 3. *Of the devil*, John viii. 44. and with an emphasis, the wicked, Psal. ix. 7."

Answ. In these grammatications, Mr. Moor sheweth how weak his cause is, and how dubious from the word *men*, and *all*; for Heb. ix. 27. it is said, *It is appointed for all men to die*, and the Holy Ghost insinuateth clearly, that Christ died for all men that die, in the

very

very next words, v. 28. *So Christ was once offered to bear the sins of many*; he saith not *all men*: observe the change of words. 2. We deny not but *all men* in scripture signifieth all descended of the first Adam by propagation. *Ergo*, It signifieth so here? This is to be proved. 3. What Mr. Moor meaneth by some not *wholly reprobated*, I know not, except he make in God, answerable thereunto, a whole and complete decree of reprobation, and so of election, and a half, and incomplete decree of both, as Arminians do. Which scripture knoweth not, and removeth all certainty of salvation, of perseverance, joy, comfort, earnest of the spirit, seal of Spirit. 4. We contend not that by *all men* here must be meant believers and regenerated persons only, and so he fighteth with his own shadow. 5. He granteth believers are called men, and I hope to prove that the elect and believers, are called *all*, and *all flesh, and us all*, etc. Though it be true, *Believers are called men, because of their human passions and carnal walking, and some more, to wit, sons of God, saints, faithful christians;* it followeth not, that here they should be called *sons of God, saints,* because Christ dieth not for them as saints, but as men, and sinners chosen to life: else Paul should not say, Eph. ii. 1. *God hath quickned you who were dead in sins,* etc. for those whom God *quickneth*, are something more than *dead in sin*; sure they are *chosen saints, new creatures,* etc. after they are converted.

    Mr. Moor ib. *Object.* 6. "*All men,* here, 2 Tim. ii. 6. intentionally, expressly, principally and especially, is meant of the first sort, for natural men, sons of Adam, sinners, unbelievers. 1. Because this sense includeth all, at first *all men,* having some in which they are such, and neither better nor worse than such, before they be born of God, Eph. ii. 1, 2, 3. Tit. iii. 3. Rom. iii. 9, 20."

    Answ. We deny not but *all men* includeth unregenerate men: but Mr. Moor proveth *idem per idem,* the same thing by the same thing; *all men* must be meant of all Adam's sons, why? *Because all includeth all,* at

first,

first, all men; that is, all includeth all, but not all men distributively, all and every one without exception. 2. 'Tis denied that *all men* includeth *all as unregenerate,* or under that reduplication; it is meant of all men unregenerate as fallen under the good-will of God's election of grace, and as stated in his eye as objects of special favour and grace. Nor doth the Lord quicken men *as dead in sins,* Eph. ii. 1. *as foolish and disobedient,* Tit. iii. 3. *as under sin,* Rom. iii. 9. for then he should quicken all dead in sin, all foolish and disobedient, all under sin; and this will prove the conversion and salvation of all and every son of Adam. The Lord quickneth dead sinners, as they lie under his free choice of election to glory.

Object. 7. "Because Christ died to make a propitiation for them, as they are sinners."

Answ. That is denied, he died for them as they were sinners, but as within the pale and under the covering of the fair and sweet shadow of eternally chusing love: otherwise, if Christ died for sinners as sinners, he died for all sinners, and for those that are finally obstinate, for these with the first come under the reduplication of *sinners as sinners.*

Object. 8. "It is nowhere said, Christ died for good men, for righteous, for believers, neither when they were such, nor as they were such; but for the unjust, ungodly, his enemies, Rom. v. 6, 8. 1 Pet. iii. 18. Gal. i. 14."

Answ. Christ neither died for sinners as sinners, nor for sinners as righteous; as Jacob neither served for his wife as a wife, nor for his wife as a sinful woman, *datur tertium.* This is an imperfect enumeration. Christ died for the ungodly, the unjust, his enemies; as freely chosen to be made righteous, and the friends of Christ: as Jacob served for a wife, that is, for Rachel, whom he freely chused before Leah, that he might make her his wife; neither when she was his wife, nor as she was his wife: and as the scripture saith, *Christ died for the ungodly, the unjust, his enemies;* so also for *his friends,* John xv. 13. *his sheep,* John x. 11. *his beloved*

beloved church and spouse, Eph. v. 25, 26. And the places cited, Rom. v. Gal. i. 4. 1 Pet. iii. 18. are all restrictive of these *for whom Christ died;* as Rom. v. he died for us who are *justified by faith, have peace with God, access by faith, who glory in tribulation, rejoice in hope*, Gal. i. 4. *He gave himself for us*, the churches of Galatia, to whom Paul prayeth, *grace and peace.* 1 Pet. iii. 18. for those *that he was to bring to God.* And in no place of scripture, nor yet, 1 Tim. i. 15. is it said, *Christ died for sinners, as sinners*, but only for those that were sinners; which can never prove the Arminian conclusion, that he died for all sinners.

Moor, p. 57.

Object. 8. "He saith not, pray for some of all sorts, but for all men, and nameth but one sort."

Answ. His naming one sort, inferreth, we should exclude no sort out of our prayers; seeing this one sort were persecutors, that may seem farthest from our prayers.

"Moor. We are not to pray for such as are known to sin against the Holy Ghost, because they cast aside the sacrifice and ransom of Christ's blood, and there is no more sacrifice for them, and so they are blotted out of the hopeful book of life, and separated from all men of which they were once, being now reprobated of God, Jer. xvi. 5. 1 John v. 16.

Answ. But either Christ did bear *on his body on the tree,* that sin of casting *aside the sacrifice of Christ*, or not; if the first be said, Christ died for them, and we are to pray for them, and further such as sin against the Holy Ghost, as such, must come under the reduplication of *God's enemies, the ungodly sinners, disobedient, dead in sins and trespasses*, in the highest degree, and so Christ must have died for them under that sin; or then there is a sin of some of the sons of Adam, that Christ did no more *bear on his body on the tree,* than the sin of devils; which should render that sin intrinsically unpardonable, even in relation to Christ's blood, which Arminians cannot bear. 2. A blotting out of the book of life, and time-reprobation, here

asserted

asserted by Mr. Moor, is the highest indignity done to the unchangeable love and grace of God, and gross Arminianism.

Pag. 58. *Object.* 9. "Praying for their brethren could not be doubted of, but the doubt was to pray for opposers and persecutors; the apostle saith, thus to pray for all men was good, according to Mat. v. 44, 48."

Answ. To pray for all ranks of men, Nero and others, was the doubt: but Mat. v. which saith, we must *pray for, and bless our enemies*, with submission to God's decree, and in imitation of God, who causeth the sun to shine on the unjust, cannot infer that we are to pray for all and every one absolutely, as Arminians dream, *that Christ died for all absolutely.*

Object. 10. "The motives to pray for all men are from only God's good-will to man, and what Christ hath done to ransom us, like Mat. v. 44, 45. Motives to pray for believers are sweeter, as their uprightness with God, faith in Christ, love in the saints, fellowship to the gospel."

Answ. The thing in question is not concluded; we say not we are to pray for the salvation of none but believers only, and that Christ died for none but those that already believed: we are to pray for all ranks, believers or unbelievers, as Christ died for thousands of both, but ever in order to faith, and election to glory. It is a blasphemous comparison to say, the gracious good-will of God to chuse men to glory, and the highest and most matchless love of Christ, John iii. 16. & xv. 13. Eph. v. 25, 26,27. Acts xx. 28. Tit. iii. 3, 4. is but a common motive to induce us to pray for all men, and such belly-blessings as a shining sun, and raining clouds, which God bestoweth on blasphemers, apostates, and crucifiers of the Lord Jesus, Psal. lxxiii. 1, 2. Jer. xii. 1. Job xxi. 1, 2, 3, 4, 5, 6. Yea, the giving of Christ to die for sinners, is an argument to prove that far more Christ will give us all other things, Rom. viii. 32. even righteousness, faith, love, and all graces; and therefore there can be no sweeter motive to move us to

pray

pray for all men conditionally, than because for any thing our charity is to deem on the contrary, they may, even though persecutors, be within the circumference and sweet lists of God's free love, and greatest good-will, and affection of election and redemption, Rom. ix. 11, 12, 13. Eph. i. 9. John xv. 13. and iii. 16. Gal. ii. 20. and we are to pray for them under this reduplication and notion, as freely loved of God, and redeemed of his rich grace, and in no other consideration; which is the far sweeter motive than any inherent uprightness, faith, or love that can be in us.

Object. 11. "We are to pray without wrath, v. 8. which is incident, when we pray for those that cross and persecute us, not when we pray for believers."

Answ. Non concluditur negatum, ergo, we are to pray for all, and every man, because we can hardly pray without wrath and grudging for such as Nero. 2. If believers injure us (as they often do now a-days) he knows not his own heart, who is not tempted to wrath in praying for them. 3. Verse 8. All prayers in general must be without wrath, and with pure hands, and not prayers only for persecutors.

Object. 12. "The thing prayed for is, that we may lead a quiet and peaceable life, that so the gospel might run and be glorified. 2 Thes. iii. 1. John xvii. 22, 23. But things to be prayed for to the believers are higher, as increase of love, sincerity, filling with the fruits of righteousness, Phil. i. 9, etc."

Answ. All these prove this place will prove only, we are to pray for magistrates under whom we have peace and the gospel, not for believers, and so not for all Adam's sons; as the next words, page 59. prove.

Moor, p. 59. *Object.* 13. "Here is a ground to preach the gospel to all men, and to every creature, Mat. xxviii. 20. Mark xvi. 15. And how far to all men, John xvi. 12. 1 Cor. iii. 12. Heb. v. 12. *even tho' they hate and persecute us.*

Answ. If every creature be no synecdoche, it must warrant us to preach to devils. 2. It is evident by the

story

story of the Acts, that the apostles obeyed not this command, in the letter, as Mr. Moor presseth it; there be many nations, and thousands of people, to whom the apostles never preached the gospel, neither to fathers nor sons. 3. God's decree is no warrant to them to preach the gospel, except God confer miraculously the gift of tongues; and this strongly proveth the contrary: the Lord never yet sent the means of the knowledge of the truth to all and every son of Adam, then he cannot will all and every son of Adam to be saved; and Christ died not for all and every creature, then he commanded not to preach the gospel to all and every creature, but only to every creature; that is, *to all nations, Jews and Gentiles*, now, when *the partition wall is broken down.*

Object. 14. "He sheweth the will of God touching the Mediator, to save and ransom all. 2. To bring all to the knowledge of the truth. 3. By this knowledge sin is removed, death abolished, enmity slain, peace obtained, so far for all men, that God hath given all over to the dispose of Christ, and made him Lord and Judge of all. 4. The other part of God's will, Jesus Christ performeth, to wit, to preach the gospel to all, and will perform it in due time. 5. The gospel may be preached to all, v. 7. 6. Prayers made for all, v. 1, 2, 3, 4. and here is no more than Christ doth to all men.

Answ. Here be fair positions, but not a word to prove, that this is God's will concerning all and every son of Adam. He supposeth all this as granted, because he saith, not because the text saith it; and therefore we deny what he proveth not.

Mr. Moor alledgeth that, John i. 29. *Behold the Lamb of God that taketh away the sins of the world.*

Answ. The word world is the nations and Gentiles, and believers are elect of both Jews and Gentiles, John iii. 16. *God so loved the world*, Rom. xi. 12. *If the fall of them be the riches of the world; if the casting away of them be the reconcilement of the world;* of the Gentiles, and especially of Jews and Gentiles. Mat. xxiv.

14.

14. *And this gospel of the kingdom shall be preached in all the world, for a witness to all nations;* that is, Jews and Gentiles. A personal witness to every single man it cannot be, except every single man heard it, Rom. x. 14. *How shall they believe in him of whom they have not heard?* John xv. 22. Rom. ii. 12. So is the word *all nations*, taken, Mark xiv. 9, 10. And the word *world*, Mark xvi. 15. (2.) *Taking away of sin*, is the actual, free, complete pardoning of sin; so as *Judah's sin is sought, and not found*, Jer. l. 20. As 2 Sam. xxiv. 10. David having numbred the people, prayeth, *O Lord, take away the iniquity of thy servant.* Any Arminian in conscience, answer, Did David pray for no more, than is due to Judas, Cain, and all mankind, of whom many never, in faith, can pray, as David here doth? Or doth he not seek the effectual pardon of his numbring the people? Job vii. 21. *And why does thou not pardon mine iniquity, and take away my transgression?* Isa. xxvii. 9. *This is all the fruit, to take away his sin*: This cannot be the potential and ineffectual removing of sin, common to all the world, but proper to the church, and brought to pass by particular afflictions on the church, Rom. xi. 27. *This is my covenant with them, when I shall take away their sins.* These words are not fulfilled, till all *Israel be saved*, both elect Jews and Gentiles, and the Jews converted. But Arminians say, tho' the Jews were never converted, and not a man of Israel saved, *yet the Lamb of God taketh away the sins of the world:* so Isa. vi. 7. *Thine iniquity is taken away, and thy sin purged*: this is no half pardon, such as Isaiah had before the Lord touched his lips. 1 John iii. 5. *And ye know that he was manifested to take away our sins.* John speaketh of the taking away of the sins of us, John and the saints, who were loved, v. 1. with a wonderful love to be called the sons of God; us, whom the world knoweth not; v. 2. Us, who shall be like Christ, when he appeareth. Arminians are obliged to give us parallel places, where the redemption of all, and every man, and Christ's naked power and desire to be friends with all men, and to make any covenant of

grace,

grace, or works, as he pleaseth, is called, *The taking away the sins of the world;* and yet the whole world may possibly die in their sins, and not a man be saved. The taking away of the world's sins, to us, is the complete pardoning of them, remission of sins in his blood, Eph. i. 7. Col. i. 14. *Blotting out of transgressions,* Isa. xliii. 25. *as a thick cloud,* Isa. xliv. 22. *A not remembring their sins,* Isa. xliii. 25. Jer. xxxi. 24. Such a taking away of sins, as is promised in the covenant of grace to the house of Judah, to the church under the Messiah, that heareth the gospel, Jer. xxxi. 34. Heb. viii. 8, 9, 10, 11, 12. Rom. xi. 26, 27. Isa. lix. 20. This is the *taking away of the sins of the world;* a new world, *in whose inner-parts the Lord writeth his law,* and with whom *the Lord maketh an everlasting covenant, never to turn away from them,* Jer. xxxi. 33, 34, 35, 36, 37. in whom the *Lord putteth his Spirit, and in whose mouth he putteth his word, and in the mouth of their seed, and their seed's seed,* Isa. lix. 20, 21. The Arminians taking away of sins, is of all, and every one of Adam's seed, of such as never heard of a covenant, of a word, of a Spirit, of a seed, a holy seed, of a new heart, finally, the taking away of the sins of the world, is the removing of them as far from us, as the east is from the west, Psal. ciii. 12. bestowed on these *that fear the Lord,* v. 11. and are pitied of the *Lord, as the father pitieth the son;* and the *subduing of our iniquities, and the casting of our sins in the deeps of the sea,* Mic. vii. 19, 20. a mercy bestowed only *on the remnant of the Lord's inheritance.* The Arminian taking away of sin, is a broad pardon of sins to all the world: let them shew scripture for theirs, as we do for ours, and carry it with them.

Object. 15. "Tho' reconciliation be purchased to all and every one, yet it is not necessary that it be preached to all, and every one; but only it is required that God be willing it be preached to all: now, it is free to God, before he be willing, to make offer of the purchased reconciliation to all, to require afore hand, such acts of obedience, and duties, which

"being

"being performed, he may publish the gospel to them; or being not performed, he may be unwilling to publish the gospel to them. Yea, though reconciliation be purchased to all, yet it is free to God, to communicate the benefits of his death, upon what terms he thinketh good: and Christ died (saith Mr. Moor) to obtain a lordship over all, and a power to save believers, and destroy such as will not have him to reign over them, as we heard before.

Answ. 1. We have in this doctrine, that argument yielded. God commanded to preach to all, and every one; *Ergo*, Christ died for all, and every one. For, 1. The consequence is true absolutely, by the Arminians doctrine, Christ absolutely died for all, and every one, without prescribing any condition to those for whom he dies: he saith not, *My son dieth to purchase reconciliation to all, upon condition all believe, or perform some other duty*: but believe they, or believe they not, the price is paid, and salvation purchased for all, without exception. But the antecedent is not true, but upon condition. God is not willing the gospel be preached to all, but to such as perform such conditions.

2. If they perform not the condition, Christ should have said, "Preach not the gospel to all nations, nor to every creature; but only to such as ye find fit hearers of the gospel, and have performed such acts of obedience, as I require." For conditional threatnings are set down in the gospel, as well as conditional promises: he that believeth shall be saved, he that believeth not shall be damned. But in Old or New Testament, Arminians never shew us where the preaching of the word of grace is referred to our free-will: "Do this, O Ammonites, O Indians, and the glad tiding shall come to you; if ye do not this, ye shall never hear the gospel." Arminians say, God sendeth his grace and gospel, both *genti minus dignae et indigniori negat*, to the unworthy nation, and denieth both to the worthier.

3. Arminians say, in Script. Synod. Dordr. p. 6. *Lex non lata, aut non intellecta, cumintelligi non possit, non*

obligat:

obligat: a law not made, or not understood, when it cannot be understood, doth not oblige. Then God cannot deny a salvation, and the benefit of a preached gospel to Indians, tho' both were purchased in Christ, if they never heard (as hundreds of nations could by no rumor, hear, or dream of Christ and the gospel) of Christ.

4. How can God, with the same natural, and half-will, equally will that all be saved; when he absolutely, without merit, or condition, willeth the means of salvation to some, and denieth the means of salvation to the far greatest part of mankind, for want of a condition unpossible; because it neither was, nor could be known to them?

5. By the Arminian way, *Sin original, is no sin; it bringeth wrath and condemnation on no man.* God beginneth upon a new score, and the reckoning of the covenant of grace, to count with all men; and God is so reconciled to all mortal men, and transacteth with them in such a way of free-grace, *That he will punish no man, for any new breach, except committed actually by such as are come to age as have the use of reason, and are obliged to believe in Christ.* Page 285, 286, 287. Dordr. Scrip. Synod. Yet hath God decreed never to reveal any such gracious transactions to millions of men, that better deserve to hear these secrets of grace, than thousands, to whom they are proclaimed in their ears, ere they can discern the right-hand by the left. This, Arminians say, was God's dispensation, Mat. xi. with Capernaum, and Tyrus, and Sidon. But, it will be found, that Arminians deny the prescience and fore-knowledge of God.

6. Most abominable, and comfortless, must the doctrine of the death of our Lord Jesus be, if Christ died only to be a Lord, and such a Lord, as he might have power without impeachment of revenging justice, to save men, upon a new transaction, either of grace or works; and to destroy his enemies that would not accept of that new transaction; yet so, as when Christ hath died, and taken away the sins of all, and is made Lord and King

of

of dead and quick, all mankind may freely reject all covenants Christ maketh, or can make, and be eternally lost, and perish.

For, 1. Christ's princedom and dominion, that he hath acquired by death, is not a free-will power or possibility, by which he may, upon such and such conditions kill, or save, tho' all may eternally perish. But Christ *is made Lord of quick and dead,* by dying, Rom. xiv. 9. that he might be Judge of all; but so, that we should *not live and die to ourselves, but that, whether we live or die, we should be Christ's*; tho' we change conditions, yet not matters in both, *we should be the Lord's,* v. 7, 8. as Christ lived again after death, that he might be the husband of his own wife, the church, that he died of love for.

2. Upon what terms Christ was, by death, made a Lord, and acquired a princedom, upon these terms he was made a Prince over his church; for Lord, and Prince, and King, are all one; but the Lord maketh David, that is, *Jesus the Son of David,* Prince over his people: not with power to save or destroy his redeemed flock, and so as all the flock may eternally perish. Ezek. xxxiv. 22. *Therefore will I save my flock, and they shall no more be a prey.------v. 23. And I will set one shepherd over them, and he shall feed them, and my servant David he shall feed them, and he shall be their shepherd.* v. 24. *and I the Lord, will be their God, and my servant David a prince among them; I the Lord have spoken it.* v. 25. *And I will make with them a covenant of peace.* Now, was Christ, by the blood of the eternal covenant, brought back from the death, and made a Shepherd of souls, to the end he might have power to destroy all the flock? Ezekiel saith, to feed them; the apostle, *to make the saints perfect in every good work, working in them (actually and efficaciously) that which is well-pleasing in his sight,* Heb. xiii. 20, 21. It is true, Christ obtaineth, by his death, a mediatory power to crush, as a potter's clay vessel, with a rod of iron, all his rebellious enemies. But, 1. This is not a power to crush any ene-

mies,

mies, but such as have heard of the gospel, and will not have Christ to reign over them, in his gospel-government; but not to crush all his enemies, that never heard of the gospel, and so are not evangelically guilty in sinning against the Lord Jesus, as Mediator; for they cannot be guilty of any such sin, Rom. x. 14. John xv. 22. He had, and hath power, as God equal with the Father to judge and punish all such as have sinned without the law. 2. It is not merit, or acquired by way of merit of Christ's death, that a crown is given to Jesus Christ, for this end, to destroy such enemies as are not capable of sinning against his Mediatory-crown; especially, when, as God, he had power to destroy them, as his enemies, tho' he had never been Mediator.

Yea, Acts v. 31. 'tis said, *him* (whom ye slew, and hanged on a tree) *hath God exalted with his right hand, to be a Prince and Saviour* (not to destroy all his subjects, upon foreseen condition of rebellion, to which they were, thro' corruption of nature, inclinable; but) that he might, by his Spirit, subdue corruption of nature, and *give repentance to Israel, and forgiveness of sins.*

3. By what title Christ is made a King and Lord, by the same he is made Head of the body the church: for, Eph. i. 20, 21, 22, 23. *By raising him from the dead, God conferred a headship upon him.* Now, he was not made Head of the body, that he might destroy all he members, or most of them, as Arminians must say; but his Headship is for this end, that the whole body, *by his Spirit fitly joined together, might grow up in love,* Eph. iv. 16. and that the members might receive life and spirit from him.

4. By the same title he is made Lord, by which he is made King, Governor, and Leader of the people; for power of dominion and Lordship is nothing but royal power. Now he was made King, not on such terms, as he might destroy all his subjects (for all mankind are his subjects, to Arminians) but he is made King, Psal. lxxii. 11. *That all nations may serve him;*

that

that he should deliver the poor, needy, and helpless; and redeem their souls from violence, and esteem their death precious: and he reigneth and prospereth as a King, *that in his days Judah may be saved, and Israel dwell safely,* Jer. xxiii. 7, 8. And God raiseth the horn of David, Luke i. and so setteth Christ on the throne, to perform his mercy promised to our fathers, and remember his holy covenant. Ver. 69, 70. *That we might serve him in holiness and righteousness.* Now, by the Arminian way, he is set upon the throne of David, to execute vengeance on all his subjects, and that he may utterly destroy all, if all rebel, and not to save one of Judah and Israel; for he may be a King without any subject, suppose all his subjects were cast in hell: yea, he groweth *out of the root of Jesse,* a royal Branch of king David's house; not that these wars may be perpetuated between God and all the children of men, but that *the wolf should dwell with the lamb, and the leopard ly down with the kid, and the calf and the young lion together, and a little child should lead them; and the earth should be filled with the knowledge of the Lord, as the waters cover the sea,* Isa. xi. 1, 2, 6, 7, 8, 9. And Christ is given for a *Guide and Leader of the people*; sure, for the good of the flock, and that he may *carry the lambs in his bosom,* Isa. xl. 11. *That they should not hunger nor thirst, that neither the heat nor the sun should smite them; because he that hath mercy on them, doth lead them, and by the springs of water doth he guide them,* Isa. xlix. 10. Salvation is engraven on the crown of Christ: by office, Christ must be a destroyer, and a Lord-crusher of his people, as a Jesus, and a Saviour, by this conceit.

5. And what more contrary to the intrinsical end of Christ's death, than that he should obtain no other end by dying, but a placability, a possible salvation, a softning only of God's mind, by which justice should only stand by, and a door be opened, whereby God might be willing, if he pleased, to confer salvation, by this or that law, a covenant of grace, or of works, or a mix'd way, or by exacting faith in an angel, or an holy

man;

man; and this possible salvation, this virtual or half reconciliation, doth consist with the eternal damnation of all the world; whereas the genuine con-natural end of Christ's death is, John x. 10. *That his sheep may have life, and have it more abundantly;* he suffered, *the just for the unjust, that he might bring us to God,* 1 Pet. iii. 18. and in the very act of suffering (to speak so) or in that he was stripped and died, *The chastisement of our peace was on him,* Isa. liii. 5. This cannot be such a possible heaven, a fowl flying in the air, a *may be* as far off as a *never-may-be,* which may consist with an inevitable hell: so as Christ died not, but on a poor *hopeless venture,* and a *forlorn contingency,* that might as soon fill hell with the damned souls of all the world, as grace paradise with redeemed ones.

6. His coming in the world hath no such Arminian end, that we read of, as a possible saving, or an obtained salvation, that thousands, yea not one in the world may ever enjoy; but he came to seek, and actually, and intentionally, *to save that which was lost,* Luke xix. 10. *to save sinners,* 1 Tim. i. 15. *and Paul the first of sinners; and not for wrath, but that we might obtain salvation by our Lord Jesus Christ.* 1 Thess. v. 9.

7. Nor did he die so that we should not *live to ourselves, but unto righteousness; but that we might be,* 1 Pet. ii. 24. *redeemed from this present evil world,* Gal. i. 4. *from our vain conversation,* 1 Pet. i. 18. *That he might redeem us from all iniquity, and purify to himself a peculiar people, zealous of good works,* Tit. ii. 14. *That we should glorify God in our bodies and spirits, which are God's,* 1 Cor. vi. 20. *That he might present to himself a glorious church, not having spot nor wrinkle, or any such thing; but that it should be holy and without blemish,* Eph. v. 27. Now, Christ may obtain the native and intrinsical end of his death; tho' all the redeemed ones (say the Arminians) *live to themselves, and never be redeemed from the present evil world,* nor from their vain conversation, and live and die to themselves, and walking in their lusts.

8. And upon what ground Christ is made Lord, he

is

CHRIST DYING AND DRAWING SINNERS TO HIMSELF. 459

is made also a husband to the church; for the husband, as an husband, is made head of the wife. Now, the intrinsical end, that so the specific acts of this husband, who is joined to us by the marriage-covenant of free grace, must be free love to his spouse; as Paul expoundeth it, Eph. v. 25. And the native fruit and end of marriage is, that the spouse might have interest in the righteousness, glory, spirit, wisdom and sanctification, the kingdom and throne of the husband and Lord, not that he might condemn and destroy his spouse.

9. It is a reasonable conceit, that after Christ died, he had a freedom to transact for our actual saving and glorifying in what terms he will, law or gospel, grace or works; because he died the surety of the covenant of grace, Heb. vii. 2. and made his testament, and last will, and confirmed it by his death as our friend, and bequeathed to his poor friends the promise of an eternal inheritance, Heb. ix. 15. and so he died as the Mediator of the New Testament, and sealed the covenant with his blood, which is therefore called the *blood of the eternal covenant*, Heb. xiii. 20. Zech. ix. 11. And *therefore neither the first testament was dedicated without blood*, Heb. ix. 18, 19, 20, 21. and Christ by his blood *entred into heaven*, as a priest to intercede for us, v. 23, 24. And this Arminian way overturneth the whole gospel, which is a bargain of blood between the Father and the Son Christ; and Christ dying, and justifying, *pardoning the iniquities of his people*, making them heirs of the same covenant and kingdom with himself, is in this indenture of free grace, the chief man: now, impossible it is that this can be an effect of Christ's death, that he may set up a covenant of grace and a gospel-way to heaven, or set up another way; when as by the gospel covenant only God gave Christ a body, indented with him to do the work, to make his soul an offering for sin; and God promised to him, if he would die, *a seed, and that the pleasure of the Lord should prosper in his hand, that his soul should be satisfied, that he should justify many, intercede for many,*

Isa.

Isa. liii. 10, 11, 12, 13. Now, if all might eternally perish, notwithstanding that Christ died for them, and it were free to Christ to make such a covenant after his death, in which not one man possibly may be saved; Christ then should do his work, and yet not have his wages, nor have a seed, nor justify his people, nor have a willing people to serve him; yea, then should Christ offer the sacrifice of his body, as our priest on earth, in shedding his blood, and yet not enter into heaven, and the holy of holiest, to intercede for us, as our high priest there also.

10. All the offices and relations of Christ, and comfortable promises of the gospel, shall be overturned; for it is in the free-will of man, that Christ be King, or no King; Head, or no Head of the church; a Husband, or no Husband: clear it is, Christ is a Gospel-King; now if his death might stand and attain its intrinsical end and effect, which is a meer possible reconciliation, and a salvation to his people standing only in a (may be) or a (may never be) then Christ is a Gospel-King, without a kingdom of grace, the fruits whereof are *righteousness, joy of the Holy Ghost, and peace*, Rom. xlv. 17. *He is a King,* but *Judah shall never be saved in his days*; there shall be no righteousness, no peace, no joy in his kingdom; he is a Redeemer and a Saviour, but his people are all eternally lost, and die in bondage and misery, and in their sins; he is a Saviour, but saves not his people from their sins; he is the chief corner-stone, but no other living stones are built on him; he is a Head, but hath not a living body quickned by his Spirit, nor a body that is the fulness of Christ; he is a Husband, but the essence of his marital and husbandly power standeth in that he hath power to destroy his spouse eternally, That he hateth his own flesh; he is a Shepherd, and a good Shepherd, and layeth down his life for his sheep, but the roaring lion devoureth all his flock; he carrieth *not the lambs in his bosom, he feedeth them not in the strength of the Lord, he causeth them not lie down safely, he leadeth them not to the living waters,* they hun-

ger

ger and starve eternally; he is the *vine-tree, but no man bringeth forth fruit in him;* he is an eternal Priest, but the sins of all he offereth for, remain in heaven before the Lord for ever; he is the promised seed, and by death triumpheth over devils and principalities and powers, but the *serpent's head is not bruised, Satan is not cast out.* Satan reigneth and ruleth in all mankind, *he hath much in Christ,* all the world of elect and reprobate; all Adam's sons live and die in sin, and are *tormented with the devil and his angels* eternally; such a thing as life eternal and the kingdom of heaven is for no use offered or purchased to the Redeemed, who *stand before the throne, and sing praises to the Lamb*: he is the Lord and builder of his house the church; but he hath no church, but that which cannot be called a church: I know no article of the gospel, that this new and wicked religion of Universal atonement doth not contradict.

11. To believe in Christ, is to believe that omnipotency can save Judas, Pharaoh, and all, every mortal man, so they believe in Christ; but Christ hath purchased sufficient grace to no mortal man, because in the obtaining of eternal life to all the world, as Arminians say, neither faith, repentance or grace to believe and repent, hath any place. God might after Christ's death have required nothing for our actual salvation, *but abstain from eating the fruit of such a tree, and ye have life eternal in Christ.*

12. How can Christ's satisfaction be imputed to any man, seeing it is a meer possible salvation, or a power to save, that may, and doth stand, with the damnation of millions that Christ died for?

13. Christ, dying, had in his eye the sanctification, the giving of the Spirit, the raising to life, the eternal glory of not one man more than another, not of Peter, of Moses, more than of Cain or Judas; though he said, John xvii. 19. *For their sakes sanctify I myself.* And v. 24. *Father, I will that those whom thou hast given me, should be where I am, that they may behold the glory that*

thou

thou hast given me. I pray not for the world, but for them that thou has given me.

14. Christ hath died, yet he must, by the Arminian way, make no testament, appoint no certain heirs, but win the dead man's legacy by free-will, and have it who will.

15. Christ obtained by his death that the gospel should no more be preached than the law, or faith in an angel, that men may be saved.

Use. All the doctrine contrary to Universal Atonement, doth highly advance Christ; for by it the Lord Jesus, as Mediator and our High Priest, must be essentially grace, and essentially an ambassador of grace. It is kindly to Christ to save, salvation belongeth to Christ as Christ; enjoy him as a Saviour, and ye cannot perish; be joined to him as a Husband, and he cannot but love and save his spouse; submit to him as a King, and ye must share with him in his throne, his King's-royal crown was never ordained for another end, but that the lustre of the precious stones in that crown should shine on the face and souls of his redeemed ones; Christ came not to destroy, but to seek and save the lost. Get an union with Christ by faith and the spirit of the Lord Jesus, and he will save you (to speak so) whether you will or no; ye complain of corruption, he is a King over the body of sin, he is a Priest to sacrifice lusts. To preach Christ a dying Redeemer of all and every one of mankind, when millions redeemed do eternally perish; is to steal away Christ from the people, as thieves in Jeremiah's days *did steal the word of the Lord;* it is to make the Lord Jesus as weak and powerless a priest, as ever any son of Aaron; for his blood no more can take away their sins, than the blood of bullocks or goats could do it; it is to enthrone free-will, and dethrone the grace of Christ, and to put shame on the Lord Jesus and his blood. And though these enemies of the cross of Christ, now croud in, in England, under the name of the godly party; yet it was a good observation of that learned and gracious servant of Christ, Doctor Ames, who conversed with the Arminians, that he could

never

never see a proof of the grace of Christ, in the conversation of such men as, in doctrine, were declared enemies of the grace of Christ.

Now for the word, all, and the world, and all nations, it may be demonstrate from Christ's will in the scriptures, that if universal atonement, and redemption of all and every one, can be proved from these grammatications: then with the like strength I can prove, 1. The conversion of all and every mortal man to saving faith. 2. The eternal salvation of all and every man. 3. The eternal perishing of all and every one, which must be infinitely absurd and blasphemous: and if the goodwill of God cannot be extended to the end, and the efficacious and only saving means tending to this end, which are salvation and saving faith; with no colour of reason can it be extendeded to one means of redeeming all and every one, rather than to another.

1. There is an universal conversion, and saving illumination, which is called in the text, *a drawing of all; and I, when I am lifted up on the cross, will draw all men to me.* Here is a drawing of all men, and so an effectual conversion, but not of all and every man, as Mr. Den (*Drag net*, p. 80.) saith; 1. Because, v. 33. this drawing is by the power of Christ, *lifted up on the cross*, and by the *Holy Spirit given by Christ*, John vii. 39. and xiv. 16, 17, and xv. 26, 27. and xvi. 7, 13, 14. Now, it can be no gospel-truth, that Christ draweth, by the lifting of himself on the cross, and by his death, all and every man to himself, even thousands and millions of the sons of Adam, that never heard one letter or the least sound of the gospel, or of his lifting up on the cross; for sure, Christ's death-drawing must be by proposing the beauty and loveliness of Christ crucified, which thousands never heard of. 2. This drawing must be all one with the drawing which effectually produceth running, Cant. i. 4. after Christ; and which is, John vi. 44. Now, when Christ saith, *no man can come except he be drawn*; he clearly sheweth, that the drawing of the Father is a peculiar privilege of some, and not

com-

common to all; as the other two expressions beside, of being taught of God, and hearing and learning of the Father. 3. Because all the drawn are raised up by Christ their life and head at the last day, v. 44. 4. The adversary cannot show any drawing of Christ, or to Christ, that is common to all, and every one of mankind.

So, *All Israel shall know the Lord,* as it is Heb. viii. 10. *For this is the covenant that I will make with the house of Israel (saith the Lord) I will put my laws into their minds, and write them in their hearts; and I will be to them a God, and they shall be to me a people.* v. 11. *And they shall not teach every one his neighbour, and every man his brother.* [Gr. hoti pantes eidesousi me.] *They shall all know me, from the least of them, even to the greatest*: when was this covenant made? Under the Messiah, when both the Jews to whom this apostle wrote, and the Gentiles came in. After those days, Arminians cannot deny, but the putting of the law in the mind, and writing it in their hearts, and this knowing of the Lord, not by the ministry of men, but by the inward teaching of the Spirit, must be saving conversion; and there is no more reason to expound Israel, all Israel, both Jews and Gentiles, of all of every kind, and some few (except they flee to our universality of the elect) in the matter of conversion, than in the matter of redemption by Christ, when it is said, *Christ gave himself a ransom for all,* 1 Tim. ii. Because it is their constant doctrine, to make all and every one of Adam's sons, as many as Christ died for, to be the parties with whom the covenant is made; so in the same covenant, it is said, John vi. 45. [Gr. Kai esontai pantas] *They shall be all taught of God,* as Jeremiah saith, chap. xxxi. 34. [Heb. *ki culam*] etc. *Because they shall all know me, for I will forgive their iniquity, and remember their sin no more*: except they admit an universality of the redeemed of God. Then, as they contend for an universal redemption, and all and every one of mankind, in Christ, to be taken in within the covenant of grace (for they expound all those of

the

the visible church) there is as good reason, that we prove from the grammar of [Heb. col.] and [Gr. pantes] all, an universal regeneration, and an universal justification of all, as they can prove an universal redemption; so is the same promise, Isa. liv. 11. and clearly, Rom. xi. 26. *All Israel shall be saved.* He meaneth Jews and Gentiles, when the fulness of the Gentiles shall come in; here is universal salvation of all.

So, by John Baptist's ministry, all and every one of his hearers must be converted, why? As Arminians expound many that Christ died for, Mat. xx. 28. *To be all and every man without exception.* 1 Tim. ii. 6. Heb. ii. 9. 1 John ii. 1. so they are debtors to us for the same liberty, Mal. iv. *He shall turn the hearts of the fathers to the children.* Luke i. 16. *Many of the children of Israel shall he turn to the Lord their God*: these we must expound, by the Arminian grammar, of the conversion of all and every one, that heard John preach; contrary to Luke vii. 29, 30. for Pharisees and lawyers were not converted. Yea, it is said, Isa. xl. *Every valley shall be exalted, and every mountain shall be made low, and the crooked shall be made straight, and rough places plain, and the glory of the Lord shall be revealed, and all flesh shall see it together.* Mat. iii. expoundeth it of the preaching of repentance, and the coming of the kingdom of God, by the ministry of John; so doth Mark ii. 3. and John i. 23. And the filling of valleys, and making straight crooked things; is sure the humbling of the proud, and the exalting of the humble, and the conversion of the disobedient: but who can say that all and every mountain was made low? by John's ministry, or Christ's either? Was the gospel preached to all and every man? Or the heart of every son, converted to the Father? Or, did all flesh see or enjoy the salvation of God? Then they must flee to our exposition: yea, the seeing of the salvation of God, is no less the saving of all, which Arminians cannot say. Mr. Denne saith, "That the seeing of God, is in that *when they knew God, they glorified him not as God*, Rom. i. 21. And *they liked not to retain God in their*

know-

"knowledge, as that is, *They have both seen and hated both me and my Father;* and Mat. xiii. 13. *And seeing, they see not;* but (saith he) it is not to be understood of saving knowledge.

Answ. 1. This is contrary to the scope of the prophet Isaiah, and of the Evangelists, who aim at holding forth the fruits of the gospel in John Baptist his ministry, which was the conversion of souls, as Malachi saith, *and the bringing down the proud, and in turning many of the children of Israel to the Lord their God;* and in going before Christ in the spirit and power of Elias, *to turn the hearts of the fathers to the children, and the disobedient to the wisdom of the just, and to make ready a people prepared for the Lord,* Luke i. 16, 17. Which is a clear exposition of laying every proud mountain level to Christ, and of fitting souls for the Messiah; which no man can say, by teaching such a knowledge of Christ, as idolatrous heathens had of God as Creator, or blind and obstinate Pharisees had of Christ and his Father, whom they both saw, and hated, John xv. Rom. xxi. That seeing of the salvation of God, is neither conversion, nor preparation of a people for Christ. 2. The phrase of seeing God, and the salvation of God, being set down as a powerful fruit of the gospel, hath never in scripture so low a meaning, as is not wanting to natural men, and Atheists, and Pharisees: but is meant of an effectual knowledge of God, and the enjoying of God, as Job xix. 25. *I shall see God.* Psal. cvi. 5. *That I may see, that is, enjoy the good of thy chosen.* Isa. liii. 17. *Thine eyes shall see the King in his beauty.* Isa. lii. 10. *The ends of the earth shall see the salvation of our God.* Mat. v. 8. *Blessed are the pure in heart, for they shall see God.* John iii. 3. *Except a man be born again, he cannot see the kingdom of God.* Acts xxii. 14. *Then Ananias said to Saul, The God of our fathers hath chosen thee, that thou shouldst know his will, and see that just One.* Heb. xii. 14. *Follow holiness, without which no man shall see the Lord.* But if Mr. Denne and others will contend, that this seeing of the salvation of God,

is

is the revelation of the literal knowledge of Christ, that saving thing which is bestowed on the nations by the ministry of John, and the coming of the Messiah; they must with us confess a large synecdoche and figure in this, when it is said, *All flesh shall see the salvation of God;* because there are thousands that live and die in the region and shadow of death, to whom the least taste of literal knowledge of Christ, or of his name, never came, Psal. xxix. 9. *In his temple shall every one speak of his glory*; not every one, but converts only, can utter the glory of God savingly, in the temple of the Lord; otherwise many speak, and do in his temple, to his dishonour, Jer. vii. 4, 10, 11. Ezek. xxiii. 38, 39. Acts ii. 4. *They were all filled with the Holy Ghost.* 17. *And it shall come to pass in the last days (saith God) I will pour out my Spirit upon all flesh.* Now it is clear, this is a prophecying of all flesh within the church: *your sons and your daughters shall prophesy, your young men shall dream dreams,* etc. Now, all flesh did never prophesy, nor was the Holy Ghost on Ananias and Sapphira. Rom. iv. Abraham is called *the father of us all.* A spiritual father by faith, he is to those that are of the faith of Abraham: now, Arminians will not suffer us to expound *us all* in the matter of redemption of us all, the elect of God, and believers; but of all and every one within the *visible church,* John i. 16. *And of his fulness have all we received, and grace for grace.* There is as good ground for saving grace given to all in Christ, as for universal redemption, except the words be restricted. For Arminians have ground from the words to alledge, All *we, among whom Christ dwelt, have received grace, all we who saw his glory, as the only begotten Son of God,* v. 14. which sight is the sight of saving faith, *not given to all and every son of Adam.* 14. *And he dwelt personally in the flesh and nature of all Adam's sons.* So it is said, 1 Cor. xii. 13. *For by one Spirit we are all baptized into one body, whether we be Jews or Gentiles, whether we be bond or free, and have been all made to drink unto one*

Spirit

Spirit [Gr. he meis pantes.] How can Arminians decourt from a spiritual communion, in both sacraments, all Jews and Gentiles in the visible body of Christ, except they restrict all [Gr. pantes,] as we do? And 2 Cor. iii. 18. *But we all with open face* [Gr. he meis de pantes,] *beholding as in a glass the glory of the Lord, are changed into the same image, from glory to glory, even as by the Spirit of the Lord.* Now, Paul speaketh of all under the gospel, and under the glorious ministration of the Spirit, opposite to the condition of the children of Israel, who were under the law, which was the ministration of death, v. 6, 7, 8. whose minds are blinded, through the vail that was, and yet is over the hearts of that stiff-necked people, in reading of the Old Testament: whereas this vail is taken away in Christ, and we all under the gospel have the Spirit, and are free, and see the glory of the Lord, and are changed into the same glory, being in the suburbs of heaven; all of us having our faces shining with the rays and beams of the glory of the gospel, in the face of God, in a more glorious manner than the face of Moses did shine when he came down from the mount, with a glory that was to be done away: whereas this is eternal, v. 9, 10, 11, 12. compared with v. 17, 18. Now, let Arminians speak, if they think all and every one that heareth the gospel are partakers of this vision of God in the kingdom of grace? And, Eph. iv. Christ ascending on high, gifted his church with a ministry, v. 13. *Till we all come in the unity of the faith, and of the knowledge of the Son of God, into a perfect man, unto the measure of the stature of the fulness of Christ.* When we (to decline the absolute universality of the redemption of all and every one) do say, *We all,* and *he tasted death for all men, and Christ gave himself a ransom for all;* all must be restricted according to the scope, the antecedent and consequent of the text; we cannot be heard. Mr. Moor saith, We make the *Holy Ghost to speak untruth,* because we expound, *all men,* to be *few men*: yet must they either use the same restriction, and acknowledge an universality of converted

and

and saved men, and so expound, all, to be few, as we do; or they can no more decline the *universal salvation of all, and every one,* than we can decline the catholic redemption of *all and every one.* So, they must say, That the number of the perfected saints, that attain *to the fulness of grace and glory, and to a perfect man in Christ,* is equal to that visible body, the church, gifted with apostles, evangelists, prophets, and pastors, and teachers. For, all the like places Arminians expound of the body, of the whole body of the visible church, externally called: now, this is most absurd, that all and every one should be saved, to whom apostles and pastors were sent to preach the gospel; then need force all must be restricted to the chosen flock only: so, Luke xvi. 16. *The kingdom of God is preached,* [Gr. kaì pâs eis auten biazetai] *and every man presseth violently to it.* The meaning is not as Mr. Denne (Denne Dragnete p. 96.) saith, that every one is pressed by command, and gospel-exhortation to repent: for, (1.) From John Baptist's time, all and every one heareth not the gospel, Mat. x. 5. (2.) Mat. xi. v. 12. is clearly expounded by an active verb, these that take heaven violently, [Gr. árpázou sin autèn,] *take it by force:* but do all and every son of Adam take heaven by force? No, then, there must be an all, and a catholic company of converted and saved persons, by this conceit. And, 1 Thes. v. 5. *Ye are all* [Gr. pántes humeîs] *the children of light, and the children of the day; we are not of the night, nor of the darkness*: these all, that are called the children of the day, are opposed, in the fore-going verses, to the children of darkness, on whom the last day cometh suddenly, as child-birth pains on a woman. 2. All these are the children of light, who are exhorted *to be sober, not to sleep,* v. 6, 7, 8. *And whom God hath not appointed for wrath, but for salvation, by the means of our Lord Jesus.* But these be all the visible church of Thessalonica; *Ergo,* there were no children of darkness among them, which is absurd; and will be denied by Arminians. When Christ speaketh to the multitude, he saith, Mat. xxv. 8. *All ye are*

brethren:

brethren: they must be brethren, by the new birth. v. 8. *Call no man your father on earth*, etc. Phil. i. 7. *Ye are all partakers of my grace.* Now, he speaketh of these in whom Christ had begun the good work, *and would perfect it unto the day of Christ*, v. 6. Such, the Arminians do say, were all the visible saints at Philippi. Then, by this, all and every one of them were converted, 1 Cor. xi. 4. *The head* [Gr. pantòs andròs] *of every man is Christ*, of every man without exception? No, these of whom Christ is head, these are his body, the church, that have life from him, and are knit to him by the Spirit, and among themselves by spiritual ligatures, Eph. i. 22, 23. and Christ's fulness, Eph. iv. 16. Col. i. 18. Gen. xxi. 6. *All that hear shall laugh with me*; Sarah meaneth the laughter of faith: then, must all that hear of Sarah's bearing of Isaac in her old age, believe in Christ, as Sarah did? Psal. lxv. 2. *O thou that hearest prayer, unto thee shall all flesh come:* A figure there must be in the word flesh; and if there be no figure in the particle [Heb. col] then must all flesh, and all Adam's sons put up prayers to God, contrary to experience, and to scripture, Psal. xiv. 4. Psal. liii. 4. Jer. x. 25. So Psal. lxxii. 12. *All nations* [Heb. col gojim] *shall serve him;* it is meant of Christ, and in the letter cannot be true, if many refuse him to be their king, Psal. ii. 3. Luke xix. 14. Psal. cx. 1. So it is said, Psal. xxii. 27. *All the ends of the world shall remember, and turn to the Lord; and all the kindreds of the nations shall worship before thee.* Now, that he meaneth of spiritual turning to God, and of repentance, is clear, v. 18. *For the kingdom is the Lord's, and he is the governor among the nations*, v. 13. *A seed shall serve him, it shall be counted to the Lord for a generation.* Except there be a restriction of this *(All)* how will Arminians eschew this, that all, and every man of the heathen, shall repent, and be a holy seed devoted to the Lord, as his righteous ones? For, sure, the same expression of all nations, Isa. xl. 16. are taken for all and every one of mankind, Psal. lxvi. 9. All nations, [Heb. col go-

jim]

CHRIST DYING AND DRAWING SINNERS TO HIMSELF. 471

jim] *whom thou hast made, shall come and worship before thee, O Lord, and shall glorify thy name,* Isa. lxvi. 23. *And it shall come to pass, that from one new moon to another, and from one sabbath to another, shall all flesh come to worship before me, saith the Lord.* Let Arminians speak, if all flesh, that cometh before God, from sabbath to sabbath, under the New Testament, to worship, be as large and comprehensive as the same expression, Isa. xl. 6. *All flesh* [Heb. col baser] *is grass.* Sure, the latter comprehendeth all Adam's sons, without exception, even including infants; the former cannot bear so wide a sense. So, Gen. xii. 3. *In thee shall all the families of the earth be blessed.* Gen. xxii. 18. If the meaning be, that, without any figure or exception, all and every family be blessed in Christ; then shall I infer, that all the families of the earth, without exception, are justified by faith in Christ, Gal. iii. 10, 11, 12, 13, 14. and that the *nations of the earth,* without exception, *are heirs of the promise, have right to strong consolation, are fled for refuge to lay hold on the hope laid before them, and have anchored their hope up within the vail, whither the Fore-runner Christ hath entred;* for of these nations the apostle expoundeth the promise, Heb. vi. 13, 14, 15, 16, 17, 18, 19, 20. So Isa. xxvii. 6. *Israel shall blossom and bud, and fill the face of the world with fruit;* then, shall there be none on earth, but the blossoming Israel of God? Rom. xi. 26. *And so all Israel shall be saved, as it is written, There shall come out of Zion a Deliverer,* etc. These that Paul calleth all Israel, Isa. lxix. 20, 21. *calleth Jacob and the seed, and the seed's seed.* Isa. lix. 19. *So shall they fear the name of the Lord from the west, and his glory from the rising of the sun.* Mal. i. 11. *For, from the rising of the sun, even to the going down of the same, my name shall be great among the Gentiles, and in every place incense shall be offered unto my name, and a pure offering; for my name shall be great among the heathen, saith the Lord of hosts.* If from the East to the West, and in all places of the Gentiles, men fear the name of the Lord; then sure, the whole inhabitants

habitants of the earth, between the rising of the sun to the going down of the same, must be converted to Christ, and offer prayers, praises, spiritual service to Christ, except some restriction be made; the most part from the East to the West, are enemies to the gospel. And how would Arminians triumph, if so much were said for universal redemption, as is said for universal regeneration and conversion of all, except we say there must be a figure, a synecdoche, of all or many? Or Christ's all, and universality of converted ones, must be here meant? John i. 9. *That was the true light, that inlightneth every one that cometh into the world.* What? even infants who come into the world, and all and every one of Adam's sons? It cannot be true, in any sense; except it be meant of the light of the gospel, that yet never came to the half part of the world: for, v. 10. *The world knew him not;* and v. 6. *There was a man sent from God whose name was John,* v. 7. *The same came for a witness, to bear witness of the Light, that all men through him might believe.* Can any divinity teach, that God intended, that all and every mortal man should believe by him, that is, by the ministry of John, the morning-star, which was to fall, and disappear, and shine no more, at the rising of Christ the Sun of righteousness? 1 John ii. 27. *Ye need not that any teach you, but the anointing that ye have received teacheth you all things.* Why should then fewer have the Spirit of holy unction in them than the world, for whom Christ is a propitiation, and all the visible saints that John writeth unto 1 John i. 2. & ii. 1, 2, & iv. 9. *God sent his only begotten Son to the world, that we through him might live.* Nor need we flee to that exposition ever and anon, that *Christ died for all,* that is, all ranks of men: for, all, is put in scripture ordinarily for many; as Deut. i. 21. Psal. xvii. 18. Jer. xv. 10. and xix. 9. and xx. 7. and xxiii. 30. and xlix. 17. Ezek. xvi. 27. Exod. xxxiii. 10. Col. i. 28. Isa. lxi. 9. Gen. xli. 57. Mark. xiv. 4. John iii. 26. Acts xvii. 31. and x. 38. Mark i. 37. 2 Cor. iii. 2. Luke xxiv. 47. and iv. 15. Isa. ii. 2, 3. Otherwise,

I could say, Christ died for no man, because the scripture ascribeth an universality to the wicked, Jer. vi. 28. & ix. 2 Mic. i. 7. 1 John ii. 15, 16. and 1 John v. 19.

And surely, that election and redemption move both in the same sphere and orb of the free-love of God, is clear to me from that place, John iii. 16. on which Arminians confide much; for God's love to save mankind, by the death of Christ, is the very love of election to glory, of such certain persons, as the Lord therefore gives grace to believe; because they are ordained to eternal life: so, that the [Gr. hosoi] as many, and the number of believers, and of the chosen to life are equal, Acts xiii. 48. John x. 26. Rom. viii. 29, 30.

1. That love cannot be a general, confused, antecedent, conditional love, offered to all the world, on condition they believe; for that the scripture freeth thousands of the sin of unbelief of that love, if Christ come not to them, and speak not, John xv. 22. And, Paul saith, Rom. i. 14. *How shall they believe in him of whom they never heard?* Now, the loved world, John iii. 16. is obliged to believe.

2. That love that is the cause of Christ's death, is, John xv. 13. the greatest love that is; it is such a giving love whereby God gives his Son, that with him he cannot but give his Holy Spirit, faith and salvation, *yea, and all things*, Rom. viii. 32. But the conditional general love is not the greatest love, for the Lord beareth not the greatest love to all and every man, nor gives he faith and salvation to all and every man; yea, the known and believed love of God, in sending his Son to die for us, is proper to the believer, 1 John iv. 6, 9, 10. We have known and believed the love God hath to us; *God is love, and he that dwelleth in love,* (it is a noble princely palace to lodge in) *dwelleth in God, and God in him.* This cannot be said of the love that God beareth to the reprobate, yea, and to the fallen angels; for Arminians say, that God loved them with such a love: but that love to devils is now dried up long ago, and so that to Pharaoh, Judas, Cain, now in hell; but this love is gone. So dream

they,

they, that love in God is like summer-brooks, that go dry in time of drought; but the truth is, God's general love to Arminians, is a faint desire, and a wish that all and every one, men and angels, be saved: and bestowing on them means, 1. Which the Lord knows shall plunge them deeper in hell, and make their everlasting chains heavier and more fiery; better he love them not. 2. Such means as can be demonstrated free-will, without God, or any determination or bowing to one hand, rather than to another, can, and may absolutely master and over-master equally to conversion, or obstinacy, or to final rebellion, to salvation, or damnation, to make themselves free princes and lords of the book of life, and the writing pen of eternal election and artists, causes, and masters of the decrees of election, or reprobation. For, 1. Let God do what he can, or omnipotency, or sweetness of free-grace, all that is possible, free-will hath the free and absolute casting of the balance to will, receive Christ, *open to the King of glory*, and be converted, or to the contrary. 2. In election and reprobation from eternity, (as Arminians in their last apology go no higher than time, *capta est in tempore electio, contra quam creditum est*, etc.) God doth no more in his general decree for chusing of Jacob or Peter, than of Pharaoh, Esau or Judas; but chuseth all indefinitely who shall believe. But for the assumption that Peter, John, Pharaoh, Judas, Esau, believe, or not believe, the eternal decree of God does nothing; his means, gospel, his inward grace (such grace as they can grant) do no more, nor can do any more to determine the will to either side, to believing or not believing, than he can work contradictions, or make free-will, and free obedience to be no free-will, and no obedience: for it is repugnant (say they) to the nature of free-will, that it should be determined by God; and obedience, such as is required of us now who are under commandments, threatnings, promises, were no obedience at all; for if the Lord should determine the will (say they) and therefore God's last decree of chusing those to life, whom he foresees shall expire in

faith,

faith, and persevere to the end, and of rejecting such, as he foresees shall go on in final obstinacy against the gospel, is not any scriptural decree of election or reprobation; nor hath God any liberty, in this, to chuse this man, not this man, but all men chuse God, and are foreseen finally to believe, or not believe, before, and without any free decree of God; so that the number of chosen angels or men is in the power of the creatures free will, not in the liberty of the former of all things; so as we chuse God, but God chuseth not us. But, 2. So none are within the compass of election or reprobation, but such as hear the gospel; and so all the heathen are saved or damned by chance, or without any will or decree of God, or they must be neither capable of salvation, nor damnation; contrary to scripture and experience; for terrible judgments temporal, and great external favours befal Indians, Americans, and such as never heard of Christ, and not without the counsel of God's will, if there be a providence that rules the world. 3. God doth nothing in the election of Peter, more than of Judas; nor can grace and mercy have place in the chusing of the one, rather than the other; but as free will is foreseen to play the game, ill or well, so go the eternal decrees of election and reprobation, and there can be no such thing as that grace and the free pleasure of God, who hath mercy on whom he will, or because he will, and hardens whom he will, can have any place here.

4. The scripture nowhere speaks of any love of God in Christ to man, but such as is efficacious in saving; any other love is lip-love, not real; and so to alledge this one place, without authority of the word, is *petitio principii*, a begging of the question: for the love, Ezek. xvi. 8. called the time of loves, was such as saved, all that were to be saved, amongst the people of God; and cannot be understood of such a love as God did bear to the heathen, and the Canaanites; for it separates them from all the world: so Deut. vii. 7. Psal. cxlvi. 19, 20. Isa. li. 1, 2, 3. Isa. lii. 3, 4. Psal. cxxxvi. 13. Psal. cxxxv. 4. Zech. iii. 2. 1 Kings xi. 13. 2 Chron.

vi. 6.

vi. 6. Isa. iv. 8, 9. Deut. xiv. 2. Isa. xliii. 20. Dan. xi. 15. 1 Chr. xvi. 13. Ezek. xx. 5. Acts xiii. 17. Ye shall not find that the love of God in Christ can consist with reprobation, or damnation, in all the scripture; but by the contrary, it is a love that Christ hath *to his wife, in giving himself for her; sanctifying, washing and presenting her, without spot or wrinkle, before God;* and a husband-love, Eph. v. 25, 26. *a love saving, by the washing of regeneration, and renewing of the Holy Ghost,* Titus iii. 4, 5,6. *a great love, quickning us together with Christ, saving us by grace, raising us up, and making us sit together with Christ, in heavenly places,* Eph. ii. 4, 5. a love causing *washing of us,* and advancing us to be *kings and priests to God,* Rev. i. 5, 6. a love to Paul in particular, and working life in Paul, Gal. ii. 20. *I live no more, but Christ liveth in me; and the life which I now live in the flesh, I live by the faith of the Son of God, who loved me, and gave himself for me.* It is the *love of God our Father, who hath loved us, and hath given us everlasting consolation, and good hope through grace,* 2 Thes. ii. 16. *An everlasting love,* Jer. xxxi. 3. a love *before the foundation of the world,* Eph. i. 3, 4. *before we do good or evil,* Rom. ix. 11. Not a love that falls to nothing by a consequent act of hatred; nor a love to which the hatred of reprobation may succeed every hour, and out of which we may be decourted: a love that puts the honour of sons on us, 1 John iii. 1. It is a saving and a pitying love, Isa. lxiii. 9. a love which the Lord *rests in,* Zeph. iii. 17. a love *continuing to the end,* John xiii. 1. a love that *makes us more than conquerors,* Rom. viii. 37. It is a separating love, that differenceth the loved of God, from all others, Psal. lxxxvii. 2. Psal. cxlvi. 8. otherwise all the world should, in regard of this *general, and antecedent, and conditional love of God,* be so the beloved of God, as Christ (in the song of Solomon) esteemeth the spouse his love, his well-beloved. 'Tis a love better than life, Psal. lxiii. 3. and the dowry Christ bestoweth on his spouse, Hos. ii. 19. Now the scripture nowhere speaketh of that conditional love, which the Lord

CHRIST DYING AND DRAWING SINNERS TO HIMSELF. 477

Lord beareth to heathens, reprobates, and to all men and angels.

5. Such as the Lord so loved, as he hath redeemed them from perishing, he hath redeemed them from sin and Gentilism; to wit, from this present evil world, Gal. i. 4. Yea, the blood of the Lamb, *unspotted, and undefiled, hath bought them from their vain conversation, received by tradition from their fathers*, 1 Pet. i. 18. yea, *from fornication, that they should be members of Christ, temples of the Holy Ghost*, 1 Cor. vi. 20. Yea, *Christ bare their sins in his own body on the tree*, that they should live to righteousness. Now, all and every one of mankind, heathens and Turks, are not thus bought with a price, and delivered from idolatry, blasphemy, killing of children to their God, from the world of Gentilism. 1. They live in these sins, as serving God in them; the gospel never forbade them any such sins, in regard they never heard the gospel. 2. They cannot sin on a new score, or a new reckoning; these being to them, no sins against the gospel; but against the law written in their heart. 3. There is a price then given for all the reprobate *vice reproborum*, it is as good as they had paid the price to redeem them from sin and unbelief; yea, from final impenitency against the gospel: if this be a sin, as it is the sin of sins, Christ must bear it on the tree, 1 Pet. i. 24. *The Lamb of God must take it away,* John i. 29. except it were possible final unbelief were pardonable without shedding of blood, Heb. x. Now, here the ransom paid, but the captive is never delivered, for the *reprobate die in their sins*, John viii. 21. There be some say, "There is a ransom given for these gospel-sins of the reprobate, conditionally, so they believe."

Answ. That is, they are freed from final impenitency, so they be freed from final impenitency: is this a wise bargain? 2. Where is there, in all the world, a warrant that Christ laid down his life for his sheep conditionally; so he foresaw they would be his sheep; so they would believe and repent? Now, this he could not do; for Christ, out of deliberation, and his Fa-

ther's

ther's eternal counsel, absolutely gratis, freely died for these; he died not for those, that he foresaw would never fulfil the condition, *nunquam posita conditione, nunquam ponitur conditionatum.*

6. Christ bought, by his blood of the eternal covenant, all the jewels of the covenant, all *things that belong to life and godliness*, and *all spiritual blessings*, 2 Pet. i. 3. Eph. i. 3. *A new heart, and a new spirit*, Ezek. xxxvi. 26. Jer. xxxi. 33, 34, 35, 36. Ezek. xi. 19, 20. He bought all that God giveth to us, then he must have purchased faith, Phil. i. 29. John vi. 29. and if he was made *a prince to give repentance and remission*, then to give faith, for it is a grace above nature; and out of this fountain, *we have grace for grace*, John xiv. Now, this is not given to all men.

7. All these graces are particular, 1. Election to glory is particular, *Few are chosen*, Mat. xxii. 14. John x. 26, 29. Eph. i. 4. Rom. ix. 11. The promise is particular to *the sons of the promise*, Rom. ix. 8, 9. *made to Christ, and his seed only*, Gal. iii. 16, 17, 18. Gal. iv. 22, 23, etc. the calling particular, Isa. lv. 1, 2. Mat. xi. 27, 28. Acts ii. 39. the covenant particular, and takes in only the house of Judah, the elect, and such as cannot fall away, Jer. xxxi. 34, 35, etc. and xxxii. 39, 40. Isa. liv. 10 and lix. 19, 20. *The surety of the covenant, Christ*, Heb. vii. 22. promised to be king over the house of David, over his people only; the intention of God particular to a foreknown people only, Rom. xi. 1. The circumference and extent of grace then cannot be so wide, as to take in all; nor can redemption be universal, because conditional. For, 1. Arminians make election conditional, but they deny it in words to be universal. Further, glorification is conditional, justification conditional, upon condition of faith; but because the condition never is, *All men have not faith*; therefore glorification and justification is particular, and redemption on the same ground must be particular; none are actually redeemed, but the believers: so as glorification actual (the decree of glorifying is another thing, and absolute) and election to glory are commensurable,

the

the one not larger than the other, Rom. viii. 29, 30. How can redemption, which is a mid-link between both, be of a wider sphere to take in all? For, 1 Thess. v. 9. God's counsel set us on Christ as Redeemer, and gives us to Christ.

8. These two (Christ redeemeth all) and (Christ intendeth to redeem all) are most different: now God's intention to redeem all if they believe, suspendeth either redemption, or the intention of God to redeem: if the former be said, redemption of all, is no redemption, except all believe, but all do not believe: if the latter, God must wave and hang by his intention in millions of souls, and cannot fix his foot to be peremptory in his intentions, except they believe; and he seeth they shall never believe, *for he knoweth what is in man, and beholdeth the thoughts afar off.*

Yea, as I said elsewhere, if we speak properly in reference to God, the very promises of the gospel are not conditional; because both the condition, and the thing that falls under the condition, depend on his own absolute will, and free gift. If a father promise to his child an inheritance upon condition the child pay him then thousand crowns, and the father do only give and can give the child these ten thousand crowns; we cannot say, this is a bargain between the father and the son, that leans upon conditions; especially if we suppose, as the case is between God and the creature, that this father can and doth indeclinably determine the will of his son to consent, and to give back again to his father this sum of money, and to consent to the bargain; there is here no condition relating to the father, but he does all freely. Believing is a condition, and life eternal is *conditionatum*, a thing that falleth under promise, but both depend upon the absolute, free and irresistible will of the Lord; as there is no condition here properly so called, either laid upon the will, or limiting the external action of God.

9. Hence the promises of the gospel are indefinite, not universal, and in the Lord's purpose and intention made

with

with the elect only, not with the reprobate at all; for when God saith, If Judas, Cain, Pharaoh, believe, they shall be saved, the Lord's purpose being to deny to them the grace of believing, without which it is unpossible they can believe, the promise in God's purpose is not made with them: he that so willeth what he promiseth, upon a condition, which he that so willeth only can do and work, and yet will not do or work the condition: he doth indeed not will to the party, what is so promised: if John send Peter to work in his garden, upon condition, that if he work, he shall give him a talent a day, and in the mean while John only can give to Peter strength of legs, and arms, and body to work, can determine his consent to the work, and yet refuse to give strength, and to win his consent to the work; sure he never willed either to give him a talent for his work, nor intended he should work at all. Hence I argue, it is against the wisdom of God, to intend and will that the reprobate be redeemed, pardoned, saved, upon a condition, which he himself only can work by his grace, and absolutely and irresistibly will not work. Now, in scripture such a thing is argued not to be done, because *the scripture must be fulfilled*, and the decree of God and his will fulfilled; as Christ's bones, upon this ground could not be broken; and such a thing is done, that the scripture, and so the will and decree of God, might be fulfilled; so that which is never done, is simply God's will it shall never be done; that which is done, is simply God's will it must be; I mean either his permissive or approving will. And the will of God revealing what is the duty of reprobates, tho' it never be done, argues it was not simply the will of God; hence that *voluntas signi*, in which God reveals what is our duty, and what we ought to do, not what is his decree, or what he either will, or ought to do, is not God's will properly, but by a figure only; for commands, and promises, and threatnings revealed, argue not the will and purpose, decree or intention of God, which are properly his will.

10.

10. It is against the wisdom of God, to intend the actual redemption and salvation of all, and every one; and not to will, nor work such conditions, which only he himself can work, and are in his power only, and without the which, the creature cannot be redeemed and saved: but he neither will, nor doth work faith in all; then he never intended the actual redemption and salvation of all and every one.

Hence, whatever wanton and lascivious reason can object against absolute reprobation, the absolute redemption of some few, a particular atonement of some few, equally fighteth with the opinion of adversaries, as against ours. They say,

1. "God intends the eternal destruction of the innocent, sinless and greatest part of mankind.

2. "Mercy, bowels of compassion, by your particular, absolute redemption, is extended to few; and all the rest of the lost world, left to sink eternally, notwithstanding of the infinite and boundless love and man-kindness of God." 'Tis answered, these fall with equal strength of wanton reason, upon conditional and universal redemption, or God's conditional and universal will to save all, and every one: for, say that the father did foresee, if he beget twenty sons, that eighteen of them shall be cast in a river of fire, to be burnt quick, where they shall be tormented ten thousand years, ever dying, and not able to find death, to end their miseries; and that they may be kings in great riches and honour, upon a condition of such and such a carriage of them in their education and young years, which this father can easily work with one word; yet he willingly begets these children, he can work such a condition in them, as they may all be kings, yet deliberately this he will not do, but acts so upon the will of these children, as he knows indeclinably the greatest part of them all shall be tormented for ten thousand years in this extreme fire: who can say, 1. That this father, *quantum in se*, as far as he can, hath redeemed all, and every one of his children, from ten thousand years pain? Who can say, this father intended and

willed

willed the life and honour of these eighteen children, when as he might, with no pain to himself, most easily have wrought the condition in them, which he wrought in others, and would not? Hence, if there must be a mystery in the gospel, and the Lord's ways and thoughts must be above ours, as far as the heaven is above the earth, if the Lord did foresee the greatest part of mankind, and many legions of angels, should be cast in chains of darkness, and in a lake of fire and brimstone for ever and ever; 1. Vain reason would say, why did he create them, if he foresaw their misery would be so deplorable? And how can he earnestly and ardently, with prayers, obtestations, wishes, threatnings, precepts, promises, desire their eternal salvation? 2. If he could have hindred them to sin (as no question he could) without hurting Adam's free-will, and without strangling the nature of free obedience, in reference to threatning of ill, and promising of good, and life, as we see all angels, being equally under one law, he kept some from sin, of free-grace, and permitted others to fall in eternal misery; if he could have hindered them to sin, how created he them, and gave them a law, which, he saw, they would violate, and make themselves eternally miserable? 3. When the same gospel was preached to some, yea, and to a huge multitude within the visible church, if the Lord willed all and every one to be saved, and gave his Son to redeem all and every one; was there not an eternal and absolute will, most unlike and disparous to some, beside others; when as he took a way of working, with the gospel preached, on some, which he saw would eternally, indeclinably, inevitably save them, and a contrary way of working with others, which he foresaw would be fruitless, ineffectual, and null, and tend to their sadder condemnation: now, can he will both the redemption and salvation of these that he moveth ineffectually to obey, and also efficaciously to obey? Corvinus saith in this, "he willeth all, *ex aequo*, equally to be saved, in regard of his affection and will to all; but he willeth not all equally to be saved, *ex parte boni voliti*, in re-
"gard

secundo, efficaciously, effectual, and denies both to other nations and people; and with this distinction, he willeth, and willeth not, equally, *ex aequo*, the salvation of all." But this is *petitio principii*; the disparity of favours bestowed on persons and nations, do argue, in scripture, disparity of good-wills in the Lord; as, because God sent his law and testimonies to *Israel and Jacob, and dealt not so with every nation*, Psal. cxlvii. 19, 20. Every page almost in the Old Testament, and the Lord's Spirit, and all divines argue, that the Lord chose Israel, and loved and saved them, and with a higher and more peculiar love, as his chosen people, than he loved all the nations, Deut. vii. 7. Psal. cxxxii. 12, 13, 14. Psal. cxxxv. 3, 4. Because he bestowed on them the means of salvation, his law and his testimonies, which he denied to the nations; then the nations were not his beloved and chosen ones.

10. That will of God, called *voluntas signi*, the revealed will of God, that precepts, promises, and threatnings hold forth, do not express to us the decree, intention and purpose of God, that he willeth the thing commanded to be, but only that he approves of the thing commanded, as just and good, whether it be, or be not, whatever the event be: then God's revealed will is no more formally, but his approbation of the moral goodness and obedience of elect and reprobate, whether they obey or not.

11. These that Christ offered his body for as a priest, for these as a priest he intercedes and prays; for these two cannot be separated: but he prays not for all, not for the world, John xvii. 9. *I pray for them, I pray not for the world*.

12. These for whom Christ is a priest to offer his body, for them he is a king to make them kings, and to save them, and a prophet to teach them; but he is not king and prophet to any but to his people, kingdom, conquest, disciples, seed, children, subjects.

13. These

13. These that Christ died for, cannot be condemned, Rom. viii. 33, 34. but are chosen, and cannot be impeached; but the reprobate can be condemned and impeached.

14. Those whom God wills to save, and whom he redeemed, to these he willed the means of salvation; but he wills not the means, nor that the gospel be preached to the Gentiles, Mat. x. 5. nor to Asia, nor Bithynia, Acts xvi. 6, 7.

15. All that Christ died for, are justified and reconciled by his death, and shall much more be *saved by his life*, Rom. v. 9. 1 John i. 7. and God required not one debt twice. If Christ sustained the person of all the elected, as he died for his friends, John xv. 13. for his *sheep*, John x. 11. *for his church*, Eph. v. 25. *for many*, Mat. xx. 28. *for his enemies*, Rom. v. 10. *for the ungodly, and unjust*, 1 Pet. iii. 18. *for his brethren*, Heb. ii. 1 John iii. 16. and not for their good only, so as they might all and every one have perished eternally, that Christ died for; then cannot they die eternally, for then Christ should first have paid their debt, and they must pay for that debt over again, eternally in hell; then might Christ be a Redeemer, a King, a Priest, a Husband, a Saviour, and Head, and have no ransomed ones, no subjects, no Israel that he interceeds for, and offers his soul, no spouse, no saved people, no members, no church.

Artic. 4. *Places of scripture seeming to favour universal atonement vindicated.*

For the fourth particular, and the clearing of places alledged; we are, 1. To consider if the place, John iii. 16. prove any thing against us. 2. If all men, and all the world that are said to be redeemed, be concludent against us. 3. There be some particular places to be considered.

1. The Greek word (Kosmos) world, must be a figurative speech, the whole for the part; otherwise in its latitude it comprehends the angels, Acts xvii. 24. Rom. iii. 6. 1 Cor. vi. 2. Rom. i. 20. John xvii. 5. Now 'tis certain, God hath not so loved angels good and bad,

that

that he hath given his only begotten Son for them, Heb. ii. 16. therefore it must sometime signify, a great part of the world; as John xii. 19. *The world goes after him.* 1 John v. 19. *The whole world lies in evil.* The adversary yieldeth, that the world here, is not all, and every one of mankind, without exception. I deny not but it signifieth so, Rom. iii. 13. *That all the world may become guilty before God.* But the Arminians take on them a hard task, *duram proviciam*, to prove that it is so taken here. For, 1. The Greek word houto, *God so loved the world*, is the highest love that ever was, above God's love to the angels, Heb. ii. 16. So God must carry the most superlative love, that is, than which there is none greater, John xv. 13. Such a love as is manifested to us, to the beloved John the apostle, and all the saints, 1 John iv. 9. to Cain, Judas, and all the heathen; and God's love giving his Son, differenceth men from angels, but not one man from another; the contrary of which Paul saith, Gal. ii. 20. and must Paul say no more? *Who loved me and gave himself for me*, than Judas, Pharaoh, all the lost heathen, who never heard of Christ, can and may say? Believe it who will, it sound not like Christ's love.

2. They have two sorts of love in Christ's dying for men to make out two redemptions; one general, one potential, or half a redemption, where life is purchased, never applied, standing with the eternal destruction of the greatest part of mankind; another special, in which men are redeemed from sin, preached to few, applied to far fewer.

3. Two reconciliations, two non-imputations of sin; one, 2 Cor. v. another Rom. iv. and so two justifications; one Rom. v. and two blessednesses, and two salvations, or deliveries from wrath, and the curse of the law.

4. This giving love, with which God must give all other things, saith, the gospel, Rom. viii. 32. must be bestowed on heathens, that never heard such a thing.

5. God by this must intend life eternal, as an end, to all the heathen; faith as a mean, which are clearly intended to this loved world; and yet God forbids

Paul

Paul and his apostles to preach the word of faith to them, Acts xvi. 6, 7. Mat. x. 5. and contrives businesses so, that the hearing of the word of faith, and of this highest love, and rarest gift, and given Redeemer, shall be simply unpossible to them.

6. Therefore better by the (world) understand the elect of Jews and Gentiles, opposed every where in the New Testament, to the narrow church of Judea; the gospel world, the Messiah's world, larger than the little world of Moses; yea, all nations, Mat. xxviii. 19. *Every creature*, that is, most of all the nations, Mark xvi. 15. all the world, the hearing world, almost all the nations, Col. i. 6. sure not every individual person; as they would have this loved world to include.

Object. "But [Gr. pas] that every one that believes etc. These words, limit, and draw narrow the world, and so divide it in believers, and not-believers; and by your exposition, some of the elect world believes, and are saved; some believes not, and perishes, which is absurd; therefore the (world) must be comprehensive of all, elect, and reprobate."

Answ. 1. I shall deny that [Gr. pas] *whosoever*, is here a distributive or dividing particle: if he had said [Gr. hostis or hoste] as Gal. v. 4. 1 Cor. xi. 27. there had been some colour for this; but I deny that [Gr. pâs or pántes] all must be restrictive here, more than 2 Thess. ii. 11, 12. *God gave them over to the efficacy of error to believe a lie, that* [Gr. hinà pántes] *all those might be damned, that believe not the truth, but have pleasure in unrighteousness.* It follows not, that [Gr. pantes here,] that all, *or whoever believe not the truth*, should be fewer in number than those that are given over to the efficacy of error: yea, the number of the one and the other is equal; so, John v. 22. *The Father judgeth no man, but hath committed all judgment to the Son.* Ver. 23. [Gr. hina pantes] *That men should honour the Son, as they honour the Father who sent him.* I see no ground to say, that some may honour the Father, and be raised from the dead and quickened, as ver. 21. *who do not honour the Son;*

Son; and therefore it ought not to be translated, *God so loved the world,* etc. *that whosoever believes should not perish*; but far more agreeable to the original, God so loved the world, *that every one believing should not perish*; as in multitude of places it is translated, *unusquisque, non quicunque*: and therefore faith is not set down here so much *ad modum conditionis,* as *ad modum medii,* as a condition, as a means of bring this loved world to glory: as if ye would say, he so loveth letters, as all learned are dear to him; so God so loved his chosen world, that he gave his Son to die for them, (now this love is eternal) that all these believing, in their own time, might never be lost, but have eternal life. Nor can Arminians take the word (world) for all and every one of mankind, for they exclude all infants dying so, as uncapable of faith; and they say, these words contain God's special decree of election, and reprobation; to wit, John iii. 16. God decreed to save all that believe, and God decreed all that believe not should perish. Now, from election and reprobation, they exclude all the heathen, and all their infants, and all infants whatsoever, and such as never heard the gospel: so I fear they make as narrow a world here, as we do; let them see to it: whereas Arminians say, that the word world, never signifieth in scripture the elect only; what then? Let me answer. 1. Their world of elect and reprobate, excluding the best part of mankind, all infants, all that never heard the gospel, sure, is not in the scripture, nor speaks it of such a world. 2. This is a begging of the question; for, John i. 29. The world whose sins the Lamb of God takes away; the reconciled world, to *whom the Lord imputes no sin* [Gr. me logizômenos autôis ta poraptô nata autôn] 'tis the same word that is ascribed to Abraham's believing, Rom. iv. 3, 4, 5. and that David speaks of, Psal. xxxii. 2. Rom. iv. 6. *The imputing of righteousness,* and of *faith to righteousness*; that in which blessedness coming through Christ consisteth, Rom. iv. 8, 9, 10, 11. This world is the only believing elect world, the loved world, John iii. 16. the world saved, v. 17. the world of which Christ is Saviour,

John

John iv. 42. the world that Christ giveth his life unto, John vi. 33. and for whose life he giveth his life, v. 55. the world of which Abraham, but much more Christ, is heir, Rom. iv. 13. the reconciled world, occasioned by the Jews falling off Christ, Rom. xi. 15. All these are the elect, believing, and redeemed world; this they can never disprove.

The other ground of our answer to all the places on the contrary, is, that the Heb. word col, and Gr. word pantes, Christ died for all, doth never signify all and every one of mankind, by neither scripture, nor the doctrine of adversaries: but is, as all divines say, to be expounded according to the subject in hand, *secundum materiam substratum*.

Hence our 1st rule, all, often signifieth, the most part, Mark i. 64. [Gr. pantes] *They all condemned him to be guilty of death*; [Gr. holon] *the whole council*, Mat. xxvi. 59. yet Joseph of Arimathea consented not to his death, Luke xxiii. 51. and the flood *destroyed* [Gr. hapantes] *them all*, Luke xvii. 27. yet eight persons were saved; so *all Judah*, Jer. xiii. 19. [Heb. cullah] *was carried unto captivity*. [Heb. col] All is often the same with many, *all the sheep of Kedar shall be gathered to thee*, [Heb. col] that is, many: and Gen. xli. [Heb. vecol] *and all the land came to Egypt*: when the matter bears a clear exception, and other scriptures expound it; then sure Christ's dying for all, must be expounded for his *giving himself a ransom for many*. Mat. xx. 28. compared with 1 Tim. ii. 6. [Gr. antilútron hupér panton] is here, and there [Gr. lutron antipollon,] so the law saith, *all do that which the most part do; men's will do not limit what God speaks;* but let the text itself be diligently considered, Exod. ix. 6. *All the cattle of Egypt died*, that was in the field. Christ gave himself a ransom for all, capable of a ransom; Arminians say, that the finally obdured, those that sin against the Holy Ghost, and infants of heathen, or any dying infants cannot be ransomed by Christ, Exod. xxxii. 26. *All the sons of Levi came to Moses:* not all without exception; many adhered to Aaron in his idolatry, ver. 29.

Deut.

Deut. xxxiii. 9. So Mat. iii. 5. *Then went out to him Jerusalem, and all Judea, and all the country near to Jordan.* Now, this signification being applied to our use, Christ *giving himself a ransom for all men;* his dying for all, can be no larger than the saving of all, the believing of all flesh, and the blessing of all nations in Christ: but, Gen. xviii. 18. all, *In him* [Heb. col gojei] *all the nations of the earth shall be blessed.* Gen. xxii. 18. *In thy seed all the nations of the earth shall be blessed.* The whole world, that John saith Christ is a propitiation for, 1 John ii. 1. cannot be larger than this; now, this cannot carry any tolerable sense, that all and every man of the nations are actually blessed in Christ, more than all and every one are redeemed, reconciled, received in favour within the covenant of grace: and therefore Arminians have as good reason from col and pantes, all that are said to be ransomed, are actually saved, and hell shall be empty and to no purpose; as to contend with an universal redemption. As a wicked pamphlet printed of late saith, all the creation of God, men and angels are redeemed, and shall at length be saved in Christ. Now, we can undeniably prove, that all and every nation, and all and every man descended of Abraham, are not blessed in Christ. (1.) Rom. ix. 7. *Because they that are the seed of Abraham, they are not all children; but in Isaac shall thy seed be called.* v. 8. *They which are the children of the flesh, are not the children of God, but the children of the promise are counted for the seed.* Now, Christ hath a spiritual seed of a more narrow compass than all the nations of the earth. Isa. liii. 10. *He shall see his seed.* Christ marrieth not with the cursed seed; and many nations, such as for many generations never heard of Christ, are under the law, and under a curse; but the nations are blessed and all nations (say they) *quantum ad Deum,* in God's intention, in the covenant of grace that God made with all the nations, if they would embrace and receive Christ; but that they are not actually blessed, fully redeemed and saved in Christ is their fault.

Answ. The scripture expounds scripture better than Arminians, and the apostle, Heb. vi. resolveth us, that all

the

the nations of the earth, v. 17. are the *heirs of the promise, those who have fled for refuge to lay hold on the hope set before them, who have anchored their souls by hope within the vail, and have Jesus for their Forerunner,* v. 17, 18, 19, 20. 2. He expounds the blessing of Abraham and of his seed, not of any conditional and far-off intention of God, but of God's actual blessing of Abraham and his spiritual seed whom the Lord multiplied, v. 14. Nor was it ever fulfilled in all the nations of the earth, they were never heirs of the promise; our exposition is made good, and by it the promise and oath of God fulfilled and his covenant accomplished; not by the Arminian gloss. 3. Paul expoundeth Abraham's seed, Gal. iii. 16. to be Christ and his seed, Rom. xi. 26. *So all Israel shall be saved,* this was the Israel to whom the covenant by oath and promise was made. *For the redeemer shall come out of Zion, and shall turn away ungodliness from Jacob.* 27. *For this is my covenant unto them, when I shall take away their sins.* Acts iv. 33. *Great grace was on them all,* yet not on Ananias and Sapphira who were of that visible number. Isa. xl. 5. *And the glory of the Lord shall be revealed, and all flesh shall see it,* Psal. lxxxvi. 9. *All nations, whom thou hast made, shall come and worship before thee, and shall glorify thy name, O Lord:* that is expounded, Isa. ii. 1. *All nations shall flow to the mountain of the Lord's house.* What? All nations without exception? No, v. 2. *Many people shall say, come ye, and let us go to the mountain of the Lord's house.* Hag. ii. 7. *And the desire of all nations shall come;* did all nations *quantum in se,* so far as lay in them, desire Christ? No such thing.

2. All skilled in the mother languages, and all divines say, that the particle all is taken *pro singulis generum, vei pro generibus singulorum;* all and every one of kinds, and for the kinds of all, tho' not absolutely excluding any kind.

1. The word all is, *in materia necessaria,* in a necessary matter, taken for all, and every one, *God made all nations of one blood,* Acts xvii. 26. *He knows the hearts*

of

of all men, Acts i. 24. Rom. iii. 12. *All have sinned,* Rom.v. 12. 2 Cor. v. 10. 1 Tim. iv. 10. Jam. i. 5. Phil. i. 10, 11.

2. All, without exclusion of particular men, in a contingent matter sometime so taken, Mat. xxvi. 33. *Though all be offended,* Luke vi. 26. Revel. iv. 26.

3. When all is spoken of God's works for men, or in men, especially works of mere grace, opposite to sense, as Mr. Moor imagines: so our text; *I, when I am lifted up from the earth, will draw all men to me,* cannot be meant of all men without exception. 1. Because 'tis a clear restriction of calling of multitudes, under the Messiah's kingdom, after his death, and cannot but speak against an universal drawing in the times of the Old Testament. 2. Christ draws not all to himself by the gospel, because thousands hear not of him; not virtually, for we read of our calling or drawing of Christ, lifted up on the cross, and crucified, by the works of nature: so God blesseth all nations, not all and every one; *God saveth all Israel, and turneth iniquity away from Jacob, and forgiveth the sins of Israel;* and God only saveth, and only pardoneth believers. But will Mr. Moor say, "God saveth and pardoneth all, and every man in Israel?

Rule 3. There is hence a third rule, *That many is placed for all the elect,* as Mat. x. 28. *He gave himself a ransom for many.* Mark xiv. 14. *This is my blood of the New Testament, that is shed for many;* as Rom. v. 15. *Through the offence of one, many were dead,* that is, all were dead: so the *sheep of Christ,* John x. 11. the *scattered sons of God,* John xi. 52. *His people,* Mat. i. 21. *His brethren,* Heb. ii. that he died for, must be exclusive of those that are not his sheep, not his brethren, not his people, not the sons of God. When there is mention of a singular privilege bestowed on friends, whom Christ is to make friends, John xv. 13. tho' it be bestowed on them in regard of their

pre-

present ill-deserving, when they are enemies, Rom. v. 18. *Sinners*, 1 Tim. i. 15. *Unjust*, 1 Pet. iii. 18. *Lost*, Luke xix. 19. as the necessity of the prerogative of redemption and ransom of free-grace cleareth; as, *In thy seed shall all the nations of the earth be blessed.* Paul expoundeth it exclusively, *in thy seed only*, Gal. iii. 16. So Deut. x. 20. *Thou shalt fear the Lord thy God, and serve him.* Christ expoundeth it, Luke iv. 8. exclusively, *Thou shalt serve only the Lord*, because 'tis the prerogative of God, to be worshipped, as 'tis the prerogative of grace, to be the ransomed and redeemed of God, Deut. xxi. 8. and vii. 8. Exod. xv. 15. Luke i. 68. Gal. iii. 13. 1 Pet. i. 18. Rev. v. 9. and Rev. xiv. 4. Isa. i. 24. and xliv. 23. and xxxv. 10. and li. 10. Jer. xxxi. 11. And the manner of Christ's dying, in regard of application, is exclusive, by confession of party, as is clear, Luke ii. 11. and i. 68, 69, 70. Luke ii. 30, 31. Heb. ii. 17. Rom. viii. 34. Rev. v. 9.

Rule 4. In the matter of our redemption, especially in the New Testament, and prophecies of the Old of the same subject, Christ died for all *pro generibus singulorum*, for men of all nations, some of all kinds. 1. Because God speaks so of our salvation, as Joel iii. 28. which was fulfilled, Acts ii. 17. *And it shall come to pass in the last days, (saith God) I will pour out my Spirit on all flesh;* that is, people of all nations, as v. 9. *Parthians, and Medes, and Elamites, and the dwellers in Mesopotamia, and Judea, Cappadocia,* etc. And of all sexes, v. 17. *Sons and daughters.* Of all ages, *young and old.* All conditions, *servants and handmaids.* Verse 5. *And there were dwelling at Jerusalem Jews, devout men out of every nation under heaven;* nor will this include all and every nation without exception. Erasmus would ask of those that will not admit an hyperbole in scripture, if there were English and Scots there? *Ye tithe every herb,* that is, herbs of all kinds, Luke xi. 42. *Christ cured every disease,* Mat. iv. 23. *Ye shall eat of every tree of the garden,* Gen. ii. 16.

[Heb.

[Heb. micol] all this master's goods are in his hand [Heb. vecol-tob] Gen. xxiv. 10. Now, *thus God will have all to be saved, and Christ is the Mediator of all men*, 1 Tim. ii. which is not to be understood of all and every man, but of kings and low men, and all conditions of men; the word [Gr. pantes] is thrice used in the text. 1. We are nowhere, but in this place only, commanded to pray for all men; for if for the eternal salvation of all and every one without exception, is the doubt. You shall not find a warrant in the world to pray that all mankind may be saved absolutely; for God hath revealed in his word, that he hath decrees of election and reprobation of men. 2. And hath expressly forbidden to pray for their salvation, *that sin to death*, 1 John v. 16. And what faith have we to pray for such? For the salvation of magistrates, in that notion only, we may pray; for the peace of Babylon, and for peace of heathen princes, the church being under them. 3. God will have all men to be saved, no otherwise than *he will have all to come to the knowledge of the truth*, that is, of the gospel. Now, how he will have all men without exception *to come to the knowledge of the gospel*, since this natural, antecedent and conditional will to save all, was in God toward the fallen angels and the Gentiles in the time of the Old Testament, when the law of God, and his will touching salvation, through the Messiah to come, was only revealed to the Jews, Deut. vii. 7. Psal. cxlvii. 19, 20. let Arminians see; for sure the gospel is not, and hath never been preached to all and every rational creature, and to all men, yet he wills all men (by Arminians grounds) to come *to the knowledge of the gospel*. Now, we know not how God, who hath this natural will eternally in him, as they say, willeth the *heathens to come to the knowledge of the gospel*, except he send apostles with the miraculous gift of tongues, to them, to preach in their language. 4. He instances in a specie of the all he spoke of, v. 1. in magistrates, tho' heathen. Thanksgiving here for all and every man must also be commanded, as well as prayer, even for Julian and the greatest scourges and blood scorpions,

that

that lay heaviest stripes on the back of the church: Sure we have no faith to believe this, in reference to their salvation.

5. Paul must here speak of the Lord's effectual will. Whom he saveth, and will have to be saved, and to hear the gospel, they must be saved. So, the apostle, 2 Pet. iii. 9. (8.) *The Lord is long-suffering*, [Gr. eis hemàs mê bouloménos tinàs apolesthai allà pantàs] *to us, willing none* (of us, to whom he is long-suffering) *to perish, but will have all us, to whom he extendeth this long-suffering, to come to repentance.* For, he gives a reason why the day of judgment comes not so quickly, but is so delayed, that lustful men scoff at it; because God waits till all the elect be gathered in; they should perish, and should not come to the knowledge of the truth, if the Lord should hasten that day, as Mat. xxiv. *For the elect's sake, the ill days are shortned;* not for the reprobate. So, for this reason, Paul, v. 7. is appointed *a preacher of the Gentiles in faith and truth;* this must be the Gentiles that believe, and come to the knowledge of the truth: nor did Paul bear this testimony to all and every one of the Gentiles; yet Arminians say, God will have all and every one of Jews and Gentiles saved and ransomed: as also, he restricts the peaceable and godly life to the church, taking in himself, [Gr. hiadiagomen,] *etc. that we may lead*, etc.

6. His reason; *There is one God:* so much as of all orders in the christian church, there is one God. The king and magistrate, as touching his office, hath not one God, and the poor another God; the Jews have not one God, and these I preach to, the Gentiles, v. 7. another; the husband hath not one God, and the wife another; for these three orders, magistrates, and these that are under them, Jews, Gentiles, husband, wives, are in the text. And if that poor argument of Mr. Moor's had blood or nerves, because *there is one God;* and because he names [Gr. Anthropoûs] men, therefore God will save all; and the ransom must be as wide and spacious as the reason, *God is God to all and every one*

one, and all and every man is a man; it may prove, that these that blaspheme and sin to death, these of Bythinia, and Samaria, and all the Gentiles, that the *Lord winked at,* and did not invite to repentance, Acts xiv. 17. they left off to be men; and God was not a God in relation to them, as to the work of his hands: for, sure, God is not in covenant with all and every one of mankind; for thousands, that are men, are without the covenant. I demand of this universal will of God, to save all and every one, and the ransom for all and every one, was it ever heard of, in one letter in the Old Testament, except by prophesying what was to be under the New? Never. Now, was there not one God, and one Mediator, in the Old as in the New? And natural and universal desires and wills in God to save men as men, and that God should save men as one God, do not rise and fall in God; but sure his will, called his command, and revealed in the gospel, is larger under the gospel, nor it was before the Messiah's time; otherwise, God no otherwise willed all men to be saved, amongst the Jews, as their God, in covenant with them, than he willed all the Gentiles, and every man of the heathen to be saved; which contradicts Old and New Testament broadly; for, in the time of the Old Testament, God willed not *Moab, Ammon, Tyre, Sidon, Philistines, Egyptians, to come to the knowledge of the truth, and gospel,* 2 Sam. vii. 23. Deut. iv. 34. Psal. cxlvii. 19.

7. God no more wills all and every man to be saved, and come to believe, so they will all and every one believe; than he wills all and every one to be damned, so they believe not and refuse the gospel; the one will is as universal as the other.

8. It is no justice, that the ransom should be paid for all and every one, and the captives remain in prison eternally: it is against the law, Exod. xxi. 30. Exod. xxx. 12, 15. Yea, the Lord's ransomed, Isa. xxxv. 9, 10. *must obtain everlasting joy in Zion.* Isa. li. 10, 11. *They shall obtain joy and gladness, and sorrow and mourning shall fly away.* And, Hos. xiii. 14. 1 Cor. xv.

54. *They are ransomed from the grave.* Let them find in all the Old or New Testament, any *ransomed of the Lord, and ransomed from the grave, cast in utter darkness, where there is weeping and gnashing of teeth*: they are *redeemed from all iniquity, purified as a peculiar people,* Tit. ii. 14. 1 Pet. i. 18. Gal. i. 4. 1 Pet. ii. 24.

9. This ransom is to be testified *in due time,* or as 1 Pet. i. 20, 21. *was manifest in these last times,* [Gr. di hemâs tous de autu piste uóntas] *for you* (the elect of God) *that believe by him.*

Rule 5. [Heb. col] or [Gr. pantes] his undeniably expounded of *all that are saved only;* and is restrictive: such a physician cured all the city; that is, no man is cured but by him. Exod. xxviii. 14. Jethro saith to Moses, *what is this that thou doest? thou sittest alone,* [Heb. vecol-hagnam nitzab] *and all the people stand by thee, from morning till evening,* (for judgment:) the scope of Jethro is to condemn Moses, in wearing out his spirit, and taking the burden of judging all the people himself alone, Numb. xi. 13. And his words bear not, that all the people without exception came for judgment, that had been unpossible; but because there was then no other judge but Moses, the sense is clear, all that were to be judged, they were to be judged by no other, but by Moses only. Rev. xiii. 8. *And all that dwell in the earth worshipped the beast*; that is, all seduced to popish idolatry, were seduced by the beastly vicar of Christ, and his limbs. John xi. 48. *If we let him alone, all will believe in him;* that is, none will believe in us, nor follow us; and all seduced men shall be seduced by him. John iii. 26. John's disciples, a little emulous, that Christ drew all the water from their master's mill; say, *behold he baptizeth, and* [Gr. pantes] *all men come to him;* that is, there be now no comers, nor followers of men, but such as follow this Jesus. That Christ in this sense should be the Saviour of all men, that he should have a negative voice in the salvation of all, that all the ransomed ones should come through his hands, is no other thing than Peter saith, Acts iv. 11.

11. *That there is no other name under heaven, by which men may be saved, and none comes to the Father but by him*, John xiv. 6. Then all that come to God, come by him only. Christ is the heir of blessings, and *in him all the kindreds of the earth are blessed*, Acts iii. 24. but it follows, as well all and every mortal man are glorified, as redeemed, by this logic; *out of his fulness, we all,* [Gr. pantes] *all that receive, do receive from him*, John i. 16.

Upon this is grounded the common nature of all that Christ assumed, that no man should be saved, but by a man. Hence, (say Arminians) "Look how far the nature of man extends, the ransom extendeth as far: but (saith Mr. Moor) the nature is common to Adam's sons, all and every one, as men contradistinguished from angels," Heb. ii. 9, 16. But there is a wide difference between the fitness and aptitude that man should die for man, not an angel for a man, and the intention and good-will of God, that Christ should either take on him the nature, of man to die for mankind, rather than for angel-kind, Heb. ii. 16. And why he should die for this man Peter, or John, not that man Pharaoh or Judas; the reason of the former was the infinite wisdom of God, seeing a congruity of justice in it, that the nature that sins should suffer for sin. Whether Christ, having a soul of a spiritual nature as angels, might have fitly been a suffering Saviour for them, (which may be thought possible) is another question. But the reason of the other is only the grace of God. Who could give a hire, or a price to Christ, to move him to die for you, and effectually, and savingly, by gifting you with faith, and not for another? All the Jesuits, Arminians, Papists, Socinians, for themselves, if provoked, shall not answer, except there be a fountain-well, that solveth all, touching men and angels; *he hath mercy on whom he will, and hardens whom he will; and who hath given to him first, and it shall be recompensed?* And with as good reason; because Christ is glorified at the right-hand of God, in man's nature, common to all Adam's sons,

may

may they infer, that *all and every man is risen again from the dead with Christ;* as Col. iii. 1, 2. and *all, and every man, is set with Christ in heavenly places,* Eph. ii. 6. and so all and every man must be glorified with Christ. For, as Christ died, in a nature common to all men; so, in a nature common to all, he rose again, ascended to heaven, is glorified at the right-hand of God. But, the truth is, Christ assumed that nature that is common to all men, but not as common to all men, but *as the seed of Abraham,* Heb. ii. 16. *as the flesh and blood of the children,* v. 14. *of his brethren, not according to the flesh, but according to the Spirit*, that are, or were to be born again.

And it is true, *Jesus,* Heb. ii. 9. *is made a little lower than the angels.* I hope, the comparison is not with all and every one of the angels; he was never made a little lower than all the angels, even evil angels. Nor (2.) *hath he tasted of death for every man;* that is, for all and every son of Adam. 1. We know no grace as common to all and every one of Adam's sons, as nature. 2. Because the scripture makes nature, wrath, sin, death, common to all. Rom. v. 14, 15, 16, 17, 18, 19, 20, 21. Rom. iii. 9, 10, 11, 12, 13, 14, 15. Job xiv. 4. Psal. xv. 5. Eph. ii. 1, 2, 3. Heb. ix. 27. But for grace, the word of the covenant, a covenant of grace, reconciliation with grace and favour with God, justification; we know no such things common to all and every one of Adam's sons; for then all must be born, the covenanted, justified, reconciled, beloved with the greatest love that is, John xv. 13. ransomed and redeemed *in Christ's blood, a people near in the beloved, chosen as peculiar to God,* as well as heirs of wrath. (2.) That some sins against the first covenant are taken away in Christ, and not all, as 1 John i. 8. or some half-redeemed in Christ's blood, not wholly, we know not. (3.) That Christ should taste death for all, it being as good, as if all in person had not only sipped, but drunken death out to the bottom, and yet, that the greatest part must drink death to

the

CHRIST DYING AND DRAWING SINNERS TO HIMSELF. 499

the bottom again, is no gospel-truth. (4.) Nor is the apostle's argument of weight to exalt Christ, as he intendeth, Heb. ii. to say, Christ so *tasted death for all*, as all and every one, notwithstanding many never have, either saving faith, or fruit of his death, but eternally perish; whereas, clear it is, that these [Gr. pantes] *all that be died for*, are the many sons he actually *brings to glory*, v. 10. these who are one with him, as the sanctifier Christ, and the *sanctified*, v. 11. *His brethren, whom he is not ashamed to own*, v. 11. *The church*, v. 12. *The children that God hath given him*, v. 13. *The children partakers of flesh and blood*, v. 14. *These for whom he, through death, which he tasted for all, destroyed him that had the power of death, that is, the devil;* if the devil reign in the sons of disobedience, Eph. ii. 2. If they *be born of the devil*, John viii. 44. *Taken captives at his will*, 2 Tim. ii. 26. Let Arminians see how Christ, by tasting death for them, as they fancy, Heb. ii. 9. hath for them, by death, *Destroyed the devil*, v. 14. *Loosed his works*, 1 John iii. 8. *Triumphed over devils*, Col. ii. 15. *Judged and cast out the devil*, John xii. 31. John xiv. 30. Yea, these *All*, these *are delivered from bondage of death*, Heb. ii. 15. *The seed of Abraham*, v. 16. *His brethren, that he is made like to in all things, except sin.* Heb. ii. 17. *His people*, v. 17 The *tempted*, that Christ *succoureth*, v. 18. I defy any Divine to make sense of that chapter, as Arminians expound *tasting of death for all men.*

And the second Adam must come short of the first Adam, Rom. v. by the Arminian exposition; and the comparison must be as the legs of a cripple, both here, and 1 Cor. xv. *For, by the first Adam many be dead.* What be these many? All and every one of mankind, that are the natural heirs coming forth of the loins of the first Adam: then, who be the [Gr. *polloi*] many to whom the grace of God hath abounded? v. 15. Sure the second Adam is no dry tree, no eunuch; the scripture saith, *He hath a seed*, Isa. liii. 10. *many sons*, Heb. ii. 10. *Children that God hath given him, that*

are

are for signs and wonders, Isa. vii. 18. Heb. ii. 13. A seed in covenant with God, David's spiritual seed, who shall never fall away, Psal. lxxxix. 28, 29, 30, 31, 32, 33, 34, 35, 36, 37. Then, as all the first Adam's sons and heirs were through his offence dead; so all Christ's spiritual seed and heirs have grace communicated to them, v. 15. This is far from grace abounding to all and every one of the heirs of the first Adam. Then, as the first Adam killed none but heirs naturally descended of him; so the second Adam derives grace, and the gift of life, to none but to his spiritual heirs. Make an union by birth, between the first Adam and all his, and between the second Adam and all his, and stretch the comparison no farther than Paul, and let Arminians enjoy their gain by this argument.

2. Verse 16. Sin and judgment to condemnation, not intended only, but real and efficacious, came on all by the first Adam; for all that live, incur sin, and actual condemnation by the first Adam; *but the first gift is of many unto justification:* then justification, not intended only, which may never fall out, but real; not virtual, or potential, or conditional, if their fore-fathers have not rejected the covenant; but efficacious and actual, came upon all the heirs and seed of the second Adam.

3. Paul compareth v. 15. the offence [Gr. tû henos] of one, the first sin of Adam that came on all, with the justification [Gr. ekpollônparaptomàton] from many offences. The justification spoken of here, which we have in the second Adam, is not a pardon of sin original, and of a breach of the first covenant, so as we begin to sin, and God reckons with us on a new score: but the justification here, *is from many offences*, and the blood of *Jesus purges us from all sins*, 1 John i. 8. This justification runs not up from the womb, as the offence of Adam doth, For, 1. Where are there two justifications in Christ's blood? 2. Where is there in scripture a righteousness of all and every one, a justification in Christ's blood, by nature, or from the belly, and that of Turks, Indians, Americans, and their seed, and of all infants, in all the scripture?

4.

CHRIST DYING AND DRAWING SINNERS TO HIMSELF.

4. Verse 17. By one man's offence, there was a cruel king, death the king of terrors, who hath a black sceptre, set over all and every man without exception. Here we grant an universal king, the first and second death; as when a conqueror subdues a land, he setteth over them a little king, a lieutenant in his place: now, the other part of the similitude, and the antitype, is, *So much more, they that receive abundance of grace, and of the gift of righteousness, shall reign*, shall be kings *in life* (eternal) *through one Jesus Christ*, v. 17. See, the heirs and sons of the second Adam are, not all and every one of the mortal stock of Adam, redeemed, reconciled, saved, but [Gr. hoi lámbanóntes tèn perisseian tès cháritos] these *that receive abundance of grace, and of the gift of righteousness*, only. I appeal to the conscience of Arminians, if Turks, Jews, Tartarians. Americans, Indians, all heathen, and all infants come in as (Gr. lambanóntes] and as these that for the present are under the fat drops of the second Adam, and *receive abundance of grace and righteousness:* for their universal righteousness is poor and thin and may be augmented. 2. If they receive it conditionally, so they believe, then it is not universal. 3. Then they are not [Gr. lambanóntes] all are not believers by nature, all are not, by this, within the new covenant actually: they have but a far-off venture, and a cast of abundance of grace. Farther, Paul, by this, makes glory as well as grace universal, and all and every one must be born heirs of heaven; for Paul saith of heirs of the second Adam [Gr. basileúsousin en zoê:] here be kings for a king; there was one catholic tyrant, death, set over all men; but there be here heirs of the second Adam made kings of life and glory through Jesus Christ. v. 18. If it be said, It is life conditionally, if they believe; consider then, if the second Adam be not weaker than the first: the first indeclinably, really, without a miss, transmitted death to all his: the second Adam cannot transmit life to the thousandth part of his; but as he misseth in the far greatest part of his heirs (if all mortal men be his heirs) he may miss in all, if free-will so think good. Arminius (Anteperkins)

saith,

saith, "*Constare potuit intiger fructus mortis, etc.* The fruit of the second Adam's death might stand entire, though all and every one of mankind were damned." If this be a potential justification, it is good, it is not Paul's justification, Rom. viii. *Whom he justified, them he also glorified.* Nor speaketh the scripture of any such justification, but of such as makes the party justified, blessed, Rom. iv. 6, 7. as hath faith joined with it, Rom. iii. 26. Rom. v. 1. as *cleanseth us from all our sins*, 1 John i. 8. (5.) The *reconciled shall much more be saved*, Rom. v. 10. they are friends, not enemies, (enemies and reconciled are opposed in the text) and then they cannot be strangers, nor far off, but built upon the *foundation of the prophets and apostles;* who of enemies are reconciled, Eph. ii. Col. i. 19, 20. and so shall *far more be saved by the life of Christ:* but all and every one of mankind shall not much more be saved by the life of Christ. 6. There is all (*all men*) under condemnation, and an (*all men*) justified: let any of common sense judge, if ye ought not in equity to compare the heirs, sons, seed, of the first and second Adam together; and then let the two *Alls* run on equal wheels, and see what Arminians gain by this. For, if ye compare all in the loins of the first Adam on the one side, with all in the loins of the second, and yet never in the second Adam, but as great strangers to Christ, as those that are out of Christ, *enemies, sons of the bondwoman, strangers to Christ, without God and Christ in the world*, on the other side; the sides are unequal, and beside the Holy Ghost's mind; except ye shew us a second birth, a communion supernatural of justification, of free-grace, of sonship, of redemption, of mercy, between Jesus Christ, and all and every one of mankind, Heathens, Jews, Gentiles: this, I fear, must send all the Arminians in Europe to their book, to seek what cannot be found.

And it is as easy to answer, 1 Cor. xv. for as many in number as die in Adam, are not, by that text, made alive in the second Adam; for [Gr. pantes] *All*, noteth not equality of number: but, as the heirs of

the

the first Adam have death in heritage by him, so the heirs of the second Adam have life by him; and all in each, noteth all of each quality, not of each number; for the all quickened by Christ, (1.) Are the *fallen asleep in Christ, that are not perished,* v. 18. (2.) The all, *whose faith is not in vain, and are not in their sins,* v. 17. (3.) The all, *that have not hope in this life only, but in the life to come,* v. 19. (4.) Such as are *the first fruits,* of the same kind of *dead with Christ;* for Christ, and all his, are as one corn-field of wheat gathered into one barn, v. 23. (5.) They are quickned with the same Spirit, that Christ was quickned withal; but in their own order, life cometh to the head first: and if Paul's mind be, that Christ as Head and Redeemer raiseth all the elect and reprobate by this text, then sure the reprobate must be a part of the field, whereof Christ is the first sheaf, else the text shall not run; but, for Paul's purpose, it was enough to prove the resurrection of believers principally.

The place, 1 John ii. 1. The world and the whole world, is the world that hath an advocate established in heaven; for if we *sin, we have an Advocate, who is a propitiation, not for us Jews only,* to whom I write, but for the sins of the whole world, both Jews and Gentiles: for the propitiation and advocation are of the same circumference, and sphere; else the argument should be null: but the advocation of our High Priest, in the holy of holiest, at the right-hand of God, is for the people of God only, Heb. ix. 24. For us, as the High Priest carried only the iniquity of the people of Israel, and their name engraven on his breast: for those, for whom he hath purchased an eternal redemption, with the *sprinkling of blood, to purge the conscience from dead works to serve the living God,* v. 12, 13, 14. For those, to whom he left peace in his testament, and the promise of *eternal inheritance,* v.15, 16, 17. And for those, that look for Christ's *second appearing to salvation;* and for those, for whose faith he prays, Luke xxii. 31, 32, 33. and for whom he *prayeth the Father,* that he *may send the Holy Spirit,* John xiv. 16,

17. and xvi. 7. For all these, Christ doth as our High Priest (Heb. ix. 10.) interceed.

2. It is clear, the persons cannot be so changed, *if we sin we have a propitiation;* if we confess the blood of *Jesus shall cleanse us from all sins*: and by the sins of the whole world, he understands all that did, or should believe, of Jew or Gentile, Rom. xi. 13. 2 Cor. v. 19. John i. 29. and iii. 16. the whole world, loved, pardoned, reconciled, to whom sins are not imputed, and so blessed and justified, Psal. xxxii. 1, 2, 3, 4. And whereas the apostle ascendeth, *and not for our sins only*, etc. it is not to extend propitiation, further than advocation, confession, knowing that we know him: That is *petitio principii*; for John doth not conclude a comfort of Christ's advocation, which is undeniably peculiar and proper only to those that *have fellowship with the Father and Son*, and have *believed in the word of life, are purged from all their sins*, from a general propitiation, common to those that are eternally damned, and which may have its full and entire fruit, tho' all the world were eternally damned; it were a poor comfort to weak ones, who sin daily and *are liars if they should say, they have no sin*, that there is no better salve in heaven for their sin, than such an one, as they may no less perish eternally having it, than Pharaoh, Cain, Judas; it were better for them to want it, as have it.

2 Pet. ii. 1. *Some false teachers deny the Lord that bought them;* which is not so to be taken, as if Christ had redeemed those *from their vain conversation*, 1 Pet. i. 13. *and from the present evil world,* Gal. i. 4. for then he should have redeemed them from apostasy, and the power of damnable heresies, which he did not; but in their profession they were bought, and so the apostle more sharply convinceth them, for they were teachers in profession, but really wolves that devoured the flock, but professed themselves to be shepherds sent to seek the lost. 2. They were heretical teachers, and brought in damnable heresies, and therefore nominal christians and professed Christ to be their Lord; for if they had been without, and open enemies, they could not bring in heresies.

resies. 3. They did it covertly and privily, teaching and doing one thing, and professing another. They professed the Lord to be their Redeemer who bought them; but that they were hypocrites, is clear, ver. 1. [Gr. parisaxousi hairéseis] they shall *bring in heresies in the by, at a side, privily.* 2. *By reason of them the way of truth shall be blasphemed;* enemies shall speak ill of the gospel, because these men profess the *Redeemer who bought them*, but yet they are covetous men, v. 3. They buy and sell you [Gr. plastoîs lógios] *with decked-up and well-combed fair words*, O our Redeemer that bought us, our Saviour! O free grace! O free redemption! as Libertines now do; and yet they that deny sanctification, deny Christ, who in their profession bought them. And 'tis ordinary for scripture to affirm things of men, as they speak and profess; as the scripture calleth wolves, prophets, Jer. xxiii. because they so profess themselves; Christ called Judas friend, but he was but a face-friend, and a real enemy; so Pharisees are styled by the Holy Ghost, Mat. ix. 12, 13. *Whole and righteous, just persons that need no repentance*, Luke xv. 7. such *as need not the physician,* Mark ii. 17. because they are such only in their own conceit and vain opinion, not really. If any man say, Christ bought these, in regard that by his death he purchaseth a dominion over elect and reprobate, that all knees should bow to him, men and angels, Rom. xiv. 8, 9, etc. Isa. xlv. 23. Phil. 9, 10, 11. John v. 27. Acts. xvii. 31. So that there is a difference between buying as conquerors, and buying from our vain conversation. I think it hath truth in it, Christ by his death hath acquired a dominion; but I much doubt, if in that sense scripture say, Christ hath bought the reprobate by his blood; for so, by his death he hath bought angels, devils, all things, and all knees in heaven and earth, and under the earth; for by his death and resurrection he hath acquired this dominion, Rom. xiv. *God is the Saviour of all men,* 1 Tim. iv. 10. 'Tis not spoken of Christ as Mediator, but of the *living God the Saviour of all men,* Psal. cvi. 8,10. Mat. viii. 25. Neh. ix. 27.

Psal.

Psal. xxxiv. 6. [Heb. jaschang] is here; and the living God is given indefinitely to God as One with all the Three, but God in Christ is especially the Saviour of believers. Other places for universal grace, and the apostasy of the saints, I pass here.

ART. V.

The fifth particular is touching the faith required of the elect, and of the reprobate, within the visible church: which ere I enter in, let this one necessary doctrine, clearing that point much, be observed; that if Christ draw all men to him,

Doctrine, "He must have a singular and special good-will and liking to save sinners, in that strongly and seriously, he draweth all sorts of men to himself.

1. The promises and good-will of Christ are not concluded or locked up, as touching the revealed damnation of any sort of persons: Christ is no ingrosser, and never loved to make a monopoly of grace; he sets down his will in positive comfortable positions, John vi. 39. *This is the Father's will which hath sent me, that of all which he hath given me, I should lose nothing, but raise it up at the last day.* John v. 24. *Verily, verily, I say unto you, He that heareth my word, and believeth in him that sent me, hath everlasting life, and shall never come to condemnation.*

2. Christ had no good mind to save, that, 1. He did not send only, but the King came in person, 1 Tim. i. 15. Luke xix. 10. *The Son of man came to seek and to save,* etc. 2. He cried not afar off, but came near-hand to draw; he came so near as within the reach of his arm to save us. 3. When a rope is cast down to prisoners in a pit, if it come not within the compass of their reach, and if it be too far for a short arm, it can do no good for the help of the prisoner; therefore he came below us, and under all our infirmities, to put his shoulders under the lost sheep, Luke xv. 5. Love must sweat, and stoop low, to save.

3. Christ's good-will is held forth in as large terms, having the Lord's liberty of election and reprobation,

as

as can be; and that in six wide expressions, that no man should complain, Oh, I am a dry tree, because we are inclined to forge forced quarrels against the Lamb of God, as if he loved not us; and 'tis an answer to those that naturally complain of absolute election; as, 1. The weakest are readiest to move doubts.

Object. 1. "I am sinful, and sinfully sick, and I have jealousies of the physician."

Answ. The Physician came to force himself *on the sick*, Mat. ix. 12, 13. Sick of body, are often sick of mind, and passions of the soul rise with humours of the body; the sick are soon angry and jealous. Christ saith, he hath a tender soul for a sick sinner.

Object. 2 "But I have little grace or goodness."

Ans. I, Can ye have less (saith Christ) than a reed? 'tis far below a tree and a cedar; and I will not break a reed. But a broken reed is out of hope, it cannot do any more good; a reed is weak, but a broken reed, sure, can never grow: yea, but he cannot break the bruised reed, but pours in oil at the root of the broken reed, and makes it green, and causeth it to blossom. So the fire or light in flax must be less than the fire in timber or wood; but he will not throw water on flax that hath fire, yea, nor on smoking flax, that seems to have fire, and hath but smoke.

Object. 3. "A broken bone in a living man may be splinted and cured; but the heart is *ultimum moriens*, the last thing of life; if it be broken, the man is gone; he dies, when the last seat of life, the heart, is broken." Yea, but saith Christ, *I can bind up the broken heart,* Isa. lxi. 1. Psal. cxlvii. 3.

Object. 4. "If the man be dead and buried, then farewell he, there is an end, no more of him." Yea, but Christ, 2 Cor. i. 9. John v. 25. *Raiseth the dead, and giveth life to dry bones,* Ezek. xxxvii.

2. Some fear they have nothing but an empty profession.

Answ. Then the scripture holdeth forth the promises to visible saints, 2 Cor. vii. 1. Can ye come in among the

crowd

crowd of visible saints? This is preached to all within the wide gospel-net, and Christ's visible court, *Whosoever believeth, shall be saved*, John iii. 16. Rom. x. 9. John v. 24.

3. Say thou canst not come so near as visible professors, but thou art nothing but a publican and a sinner, and that may be thought to be without Christ's line of mercy; yet, 1 Tim. i. 15. *This is a faithful saying, and worthy of all acceptance, that Christ Jesus came into the world to save sinners.* Be what thou wilt, as unbelief estrangeth a sinner far enough from Christ, thou mayest claim blood and kin to a sinner; then Christ came to call sinners, and to save sinners. Canst thou deny thyself to be a sinner?

4. Canst thou crowd in amongst the *We*, that are the godly party? There is here room for thee, not to cast off Christ, but that thou mayest let out a warm look, and half an hope thou mayst be one of his; the gospel-grammar is fair and sweet. Art not thou amongst an *Us*, that there may be hope? 1 John iv. 9. *In this was the love of God toward us, because God sent his only begotten Son into the world, that we might live through him.*

5. The scripture calls out a longer rope yet, that thou mayest reach to Christ. Art thou not a man? If thou be not a sinner, nor a visible saint, nor a bruised reed, thou art one of mankind; see, the gospel will not have thee to despair, or to foment and harbour strange and far off thoughts of Christ, Tit. iii. 4. *But after that the kindness and love of God our Saviour, to man appeared---------he saved us.* 1 Tim. ii. 3. *God our Saviour will have* [Gr. pántas anthropous sothênai] *all men to be saved.*

6. The farthest from Christ, must be creatures that are nothing, but bits of the world; now the name world, is a srameder and a farther-off word, than the name of man, or sinners, 'tis the farthest off word; for fallen angels are members and citizens of the world, therefore the gospel is preached to the *world*: Christ is

brought

CHRIST DYING AND DRAWING SINNERS TO HIMSELF.

brought in in the gospel, as a world-lover; as if he were a whole world-saviour, *He takes away the sins of the world,* John i. 29. *He so loves the world,* John iii. 16. *He giveth his flesh for the life of the world,* John vi. 51.

In this grammar of the Holy Ghost, observe we, by the way, for resolution, The wisdom of God, in framing the words of the gospel. It cannot be said that God loved all the world, in Christ his beloved; and all, and every sinner, and all the race of mankind. Yet, laying down this ground, that God keepeth up in his mind, the secrets of election and reprobation, till he, in his own time, be pleased to reveal them; the Lord hath framed the gospel-offer of Christ in such indefinite words, and so general (yet without all double-dealing, lying, or equivocating; for his own good pleasure is a rule both of his doings and speeches.) As, 1. seldom doth the Lord open election and reprobation to men, till they, by grace, or in the order of his justice, open both the one and the other, in their own ways; and therefore he holdeth out the offer of Christ, so as none may cavil at the gospel, or begin a plea with Christ. 2. Seldom doth the gospel speak, who they be that are elect, who reprobate; yet doth the gospel offer no ground of presuming on the one hand, or of despairing on the other. For if thou be not a believer, nor a weak reed, nor a saint, yet thou art a sinner; if not that, thou art a man; if not that, thou art one of the world: and tho' the affirmative conclude not, *I am a sinner, I am a man, I am one of the world,* but it followeth not, *therefore I am elected to glory, or,* Ergo, *I am ransomed of the Lord;* Yet the negative, touching reprobation, holdeth, *I am a sinner, I am of the world, I am a man;* hence it followeth not, *therefore I am a reprobate, and therefore I have warrant to refuse the promise, and Christ offered in the gospel.* It followeth well therefore, I must be humbled for sin, and believe in Christ. There is room left for all the elect, that they have no ground of standing aloof from Christ,

(and

(and the rest never come, and most willingly refuse to come) nor have the reprobate ground to quarrel at the decrees of God; tho' they be not chosen, yet they are called, as if they were chosen; and they have no cause to quarrel at conjectures, they have as fair a revealed warrant to believe, as the elect have; they are men, sinners of the world, to whom Christ is offered: why refuse they him upon an unrevealed warrant?

4. The fourth ground of Christ's good-will to draw all men, is, That Christ goeth as far in the dispensation of free-grace, as sinners, as the chief of sinners; grace journeys all along, and can go no further than *hell and damnation*, Luke xix. 10. *The Son of man came to seek and to save that which is lost;* as if Christ would say, Is any man a sinner? (and who are not?) and a lost sinner? See and behold, I am a Saviour for that man. Christ went as low down to hell, in the freedom of grace, to save, as Zaccheus, in evil-doing, to destroy. Mary Magdalene, went as far on toward hell, as seven devils; grace in Christ went as far on, as to redeem from seven devils. Manasseh, as if he had intended to make sure work for hell, runs on to empawn soul and salvation, and gives himself to witchcraft, observing of times, to cause the streets of Jerusalem run with blood, to all abominable idolatry: mercy in the Lord went as near hell to save him. Paul goeth so far on the mouth of the furnace, as to waste the church of God, and [Gr. lomalnein] Acts viii. 3. to make heaps of dead men in the church, and there came nothing out of his nostrils for breathing and respiration, Acts ix. 1. but threatnings, that is, ripe purposes of blood; yea, murdering of the saints came out of his mouth, with every word he spoke: but Christ's free-grace pursues him hard, and outruns him. 1 Tim. i. 14. *And the grace of our Lord,* (saith he) *was more, or over-abundant in me, through faith and love.* Jer. iii. 1. *And thou hast played the harlot with many companions, or lovers; yet return to me, saith the Lord.* 'Tis here, as if Christ's rich grace, and our extreme wickedness

should

CHRIST DYING AND DRAWING SINNERS TO HIMSELF.

should strive, who should descend to the lowest room in hell, the latter to destroy, the former to save; and here Christ desires the sinner to be more wicked, than he can be gracious.

5. Christ in the gospel, as a great conqueror, sends out writs signed under his excellency's hand, come and meet me, who will, and be saved: as far as graced will can go, as far goeth the good-will of the conquering Prince, Rev. xxii. 17. 'Tis much worthy of observation, how that sweet evangelic invitation is conceived, Isa. lv. 1. *Ho, every one that thirsts;* the Heb. word, Hui, is alas, *or* ah, *every one that thirsts, come to the waters; and he that hath no silver, come, buy, and eat;* as if the Lord were grieved, and said, Wo is me, alas, that thirsty souls should die in the thirst, and will not come to the water of life, Christ, and drink gratis, freely and live. For the interjection, [Heb. Hui.] Ho, is a mark of sorrowing; as ah, or wo; every one that thirsts, Isa. i. 4. *Ah sinful nation;* or wo [Heb. Hui] *to the sinful nation.* Verse 24. *Ah, I will ease me, or alas* [Heb. Hui] *I will ease me of my adversaries.* Jer. xxii. 18. *They shall not say of Jehoiakim, Ho, or alas, or wo to my brother, ah sister.* It expresseth two things, 1. A vehemence, and a serious and unfeigned ardency of desire, that we do what is our duty; and the concatenation of these two, extremely desired of God, our coming to Christ, and our salvation: this moral connection between faith and salvation, is desired of God with his will of approbation, complacency, and moral liking, without all dissimulation, most unfeignedly. And whereas Arminians say, we make counterfeit, feigned, and hypocritical desires in God; they calumniate and cavil egregiously, as their custom is. 2. The other thing expressed in these invitations, is a sort of dislike, grief, or sorrow; ('tis a speech borrowed from man, for there is no disappointing of the Lord's will, nor sorrow in him for the not-fulfilling of it) or an earnest nilling and hating dislike, that these two should not go along, as approved efficaciously

by

by us, to wit, the creatures obedience of faith, and life eternal. God loveth, approveth the believing of Jerusalem, and of her children, as a moral duty, as the hen doth like to warm and nourish her chickens; and he hateth, with an exceeding and unfeigned dislike of improbation and hatred, their rebellious disobedience, and refusing to be gathered: but there is no purpose, intention, or decree of God holden forth in these invitations called his revealed will, by which he saith, he intendeth and willeth that all he maketh the offer unto, shall obey and be saved. But 'tis to be observed, that the revealed will of God, holden forth to all, called *voluntas signi*, doth not hold forth formally, that God intendeth, decreeth, or purposeth in his eternal counsel, that any man shall actually obey, either elect or reprobate; it formally is the expression only of the good liking of that moral and duty-conjunction between the obedience of the creature, and the reward; but holdeth forth not any intention or decree of God, that any shall obey, or that all shall obey, or that none at all shall obey. And what Arminians say of Christ's *intention to die for all, and every one; and of the Lord's intention and catholic good-will, to save all and every one;* to wit, That these desires may be in God, tho' not any be saved at all, but all eternally perish; which maketh the Lord's desires irrational, unwise and frustraneous; that we say with good reason of God's good-will, called *voluntas signi*, it might have its complete and entire end and effect, tho' not any one of men or angels obey, if there were not going along with this will of God, another will, and eternal decree and purpose in God, or working by free-grace in some chosen ones, what the Lord willeth in his approving will; and another decree, in the which the Lord proposeth to deny his saving grace, upon his absolute liberty, to others; that being left to the hardness of their own hearts, they may freely disobey, and be the sole authors of their own damnation. Now, because Arminians deny any such two decrees in God, but assert only such as depend wholly, in their fulfilling, on the free will of men and angels,

and

and all the decrees of God may be frustrated and disappointed by men and angels; as if the poor short sighted creature, not the sovereign Creator, were carver and Lord of the decrees, and master of work in fulfilling of these counsels. We reject their catholic intentions and decrees, to save and redeem all and every one, which they vainly fancy to be God; as repugnant to his will which is irresistible, and cannot miss its end. 2. To his immutability, which cannot be compelled to take a second port, whereas he cannot fail the first. 3. To his omnipotency, who cannot be resisted. 4. To his happiness, who cannot come short of what his soul desires. 5. To his wisdom, who cannot aim at an end, and desire it with his soul, and go about it, by such means, as he seeth shall be utterly uneffectual, and never produce his end; and not use these means, which he knoweth may, and infallibly doth, produce the same end in others. Now this desire of approbation is an abundantly sufficient closing of the mouth *of such as stumble at the gospel, being appointed thereunto;* and an expression of Christ's good-liking to save sinners expressed in his borrowed wishes, Deut. v. 29. *O that there were such a heart in them, that they would fear me, and keep my commandments!* Psalm lxxxi. 13. *O that my people had hearkened unto me, and Israel walked in my ways!* Which wish, as relating to disobeying Israel, is a figure, or metaphor borrowed from men, but otherwise sheweth how acceptable the duty is to God, how obligatory to the creature. 2. By the Lord's expostulations, Ezek. xviii. 31. *Why will ye die, O house of Israel?* Verse 32. *For I have no pleasure in the death of him that dies.* 3. In the Lord's crying to sinners. Prov. i. 20. *Wisdom cries, she uttereth her voice in the streets.* The Hebrew word, rinnah, is to cry with strong shouting, either for joy, Psalm lxxxi. 2. or sorrow, Lam. ii. 19. which expresseth Christ's desire to save sinners.

 6. For the ground and warrant of Christ's willingness to save and draw sinners, do but consider, 1. The words of the text, *I will draw all men to me;* It is as

if

if he would say, I will baulk no nation, nor any man, upon a national respect; the first covenant to the Jews, suffered a mighty exception. What, is God the God of the Jews only? Have all the nations of the earth done with their part of heaven and salvation, but only the narrow trinket, and bit of the earth, in poor little Judea? This made the gospel despised, and liable to sad and heavy calumnies; Christ must have narrow bowels, and must be ebb, short, and thin, in free grace, if the matter be so. Nay, but Christ hath mercy for all men; *I will draw all men*, that is, multitudes of Jews and Gentiles: for, that Christ draweth all and every one without exception, and that by his death, is against scripture, and experience; but he hath an all that he draws, Tit. ii. 11. *The grace of God appeared to all men* [Gr. pâsas anthropois] which grace? the teaching grace of god, *that teacheth us to wait for the blessed hope, and the appearance of the glory, and of our Saviour Jesus Christ:* sure, this must be the preached gospel: now, the gospel, by scripture, experience, consent of Arminians, never appeared, in the least sound, to all and every son of Adam; then Christ must have another all, a fair and numerous multitude, whom he saves and draws; and this saith, he had a good will to save all, and that his elect ones believe, Rev. v. 11. *And I beheld, and I heard the voice of many angels round about the throne, and the beasts, and the elders, and the number of them was ten thousand times ten thousand, and thousands of thousands*, v. 12. *Saying, Worthy is the Lamb.* Rev. vii. 9. *After this, I beheld, and lo, a great multitude, which no man could number, of all nations and kindreds, and people, and tongues, stood before the throne, and before the Lamb, clothed in white robes, and palms in their hands.* It is true, in civil assemblies and judicatures, Christ hath a few number; yet he hath a fair and numerous offspring of children, and when they are gathered together, they are a fair beloved world. In the Hebrew many and great, are often one and the same. As one ruby is worth ten hundred, one sapphire worth
                                                                                                thousands

thousands of common stones; so, one saint is more than ten thousand wicked men: then all together they must be an *all, a world, a whole world of ransomed ones, bidden ones,* Psal. lxxxiii. 4. *of the Lord's jewels,* Mal. iii. 17. and of *Christ's precious ones,* Isa. xliii. 4. they are the flower, and the choice of mankind.

2. Christ is willing to take away all heart-exceptions of unbelief from men: as, 1. "Can God be born of a woman, to save men, not angels?" Believe it, saith the Lord's Spirit with a sort of oath, Heb. ii. 16. *Verily, he took on him the seed of Abraham, not the nature of angels.* Halt not at Christ's man-kindness, and not angel-love, to the excellenter child by nature, the angel when he fell: and it is to remove our doubts, that God is brought in promising, and swearing the covenant; Christ is a sworn covenanter, Heb. vi. 13. When God made promise to Abraham; *because he could swear by no greater, he sware by himself.* Ezek. xxxiii. The people slandred the Lord, he delighted so to have the people pine away in their iniquities, that he would punish them for no fault; *but the children's teeth should be set on edge, for the sins of the father, and the grapes that they ate not themselves.* The Lord answers that calumny, Ezek. xviii. and here, *As I live, I delight not* (so as you slanderously, and blasphemously say) *in the death of a sinner; by my life, I desire you may repent and live;* nor have I pleasure to punish innocent men, for no sin at all.

And the second exception is, "But Christ's heart is not engaged with a heart-burning purpose, or desire to save man; the purpose of saving came upon him but yesterday." Yea, but (saith Christ) it was not a yesterday's business, but was contrived from eternity, Prov. viii. before the Lord made sea, or land, v. 30. *I was by him as one brought up* (as a son nourished) *with him, I was daily* (when there was neither night nor day) *his delight, rejoicing in the habitable earth, and my delights were with the sons of men.* Two words express Christ's old and eternal love to men, his de-

lights

lights were with the sons of men. As Christ was his Father's delight, from eternity; so was Christ feasting himself on the thoughts of love, delight, and free-grace to men; sure not to Pharaoh, Judas, and all the race of the wicked, and with such a love as (if free-will please) should never enjoy one son of Adam. 2. I was (saith Christ) *playing and sporting, in the habitable earth;* the Hebrew word *schahak,* is to *play in a dance.* It is, 2 Sam. vi. 21. spoken of *David's dancing before the ark;* & 1 Sam. xviii. 7. *The women in Israel playing, answered one another in their songs.* It holds forth this, that it resolves the question, that Augustine loosed to a curious head, asking what the Lord was doing before the world was; he was delighting in his Son Christ, and the thoughts of the Lord Jesus, in that long and endless age, were solacing him; and they were skipping, and passing time, in loving and longing for the fellowship of lost men; and since God was God, (O boundless duration!) the Lord Jesus, in a manner, was loving, and longing for the dawning of the day of the creation, and his second coming again to judgment; the marriage-day of union with sinners. Christ was (as it were) from eternity with child of infinite love to man; and in time, in the fulness of time, it blossomed forth, and the birth came out, in a high expression of love; the man-child, the love of Christ was born, and saw the light, Gal. iv. 4. Tit. iii. 4. when Christ was ripe of love, to bring forth free salvation; glory, glory to the womb and the birth!

And a third exception is, "But sinners disobliged Christ, and provoked him as his enemies: can it be, that in time, seeing how undeserving we were, he could heartily and seriously die for man, offer himself to all? God may have mercy on the work of his hand, but he cannot have mercy on sinners."

Answ. 1. It is true, the gospel is contrary to nature, and not one article more thwarteth and crosseth carnal wisdom, than that of imputed righteousness; that crosseth moral philosophy so much, as we can more easily believe the raising of the dead, or any the great-

est

est miracle, the drying up of the Red-sea, than believe the gospel; for we believe the gospel for miracles as motives, not as causes of faith, not miracles for the gospel; and if at the first we believe the gospel for miracles, then we naturally rather believe miracles, & the dividing of the Red-sea, and the raising of the dead, than we can believe that Christ came to die for sinners.

2. Consider with what a strong good-will Christ died, Luke ix. 51. *And it came to pass, when his time was come that he should be received up, he stedfastly set his face to go to Jerusalem.* He hardned his face, he emboldned himself to go to Jerusalem to suffer; he mended his pace, and went more swiftly, with a strong fire of love, to expend his blood. Luke xii. 50. *I have a baptism to be baptized with,* [Gr. kai pós synechómai] *how am I fettered or besieged* (as the word is used, Luke xix. 43.) *till it be perfected*?

3. What could move Christ to lie and fancy Were his weeping and tears counterfeit? Were his dying, bleeding, sweating, pain, sorrow, shame, but all shews for the market, and to take the people? Isa. liii. 4. [Heb. achen] *Surely, really, he bare our sorrows.*

4. His offer must be real, John vii. 37. for with vehemency he speaks [Gr. eistéke kai ekraxe] *He stood and shouted in the temple, If any man thirst, let him come to me and drink.* Here is a dear fountain to all thirsty souls, and most free: Christ thirsteth and longeth to have thirsty sinners come gratis and drink.

"But I doubt he bears not me in particular at good will; are the promises made for me? Did he love me before the world was? Did Christ dying intend salvation for me?"

This doubt draweth us to the fifth particular, (that so I may hasten to the uses) which is, what sort of faith it is that God requireth of all within the visible church, for the want whereof reprobates are condemned.

Asser. 1. Saving faith, required of all within the visible church, is not, as Antinomians conceive, the apprehension of God's everlasting love of election to glory of all and every one that are charged to believe. Salt-

marsh

marsh, in an ignorant and confused treatise, tells us, "To believe now, is the only work of the gospel,--that is, That ye be persuaded of such a thing, that Christ was crucified for sins, and for your sins.------- So as salvation is not a business of our working, and doing, it was done by Christ with the Father.--- All our work is no work of salvation, but in salvation we receive all, not doing any thing, that we may receive more; but doing because we receive so much, and because we are saved; and yet we are to work as much, as if we were to be saved by what we do, because we should do as much, by what is done already for us, and to our hands, as if we were to receive it for what we did ourselves: so here is short work, *(saith the man*)* believe and be saved-- ----There are yet these grounds why salvation is so soon done, 1. Because it was done before by Christ, but not believed on before, by thee, till now. 2. Because it is the gospel-way of dispensation, to assure, and pass over salvation in Christ, to any that will believe it. 3. There needs no more on our side to work or warrant salvation to us, but to be persuaded that Jesus Christ died for us, because Christ hath suffered, and God is satisfied; now suffering and satisfaction is that great work of salvation." And the man† taking on him to determine controversies of Arminians touching the extent of free grace, whether Christ died for all, (in which questions I dare make apology for his innocency, that he is not guilty of wading too deep in them) he would father on the reformed churches of Protestant Divines, that we make this a rational way of justice, "That God will meerly and arbitrarily damn men, because he will, so as God hath put every one under a state of redemption and power of salvation; and they are damned, not from their own will, but from God's." The opinion by Arminians is fathered upon that apostolic light of the church of Christ, eminent and divine Calvin; and Saltmarsh will

but

---

* Page 193, 194.   † Page 199, 200, 201, 202.

but second them, that he may appear a star in the firmament, with others of some great magnitude.

But (saith he*) the other way is, "Christ died only for his, but is offered to all, that is, who are amongst this all, might believe; and tho' he died not for all, yet none are excepted," (that is, as he saith, all and every one to whom Christ is preached, elect or reprobate are to be persuaded that Christ died for them in particular) "and yet none are excepted but they that believe, and none believe but they to whom it is given." And having shown some dreams of his own touching these controversies, he concludeth with a truth I believe easily, "Thus have I opened, tho' weakly, the mystery." Weakly, but wilfully and daringly.

But faith is formally no such persuasion, as to be persuaded, every man is loved with an everlasting love, chosen and redeemed in Christ; for it changeth the whole gospel in a lie, Christ obligeth no man to believe an untruth: now, all are charged to believe in the Son of God, and elect and reprobate (as there be of both sorts within the net of the kingdom) are not loved with an everlasting love, nor did Christ die for them all.

2. 'Tis meer presumption, not faith, that all hypocrites, fleshly men, slaves to their lusts, idolaters, covetous men, remaining such, never broken with any law-work, should immediately believe Christ is their Saviour, died for them, and the Father loved them to salvation, before the world was. True it is, before a sinner believe, he is an unpardoned, an ungodly and guilty sinner; but that he is broken, yea, or unconverted before he believe, (I speak of order of nature) 'tis as impossible, as that a thistle can bring forth figs; for then he should believe, having no new heart in him, which is the only principle of faith.

3. 'Tis a more ingenuous opinion, that Christ died for all and every one, tho' it have no truth in itself, than to hold that he died for the elect only, and yet oblige

men

---

*Pag. 202, 203.

men (as Antinomians do) against their conscience to believe he died for all and every one that are in the practice of believing.

4. *He that believeth not, maketh God a liar;* then that which is to be believed, must be an evangelic truth.

5. Faith layeth bands on all within the visible church, to *be knit together in love, unto all riches of the full assurance of understanding, to the acknowledgment of the mystery of God, and of the Father, and of Christ,* Col. ii. 1, 2. to be persuaded that *nothing can separate us from the love of God in Christ,* Rom. viii. 37, 38, 39. *To full assurance,* Heb. x. *without wavering or declining or bowing like a tottering wall.* Now, sure all and every one of the visible church, to whom the command of believing comes, reprobate or elect, are not holden to have a full assurance that they are chosen in Christ to salvation, and redeemed in his blood.

Asser. 2. The object of saving faith, required of all within the visible church, is, 1. Christ's faithfulness to save believers, Heb. x. 23. *Let us hold fast the profession of our faith without wavering;* and the apostle backs it with an argument, that saving faith must lean upon, *(for he is faithful that hath promised)* and Paul, 1 Cor. i. 9. presseth the same, *God is faithful, by whom ye were called into the fellowship of his Son Jesus Christ our Lord.*

2. We do not read in the Old or New Testament, that the decree, purpose, or intention of God to save and redeem persons in particular, is the object of that saving faith required in the gospel. For the second object of this faith is the truth and goodness of that mother-promise of the gospel, John iii. 16. and v. 25. that gospel-record, 1 John v. 10, 11, 12. *He that believeth, hath life eternal; and Jesus Christ came into the world to save sinners,* 1 Tim. i. 15. *To seek and to save the lost,* Luke xix. 10. That he came to save me in particular, is apprehended by sense, not by faith; for the election of me by name to glory, and the Lord's intention to die for me, is neither promise, nor precept, nor

threat-

CHRIST DYING AND DRAWING SINNERS TO HIMSELF. 521

threatning; if it be a history that I must believe, 'tis good, shew me histories of particular men now to be believed, except of the Antichrist, the second coming of Jesus Christ to judge the world. Election to glory is not held forth as a promise, *If ye do this, ye shall be elected to glory;* nor is the contrary holden forth as a threatning, *If ye believe not, ye shall be reprobated;* nor does the Lord command me to be *chosen in Christ to salvation, before the foundation of the world;* nor doth he command all men within the visible church to believe they are chosen to salvation, or that any one elect person should believe a thing as revealed, which is not revealed. When he is pleased to give to any elect person *the white stone, and the new name,* and to give him faith, by which he chuseth Christ for his portion, he is then, and never till then, to believe; or rather by spiritual sense to apprehend that he is chosen to salvation from eternity. So election is neither precept, nor promise, but a truth of God's gracious good-will and pleasure hid in God's mind, till he be pleased to reveal it by the fruits thereof.

There can be no such imaginable double-dealing in the world, as Arminians lay upon God: for they make the Lord to say thus, as imagine a king should speak to twenty thousand captives, "I have a good-will, purpose, hearty intention, and earnest desire to make you all and every one free princes; and I pray, wish, obtest, and beseech you subscribe such a writ to grace for that end, but I only can lead your hand at the pen, and give you eyes to see, and a willing heart to consent to your own happiness; and if you refuse to sign the bill of grace, you shall be tormented for ever and ever in a river of fire and brimstone: again, I have a like good-will to my own justice, and purpose so to carry on the design, as that sixteen thousand of you shall have the benefit of my hand, or of one finger to lead your hand at the pen, or any efficacious motion to act upon your will, to obtain your consent to subscribe the writ: yea, by the contrary, though I, of exceeding great free-

"love,

"love, will, intend, decree, and purpose you be all princes of glory; yet I purpose that these sixteen thousand, whose salvation and happiness I extremely desire, shall for their former rebellion, which I with the like desire of spirit could, and I only might have removed, never be moved to consent to this bill of grace." Now, were not this the outside of a good-will? And should not this prince be said rather to will and desire the destruction of these sixteen thousand, and not their honour and happiness.

Asser. 3. This is the mystery of the gospel in which I must profess ignorance; and that the *Lord's thoughts are not as our thoughts, nor his ways as our ways:* he hath by preaching of the gospel, engaged thousand thousands within the visible church, to the duty of their fiducial adherence and heart-resting in Christ, as they would be saved; and yet hath the Lord never purposed to work their hearts (and he only can do it) to this heart-resting in Christ by faith, nor hath he purchased either remission of sins or pardon for them. If any object, How can Christ in equity judge and condemn them for not believing pardon and salvation in his blood, when as neither pardon nor salvation are purchased in this blood to them, nor purposeth he to give them faith? Yet we may plead for the Lord: we conceive of the decree of God, as of a deep policy and a stratagem and snare laid for us; whereas the Lord lies not in wait for our ruin, nor carries he on a secret design in the gospel to destroy men. If Christ should say in the gospel-precepts, promises, or threatnings, I decree, purpose, and intend to redeem all and every man; but I purpose to carry on the design so, as the far greatest part of mankind inevitably shall be lost; it should be a stratagem: but the gospel, as the gospel, revealeth not any decree or intention of God, touching the salvation or damnation of men, intended from eternity; indeed, the gospel, as obeyed or disobeyed, reveals God's intentions and decrees; the gospel revealeth nothing but the Lord's complacency, approbation, and good-liking of the sweet connexion between faith and salvation;

the

"love, will, intend, decree, and purpose you be all princes of glory; yet I purpose that these sixteen thousand, whose salvation and happiness I extremely desire, shall for their former rebellion, which I with the like desire of spirit could, and I only might have removed, never be moved to consent to this bill of grace." Now, were not this the outside of a good-will? And should not this prince be said rather to will and desire the destruction of these sixteen thousand, and not their honour and happiness.

Asser. 3. This is the mystery of the gospel in which I must profess ignorance; and that the *Lord's thoughts are not as our thoughts, nor his ways as our ways:* he hath by preaching of the gospel, engaged thousand thousands within the visible church, to the duty of their fiducial adherence and heart-resting in Christ, as they would be saved; and yet hath the Lord never purposed to work their hearts (and he only can do it) to this heart-resting in Christ by faith, nor hath he purchased either remission of sins or pardon for them. If any object, How can Christ in equity judge and condemn them for not believing pardon and salvation in his blood, when as neither pardon nor salvation are purchased in this blood to them, nor purposeth he to give them faith? Yet we may plead for the Lord: we conceive of the decree of God, as of a deep policy and a stratagem and snare laid for us; whereas the Lord lies not in wait for our ruin, nor carries he on a secret design in the gospel to destroy men. If Christ should say in the gospel-precepts, promises, or threatnings, I decree, purpose, and intend to redeem all and every man; but I purpose to carry on the design so, as the far greatest part of mankind inevitably shall be lost; it should be a stratagem: but the gospel, as the gospel, revealeth not any decree or intention of God, touching the salvation or damnation of men, intended from eternity; indeed, the gospel, as obeyed or disobeyed, reveals God's intentions and decrees; the gospel revealeth nothing but the Lord's complacency, approbation, and good-liking of the sweet connexion between faith and salvation;
the

the just contentation between unbelief, disobedience, and eternal damnation: so the gospel reveals duties, but not the persons saved, or damned; the Lord's working with the gospel, or the efficacy of the gospel (which is a far other thing) reveals the persons.

Now the difficulty is, How the Lord can command the reprobate to believe life and salvation in Christ, when there is no life and salvation either intended to them, or purchased for them?

To which I answer, 1. God gave a law to all the angels created in the truth, *If ye abide in the truth, ye shall be eternally happy:* ye cannot say that the devils in that instant were to believe that God intended and decreed them for eternal happiness, and to give them efficacious grace, by which they should abide in the truth, as their fellow angels did; God's command and promise did reveal no such intention of God. So the Lord said to Adam and to all his seed, If ye keep the law perfectly, ye shall have life eternal; according to that, *Do this and live:* yet was not Adam then, far less these that are now under the law, to believe that God ordained them from eternity, to eternal life, legally purchased; or that any flesh should be justified by the works of the law.

Arminians tell us, That there be numbers judicially blinded and hardned within the visible church, who cannot believe, and whom the Lord hath destined for destruction; yet the word is preached to them, they hear and read the promises of the gospel, and the precepts: whether are they to believe that God intended from eternity to them salvation and grace to believe? I think not: for they teach, that Christ neither prayeth for, nor intendeth to die for the unbelieving and obstinate world as such, nor decreed their salvation. And except men may fancy senses on the words of God's Spirit; where learned they to expound the word *world* (when it makes for them) for all and every one of mankind; and when it makes against them, for the least part of mankind, and that either within the visible church only, or yet without the visible church? For in

both

both, Satan's world of disobedient ones is the far greatest part, seeing *the whole world lies in sin*, as John saith. Let it be also remembered, when Arminians say, *The Lamb of God taketh away the sins of the world*, that is, of all and every mortal man, they mean Christ takes not away, nor sheddeth he his blood, for the sins of the rebellious world; so the world's rebellion, contumacy and infidelity against Christ, must be pardoned without shedding of blood: and if Christ did bear all the sins of the world on the cross conditionally, and none of them absolutely; then our act of believing must be the only nearest cause of satisfaction for sins: but why then, if Christ satisfied on the cross for the final impenitency and unbelief of the rebellious world conditionally, so they believe and be not rebellious; but Arminians should say right-down, Christ died for the rebellious and contumacious world, and he prays for the contumacious world as such, but conditionally; for he prays and dieth for the not-rebellious world of all mortal men, not absolutely, but conditionally, so they believe in Christ; if they believe not, neither the prayers of Christ, nor his death, are more effectual for them than for devils.

To all these we may add, That the Lord, in commanding reprobates to rest on Christ for salvation, though no salvation be purchased for them deals sincerely and candidly with them: for, *First*, He commands them to believe no intention in God to save them by the death of his son, nor saith he any such thing to them, but only commandeth them to rely on Christ as an all-sufficient Saviour. *Secondly*, God commands all the reprobate, even by their way, to believe that Christ in his death intended their salvation, justification, conversion: and yet, whereas God taketh ways effectual, and such as he forseeth shall be effectual for the efficacious working of justification and conversion, and actual glorification of some few; yet he taketh ways which he knoweth shall be utterly ineffectual for the salvation, justification, and conversion of all these reprobates, and yet commandeth them to believe that he decrees and intendeth their

sal-

salvation and conversion, with no less ardency and vehemency of serious affection, than he doth intend the salvation and conversion of all that shall be glorified. Sure this we would call double-dealing in men; and the scripture saith, He is *a God of truth*, Deut. xxxii. *and the Lord who cannot lie.*

Object. "If a rich inn-keeper should dig a fountain in his field for all passengers, thirsty and diseased, which were able to cure them, and quench their thirst; and invite them all to come and drink and be cured, upon condition they come and believe the virtue of the water to be such; and yet should intend and decree absolutely and irresistibly the tenth man invited, should never be cured; this inn-keeper should not deal sincerely with them. So you make God to deal with sinners in the gospel: he doth all, in inviting sick sinners to come and drink life and salvation at Christ the fountain of life, which expresseth with men who speak as they think, their sincere intention; but he intendeth no such thing."

Answ. Make the comparison run as it should do, and it maketh more against Arminians; say that this inn-keeper had dominion over the heart and will, as the Lord hath, Prov. xxi. 1. Psal. cxix. 36, 37. Heb. xiii. 20, 21. Mat. vi. 13. and that he could and doth, without straining of the heart, work in all the passengers, a sense of their disease, grace actually to come and drink, and yet he taketh a dealing with the souls of some few, and causeth them come to the waters and drink, and healeth them, and he useth such means, and so acts upon the will of the far most part, that they shall never come, never be sensible of their disease, and yet he invites them to come to the waters and drink; 'tis clear, this inn-keeper never intended the health of all and every one of the passengers, but only of these few that come and drink; nor doth invitations with men, upon condition which the party invited is obliged to perform, but doth never perform, and which the inviter only of grace can work in the invited, but doth not work

them,

them, as being not obliged thereunto, speak any such intention.

Again, let it be considered, that here, 1. God lies in wait for no man's destruction. 2. God is not obliged to reveal his eternal purpose and intentions touching men's salvation and damnation, but in the way and manner seems best to him. 3. God never saith in all the gospel, that from eternity he hath passed a resolve to save all mankind, if they will; and to yield them the bridle on their own necks, that they may be indifferent and absolute lords of heaven and hell. 4. Nor should the gospel be framed in such wisdom, if the Lord had set down particularly the names of all the elect and reprobate in the world, and have proponed salvation upon condition of obedience and faith to some few; it should evidently have raised a hard opinion in the minds of thousands touching Christ.

Asser. 4. The third object of faith, is, the sufficiency and power of Christ to save. 1. The scripture maketh the object of coming, which is believing, John v. 40. John vi. 35. Mat. xi. 27. to be Christ's ability and power, Heb. vii. 25. *to save them to the uttermost, that come unto God by him, seeing he ever liveth to make intercession for them.* What the scripture presseth us to believe savingly, that we must be inclined to mis-believe; and for the mis-believing thereof, the reprobates are condemned, and not because they believe not the Lord's intention to save all, or his decrees of election and reprobation. But the scripture presseth faith in the power of mercy, Rom. iv. 21. Abraham *staggered not, but was strong in the faith, giving glory to God, being fully perswaded that what he had promised, he was able also to perform.* Now, Abraham is commended for that he savingly, and for his justification, believed the power of God in the gospel promise, that God was able of his mercy to give him the son of promise in his old age; otherwise, to believe simply the power of God to give a child to a mother who is past the natural date of bearing children, is but the faith of miracles, which of itself is not saving, and may be in

workers

workers of iniquity, Mat. vii. 21, 22. So this power, then, is the power of saving, conjoined with the mercy and good-will of Christ. 2. The scripture holds forth to our faith the power of God *to graff in the Jews again in Christ,* Rom. xi. 23. to make a weak believer stand, Rom. xiv. 4. *to keep the saints from falling, and to present them faultless before the presence of his glory with exceeding joy,* Jude v. 24. 3. The good land was a type of the heavenly rest, Heb. iv. 1. Heb. iii. 19. *some entred not in through unbelief:* why, what unbelief? The story sheweth us, Psalm xciii. 7. Numb. xiv. 9. Numb. xiii. 28. they doubted of the power of God, and believed the report of the unbelieving spies, who said, *The people be strong that dwell in the land, the cities are walled and very great, and moreover we saw the children of Anak there.* Joshua and Caleb, chap. xiv. 9. said, *They should be bread for them, and their strength was gone;* then the question was, whether God was able to give them that good land? So then, men enter not into the heavenly rest, because they believe not that *Jesus is able to save to the uttermost those that come through him to God,* Heb. vii. 23. 4. The scripture is as much in proving the all-sufficiency, power, and perfection of Christ our Saviour, to save, as in demonstrating his tenderness of mercy and good-will to save; as in the epistle to the Hebrews, the apostle laboureth much for to prove the Godhead of Christ his excellency above angels, and that the angels were to adore him; his dignity and greatness above Moses and all the mortal and dying priests; the virtue of his blood above all the bloods of bulls and goats, *to purge the conscience from dead works,* to expiate sin, *to sanctify his people, to open a way, a new and living way to the holy of holiest, by his blood, that we with full assurance may draw near to God;* that he with one sacrifice, never to be repeated, did that which all the thousands of reiterated sacrifices were never able to do; that he is no dying priest, but *lives for ever to interceed for us at the right-hand of God.* And for what is all this, but that we should believe the all-sufficiency

of

of Christ to save, and because we have too low thoughts of Christ, as conceiving him to be but a man, or less than an angel, or a common priest, that can do no more by his blood, as touching remission of sins, than dying priests could do with the blood of beasts; and that he is dead, and now, when we sin, he cannot advocate for us at the right-hand of God; and that his redemption he brings in, is not eternal? Yea, all this saith, that saving faith rests upon Christ as God, as able and compleatly perfect and sufficient to save, tho' sinners do not, in the formal act of faith, believe his good-will, decree, and intention to redeem and save them by name.

5. I should think, that these who have high and precious thoughts of the grace, tender mercy, perfection and sufficiency of Christ to save all that believe, and fiducially rely on Christ as a Saviour sealed for the work of redemption, though they know not God's mind touching their own salvation in particular, have such a faith as the gospel speaks of, and do savingly believe that Christ came to *seek and to save that which is lost, to save sinners;* that Christ is the Son of the living God, *the Saviour of mankind:* and this no devil, no temporary believer, no hypocrite can attain unto.

Object. 1. "But I believe not then that I am in particular redeemed: and, without that, I am a stranger to Christ; for devils and reprobates may believe all the general promises of the gospel."

Answ. 1. 'Tis true, in that act formally you believe not you are redeemed in particular; yet virtually and by good consequence you believe your own redemption in particular, and so you are not a stranger to Christ. 2. 'Tis true, devils and reprobates may yield an assent of mind to the general promises, as true: but 'tis denied that they can rest on them as good, as worthy by all means to be embraced; or that in heart and affections they can intrust the weight and burden of their soul on these general promises, or that there is any taste of the honey and sweetness of Christ in these promises to their

soul,

soul, as it is with the souls that fiducially rest upon Christ in these promises.

Object. 2. "Suppose I know of a ship offering to carry all to a land of life, where people are never sick, never die, have summer and day-light, and peace and plenty for ever, upon condition I should believe the good-will of the ship-master to carry me to that land; if I know nothing of his good-will to me in particular, I have no ground to believe I shall ever enjoy that good land: so here, if I know nothing of Christ's good-will to me, how can I believe he shall carry me to the heavenly Canaan?"

Answ. Yea, suppose, what is in question, that to be persuaded of the good-will of Christ the owner of the ship to carry you in particular, is the condition upon which he must carry you, but that is to be proved; there is no other condition, but that you rest on his good-will to carry all who so rest on him, and that is all.

Object. 3. "But I cannot believe."

Answ. You are to believe you cannot believe of yourself, and of your own strength; but you are not farther from Christ, that you are far from yourself.

Object. 4. "'Tis comfortable that Christ the Physician came to heal the sick; but what is that to me, who am not sick, nor of the number of these sick, that Christ came to heal, for any thing I know?

Answ. 'Tis true, 'tis nothing to you that Christ came to heal the sick, and to cure the distemper of sin that is on them; you want nothing but that the Spirit working with the law, let, you see your lost condition, and the gospel-offer be considered, and compared with your estate. But whether you be of the number of these sick that Christ came to heal, is no lawful doubt, and comes not from God; for what that number is, or whether you be one of that number or no, is a secret of the hid counsel of election to glory: a negative certainty, that, for any thing ye know, you are not of the contrary number, nor are ye excluded out of that number, is enough for you to father kindness upon

Christ,

Christ, though he should say, from heaven, Thou art not a son.

Object. 5. "I shall never have a ground of assurance to believe Christ's good-will, nor either hope or comfort in the gospel-covenant or promises, if Christ died for a few elected and chosen absolutely to glory: for all must be resolved on doubtsome, hopeless, sad and comfortless grounds, by your way, thus:

"These for whom Christ laid down his life, and have ground of assurance of hope and comfort in Christ's death and in the gospel-promises, are not all men and all sinners, but only some few handful of chosen ones, by name, such as Abraham, David, Peter, Mary, Hannah, etc. and not one more, not any other.

"But I am not of thee few handful of chosen ones by name, I am Abraham, David, Peter, Mary, Hannah, etc. and of no other number; therefore I have ground of assurance of hope and comfort in Christ's death and in the gospel-promises.

"Now, the proposition is poor, comfortless, and a very hopeless field to all within the visible church? and the assumption to the greatest part of mankind evidently false, because many are called, but few are chosen: and so the syllogism shall suggest a field of comfortless and hopeless unbelief and doubting, yea, of despairing, to the far largest part of mankind; whereas the doctrine of the Lord's good-will to save all and every one of mankind, and of redeeming all, and covenanting in Christ with all, removes all ground of unbelief and doubting, from any; offereth grounds of faith, hope and comfort in the gospel, of peace to all."

Answ. 1. We shall consider what certainty and assurance of faith Arminians furnish to all and every one from the gospel.

2. What the scripture speaks of the assurance, hope and comfort of all and every one. And,

3. The argument shortly shall be answered. As for the first, That Arminians may make their syllogism of

as-

assurance, hope, and comfort in Christ's death, as large as Christ's death; they must extend the gospel-comfort and hope to the heathen, who never heard of these comforts: now, how this can be, let us judge. A very learned and eminent divine *(a)* sheweth from the matter itself, and confession of Amayrald *(b)* an Arminian, that twelve apostles could not in so short a time have gone through the whole world; yea, they must have passed many particular nations, who never by any sound heard of the gospel: and Arminians yield to us, that this was done *arcana Dei dispensatione, by the secret and unsearchable providence of God*; they would say, if they would speak truth, by the Lord's absolute, highest, independent and unsearchable good pleasure, in his decrees of absolute election and reprobation. 2. Again, they are made excusable, and freed from all guiltiness of unbelief, and hopelessness of comfort or ground of comfort in the gospel-promises, who never heard of the gospel; yea even these who heard but the gospel, as the Athenians, Acts xvii. *who judged Paul to be a babler and Festus, who thought him mad,* and the Grecians, *who esteemed the preaching of the gospel foolishness,* 1 Cor. i. and so most have heard the gospel, yet are not condemned so much for doubting of the sufficiency of Christ's death, seeing they believed Christ to be a false prophet, as for their not hearing men sent of God, Christ and the apostles, speaking with the power of God, and endued with the power of working miracles. 3. But what assurance, hope and comfort of salvation do Arminians give? One Thomas Moore has written a book, intituled, *The universality of God's free grace in Christ to mankind; that all might be comforted, encouraged, every one confirmed and assured of the propitiation and death of Christ for the whole race of mankind, and so for himself in particular:* hear then what

Arminians,

NUMB. V.   4 B

(a)   Freder. Spanhemius, a professor in Leyden, to 3. page 750. Ans. to the 3d Query.
(b)   Amayrald, ch. 12. Defen. Decr. de Reprobat.

Arminians, and Mr. Moore saith, "comfort ye, comfort ye my people, saith the Lord; comfort and encourage with the joy of the Holy Ghost, with the lively hope of eternal life, with the comforts of the scripture, Scipio, Aristotle, Cato, Regulus, Seneca, all the Turks, Americans, Indians, Virginians; such as worship the devils, the sun and moon; such as have no hope, and are without God, and without Christ in the world; bid them be assured Christ died for them, prays and interceeds for them, intends and wills their salvation upon good condition, no less than the salvation upon good condition, no less than the salvation of his chosen people."

But, 1. The object of this faith, hope, and comfort, may stand and consist, though all and every one of the race of mankind should believe it, with no les certainty of eternal damnation than Indians, all the reprobate and condemned devils are under: now, saving faith removeth all hazard of damnation, John iii. 16. John v. 25. John xi. 26. 1 Tim. i. 15, 16. Gal. ii. 10. but thousands believe, yea, the damned devils, who assent to the letter of the gospel, and gave testimony that Jesus is the Son of the living God, by the judgment of the Arminians, believe that Christ died for all and every one of the race of mankind. Ergo, all the reprobates may have this faith, assurance, comfort and hope. 2. Saving faith, bringing peace, justification, rejoicing in tribulation, purifieth the heart: but I am not a whit nearer peace, that I believe that Christ intendeth to redeem, save, justify all and every one of mankind, upon condition they believe; for this remaineth ever a hole in the heart; God either efficaciously intendeth to save all, or inefficaciously, committing the event to the good guiding of free-will, which once lost all mankind: now the former neither can be known to any living; 'tis a doubt to Arminians, if it be known to God himself: Arminius (Anti-Perkins) saith, "*Deum posse excidere fine suo, quia non semper intendit sinem secundum praescientiam*; God may fail and come short of his end, because he doth not, especially in events that fall out freely, and may not

"fall

"fall out, intend the end according to foreknowledge." See then here the Arminian courage, hope and comfort: God intendeth to redeem and save me in Christ; but ah! it is as the blind man casteth his club, or shoots his arrow, he winks and draws the string; it may come up to the white, but it runs a hazard to fall short and wide. Again, 'tis false that God intendeth efficaciously to save all; therefore Bellarmine and Arminius say, the Lord doth here, as politicians, who have two strings in their bow: for God (say they) lieth at the wait between two ends, and intendeth either the obedience, conversion and salvation of all; or, if he miss, he has another string in his bow, and intends the declaration of the glory of his justice, if free-will shall thwart and cross the former intention of God; and this is the latter intention, all and every man is to believe that God intends his conversion and salvation ineffectually; but ah! this is cold comfort, and dubious, hazardsome and far off hope; the poor man is here between hope to be saved, (if the fortune, or loose contingency of free-will be lucky) and fear to be eternally thrice more miserable than if God had never borne him any good-will (if free-will miscarry, as it doth in the far greatest part of mankind) for Arminians do not say, one man is more saved, by their pendulous and venturous good wishes and doubtsome intentions to save all and every one, than we do by the Lord's most wise, stayed, poised, fixed, and absolute decrees; so it is but a toom and an empty spoon, they thrust in the mouths of the whole race of mankind, when they will them thus to *hope for salvation*.

2. By this means, God intending two ends, either the salvation or damnation of all and every one, he puts all mankind upon large as great fear and despair, as upon comfort and hope; and he intends and wills the destruction of all mankind more efficaciously, and with far greater success, than he wills their salvation: only, here is a comfort men may take to hell with them, and an east-wind hope they may feed on; God primarily, antecedently, and first wills my salvation, but seconda-

rily

rily and with better certainty of the black event, he wills, in justice, my damnation, and the eternal destruction of the far greatest part of mankind; and this is the Arminian comfort, and white hopes that the tenet of Arminian universal grace, liberally bestows on all; much good do it them.

3. They stand not to make God to fluctuate between two ends; either this or that, justice or mercy: mercy is the port, God desires to sail to, and to carry all to heaven; but because he cannot be master of tide and wind, and free-will bloweth out of the east, when God expecteth a fair west-wind, the Lord is compelled to arrive with a second wind, as a crossed seaman must do, and to land his vessel in the sad port of revenging justice, and make such a sea-voyage, as against the heart of God (what will ye say of the destiny of free-will's ill luck?) must cast the far greatest part of mankind, as ship-broken men, into an eternal damnation; and except God would have strangled free-will, and destroyed the nature of that obedience which is obnoxious to threatnings and rewards, he could not for his soul mend the matter. And here, good reader, you have the Arminian hope and consolations, if you list to hearken to the Arminians of England, now risen to comfort all mankind in these sad times. 3. Saving faith layeth hold on salvation, righteousness and everlasting redemption, as proper heritage; faith being a supernatural instinct, that layeth a peculiar claim to Christ, as the natural instinct in the lamb claimeth the mother: 'tis property that faith pursueth. Let experience speak, if there be not a peculiar warmness of heart in a believer at the sight of Christ: now, to believe a common salvation hanging in the air, the heaven of Turks and Arminians, and the righteousness, and redemption of Indians, of Seneca, and Catiline, Clodius, and Camillus, I confess must be far from such a property.

4. Saving faith is the first dawning, the morning-sky and the first day-light of the appearance of election to glory, Acts xiii. 48. The man never hath a fair

ven-

CHRIST DYING AND DRAWING SINNERS TO HIMSELF. 535

venture of heaven, nor cometh in handy grips with eternal love revealed, till he believe; because the poor man's believing is his act of chusing God for his portion, and so cannot be an assent to a common good, general to all men, Heathens, Pagans, Jews, Turks, and believers: faith makes him say, *I have now found a ransom*, I have found a pearl of great price, I make no other choice, my lot is well fallen on Christ; whether Christ cast his love or his lot upon me from eternity, I cannot dispute; but sure, I have chosen him in time. Now, for the second, the scripture sheweth us of *an hope of righteousness by faith;* this we *wait for through the Spirit,* Gal. v. 5. and *of the hope laid up for the saints in heaven,* Col. i. 15. and *Christ in the saints the hope of glory,* v. 27. and *of the hope of the appearing of our life Christ,* Tit. ii. 13. Which *hope maketh a man to purge himself, and to be holy,* 1 John iii. 3. and *of a rejoicing in hope of the glory of God,* Rom. v. 2. Rom. xii. 12. *the hope to come, for which the twelve tribes of Israel serve God instantly,* Acts xxvi. 7. and *that lively hope unto which we are regenerated by the resurrection of Jesus Christ from the dead,* 1 Pet. i. 5. and *the hope that we have through patience and comfort of the scripture,* Rom. xv. 4. and the hope which is not confined within the narrow sphere and region of time and this corruptible life, 1 Cor. xv. 19. *the hope which experience bringeth forth,* Heb. v. 4. Now, whether we take hope for the object of hope, the thing hoped for, or the supernatural or gracious faculty of hoping; in neither respects have Seneca, Scipio, Regulus, Jews, Turks, Americans, and such as never by any rumour heard of Christ any hope from scripture: Paul saith of them, and of the Ephesians in their condition, Ephes. ii. 12. *At that time ye were without Christ, being aliens from the commonwealth of Israel, and strangers from the covenants of promise, having no hope, and without God in the world;* and for the grace of hope, the scripture saith, *'tis an anchor cast in heaven by these who* upon life and death *make Jesus their city of refuge,*

Heb.

Heb. vi. 19, 20. it is a *fruit of the Spirit*, Gal. v. 5. Wherever it is, it *makes a man purify himself*, 1 John iii. 2. 'tis a *lively hope;* and a fruit of predestination, *and of the sprinkling of the blood of Jesus*, 1 Pet. i. 3, 4, 5. Now, such a hope as Arminians allow to heathens and Indians, to reprobates, who believe that Christ died for all and every one, and such as perish eternally, we gladly leave to themselves; and if our doctrine of particular redemption furnish ground of despair, as opposite to this hope, we profess it: but let Arminians answer this of their own way; so God must speak to the most part of the christian world, "Be of good courage, hope for salvation in Christ, be comforted in this, that Christ died for you all without exception, and be fully assured and believe there is a perfect ransom given for you; and salvation and righteousness purchased to you in Christ's blood; but I have decreed so to act upon the wills of the far greatest part of you, that you shall have no more share in that redemption and purchased salvation than the damned devils; whereas, if I had so drawn you, as I have done others, as sinful by nature as you are, you should certainly have been eternally saved in Christ's blood;" and the like. And far more I could say, of the dream of the middle science and knowledge of God; for Arminians spoil the Almighty of all grace, compassion, mercy, or power to save: for this is the gospel, and no other, that God must utter, by their doctrine; "I have chosen out of grace and mercy all to salvation, who shall believe, and have given my Son, to give his life and blood a ransom for all and every one; and I will, desire and wish, that all mankind were with me in eternal glory, and that my revenging justice had never been experimentally known to men or angel, and that death, hell, sin, had never had being in the world: but the far greatest part of mankind were to sin, and finally and obstinately to resist, both my general universal grace given to all, and my special and evangelic calling, and that they were to do before any act of my knowledge, free

"de-

"decree, strong grace, or tender mercy; and I cannot bow their wills indeclinably to final obedience, nor could I so powerfully, by moral swasion, draw them to a constant faith and perseverance, except I would act against that which is decent and convenient for a law-giver to do, and destroy the nature of that free obedience that lieth under the sweet droppings of free reward, which must be earned by sweating, and under the lash and hazard of eternal punishments to be inflicted, (which I will not do) yea, though in all things even done by free agents, as translations of kingdoms from one prince to another, and bringing enemies against a land, which are done by free agents, I do whatever I will, and my decree stands and cannot be recalled, Dan. iv. 35. Isa. xiv. 24, 25, 26, 27. chap. xlvi. 10, 11. Psal. cxv. 3. Psal. cxxxv. 6. Yet in matters of salvation or damnation, or of turning the hearts and free actions of men and angels, that most highly concern my glory above all; I cannot but bring all the arrows of my decrees, to the bow of that slippery contingent indifferences of the up and down free-will of men and angels; and here am fast fettered, that I can but dance as free-will pipeth, and say amen to created will in all things good or bad. I cannot out of the abundance of my rich grace and free mercy (though earnestly and vehemently I desire it) save one person more than are saved, or damn one more than are damned, or write one more in the book of life, and bestow on them the fruits of my dear Son's death, than such as, in order of nature, were finally to believe before any act of my middle science, or my conditional free decree, or drawing grace; therefore am I compelled (as a merchant, who against his will casts his goods in the sea, to save his own life, because the winds and storms over-master his desire) to take a second course, contrary to my natural desire, and gracious and mild inclination to mercy, to decree and ordain that all who before the acts also of my middle science, free decree and just will, were finally to resist my calling,

"shall

"shall eternally perish; and to will that Pharaoh should not at the first or second command obey my will, and let my people go: and therefore, with a consequent or constrained will, to suffer sin to be, to appoint death and hell, and the eternal destruction of the greatest part of mankind, to be in the world, for the declaration of my revenging justice, because I could not hinder the entrance of sin into the world, nor master free-will as free, if my dispensation of the first covenant made with Adam in paradise should stand: whereupon I was compelled to take a second harbour, and a second wind, like a sea-man, who is, with a stronger cross wind, driven from his first wished port; and to send my Son Jesus Christ into the world to die for sinners, for that I could not better do, and out of love to save all, offer him to all, one way or other, though I did foresee my desire and natural kindness to save all, should be far more thwarted and crossed by this way; because need-force my consequent will must needs prepare a far hotter furnace in hell for the greatest part of mankind, since thousands of them must reject Christ, in resisting the light of nature, and the universal sufficient grace given to all; which if free-will should use well, would have procured to them more grace, and the benefit of the preached gospel. But a heavier plague of hardness of heart, and far greater torments of fire, than these, I foresee must be the doom of such, within the visible church, as resist my calling, or having once obeyed, may, according to the liberty of independent free-will, persevere if they will; and notwithstanding of the power of God, by which they are kept to salvation, the promises of the eternal covenant, the efficacy of Christ's perpetual intercession, of the indwelling of the Holy Ghost, that everlasting fountain of life, etc. may fully and finally fall away, and turn apostates: and therefore all their hope of eternal life, their assurance of glory, their joy, their consolation and comforts in any claim to life eternal, and the state

"of

"of adoption, is not bottomed on my power to keep them, my eternal covenant, my Son's intercession, (I can do no more than I can) but upon their own free-will, if they please (and 'tis too pleasant to many) they may all fall away, and perish eternally, and leave my son a widow, without a wife, a head without members, a king without subjects."

And if Arminians will be so liberal or lavish of the comforts of God, proper to the Lord's people, Isa. xl. 1. chap. xlix. 13. the proper work of the *Holy Ghost the Comforter*, John xiv. 16. chap. xv. 26. chap. xvi. 7. the *consolations of Christ*, Phil. ii. 1. *the everlasting, the strong consolations*, 2 Thess. ii. 16. Heb. vi. 18. *the heart-comforts*, Col. ii. 2. *wherewith the apostles are comforted*, 2 Cor. i. 4, 6, 7. *coming from the God of all comfort, the Lord that comforteth Zion*, Isa. li. 3. 2 Cor. i. 3. Isa. li. 12. *Blessing promised to the mourners*, Mat. v. 4. We desire Mr. Moore and other Arminians to enjoy them; but for us, we allow neither assurance, courage, hope, nor comforts in Christ or his death, but on the regenerate and believers: and this makes the doctrine of universal redemption more suspicious to us, as not coming from God, that they allow to all (even dogs and swine) the Holy Ghost, and the gracious privilege of the saints. Therefore, *Thirdly*, we answer, That the assumption is not ours, but theirs. Let the assumption be, But I believe, and the proposition be corrected thus, These for whom Christ laid down his life, are some few chosen believers; but I am chosen and a believer: ergo. etc. and we grant all, so the assumption be made sure.

But I have no assurance, hope, nor comfort to rest on a general good will that God beareth to all, to Judas, Pharaoh, Cain, and to all mankind, no less than to me. For I am of the same very metal, and by nature am an heir of wrath as well as they.

2. The far-off good-will, that all be saved, and that all obey; the Lord from eternity did bear it to the fallen angels, as well as to me. O cold comfort! And it works nothing in order to my actual salvation, more than

than to the actual salvation of Judas the traitor: it sets on moving no wheels, no causes, no effectual means to procure the powerful application of the purchased redemption to me, more than to all that are now spitting out blasphemy against eternal justice, and are in fiery chains of wrath, cursing this Lord, and his general good-will to save them.

But the fountain good-will of God, to save the elect, runneth in another channel of free-grace, that separates person from person, Jacob from Esau; and sets the heart of God from eternity, and the tender bowels of Christ, both from everlasting, and as touching the execution of this good-will in time, upon this man, not that man, without hire-money or price; 1. Because angels or men can never answer that of Rom. ix. 13, 14, 15. *As it is written, I have loved Jacob, and have hated Esau, and that before the one or the other had done good or evil.* Then the natural Arminian objecteth what our Arminian does this day, that must be unrighteousness, to hate men absolutely, and cast them off, when they are not born, and have neither done good nor evil. Paul answereth, It followeth in no sort that *there is unrighteousness with God*, because, verse 15. all is resolved on the will of God, because it is his will; for he saith to Moses, *I will have mercy on whom I will have mercy, and I will have compassion on whom I will have compassion:* and upon this he infers, Then the business of separating Jacob from Esau runs not upon such wheels as running and willing, sweating and hunting by good endeavours; Jacob did here less, and Esau more: but all goes on this, on God's free goodness and mercy; all the difference between person and person, is, God has mercy, because he will, not because men will. Now, because Arminians say, This is not meant of election and reprobation, but of temporary favours bestowed on Jacob, not on Esau; he alledgeth the example of Pharaoh, a cruel atheist and a tyrant, who never *sought justification by the works of the law:* the reason why Pharaoh obtained not the mercy that others obtained, *I, saith the Lord,* ver. 17. told Pharaoh

to

to his face, *For this purpose I raised thee up, that I might make an example of the glory of my power, and name,* that is, *the glory of justice in thee,* to all the world who hears of thee: and then, verse 18. he returns to the Lord's free-will, and unhired and absolute liberty in differencing person from person. Why has he mercy upon this man, and not on that man, if there had been such a conceit, as a general catholic good-will in God, to Pharaoh, to Esau? The apostle should now have denied any absolute will in God to separate one person from another. Arminians can instruct the Spirit of the Lord, and the apostle to say, He has an equal general good-will and desire to save all and every one; Esau as well as Jacob; Ishmael as Isaac, the son of promise; Pharaoh as Moses, or any other man: but then, two great doubts should remain; how then hated he Esau, when he was not yet born, and had not done good or evil? All the Arminians on earth, answer that. 2. But the doubt is not removed: how is it, that God loves Jacob, blesseth, and hath mercy on him, and hateth Esau, and yet Esau has neither done good or ill? Arminians answer, "In an antecedent general good-will, God indeed loved Esau as well as Jacob; Pharaoh, as well as another man: but here is the thing that makes the separation, Jacob runneth and willeth; Esau is a wicked man; Pharaoh, and others like him, bloody tyrants: and God sheweth mercy with another posterior and consequent will on Jacob, because he runs and wills, and has mercy on him, because he pays well for mercy; and has not mercy on Esau, because he neither runs nor wills." Now this is to contradict God; therefore we must bear with it, that men of corrupt minds, destitute of the truth, rising up to plead for universal atonement, contradict us. But Paul resolves all the mercy bestowed on this man, not on that man, v. 18. on this saying, [Gr. Thèlei] *he will; therefore hath he mercy on whom he will have mercy, and hardeneth whom he will.* (2.) Unpossible it is, that conversion should be grace, and matter of the praise of the glory of the Lord's grace

to

to Peter rather than to Judas, except the grace of God separate Peter from Judas, by moving effectually the one to believe, and not moving the other. All the wit of men cannot say, but I may glory in my own free-will, that I am efficaciously redeemed and saved, rather than another; except grace efficaciously move me in a way of separating me from another, if he had a like good-will to save me, and Judas and all the world; but he committed the casting of the balance, in differencing the one from the other, to free-will, so as the creatures free-will made the consequent will of God different toward the one and toward the other.

3. *The God, who is willing to shew his wrath, and to make his power known, in enduring with much long-suffering the vessels of wrath fitted to destruction, that he might make known the riches of his glory on the vessels of mercy, which he had afore prepared to glory*, Rom. ix. 22, 23. is also willing, because he is willing, to declare these two ends equally; in some, because he will, the glory of power, justice and long-suffering; in others, the glory of grace and mercy, because he will. Nor did I ever see a reason wherefore God should carry on the two great state-designs of justice and mercy, in such an order, as he should incline more to declare and bring to pass the design of mercy than the design of justice; for, out of the freedom of high and deep sovereignty, he most freely intended both these glorious ends. Now, as the attaining of his freely intended end of manifested mercy in some, both angels and men, makes visible in an eminent manner the glory of justice in other some; so the attaining of his freely intended end of pure grace in the elect, doth highly endear Jesus Christ, that we should prize the blood of the covenant, the riches of free-grace to us whom he hath freely chosen, leaving others as good as we to perish everlastingly. And as Arminians cannot deny, but that the Lord might so have contrived the business, as all that are saved, and to praise the Lord that sits on the throne in heaven, might have been damned, and should blaspheme eternally in hell the holy just Judge of the

world;

CHRIST DYING AND DRAWING SINNERS TO HIMSELF. 543

world; as he can make a revolution of all things in heaven and in earth to a providence contrary to that which is now; so they cannot deny an eminent sovereignty, deliberate and fixed free-will in God, before any of the elect and reprobate were placed in such a condition of providence, in which he foresaw all that are saved or damned, should be saved or damned; and that this will was the prime fountain cause of election and reprobation.

4. Paul shewing, Rom. xi. that God *concludes all in unbelief, that he might have mercy on all*; and shewing a reason why the Lord was pleased to cast off his ancient people for a time, and to *ingraff the Gentiles, the wild olive*, in their place; saith, *O the depth!* And another reason he cannot find, but bottomless and unsearchable freedom of grace and free dispensation to some people and persons, and not to others. I confess it had been no such depth, if the Lord from eternity had equally loved all to salvation, but, through the running and willing, or not-running and not-willing of the creature, had been put upon later, wiser and riper thoughts, and a consequent will to save or not save, as men and angels in the high and indifferent court of their free-will shall think good; there had been no other depth than is in earthly judges, who reward well-doers, and punish ill-doers; or in a lord of a vineyard, who gives wages to him that labours, and no wages to him that stands idle and doth nothing: this is the law of nature, of nations, and no depth; 'tis but God rewarding men according to their works, and God shewing mercy in such as co-operate with, and improve well the benefit of God's antecedent will, and not shewing mercy on such as do not co-operate therewith, but out of the absoluteness of indifferent free-will are wanting thereunto. But the great and unsearchable depth is, How God should so carry on the great designs of the declaration of the glory of pardoning mercy and punishing justice, as there should be some persons and nations, the Jews first, and not the Gentiles, as of old; and now the Gentiles, taken into

Christ,

Christ, and the Jews cast off; and again, the Jews, with the riches of the world of elect, both Jews and Gentiles, who are chosen and must obey the gospel, and be called, without any respect to works, but of grace, Rom. xi. 5, 6, 7. and when the children had neither done good nor evil, and were not born, Rom. ix. 11. and these who were nearest to Christ, and did work more for the attaining righteousness and life, than other strangers to Christ, and Gentiles, Rom. ix. 30, 31, 32, 33. Rom. x. 1, 2, 3, 4. Rom. xi. 1, 2, 3, 4, 5, 6, 7, 8. etc. rejected; and there should be others, as good as these by nature, that the Lord should have mercy on: now, in both these, *First*, God is free in his grace: *Secondly*, Just in his judgments, though he neither call, nor chuse according to works: *Thirdly*, The damned creature most guilty: and, *Fourthly*, The Lord both justly severe, and graciously merciful: *Fifthly*, None have cause to complain or quarrel with God; and yet God might have carried the matter a far other way: *Sixthly*, The head cause of this various administration, with nations and persons, is the deep, high, sovereign, innocent, holy, independent will of the great potter and former of all things, who *has mercy on whom he will, and hardneth whom he will;* and this is the depth without a bottom. No creature, angel or men, can so behave themselves to their fellow-creatures, and yet be free, just, holy, wise, etc. But sure, one creature can deal with his fellow-creature according to the rules and road-way of an antecedent and consequent will; so may the king deal with his people, the governor with those he governs, the father with his children, the commander with his soldiers, the lord of a vineyard with his hired servants; all these may order their goodness, mercy, rewards, punishments, in a way level with the use, industry, improvement of free-will, or the rebellion, unjustice, wickedness and slothfulness of their underlings; but no master nor lord can call labourers to his vineyard, and exhort, obtest, beseech them all to labour, and promise them hire, and yet keep from the greatest part of them the power of stirring arms or

legs,

legs, of free consenting to labour, and suspend his so acting on the greatest part of them, as they shall willingly be carried on to wilful disobedience, and to be the passive objects of his revenging justice, according to the determinate counsel of the lord of this vineyard, because so he willed out of his absolute sovereignty to deal with some, and deal a just contrary way with the least part of the labourers, because he purposed to declare the glory of his grace on them; either there is here an unsearchable depth, or Paul knew nothing: and this calms my mind, and answereth all that reason can say for universal atonement. And the

1st *Use* I aim at, is, That no doctrine so endeareth Christ to a soul, as this of particular redemption and free-grace separating one from another, Psal. cxlvii. 12. *Praise the Lord, O Jerusalem:* and, amongst many grounds, here is one, verse 19. *He sheweth his word unto Jacob, his statutes and his judgments to Israel,* verse 20. *He hath not dealt so with any nation:* And he speaketh not of the measure, as if God had revealed the same grace in nature, but in an inferior degree, to other nations, for he saith, *As for his judgments, they have not known them;* and then, being full of God, for this separating mercy, he addeth, *Praise ye the Lord.* Christ esteems this the flower of grace, the grace of grace, and blesseth his Father for it, Mat. xi. 25. *I bless thee, O Father, Lord of heaven and earth, because thou hast hid these things from the wise and prudent, and hast revealed them to babes.* Now, because Arminians say, The pride of the self-wise, and the humility of babes, are the causes separating the one from the other, and so free-will is to share with the Father in the praise of the revealed glory of the gospel, and the discovered excellency of Christ to babes, rather than to wise men; a literal revelation no doubt was common to all babes and prudent, the swelled Pharisees, and humbled sinners; Christ praiseth the eminency, the blossom of grace, the bloom of free-love, and that the free-will of the humble and the proud made

not

not the separation, but the good pleasure of God, ver. 27. *No man knows the Son but the Father; neither knoweth any man the Father but the Son, and he to whom the Son will reveal him.*

2. That which is common to all, shall never leave an impression of wonder and thankful admiration. (1) and (we) are swelled, lofty and proud things; and the Spirit of God commends grace highly, in that it falls upon pronouns and persons, and not on others, 1 Cor. xv. 9. [Gr. Ego] *I am the least of the apostles,---------ver. 10. By the grace of God I am that I am: and his grace* [Gr. eis eme] *toward me was not in vain; but I laboured more abundantly than they all;* [Gr. houk ego dè] *but not I, but the grace of God* [Gr. he sen emói.] *in me,* Tit. iii. 3. [Gr. Kaì hemeis] *For we ourselves also were sometime out of our wits, disobedient, etc.* ver. 4. *But when the kindness and man-love of God our Saviour appeared,* ver. 5-------[Gr. esosen hemâs] *he saved us,* 1 Tim. i. 15. [Gr. Ego] *I am the chief of sinners;* ver. 16. *But for this cause I obtained mercy,* [Gr. hina en pro ó] *that in me first Jesus Christ might shew forth all long-suffering.* Gal. ii. 20. *I am crucified with Christ, but I live,* [Gr. ouk etì egò] *yet not I, but Christ lives in me.* [Gr. en emoì] *and the life that I now live in the flesh, I live by the faith of the Son of God, who has loved me, and given himself for me;* [Gr. mè huper emû] Ephes. ii. 1. [Gr. Kaì humâs] *And you, who were dead in sins and trespasses, hath he quickned,* ver. 4. *For his great love wherewith he loved us,* [hemâs] ver. 5. *Even when we were dead in sins and trespasses, he hath quickned us* [hemâs] *together with Christ.* ver. 13. *But now in Christ Jesus, ye who sometimes were far off, are made near by the blood of Christ.* The passing by my father and mother, and brother and sister, neighbour and friend, and taking me, is a most endearing favour.

Of all in Scotland and England, all in Europe, all Adam's seed, that ever were masters of a living soul, in the womb or out of it; the Lord passed by so many thousands and millions, and the lot of free-grace fell upon me precisely by name, and upon us, and not u-

pon

pon thousands besides, no less eligible than I was. What thoughts will you have of the free lot of love that fell upon you, ever since God was God, when Christ shall lay such a load of love, such a high weight and mass of loved on you! Ye shall then think, O how came I hither to sit in heavenly places with Christ! That body, that is trimmed, clothed, and doubly embroidered with pure and unmixed glory, is just made of the same lump of earth, with the body of Judas or Cain, that are now flaming and sinking to the bottom of the black and sad river of brimstone. The Lord saith, Ezek. xviii. 4. *Behold, all souls are mine:* and when your soul shall be loaden with glory, and thousands of souls blowing and spitting out blasphemies on the majesty of God, out of the sense of the torment of the gnawing worm that never dies; and ye consider the soul of Judas might have been in my soul's stead, and my soul in the same place of torment that his is now in; what wonder then John cry out, *Behold, what love!*

4. How much love for extension, and intension; for one man, and every one in covenant! Psal. cvi. 45. *Multitudes of mercies,* and Psal. cxxx. 7. *Plenteous redemption;* one David must have *multitudes of tender mercies*, Psal. li. 1. Psal. lxix. 13, 16. 'Tis not one love, but loves, *many loves*, Ezek. xvi. 8. Cant. i. 2. He gives many salvations to one, as if one heaven, and one crown of glory, were not enough; Eph. ii. 4. He is rich in mercy; *and he quickned us, when we were dead in sins*, [Gr. dia pollen agapèn] *For his multiplied love:* every man has a particular act of love, a particular act of atonement bestowed on him. Can ye multiply figures with a pen, and write from the East to the West, and then begin again, and make the heaven of heavens all circular lines of figures; it should weary the arm of angels to write the multiplied loves of Christ. Christ's love desires to engage many: how many millions be there of elect angels and men? Every one of them, for his own part, must have a heaven of love; and Christ thinks it little enough that

the

the first-born's love be on them all, and that they all be first-born: Col. i. 20. *It pleased the Father, by Christ, to reconcile all things in heaven and in earth to himself:* all the angels are Christ's vassals, and he is their head, Col. ii. 10. Then Christ must have two eyes, yea, seven eyes, to see for every one, and two legs for every angel to walk withal; Christ must have a huge host, and numerous troops in his family. (2.) Who then can number the sums of all the debts of free-grace, that angels and men owe Christ, and when they shall be paid? Though sins shall be acquitted, yet debts of undeserved love shall stand for ever and ever. O how unsearchable are the riches of Christ's grace! Know ye, O angels, O glorified spirits, where is the brim, or where is the bottom of free-grace? Yet not one sinner can have less grace than he has, he has need of all; he has no oil to spare, to lend to his neighbour, Mat. xxv. Our deep diseases, and festered wounds, could have no less to cure them, than infinite love, and free-grace, passing all knowledge. It was a broad wound, that required a plaister as long and broad, as infinite Jesus Christ.

Paul bows his knee to the master of the families of heaven and earth, for this act of grace, to weigh the love of Christ, Eph. iii. 18. *I pray* (saith he) *that ye may comprehend, or overtake the love of God.*

2. How many are set on work to compass that love? as if one man could not be able to do it: Yet I pray, that ye with all the saints may comprehend what is the breadth; 'tis broader than the sea, or the earth: and what is the length of it? 'tis longer than between east and west; though ye could measure between the extremity of the highest circle of the heaven of heavens: and then it hath depth and height more than from the centre of the earth to the circle of the moon, and up through all the orbs of the seven planets, and to the orb of stars and highest heavens: who can comprehend either the diameter or circumference of so great a love? Love is an element, that all the elect, men and angels, swim in; the banks of the river swell a-
bove

bove the circle of the sun, to the highest of the highest heavens.

Christ's love in the gospel takes all alive, as a mighty conqueror; his seed for multitude is like the *drops of dew that come out of the womb of the morning*, Psal. cx. And they are the dew of the youth of Christ; for Christ, as a strong and vigorous young man full of strength, who never fails through old age, brings in the forces of the Gentiles, like the flocks of Kedar, Isa. lx. 5, 6.

5. Christ's love outworks hell and devils. Can ye seal up the sun that it cannot rise? or can ye hinder the flowing of the sea? or lay a law upon the winds that they blow not? far less can ye hinder Christ's wilderness to blossom as a rose, or his grace to blow, to flow over banks, or to fly with eagle's wings. O how strong an agent is Christ's love, that bears the sins of the world! John i. 29. It works as fire doth, by nature, rather than by will; and none can bind up Christ's heart, or restrain his bowels, but he must work all to heaven that he has loved.

Use 2. We are hence taught to acknowledge no love to be in God, which is not effectual in doing good to the creature; there is no lip-love, no raw well-wishing to the creature, which God doth not make good. We know but three sorts of love that God has to the creature, all the three are like the fruitful womb; there is no miscarrying, no barrenness in the womb of divine love. 1. He loves all that he has made, so far, as to give them a being, to conserve them in being as long as he pleaseth: he had a desire to have sun, moon, stars, earth, heaven, sea, clouds, air; he created them out of the womb of love, and out of goodness, and keeps them in being; he can hate nothing that he made: now, according to Arminians, he wished a being to many things in their seed and causes, as he wished the earth to be more fruitful before the fall than now it is; so that, against God's will, and his good-will to the creatures, he comes short of that natural antecedent love, that he beareth to creatures: he could have

have wished death never to be, nor sickness, nor old age, (say Arminians) nor barrenness of the earth, nor corruption. Nay, but though these have causes, by rule of justice, in the sins of men, yet we have no cause to say, God falls short of his love, and wished and desired such and such a good to the creature, but things miscarried in his hand; his love was like a mother that conceiveth with many children, but they die in the womb; so God willed and loved the being of many things, but they could not be; the love of God was like the miscarrying womb that parts with the dead child: we cannot acknowledge any such love in God.

2. There is a second love and mercy in God, by which he loves all men and angels, yea, even his enemies; makes the sun to shine on the unjust man, as well as the just, and causeth dew and rain to fall on the orchard and fields of the bloody and deceitful man, *whom the Lord abhors;* as Christ teacheth us, Mat. v. 43, 44, 45, 46, 47, 48. Nor doth God miscarry in this love; he desires the eternal being of damned angels and men; he sends the gospel to many reprobates, and invites them to repentance, and, with longanimity and forbearance, suffereth pieces of forward dust to fill the measure of their iniquity; yet does not the Lord's general love fall short of what he willeth to them.

3. There is a love of special election to glory; far less can God come short in the end of this love: for, 1. The work of redemption prospereth in the hands of Christ, even to the satisfaction of his soul; saving of sinners, (all glory to the Lamb) is a thriving work and successful in Christ's hands, Isa. liii. 10, 11. *He shall see of the travel of his soul, and be satisfied.* 2. Christ cannot shoot at the rovers and miss his mark: I should desire no more, but to be once in Christ's chariot paved with love, Cant. iii. Were I once assured I am within the circle and compass of that love of election, I should not be afraid that the chariot can be broken or turned off its wheels; Christ's chariot can go through the Red-sea, though not dried up: he shoots arrows of love, and cannot miss; he rides through hell and the

grave,

grave, and makes the dead his living captives and prisoners. 3. This love is natively of itself active; Hezekiah saith in his song, Isa. xxxviii. 17. *Behold, for peace I had bitterness, but thou hast in love to my soul (delivered) me from the pit of corruption;* but in Hebrew it is, *Thou hast loved my soul out of the pit of corruption, because thou hast cast all my sins behind thy back:* he speaketh of God's love, as if it were a living man, with flesh and bones, arms, hands, and feet, went down to the pit, and lifted up Hezekiah's soul out of the pit; so has the love of Christ loved us out of hell, or loved hell away to hell, and loved death down to the grave, and loved sin away, and loved us out of the arms of the devil: Christ's love is a pursuing and a conquering thing. I shall never believe that this love of redemption stands so many hundred miles aloof on the shore, and the bank of the river and lake of fire and brimstone, and cries afar off, and wisheth all mankind may come to land and shore, and casteth to them, being so many hundred miles from them, words of milk, wine and honey, out of the gospel, and crieth that Christ loveth all and every one to salvation; and if wishes could make men happy, Christ earnestly wishes and desires, if all men were alike well-minded to their own salvation, that all and every one might be saved, that there were not a hell, but he will not put the tip of his little finger in their heart to bow and incline their will; and Christ crieth to the whole world, perishing in sin, I have shed my blood for you all, and wish you much happiness; but if ye will not come to me to believe, I purpose not to pass over the line of Arminian decency or Jesuitical congruity, nor can I come to you to draw your hearts, by way of efficacious determination; if ye will do for yourselves and your own salvation, the greatest part of the work, which is to apply redemption, by your own free-will (though I know you cannot be masters, of yourselves, of one good thought, and are dead in sins) as I have done the other lesser part, purchased salvation for you, or made you all reconcileable and saveable, 'tis well; otherwise,

I love the salvation of you and every one, but I will not procure it, but leave that to your free-will; chuse fire or water, heaven or hell, as the counsels of your own heart shall lead you; and I have done with you: oh such a love as this could never save me! If the young heir had wisdom, he should pray that the wise tutor lay not on the falling or the standing of the house on his green head, and raw, glassie, and weather-cock free-will; we shall cast down our crowns at the feet of Him that sitteth on the throne, because he has redeemed us out of all nations, tongues, and languages, and left these nations to perish in their own wicked way: sure, in heaven I shall have no Arminian thoughts, as now I have, through corruption of nature; I shall not then divide the song of free redemption between the Lamb and free-will, and give the largest share to free-will: my soul, enter not into their counsels or secrets, who thus black Christ, and shame that fair, spotless and excellent grace of God.

Use 3. Here is excellent ground of encouragement to the elect to believe; for the fear of reprobation from eternity is no ground that thou shouldst not believe.

Object. 1. *I fear that I am a reprobate.*

Answ. If thou wilt know the need that a reprobate man has of that saving Saviour Jesus Christ, thou wouldst upon any terms cast my soul upon Christ; which if thou do, now thou hast answered the question, and removed the fear that thou art a reprobate; for a reprobate cannot believe.

Object. 2. *But sin and unworthiness inclines more to reprobation, than to be loved eternally of God.*

Answ. Not a whit, except the Lord had revealed reprobation to thee; sinful clay, nothing but the great Potter may wash the clay, and frame thee a vessel of honour.

Object. 3. *But sin continued in, such as may sin, is the first morning-dawning of reprobation; as faith, and sorrow for sin, is the first opening of election to glory.*

Answ.

CHRIST DYING AND DRAWING SINNERS TO HIMSELF. 553

Answ. Sin, finally and obstinately continued in, is a sign of reprobation; but say you had obstinately gone on in sin (as I love not to cure spiritual wounds by smoothing and lessening them) yet your duty lies on you, in a sense of your need of Christ, to come to Christ; the event is Christ's. You may say, it is fitting, Lord, I be a reprobate; but many thousands of bad deserving as I am, are singing the praises of free-grace before the throne.

Object. 4. *But, if my sin evidence to me reprobation, it is a cold comfort to go to Christ and believe; for sure, I have obstinately gone on against Christ, and refuted his call.*

Answ. Tho' we are not to lessen the sins of any, yet a physician may say, it is not so desperate a disease as ye say it is; so may we say, it is a strong disease that overcomes the art of Christ; tho' it falls seldom out, never to my observing, that any finally obstinate can attain to wide, broad and anxious wishes to enjoy Christ, with some seen and acknowledged need of Christ.

Object. 5. *But, what encouraging comfort have I to believe, since I have gone further on in obstinacy than any?*

Answ. There cannot be such an encouraging comfort in a non-convert as is satisfactory; no work can be in a non-convert, of that strain with such as are in converts. Ye are not to look for so much in yourself as in others; but he is far behind, who may not follow.

Object. 6. *Nay, I find nothing in me, that may qualify me for Christ.*

Answ. Fit and sufficient qualifications for Christ, is the hire of merit, that we naturally seek in ourselves. Antinomians do not a little injure us, because we teach, That obstinate sinners, as obstinate and proud, are not immediately to believe; not that it is not their duty to believe, but because believing is physically incompatible with these persons that are to believe, since believing is the going of the sinner out of himself to Christ: and a proud, obstinate and rebellious sinner,

never

never broken, nor in no sort humbled, under that reduplication, stays in himself. But, we are far from exhorting any to stand aloof and afar-off from Christ, because they cannot be prepared sufficiently for him, or because they have not a present to bring the King. Yea, come, as ye are bidden, kiss the Son, but tremble and stoop: faith is a lowly thing; merit or hire sufficient, in half or in whole, penny, or penny-worth, to give to Christ, before a sinner come to Christ, or after, we utterly disclaim.

Object. 7. *But, I have low thoughts of Christ, and am afraid he will cast me away; how then can I have low thoughts of myself, and be humbled, ere I believe?*

Answ. There be not any of us, who teach, that saving-humility goeth before faith. It is one thing to be broken and plowed; another to be humble and harrowed; the law must break the rocky ground, ere ye believe; but Christ must break the clods, and harrow and soften the soul; true humiliation followeth faith.

Object 8. *But base thoughts of Christ, which I find in myself, are most contrary to faith; I think Christ not so meek a lamb, as to put a wolf, or tyger, or a leopard in his bosom.*

Answ. Not any, but they have too low thoughts of Christ, ere they can come to him; for the gospel, in whole and in part, is medicine. Christ has a healing tongue; medicine is relative to sickness; Christ would never have said to unbelievers, John vi. 39. *Him that cometh, I will in no way refuse,* if men had not naturally had such thoughts of Christ, as he is rough, and strange, and lordly, and so far from meekness, that he casteth thousands of poor sinners out that come to him; so Christ's tongue, in speaking these words, is good physic: all of us have jealous and strange thoughts of Christ; ye may know the disease by the physic; *contraria contrariis curantur.* The weary and loaden sinners take Christ to be rough, and not meek; therefore saith Christ, *Come unto me, all ye that are weary, and loaden, and*

I

I will ease you: if he be a shepherd, we naturally think, if we cannot go on our own feet, he hath a club to beat us: therefore, Isa. xl. 11. the Lord saith, Not so, he will not beat those that want legs of their own to follow him: *but he shall carry the lambs in his bosom, and gently lead those that are with young.* Yea, if converts and weak ones had not jealousies, ah, Christ is above us, and so lordly, so just, that if we be not as strong as others, he will break us; it had not been prophesied of him, Isa. xli. *A bruised reed shall he not break, a smoking flax shall he not quench.* Now, precious thoughts of Christ ye cannot have, till ye come to Christ, and buy from him a new mind, and new thoughts, without money.

Object. 9. *But believing is fruitless, and unpossible, if I be excluded from the number of those that Christ died for; for then I am to believe remission of sins without shedding of blood; and Christ shed no blood for me.*

Ans. You are neither to lay such a supposition down, that either you are excluded from the number of those that Christ died for, or included in that number; neither of the two are revealed to you, and *secret things belong to the Lord:* it is enough to you, that 1. You are not excluded, for any thing that is revealed to you. 2. That thou hast need of Christ, and art a guilty sinner. 3. That thou art commanded to believe. As for Christ's not shedding of his blood for thee; say it were so, it is no more absurd that you are obliged to believe on Christ, as an all-sufficient Redeemer for remission of sins, (tho' remission be not purchased to you in Christ's blood) than that you are obliged to believe that God will infallibly save you, when as God has peremptorily reprobated you, upon foreseen final impenitency; and has decreed not to work in you to believe, and has not purchased by his blood, the grace of believing; without the which, he seeth believing is unpossible. Let Arminians answer the one doubt, and we can answer the other: only, their way maketh God to say, He willeth the salvation of reprobates; which in very truth, he willeth not: for, it is *protestatio facto con-*
traria:

traria: a will contrary to his dispensation toward them, and so no will: whereas, we acknowledge God, in his promises, commands, charges to be most sincere; and that the promises belong only to the children of the promise, not to the reprobate.

Object. 10. *But, it is unpossible I can be fitted with sorrow for sin or repentance, before I believe in Christ.*

Answ. We teach not, that you must first repent, then believe; or first believe, then repent; but that some legal acts of sorrow, and bruisings of spirit, and self-despair go before faith; then acts of believing, and then evangelic repentance, in seeing by faith, *him whom ye have pierced with your sins*, and the mourning for piercing of him, Zech. xii. 10. But, your need, beggarliness, sinfulness, may well be a spur to chase you to Christ, seeing Christ heightneth his fair grace, by occasion of your black sins, Rom. iii. 5. 20, 22. Rom. iii. 24, 25.

If Christ have such a good will to draw all men; ah! shall he draw all men, and such a fair number of all ranks, and not draw me? Lord Jesus, what ails thee at me? When offices of estate are distributed, and livings and pensions given to men, there be some male-contents; this man is preferred, not I. It were good there were spiritual male-contentedness with self-discontent, at our own rebellion, and no envying of others: O that Christ, who draws all men, would draw me, and he that has love for so many, would out of his love cause me say, *Whither is thy beloved gone, O thou fairest among women? whither is thy beloved turned aside, that we may seek him with thee?* Say there were a free gold-mine in India, that loadeth with gold all ships, and enriches multitudes that go thither, and it hath never drawn thee to make a voyage thither; blame thyself if thou be poor, when many are enriched. 1. Hath not Christ knocked at the door of thy soul, with a rainy head, and frozen locks, and thou hadst rather he should fall into a swoon in the streets, as open to him, and lodge him; and hast had open back-doors for harlot-lovers? O be ashamed of slighting free-love. 2. Despised love turneth into a

flame

flame of gospel-vengeance; a gospel-hell is a hotter furnace, than a law-hell.

No man should spin hell to himself, out of the wool of unbelieving-despair: if Christ be so willing to redeem and draw his own All, and can go as near hell as to save one who had seven devils; have noble and broad thoughts of the sufficiency of Jesus to save. 1. Consider and say, with feeling and warmness of bowels to Christ, All the redeemed family that are standing up before the throne now in white, and are fair and clean, without spot, were once as Black-moors on earth, as I am now: some of them were stables of uncleanness to Satan; now, they are chaste virgins, who defiled not themselves with women, before the Lamb. The mouths that sometimes blasphemed, are now singing the *new song of the Lamb, of Moses the servant of the Lord.* 2. What love is that, that there is a hole in the rock, for ravens of hell to fly into, as doves of heaven; and a chamber of love in the heart of Christ, for pieces of sinful clay? Fair Jesus Christ can love the black daughter of Pharaoh; he has found in his heart to melt in love and tender compassion toward a forlorn Amorite, a polluted Hittite; it breaks his heart to see the naked foundling cast out into the open fields, dying in gored blood: Christ can love where all do lothe. It is much he can love a sinner, thou art but a sinner; he has not blotted thy name out of the New Testament: imagine thou heard him say, *Sinner, come to me; lost man, suffer me to love thee, and to cast my skirt of love over thee:* do but give him an hearty (ay, Lord) consent, and take him at his word. Never rest, till thou be at such a nick of the way to heaven as no backslider can attain to. We are too soon satisfied with our own godliness, and go not one step beyond these that have cast out of themselves one devil, and the next day take in seven new fresh devils, and *the end of these men is worse than their beginning;* they are redeemed, and bought and washen in profession, and righteous in themselves; those that have no more, must fall away. A sheep in the eyes of men,

and

and a sow at the heart, must to the mire again. Sit not down till ye come (1.) To be willing to sell all, and buy the pearl. 2. Till ye attain to some real and personal mortification, that is, a subduing of lusts, a bringing under the body of sin, a heart-deadness to the world, (from this) because your Lord died for you, and has crucified the old-man: I mean not a mortal mortification of Antinomians, to believe Christ has crucified your lusts for you, as if you were obliged, by command of the letter of law and gospel, to no personal mortification, that ye may be saved: never think ye are redeemed, till ye be redeemed from the walking in the way of the present *evil world, from all iniquity, from your vain conversation:* draw not breath, rest not till ye come to this, as ye would not turn back-slider in heart.

Use 7. Redemption believed, maketh men crown Christ as their king; and such to whom Christ is made redemption, must assert and confess Christ a perfect Redeemer, the king of his church. Those that are impatient of his yoke of government, would set another king over Christ, a magistrate, who by office ruleth, not by the word, but by civil laws, testify they are unwilling to have Christ their Lord, in their life, who will not have him their Lord in the church, and his ordinances. The great controversy that God has with England, is slighting religion, the not building the temple, the increase of blasphemies and heresies; fear that Christ reign over them, John xxxiii. *If I be lifted up from the earth, I will draw all men unto me.*

The fourth considerable article in the drawing, is the *terminus ad quem*, the person to whom all men are drawn. It is (saith Christ) [Gr. pros hemauton] to me: this is not a word which might have been spared; as there is no redundancy, nothing more than enough in the gospel, so Christ is no person who may be spared; but whoever be one, Christ must be the first person; take away Christ out of the gospel, and there remained nothing but words; and remove him from the work of redemption, it is but an empty shadow; yea, remove Christ out of heaven, I should not seek to be

there

there. This a noble and divine TO ME, *I will draw all men to Me.* 1. It concerneth us much what we leave. If we leave the earth, it is but a clay footstool, and a mortal perishing stage, and the house of sorrow, and my dying fellow-creature: if we leave sin, we leave hell, the worm that never dieth; vengeance and eternal vengeance is in the womb of sin; to leave father and mother, and all the idols of a fancied happiness, is nothing: but to whom we go; to Christ, or not; to such an one as God, the substantial and eternal delight of God; O that is of high concernment!

2. This (to Me) coming out of the mouth of Jesus Christ, is all and all; 'tis heaven, 'tis glory, 'tis salvation, 'tis new paradise, 'tis the new city, 'tis the new life, 'tis the new precious elect stone laid in Zion, the new glory, the new kingdom: there is a greater emphasis, an edge and marrow of words and things, in this (to Me) than in all the scripture, in all earth and heaven, and all possible and imaginable heavens. 1. Why is Israel loosed? Here the cause, Psal. lxxxi. 11. *Israel would none of me.* Why drink thy rotten waters and cisterns of hell? Oh here is the cause, Jer. ii. 13. *Be astonished, O heavens!* Why? *For my people have committed two evils;* (ah, these two are hundreds, and millions) *they have forsaken me the Fountain of living waters.* Is not Christ crying in all the gospel, *who will have me? Who will receive me?* Is not this the gospel-quarrel, John v. 40. *Ye will not come to me, that ye might have life?* 'Tis no sport to die in sin, 'tis a sad fall to fall into hell, John viii. 21. *Then said Jesus again unto them, I go my way, and ye shall seek me, and shall die in your sins; whither I go, ye cannot come.*

3. If ye look to any other, it cannot save you, but one look on him would make you eternally happy; and you have it, Isa. xlv. 22. *Look unto me, and be saved, all the ends of the earth; for I am God, and there is none else;* come and have heaven for one look, for one turning of your eye: and when destruction com-

eth,

eth, that the church shall be like two or three olive-berries left, and all the rest destroyed; what shall save the remnant? Isa. xvii. 7. *At that day shall a man look to his Maker;* and when Jerusalem is saved, and the Spirit of grace and supplication is poured on the house of David, Zech. xii. 10. *And they shall look upon me whom they have pierced, and they shall mourn for him, as one mourneth for his only son.*

4. You are poor and naked; then saith Christ, Lean and hungry, and ye that want bread, and ye that sweat, and give out money, Isa. lv. 2. *Hearken diligently unto me, and eat ye that which is good, and let your soul delight itself in fatness.* v. 3. *Incline your ear to me, and hear, and your soul shall live; and I will make an everlasting covenant with you, even the sure mercies of David:* then a soul dies a soul's death; he is lean, he eateth dirt, he has no bread, until he comes to Christ, Rev. iii. 18. *I counsel thee to buy of me.* O this noble Me! this brave, celebrious, this glorious Me! *I counsel thee to buy of Me* (and not of others, who are but cozening hucksters) *gold tried in the fire;* gold buyeth all things, and is not bought: but this is not a common merchant; *and buy of me white raiment, that thou mayest be clothed.* But thou mayest have a burden on thee heavier than thy back or bones can stand under; then hear him, Mat. xi. 18. *Come unto me, all ye that labour and are laden, and I will give you rest:* and because all are thirsty for some happiness, the desires are gaping for some heaven, Christ crieth at Jerusalem with a loud voice, with a good-will to save, John vii. 27. *If any man thirst, let him come to me, and drink.* John xi. 26. *He that liveth, and believeth in me, shall never die.*

5. What greater reason than to hear this, Cant. v. 2. *Open to me, my sister, my dove, my love, my undefiled!* And wisdom's voice is sweet, Prov. vii. 14. *Hearken unto me therefore, O ye children, and attend to the words of my mouth.* Isa. xlix. 1. *Listen, O isles, to me;* so he speaketh to his redeemed, Isa. xlviii. 16. *Come ye near to me.* And,

6. There

CHRIST DYING AND DRAWING SINNERS TO HIMSELF.

6. There is nothing more fitting than that his oath stand, that the knee that will not bow to him shall break, Isa. xlv. 23. *I have sworn by myself.* Rom. xiv. 11. *For it is written, As I live (saith the Lord) every knee shall bow to me, and every tongue shall confess to God.*

7. What greater honour can be, than such alliance? than that Christ speak so to his bride, Hos. iii. 3. *And I said unto her, Thou shalt abide for me many days, thou shalt not play the harlot, and thou shalt not be for another man, so will I be for thee;* and Hos. ii. 19. *And I will betrothe thee unto me for ever; yea, I will betrothe thee unto me;* v. 20. *I will even betrothe thee unto me in faithfulness.*

8. In him is that which may be ground of faith and confidence, Luke x. 22. *All things are delivered to me of my Father.* Mat. xxviii. 19. *All power is given to me in heaven and in earth:* there is a great trust put upon Christ, John xvii. 6. *Thine they were, and thou gavest them me.* Heb. ii. 13. *Behold, I, and the children that God hath given me.* Luke xxii. 29. *The Father has appointed a kingdom* to Me.

This *(to Me)* hath yet a greater edge and fulness of Christ's soul-taking and drawing expressions: *1st,* To Christ, we are drawn as to a friend; approaching to Christ, is expressed by coming to him. 1. We come to him, as to our home: the man that cometh to Christ, is in a friend's house; Christ will not cast him out, John vi. 39. The man may throw down his loads and burdens, and cast himself and his burden on him, and find rest for his soul; he doth not stand, nor run any more, but sit down under the shadow of the tree of life, Cant. ii. 3. *I sat down under his shadow with great delight;* Hebrew, *I lusted or desired him, and sat down, and his fruit was sweet in my mouth.* And how did Christ take with the soul? O most kindly! v. 4. *He led me into a house of wine.* What do you think of a house of joy? Every stone, every rafter, every piece of covering, wall, and floor, is the cheering consolation of the Holy Ghost; and what further? *His banner over me is love;* the colours and ensign of this christian, is, The love of Christ, v. 6. And what

what love-rest is here? *His left-hand is under my head, and his right-hand doth embrace me.* What a bed of love must that be, to lie in a corner, in a circle infolded in the two everlasting arms? The left arm is near the heart: such a soul must lie with heart and head upon the breast and heart of Jesus Christ; and above, and underneath for pillow, for covering, for curtains, arms of everlasting love: an house all made, within and without, of eternal joy and consolations, is incomparable; such a chamber of a king, such colours and hangings as love, such a bed as the embracings of Christ, you never heard of.

2. Life is the sweetest flower of any being, it is a taking thing now, 1 John v. 12. *He that hath the Son, hath life;* all out of Christ are dead men: so we come to Christ as our life, 1 Pet. ii. 4. *To whom coming as to a living stone, disallowed indeed of men;* but that's no matter; *chosen of God, and precious.* Where read we, but here, of a stone with life, and so noble a life as an intellectual life, and then the life of God? O death, come to thy life, that *is hid with Christ in God,* Col. iii. 3. Here a breathing living stone, and then a chosen one, of great price. Should all the crowned kings since Adam to the dissolving of this world, sell themselves, their globe of the earth, and all their precious stones, they should not buy a day's glory in heaven; but say that they should sell the earth and the heavens, and oppignorate or lay in pledge sun and moon and stars, if they were their moveable inheritance, and sell them all millions of times, they should be far from any comparable buying of the elect precious stone that is digged out of mount Sion, Job xxviii. 13. *Man knoweth not the price of wisdom,* of this wisdom. Ver. 18. *No mention shall be made of corals or of pearls; for the price of wisdom is above rubies.* ver. 19. *The topaz of Ethiopia shall not equal it, neither shall it be valued with pure gold;* there's no talking, no bidding in this market, so precious is the stone; but 'tis the stone living and breathing out heaven, and God infinitely more excellent than heaven.

3. To

3. To Me (saith Christ) because no excellency can be comparable to him, who only can give God to the sinner, John xiv. 6. *No man cometh to the Father, but by me;* it must be an incomparable privilege to come by Jesus Christ, to God. GOD, GOD is All in all; I cannot savingly be drawn to any but to him, who can reveal God to me. Christ is the bosom, the heart, the only new and living way and door to God; all creatures, angels, men, saints, are strangers to God. The substantial, the essential, the living intellectual image, and being, God must reveal God. Christ saith to Philip, John xiv. 9. *He that hath seen me, hath seen the Father:* open Christ, and you open God; enjoy Christ, and you enjoy God; come into Christ, and you come to a new world, to a new all, to a new infinite ocean, and you fall in the bosom of a Godhead.

4. To me] as to all perfection and compleatness of fulness; they are but all streams and shadows, and emptiness, while you come to Christ; poor nothing is an empty bottom to a sinner, John i. 16. *Out of his fulness have all we received, even grace for grace;* this is fountain fulness, God's fulness, Col. ii. 9. For in Christ is fulness itself. 2. Not fulness going and coming; there is a fulness in the sea, but it is ebbing and flowing; a fulness in the moon, but decreasing and growing; a fulness in the creature, but going and coming, up and down: but in Christ there dwelleth a fulness; it is with Christ new moon and full moon, and dawning, and noon day all at once. 3. All fulness dwelleth in Christ: there is fulness of beauty in Absalom, but not of truth and sincerity; fulness of wisdom in Solomon, but not fulness of constancy; he gave his heart to pleasure and folly; fulness of policy in Achitophel, but not fulness of holiness and faithfulness to his prince; yea, it was fulness of folly to hang himself; fulness of strength in Samson, but not fulness of faith and soundness and courage of mind; he was strong in body, but soft and impotent in mind, and was overcome by a woman; there is an Hiatus, a hole

and

and some emptiness in every creature: and angel's fulness fitteth neighbour to pure nothing; the angel may be turned into nothing, and is by nature capable of folly: but in Christ there is all fulness. 4. But, as every fulness is not all fulness, so every fulness is not the fulness of the Godhead; then, to Me] it is as much as the elect are drawn to Christ, as the choicest, the rarest amongst all.

2. So, amongst all choice things and all relations, he is the first, and most eminent and glorious. Among kings, Rev. i. 5. *The Prince of the kings of the earth;* Rev. xix. 16. *The King of kings, the Lord of lords;* among prophets, the *Prophet, raised out of the inward part of the brethren,* Deut. xviii. 18. Among priests, the highest and greatest, the eternal Priest, *after the order of Melchizedeck,* Heb. iii. 1. Heb. vii. 17. Among gods, he stands, he's alone *the only wise God,* 1 Tim. i. 17. Among angels, *the Angel of the Lord's substantial presence, the archangel, the head of angels,* Isa. lxiii. 9. 1 Thess. iv. 16. Col. ii. 10. Among beautiful things, *the Flower of Jesse, the Rose of Sharon, the Lily of the valleys, fairer than the children of men,* Isa. xi. 11. Cant. ii. 1. Psal. xlv. 2. There is such grace created in no lips, yea, uncreated grace is in no face, but in his only; among shepherds, *the chief Shepherd,* 1 Pet. v. 4. Among armies, the *Standard-bearer, and chief among ten thousand,* Cant. v. 10. Amongst creatures, *the first-born of every creature,* Col. i. 15. Amongst heirs, *the heir of all things,* Heb. i. 2. Among *those that were dead, and is alive again,* and the fruit that groweth out of death; *Christ is the first born from the dead,* Col. i. 18. and *the first fruits of them that sleep,* 1 Cor. xv. 20. Among sons, he is God's *first begotten Son,* Heb. i. 6. *his only begotten Son,* 1 John iv. 9. Among saviours, none to be named a Saviour under heaven but he only, Acts iv. 12. *Neither is there salvation in any other:* the first among brethren, Rom. viii. 29. *the first-born among many brethren.* In a word, He is the choice and the first of the flock, the flower, the first glory, the standard-

bearer

bearer of heaven, the heart, the rose, the prime delight of heaven, the choicest of heaven and earth, the none-such, the chief of all beloveds. Some have one single excellency, some another; Abraham was excellent in faith, Moses in his choice of Christ above all the treasures of Egypt; David in his sincerity, having a heart like God's heart: but Christ hath all eminency of grace in one. Some are gods, that shall die as men; Christ the Prince of life was dead, but can die no more: some are wise, but he is wisdom itself: some are fair, but Christ is the beauty and brightness of the Father's glory. We are apt to have low and creeping thoughts of Jesus Christ, and to undervalue Christ.

3. There's need of an angel-engine framed in heaven, of a tongue immediately created by God, and by the infinite art of omnipotency, above other tongues, to speak of the praises of Christ; and that pen must be moulded of God, and the ink made of the river of the water of life, and the paper fairer than the body of the sun, and the heart as pure and innocent as sinless angels, who should write a book of the virtue and super-eminent excellency of Jesus Christ: all works, even uttered by prophets and apostles, come short of Christ. Imagine that angels and men, and millions of created heavens of more than now are, should build a temple, and a high seat or throne of glory, raised from the earth to the highest circumference of the heaven of heavens, and millions of miles above that highest of heavens, and let the timber not be cedar or almug trees, nor the inside gold of Ophir seven times refined, but such trees as should grow out of the banks of the pure river of water of life, that runneth through the street of the New Jerusalem, and overlaid with a new sort of gold that was found above the sun and stars, many degrees above the gold of Ophir; and let the stone not be marble, nor sapphires, nor rubies, nor digged out of the excellentest earth imaginable, but more refined than elementary nature can furnish; let every stone be a star, or a piece of the body of the

sun

sun, and let the whole fabric of the house exceed the glory of Solomon's temple, as far as all precious stones exceed the mire in the streets; and let Jesus Christ sit above in the highest seat of glory in this temple, as he dwelt in Solomon's temple; the chair should be but a created shadow, too low and too base for him. This is not yet like the Lord's expression by the apostle, shewing how eminent and high Christ is, Phil ii. 9. *Wherefore God also hath more than exalted him;* he saith not, [Gr. ho Theòs autòn hupsose,] God hath heighted or exalted Christ; but God hath [Gr. huperupsose] over-heighted and super-exalted him, and hath gifted to him [Gr. hónoma tò huper pân onoma] *a name above all names,* that is, real honour above all expression, above all thoughts: if such a temple and seat of majesty might be named, it should not be above every name, nor a glory above every glory that can be named, *either in this world, or in the world to come.*

To me] conversion is the drawing of a sinner to Christ, 'tis a supernatural journey, 'tis not a common way to come to this eternal wisdom of God, as saith Job. xxviii. 7. *A path which no fowl knoweth, and the vulture's eye hath not seen: where is the place of understanding?* ver. 21. *Seeing it is hid from all living, and kept close from the fowls of the air.* Verse 22. *Destruction and death say, We have heard the fame thereof with our ears.* Verse 23. *Where is it then?* Nature's dark candle cannot shew it. Verse 24. *God understandeth the way thereof, and he knoweth the place thereof.* Prov. xv. 24. *The way of life is on high;* the way of the life of all excellent lives, is an high and an exalted way, every man knows it not.

2. Christ saith, by way of exclusion, that he getteth not one soul to him, but by strong hand and violence; never man comes to Christ on his own clay-legs, and with the strength of his own good-will, John vi. 44. *No man can come to me, except the Father, which hath sent me, draw him.*

3. There be other acts of God, of an high reach, in these that come to Christ; as there must be resigning

over,

over, a making over of the Father to the Son, ver. 29. *All that the Father giveth me, shall come:* the Father's making over of any soul, or his giving one to Christ, is not by way of alienation, as if the man belonged no more to the Father, or were no more under the tutory and guidance of the Father, but under the Son. Famulists teach us, 'That there be distinct seasons of the working of the several persons of the Trinity, so as the soul may be said to be so long under the Father's, and not the Son's; and so long under the Son's work, and not the Spirit's.'

We know no such distinct posts to heaven, nor such shifting from hand to hand; the saints have many bouts in their way to glory, but all the Three jointly at the same season help at the lifting of the dead out of the graves, John vi. 39, 44, 45. John v. 24, 25. All the Three, in one dead lift, open blind eyes, and convert lost sinners, Matth. xi. 25, 26, 27. Eph. i. 17, 18. Matth. xvi. 17. John xii. 32. 2 Cor. iii. 14, 15, 16, 17. John xiv. 23. John xvi. 7, 8, 9, 10. John xiv. 16. Eph. ii. 1, 2, 3, 4. 1 John ii. 27. 1 John v. 6, 7. *Grace, mercy, and peace,* cometh at the same season, to the *seven churches,* from all the Three; *from Him which is, and which was, and which is to come, and from the seven Spirits that are before the throne, and from Jesus Christ, who is the faithful Witness,* etc. 2 Cor. xiii. 14. Rev. i. 4, 5. Then the Father so giveth the elect to the Son, as I should not desire to be out from under the care and tutory of the Father; the Father maketh them over, and keepeth them in his own bowels, and in the truth, John xvii. 2, 10, 11. So there is the Father's teaching, and the hearing and learning from the Father, John vi. 45. *It is written in the prophets, And they shall all be taught of God: every man therefore that hath heard, and hath learned of the Father, cometh unto me.*

In the uses of the doctrine, I have three things to speak of; 1. What a sin they be under, who resist the right-arm of the Father. 2. What free-will and moral honesty can do, or how nothing they are, to work a communion with God. 3. These are to be refuted,

who

who think we are neither to pray, nor to do, to *work out our salvation in fear and trembling,* but when the Lord by saving grace acteth in us, and draweth irresistibly. Now, to the end that this common gospel-sin may be the better seen in all its spots, consider, 1. What is in Christ the Drawer. 2. What is in grace, by which sinners are drawn.

    1. In Christ the Drawer. There be many drawers suiting us: the world is the *tail of the great red dragon, and his tail drew the third part of the stars of heaven, and did cast them down to the earth,* Rev. xii. 4. Glorious professors, like glistering stars up in heaven, are drawn away after the dirty world. Should there be more power in Satan's tail to draw down stars from heaven, than there is beauty and sweetness in Christ's face to ravish hearts, *and are drawn away, and worship other gods, and serve them;* yet they are but bastard-gods: Christ has a true, real Godhead in himself. Why will you not be drawn after the smell of his precious ointments? And, Acts v. 37. *Judas of Galilee arose, and drew away much people after him,* and they were destroyed. And, Jam. i. 14. *Every tempted man* (and who is not tempted?) *is drawn away of his own lust;* and this is a mother with child of death and hell: supposed goodness is an angle, a vast net, that draws millions of souls to eternal perdition; every man has a soul-drawer about him, devils and false teachers are pulling at and hailing souls. O be drawn by Christ; he is the rose without a thorn, the sun without a cloud, the beauty of the Godhead without a spot, he draws his Father's heart to love him, and delight in him: Christ's love, and the art of free-grace, are good at drawing of souls: there is not a soul-drawer comparable to him: ah! our hearts are as heavy as hell; suppose that hell were of the bigness of ten worlds, all of sand, iron or the heaviest stones in the world: nay, all fancies that pretend loveliness are but lies, and Christ true; every piece of fair clay is hell, and
Christ

Christ heaven; every beauty blackness, and he all loves, Cant. v. 16.

2. For alluring souls in a moral way, nothing like Christ in the gospel; David is called by the Holy Ghost, *the sweet singer of Israel:* when Christ speaketh to hearts, he sings like heaven, and like the glory of a new unseen world. Deut. xxxii. 16. Joseph was blessed of the Lord, *for the good-will of him that dwelt in the bush:* 'Tis most alluring in Christ, that he is the bird in the bush, the bird of paradise, the turtle in our land, Cant. ii. 12. that singeth the sweet gospel-hymns, and psalms of good tidings from Sion, peace, peace from heaven to the broken-hearted mourners in Sion; all the gospel is a love-song of Christ dying for love to enjoy sinners of clay, and to have them with him in heaven. Are not these love-songs of the bird whose nest was in the bush? *If any man thirst* (saith Christ) *let him come to me and drink; and whosoever will, let him take of the water of life freely.* If this cannot draw to Christ, the law, curses, rewards, cannot draw; Christ pipeth a spring of joyful news, but few dance, Mat. xi. 16.

3. The lower that high love descendeth, the sweeter and the more drawing, and the greater guiltiness not to be drawn. Christ came down from a Godhead, and emptied himself for us, *to be a worm, and no man,* Psal. xxii. 6. *The last of men,* Isa. liii. 3. a doubt it was, if he were in the number of men, and so the word importeth; *and he dwelt in the bush;* he made not his nest among cedars, but in the bush [Heb. Seneh] a bush whence cometh Sinah or a desert and wilderness, such as was in Arabia. Christ taketh it hard, and weepeth for it, Mat. xxiii. 37. Luke xix. 42. that he came down as a hen in the bush, (O but Christ has broad wings, far above the eagle!) and would have made sinners in Jerusalem his young ones, to nourish them with heat, from his own bosom and heart; but they would not be drawn: and when he appeareth in a time of captivity, Zech. i. to save his people out of captivity, many would not be saved; he is seen, ver.8. *amongst the myrtle-trees in the bottom.* It is true, the myrtle-tree

is far above the briar and the thorn, Isa. lv. 13. Yet 'tis as much, as Christ dwells among the bushes, and came down to the lowest plants; for the myrtle is a bush rather than a tree, and grows in valleys, deserts, in the sea-shore: Christ is a young low plant, and *a root out of a dry ground.* 'Tis a matter of challenge, that none believed his report, and few were drawn by the Lord Jesus, who is God's arm; all the strength of God, and the drawing power of grace being in Christ, and in Christ who came down so low in his love to us. Low, stooping love refused, is a great deal of guiltiness; salvation itself cannot save, when love, submitting itself to hell, to death, to shame, to the grave, cannot save you think little to let a love-song of the gospel four times a week pass by you; but you know not what a guiltiness it is.

4. The greater the happiness you are drawn to, the higher is the sin. Should Christ draw you to the mount burning with fire, to the law-curses, to the terrible sight of the fiery indignation of God, men would say it were less sin to refuse him; but he draws you, Heb.xii. 22. *To mount Sion, to the city of the living God, the heavenly Jerusalem, and to an innumerable company of angels, to the general assembly and church of the first-born, which are written in heaven, and to God the Judge of all, and to the spirits of just men made perfect; and to Jesus the Mediator of the new covenant, and to the blood of sprinkling.* And he addeth, *Despise not this;* he is a speaker from heaven: 'tis but one house, one family, which is in earth and heaven; they differ but as elder and younger brethren. Paul, Rom. xvi. 7. putteth a note of respect on Andronicus and Junia, *Who* (saith he) *also were in Christ before me.* There is more honour put on them that are in glory before us, than on us: as the first-born of nature and grace, so the first-born of glory are honoured before us (we should not weep for our friend's crown and honour, when they die) yet they be all one house; then to be drawn to Christ is to be drawn to heaven. He should deservedly weep for ever, and gnash his teeth

in

in hell, who in right-down terms refuseth to be drawn to heaven.

There is another ground of shewing what a high provocation it is, to resist the gospel-drawings of Christ's arm, and it is the way of resisting the operation of grace. Interpreters say on the text, that Christ's drawing, when he is lifted upon the cross, is a clear allusion to the manner of Christ's crucifying; for he, with is two arms stretched out, holdeth out his breast, openeth his bosom and heart, and crieth, Who will come and lodge in Christ's heart? And again, favours profered by a great friend in his death, ought not to be refused; and the sour tree of the cross was Christ's dead-bed; here he made his last will: and, which no dying friend doth, Christ dying, left his heart, and bowels of tender love to his dear friends; he died drawing and pulling in sinners to his heart. What a sin must it be, to meet his love with hatred and disdain? 2. Grace moveth in a circle of life, the spring and fountain is the heart of Christ, and it reflecteth back to Christ's heart; he resteth not with stretched-out arms, to pull, while he have his friends and church in at his heart. 3. The motion of free-grace is a subduing and conquering thing, and strong to captivate our love: when you see Christ dying and leaping for joy to die for you, and when ye see him set on his head a cup of thick wrath, of death and hell, and see him smile and sing, and sigh and drink hell and death for you, it layeth bands of love on the heart. What iron bowels must we have, who would break the cup on his face, and despise his love? Grace applied to the heart maketh it ingenuous, free, thankful; how can the sinner withhold his love, without the greatest guiltiness that ever devils committed? for they cannot resist Christ's drawing-love. O what sweetness of strongest and captivating love, to see Christ and the tear in his eye, and his *face foul with weeping,* and his *visage more marred than any of the sons of men,* Isa. lii. 14. and a flood of blood on his body, Luke xxii. 44. and yet good-will, and joy, and delight to do and suffer God's will for us, sitting on on his brows, Psal. xl. 6, 7, 8. Heb. x. 5, 6, 7. Now, when Christ is burnt up with love, and sick of tender kindness; to cast water on this love, by resisting it, is the highest gospel sin that can be, except despiting of the Holy Ghost. And a third ground of aggravating to the full, this sin of resisting Christ's drawing, I take from the judgment and the plague and gospel-vengeance on such as Christ draweth, and they will not be drawn, and is the sin of the times: I refer these to two heads.

1. This gospel-despising of Christ, now reigning in the age and kingdoms that we now live in, cometh near to the borders of the sin against the Holy Ghost; for the more men be convinced and enlightned, if they be not drawn to Christ, they are the nearer to this sin, Heb. vi. 4, 5. Chap. x. 26, 27. Now, may we not think hardly of these who are convinced of many gospel-truths, and yet oppose them? Doth not Christ's love come near them, and they flee from it? Now, but to neighbour or border on the coasts of a sin, like to the sin against the Holy Ghost, may cost men as dear as the loss of their soul, and the next furnace for torment and pain, to these that sin against the Holy Ghost.

2. The temporal plague that cometh nearest eternal, is the judgment of God on the Jews that refused and resisted Christ: see what expression is put on the last judgment, that same is on the judgment of Jerusalem's destruction for resisting Christ: for, 1. It is hell-like, when mothers shall wish their children had never been born; and when they shall, as damned, in the day of judgment, pray, *Mountains fall on us, and hills cover us*, Luke xxiii. 29, 30.

Use 2. If Christ draw all men to him, then they are far wide, who think, that free-will and moral honesty can bring men to heaven; there be no moralists in heaven, who were pure moralists on earth, and had nothing of the gospel-drawing, and of supernatural work in them: civil saints can never be glorified saints; thousands are deceived with this: they think their lamp can shew them light to know the bridegroom's

cham-

chamber-door. But take these for marks of deluded men;

1. Such men will shout and cry at adultery, as he that took Abraham's wife from him: and a Cain may be madded with murdering his brother; but was Cain touched for gospel-sins? Is Judas wakened in conscience for that which is the special condemning gospel-sin, the cause of condemnation and dying in sin, John iii. 36. John xvi. 9. Chap. viii. 24. No, but for murdering his master: it is the light of the Spirit that seeth spiritual sins spiritually.

2. Profession looketh like paradise and the rainbow; it is big in its own eyes, and the fairest for variety of colours; but it is a self-plague, and doth carry millions of souls to hell, without din and noise of feet; it is Christ acting judicially on the hypocrite, within pistol-shot of a besieged soul, making fireworks under the earth; and when all within are sleeping, Christ springeth a powder-mine, and burneth up all forward: gospel-fire-works make more than ordinary fury in the soul: open, open to Christ; multiplied fastings, and taking Christ's crown from him, are dreadful.

3. They had never a sick night for the want of Christ: gospel-profession is a light to let men see to sin, a candle to let men see to go to hell, and lie down in sorrow with art. Ah! what comfort is it, that I go to hell, no man seeing me, and by stealth, and my back to the pit? What a poor comfort, to go to eternal perdition, fasting and praying monthly, multiplying days of thanksgiving, and withal, plundering Christ of his royal crown, following the sins of prelates, whom God cast out before us, exercising rapine and unjustice, giving new laws to Christ, and planting plants, which God will root out? The manner of perishing is a poor accident of death. O but heart-boiling of love, a faint pulse, a pale and a lean sinner dying for the absence of Christ, no man but the spirit and physician knoweth what ails him, are sweet diseases. Let the love of Christ absent be in the man's soul a deep river. How sweet were it to be drowned

in

in that river, and to die an hundred deaths in one day, because he whom the soul loves is gone away! O watchmen, know you not where he is? O daughters of Jerusalem, *can you tell him that I am sick of love?* O shepherds, where is Christ's tent? where dwells he? What is profession to this? a shadow, a straw, nothing, vanity.

2. What a deceitful thing is it, to make free-will the great idol, and to hire a house in heaven for the income and rent of merit? Can it be imagined, that the love of Christ can be hired? so much as it should have of hire, so much it should want of free-love: how can the heart of God be taken with the merit of man? Grace is the flower, and the freeness of grace like the beautiful bloom of the flower; and this freeness is so taking, that it lays bands and chains on the heart: were there a good deserving in the man to buy grace, the cord should be as a single and untwisted thread.

Use 3. Christ so draws all men to him, that drawn man's will is not forced, as we have seen; and therefore Libertines err foully, who make the drawn party, blocks and stones, and meer patients: hence these positions of Famulists and Libertines.

(a) 1. "In the saving and gracious conversion of a sinner, the faculties of the soul, and the working thereof, in things pertaining to God, are destroyed, and made to cease.

"*(b)* 2. And, instead of these, the Holy Ghost doth come and take place, and doth all the works of these natural faculties, as the faculties of the human nature of Christ do.

"3. The *(c)* new creature, or the new man mentioned in scripture, is not meant of grace, but of Christ.

"4. Christ

(a) A short story of the rise, reign and ruin of the Antinomians, etc. Error 1. page 1.
(b) Rise, reign, Er. 2. p. 1.
(c) Rise, reign, Er. 7. p. 2.

CHRIST DYING AND DRAWING SINNERS TO HIMSELF.

"4. Christ (d) worketh in the regenerate, as in those that are dead, and not as in those that are alive; or, the regenerate, after conversion, are altogether dead to spiritual acts.

"5. There (e) is no inherent righteousness in the saints, or grace, or graces are not in the souls of believers, but grace in Christ himself working in us; who are mere patients in all supernatural works.

"6. Faith, repentance (f) new obedience, are gifts, not graces-----all the elect are saved, and receive the kingdom, as little children do their father's inheritance, passively. Mr. Towne saith, in sanctification as well as in justification, we are mere patients, and can do nothing at all. Assertion of grace, p. 11, 68.

"7. The Spirit (g) doth not work in hypocrites by gifts and graces, but in God's children immediately.

"8. We may not (h) pray for gifts and graces, but only for Christ.

"9. The efficacy (i) of Christ's death, is to kill all activity of graces in his members, that the might act all in all.

"10. All the activity of a (k) believer, is to act sin.

"11. We are not bound (l) to keep a constant course of prayer in our families, or privately, unless the Spirit stir up thereunto.

"12. If Christ will (m) let me sin, let him look to it, upon his honour be it.

"13.

(d) Rise, Reign, Er. 14. p. 3. (e) Rise, Reign, Er. 15. p. 3. (f) Ro. Towne's assertion of grace, p. 11, 12. (g) Rise, Reign, Er. 18. p. 4. (h) Rise, Reign, Er. 23. p. 5. (i) Rise, Reign, Er. 35. p. 7. (k) Rise, Reign, Er. 36. p. 7. (l) Rise, Reign, Er. 49. p. 9. (m) Rise and Reign, unsavoury speech, 4. p. 19.

"13. The new heart, and the walking in (n) God's commandments are no condition of the covenant of grace: where is there one word, that God saith to man, Thou shalt do this? If God had put man upon these things, then they were conditions indeed; but when God takes all upon himself, where are then the conditions on man's part?-----------If there be a condition, he that undertaketh all things in the covenant, must needs be in the fault: *If the Lord work not in us a clean heart, and cause us not walk in his commandments, 'tis then the Lord's fault* (absit blasphemia) *if we sin against the covenant.*

"14. The (o) blessedness of a man, is only passive, not active, in his holy and unblameable walking."

To the end that these errors may the more fully be discovered, we are to enquire, in these assertions, what activity we have in works of grace.

Asser. 1. In the first moment of our conversion, called *actus primus conversionis*, we are mere patients,

1. Because the infusion of the new heart, Ezek. xxxvi. 26. the pouring of the *Spirit of grace* and supplication on the family of David, Zech. xii. 10. and of *the Spirit on the thirsty ground*, Isa. xliv. 3. is a work of creation, Eph. ii. 10. Psal. xv. 10. *a quickning of the dead.* Eph. ii. 1, 2, 3, 4. John v. 25. 2 Cor. iv. 6. and the wilderness is not here a co-agent for the causing roses to blossom out of the earth.

2. The effect is not wholly denied of the collateral

cause,

(n) D. Crispe's Christ alone exalted, Sermon 6. of the N. covenant, pag. 163, 164. The life and light of man, chap. 1. p. 4. The will, mind and end of the internal operative Spirit, and life, is to be a living active Lord God in a dead passive creature; as, I live, yet not I, but Christ liveth in me.

(o) Ro. Towne's assertion of grace, against Dr. Taylor, pag. 47, 48, 49.

cause, and ascribed wholly to another. If Peter and John draw a ship between them, with joint strength, you cannot say, the one drew the ship and not the other: but Christ said, *flesh and blood* maketh no revelations of Christ, *but his Father* only, Mat. xvi. 17. Mat xi. 25, 26, 27. Jam. i. 18. John i. 18. Then *neither blood, nor the will of man,* contribute any active influence to the first framing of the new birth; nor can clay divide the glory of regeneration, with the God of grace, *who maketh all things new.*

Asser. 2. The soul or its faculties are not destroyed in conversion: Peter's will which he had when he was young, was the same when converted, but renewed, John xxi. 18. The saints, that Peter writeth to, are *not to run to the same excess of riot,* as of old, when *they wrought the will of the Gentiles,* 1 Pet. iv. 3, 4. Paul and Titus were the same men, when *disobedient and serving divers lusts,* and when converted, and now washen, regenerated, and justified heirs, Tit. iii. 1, 2, 3, 4. Paul the same man, a persecutor, and an apostle; but grace made a change, 1 Cor. xv. 9, 10. The same mind and spirit remaineth in nature; but they *are renewed in the spirit of the mind,* Rom. xii. 2. Eph. iv. 23. It is the same heart, but *turned to the Lord,* 2 Cor. iii. 15, 16. Christ but removeth the scum, and the dross, and the false metal, and frames the man a new vessel of mercy.

Asser. 3. The person of the Holy Ghost is not united to the soul of a believer, nor are there two persons here united or made one spirit by union of person with person; but the person is said to come to the saints, and to dwell with them, and *to be in them,* John xiv. 16, 17. and *God hath sent the Spirit of his Son in our hearts, crying, Abba Father:* not that the Holy Ghost, in proper person, doth in us formally, and immediately believe, pray, love, repent, etc. we being mere patients, in understanding, will, affections, memory, as Libertines teach: but the Holy Ghost cometh to the saints,

and

and dwelleth in them, in the spiritual gifts, and saving graces, and supernatural qualities created in us, by the Holy Spirit, and acted, excited, and moved as supernatural and heavenly habits, to act with the vital influence of our understanding, will, and affections.

I prove the former part: 1. Because such an union of the person of the Holy Ghost in us, believing, loving, joying, praying, and immediately in us, were that blasphemous deifying and godding of the saints†, so as believing, loving, praying, were not our works, but the immediate acts of the Holy Ghost; and either the faint manner of believing, or the cold slacked loving, and praying of saints, or their not-believing, and sinful omission of the acts of faith, love, praying, rejoicing, could not be more imputed to saints, as their sinful defects, and transgressions, (but must be laid on the Holy Ghost's score) than we can impute the splitting of a ship, to the ship itself, and not to the negligent and wilful pilot, who of purpose dasheth the vessel on a rock: but we must not in reason blame the ship, but the pilot; for the loss of the ship, is the only and proper fault of the man that steered the ship, and the ship is innocent and harmless timber: now, what sin can be in the saints in these supernatural acts, if the Holy Ghost immediately in his own person, steer the helm, and only without us, act these in us? We might with as good reason say, The shop that a man worketh in, doth make the portrait, which is a great untruth, since the artificer in the shop doth it, as say that the saints do pray, believe, rejoice, if the Holy Ghost immediately do all these in them, as in a shop.

2.

---

†Henry Nicholas a German, a blasphemous Libertine, saith, c. 34. Sent. 10. "God hath raised up me H. N. the least among the holy ones of God, which lay altogether dead, and without breath and life among the dead, from the death, and made me alive through Christ; as also anointed me with his godly being, meaned himself with me, and godded me with him, etc."

2. Upon the same ground, the Lord's coming down and filling John Baptist from his mother's womb, and the apostles and Stephen full of the Holy Ghost, should be the Holy Ghost's personal filling of them, and his immediate acting in them, without any action of them, in preaching, praying, and their heavenly bold confessing of Christ before men; and there should be no difference between the ark and temple of Jerusalem, filled with the immediate presence of God, in the Lord's manifestation of his glory there, and these saints filled with God, in these works of free-grace. I shall not believe that the person of God can be said to be united to either ark, temple, apostle, or martyr; all the union is in the effects and manifestations of graces, or tokens of divine presence, which are creatures rising and falling with time.

3. That excellent and living ark, the most glorious and admirable thing that heaven hath, the Lord Jesus, is God and man, two natures united in one person. But both the word of God making that HE, that same holy thing, *born of the Virgin Mary, the Son of God*, Luke i. 35. and that same He, and person, who came of the Jews, *according to the flesh, to be God blessed for ever*, Rom. ix. 5. Heb. vii. 3. Mat. xvi. 13, 16. And the third general council, called that of Ephesus, and after the council of Chalcedone, verses 4 and 5, do evidence to us, that *Christ cannot be two persons*, as Nestorius dreamed, and one person. Paul spread the gospel from Jerusalem to Illiricum, about ten hundred miles. I know not he, *but the grace of God that was with him,* 1 Cor. xv. 9, 10. not he, but the Lord: true, but the question now is, Whether Paul and the Holy Ghost, in all these works of grace, were two persons become one spirit by union, as some dreamers affirm; because both did the work? I believe not. God and clouds rained down manna to Israel; O but Christ's Father (John vi.) *gave the manna:* but the question is, If the person of God were united with the clouds or any second causes producing manna? So the Lord ma-

keth rich and poor, killeth and maketh alive, maketh snow, frost, fair weather, drought, and rain, the sun to rise, and go down, and that in his own person, Father, Son, and Spirit; *He, He* only, made heaven, earth, sea, and all creatures, and the world: the Greek word Autos, Acts xvii. 25. and the Hebrew word Hu, Psal. xxxiii. 9. do prove him to be a person who doth all these: but we cannot say that the person of God must be united with clouds, ship, sea, sun, heavens, men fighting, and men saving and killing; and that God personally filleth all creatures; only God, in the immensity of his nature, is all these, and every where, and is in them by his operation: so the Holy Ghost is with the saints, and dwelleth in them, not by union of his person to them, or the immensity of his essence, which is, as David saith, every where, Psal. cxxxix. 7. *Whither shall I go from thy Spirit?* But so he is in heaven, in hell, in the sea. 2. But he dwelleth in the saints, in regard of the works, operations, gifts, and graces of the Holy Ghost.

1. Because the Holy Spirit is in them, in that they have in them the fruits of the Spirit, Gal. v. 22. such as love, joy, peace, long-suffering, gentleness, goodness, faith; now these are not the Holy Ghost, who is eternal, and God uncreated, but are created in time, out of meer nothing, not out of the potency of the subject; but, ere God produce grace, so knotty and so rocky are we, and so contrary to grace, that he must fall upon a new and second creation, Eph. ii. 10. Col. ii. 10. Psal. li. 10. The same word that is used for *creating heaven and earth*, Gen. i. 1. is here used; it is not like the repairing of a fallen house, where the same timber and stones may do the work, or the repairing of decayed nature, when a healthy body recovereth out of a fever; grace is a rare and curious workmanship.

2. We are said *to grow in grace*, 2 Pet. iii. 18. and by *grace to increase to the edifying of the body in love,* Eph. iv. 16. and to *the measure of the stature of the fulness of Christ,* 13. and *to add grace to grace,* 2 Pet. i.

i. 5, 6, 7. *and to go on to perfection*, Heb. vi. 1. Phil. iii. 12. But the person of the Holy Ghost is not capable of growing, or addition, nor like the morning-light, or the new moon, that can grow and advance in perfection, being God blessed for ever.

3. If there be an union of the person of the Holy Ghost with the soul, and not an indwelling by graces, the believer, as a believer, must live by the uncreated and eternal life of the Holy Ghost, or a created life. *Creatum vel increatum dividunt omne ens immediate, sicut finitum & infinitum:* not the former, neither any man, nor the man Christ can in any capacity be elevated so above itself, as to partake of the infinite life of God. How the manhood of Christ partaketh of the personal subsistence of the Godhead, is incomprehensible to me, except that it is not by such an union as my singular nature standeth under personality created, and is by assumption rather than union. However, if there be an union of the person of the Holy Ghost to our souls, it cannot be conceived, nor doth the scripture speak of it; if the saints live the life of God, it must be by created graces, and this is that we conceive.

4. The person of the Holy Ghost immediately acting in the saints, without them or any active and vital influence of the natural faculties, cannot be guilty of sin, because David and Christ are absolved of sin in this. *They laid to my charge things that I knew not,* that is, things that I never acted, crimes in which I had no action or hand: but we are blamed in the word; for all the omissions of holy duties; and the Holy Ghost cannot be blamed, for he bloweth when, and where he listeth, and is under no law in his motions of free-grace; then he who cannot be blamed in not acting, cannot be united as one Spirit, person with person, with him who is justly to be blamed in not acting.

Asser. 4. It must evidently follow that there is in the saints a grace created, that is neither Christ, nor the Holy Ghost in person: for what reason any hath to fancy an union of the person of Christ or the Holy Ghost

in

in the saints, the same reason have they to say that all the three are united to the person of the believer in all supernatural actions; for the Father is said *to draw men to the Son,* John vi. 44. and Christ *to reveal the Father,* and to draw men, John i. 18. John xii. 32. and the Holy Ghost *to reveal the deep things of God,* 1 Cor. ii. 10, 11. Now all the three in person do these, but all the three persons are not united to believers in person; this were a mystery greater than *God manifested in the flesh,* and unknown to scripture.

2. If Christ be all the grace of believers, faith in Christ, and the love of Christ should be Christ.

3. Then should a believer, having a new heart and a new spirit, be christed, or godded; and God should be incarnate in every believer, and how many Christs should there be? and the new heart in one saint, and the grace given to Paul, should be the new heart given to Peter; whereas God hath given grace to every man, according to his measure; and *there are diversity of gifts, but one Spirit,* 2 Pet. iii. 15. Phil. i. 9. Eph. iii. 3, 4, 5. 1 Cor. xii. 3, 4, 5, 6. Eph. iv. 19.

Asser. 5. The grace of God and our free-will in a four-fold sense may be said to concur in the same works of grace.

1. When free-will receiveth no more from grace and the Lord's drawing, but only literal instruction; and if by our industry an habit of the knowledge of the letter of the word be acquired, it is necessary only to the easier believing, as Pelagius said, I may believe without preaching the gospel, by reading, but more easily by fair and powerful preaching, and by grace helping and assisting preaching, but yet without grace, but with greater difficulty, as I may go a journey on foot, but more easily on horse-back; then a horse is not simply necessary for the journey; and a ship may fail more easily and expeditely with sails, yet also without sails, with the help of oars, though with more difficulty. Thus Christ and his grace may be spared, we may fail to heaven by nature's sweating and free-will's industry, though the sails of grace could more expeditely promove

our

CHRIST DYING AND DRAWING 583
SINNERS TO HIMSELF.

our journey. Now, we think not that Christ draweth when men speak but the bare letter of the gospel, and softly request the dead with only sound of words, and syllables to live, and orators with golden words do pray and persuade the blind to see, and the cripples to walk; but 'tis long ere words fetch a soul to dry bones that they may live, or tie the broken eye-strings, or add vital power and life to eyes and ancle-bones.

2. Grace and free-will (as Bellarmine and the rest of the Jesuits with Arminians teach) may be thought to be two joint causes, the one not depending on the other, as two carrying one stone or burden, neither he helpeth him, nor he him, but both join their independent strength to one common effect. Bellarmine and Grevinchovious, with the like comparisons, do prove that we may storm heaven by the strength of free-will, without dependence on Christ; for three untruths are here taught. 1. That grace determineth not free-will; a saying destructive to providence: if God determine not all second causes, he is not master of all events, nor hath he a dominion of providence in all things that fall out, good and evil. 2. Grace doth not begin in all things that concern salvation, nor doth the *Lord work in us to will and to do,* if we will not do without any prior dependence on the influence of the grace of God; we as much work in ourselves willing and doing, as the Lord doth, and the Lord in his grace shall follow, and not lead our will. 3. Grace doth not confer any help on the will, to actuate it, and to strengthen it in going good, in believing, repenting, loving God, hoping, (as Grevinchovius saith) but will and grace do both jointly meet in one and the same effect, in which, 4. Free-will divideth the spoil with Christ. And what need we say, *Worthy is the Lamb, who has redeemed us,* if free-will in the application of redemption share equally with the grace of Christ?

3. The third way is, That free-will is said to believe, repent, love God, by a mere extrinsical denomination, because it carrieth that grace which formally and only
doth

doth perform all these supernatural actions; so grace doth all, and free-will is a mere patient, that conferreth no vital, subordinate and active influence in these acts: as we say, the apothecary's glass healeth the wound, because the oil in the glass worketh the cure; when the glass doth actively contribute nothing to the cure; or the ass maketh rich, when it carrieth the gold that enricheth only. This sense Antinomians hold forth make us mere patients and blocks in the way to heaven; and this sense Jesuits, especially Martinez de Repalda†, falsely chargeth upon Luther and Calvin; and the council of Trent, inspired with the same lying spirit, saith the same.

4. The fourth sense is, That grace and free-will doth work so, as grace is the principal, first inspiring and fountain cause: 1. It being a new supernatural disposition and habit in the soul, John xiv. 23. 1 John ii. 27. 1 John iii. 9. John iv. 14. Isa. xliv. 3, 4. Ezek. xxxvi. 26, 27. Deut xxx. 6. a good treasure or stock of grace, Mat. xii. 35. Luke vi. 45. And also actually it determineth, sweetly inclineth and stirreth the will to these acts; yet so as free-will moveth actively, freely, and conferreth a radical, vital, and subordinate influence, and is not a mere patient in all these, as Antinomians dream, Psal. cxix. 32. *I will run the way of thy commandments, when thou shalt enlarge my heart.* John xiv. 12. *He that believeth in me, the works that I do, he shall do, and greater than these.* Mat. xii. 50. *He that doth the will of my heavenly Father, the same is my brother,* etc. 1 Cor. ix. 24. *So run that ye may obtain.* Rev. ii. 2. *I know thy works and thy labour.* 1 Thess. i. 3. *Remembring without ceasing your work of faith, and labour of love, and patience of hope.* 2. We are not dead in supernatural works, and mere blocks, Rom. vi. 11. *We are alive unto God in Jesus Christ,* Eph. ii. 1. *He hath quickned us,* Rev. ii. 3. *For my name's*

sake,

†Martinez de Repalda, de ente supernatu. Tom. 1. disp. 29. sect. 1. n. 3, 4. Concil. Tridenti. sess. 6. c. 5. c. 4.

sake, thou hast laboured, and hast not fainted. 1 Cor. xv. 58. *Be ye stedfast, unmoveable, always abounding in the work of the Lord.* There is activity in the spirit to *lust against the flesh,* Gal. v. 17. Rom. vii. 15. Nor is the blessedness of the saints only passive in receiving; though to be justified, and receive Christ's righteousness, be the fountain-blessedness, Psal. xxxii. 1. Rom. iv. 6, 7. Gal. iii. 13. But the scripture speaketh of a true and solid blessedness in the action, Psal. cxix. 1. *Blessed are the undefiled in the way.* Isa. lvi. 3. *Blessed is the man that doth this.* James i. 12. *Blessed is the man that endureth temptation.* Psal. cxix. 2. *Blessed are they that keep his testimonies.* Psal. cvi. 3. *Blessed are they that keep his judgment.* Rev. xxii. 14. *Blessed are they that do his commandments.* Mat. v. *Blessed are they that mourn, that hunger and thirst.* Then there must be a part of blessedness in sanctification, as in justification; though the one be the cause, the other the effect.

Asser. 6. The Lord's working in us the condition of the covenant of grace, such as faith is, by his efficacious grace, doth not free us from sin, when we believe not; nor involve God in the fault, when he worketh not in us to believe, as Crispe imagineth. Here let me by the way remove the arguments of Dr. Crispe (Serm. 6. pag. 160.) by the which he imagineth, that there is no condition at all in the covenant of grace.

Arg. 1. "The covenant should not be everlasting, if it depended on a condition of faith to be performed by us; for we fail in our performances daily, and the covenant is annulled and broken so soon as the condition is broken.

Answ. 1. We speak not so, that the covenant of grace depends on a condition in us: dependency includes a causality in that of which the thing has dependency; we know nothing in us, either faith or any other thing that is the cause of the covenant of grace, or of the fulfilling of it: a cause is one thing, a condition caused by grace is another thing; for the perpetuity of the covenant, there is not required a condition always in act.

1. If at the eleventh or twelfth hour, you come to Christ, the nature of this covenant promiseth you welcome. 2. Particular failings, and acts of unbelief, do well consist with the habit and stock of faith that remaineth in him that is born of God; nor is the act so tied to a time. But, 3. There is by tenure of the covenant a privilege two-fold here. (1.) If by the law a man step a hair-breadth wide off the way, the door of paradise is bolted on him, and in again can he never enter, he must seek another entry, the man has done with heaven that way, the law knoweth not such a thing as repentance; but the covenant of grace being made with a sinner, a slip, an act of unbelief doth not forfeit the mercy of this covenant: but Christ saith, if you fall, there is place to rise again; if you sin, there is an Advocate, there is a blood of an eternal covenant; the covenant stands still to make up room for repeated grace, for a thread and continued track of free-grace and mercy, all along your foot never go out of the traces of renewed pardon while you be in heaven: though the child of God ought not to sin, yet can he not out-sin the eternity of the new covenant, nor can he sin an eternal Priest out of heaven. (2.) The law requireth a stinted measure of obedience, even to the superlative, with all the soul and the whole strength; any less is the forfeiting of salvation; but the covenant of grace stinteth no weak soul, Christ racketh not, nor doth he (as it were) play the extortioner, and say, either the strongest faith, or none at all; he maketh not Abraham's foot a measure to every poor sinner: many smoking flaxes, and broken reeds on earth, are now up before the throne; mighty cedars, high, tall, green, planted on the banks of the river of life. If Adam be the first in heaven, what though I be the last that enter in, though I close the door in the lowest room, so I see the throne, and him that sits on it, it is enough to me.

Dr. Crispe's 2d Arg. "All the tie of the covenant lieth on God, not any on man, as bond or obligation for the fulfilling of the covenant, or partaking of the "be-

"benefits thereof, Heb. viii. 10. Ezek. xxxvi. 25, 26. Jer. xxxi. The Lord promiseth to do all, and the new heart is but a consequent of the covenant; where is there in all this covenant, one word that God says to man, Thou must do this? If God had put man on these conditions, then they were conditions indeed: but when God takes all upon himself, where are then the conditions on man's part? Give me leave, suppose there should be a fault of performing in this covenant, whose were the fault? Must not the fault or failing be in him who is tied and bound to every thing in the covenant, and saith, He will do it? If there be a condition, and there should be a failing in the condition, he that undertaketh all things in the covenant must needs be in the fault,-----God saith not, Make yourselves clean, get you the law of God in your mind, get you power to walk in my statutes; and when you do this, then I will be your God, and enter in covenant with you."

Answ. 1. We never teach that the making to ourselves a new heart is an antecedent condition required before the Lord can make the new covenant with us, as this man would charge Protestant Divines; but that it is a condition required in the party covenanting, which is *conditio faederatorum, non faederis*, and such a condition without which 'tis impossible they can fulfil the other condition, which is to believe, and so lay hold on the covenant: but it is clear, Antinomians think the new heart no inherent grace in us, but that Christ is grace working immediately in us as in stones, and the new heart is justification, without us, in Christ only. Let Crispe shew where the making of a new heart is commanded to us, as a consequent and an effect of the covenant; surely the new heart, the washing of us with clean water, be it an antecedent, or be it a consequent of the covenant of grace, it is a promise that God doth freely and of mere grace undertake to perform in us, Ezek. xxxvi. 26. *A new heart will I give you:* so, Jer. xxxii. 39, 40. Jer. xxxi. 33. Ezek. xi. 19. Isa. liv. 13. John vi. 45.

45. Ezek. xxxvi. 32. *Not for your sakes do I this, saith the Lord God, be it known unto you; be ashamed and confounded for your own ways, O house of Israel.* ver. 22. *I do not this for your sakes, O house of Israel, but for mine holy name's sake, which ye have prophaned amongst the heathen, wither ye went.* And Crispe saith, "The covenant in the Old Testament had annexed to it divers conditions, of legal washing and sacrifices, where the new covenant under the New Testament is every way of free-grace." He is far wide; conditions wrought in us by grace, such as we assert, take not one jot or title of the freedom of grace away: and though there be *major gratia*, a larger measure of grace under the New Testament, yet there is not *magis gratia*, there is no more of the essence of free-grace in the one, than in the other; for all was free grace to them, as to us. Why did the Lord enter in covenant with the Jews more than with other nations? Deut. vii. 7. *The Lord loved you, because he loved you.* Was Jerusalem, Ezek. xvi. holier than the Ephesians, Eph. ii. *No, their nativity was of the land of Canaan, their father an Amorite, their mother an Hittite*, Ezek. xvi. 5. *Thou wast cast out in the open field, to the lothing of thy person, in the day that thou wast born.* ver. 6. *And when I passed by thee, and saw thee polluted in thine own blood, I said to thee in thy blood, Live:* and, to cause grace have a deeper impression and sinking down into the heart's bottom, he repeateth it again, *I said unto thee in thy blood, Live.* And will Crispe say that this is not a history of free grace, as far from bribe or hire of merit as in the world? or, will he say, it was God's meaning, first, *Wash you with holy water, and sacrifice to me, and perform all these legal conditions to me, while you are Amorites and Hittites by kind; and that being done, I'll enter in covenant with you; when he have done your work, I'll pay your wages, and be your God.*

2. This argument militateth strongly against every gospel-duty, and the whole course of sanctification; God must so be the cause, and only cause of our all sin-

ful

ful omissions, and sins under the covenant of grace, in that he promiseth to work in us to will and to do, and to give us grace to abstain from sin, but does not stand to his word, as Antinomians teach; which is an argument unanswerable to me, that 'tis the mind of Antinomians, that no justified person can sin, but in that they omit good, or commit ill, God is in the fault, not they; and that the justified are meer blocks in all the course of their sanctification; in all the sins they do, they are patients; God should more carefully see to his own honour, and not suffer them to sin: so they and the old Libertines, go on together. For say, that the new heart, that to will and to do, to persevere stedfastly in the grace of God, were no conditions of the covenant (sure, believing in the Lord Jesus is clearly a condition of the *righteousness of faith, as doing is of the righteousness which is of the law,* Rom. x. 3, 4, 5, 6, 7, 8. Gal. iv. 22, 23, 24, 25, 26, 27, 28.) say that to repent, pray, love God, and serve him, were not from God through the tye of the new covenant; yet God's promise, his single word, when he saith, He will do such and such things, is as strong a tye as his covenant and oath, when he knoweth 'tis impossible these things that he saith he will do, can be done, except he, of his meer grace, work them in us. Now, the Lord clearly promiseth, that he will give repentance, Acts v. 31. Sorrow for sin, the Spirit of grace and supplication, Zech. xii. 10. a circumcised heart to love and serve the Lord Deut. xxx. 6. Ezek. xxxvi. 26. Perseverance in grace, Jer. xxxii. 40, 41. Isa. liv. 10. chap. lix. 20, 21. Psal. i. 3. John iv. 14. Chap. x. 28. Phil. i. 6. Eph. v. 26, 27. 1 John ii. 1. Then let D. Crispe or any Libertine say, when the saints sin, in not praying, in not sorrowing for sin, in not willing and doing, in their sins and falls in their christian race to heaven, let me speak in the words of Crispe, "Whose fault is it, or failing, not to perform the word or promise of God? God undertaketh by promise, yea by his simple word, to fulfil what he promiseth, and saith, He will work all these in us, yea to will and to do; *Ergo*, if it be not done, the fault

"cannot

"cannot be man's, but it must be *(which I abhor to write or speak)* the Lord's."

3. God takes all upon himself, *in genere causae gratiofae. Liberrimae independentis, primae, non obligatae ad agendum exulla lege;* in the kind of a cause that worketh by meer grace, freely, independently, without any law above him to oblige him to do otherwise with his own, than he freely willeth, decreeth, promiseth; for men carnally divide God's decree, which is most free, from his promise, which is as free as his decree: but it followeth in no sort, (as Arminians and Jesuits object to us) therefore men, who do not believe, pray, walk holily, are not in the fault, being under a law to obey; for sinful inability to obey, can ransom no man from the obligation of obedience: and most blasphemous it is, that because God undertaketh in the covenant, that we shall walk in his commandments, as he doth promise, Ezek. xxxvi. 27. and that we shall fear him, Jer. xxxii. 39, 40. that God should therefore be in the fault, and we free of all fault, when in *many particulars we offend all,* James iii. 2. and we fear not God, in this or this sin; as is possible, and may be gathered from Joseph's speech to his brethren, who says he would not wrong them, for he feared God; and Job's word, that *he durst not despise the cause of his servant, because he was afraid of God.* Yet God promiseth, that he will keep Joseph, Job and all the elect, in the way of God's commandments, that they shall not fully fall away from him: God never, by promise, covenant, oath, or word, undertaketh to keep his elect from this or this particular breach and act of unbelief, against the covenant of grace.

4. The fault against the gospel, or any sin in a believer, must justly be imputed to him, because he is tyed by the evangelic law not to sin in any thing; the gospel granteth pardons, but not dispensations in any sins: and it can in no sort be imputed to God, because if any believer fall in a particular sin or act of unbelief against the covenant of grace, the Lord neither decreed

nor

nor did ever undertake by covenant or promise to keep him by his effectual grace from falling in that sin; for the Lord would then certainly have keeped him, as he did Peter, and doth all the elect that are effectually called, that in mighty temptations their faith fail them not. Nor is the act of believing, that is wanting in that particular fall, such a condition of the covenant, as Christ either promised to work, or the necessary condition of the covenant of grace, or such a condition, the want whereof doth annul and make void the eternal covenant of grace.

5. I here smell in Antinomians, that God must be in fault, as the author of our unbelief, our stony hearts, our walking in our fleshly ways, because God hath promised to give us faith, and a heart of flesh, to walk in his ways; as the old Libertines said, God was the principal and chief cause of sin, and that 'God did all things, both good and ill, and the creatures did nothing.' So Calvine, in institut. Adversus Libertinos, chap. 14. in epus. p. 446. Mr. Archer down-right saith, 'God is the author of sin.' What end is there of erring, if God leave us? It is true, the tie, and all the tie of giving a new heart, and the Spirit of grace and supplication, lieth on the Lord, who promised so to do, Deut. xxx. 6. Ezek. xi. 19, 20. chap. xxxvi. 26, 27. Jer. xxxi. 33, 34, 35, 36. But yet so that we are under the obligation of divine precepts to do our part, Ezek. xviii. 31. *Make a new heart, and a new spirit; for why will ye die, O house of Israel?* Jer. iv. 4. *Circumcise yourselves to the Lord, and take away the fore-skin of your heart*, Eph. iv. 23. *Be renewed in the spirit of your mind,* Rom. xii. 2. Rom. xiii. 14. and 1 Thess. v. 17. *Pray without ceasing.* Psal. l. 15. *Call upon me.* Mat. xxvi. 41. *Watch and pray*: therefore all the tie and obligation of whatever kind cannot so free us from sinful omissions, nor can the tie ly on God; evangelic commandments are accompanied with grace to obey, and grace layeth a tie on us also to yield obedience.

'Tis a foul and ignorant mistake in Crispe, to make *the covenant nothing but that love of God to man,*

which

which he cast on man before the children had done good or evil, Rom. ix. 1. That love is eternal, and hath no respect to faith as to a condition; but 'tis not the covenant itself, because it is the cause of the covenant. 2. To the love of election, there is no love, no work, no act of believing required on our part; yea, no mediator, no shedding of blood; we are loved with an everlasting love, before all these: but the covenant, though as decreed of God, it be everlasting, (as all the works of creation and divine providence, which fall out in time, and have beginning and end, are so everlasting; for God decreed from eternity that they should be) yet it is not in being formally, while it be preached to Adam after his fall; and there is required faith on all the saints part, *to lay hold on the covenant,* Isa. lvi. 4. and to make it a covenant of peace to the saints in particular. 2. Faith is the condition of the covenant. 3. Christ the Mediator of it. 4. *Christ's blood* the seal of it. 5. *The Spirit* must write it in our heart: but the love of election is a compleat, free, full love, before our faith, or shedding of blood, or a Mediator be at all.

Object. "We are not saved, nor justified, nor taken in covenant by faith, as a work, (saith Crispe) for then we should not be saved by grace, and grace should not be grace: but we are justified by faith, that is, by that Christ which faith knoweth, according to that, *By his knowledge shall my righteous Servant justify many;* therefore faith is no condition of this covenant."

Answ. The contrary rather followeth: 1. Seeing Crispe doth say, None under heaven can be saved till they have believed; we are not taken in covenant by faith; neither we nor scripture speak so; taking us in covenant, is before we can believe; but we lay hold on Christ and righteousness by faith, not as a work, but as a necessary condition required of us. 2. I leave it to the consideration of the godly, if believing in him who justifieth the ungodly be no condition; (a work justifying, I do not think it) but only I believe and

know

know that Christ justified me before I believed, from eternity, as some say, when I was conceived in the womb as Crispe saith; and that the threatning, *He that believeth not, is condemned already,* carries this sense, He that believeth not that he is not condemned, he is already condemned: Who can believe such toys?

2. Believing is a receiving of Christ, John i. 22. Christ's dwelling in the heart, Ephes. iii. 17. Then to believe, must be to know that Christ was in me before I believed, and that I received him from eternity, or from my conception.

3. To believe, maketh me a son born, *not of flesh and blood,* John i. 12, 13. and Gal. iii. 26. and by faith we receive the Spirit: this then must be nothing else but I know by the light of faith, I was a son before, and had received the Spirit, before I believed. What more absurd?

4. And by faith I live not, Christ liveth in me, and I am crucified and mortified; that is, by faith I know that I did live the life of God, and was crucified to the world: whereas I was dead in sins, before I believed.

5. And, because believing is somewhat more than a naked act of the mind, it being a fiducial adherence unto, and an affiance, acquiescence, and heart-reliance, and staying on Christ, or a rolling of ourselves on God for salvation, as is clear in the original holy languages of scripture, Psal. xviii. 18. Isa. xxvi. 3. Psal. cxii. 8. Isa. x. 21. Mic. iii. 11. Psal. xxii. 8. Psal. lv. 22. 1 Pet. v. 7. Cant. viii. 5. John i. 12. 'Tis too hungry a notion of faith, to make it nothing but a knowing of that which really was before; for heart-adherence is not an act of the mind, and so not an act of knowledge, but of the will and affection, in which there is no act of knowledge formally, though it presuppose an act of knowledge.

6. Then wicked men must be in their sins, not justified in his blood, because they will not know that Christ died for them in particular, and that Christ bore their sins on the cross, and justified and pardoned them long ago;

ago; all which to believe, is to hold a lie in the right-hand. But to return.

Asser. 7. How the Lord worketh in us to will and to do, the power and the act, and yet we are guilty in our omissions of good, or in our sinful and remiss manner of working with the grace of God, is a point more mysterious than I dare undertake to explain. If these may give light, I offer them to the reader.

Pos. 1. Grace, free-grace, is the great and master-wheel, that carrieth about heart, senses, foot, and hand; and not that only, but seed and tree and fruit, the flower, the principle dependeth necessarily on free-grace: and for a third, the state and condition is higher than either principle, or seed, or fruit; to be an heir of glory, is more than a supernatural principle of gift, and more than one single action above nature. Grace must make the principle gracious, and grace must in-act and quicken the principle to bring forth; and grace's policy makes natural men, citizens of heaven, *sons of God*, heirs of life, John i. 12, 13. Gal. iv. 4, 5.

Pos. 2. This must stand as a ground, That there is not any gracious act performed by the members, but the head Christ is so interested in it, that, as even the finger and toe, in the natural body, cannot stir without the motion takes its beginning from life and head; so neither can the mystical body, or any joint or member of it, act or move in its supernatural orb of grace, but every individual act of grace must pay the rent of glory to the mystical head, whose predeterminating influence does act and steer the ship: for Christ is not only the compass, and day-star, according to which spiritual motions are directed, and hand and finger, foot, (and all see with the visive power seated in the head, for they have no faculty of seeing in themselves) and the saints in these actions stir with the light in the two eyes, or seven eyes and lamps that are in the Head Christ; but also the real motions of grace, in their physical, as well as in their moral sphere, are shapen and acted by Christ. It is not much (though it

be

be a wonder) that a huge great ship, made up of so many pieces of dry dead timber, can move regularly through so many circles, compasses, turnings of many coasts, countries, change of winds, ten thousand miles, to a certain harbour, when timber is acted and moved with the borrowed art and reason of a man stirring the helm; so there is a [Gr. lógos,] a reason, a wisdom in him, *Who is made our wisdom*, to act the saints in their heavenward motion, that are carried through so many sea-circles, turnings, contrary winds of temptations, afflictions, various soul-dispensations of sweet and sour, absence, presence, going and coming again of Christ, to such a determinate home as heaven: for the Father must thank the steersman Christ, his Son! that the broken bark and all his poor friends are landed, with the borrowed art of Christ; and no more thanks or praise to us, than to dead timber. *That we should be* [Gr. eìs tò einâi hemâs,] *to the praise of his glory,* Eph. i. 12. as if our passive being (it is a borrowed expression, for we are co-agents with and under Christ, in the work) were destinated to the praise of the glory of his grace: but we are so drawn, as Christ is great Lord moderator and author; and God in the second and new world of grace, as God creator is in all actions of nature, John xv. 5. *Without me,* (as your vine-tree, in whom you grow, and a stock in whom you bring forth fruit, every blossom of life, every apple) *ye can do nothing.* Phil. ii. 13. *For it is God that worketh in you to will and to do, according to his good pleasure.* 2 Cor. xiii. 3. *Since ye seek a proof of Christ speaking in me, which to you-ward is not weak, but is mighty in you;* then every word that Paul spoke, Christ in him spoke it not formally, as if Paul had been a meer patient, but efficaciously, Rom. xv. 18. *For I will not dare to speak of any of these things which Christ hath not wrought by me, to make the Gentiles obedient by word and deed.* Isa. xxvii. 23. *I the Lord do keep it,* (the church, the garden of red wine) *I will water it every moment, lest any hurt it, I will keep it night and day.* Keeping and watering every moment, is grace actual

every

every moment, to make his tender vines grow, and preserving his own from succumbing under every temptation.

2. There were no ground for Adam thankfulness and praise, that he stood one moment, or that he gave names to every thing according to their nature, or ever heard with patience the command of God, *Thou shalt not eat,* if in every act of obedience, he had not need of the actual predeterminating influence of God; nor were there ground for this prayer in faith, and in patient submission to God, as to one to whom we owe the praises, of the not-failing of our faith, *Lead us not into temptation, but deliver us from evil;* nor were there any glory due to Christ's advocation and intercession, that we fall not fully and finally off Christ and from Christ, and the state of grace, when we are tempted, if free will, not the actual influence of predeterminating grace, did keep the saints, and stir them to every act.

3. Who is the author and finisher of our faith? Christ; and who perfecteth the good work once begun, but Christ? and who but he bringeth many children to glory? Not we. When the soul is distempered under desertion, the soul is so tender and excellent a piece, love so curious and rare a work of Christ, that let all the angels in heaven, seraphims, and dominions, and thrones, set all their shoulders and strength together, they cannot with angel-tongues (let them speak heaven, and Christ, and glory) calm a soul-fever; and words of silk, and oil dropped from the clouds, cannot command the love-sickness of a sad soul. Will ye look to heaven while your sight fail, and weep out two eyes, while Christ's time come, you cannot find ease for a broken spirit; when Christ breaketh, can angels make whole? The conscious is a hell-fever. *The comforter is gone:* can you with a nod bring the physician back again? Can golden words charm and calm a fever of hell? Can you with all the love-waters on earth quench a coal of fire that came from heaven? Send up to heaven a mandate against the decree and

dis-

dispensation of God, if you can; if the gates of death can open to thee; or if thou hast seen the doors of the shadow of death; or can do such great works of creation, as to *lay the corner-stone of the earth, or hang the world on nothing*, which Job could not do, chap. xxxvii. chap. xxxviii. But who can command soul-furies? Only, only Christ.

The soul is down amongst the dead, wandring from one grave to another. Can you make a dead spirit a gospel-harp to play one of the springs of Zion, the songs of the Holy Ghost? Christ can do it. Can you cry and find obedience to your call, *O north, south-wind, blow upon the garden?* Christ hath his own wind at command; he is master of his own mercies. Can you prophesy to the wind to come and breathe on dead bones? Christ only can. Can you breathe life, soul, and five senses on a coffin? Could you make way for breathing in the narrow and deep grave, when clods of clay closeth the passage of the nostrils? Christ can; Isa. xxvi. 19. *Thy dead men shall live, together with my body they shall arise: awake and sing, ye that dwell in the dust, for thy dew is as the dew of herbs, and the earth shall cast out the dead.* Can you draw the virgins after the strong and delicious smell of the ointments of Christ? But if he draw, the virgins run after his love, Cant. i. 3. Christ indicts war: are you a creator to make peace? He cries hell, and wrath; can you speak joy, and consolation? are you an anti-creator, to undo what Christ does? Christ commandeth fury against a people, or person; can men, can angels, can heaven countermand?

Pos. 3. The Lord's suspending of his grace cometh under a twofold consideration. 1. As the Lord denieth it to his own children. 2. As to wicked men also. As he witholdeth grace, especially actual and predeterminating; it falleth under a threefold respect,

1. As it is a work of the free and good pleasure and sovereignty of God.

2. As it is a punishment of former sins.

3. As from it resulteth our sin, even as the night hath

its

its being from the absence of the sun; death from the removal of life.

Asser. 4. The Lord's denial of grace, is seen most eminently in two cases: 1. In the parting asunder of the two decrees of election and reprobation.

2. In God's withdrawing of himself and his assistance, in the case of trying the saints.

In the former, the Lord has put forth his sovereignty in his two excellentest creatures, angels and men. If we make any cause in the free-will of angels (I speak of a separating and discriminating cause) why some angels did stand, and never sin, some fall, and become devils; we must deny freedom of God's grace in the predestination of angels: now the scripture calleth them elect angels; how then came it that they fell not? From free-will? No: angels are *made of God, and for God, and to God;* then, by the apostle's reason, they could not give first to God, to engage the Almighty to a recompence, they could not first set their free-will to work their own standing in court, before God did with his grace separate them from angels that fell, Rom. xi. 36. Isa. xl. 13. 2. Make an election of angels, as the scripture doth; when some are called elect angels, and some not, then it must be an election of grace: an election of works cannot be; because angels must *glory in the Lord*, that they stand when others fell, Rom. iv. 2. as men do, Prov. xvi. 4. Jer. ix. 23, 24, 2 Cor. x. 17. Rom. xi. 36. For no creature, angels or men, can glory in his sight; for angels are for him and of him, as their last end, and first author, Rom. xi. 36. Then they gave not first to God, to engage the Lord in their debt, ver. 35. for, if so, then glory should be to the angels: but now, upon this ground, that none can engage the Lord in their debt, Paul, ver. 36. saith, *To him be glory for ever;* because none can give to him first, and all are for him, and of him; then so are angels.

3. Angels are associated in the element and orb of free-grace, to move as men, with grace's wings to fly over the lake prepared for the devil and his angels,

whereas

whereas others fell in; otherwise Christ, the Lord treasurer of free-grace, cannot be the head of angels, Col. ii. 9. as of men, Col. i. 8. Eph. i. 20, 21, 22, 23. For as art, not nature, can prevent a dangerous fever, by drawing blood, or some other way; even as the same art can recover a sick man out of a fever, whereas another sick of that same disease, yet wanting the help of art, dieth: so the same grace, in nature, specie and kind, not free-will hindred the elected angels to fall; whereas, by constitution of nature and mutability, being descended of that first common poor and base house, the first spring of all the creation of God, mere and simple nothing, the mother of change and of all defects natural and moral, in every the most excellent creature; they were as an humorous gross body, in which the vessels are full, and in a nearest propension to the same fever that devils fell into, *even to the ill of the second death,* if the grace of God had not prevented them.

2. In men, God has declared the deep sovereignty and dominion of free-grace, in calling effectually one man, Jacob, not Esau; Peter, not Judas; in having mercy, in time, *on whom he will, and hardning whom he will.* I humbly provoke all Arminians, all Libertines, who dash themselves the contrary way against the same stone, to show a reason why one obeyeth and actively joineth with the draught and pull of the right arm of Jesus Christ, John xii. 32. and his Father, John vi. 44. and another refuseth, and actively and wilfully withdraweth from the call of God, if the omnipotency of never-enough praised grace be not the cause, the adequate, highest, and principal cause. I deny not but corrupt and rebellious will is the inferiour, culpable, and only culpable and moral cause, why Judas denieth obedience to the holy call of Christ.

It is a sweet contemplation, that angels and men sing the same song and psalm of free-grace in heaven, to the Lamb, to him that sitteth on the throne; and a question it is, if a more engaging and obliging way to free-grace could be devised, than that as many as are in

the

the glorified troops and triumphing armies in heaven, clothed in white, should be also the sworn subjects, and the eternal debtors of the freest grace of him who is the high Lord Redeemer, and Head of angels and men.

But in the engagement itself of the wind of the Spirit, for the trial of the saints, there is a great ground of admiration; as, 1. The blowing of the soft and pleasant breathings of the south-wind of free-grace, lying under the only work of sovereignty, when, and where, and in the measure the Lord pleaseth, is a high and deep expression of the freedom of grace; for in one and the same prayer (the like by proportion may be said of the acts of faith, love, patience, hope) we often begin to pray, with sad and fleshly complaints of unbelief, as is evident in many psalms and prayers of the saints in scripture, Jeremiah, Lam. iii. of Job, of David; yet going on, the breathings of the Holy Ghost will fill the fails, and he returneth; therefore this is a ground, yea, a demonstration to me, then, when I find no motion of the Holy Ghost, no spiritual disposition, but mere deadness, I am not to abstain from praying, because I find the Spirit not acting nor stirring in me, as Antinomians say: but, 1. I am to act and do, though the principle of motion be natural; as if the first stroke on flint make not fire, we are to strike again and again; and if the fire blowing of the bellows kindle not the sticks, *let us be doing, and the Lord will be with us;* a kindling and a flame may come from heaven. Say that the Lord were wanting to me in a dead and low ebb; he will not once roll about the sight of his eye, nor let out one blast or stirring of air and wind of the Spirit toward me; yet my deadness is my sin, and freeth not me from an obligation to pray and to seek to God. The door is fast bolted, shall I not therefore knock? Access is denied, and the *Lord in anger shutteth out my prayer*, Lam. iii. 8. May not I look and sigh, and groan towards his holy temple? Deadness is not the Lord's revealed will, for-

bid

bidding me to pray, because I am dead and indisposed.

2. Deadness and indisposition is a sin; then must we confess to God, and tell the Lord, when we are indisposed to pray, that we cannot pray; and let the dead and the blind but bow his knee, and lay a dead spirit, and naked wretched soul, a pair of blind eyes before God: for we are commanded to confess this to God, as may be gathered from Rev. iii. 17. 1 John i. 9. Prov. xxviii. 13. Psal. xxxii. 5.

4. We are expresly commanded in the day of trouble, and of our temptation, to pray, and seek help from God under our temptations, Psal. l. 15. Mat. vi. 13. 1 Thes. v. 17. as the saints have done, Psal. xviii. 6. Psal. xxxiv. 6. Psal. lxi. 2. 2 Cor. xii. ver. 7, 8, 9. If then we judge the no-breathing of the Holy Ghost a temptation, and a cause of humiliation, as it is, and the saints do judge it; then are we to pray, tho' most indisposed. Why doth David complain that he was as a bottle in the smoke, and pray so often that God would quicken him, if under a dead disposition we were not to pray?

4. If often the saints, beginning to pray, do speak words of unbelief, and from a principle of nature; and if words flowing from the deadness and misgivings and rovings of the flesh, interwoven in with the spiritual and heavenly ravishments of the Spirit of grace and supplication, in one and the same complaint and prayer to God, as Psal. xxxviii. Psal. cii. Psal. lxxvii. Psal. lxxxviii. Lam. iii. Jer. xx. Job viii. chap. xvi. chap. xix. and in many other passages, where the Spirit and the flesh have dialogues and speeches by turns and by course: then may and ought the saints to pray under deadness, and do as much as their present indisposition can permit them; and the Spirit is seen to come and blow, not by obligation of covenant or promise, on God's part, as Jesuits and Arminians with Pelagians have taught, but in ordinary free practices of grace; as Philip was commanded to come and preach Christ to the eunuch, while he was reading the book of the pro-

phet

phet Isaiah, not because he was reading scripture, or because such a promise is made to those who read scripture, as the angels revealed the glad tidings of the birth of Christ, while the shepherds were attending their flocks in the field; not because they were so doing, as if a promise of the gospel belonged to men because they wait on their calling: and Ananias is sent to preach Christ to Saul, and open his eyes, while he was praying, not because he was praying, but of mere free-grace, which moveth in this ordinary current and sphere of free-love, congruously to the Lord's freely intended end to save his people: even as the Lord joineth his influence and blessing to give bread and a harvest to the sower, Isa. lv. yet not that he hath tied himself by a promise to give a good harvest to every industrious husbandman; yet this ordinary practice of grace, with the commandment of God, is enough to set us on work to pray, to believe, to acts of love to Christ, in the saddest and deadest times.

5. It should be no sinful omission in us, not to pray when the Spirit stirreth us not, if our deadness should free us from all sin, because we cannot run, when the Bridegroom doth not draw. Christ's drawing goeth along with the secret decree of election, but is not to us a signification of the Lord's revealed will, that we should not follow Christ, when he suspendeth the influence of his drawing power.

6. Now, as in nature, men may so dare the Almighty in his face, that God in justice may deny his influence to natural causes; as when malice opposeth the Spirit of God in the Prophet of God, that the Lord refuseth to concur with the oil in Jeroboam's withered arm, that he cannot pull it again to him: 2. When the Lord is put to a contest with false gods to work a miracle, as in his refusing to concur with the fire in burning the three children; for in all causes natural, or moral, or whatever they be, God has a negative voice and more: 3. When the ax or the saw boasteth itself against him that lifted it; the Lord may use his liberty: so (to come to the second consideration) when

Peter

Peter proudly trusteth in himself, *I will die with thee, ere I deny thee;* the Lord, to punish his pride, must deny his assisting grace, when Peter is tempted, that he may know that nature is a sorry undertaker; that the man rideth to heaven on a withered reed, who aimeth to climb that up-hill-city on his own fleshly and clay-strength; and God, to show a black spot on a fair face, in heaven, will have it said, There standeth David before the throne, who once committed adultery, and, to cover the shame of it from men, killed most treacherously an innocent godly man: God here, out of the ashes of our sin, will have a rose of free-grace, that filleth the four corners of heaven with its smell, to grow green up in the higher paradise, for a summer of eternity; and will have no tenants in heaven, but the free-holders of grace. It is a question whether there be more grace or more glory in heaven; for the crown of glory is a crown of grace: that vast sea of the redemption of grace issued from under our sinful falls.

7. Yea, upon this reasonless and fleshly ground, if we omit praying, and so believing, loving, repenting, mortifying our lusts, when the Spirit stirs us not to these acts, and say, *If God will suffer me to sin, let him see to it;* then, upon the same ground, all the justified saints (I should think them devils, not saints) might sin, murder, blaspheme, whore, oppress, commit sodomy, incest, as Lot, deny Jesus Christ, as Peter did and say, As we are not to pray, nor obliged to a constant course in prayer, when Christ draweth not, and when the Spirit moveth us not (as Antinomians say with Mr. Crispe and others, error 49. page 9, 10. Rise, Reign) so neither are we to abstain from murder, denying of Christ, blasphemy, sodomy, when the Spirit of Christ draweth us not, and moveth and stirreth not our soul to abstinency and a holy fear and circumspection that we commit not such abominations; and Peter might say, *I am not obliged to a constant course of confessing Christ before men, unless the Spirit stir me thereunto;* and David or any saint might say, *If the Lord will suffer me to murder the innocent, let him see to it:* for the Lord's

draw-

drawing, and the Spirit's stirring is as necessary in a holy eschewing of sins of commission, as in sins of omission; and by as great, and an every way equal necessity, if the Lord withdraw himself and the Spirit stir not, we must fall in such abominations, when tempted by Satan and the flesh, as in the sins of sinful omitting of praying, praising, believing, when the Spirit stirs us not thereunto; but the truth is, this necessity can neither lay the blame on the holy and spotless dispensation of God, nor free us from guiltiness, because, between God's withdrawing influence and the sin, there doth intervene an obliging law that forbids sin, and our free-will and reason acting the sin freely. But we are commanded, 2 Tim. i. 6. *To stir up the grace of God in us,* [Gr. anazopureis] 'tis an allusion to the priests, who were to keep in the fire that came from heaven; grace is resembled to fire under ashes, which with blowing of bellows is made to revive and burn again. It is the prophet's complaint, Isa. lxiv. 7. *There is none that calleth upon thy name, or stirs up himself to lay hold on thee;* the habit of grace may be warmed, blown upon, and kindled, that as fire makes fire, so grace may put forth itself in acts of grace, and the seed of God in the saints, 1 John iii. 9. may bring forth births like itself; motion here produceth heat.

Object. "But the actual predetermination of grace, is not in your hand; and without this, acts of praying and believing are impossible to me."

Answ. If this were a sufficient reason, then all works of nature, whatever the creature doth, were impossible; for the plow-man should not go to till, sow, and reap, because, without the blessing of the common and natural influence of the first cause, he could do none of these things.

2. Because the saints know not the counsel and mind of God in his decree of joining of his supernatural influence, or his suspending of the same, to this or this act of praying, believing, hoping, loving of Christ, etc. Therefore, upon all occasions, the saints, whatever be their present deadness and indisposition, are to pray, be-

believe, and *to stir up themselves to lay hold on God;* 1. Because, as, in natural and moral actions, men are not to neglect plowing, earing, journeying, eating, drinking, sleeping, buying, and selling, upon this ground, because they are ignorant, whether, in the work, the Lord shall be pleased to join his influence, as the first cause, without whom all inferior causes can do nothing: so are not the saints to neglect to pray, because they are dead and indisposed, upon the ground of their doubting and not knowing whether the *Lord of grace* will be pleased to add his actual assistance of grace, to work in them to will and to do; for the Lord may be pleased to add his supernatural influence in a moment; his wind bloweth when it listeth, his grace moveth swiftly, when, and where he pleaseth: our good disposition is neither rule, condition, work nor hire to move him to work.

 2. It is all one, as if we wilfully neglected to pray, and resisted the predeterminating grace of God, when we know not whether the Lord shall deny his influence or no, yet we disobey the Lord commanding, and so obliging us to pray; for, as if we had his influence at our elbow attending us, so we are to pray, and set to work: yea, our voluntary refusing to pray, we only conjecturing evil of God, and of his free-grace, without ground, must come from sinful wickedness, not from impotency and weakness; for, who told you that Christ would be wanting in his influence? You knew it not from any word of God; and shall you fancy a jealousy against Christ's love without any warrant? Even as a servant commanded to lift a burden, upon a sluggishness should say, It came thither in a cart and two horses, when he would never move an arm to take a trial what he could do, though the burden were above his strength, when he will not do as much as he can, his disobedience is wilful: therefore we may say, if we speak of a voluntary, wilful and groundless forsaking of God, in order of time, we first forsake God ere he desert us; but in order of nature, God first forsaketh us, that is, he withdraweth his heavenly influence from
us,

us, but so as, before and after the act of withdrawing, we are willing that God should withdraw, and be gone; for we love in all the acts of sinning to have a world of our own.

3. We are to believe in the general, we being within the covenant, the Lord will keep his promise, Deut. xxx. 6. *And the Lord thy God will circumcise thine heart, and the heart of thy seed, to love the Lord thy God, with all thy heart, and with all thy soul, that thou mayest live.* Ezek. xi. 19. *And I will give them one heart, and I will put a new spirit within you.--------*v. 20. *That they may walk in my statutes,* Ezek. xxxvi. 27. Then are we so to set to these duties of walking in the Lord's way, as we are to believe he will not deny actual grace, necessary for our perseverance, because it is his express promise, Jer. xxxi. 33, 34, 35, 36. Jer. xxxii. 39, 40. Isa. lix. 19, 20, 21. Isa. liv. 10, 11. Ezek. xxxvi. 26, 27. 1 John ii. 1, 2. Mat. xvi. 18. Luke xxii. 31, 32. though in acts not fundamental, and simply necessary for our being in the state of grace, the Lord hath reserved a latitude of independent sovereignty to act the soul in these and these particular acts, as seemeth good to him, that every new breathing of the Spirit of Jesus, may be a new debt and obligation of free-grace, to Christ.

We are absolutely to pray for the breathings of Christ's Spirit, to go along with us, in all the particular acts of a gracious and spiritual walking; but we know the Lord's absolute good pleasure is his rule he walks by: so here, our desires may be absolute in seeking, where the Lord gives upon condition of his own good-will; nor are our desires in prayer to be conformable to God's decree, or free pleasure, but to his revealed will.

Grace is the colours of the inhabitants and citizens of the house of the lower and higher rooms of the new Jerusalem; all the way, and all the home the saints walk in, is white; Christ keeps not his spouse in a close chamber; it is not one great act of free grace only, when all were in one day redeemed on the cross, but daily Christ weareth his church as a bracelet about his

neck,

CHRIST DYING AND DRAWING SINNERS TO HIMSELF.

neck, as a seal on his heart, as his royal diadem, and a crown of glory on his head, as his love-ring on his hand; this day grace, to-morrow new and fresh supply of grace; the next hour grace; he has strewed all the way to heaven with new grace; every day new wine, new spikenard, new perfume, new ointments.

When will Christ grow old and gray-haired? Never: will his heart ever grow cold of love? No: will be tire of love? Will he wear out of delight in the spouse that lieth for eternity between his breasts? No, no: the love of Christ is always green, as young-like, as fair and white to day, as from eternity; this rose is not altered a whit. Who knows how grace and love in Christ's breast solaced themselves in these infinite revolutions of ages, before the creation? How Christ's heart was cheering itself, and rejoicing to have the first day of the creation dawning, that he might enjoy the love of the sons of men, not then created, Prov. viii. 30, 31. as if grace and love had thought long to find a channel with wide banks to flow in; as if Christ, having infinite love with him, in that long, long age (to borrow that expression) should say, when shall time begin? And sinful men, and my mystical body, and desired spouse my church, have being in the world, that I may out that grace on her? I have love within me and lying beside me; I rejoice to have a lover: as if grace in Christ, had been in too narrow banks, in the infinite acts of the infinite mind of God and the heart of Christ, and longed to have men and angels to give a vent to his love.

And that long *AEvum*, the ages that were before the world was, brought it green to us; that long, long, endless and vast duration, when time shall be no more, cannot make Christ's love change the colour, or grow less, or root one saint out of his heart; when God leaveth off to be God, grace will leave off to be grace. Make Christ repent of grace, if you can: as Christ has washen his spouse, and, in regard of the guilt of sin, has made her all fair and spotless; so doth he daily

lick,

lick, and purge, and cleanse her, in regard of the inherent blot, while she be fair as the sun, and all a new heaven.

Asser. 7. In the third consideration, from the suspension of divine influence cometh our sin, as a necessary consequent, and result; yet so as the Lord's suspension, and our transgression, fall both in the bosom of divine providence: the Lord knoweth why he withdraweth his grace, that we might know how weighty a thing great heaven is laid upon our poor shoulders, and that we would make soul work out of all we have received; and the stock the second Adam has given us if we had not Christ to steer the ship, to lead the minors to heaven, to keep the inheritance to the little heirs of Christ, should evanish to nothing.

Posit. 9. If we consider the Lord's denial of grace, from wicked men; they cannot turn to God, but that impotency lay in the womb of will; it is not weakness only, but also willingness, Mat. xxiii. v. 37. *I would have gathered you,* (saith Christ) *ye would not.* John v. 6. Christ saith to the sick man, *Wilt thou be made whole?* then there was a stop in his will, as well as in his weakness. Jer. xliv. 19. *As for the word that thou hast spoken to us in the name of the Lord, we will not hearken to thee.*

2. Love and delight to do ill, is from the strength and marrow of the will, not from weakness only: the servant that would not leave his master, because he loved him, is a slave for ever, through love to slavery, rather than through impotency to be free. In those that delight to do evil, will hath a strong influence in the evil they do: every sinner esteems his prison of hell, a heaven; his fetters of sin on his legs, as a gold chain about his neck.

3. It is a journey of a hundred miles to Christ; it is impossible to the natural man to compass it, yet he may walk two of these hundred miles, tho' not as a part of the way; he will not so much as cast a sad look after Christ, he will not bestow one sigh of Christ, nor know his own weakness, nor despair of his own hability, nor

lie

lie at the water-side, and cry, *Lord Jesus, come carry me over;* he positively hates Christ: were it possible, that the unrenewed man had the two eyes of a renewed man, to see the beauty and high excellency of Jesus, tho' he had still his own lame legs, he would weep out his eyes for a chariot to carry him to Christ, he would send sad love-challenges after Christ: could those that are scorched in hell-fire, and hear the howling of their fellow-prisoners, and see the ugly devils, the bloody scorpions with which Satan lasheth miserable souls, and the huge, deep, broad furnace of eternal vengeance; have but a window opened to see heaven, the throne, the tree of life, the glory of the troops clothed in white, and hear the musick of those that praise him that sitteth on the throne; or, say but one of the apples of the tree of life were sent down to hell, and that the damned had senses to taste and smell a grain-weight of the glory that is in it, what thoughts would they have of Christ and heaven? It is like they would hate themselves, and send up sad wishes at least, for the continuance of that sight. O could but natural men see Christ with his own light, it may be they would make out for him. But when all is said of this subject, the grace of God is a desirable thing; better have Christ's heart and love and soul toward you, than what else your thoughts could imagine, above or below heaven,

If I be lifted up from the earth, I will draw all men to me.

Article 5. I come now to the fifth article, the condition of Christ's drawing: [Gr. eân hypsosthô ek tês gês] *If I be lifted up from the earth.* This particle [Gr. eàn] (*if*) is not, as in other places, a note of doubting, or of a thing of a contingent and uncertain event: yea, it signifieth here, that Christ was not on any deliberation; *shall I die, or shall I not die, for lost man?* Christ is not wavering, dubious and uncertain in his love; love in Christ is more fixed and resolved upon, than the *covenant of night and day,* and the standing of mountains and hills, Jer. xxxi. 35. Isa. liv. 10. In other places of scripture, it is not a matter of debate; as John

xiv.

xiv. 3. *If I go away* [Gr. eàn poreutho] Christ made no question whether he would go to his Father, 1 John ii. 1. [Gr. eàn tis amárte] *If any man sin, we have an advocate;* there is no doubt but the saints sin; and *if we say we have no sin, we deceive ourselves, and the truth is not in us,* 1 John i. 8.

To be lifted up from the earth, is expounded to be crucified, v. 33. This is Christ's metaphrase of the kind of death which he suffered.

Crucifying was a cursed, shameful and base death, Deut. xxi. 23. yet Christ expresseth it by a word of exaltation, Phil. ii. 9. Lifting up from the earth: Christ's death is life, his shame glory; there be pearls and sapphires of heaven in Christ's hell; and Christ keepeth warm breath of life and hot blood in the cold grave: when he is in an agony, which materially was hell, a glorious angel of heaven is in that hell with him to comfort him: when he is born a poor man on earth, and lies in a horse's manger, there is a new bon-fire in heaven for joy that a great prince is born, a new star appears; the weakness of Christ is stronger than men; the blackness of Christ's marred visage is fair in Christ's poverty, when he has not to pay tribute to the emperor Caesar, the sea pays tribute to the king and prince of kings, Jesus; a fish yields him a piece of money: the lowest and basest reproaches of Christ, his cross and sufferings, drop the honey, the sweet smell of heaven; Christ's thorn is a rose, his sadness joy; O what must immediate rays of glory that come from his face be? The very second table of heaven must be exceeding fatness, the back-parts of the glorious king that sitteth on the throne must be desireable; the fragments and the broken meat of the Lord's higher table must be incomparably dainty: all the earth to these are but husks; the reproaches of Christ must be not so sour as they are reported of. 2. He maketh it the cause of Christ's drawing all men to him. 1. The Holy Ghost will express the cursed and shameful death of Christ, by a word of glory, to be lifted up.

1. The

CHRIST DYING AND DRAWING SINNERS TO HIMSELF.

1. The dying of Christ, is a leaving of the earth.

2. It is a matter of exaltation, that Christ was thus abased: of these two only in this place in the New Testament, and John iii. 15. is Christ's dying so expressed. It is considerable, that in this manner of death, Christ will hold forth to us, that the dying of Christ is in a special manner a leaving of the earth; so Hezekiah, Isa. xxxvii. 11. *I shall behold man no more with the inhabitants of the world;* that is, I must leave the earth, and see the sun no more: and Christ, John xiii. 1. *Jesus knew that his hour was come, and that he should depart out of this world unto the Father:* hence his own word to the repenting thief, Luke xxiii. 43. *To-day thou shalt be with me in paradise.* John viii. 21. *I go my way, and ye shall seek me, and shall die in your sins: whither I go, ye cannot come.*

Doct. Christ choosed a kind of death which was a visible leaving the earth, and a going to heaven, ere he came down again off the cross; for that day his soul was in paradise: as the serpent was lifted up in the wilderness, John iii. 15. Christ's motion of death is from the earth; Christ was tired of the earth, and had his fill of it, he desired no more of it. It is not a place much to be loved by you, saints; for your dear Saviour had but few and sad days on the earth, he was served as a stranger here, and has now left the earth, and gone to the Father. Consider but a few reasons to move you to leave the earth, 1. The earth was Christ's prison, he could not escape out of it, till he paid his sweet life for it: only two that we read of, Enoch and Elias, left the earth, and went to heaven and *saw not death;* these that *shall be changed, and shall not die,* at Christ's coming, have this privilege; but otherwise, all have a bruise in the heel, ere they go out of earth. 2. When Christ was on his journey, he was not so much in love with the earth as to repent and turn back again; as Christ's head and face was toward heaven, so his heart and soul followed, he went from the cross straight-way to paradise. 3. What doth Christ leave? The earth: it is thy fellow-creature of God.

But,

But, 1. The foot-stool for the soles of Christ's feet, Isa. lx. 1. Matth. v. 35.

2. A foot-stool of clay, far from the throne of glory, *the office-house of sin,* Isa. xxiv. 5. *The earth also is defiled under the inhabitants thereof.* Chap. xxvi. 21. *For the Lord cometh out of his place, to punish the inhabitants of the earth for their iniquity.* It is Satan's walk, Job ii. 2. *And the Lord said unto Satan, From whence comest thou? And Satan answered the Lord and said, From going to and fro in the earth, and from walking up and down in it.*

3. It is the poor heritage of the sons of men, a clay-patrimony, Psal. cxv. 16. *The heaven, even the heavens are the Lord's; but the earth hath he given to the children of men.* And oppressors are the land-lords of it. Psal. x. *God ariseth to judge,* v. 18. *that the man of the earth may no more oppress.* Job ix. 24. *The earth is given to the hand of the wicked.*

4. Yea, it is not only the slaughter-house and shambles where Christ was slain, but all the martyrs and witnesses of Jesus were butchered here: for it is said of Babylon, Rev. xviii. 24. *And in her was found the blood of the prophets, and of the saints, and of all that were slain on the earth;* then the earth is the scaffold of the lambs of Christ, where their throats have been cut.

5. 'Tis a common inn, where bed and board is free to men, devils, sons, bastards, elect and reprobate; yea, to beasts, called from their country, Gen. i. 25. *Beasts of the earth;* an earthly minded man, is a fellow-citizen with beasts; it is a home to all but the saints, 'tis their pilgrimage-inns; it is a strange land, and the house of their pilgrimage; Psal. cxix. 19. *I am a stranger in the earth;* so David; so Abraham and his, though they had the heritage of a pleasant spot of the earth by promise, even the land of Canaan; yet they *sojourned in it as a strange country;* and Heb. xi. 13. *Confessed they were strangers and pilgrims on earth.* 2 Cor. v. 6. *While we are at home in the body, we are absent from the Lord.*

6. The first doomsday fell upon the earth, for man's

sin,

sin, Gen. iii. 17. *Cursed shall the earth be for thy sake, in sorrow shalt thou eat of it all thy days.* 'Tis a cursed table to man: and the other doomsday is ripening for it, Rev. xiv. 15, 16. Antichrist's seat, the earth of the false church, is a ripe harvest for the Lord's sickle of destruction. The last doomsday is approaching, when this clay-stage shall be removed, 2 Pet. iii. 10. *The earth and the works therein, the house and all the plenishing, shall be burnt with fire:* 'Tis no long time that we are here, if we believe Job, chap. vii. 1. *Is there not an appointed time to man upon earth? Are not his days like the days of an hireling?* Job. xiv. 2. *He cometh forth as a flower, and is cut down, flieth also as a shadow, and continueth not.* Many generations of hirelings have ended their day's task, and have now their wages; many shadows are gone down, many actors have closed their game, as it may be, and some have *fulfilled their course with joy,* and are now within the curtain, since the creation.

7. It is a poor narrow room. Some, Isa. v. 8 *make house to touch house, and lay field to field, till there be want of place, that they only may be placed alone on the earth:* if they report right of the earth, who make it one and twenty thousand miles in circuit, if new-found lands add to this some poor acres, and the western beast have much of this, Rev. xiii. 8. and the other beast of the East, the Turk, the enemy of Jesus Christ, have eight thousand miles of the land, and other eight thousand miles of sea, making sixteen thousand miles of the two little globes, (I leave others to examine their geography) then it must be a base plea, and a poor lodging to contend for; it were a good use for us to argue, was the earth my Saviour's refuse and his inn, not his home, and if Christ left the earth long ago, and was tired of it, *then let us* (Heb. xiii. 13.) *go forth therefore unto him without the camp, bearing his reproach: for here we have no continuing city, but we seek one to come:* we cannot lodge, far less can we dwell in a house that shall be burnt with fire; nor is there room for us here; there is a more excellent country above, where men have no winter, no night, no sigh-

ing

ing, no sickness, no death, but they live for evermore. We are thronged here for want of room, and 'tis a narrow tent; O what a large land is that above, in which we shall not strive for acres, land, kingdoms? John xiv. 2. *In my Father's house* (saith Christ) *there are* [Gr. monaì pollaì] *many dwelling places*, houses great and fair, and numerous; all these are holden forth to us; the earth is a creature near of kin and blood to the half of us, and our body. When a son of Adam dieth, he returneth, Psal. cxlvi. 4. [Heb. leadmatho] *to his own earth;* had he no free heritage on the world, though he were no landed man, yet when he goeth to his grave, he returneth to his own free heritage, *to his own earth.*

32. *If I be lifted up from the earth, I will draw*, etc.

Here is a special condition of drawing sinners to Christ: the manner of Christ's death: his being lifted up from the earth, holdeth for a drawing of sinners up after him from the earth to heaven; hence Christ's death is a special means of heavenly-mindedness and mortification. So, 1 Pet. ii. 24. *Who his own self bare our sins in his own body on the tree, that we being dead to sins, should live unto righteousness.* Col. iii. 2. *Set your affections on things above, not on things on the earth.* 3. *For you are dead, and your life is hid with Christ in God,* etc. 5. *Mortify therefore your members that are on earth, fornication, uncleanness,* etc.

Beza, Piscator, and others think it probable that Christ uttered this prayer to his Father, in the Syriack tongue, because the Evangelist useth the word [Gr. hypsoo] to be lifted up from the earth, and the word [Heb. rum] signifieth both to cut off, as [Gr. hairest hai] doth as Daniel viii. 11. *by him the daily sacrifice* [Heb. hyram] *was taken away;* and to exalt and lift on high, 1 Sam. ii. 1. *my horn is exalted.* Psal. xcix. 2. *the Lord is high*, [Heb. veram] *above all the people.* Psal. xviii. 47. *Let the Lord be exalted.* Numb. xxiv. 7. Psal. xlvi. 11. Isa. xlix. 11. Gen. xiv. 22. So he holdeth forth such an exalting of Christ, as is to cut off and to slay; this doth come home to drawing of man from sin, and the earth, by that Spirit purchased to us by

Christ's

Christ's death: now, Christ's dying thus, being a taking of him away from the earth, and from sinners, and that in a shameful manner, he being lifted up on the cross, and he in this posture drawing us after him, 'tis a clear working in us the death of sin, and our deadness to the pleasures and glory of the world. 1. Christ died pulling his brethren out of hell and sin; he died, and his spouse in his arms; and this showeth how desirous Christ is to have an union with us; 'tis a posture of love and grace, his head bowed down to kiss sinners, his arms stretched out to embrace them, his bosom open to receive them, his sides pierced, that the doves may fly into the holes of the rock, and lodge there; Christ on the cross, broached and pierced, as a full vessel, out of whom issueth blood and water, justification and redemption from the guilt of sin, and sanctification, is a drawing lover. 2. Here is fulness of power, *To reconcile to himself all things, whether they be things in heaven, or things on earth, by the blood of his cross;* here we are made Christ's friends, to *do whatsoever he commands us,* Col. i. 20. John xv. 15.

3. Nor is there a stronger band or cord to draw men from sin, than the faith of Christ's death, Gal. ii. 20. *I am crucified with Christ, nevertheless I live, yet not I, but Christ liveth in me, and the life which I now live in the flesh, I live by the faith of the Son of God, who loved me, and gave himself for me.* Gal. vi. 14. *But God forbid that I should glory, save in the cross of our Lord Jesus Christ, by whom the world is crucified to me, and I unto the world.* Here is reciprocation of deaths: Paul is crucified to the world, as a dead man, not in the world, nor one of the world's number: a mortified saint drawn up to heaven from the earth, is an odd person, not under tale, he may be spared well enough; the world and the town he lives in may be well without him; as Joseph was the odd lad *separated from his brethren,* and David none of the seven, miscounted in the telling *among the ewes at the sheepfolds,* and forgotten as a bastard, or as *a dead man out of thought:* and again, the world is crucified to Paul, for it looks

like

like a hanged man; it smells like a dead corps to a saint's senses. Now, thus they have not eyes more affected with the world, nor ears more taken with the music, nor a heart more overcome with the lusts of the world, nor a dead man set to a rich table, is affected with all the danties there, or with the harping of the sweetest musician; the man has escaped [Gr. miásmata tû Kosmu] *the pollutions of the world,* to him the world has sooty fingers, and dirty and picky hands, it defiles washen souls; but to the unmortified man, the world smelleth like the garden of God: lust casteth in, and welcometh to eye, and heart, and fancy, granadoes and fire-balls of uncleanness; sinful pleasure has a rosy face, profit has golden fingers, court and honour has a sweet breath, the world is not to him an ill-smelted stinking corps, fit for nothing, but for a hole under the earth: nay, but god-mammon looks like heaven; the world a poor thing; yea, the world of self is but a bag of empty wind, a fancy: (1.) It has no weight, as touching the part of it we count most of, the earth, but so many pounds of clay, the dregs, the earthy bottom of the creation: (2.) The stage that pieces of brittle clay comes upon, and weeps and laughs, and lives, speaks and dies: (3.) The flowers of it, that we are most in love withal, *The lusts of the eye, the lust of the flesh, the pride of life,* are not of God, 1 John iii. 16. (4.) It is a house of glass, or of ice, that stands for the fourth part of the year, for winter, but is removed on the spring, and is never to be seen again; for it passeth away like a figure written on the sea-shore, when the sea floweth, 1 Cor. vii. 31. (5.) The frenzies , or passements of it, pleasure, profit, honour are all sick of vanity and change to the saints that are crucified and buried with Christ, in whom lust is nailed to the cross of Christ; the world is a dead bag of despised dust; and tho' a toe or a finger of a crucified saint will make a motion and a stir, and break a wedge of the cross, because of the indwelling of a body of death, yet hear his arguing, O vain clay-god, dirty earth, I owe thee no love, because my Lord

was

CHRIST DYING AND DRAWING 617
SINNERS TO HIMSELF.

was lifted up from the earth, and has drawn me after him; I care not for this bubble of a vain life, this transient shadow, seeing Christ could not bruik it: what is the fancy of a plaistered and fairded worldly glory to me, if Jesus his face was spitted on? When is this painted globe of an empty, perishing, and death-condemned world to my happiness, seeing my Saviour was a borrowed body, a stranger, and slaughtered in the world, and had all against him, and always the wind on his face?

Now, let us consider what Antinomians say of mortification; "what is mortification (saith (a) Mr. Denne) "but the apprehension of sin, slain by the body of Christ? What is vivification but our new life? The just shall live by faith. I may know (saith the Antinomian) (b) I am Christ's, not because I do crucify the lusts of the flesh, but because I do not crucify them, but believe in Christ that crucified my lusts for me." Much of this lawless and carnal mortification is to be found in Saltmarsh his unexperienced treatise of free-grace, in which he labours to make protestant divines Antichristian-Legalists in the doctrine of mortification; for his way is, "(c) That we are to believe our repentance true in Christ, who hath repented for us; our mortifying sin true in him, through whom we are more than conquerors; our new-obedience true in him, who hath obeyed the law for us, and is the end of the law to every one that believeth; our change of the whole man is true in him, who is righteousness and true holiness; and thus without faith it is impossible to please God: for there is (saith he) (d) great deceitfulness in mortification of sin, as it is commonly taken, (he must point at Calvin, and other protestant divines; for as

Pa-

(a) Denne his doctrine of John Baptist. p. 48. (b) Rise, Reign, unsavoury speeches, Er. 7. p. 19. (c) Free-grace, p. 84, 85. (d) Free-grace, chap. 3. observ. 5. p. 60.

Papists and Arminians commonly speak and teach, we are justified by works of penance and mortification) "for the not acting of sin, or conceivings of lust, is not pure mortification; for then (e) children, and civilly moral men were mortified persons, etc. It is not in the mere absence of the body of sin, for then dead or sick men were mortified persons."

Eaton's honey-comb of justification, chap. 8. pag. 164, 165. "We mortify ourselves only declaratively, to the sight of men----------whereby the Holy Ghost seeth not us properly mortifying our sins out of the sight of God; for then he should see us robbing Christ of that glory which his blood hath freely done, before we begin; nay, but when the wedding garment hath freely purified us in the sight of God, then the Spirit enters in us to dwell, which otherwise he would not do, and enableth us to walk holily, and righteously, to avoid and purify out of our own sight, sense, and feeling, and out of the sight of other men, that sin which the wedding garment hath purified and abolished before out of the sight of God."

But this, in name and thing, is the doctrine of the old Libertines in Calvin's time, as ye may read, Calvin *opuscul instructio adversus* Libertinos, chap. 18. p. 450, 451. "The Libertines (saith Calvin) seem to be of the same mind with us, and extol mortification and regeneration, and say, We cannot be the sons of God, except we be born again; and if we belong to God, the old man must in us be crucified, the old Adam must perish, and our flesh must be mortified;" but they destroy all holiness, and transform themselves into beasts, when they explain to us their regeneration and mortification; they say, "Regeneration is the restitution of man, to that innocency in which Adam was created."

And they expound it thus; "This state of innocen-

"cy

(e) Page 66.

"cy was to know nothing, neither good nor ill, black nor white, not to know or feel sin; because this was Adam's sin, to eat of the tree of knowledge of good and evil; so, by the mind of Libertines, to crucify old Adam, is no other thing than to discern nothing, not to feel sin in ourselves, (as Mr. Eaton saith) but all knowledge of sin being removed, it is, according to the custom of children, to follow sense and natural inclination; hence they drew into their mortification all the places of scripture in which the simplicity of children is commended." Eaton just so, Honeycomb, p. 165. unto natural reason (or sense) objecting, if we be perfectly holy in the sight of God, then we may live freely, as we list, in sin. Paul answers, "Nay, that is impossible; for (saith he) how can we that are dead unto sin live yet therein? That is, as if a man be by justification restored to the case of the first Adam, or perfectly freed from all sin in the sight of God, as he is freed from the traffic and business of this life that is dead, which must needs be, if we be made perfectly holy in the sight of God from all spot of sin? Nay, he cannot chuse but shew and declare the same, by holy and righteous living to the sight of men, and mortify them to himself and to his own feeling and sense, as he is by justification dead to them in the sight of God." Consider, if Antinomians and Libertines do not both join in this, That tho' sin in our conversation and before men, as to walk after our lusts, we being once justified, is truly contrary to the law of God, yet to mortify sin to our sense, is to attain to a sense and feeling that it is no sin to us and before men, as it is no sin in the sight of God, and in the court of justice, because it is freely pardoned. This is the current doctrine of Antinomians.

Par. 2. "When Libertines saw any man troubled in conscience with sin, they said to him, O Adam, knowest thou somewhat yet? Is not the old man yet crucified in thee? If they saw any stricken with the fear of the judgment of God; hast thou yet (said they) a

"taste

"taste of the apple? beware that that morsel strangle thee not; sin yet reigns in thee." So Mr. Towne the Antinomian said, p. 103. "David confessed his sin, not according to the truth and confession of faith, but from want and weakness of faith, and effectual apprehension of forgiveness. Page 97. I can look on myself, my actions, yea, into my conscience, and my sins remain (this is the sense of the old Adam, the unmortified flesh) but look into the records of heaven, and God's justice, and since the blood-shed of Christ (Why, were not the fathers pardoned before Christ shed his blood?) I can find there nothing against me, but the band by my surety is satisfied, and cancelled; and even these present sins, which so fearfully stare me in the face, are there blotted out, and become a nullity with the Lord." I need not cite Mr. Denne, Eaton, Crispe, Saltmarsh; for Towne, and all the Antinomian race, teach that it is unbelief, a work of the flesh of the old Adam, and our weak sense, and want of mortification, that the justified person feels sin, sorroweth for sin, complains of the body of sin, as Paul doth, Rom. vii. for in that chapter (saith Crispe) he doth not act the person of a regenerate person, but of a scrupulous and doubting unbeliever: "But for the justified person, 'tis more than he ought to do, if he confess sin, crave pardon, mourn, fast, walk in sackcloth; he has peace (saith Towne, page 34.) security, consolation, joy, contentment, and happiness, except his flesh rob him of these: 'Tis legal, and bewrayeth the man to be under a covenant of works, if, upon the committee of incest, or the greatest sins, he doubt whether God be his dear Father. Rise reign, Er. 20. And after the revelation of the Spirit, neither the devil nor sin can make the soul to doubt." Er. 32.

Par. 3. "Libertines said, sin, the world, the flesh, the old man was nothing but an opinion or an imagination; and these were new creatures, that were free of that opinion, that sin was any thing, or such as believed sin to be nothing; and the benefit of Christ's death they place in taking away that opinion, by which

"the

CHRIST DYING AND DRAWING   621
SINNERS TO HIMSELF.

"the first sin of Adam entered into the world; and under this opinion, they comprehended all scruple of conscience, sense of judgment, or remorse or sorrow for sin: And when this opinion is taken away, then there is no more sin, nor the world, nor the devil, nor the flesh."*

Antinomians come well near fully up to Libertines in this; for in their writings they tell us, *That what sins justified persons fall in, being once justified, are sins* (saith H. Denne) *of our conversation, and before men, not sins in the conscience and in the court of divine justice.* Or, as Eaton saith, Honey-comb, pag. 165, 166. *Before God they are no sins, and in his sight they are perfectly abolished; yea, and become nullities,* saith Mr. Towne, assertion of grace, pag. 97. *But to our carnal sense and feeling* (saith Eaton) *they are sins, till our sense be mortified; and when we look in ourselves, our own actions, yea in our own conscience.* Now, the adulteries, murders, denying of the Lord Jesus, that David and Peter and other saints fall in after their justification, cannot be sins in themselves; but only in the opinion and sense and feeling of such as commit these sins, and in such

a

*Calvin opusc. advers. Libert. chap. 10. p. 451. "Ut autem (inquit) facilius Libertinorum turpitudo innocescat, Notandum est peccatum, mundum, carnem, Veterem hominem nihil aliud esse apud ipsos, quam id quod opinationem vocant. Sic, piodo ne amplius opinemur, ex eorum sententia non peccamus; sub hae autem opinatione comprehendunt omnem synteresin, scrupulum, deinq; omnem sensum judicii-----qui nullam habent rationem peccati, ipsum pro nihilo duccentes, novas creaturas vocant; quod ab opinatione vacui sint, sicque nullum in se peccatum habeant. En, in quo constituunt beneficium redemptionis per Christum factae; nempe quod opinationem illam destruxit, quae Adam culpa in mundum ingressa, cum haec opinatio abolita est, nullus, ex eorum sententia, superest aut mundus aut diabolus; nullum enim alium, a quo infestentur, inimicum habent."

a sense as is contrary to faith and the light of faith, that believeth free justification in Christ's death, and must be abolished and removed by perfect mortification: then all the justified are to believe, whatever sins they commit in their conversation, and before men, are no sins in themselves, or the court of divine justice, or in relation to a divine law; but they are sins in their sense or erroneous opinion. If Joseph be only dead in the opinion and in his father's mistaking judgment, then he is not really dead, but lives. 2. Under this head, Libertines said, mortification was not in *abstaining from fleshly lusts, that war against the soul;* but in removing the opinion and sense of apprehending sin to be sin. And so Saltmarsh forbiddeth, 1. Any man to doubt *whether his faith be true or no, and it is true faith;* and willeth all within the visible church to believe *God loved them with an everlasting love,* and 'tis true they are all chosen to salvation, and that Christ died for all: and that opinion makes it true, that *Christ died for them all,* and they are all justified in Christ's blood. There is here strong power in opinions. 3. Saltmarsh, Denne, Towne, say, mortification is not in personal abstinence from worldly lusts, but in faith apprehending that Christ dying on the cross satisfied for the body of sin; then if they abstain from adultery, murder, perjury, being once justified, it is of mere courtesy, and of no obligation to either the law or gospel-command; and if they commit such fleshly sins, they are only sins to their weak flesh and opinion, not in themselves; and if they lay aside that opinion and carnal sense, by the which they believe these to be sins, and believe that Christ has abolished them, then these sins are no sins, but perfectly mortified and abolished. That I do them no wrong, I repeat Mr. Eaton's words, Honey-comb, chap. 8. page 165. "The Holy Ghost seeth us not properly mortifying, cleansing and purifying our sins out of the sight of God ourselves, for then he should see us robbing Christ of that glory which his blood hath freely done, before we begin:

"but

"but when the wedding-garment, wrought by his blood hath freely purified them out of God's sight, then the Spirit (we being thus first clear in his sight) enters into us to dwell in us, which otherwise he would not do; but being entered and dwelling in us, he enableth us, by walking holily and righteously, to avoid and purify out of our own sight, and out of the sight of other men, that sin which the wedding-garment hath purified and abolished before out of the sight of God; and so we merely declare before the Spirit, that he himself and Christ's righteousness have originally and properly cleansed and purified away, and utterly abolished them out of God's sight freely." But this holy walking, they talk of, is not opposed to sinning or walking after the flesh; it is but a removing of the sinful sense and feeling or knowledge of unbelief, by which we apprehend sin pardoned to be sin, when it was no such thing, but our erroneous sense or opinion; as the taste of the forbidden apple remaining, could not rightly judge of these sins, because our life of justification is *hid with Christ in God,* and we apprehend ourselves to be under a law, and our lying, adulteries, swearing, etc. to be sins before God, and contrary to his holy law, when they were no such thing; for we being justified, are under no law, and so as clean from sin as Christ himself, but our dreaming sense judged so, but erroneously and falsely; for abolished sins are no sins.

Parallel 4. Libertines taught, That regeneration "was a clean angelic state, in which they were void of sin; and when they were rebuked for sin, they answered, *Non ego sumqui pecco, sed asinus meus,* It is not I, but my ass, or sin dwelling in me, doth the sin." And they cited the same text that Antinomians do now, 1 John iii. *He that is born of God, sinneth not.* So Antinomians. Mr. Eaton frequently, especially Honey-comb, chap. 6. chap. 7. saith, "Being justified, we are made perfectly holy and righteous from all spot of sin in the sight of God." Saltmarsh's flowings, Par. 2. chap. 29. pag. 140. "The Spirit of Christ sets a believer as free from hell, the law and

"bon-

"bondage here on earth, as if he were in heaven; nor wants he any thing to make him so, but to make him believe he is so; for Satan, sinful flesh, and the law, are all so near, and about him in this life, that he cannot so walk by sight, or in the clear apprehension of it, but the just do live by faith." So Saltmarsh abets nothing of what Libertines say; he will not have sin dwelling in the saints, but will have the justified as clear from sin, both the guilt and obligation to eternal wrath (which we yield) and from the bondage and indwelling of sin, of which Paul complaineth so sadly, Rom. vii. as the glorified in heaven. 2. If the justified sin only, he doth not really sin, but only in the dreamings and lying imaginations of his sinful flesh; because sin, Satan, and the law are near him; so that it is the devil, and the living flesh, the ass, not Paul, that makes him, Rom. vii. complain *he was sold under sin.* Crispe saith, *Paul lied when he saith so;* if Peter walk by faith, then Peter shall see his denial of Christ, and David his adultery and murder to be no sins; for they want nothing to make them as free from sin and death, as these that are now in heaven. But believe it is so, believe adultery and murder in these justified persons to be no sin, and they are no sinners; this looketh as like the devilish mortification of David Georgius, and Libertines, and the casting off their sense of discerning good and ill, and the banishing common honesty, and the principles of a natural conscience, as milk is like milk. Yea, Mr. Towne contendeth for a compleat perfection, not *only of persons justified in Christ, but also of performances; so that* (saith he) page 73. *I believe there is no sin, no malediction, no death in the church of God; for they that believe in Christ are no sinners:* and he will have a perfection, not only of parts, but also of degrees, pag. 77. This he proveth from Luther's words perverted.

Parallel 5. "Libertines (saith Calvin) because the scripture saith we are freed from the curse of the law, and made free in Christ, without all distinction, will

"have

CHRIST DYING AND DRAWING SINNERS TO HIMSELF.

"have the whole law abolished, and that we are to have no regard of the law at all."

Now I need not cite Mr. Towne and other Antinomians, who have believers freed, not only from the curse and rigor of the law, but from the law as a rule of righteousness: it is obvious to all that read their writings, to which Calvin answers well, *There is not* (saith he) *any epistle of Paul, in which he doth not send believers to the law, as to a rule of holy living, to which they all must conform their life:* yet Antinomians are not ashamed to pretend Calvin's name and authority for their opinion; when Calvin, in a learned treatise refuting the Libertines of his time, doth clearly condemn the Antinomians of our time, and proveth, from the necessity of sanctification, that we are not free from the law.

"Some a little legally biased (saith Saltmarsh (f) are carried to mortify sin by vows, promises, shunning occasions, removing temptations, strictness and severity in duties." (what aileth him at walking [Gr. akribôs,] *strictly*, Eph. v. 15. Psal. xvi. 4. Jude v. 23?) "Fear of hell and judgment,------ watchfulness, scarce rising so high for their mortification as Christ,----but pure, spiritual, (g) mystical mortification, is being planted together in Christ's death, in our union with Christ. So as a believer is to consider himself dead to sin only in the fellowship of Christ's death mystically, and to consider himself only dying to sin in his own nature spiritually; so as in Christ he is only compleat, and in himself imperfect at the best. I find (saith Saltmarsh) (h) no promise made against the never committing such a particular act of sin which a man lived in, in his unregenerated condition; there are differences made, but it puzzles both divines and the godliest to find a difference between sins committed before and after regeneration; for, take a man in the strength of natural or

"common

(f) Page 68. (g) page 66, 67. (h) page 70, 71.

"common light, living under a powerful word or preacher, by which his candle is better lighted than it was, such a man shall sin against as seeming strong conviction, as the other, if not more; this to me is that which the Libertines of New-England (i) say, That there is no difference between the graces of hypocrites and believers in their kind; and (k) now in the covenant of works, a legalist may attain the same righteousness for truth which Adam had in innocency, before the fall; and (l) a living faith, that hath living fruits may grow from the living law." I see not but all these must follow, if a regenerate David, or Peter, may commit the same act of relapse and falling in the same sin of adultery and murder after conversion, which he committed before conversion; then he must commit the same sin with the like intention and height of bensil of will after as before conversion, and he must now, after he is converted, fall again in the same act of murder, denial of Christ, being now converted, which he committed before conversion; that is, as the unconverted man, with the rankest and highest strength of lust and unrenewed will in its fervor of strength and rebellion, did murder and deny Christ, without any reluctancy and protestation on the contrary from the renewed will, or the Spirit; he may, being converted, fall in the same sin, yea, with a higher hand, and without any reluctancy from the regenerate part; this to me must infer necessarily the apostacy of the saints, as that believers may fall again in these same sins with as high and up-lifted hand against God, with as strong, full and high-bended acts of the will after, as before conversion, so as the battle of the Spirit against the flesh in this wicked relapse does utterly cease: for Perkins, who denieth a man can fall in the same sin, of which he once sincerely repented, and whom Saltmarsh judgeth a legalist and Antichristian in this point, denieth that a con-

vert

(i) Rise, Reign, Error, 16. p. 4.   (k) Error, 12. p. 3.
(l) Unsavoury speeches, Error 6. p. 19.

vert may fall in the same sin that he committed in his unregenerated state, or that a convert can fall in the same sin, every way the same with the like strength of corruption that this convert before acted in his unregenerated condition, yea, or regenerate, he having a further growth of habitual renovation in the second fall, and so a higher habitual reluctancy of the renewed part, than when he formerly fell in the same sin; and so it cannot be the same sin but a lesser, otherwise he never sincerely repented of the former sin, if this be more grievous and committed with a higher hand: now, Saltmarsh his ground is different from all Protestant divines, to wit, (m) "That the wound, pricking or sorrow for sin in an enlightned soul, leaveth no such habitual impression of remorse, as the man dare never adventure to commit the like again; for (saith he) the gales and breathings of the Spirit of sorrow for sin are like the wind, that makes a thing move or tremble while the power of the air is upon it; but as that slackens or breathes, so doth it."

But this is to say right-down, that the Spirit of grace, that *causeth sorrow according to God, and repentance which is never to be repented of,* is but an evanishing and transient act, like the blowing of the wind on a tree. The scripture maketh the Spirit that produceth mourning and remorse of sin, when the sinner *sees him whom he has pierced,* an habitual in-dwelling Spirit, and calls him, Zech. xii. 10. *The Spirit of grace and supplication;* if then the Spirit of adoption be no transient, but an habitual and inbiding grace, as is evident Rom. viii. 23, 24, 25, 26. it is a received Spirit, abiding in us helping our infirmities, teaching us what to pray; it is, Isa. xliv. 3, 4, 5, 6. *Water poured on the thirsty,* making us confess and subscribe the covenant; and if it be, as it is, the *new heart,* Ezek. xxxvi. 26, 27. *The law in the inner parts,* Jer. xxxi. 33. *The seed of God,* 1 John iii. 9. *The anointing abiding in us,* 1 John iii. 27. *A well of*

water

(m) Saltmarsh's Free-grace, page 70.

water of an everlasting spring within us, John iv. 14. I see not how a spirit groaning in us when we pray, Rom. viii. 26. Sighing, sorrowing for the indwelling body of sin, Rom. vii. 14, 23, 27. can be but a passing away motion like a blast of air; but this is the mystery of Libertines, that there is no inherent grace in-biding in the saints, no spring of sanctification, all grace is in Christ and is imputed righteousness; and so they destroy sanctification. 2. The aim of Saltmarsh is here, that if we sorrow once, and scarce that, at the beginning of conversion, we are never to confess or sorrow for sin, when that transient motion like a fire-flaught in the air is gone. But for mortification, against all contrary blasphemies, we say,

Asser. 1. Mortification is not, as Mr. Denne saith, *an apprehension of sin slain by the body of Christ:* 1. Because this apprehension is an act of faith in the understanding faculty, believing that Christ has mortified sin for me; and so Mr. Denne saith, *Vivification is to live by faith,* that is, to believe that I am justified and have righteousness and life free in Christ. Now mortification is not formally any such apprehension, it doth flow from faith as the effect from the cause; but mortification denominates the man mortified, not in his apprehending and knowing that Christ was mortified, and died for him, but in that he really himself is dead. When it is said, Col. iii. 3. *For you are dead,* Gal. vi. 14. *By Christ I am crucified to the world, and the world crucified to me:* by this fancy, the world and the sinful pleasures crucified, must be the faith and apprehension that is in the fleshly pleasures and lawless lusts, by which these lusts apprehended and know that Christ died for them; for Paul saith as well that the world is crucified to him, as he unto the world.

2. Mortification is a deadness in will and affections, and the abating, half death, the languor and dying of the power of our lusts to sin; as a believer is dead to vain glory, when contentedly he can be despised, have his name trampled on, be called a deceiver, a Samaritan; and when the apostles went out from the

coun-

council, Acts. v. 41. *Rejoicing that they were counted worthy to suffer shame;* and the saints are persecuted, *reviled, and men speak all manner of evil against them falsely for the name of Christ,* Mat. v. 11, 12. and yet are so far from the boiling and rising of sinful lusts in them, that, as if their lusts were dead, they *rejoice under the hope of glory;* then are they mortified to these lusts and the like, I say of fleshly pleasures, of unlawful gain. 2. Mortification is when the heart runs not out wantonly and whorishly upon the pleasures of the creature, we are too ready to take the creature in our bosom; but mortification is when the heart stands at a distance from creatures, as Job saith of himself, chap. xxxi. 24. *If I have made my gold my hope, or said to the fine gold, Thou art my confidence,* verse 25. *If I rejoiced because my wealth was great.* 3. It is to be from under the power or bondage to the creature or the world; the believer is above the creature, and the world is under his feet as a drudge or servant, they have no dominion over the heart; he has a wife, as if he had no wife: the man buys and possesseth not; because when he has bought houses, gardens, lands, they are no more in the centre and heart of his love, than if they were the houses and lands of another man; mortification is a lord over the creature. But there is nothing more contrary to the gospel and the grace of Christ, than that the apostles rejoicing, when they were scourged and shamed for Christ, had nothing of reality of scourging, of shame, nor of real joy and deadness to the world in their persons; only they believed and apprehended that Christ was scourged, shamed, crucified for their sins; this is but opiniative, not real mortification; the scripture knoweth nothing of imputed mortification, as contradistinguished from real, personal and inherent mortification.

3. When Paul saith, Col. iii. 5. *Mortify therefore your members, which are upon earth, fornication, uncleanness, inordinate affection, evil concupiscence-----for which things the wrath of God cometh on the children of disobedience;* his sense must be, believe and apprehend
that

that fornication, uncleanness, are mortified to your hand, and that Christ has slain the body of sin on the cross, and there is an end. Now this is to annihilate sanctification, and to make justification all; whereas justification, it alone, is no justification, being separate from sanctification, as Libertines do; and the Popish sanctification, or the moral acquiring of a new habit of holiness, and the infusion of supernatural habits, is not justification at all, yea, nor true sanctification; for they separate it from the free imputation of Christ's righteousness, to a believing sinner; the Libertine takes away sanctification, and makes justification all; the Papist takes away justification by faith and the free grace of God, and in the place thereof substitutes a supposed moral or civil sanctification, which to him is all in all. Further, if this (*mortify your members and the body of sin*) be nothing but believe that Christ has mortified the body of sin already; then, as we are justified from eternity, as some Libertines say, or as all say, before we believe remission of sins in Christ's blood; so to be mortified to our lusts, must be to believe we are mortified to our lusts long before we believe. Paul thinks not so of the Colossians; for he saith, ver. 7. chap. iii. *In which also ye walked some time, when ye lived in them;* ver. 8. *But now also put off all these, wrath, malice,* etc. Then, before they were converted, and did believe, they were not mortified nor freed from uncleanness, fornication, because then they walked in these; except Libertines say, that they were mortified, and did not walk in uncleanness, before they believed, but were delivered in themselves from walking in these lusts, only they were not in their own sense delivered; but in their own sense, though not really, they did walk in fornication and uncleanness; this is not sober divinity; for they say, before we believe we are justified, though not to, or in our own sense and feeling, till we believe: and why are we not also sanctified and effectually called before we believe? For, *whom he called and predestinated, them also he justified,* Rom. viii. 30. And the scripture never shews us of a

man

man in time justified, before he be sanctified and mortified in some measure.

4. When Paul saith, Col. ii. 6. *As ye have therefore received Christ, so walk in him;* he means, so mortify your lusts: then he must intend this, walk in Christ, that is, believe that Christ walked in Christ for you; and *put on love and brotherly kindness, and pray continually, in all things give thanks, abstain from worldly lusts, love one another, keep yourselves from idols, seek the things that are above,* etc. must have no other meaning but believe that Christ has put on love for you, that he abstains from fornication for you, gives thanks, abstains from worldly lusts for you, keeps himself from idols, seeks the things that are above, mortifies his members that are on earth, fornication, uncleanness, inordinate affection, for you; all which are blasphemies: or they can have this sense at the best, *love one another;* that is, Believe that Christ hath satisfied for your hating one another, and then ye love one another; and, *keep yourselves from idols,* that is, apprehend and believe that Christ hath died for your idolatry. Now, this is a mocking of sanctification, not a commanding of it.

Then, to do all these, and abstain from fornication, must be commanded and forbidden in some other gospel; otherwise we perform will-worship, and will obedience to God, without warrant of his word; and the grace of God in the gospel doth not teach us *to deny ungodliness and worldly lusts,* in our own person, but only to believe that Jesus Christ has and doth deny ungodliness and worldly lusts, and perform active and personal obedience for us, and to our hand; for Libertines cannot expound one gospel-charge one way, and another gospel-command another way, and that we are obliged to personal active obedience in one precept, and imputed active or *fidei-jussory,* or mediatory obedience in Christ, in another; yea, when we are in the gospel to believe with a promise of life and righteousness, and that damnation is threatned, if we believe not; so are we commanded to mortify our lusts, and seek the

thing

things that are above with promises, and forbidden to walk after our lusts, *because for these things the wrath of God comes on the children of disobedience;* then I may with equal strength of reason say, that the sense of these passages, *believe in Jesus Christ,* who justifies the ungodly, and believe the immediate testimony of the Holy Ghost witnessing to your hearts that ye are the sons of God, must be not to believe in your own persons, but believe that Jesus Christ believeth for you, on Christ that justifieth sinners; and believe that the Spirit witnesseth to Christ's Spirit, that ye are the sons of God: now, if the commands of the gospel urge us not to personal obedience, but to believe that Christ (as Saltmarsh saith) *has obeyed for us,* and that in the gospel-way, they cannot oblige us in a law-way, as they teach; so by law and gospel we shall be freed from all personal obedience and mortification. Saltmarsh and Libertines bid us be merry and believe that Christ has done all these for us.

A fleshly presumer, walking after his lusts, may believe that Christ *mortified sin for him, obeyed the law and repented for him:* so, if a hypocrite, as an hypocrite, a presumer vainly puffed up, void of all down-casting and conscience of sin, believe that Christ has repented and mortified sin, and believed for him, though he live as the devil, believing and trembling, he is not to doubt his faith.

If they say, that men believing savingly or sincerely, cannot go on in a constant walking after their lusts, never humbled for sin, never despairing in themselves, never out of love constraining them to please God, and strive *to walk in Christ as they have learned him;* for if they be such, their faith is but wild oats, and empty presumption: Then they say, 1. Men know their faith to be sound, by holy walking: 2. Men may call in question their faith, if there works bely their faith: 3. They deny that a fleshly man, as such, and never humbled, can believe. (This is our doctrine.)

Asser. 2. Never any of our divines said, that pure mortification *is the not-acting of sin, or the not-con-*

ceiving

CHRIST DYING AND DRAWING SINNERS TO HIMSELF.

ceiving of lusts; nor that it is the mere absence of the body of sin: this is a soul-slander; which, if wilful Antinomians, though in their own eyes perfectly holy, in the sight of God must answer to God for. Nor is that any argument of weight to prove that *mortification is not the absence of the body of sin, because there* (saith he) *dead and sick men were mortified persons;* except we admit such new vain divinity, that a bodily ague or sickness does extirpate the body of sin out of the soul; which mad or frantic men would not say. And if it be truth, that the body of sin dwelleth in us, in this life; this body of sin is either sin, or no sin: if it be no sin, let Libertines speak plain truth, *We deceive ourselves, if we say we have no sin;* If it be sin, then let Libertines resolve us, how Crispe, and Eaton and Denne say, We are all as holy and clean from sin, being once justified, as our surety Christ is; and as spotless on earth, as the angels and glorified that are in heaven, that stand before the throne: now, 'tis certain, neither in Christ, nor in angels, is there any spot of sin, or any indwelling body of lust. And Crispe* gives this reason why sin dwelling in the saints, is no sin; *it cannot sink* (saith he) *into the head of any reasonable person that sin should be taken away (by the Lamb of God,* John i. 29.) *and yet be left behind; it is a flat contradiction; if a man be to receive money at such a place, and he doth take this money away with him, is the money left in that place, when he hath taken it away?* Mr. Denne has a fine shift for this; he saith, There is *sin in the conscience, and sin in the conversation: Christ hath taken away sin out of the conscience of his called people,* 1 Pet. iii. 21. Heb. x. 22. *The white raiment wherewith the saints are clothed, signifieth not only cleanness before God, but also purity and cleanness of conscience, consisting in the apprehension of that glorious estate and condition in Christ's death; so there is no*

sin

*Crispe Ser. 4. vol. 3. p. 116. †Denne Serm. The Man of Sin discovered, p. 9, 10, 11, 12, 13.

sin at all in the saints, 1 John i. 8. *and the blood of Jesus Christ shall purge you from all sin; in the conscience does joy and gladness dwell, and there is no more place for sorrow and sighing; and there is sin in the conversation or hands: now a man may be strict in conversation, and yet not pure and clean in conscience; so 'tis possible a man hath been an exceeding sinner, and yet is not wholly cleansed from all wickedness in conversation. If this seem a mystery to you, that sin in the flesh (in the body, outward man or conversation) should stand with purity of conscience, take these reasons; if purity of conscience could not be found but where there is purity in the flesh, a pure conscience could not at all be found on earth, for there is none that doth good, no not one,* Rom. iii. 12. (2.) *Purity of conscience ariseth not from purity of conversation; but the original of purity of conversation is from the conscience's apprehension that all our impurities and sins were laid on Christ. And in regard of sin in the conversation,* if we say we have no sin, we deceive ourselves, 1 John i. and 1 John iii. 9. He that is born of God, doth not commit sin.

Answ. 1. Sin in the conversation and outward man, is essentially sin; to kill my neighbour with my hands, to speak with an unbridled tongue, to the apostle James, argueth a vain religion, and must be pardoned, else such sins condemn; for he that offends in one, is guilty of the breach of the whole law. Ergo, Sin in the conversation must be sin in the conscience; and the distinction must be vain, for the one member is essentially affirmed of the other.

Now when John saith, *If we say we have no sin, we deceive ourselves;* he must mean of sin in the conscience, and of sin before God, and not in the flesh and conversation only; because if sin in the conversation be no sin, then when we commit sin in the conversation, we fail against no law of God, and do nothing that can bring us under eternal condemnation; and if in committing sin in the conversation, we do nothing contrary to God's law, we may well say we sin not, and yet not lie in saying so.

2.

2. John must understand sin in the conscience, and in the sight of God, when he saith, *If we say we have no sin, we lie;* because that of that same sin of conversation of which Mr. Denne supposeth John to speak, he addeth in the next words, 1 John ii. 1. *If we sin, we have an Advocate;* but the sin which has need of an advocate, has need also of a pardon, and is a sin against the law, and in the sight of God, and in the conscience.

3. By this we may be pardoned, pure in conscience, justified in Christ's blood; and yet before men, in the flesh, outward man and conversation, under sin, and yet not be guilty before God; so drunkenness, murder, sodomy, incest, denying of the Lord Jesus Christ before men, shall be no sins before God; for that which is pardoned, is no more sin than if it never had been committed, as Libertines say, and is no more sin than any thing that ever our Saviour Christ did, or the elect angels. Now the sins which they call sins of conversation, and the apostle Peter's denial of Christ, and all the sins of the justified saints, their murders, adulteries, parricides, etc. are pardoned, before they have the being or essence of sin, ere they be committed; ergo, when they are committed they are no more sins before God, and in the court of conscience, and no more capable of pardon than they were before they had any being, and were not as yet committed at all: the murder that David is to commit some twenty years before ever he be king of Israel, and shall commit, it is no more his sin to be charged on him in the sight of God, than original sin can be charged on David before David or his Father Jesse be born; what may be charged as a sin on David, in regard he is not yet born, is no more his guiltiness, as yet, than the guiltiness of any other man: now, David's murder, Peter's denial, they being justified from these sins, and pardoned ere the sins have any being in the world, cannot be sins at all, nor such as are charged on mankind, Rom. iii. Psal. xiv. *There is none that doeth good, no not one;* for this sin *stops the mouth of all the world*, makes them
silent,

silent, guilty and under condemnation before God, v. 19, 20. And how Mr. Denne can cite this, to prove that there be some sins of conversation distinct from sins in the conscience, let the reader judge; yea, to my best understanding, by these reasons, while I be resolved otherwise, Libertines must hold neither the elect before or after justification can sin any at all.

4. It is most false, that a man, strict and upright in conversion can have a full and polluted conscience, if you speak of true sincere strictness and uprightness of conversation, as the scripture speaketh, Psalm l. 23. *To him that ordereth his conversation aright, I will shew the salvation of God,* Psal. xxxvii. 14. The wicked draws his bow to slay such as be of *upright conversation;* the principle of a sound conversation is the grace of God, 2 Cor. i. 12. the sound conversation is heavenly-mindedness, Phil. iii. 20. *and is in heaven,* and must be, *as becometh the gospel of Christ,* Phil. i. 27. *a good conversation,* Jam. iii. 13. we are *to be holy in all manner of conversation,* 1 Pet. i. 15. and so even before men; God beholds the sins that we do to men, no less than our secret sins we commit against God; and the scripture requires in our conversation that it be *holy,* 1 Pet. i. 15, *honest,* 1 Pet. ii. 12. *chaste,* 1 Pet. iii. 2. *without covetousness,* Heb. xiii. 5. *not vain,* 1 Pet. iii. 16. *not as in times past in the lusts of the flesh,* Eph. ii. 3. *but the putting off the old man,* Eph. iv. 22. *In charity, in spirit, in faith, in purity,* 1 Tim. iv. 12. Now every conversion contrary to this, argueth an unjustified and unpardoned man, and must be an unpardoned and sinful conversation, so as there is neither strictness nor uprightness, nor any thing but sin and an unpardoned estate, where this conversation is not, whatever Antinomians say on the contrary, being in this, as in other points, declared enemies to the grace of sanctification. But if we speak of a *strict and upright conversation,* in an hypocritical outside, 'tis true, many are, as Paul was, strict Pharisees, precise civilians, painted tombs without, but within *full of rot-*

tenness

tenness and dead men's bones: but this way Satan only saith, Job is a strict walker, and serveth God for hire; and the enemies of Christ join with Antinomians in this, to say, that the justified in Christ, have but sin in their conversation, not wide consciences, because they study strictness of walking with God. But purity of conversation (as the places cited prove) must be unseparably conjoined with purity of conscience; separate them who will, Christ hath joined them.

Mr. Eaton and Mr. Towne call the sins of justified persons, sins according to their sense of the flesh; *but in regard of faith they are clean of all sin, and without spot in the sight of God.* So Eaton's Honey-comb, chap. 5. p. 87. *God freeth us not of sins, to our sense and feeling, till death, for the exercise of our faith, yet in his own sight he hath perfectly healed us.* chap. 5. pag. 95. So Saltmarsh, free-grace, page 57. chap. 3. article 3. calls it the lust of sin, *The just* (saith he) *shall live by faith, which is not a life of sense and sanctification merely, but by believing of life in another.*

I should gladly know, if sin in the justified be sin really and indeed, or against any law? I believe not. 1. Eaton saith, *Sin hath lost its being in the justified.* Saltmarsh, part 2. chap. 32. *If a believer live only by sense, reason, experience of himself, as he lives to men, he lives both under the power and feeling of sin and the law:* now, he should not live; so this is the life of unbelief: ergo, He ought to believe that he hath no sin; and so he hath no sin, nor doth he sin, only the blind flesh falsely thinketh that is sin which is no sin.

But faith is not to believe a lie; then a believer may say, he has no sin; John saith, that is a lie.

Asser. 3. Mortification essentially is in abstaining from worldly lusts, and in remiss and slacked acts of sinning, and in begun walking with God, and acts of holy living, yet so as all these do flow from faith in Christ; another mystical or gospel-mortification is unknown to the gospel, Rom. vi. 4. *Therefore we are buried with him by baptism unto death, that like as Christ was raised up from the dead, by the glory of the Father, so we also*

(con-

(consider the formal acts of mortification) *should walk in newness of life,* v. 5. *For if we have been planted together in the likeness of his death, we shall be also in the likeness of his resurrection:* v. 6. *Knowing this, that our old man is crucified with him, that the body of sin might be destroyed, that henceforth we should not serve sin.* Then, as it is one thing to sin, and another thing to serve sin; so acts of mortification must be in abstaining from greedy sin, as hired servants make it their life and work to sin; and in remiss and weakned acts of sin, as a dying man's operations are less intended and heightned than of a strong man in vigor and health. As for the plenary mortification, expiring, and death of the body of sin, we think it cannot be, so long as we are in the body, Col. iii. 3. *Ye are dead;* v. 5. *Mortify therefore your members that are upon earth, fornication, uncleanness,* etc. To mortify fornication, must be the non-acting of fornication. 1. Because it is an abominable sense to imagine that we mortify fornication, when we believe that Christ abstained from fornication for us. 2. Or to believe that Christ died for our fornication and uncleanness; for both these may hold forth mortification of fornication and committing of fornication. 3. Because for not mortifying of fornication, *the wrath of God comes upon the children of disobedience,* v. 6. Now wrath comes not on wicked men, because they believe not that Christ abstained from fornication for them; many walk in uncleanness, covetousness, who are therefore under wrath, who are not obliged to believe that, because they never heard the gospel. 3. Such an abstinence from fornication is here commanded, as the Colossians and other Gentiles walked in, v. 7. and *which they had now put off with the old man,* v. 8. But the Colossians, while they were Gentiles, and heard not of the gospel, did not walk in this as in a sin, that they believed not that Christ abstained from fornication for them, and satisfied Divine Justice for their fornication; but their sin was, that in person, they committed these sins, 1 Pet. ii. 11. *Dearly beloved, I beseech you, as stranger and pilgrims, abstain from fleshly lusts that*

war

war against the soul. v. 24. *Who his ownself bare our sins in his own body on the tree, that we being dead to sin, should live to righteousness.* Rom. viii. 11. *And if the Spirit of him that raised Jesus from the dead, dwell in you, he that raised up Christ from the dead, shall also quicken your mortal bodies.* v. 12. *Therefore, brethren, we are debtors, not to the flesh, to live after the flesh.* v. 13. *For if ye live after the flesh, ye shall die; but if ye through the Spirit do mortify the deeds of the body, ye shall live.* v. 10. *If Christ be in you, the body is dead because of sin.* Gal. v. 24. *They that are Christ's have crucified the flesh, with the affections and lusts.* Gal. ii. 19. *For I, through the law, am dead to the law, that I might live unto God.* All gospel-commands, to subdue the lusts of flesh, not to serve the flesh, as debtors paying rent thereunto, to mortify the deeds of the body, not to live to ourselves, etc. were mere precepts for justification, not for sanctification and mortification of lusts, and should turn the saints into mere Solifidians and Gnosticks, empty professors, and fruitless trees, if our mortification were not in the weakning of lusts, abstinence from sin-service, and living to him who is our Ransomer. There is nothing more false, than that ever our divines taught 'to mortify sins by vows, promises, strictness, and severity of duties, watchfulness, scarce rising so high for mortification as Christ:' for, 'tis Christ, and faith in his death, that is the spring and fountain of mortification: yet is mortification formally in holy walking, and not formally in believing, for then should we be justified by mortification. For sure we are justified by faith: 2. Faith is a duty of the first table, respecting God in Christ as its object: mortification to uncleanness, vain-glory, or the like, is a duty of the second table, respecting men.

 Asser. 4. The living of the just by faith, is as well the life of sanctification, as of justification; 'tis true, the life of justification is the cause, more compleat and perfect, and the other the effect and imperfect; but our spiritual condition is not only in sanctification, but also in justification. And only enemies of free-grace, separate the one from the other: and heighten the one to feed men
on

on the east-wind, and lessen the other, as if sanctification were an accident, and some indifferent ceremony, that men walk after the flesh, and believe that Christ for them walked after the Spirit, and that is enough: nor do we teach men to weigh their state of grace in the scales of mortification, or simple not acting of sin, as mortification cometh from moral and natural principles, but as it floweth from faith apprehending Christ crucified, and from the Spirit of the Father and the Son drawing the sinner to Christ; and our blessedness is no less, in that corruption is subdued, and that dominion removed, than in that the curse is taken away. Saltmarsh, when he willeth the sinner, as a sinner, a parricide, a man-slayer, a slave to his lusts, to believe and apply Christ as his Redeemer, without any sense of sin or humiliation at all, and then saith, The man's blessedness is more *to have the curse of sin, than the corruption of sin removed,* clearly concludeth, that a man that walks after his lusts, in actual lusting against the Lord Jesus and the gospel, proud, vain, self-righteous, is, as such, a man to believe, and so blessed, and may promise to himself peace, *though he walk after the imaginations of his own heart.*

Nor is *arguing against the temptation with spiritual reason from the word,* as Joseph did, Gen. xxxix. 8, 9. and Job, chap. ii. 9, 10. and David, 2 Sam. xvi. 7, 8, 9, 10, 11, 13, 14. our own power, or contrary to the fighting by the shield of faith, the word of God; as Saltmarsh imagineth.

Asser. 5. It is to be reputed as a most blasphemous assertion, that we know we are Christ's, *not because we crucify the lusts of the flesh, but because we do not crucify them:* for, 1. Crucifying of our lusts, is a mark of our being in Christ, Gal. v. 24. Rom. viii. 13. this maketh walking after the Spirit, and *departing from iniquity, and being pure in spirit, and dying to sin,* a mark of no interest in Christ, contrary to Rom. viii. 1, 2. 2 Tim. ii. 19. Matt. v. 8. 1 Pet. ii. 4. Gal. i. 4. 1 Pet. i. 18. contrary to the whole gospel: which was

that

CHRIST DYING AND DRAWING 641
SINNERS TO HIMSELF.

that blasphemy of David George, who taught, 'Mortification was to act all uncleanness, without shame, or sense of sin; and the more men are void of the common passion that follows sin, the more mortified and spiritual they are:' and this is very like the Libertines way, who teach, (a) 'That to take delight in the holy service of God, is to go a whoring after God;' and that they are (b) legally biased, 'that would mortify the flesh by watchfulness and strictness of walking;' whereas, to put our crown on our mortification, as if we were thereby justified, is the idolatry: 'But the delighting in the law of the Lord, and taking of the Lord's testimonies for our heritage, a serving the Lord with cheerfulness and fervour of spirit,' Psal. i. 2. Psal. cxix. 111, 162. Isa. lviii. 13. Psal. cxii. 1. Rom. vii. 22. Rom. xii. 8. 2 Cor. ix. 7. Phil. iv. 4. Acts xx. 24. Jam. i. 2. are marks of a blessed condition. If any teach, 'That we mortify the flesh by watchfulness and strictness of walking, as if these did merit mortification,' we judge it cursed doctrine. But, if Libertines deny, and they do, that acts of mortification do formally consist in watchful, strict and accurate walking with God, in being not taken, nor madly drunken with the lusts of sin, but dead to pleasures, as these acts flow from the Spirit of Christ; we curse their fleshly doctrine also.

It is no consequent to say, Because (c) 'Regeneration is not a work of nature, but of the Spirit of God; and the way of the Spirit is not so gross and carnal as the divinity of former times, it being hard to trace and find the impressions of the Spirit; therefore we are not to take experience so low, and carnally, by the feelings of flesh and blood, and signs not infallible, as to write of regeneration, as philosophers do of moral virtues.

Answ. 1. Regeneration is above nature every way,

but

(a) Rise, Reign, Error 57. p. 11. (b) Saltmarsh free-grace, Chap. 5. p. 68. (c) Saltmarsh free-grace, chap. p. 71, 72.

but in this it is most suitable to nature, that as a man come to age doth not at all times, even when he is sick, in a swoon, in a deep sleep, know that he liveth; yet ordinarily life hath reflex acts on itself, so as living, man may know that he lives by many signs of life; so a regenerate man, except he be deserted, may know that he lives the life of God.

2. If Antinomians find out new divinity, less carnal, more spiritual, than in former times, how is it that christians are to live from under all rule of life; and not to pray, *Forgive us our sins, when they pray for daily bread;* and that none justified are to confess their sins and to sorrow for them; that new obedience, mortification, repentance, is to believe, that Christ has done these for us; that we are not to pray continually, but only when the Spirit stirreth us? An hundred of these false ways may be shown: is this more spiritual divinity than in former ages? Is it not the most carnal divinity that we read of? For, when Dr. Taylor objecteth to Antinomians, as a limb of their fleshly divinity, 'No action of the believer after justification is sin;' Mr. Towne answereth nothing at all, but off the way, 'No action is sin, the disorder and ataxy of the action is the sin.' But, Dr. Taylor meaned, there is no disorder in the actions of a justified man, by their way: to this Mr. Towne replieth not one word, but saith, 'Unto faith there is no sin, because there is not one spot in a justified person:' and he citeth Rev. i. 15. Eph. v. 26. Cant. iv. 7. and vi. 9. 1 Cor. vi. 11. because *Christ hath washed,* Rev. i. 5. *purged,* Heb. i. 3. *abolished,* Heb. ix. 26. *all our sins, and hath made us holy and unblamable, and unrebukable in the sight of God:* we are, like Christ, *void of sin;* which is not the removal of sin, but of the guilt; that is of the obligation to eternal wrath, and the curse of the law: *for if we say, we* (even though justified, as John the apostle was)

have

*Mr. Towne's asser. of free-grace p. 71, 72, 73.

have no sin, we are liars. Can this be any but a divinity of the flesh that Antinomians teach?

3. Sanctification is a far other thing than moral virtues: a moralist that is temperate, chaste, is never so over-clouded in his faith, as to doubt whether he be a temperate man or not; a sanctified soul will often doubt if he have any sanctification at all. 2. A sanctified man must have the use of the light of the Spirit to know his state, and *these things that are freely given him of God,* 1 Cor. ii. 12. A moralist knoweth with the light of his own sparks, what he is; Does Saltmarsh know of any desertions or over-cloudings of the Spirit, in a moral Seneca, Aristides, Plato? 3. The moralist dreams of justification by is virtues. 4. He needs only natural reason, not the breathings and stirring of the Spirit, to act according to his moral habits. 5. Nor are his habits infused from heaven, but his own conquest. 6. Nor knows he an absence or a presence of the Spirit; all which are peculiar to sanctified and justified persons.

We are not completely (saith Saltmarsh) *or perfectly mortified to sin, by our being planted into Christ, and the fellowship of his death.*

Answ. But if mortification be the faith and apprehension, that Christ mortified sin for us, then as we are perfectly justified, so are we perfectly mortified: now, Antinomians teach the former.

Let not (saith he) *mortification of sin in Christ, tempt any to a neglect of mortification of sin in the body, no more than the free-grace of God in forgiveness of sin ought to tempt any to take liberty to sin.*

Answ. 1. Surely, as to add any thing to justification, so to advance in mortification, must be as wicked and blasphemous, according to the way of Antinomians: for, if mortification be the believing that Christ has slain the body of sin, as Mr. Denne saith (and Saltmarsh seconds him as a brother) then our neglect of mortification is no sin; for we are to believe, that Christ hath removed all neglects of mortification, if mortification be faith and belief that Christ mortified sin for us.

2. I

2. I cannot neglect justification, or apprehension that Christ mortified sin for me, any otherwise, but by a remiss act of believing, or neglect of a higher measure, and a more intense and strong act of faith, and not by an abstinence from fleshly lusts: such an abstinence is no faith, or apprehension that Christ has slain and mortified the body of sin for me; for non-sinning cannot formally be believing; that were nonsense.

3. If the meaning be, that we are not to abstain from fleshly lusts, that is, from sins that the flesh or the body of sin acteth in us; this is neither mortification, nor any part thereof, to Antinomians. But I defy and provoke Antinomians to satisfy us in these, if Saltmarsh one of their patrons can,

1. Whether or no *sins of the body,* or *in the body,* as Saltmarsh calleth them here, or *sins of conversation,* as Mr. Denne saith, or sins (as Mr Towne* speaketh) *arising out of the earthly members of our flesh,* be sins against the *law of God?* If so, they involve the justified under a curse, and so they are sins formally; and the justified either cannot sin at all, which I fear is the fleshly way of Libertines, a way that my soul abhors, if I be not deceived; or then, the sins, the adultery of a justified man, the murder, the denial of Christ in Peter, is no less a breach of the *law of God,* than the denial of Christ in Judas (it may be the one with a greater bensil of will denies Christ, than the other; *sed magis & minus non variant speciem*) and so the justified do as truly and essentially sin against the law, as the unregenerate doth; then they are not as clean from sin as Christ the surety is.

2. If murders, adulteries, committed by the justified, be sins of their flesh and body; that is, such sins as they are not by any prophet or Nathan to be rebuked for; because the Spirit, that is not in their power in his actions and motions, did not assist them to abstain;

and

---

*Towne's asser. of free-grace, P. 72.

and they are under no other law, but the only irresistible action of the Spirit, to hinder them physically in all sins, to abstain from any sin? This must be Antinomians' spiritual divinity, to make no rule, no law of ordering the life and conversation of a justified man, but only the motions of a Spirit separated from the word.

3. Whether or not, when Paul said, Rom. vii. 17. *Now, it is no more I* (that sin) *but sin that dwelleth in me:* v. 18. *I know that in me, that is, in my flesh, dwelleth no good thing;* his meaning be, according to the Antinomians' divinity, that no regenerate man sinneth, but his flesh and sensitive part, which is not capable of any law, sinneth; but he who acteth the sin being above, or from under law, rule or direction, sinneth not against God, or any law?

4. Whether or no the Enthusiast's rule, which is the immediate and irresistible inspiration of a spirit, which doth press a brother to kill a brother, and has done it, as Bullinger saith of the practice of divers Anabaptists, and some of *New England* said, Tho' they resisted the *Christian magistrate*, and fired the *churches of Christ* there, yet *they should be miraculously delivered from the court, as Daniel was from the den of lions:* Whether or no this rule of the Spirit's immediate acting, without law and gospel, be the only law and rule that the justified are under and led by?

5. Whether from this spring does not flow the rejecting of all the scriptures or written law or gospel, as if they were but a covenant of works, and the walking by the Spirit separated from the word, and the denying any marks, as love to the brethren, sincerity, keeping of the commandments of God, recommended in the word, John xiv. 15. 1 John ii. 3, 4, 5. 1 John iii. 14. and if this be the spiritual divinity spoken of here?

6. Whether or no sins of the body and of the flesh or conversation (as Antinomians call them) be not sins against the *law of God,* and make the justified truly guilty, if the Lord shall enter into judgment with them, and though they that commit them be justified,

and

and so also absolved from obligation to eternal wrath, are not formally and inherently blotted and sinful in those sinful acts?

7. If they are not to be sad for them as offensive to the authority of the law-giver and the love of Christ, though they be not to fear the eternal punishment of them? For sorrow for sin, and fear for sin, are most different to us.

8. Whether the free-grace of God doth not tempt men to sin, most kindly and from the nature of free-grace, according to the Antinomians way? If the free-grace of justification do free the justified so from sinning, as their indulgence to the flesh and sinful pleasure, can be no sin in God's court, no more than there can be sin in Christ; and if they be as free, notwithstanding of all the sins they do, being once justified, as if they never had sinned, or as the sinless angels; and if the essence of sin, and all they do against the *law of God,* be as clean removed, as money 'taken away out of a place, which sure cannot be said, without a contradiction, to remain in that place, as Dr. Crispe speaketh, and that before the sin be committed? Whether can a thing in its essence be wholly removed as if it had never been, before it have any being at all? Can a rose be said to be withered and destroyed, as if it had never been, before ever that same rose spring out of the earth? Sure faith cannot fancy lies and contradictions.

However it be, Christ's death teacheth us mortification of our lusts; it is a mortified like death, for he dieth on a visible journey leaving the earth; his back was towards life, pleasure, profit. He is not dead to his lusts, whatever be his boasting, who is not *dead in or with Christ, to sin.*

For, 1. Christ's death and his contempt of the world teacheth that we should follow him. 1. He looked even straight before him, neither to the right, nor left-hand, nor behind him; the meadows, buildings, fair flowers and roses in the way of this passenger, did never allure him to stay in the way, and fall in love with any thing on this side of heaven, Heb. xii. 2. as our [Gr.

Ar-

Archegos] *the Captain of our faith* [Gr. anti tes prokeiménes auto charâs] *for the joy that was set before him, he endured the cross;* his heart was so upon the crown, and that which was his garland, his conquered spouse, that he did run his race with all his breath and wearied not; his heart was much upon the prize that he did run for.

2. He was nothing beholding to the world; he came to the house of his friends, they refused him house-room and lodging, John i. 11. *His own received him not,* and therefore he was fain to ly with *the birds of heaven and the foxes of the earth;* Christ was no landed man on earth, he had never a free house of his own above his head; he had a purse, but no free rent, no income by year, Mat. viii. 20. he had not whereon to buy a grave when he died, John xix. 41. The earth was his Father's land; but he lodged in a borrowed grave; his coat was all his legacy, yet it could not buy a winding sheet to him; the soldiers thought it too little fee for their pains in crucifying him; and it was not of much worth, when they put it to the hazard of lots, take it that wins it: his heart was never on the world, he refused a king's crown, when it was offered to him without stroke of sword, John vi. 15. *He had neither heart nor leisure to enjoy the world.* John iv. When he wanted his dinner, he begged a drink of water from a stranger, and was weary with walking on foot; yet he was the one great Bishop, the Head of the body the church; and had neither horse nor coach, and he could have made the clouds his chariot; *He became poor, that we might be made rich.* Was sweet Jesus thy Saviour a poor man in the world? Learn to be a stranger, and to want, and to be content to borrow, and to lie in the fields, and to have a dead heart to the world. 1. *O glory worldly, O all crowns, and gold,* and stately palaces, blush, be ashamed, take not such a wide lodging in the hearts of saints, go not with so broad and fair peacock wings; ye are too big in men's eyes, Christ our dear Saviour refused you. 2. Rich saints, drink at leisure, use the world at the by, as if you

used

used it not. Look with half an eye, the least half of your desire, upon this borrowed shadow; let not thy heart water, nor itch after white and yellow clay. 3. Gold, thou art not God; saints, look over crowns and court; see, see what a kingdom is above your hand; pilgrims, drink, but lay not down your burden and your staff; let it be a standing drink, and be gone. 4. Ye are longed for in heaven. 5. Your King lodged with poverty, and abasement, and shame; love the lodging the better, that he was there before you. Christ's love is languishing to have you soon out of this passing transitory world, and to be at your best home.

3. Christ did never laugh on earth as we read of, but he wept; O what a sad world! Psal. lxix. 11. *I made sackcloth my garment;* O precious Redeemer, cloth of gold is too coarse for thee. v. 20. *Reproach hath broken my heart, I am full of heaviness;* he was a man made of sorrow, Isa. liii. 3. and had experience and familiar acquaintance with grief. There be a multitude that goes laughing, harping, piping and dancing to heaven, as whole and unbroken-hearted christians; "Mystical mortification (say they) is only faith, and joy; we have nothing to do with weeping, confessing, sorrow for sin; that is a dish of the law-vinegar and gall, it belongs not to us; we are not under the law, but under grace; that sour sauce is the due of carnal men under the bondage of the law." But will Christ wipe away tears from the eyes of laughing men, when they come to heaven? believe it, there goes no unbroken and whole professors to heaven; that is far from mortification: heaven will not lodge whole souls, with their iron-sinew in the neck, never cracked by the death of Christ.

Object. 1. "But godliness is not melancholy, but joy of the Holy Ghost."

Answ. 1. True; but whom does Christ, with the bowels and hand of a Saviour, bind up, but the broken-hearted *mourners in Zion,* and *such as ly in ashes?* Isa. lxi. 1, 2, 3. Sorrow and joy may lodge in one soul.

2. Christ feasts some in the way to heaven, and di-

ets

ets them daintily; some feed ordinarily on the *fat and marrow of the Lord's house*, Psal. lxiii. 5. And *there is a feast of fat things, a feast of wines on the lees, of fat things full of marrow, of wines on the less well refined,* Isa. xxv. 6. and has not the *King a banqueting house,* a wine-cellar (Cant. ii. 4.) for some? and do they not feed upon the honey-comb, and the wine, the *spiced wine and the milk?* Cant. v. 1. Cant. viii. 2. But these that drink wine at some times, must at another time be glad of a drink of water.

2. And if there be varieties of temperature of saints, some rough and stiff, some mild, some old men, and some babes, 1 John ii. 13. And as there be some lambs, some fainting, some weak and swooning tender things, that Christ feeds like kings' sons, with wine of heaven: so there be others that are under the care of the steward Christ, who are heifers and young bullocks, like Ephraim not well broken yet, Jer. xxxi. 18, 19. and there be hoping and waiting saints, that must *bear the yoke in their youth,* Lam. iii. 26, 27. and sundry kinds and sizes of children; every one must have their own portion and diet, 2 Tim. ii. 15. Mat. xxiv. 45. One man's meat is another's poison, and yet they are both the sons of one Father.

3. Can every head that shall wear a crown in heaven, bear this wine, on the earth, being clothed with such a nature? and must every one be taken into the *King's house of wine,* and sit between the Father's knees, at the high table, and eat marrow, and drink spiced wine? are there not some set at the by-board, that must be content with brown bread and small drink or water?

4. Tho' the word should be silent, it is easy to prove that saints have not the like fare of Christ's dainties at all times; for the church, Cant. ii. 4. is taken into the *banqueting house,* and feasts on fatness of free-love; and yet again, Cant. iii. cries hunger, and seeks and finds not; and, Cant. v. 1. feasts with Christ on wine and honey and milk; but ver. 5, 6. there is a dinner of gall, hunger, and swooning; *My soul* (saith the spouse) *went out of me.*

5. How

5. How many saints go to heaven, and you never heard another word from them but complaints, want of access, straitning of spirit, deadness, absence, withdrawings of the beloved, at every slip, scourged, chastised every morning? Their complainings cannot be praised; yea, till they land, they are every sea-sick, till they be ashore, never see a fair day, nor one joyful hour, Psal. lxxxviii. 15. *I am afflicted, and ready to die,* [Heb. minnohar] *from my youth I suffer thy terrors, and am distracted sore.* For the Lord's dispensation, we may say, *who hath been upon his counsels, and who hath instructed him?* Antinomians allow daily feasts, & the strongest of the gospel-wine for daily food to all that are sinners; this we dare not do: but as we judge it a sin to stand aloof from free-grace, because *we have no money nor hire;* so to fill out the wine of the gospel more largely and profusely than the King of the feast allows, even to sinners as sinners, and all unhumbled and highminded Pharisees, is to be stewards to men's lusts, and to turn the gospel into the doctrine of licence to the flesh, and not to extol free-grace.

4. Christ in his way had no reason to glory in friends. (1.) How was he despised of them? Isa. liii. 3. *We did hide our faces from him;* all his friends thought shame of him, and fled the way for him, they refuse to give him one look of their eye. (2.) Psal. xxxi. 11. *I was a reproach among all mine enemies, but especially among my neighbours, and a fear to mine acquaintance; they that see me without, fled from me;* this is more, to be a reproach and a fear to neighbour and friend. (3.) Nature and blood went against itself, Psal. lix. 8. *I am become a stranger to my brethren, and an alien to my mother's children.*

All the saints idols are broken, to the end God may be one for all. This is a good ground of mortification; men shall be crul brethren, and redeemed ones shall have the iron bowels of an ostrich, a lion to kill you, and to consent to make war against you, that Christ's meekness may appear; friends must be sour, that Christ may be sweet; and you may be deadned in love to brethren and

and friends, yea to a forsaking father and mother, Psal. xxvii. 10.

5. No lust had any life or stirring in Christ, this cannot be in us; the old man, that has lived five thousand years and above, is not so gray haired as to die in any saint while he die; his *deceivable lusts* at best come to a staff and trembling, and gray hairs in the holiest and most mortified, but expire not till dust return to dust.

If I be lifted up, I will draw. When Christ is weakest and bleeding to death on the cross, he is strongest, Col. ii. 15. *he triumphed over principalities and powers;* there is more of strength and omnipotency in Christ's weakness, than in all the power and might of men and angels; the *weakness of God is stronger than men,* 1 Cor. i. 25. there is more of life in Christ's death, than in all the world; he was a grain of wheat cast in the earth, and sown in the grave, and there sprung out of dead Christ a numerous off-spring of children, all the redeemed ones grew out of the womb of his grave, his catholick church was formed out of the side of the *second Adam,* when he was fast asleep on the cross.

2. This makes the way of redemption so much the more admirable, that out of a way of weakness, of death and shame, the Lord should out-work sin and the devil, and rear up to himself out of dust, hell and death, glory, heaven, and eternal life: infinite glory made a chariot of shame, and from it highly honoured Christ: Omnipotency did ride upon death, and triumph over hell and devils, 1 Cor. i. 27. *God hath chosen the weak things of the world, to confound things that are mighty,* 28. and [Gr. tà agenê tû kosmu] *the base, the kinless thing that are of no noble blood,* and [Gr. ta exuthenemata] *things that are despised, the nothings of the world he hath chosen, and things that are not,* [Gr. kaì ta mo ònta] that he may make *idle and fruitless, or bring to nothing, things that are.*

Use. If the Lord Jesus at the lowest and weakest, his dying and shamed condition, be so strong as to pull his bride from under the water, and out of the bottom of

hell,

hell, up to heaven; what power has he now, when he is *exalted at the right-hand of the Majesty of God,* and has *obtained a name above all names,* and is crowned *King in Zion?* It is better to be weak, and sick, and weep and sigh with Christ, than to be strong, and live, dance, sing, laugh, and ride upon the skies with men in the world; sure his enemies will be now *less than bread to him,* and shall be his footstool.

2. Christ had cause to mind himself, and forget us, being now lifted up to the cross under extreme pain and shame; but love has a sharp memory, even in death.

Two things help our memory, and they are both in Christ: 1. Extreme love; the mother's memory cannot fail in minding her child, because the child is in her heart, and deep in her love: the wretch cannot forget his treasure, his gold is in his heart: Christ loved his church, both by will and nature, and cannot forget her, she is Christ's gold, and his treasure, Isa. xlix. 14, 15. Christ could not cast off nature, the husband cannot forget the wife of his youth; and the deeper love is rooted, the memory of the thing loved is the stronger. O but it is many years since Christ loved his redeemed Ones! 2. Sense helpeth memory; a man cannot go abroad in cold weather and forget to put on his clothes, sense will teach him to do that; a paining boil will keep a man in mind of pain: the church is a fragment and a piece of mystical Christ; he cannot forget his own body; the church is bone of his bone; the head forgets not a wound in the hand. Love did sweat up an high and mighty mountain with thousands on his back: 1. O what sweating for us, even in death, and sweating of blood! 2. O what praying, and praying more earnestly, *Lord help me up the mountain with this burden;* and all this time, he is drawing and carrying on his shoulders hell up to heaven. 3. What a sight it was to behold Christ dying, bleeding, pained, shamed, tormented in soul, wrestling in an agony with divine justice and wrath, receiving strokes and lashes from an angry God, and yet he kept fast in his bosom his re-

deemed

deemed ones, and said, *Death and hell, pain and wrath shall not part us. It pleased the Lord to bruise him, to afflict his soul, not to spare him, to smite the Shepherd;* but it pleased him in that condition, out of deep love, to draw his redeemed ones from the earth up after him to heaven. Christ was a good servant, he always minded his work, even to his dying day.

Use 1. If he in his weakest condition draw all men,

1. How easily can he with one look, blast the beauty and strength of his enemies, being a God of such majesty and glory? How weak is hell and all the iron gates of it, when Christ, at the weakest, plucks his church out of the *jaws of death,* and triumphs over death and hell.

2. It shall be nothing to him with a pull of his finger, when he appears the second time in power and great glory, to break the pillars that bear up heaven and earth; and to dissolve, with the heat and sparkles of fire that come from his angry face, the great globe of the whole world, as a hot hand can melt a little snowball of some few ounces weight; and to loose, with one shake of his arm, all the stars in heaven, especially since the world is now but an old thread-bare-worn case, and the best jewel in the case is man, who is old and failed, and passeth away like a figure; and it shall be but a case of dead bones, and of old broken earthen sheards at Christ's coming; and Christ, with no labour or pain, can crush down the potter's house, mar all the clay-vessels, and burn with fire all the work of the house, the houses, castles, towers, cities, acres, lands, woods, gold, silver, silks, and whatever is in it. Glory not in the creatures, but glory in Christ.

3. Death and the cross are the weakest things in the world; but, being on Christ's back, they are the strongest things in the world, 2 Cor. xiii. 4. *Though he was crucified through weakness, yet he liveth by the power of God:* 1. The cross was Christ's triumphing chariot; there is power and strength in Christ's tears, in his sighs, in the holes that the thorns made in his head, in the stone laid above him, when he is buried. 2. His shame,

shame, death, and burial, made the greatest turning of wheels in the earth and heaven that ever the ears of man heard. The more providence does concern God, his highness, his glory, the more special it is and accurate: not that infinite wisdom is not infinite in the care over a worm, as over an angel; but because there is more art of seen external visible providence in whole kingdoms, in kings, in the church, than toward one man or one saint; so providence must have more of the art, wisdom, special care of God toward his catholic church, and his own only begotten Son in redeeming the whole catholic church, than in caring for the lilies of the field, and the worms of the earth, or some one particular saint: what wonder then there be an eminent providence observed in the disposing of Christ's coat when he died, and in the borrowing of an ass for him to ride on, and in casting a garment on the ass for a saddle, or a foot mantle, when he rode into Jerusalem? So in Christ's suffering there is much of God; there was a more noble work in his dying on the cross, than the creating of the world. And there were four things of the greatest baseness imaginable upon Christ in this providence; for there were upon Christ, 1. The weakness of death. 2. Extreme pain. 3. The openest shame; Christ dying poor, despised, forsaken of all, friend and unfriend. 4. The curse of the law in the manner of his death; yet in all these he acted the part of a triumphing Redeemer, Col. i. 19. *For it pleased the Father that in him all fulness should dwell:* ver. 20. *And (having made peace through the blood of his cross) by him, to reconcile all things to himself, whether they be things in earth, or things in heaven.*

Use. Yea, we see Christ has never losed any thing by the cross, but has gained much, Rom. viii. 37. *In all these we are more than conquerors:* in death we die not, a dead man is more than a conqueror; and if he should not live and triumph, he could not be capable of conquering, far less could he be *more than a conqueror.* Rev. xii. 11. the saints overcome, but it is a blood vic-

tory;

tory; *they overcame by the blood of the Lamb, and by the word of their testimony:* then, if the word be an overcoming and prevailing thing, the cause overcame. But what if the persons be killed, then they are overcome? No, for the victory is personal; the *followers of the Lamb* overcame by dying, because *they loved not their lives unto death;* triumphing in the grave is admirable. Things work in a threefold consideration: 1. According to excellency of their being, *modus operandi sequitur modum essendi:* men's operations, flowing from reason, are more excellent than actions of beasts; and angels excel men in their actions. 'Tis a noble and excellent being that is in Christ, being the only begotten Son of God. What excellency of working is this, that not only the dead, but death should live, and shame should shine in glory? The dumb may speak, and the deaf hear; but that dumbness should speak, and deafness hear, is more than a miracle: here Christ causeth death, shame, cursing be immediate organs and instruments of life, glory, immortality and honour. 2. Christ was never weaker and lower than now, and never more glorious in his working, Isa. lxiii. 2. *Wherefore art thou red in thy apparel, and thy garments like one that treadeth in the wine-fat?* Rev. xix. 15. *He himself was trodden on in the wine-press, and fierceness, and wrath of Almighty God.* But, Isa. lxiii. 1. *He is glorious in his apparel, and travelleth in the greatness of his strength:* so, in his lowest condition, when he is shamed, he is glorious; when he is weak and lying on his back, he walketh, and *walketh in the greatness of his strength.* From the baseness of the instruments, in excellent works, we collect that there must be a high, noble and excellent cause, who acteth on these instruments. 3. Agents work according to the distance they are to that they work upon; a shot afar off is weaker. Now, on the cross, 1. Christ is nearer to us, and so getteth a heartier lift of us; death and blood are near of kindred to us. 2. Christ coming so near death, hath a fairer shot and visie of death, and the grave, and hell, and all our enemies, Heb. ii. 14, 15. *He died,*

that

that by death he might destroy him that had the power of death.

1. Drawing when he is on the cross, doth most extol Christ's love: death parteth company amongst men, and often parteth loves; but Christ dying, drawing his church into his bosom and heart, as not willing that the grave should part them and him, John xiv. 1. *Christ having loved his own that were in the world, to the end he loved them:* Christ died loving, and died drawing.

2. The cords of love, with which he draweth sinners, were woven and spun, in all their threads and twistings, out of the bowels and heart of Christ, out of his blood, death, and pain. Though it be sweet to Christ to draw, yet 'tis laborious and painful to Christ: it cost Christ a pained back, and holed sides, and pierced hands and feet, an head harrowed with thorns, and a bleeding body, and a bruised soul, to draw sinners; he drew while he did bleed again, he died under the work.

3. All the bones of all mankind, that have been, are, or shall be, all the strength of angels in one arm, could not have drawn one sinner out of hell. But O the strength of the merits of his lifting up on the cross! One sinner is as heavy as hell, as a mountain of iron; what burden must it be to Christ, to have millions of souls and all their sins hanging on him; *He carried on his body on the tree,* so many millions of sinners, and drew up after him so many thousand redeemed ones, as would have made the world to crack, the whole earth to groan and cry for pain like a sick woman in child-birth pain.

4. The white and red in a flower or rose, contempered together, make up a beautiful colour, and pleasant to the eye; 1. Love in Christ, 2. Lowliness, 3. And singular care to save, made up a sweet mixture in Jesus, that *Flower of Jesse,* to draw strongly sinners to him. See a father carrying seven or eight children on his back, through a deep river; he binds them all in his garment, that none of them fall in the water; he leans on his staff: how doth he with advised choice and election order every step, that he seem not to them to slip

or

or fall? And he cries comfort over his shoulder to them, *Fear not, be not dismayed, I will present you safe on dry land:* so Christ with all his children, great Jesus Christ had his offspring lapped up in his merits, and did wade through the floods of death and hell and the curse of the law with redeemed ones in his arms, crying, *Fear not worm Jacob, be not dismayed: I will help thee, the floods shall not drown thee;* and for his own condition, his faith was that he should safely swim through the sea, and the mighty waters of all his deepest sufferings, and that he and his mystical body (for Christ was a public surety, not one private man in this case) should shore on the land of praises, and this is above all doubting, when he saith, Isa. l. 7. *For the Lord God will help me, therefore shall I not be confounded: therefore have I set my face like a flint, and I know that I shall not be ashamed;* and then Christ had a most watchful and prudent care, Isa. lii. that not one penny, not one wheel in the work of our salvation should miscarry, but all should go right, nothing neglected, in doing, comforting, preaching, praying, suffering, sweating, weeping, believing, hoping in patience, in being shamed, spitted on, scourged, accused, railed on, traduced, condemned, belyed, pained, crucified between two thieves, buried in a sinner's grave; there was not one hole, one want, one stumble, one slip in all or any thing, but the work was whole, intire, and perfectly finished to God's satisfaction, Isa. liii. 11. Luke xxii. 37. John xix. 30

5. That drawing of sinners to Christ was his last work in his death-bed and departure out of this life, cryeth that he was desirous to lie in one grave with is spouse the Lamb's wife, and died inclosed in an union with saints; it saith also, O how admirable was his love! and that love was Christ's last work in this life, he died of no other sickness but love, love, love was Christ's death-work, Christ's testament, Christ's winding sheet, Christ's grave, he took his bride lapped in his love and heart to paradise with him, his last breath was love. The myrrhe, when it is withered has the

same

same smell (and a sweeter) than it had while it was green. *Christ, that bundle of myrrhe that lyeth all the night between the church's breasts,* when withered and dead, smelled of love, for he opened the graves and raised the dead, and took a repenting sinner to paradise with him, which are acts of great love; it is considerable that he is at one time a dying, a drawing, and a loving Saviour; and ask what was Christ's last act on earth, it is answered, he died in the very act of loving, and drawing sinners to his heart.

Use. We are engaged to love him, and if so, to keep his commandments, and to draw him after us; his own image, holiness in the saints takes Christ, and causes him fall in love with us, Cant. iv. 9. *Thou hast ravished my heart, my sister, my spouse, thou has ravished my heart, with one of thine eyes, with a chain of thy neck;* it is much love that ravishes Christ; yea it so overcomes him, that he professes it is above him, he must desire his spouse to look away, Cant. vi. 5. *Turn away thine eyes from me, for they have overcome me,* Cant. vii. 5. *The king is held in his galleries:* holiness makes our King, the Lord Jesus, a captive, for eternity he will delight to see the Lamb's wife his bride, when she shall be decked up with endless glory; be holy, *and the King shall desire your beauty;* engage Christ more to love you, deck yourselves with chains, with bracelets, be attired in raiment of needle-work; the braver in this apparel you are, ye are the lovelier to Christ, the wedding garment makes you fair to the King; put on the crown of grace on your head, and be highly beloved of this Prince.

Ver. 33. *Now this he spoke signifying what death he should die.*

The last article in Christ's drawing of sinners, is the exposition of the evangelist John, who openeth to us the sense of Christ's words, to wit, what was meant by Christ's *lifting up from the earth;* for it is not an ordinary phrase to express dying on the cross; therefore, saith John, he meaned by *his lifting up from the earth,* the kind and manner of his death, to wit,

that

same smell (and a sweeter) than it had while it was green. *Christ, that bundle of myrrhe that lyeth all the night between the church's breasts,* when withered and dead, smelled of love, for he opened the graves and raised the dead, and took a repenting sinner to paradise with him, which are acts of great love; it is considerable that he is at one time a dying, a drawing, and a loving Saviour; and ask what was Christ's last act on earth, it is answered, he died in the very act of loving, and drawing sinners to his heart.

Use. We are engaged to love him, and if so, to keep his commandments, and to draw him after us; his own image, holiness in the saints takes Christ, and causes him fall in love with us, Cant. iv. 9. *Thou hast ravished my heart, my sister, my spouse, thou has ravished my heart, with one of thine eyes, with a chain of thy neck;* it is much love that ravishes Christ; yea it so overcomes him, that he professes it is above him, he must desire his spouse to look away, Cant. vi. 5. *Turn away thine eyes from me, for they have overcome me,* Cant. vii. 5. *The king is held in his galleries:* holiness makes our King, the Lord Jesus, a captive, for eternity he will delight to see the Lamb's wife his bride, when she shall be decked up with endless glory; be holy, *and the King shall desire your beauty;* engage Christ more to love you, deck yourselves with chains, with bracelets, be attired in raiment of needle-work; the braver in this apparel you are, ye are the lovelier to Christ, the wedding garment makes you fair to the King; put on the crown of grace on your head, and be highly beloved of this Prince.

Ver. 33. *Now this he spoke signifying what death he should die.*

The last article in Christ's drawing of sinners, is the exposition of the evangelist John, who openeth to us the sense of Christ's words, to wit, what was meant by Christ's *lifting up from the earth;* for it is not an ordinary phrase to express dying on the cross; therefore, saith John, he meaned by *his lifting up from the earth,* the kind and manner of his death, to wit,

that

CHRIST DYING AND DRAWING SINNERS TO HIMSELF.

that he should be crucified, and die the shameful and ignominious death of the cross. It would seem that the exposition of John may be referred to the whole verse 32. What is the sense of this? If Christ be lifted up, he *will draw all men to him,* that is, if he be crucified, by that shameful and painful death, and the merits thereof, he will draw all men to him, and translate them from the kingdom of darkness to the state of saving grace; which is true in itself, but seemeth not to be the sense of the words.

1. Because the evangelists use to expound what may appear ambiguous to the hearers, as John vii. 8, 39. *But this be spoke of the Spirit.* John xx. 23. *Then went this saying abroad among the brethren, that that disciple* (John) *should not die: yet Jesus said not to him, he shall not die:* so Mat. ii. 16, 17, 18. But that Christ draweth sinners by his death, was not so much controverted; for, *to come to Christ, to believe in Christ, to be drawn to Christ,* were phrases obvious enough, and known to all.

2. It is most pertinent to the text, that *lifting up from the earth,* which is ambiguous, and may seem to allude to Elias his being carried up to heaven, should be expounded by Christ's manner of death, to wit, by crucifying.

Because the Holy Ghost expoundeth not the connexion of the conditional proposition, *If I be lifted up from the earth, I will draw all men after me,* which he must do, if the sense go thus; but only speaketh of the kind and nature of Christ's death, which was known to the Jews to be both shameful and cursed; but in his exposition, he speaks nothing of the fruit of Christ's death, but of the kind and manner of death.

Now that the evangelist expoundeth the sense of Christ's words, what he meaned, by being *lifted up from the earth,* it holdeth forth to us a necessity that the Lord speaks plain language to us in scripture, and that one scripture expounds another.

In finding the meaning of scripture, these considerations may give light.

1. The scripture in the plainest expressions is dark,

that

that is, high and deep, in regard of the matter which is deep; high, above the reach of reason, and yet the language plain, obvious, easy; that a virgin shall be a mother, the Ancient of Days a young sucking infant; that through one man, death digged a hole in the world, and sin passed on all; through a second man life and heaven entered again; are high and deep mysteries; yet is not the gospel obscure, as Papists say.

2. In mere historical narrations and prophecies, fore-telling the wars of the Lamb, the dragon and the beast, the Antichrist, their pursuing the woman travelling in birth, to bring forth a man-child; the matter subject is not profound, nor deep, yet the expressions are dark and covered, while the works of the Lord be a key to open his word. Here's the wisdom of God, that in deep and high mysteries, necessary for salvation, the Lord is plain and lower, and easier stories are foretold more darkly; articles of faith are not set down in dark and enigmatical prophecies, but plainly; whereas histories of things to come are more mysteriously proposed.

3. The scripture in no place is, in the popish sense, dark, that is, that we are not to take any sense for the word of life, and the object of our faith, but that which the church giveth as the sense, in regard the scripture is a nose of wax, with equal propension to contradictory senses, except the mistress of our faith, the witch of Babel expound it; and then it is for such formally the word of God, as she expoundeth it.

4. The Holy Ghost, the author of scripture, has concreated with the words, the true native sense, which all the powers on earth cannot alter.

Then, when we swear a covenant with the Lord in plain easy country-language, not devised of purpose to be ambiguous, or to hold forth that all sects, Antinomians, Socinians, Arminians, Prelatical Halters, Anabaptists, Seekers, etc. may save every one his own way, and his [Gr. phainómena] what he thinks good; to obtrude any authoritative interpretation on this covenant, which it holds not forth in its own simple words,

to

to the reader, is the greatest tyranny and equivocating juggling in the world, and we may easily distinguish and dispute ourselves out of a good conscience, or rather confess we had never any intent to keep it, or acknowledge it was our sin we did swear it, and because unlawful, it obliges us not.

When we accuse the scripture of darkness, we would but snuff the sun, and blow at it with a pair of bellows, to cause it shine more brightly. But the mischief is, that we either charge our souls beyond their stint, thinking to compass that world of the deep wisdom of God with our short fingers, or we stumble at the wisdom of the scripture, because it is eccentric to, and complies not with our lusts. And here's a deep not seen; God intends to carry Pharaoh and blinded reprobates to hell, through the wood of his mysterious works and word, they being blinded and hardned; and they intend the same, but in another notion; God aims at the same end materially with them, but God levels at the glory of his own inviolable justice; they level at the word, the works of God, to flatter their lusts, and take up a plea with both from the womb.

What death he should die.

Two things offer themselves to our consideration.

1. *Christ's dying.*
2. *The kind of his death, what death he should die.*

Christ came into the world, with as strong intention to die as to live, to be a pained, an afflicted man, as to be a man. In Christ's dying, these considerations have place.

1. The love of man can go no farther than death; *Greater love than this hath no man that a man should give his life for his friends,* John xv. 13. for this love can go no farther than the living lover. Now he cannot go one step beyond death; Christ went on to the first and second death, so far as to satisfy justice: love is like lawful necessity, neither of them can live, when God is dishonoured. Christ's love burnt and consumed him till he died; love followed and pursued his lost spouse through the land of death, through hell,

the

the grave, the curses of an angry God; tho' Christ's love was both ancienter than his manhood, and survived his death; love was of longer life in Christ, than his life as man; this sun of love burns hard down from heaven to this day.

2. It was a hard law that Christ subjected himself unto, that die he must; heaven, angels, the world could not save his life; this fair rose had life and greenness in abundance, and yet it must wither; this fountain of heaven had seas of waters, yet dried up it must be; this beauty of highest glory was full and vigorous, yet it must fade; the lily of the excellentest paradise, that cast rays of glory and majesty over the four corners of the heaven of heavens, and outshadowed angels, men, and the large circuit of the whole creation, must find its death-mouth, and must cast its fair and timely bloom: the love of loves must become pale and droop; that fire of love, that warms angels and men, must become cold: and there was strong and invincible necessity; thus it must be [Gr. Deî] Mat. xxvi. 54. *Christ must die.* Mat. viii. 31. *The Son of man must suffer many things.* Luke xxii. 27. *For I say unto you* (saith Christ) *that that which is written must have an end in me.* John iii. 14. *The Son of man must be lifted upon the cross.* Christ could not pass to heaven another way; death was that one inevitable pass that he behoved to go through; there was no passable ford in the river but one; there was but one strait pass and fort between Christ and his Father, his glory and a saved church; and justice kept this pass. Christ must lay out himself, his life, blood, estate and glory for his church, to gain his fort, and *save his people from their sins.* The law laid it on him; 2. Love laid it on him; 3. Our necessities and everlasting perishing burdened him.

3. Might not the dead all wonder? There was never before nor after, nor never shall be such a Christ amongst the dead as the *Lord of life:* all these in the dust could say, *O life, what dost thou here among the dead!* the worms and clay might say, *O Creator, canst thou ly*

near

CHRIST DYING AND DRAWING SINNERS TO HIMSELF.

near to us! Would not the fountains be offended, that they could not have leave to furnish a draught of cold water to their Creator, who made the seas and the rivers, and divided Jordan with his word? Would not life itself grieve at such a dispensation, that it could stay and lodge no longer in the body of the *Lord of life,* but behoved to be gone, and leave the *Prince of life* to fall, that he could not stand on his own feet? Was not bodily strength discontented, that sweet Jesus complained, Psal. xxii. 15. *My strength is dried up like a potsherd;* ver. 17. *I may tell all my bones.* Would not joy and beauty take it ill that sweet Jesus was a sad Saviour, and his face foul with weeping, and his fair countenance, that was like Lebanon, all marred, and our lovely Redeemer was put to his knees to pray with *strong cries and tears?* Isa. lii. 14. Heb. vii. 5. If there had been sense and reason in all the purples, silks, fleeces, wool, fine linens that ever the earth had, they would think themselves unhappy, that they could not cover the holy body of the Redeemer of men, and their Creator, when he complained, Psal. xxii. 18. *They part my garments among them, and cast lots on my vesture.*

4. It was too much in regard of our deservings, that the *Lord of life* should descend to a natural life, to be under the lowly condition of base clay; but that this tent of clay, that the Lord was to dwell in, should be of the finest and most precious earth that can be, would seem reason: it might be said, it were fitting for the glory of the Godhead united in a personal union with the man Christ, that the body of the Son of God should be above pain, weakness, or the law of death; that it should be more glorious than all the peerless and precious stones of the earth, yea, than the *sun in the firmament:* yea, but, Isa. liii. 2. *He hath no form nor comeliness, and when we shall see him, there is no beauty that we should desire him.* But this was incomparable condescension of love, that the Lord would take his own death upon him, and assume the manhood of sick, weak, pained, sad, sighing, and dying clay, Isa.

liii. 4. *Surely he hath born our sicknesses, and carried our sorrows.*

5. If there be any that ever tasted the sweet of life, it being the most noble and desirable of created beings, if it were from a glorious angel to a poor gnat or a base worm, they keep possession of life with all their desire; they will part with all things, men even with teeth and skin, ere they quit their life, Job ii. 4. The more excellent life is, they struggle the more to keep it; a young man will do more than an old man for it; and the old man, who has but a chip of life, the dregs of it, or the hundredth part of an hand-breadth, the twentieth part of an inch, yet holds it so long as there is so much as the fourth part of a drachm of natural vigor in him; now Christ had cause to love his life, as any man else. It was about the flower of his age, the thirty-third year of his life; and it must be a noble life that dwelt personally with the Godhead; yet when he was called to a treaty for rendering his life, he gave it not up, but upon princely and honourable quarters, even that he should see his seed, have a noble prize and a ransomed spouse, a fair crown, a rich kingdom to mystical Christ, but he parted with his noble and glorious life deliberately, intentionally, most willingly, John x. 18. there was more will, more love in Christ dying, than in dying of all men from the creation to the last judgment; O how he thirsted and longed to pay that ransom! he had it by him, to give it out on demand; he did not first die, and bow his head, but he first bowed his head, and beckned with his hand, and called upon death, and then rendered his spirit.

6. O what a wonder! this rose of life on the cross withereth in its full beauty, the sun of life would shine no more on it. The prime delight of the sons of men, the second Adam from heaven fades, and life can breathe no more, and beauty shine no more, and greenness blossom no more; and when most low, clothed with a curse, most lovely, most lordly and princely, because in the act of redeeming.

7. Christ's

2. As a punishment inflicted of God for sin, as a ransom paid to justice: 3. As the crown and end of Christ's journey.

In the first notion, Christ's death, as coming from wicked men, wanted three ingredients that all the wicked world and hell could not give it: 1. All the world cannot add a curse to the death of any man, God only is the master and Lord of cursing and blessing: God cast this in from heaven of his own; for, 2 Cor. v. 21. *God made him sin,* Isa. liii. 6. *Jehovah the Lord laid on him the iniquities of us all.* Who said that, *Cursed be every one that abideth not in all that is written in the law to do it?* Gal. iii. 10, 13. Deut. xxi. 23. Deut. xxvii. 26. The only lawgiver who can dispense curses, he made Christ's death a curse: one death has not a curse more than another, and Christ's death of the cross had not a ceremonial curse only in it, for that was common to the deaths of all that hangeth on a tree, Deut. xxi. 23. But the curse of the moral law which is upon the sinner, Deut. xxvii. 20. Gal. iii. 10, 13. was laid upon Christ; and this is heavier than ten million deaths of the cross: O how many thousands and what millions of talents-weight of gall and vengeance did the Lord from heaven add to the cup of Christ? 2. Because Christ was made sin, he behoved to be made the sinner; and from Christ's person his death had the sweet perfume of infinite merit, and a sweet smell of a savour of rest to God, above all sacrifices and offerings that ever were offered to God; infiniteness and merit, this Christ gave to his own death. 3. The Lord gave it a third ingredient, that it had acceptation even in the point of law and justice, which no man could give; to feel a smell of everlasting love, peace, reconciliation in blood, *is the sure mercies of David;* O but it was white blood to God, crying blood, or rather singing blood, that sings the sweet gospel song! *Abel's blood cried* a song of vengeance; *Ye are come to the blood of sprinkling,* [Gr. chreitona laloenti] *that sounds*

bet-

better things than the blood of Abel, Heb. xii. 24.

In the second notion that Christ came under the law of dying *(for it is appointed for all men to die)* speaks much love. To come to sleep, which is death's brother: to come under pain, weakness, bleeding, that are the near blood-friends of death, is great love expression: but to die, the lowest, and the saddest and sourest of bodily infirmities, and then for other men's faults, it sets out of the love of God.

In this respect, Christ dying was a ransom for justice; there be four of the saddest things in a ransom that are here.

1. To give person for person, is the hardest bargain; by the law of nations, they are meeker wars where moneys and gold may buy a captive. God in this bargain could send captives away for *neither silver, nor gold, nor any corruptible thing,* 1 Pet. i. 18. A gift, a reward will not bow justice; *rubies, sapphires,* let ten earths be turned into gold of Ophir, they cannot buy the offended law of God; therefore, it must be man for man, person for person, or nothing; a man is more precious than gold.

2. If you must have man for man, then let proportion of common justice be kept; a soldier for a soldier, a servant for a servant, a free-man for a free-man, a master for a master; ye cannot demand a king to ransom a servant: *Yea,* (saith justice) *but I will;* they are but men and slaves, and servants of sin. Their father Adam was indeed a King, but by law he is fallen from the crown, and all his children are traitors and born servants; therefore justice would have no less ransom than one of the king's line, one of the blood-royal; and more, the only heir of the crown of heaven and earth, *the King of kings and Lord of lords:* he is more than an over-ransom and over-sum; this is hard: but infinite wisdom cannot be against justice; but it was the strictest justice that ever was, the King's Son for the traitor's son, the prince for the slave, the *Lord of lords* for the poor clay-subject.

3. But the ransom King must have honourable con-

ditions

ditions like himself; if he must be a captive, let him have some freedom befitting his birth and condition. Now, because this bargain was to be stretched out to the utmost line and border of strict justice (as also it wanted not deepest mercy shining in glorious rays through justice) therefore the King standing a ransom, was as far below his place, as a servant is below a king. Phil. ii. 6, 7. You have the lowest and the highest steps, *Who being in the form of God, thought it not robbery to be equal with God, but made himself of no reputation, and took upon him the form of a servant;* a King and God made a servant, Mat. xx. 28. *For even the Son of man came not to be served, but to serve, and to give his life a ransom for many;* see here, the *Son of God* a ransom in his own person, and the lowest of ransoms, a servant far below a king.

4. It is not universal in these persons that are given to ransom others; but poor souls, if they be turned in servants, their life should be spared; but Christ was such a ransom, as must lay down his life for the captives, Mat. xx. 28. No ransom can come lower than a man, and an innocent man's death; if the captive be wounded and sickly, the man that goes a ransom for him, by no law should be sickly and wounded also. 1. It is not ordinary, that he that stands as a ransom for captives, should take their natural infirmities, their body, sighs, sadness, sorrow, wants, and be like them in all things; but Christ was like us in all things except sin. 2. And what greater hardship can you put on a ransom captive than death? All these Christ did undergo for us.

The third and last consideration of Christ's death, is as it was the end of Christ's journey, and all his labours in the flesh; and this I desire to be considered in these respects.
1. As death is Christ's last enemy.
2. In the concomitants of it.
   1. As in his triumph of victory.
   2. His welcome to his Father.

1. As death was Christ's last enemy, dying was to him, as to man, the last day and moment of his week,

week, when he entered into his sabbath and rest, and died never to die again: the world and devils chased him into the grave; and when he was there he was in his own land, in paradise, in a kingdom: death was the wearied way-faring man's home, the end of his race, and at this place was the forerunner's gold his garland, and prize, even the glory set before him, for which he *endured the cross, and despised the shame;* he then sat down; it was Christ's landing port after a stormy sailing. 2. He had no more to do in the merit of redemption, in the way of satisfying justice; for Christ's burial, or lying in the grave, was but his Mora, his lodging all night with death, or a continuation of his death. When he died, all was finished; the law of God for satisfaction could crave no more: as the last enemy of the body is death, 1 Cor. xv. 26. so it was the head Christ's last enemy on earth. 3. Heaven was Christ's place of refuge, his sanctuary and his asylum; when Christ was in the other side of death and of time, he was in his castle, in his strong fort; enemies can neither besiege him nor take him; he cares not for the world's feud, or for death or the grave, Rev. i. 18. There was no more law against Christ after his soul was in paradise; the believer has a perfect acquittance of all crosses, when he is once in the land of glory.

2. There be two considerable concomitants in Christ's death, 1. His victory. 2. His welcome. His victory was in his very act of dying, that death and the justice of a divine law had their will of Christ, and could demand no more of him for all engagements, and to answer the bill, but death, and such a death; it was a sort of overplus, and abundance of ransom to God, that death was put to the worse, and could in justice never arrest any believer or saint after Christ. O death, what wouldest thou have more! Or, what canst thou demand in law? 2. Christ, and all his, legally were crucified, and died; and Christ, and all his, were not destroyed under death, but Christ lived, and all his with him, John xiv. 19. When two strong enemies do con-

flict

flict, and put out their strength one against another to the full, and the one lives in his full strength, the other must be foiled. Christ after death lived, and can die no more, and is strong and omnipotent: Now, death did all it could against Christ, in that he died; then he must be the victor, and death the vanquished party; death was Christ's land-port, his shore after sad sea-sailing, his last stage in which he posted to glory; and he came into paradise and his Father's kingdom in a sweat of blood (and the cross accompanied him in over the threshold of the gates of heaven) so he was welcomed, he, and all his seed (who then were legally in him) as one that had acquitted himself bravely and honourably in the business that most highly concerned the Lord, and the glory of all his blessed attributes, mercy, justice, grace, wisdom, power, sovereignty, etc. There was a most joyful acclamation in heaven, a welcome and embracing, and a hand-shaking (as we say) 1. Between the Father and the Son; and this is a sweet meditation, Dan. vii. 13. *I saw in the night-visions, and behold, one like the Son of Man, came with the clouds of heaven, and came to the Ancient of Days, and they brought him near before him;* v. 14. *And there was given him dominion and glory, and a kingdom, that all people and nations and languages should serve him.* Now, who be these that brought Christ to the Father when he ascended? who but the holy *angels, his ministering spirits,* or servants; they attend his ascension to heaven, as the estates of a king wait on, and convoy the prince and heir of a crown, in his coronation-day, Heb. i. 6, 14. The disciples, Acts i. 10. *see two men in white apparel,* at his ascension, go up to heaven: sure, there must have been a host of them, as there were at his birth, and shall be at his second coming. And it is little enough that the peers of heaven, such a glorious parliament of the high-house, bear the tail of his robe-royal, and attend to welcome to heaven their *Lord Creator,* and their Head Christ, by whom they stand in court; they are the servants of the bridegroom: it was much joy to them, when Christ

re-

returned a triumphing Lord to heaven, having done all gloriously and completely. The Father after his death made him a great Prince, and *gave him a name above all names,* and *set him at the right-hand of the majesty of God.* 2. And, if the Lord shall say to sinful men, *Well done, good servant, enter into the joy of thy Lord;* far more, being infinitely satisfied with the travels and service of his Son, he must say, *Well done, well suffered, O Son of my love, enter into the joy of thy Father's soul:* for the Father's soul ever delighted in him, Isa. xlii. 1. 3. And to see the Father embrace his Son in his arms after the battles, and put the crown on his head, and set him down at his right-hand, and exalt him, as an eternal Prince for evermore, and accept all his labours, and his faithful and most successful acquitting of himself, in all his offices, as *Redeemer, King, Priest,* and *Prophet,* must be a joyful sight.

Use 1. No believer takes it ill to die; death sips at every blood, noble or low, and would but drink the blood of this celebrious and eminent *Prince of the kings of the earth:* 1. For, besides that God hath stinted our mouths, and the ship cannot pass farther than the length of the cable: here is the matter, Christ, for imputed sin, behoved to bleed to death. 2. Only Enoch and Elias were reprieved, by the prerogative of free-grace; we are by birth and sin, but some ounces or pieces and fragments of death, and it is appointed for all men to die: there is more reason we should die, than the *Lord of life;* for life was essential to the Prince of life, but life is a stranger to us; man is but man, but a handful of hot dust, a clay-vessel tunned up with the breathing of warm wind, that smokes in and out at his nostrils, for a inch of fleeting away time. And sin adds wings to the wheels of his life, and lays a law of death on man; and if Christ had not come into his clay-city, he had been under no law of death; he dies for us; then we should far rather have died, *propter quod unumquodq; tale,* etc. Now, because your Redeemer laid his skin to death, and was willing to kiss death, believers are

to

to esteem of death as the cross that Christ went through; love the winding-sheet and the coffin the better, that they were the sheep-bed and night-clothes that your Saviour slept in. 3. And Christ had the more cause to be willing to die, that he was little beholden to this life; it looked ever with a frowning face on Christ: 1. The first morning-salutation of this life when Christ was new born, it boasted and threatned Christ with the cutting of his throat in the cradle, and banishment out of his own land to Egypt. 2. He had good hap all his life to sufferings, he had ever the wind on his fair face, and the smoke blowing on his eyes, as if his whole day had been a feast of tears and sorrow: yea, life and the sad and glooming cross parted both together with Christ, as if the world had sworn never to lend the Son of God one smile, or one glimpse of a glad hour. 3. Christ thought himself well away and out of the gate (as he foretelleth, when the people mourned for his death, Luke xxiii. 5. 28, 29, 30, 31.) before the destruction that came on the city of Jerusalem, that killed many of the *Lord of the vineyard's servants,* and at last killed the righteous Heir. 4. You may remember Christ's message that he sent to Herod, Luke. xiii. 32. *I do cures to-day, and to-morrow, and the third day* [Gr. leleîumai] *I shall be perfected;* Heb. ii. 12. *It became him, for whom are all things, and by whom are all things, in bringing many sons to glory, to make the Captain of their salvation perfect through sufferings;* (Gr. dià pathemàton teleiôsai) death made Christ perfect; for the Lord put the fair crown of redemption on Christ's head with a very black hand; it was a black boat-man that carried our Prince Jesus over the water to paradise; but sweet Jesus would have it his perfection, his crown, his glory, to be swallowed up in death's womb for us. It is considerable, that death perfecteth the head, 1. As a Priest; he had been an unperfect sacrifice, if he had not died; and being offered dead to God. Christ's dead corpse had an infinitely sweet smell in the nostrils of a just God; never sacrifice never burnt-offering like this, which perfected all. 2. He had not been a perfect King and Conqueror, had he not pursued the enemy to his own land, and made the enemy's land the feat of war, and triumphed dead upon the cross. 3. He had not been a perfect Redeemer, had he not died, and paid life for life: no satisfaction without death, *no remission of sins without blood,* Heb. x. But, it was the heart-blood, and blood with the life, that was shed to God. Now, these same befal the dying saints: 1. While the saints are here, they are from home, and not at their Father's fire-side; and this world, their step-mother, looks ever asquint on them, John xiv. 33. And the cross gets a charge from God concerning a saint, wait on him as his keeper, while he die, leave him not; the cross follows the house of Christ, and all the children of the house; it is kindly to all the second Adam's seed; it is an income by year that follows the flock: every child may in his suffering say, my Father the Prince of ages, even the Head of the house, my brother Jesus, and all our kin, were sufferers; the sad cross runs in a blood to us; Psalm xxxiv. 19. Mat. xix. 24. This is not our home, I would I were ashore and at home, in my Father's house.

2. The Lord takes the righteous away from the ill to come, Isa. lvii. When Christ was taken away, vengeance came to the full on the Jews, when he was in heaven. Christ's followers, that die, out-run many crosses; as we see a man upon his life chased by his enemies, gets into a strong house, and with speed of foot wins his life; sad days pursue the saints, and they escape to their castle, before the affliction can reach or overtake: there be some Cruces, posthumelate-born crosses, calamities and ill days, that come on the posterity of the godly; the Lord closeth their eyes that they never see them. The grave is a house, the devil and the world and afflictions cannot besiege; sure, when a saint is in heaven, he is beyond doomsday, death, and tears; he defies the malignants of this world then, and the wars and blood that his own brethren can raise against him.

3. What

3. What shall we say, that as Christ thought himself maimed, and he wanted a piece, or an arm or leg of a Saviour and a perfect Redeemer till he died, and then when he died, he was perfected? Indeed, our redemption had been lame and unperfect, had not Christ died; and his escape through death and the land of darkness, the grave, to his Father's old crown, that he had *with him before the world was,* was a perfecting of Christ, 1. So, dying, to a saint, is the sun-rising, the morning birth-day of eternity, the opening of the prisoner's door, the coronation-day, the marriage-night. 2. He is ever a lame man, he wants incomparably his best half, so long as he wants Christ in a fruition of glory: all the travelling and way-faring men, in their journey toward heaven, are but sick men; for sickness is but a lameness of life, a want of so many degrees to make up a perfect life (because good health is but the flower and perfection of life) and the only perfect life, Col. iii. v. 3, 4. is the life of glory, then all the saints, yet wanting the life of heaven, must be crazy, weak, groaning men, not healthy in a spiritual consideration, while they be in heaven. 3. When a saint dies, he but takes an essay of the garment and robe of glory (though death make it seem strait and pinching) and enters in the joy of his Lord, Rev. xvi. 15. There is both word and writ, and from a land where there can be no lies, from heaven, *Blessed are the dead that die in the Lord, that they may rest from their labours,* [Gr. hine anapáuson de ek tòn ko pon autòn] that the travellers may over-rest, or exceedingly breathe, and refresh or comfort themselves after much toil and sweating in the way; therefore is death, 2 Tim. iv. 6. [Gr. analysis] an unfolding of the net, or of the tent, that the man may go out, or a taking up the burden and laying it down in another inn, or a loosing the cables of ships to sail, or an untying of cords of a tabernacle to go to a choicer place.

Use 2. From Christ's dying, we learn to die to sin, and live to him that died for us, 1 Pet. ii. 24. Rom. vi. 2, 6. 2 Cor. v. 15. Mortification to this goodly and god-

like

like idol the world, is a special lesson of the death of Christ, Gal. vi. 14. It is a great distance, and many miles about and off the road-way to heaven, to go through such a thorny, thick, and bushy wood of honours, riches, pleasures worldly; it is a shorter and easier way to stand at a distance from the silken and golden creature, and despise the fairest created excellencies that fill both sides of the sun. Antinomians would have us rest satisfied with moral mortification, in the brim of the imagination, to believe that Christ dying, mortified sin and the body thereof on the cross, and there is an end; and that we are obliged by no command, no precept, no law, to a personal mortifying of our lusts, to walk in new obedience; and that all that we do is arbitrary and free to us, coming on us by the immediate Spirit's impulsion: for, say they, "Christ works in the regenerate as in these that are dead, not as in these that are alive; and that after conversion we are altogether dead to spiritual acts." (say they) contrary to 1 Cor. xv. 10. Phil. ii. 13. Rom. vi. 11. Gal. ii. 20. 1 Pet. ii. 5, 24. And, "That it is the efficacy of Christ's death, to kill all activity in his members, that he might act all in all: yea, and that there is not any command in the gospel, (all is but promises) Christ is obliged to do all in us; and if he suffer us to sin, let him see to his own honour: yea, to act by virtue of, or in obedience to a command, is a law-way, and we have nothing to do, with the law." But, the gospel teacheth us a real and personal mortification, and that we are *to be holy as he is holy, perfect as he is perfect;* that is a new covenant command, Gen. xvii. 1. *That we should walk before him and be perfect, that we should walk after the Lord,* Deut. xiii. 4. *walk in all his ways,* Deut. v. 33. *take diligent heed to walk in his way,* Josh. xxii. 5. Psal. cxix. 93. Prov. ii. 7, 20. Isa. ii. 3. *walk in the steps of that faith of our father Abraham,* Rom. iv. 12. *according to this rule of the gospel,* Gal. iv. 16. *and worthy of the vocation,* Eph. vi. 1. *worthy of the Lord,* Col. i. 10. *in light,* 1 John i. 7. *even as he walked,* 1 John ii. 6.

af-

CHRIST DYING AND DRAWING SINNERS TO HIMSELF.

after his commandments, 2 John vi. *honestly, as in the day,* Rom. xiii. 13. *in love,* Ephes. v. 2. *as children of the light,* v. 8. *as we have received Christ,* Col. ii. 6. *in wisdom,* v. 4, 5. *as wise men,* Ephes. v. 15. And the gospel forbids and condemns *walking as the Gentiles do in the vanity of the mind, having the understanding darkened, being alienated from the life of God.* But observe, by Antinomian's fleshly doctrine, no gospel-command under pain of eternal death, be it a command of believing in him *that justifieth the sinner,* or of holy walking as a fruit and witness of our faith and justification, obligeth these that are in Christ; as if, in regard of any scriptural command of law or gospel, we might live as we list, and follow the inspiration and leading of a lawless spirit, separated from all word, either law or gospel, either commanding or conditionally promising or threatning. *We are not so to live after the flesh in lasciviousness, lusts, excess of wine, revellings, banquetings and abominable idolatries,* 1 Pet. iv. 3. *not after the flesh,* 2 Pet. ii. 10. Rom. viii. 13. *If ye live after the flesh, ye shall die.* There is a gospel-threatning as a promise of life; yea, the arms, colours, the badge of gospel-grace, is to *deny ungodliness,* Tit. ii. 11. *Not to walk in darkness, nor hate our brother,* 1 John ii. 8, 9. *for this is the new commandment;* and that the gospel has commandments, is clear, Mat. xv. 3. John xv. 12. Rom. xvi. 6. Ephes. vi. 2. 1 Tim. i. 1. *The holy commandment,* 2 Pet. ii. 21. 1 John iii. 23. Rev. xxii. 14. Prov. ii. 1 John xiv. 21. 1 Thess. iv. 2. 1 John ii. 4. & 3.24 And, *he that keepeth his commandments, dwells in him, and he in him.* John xiv. 15. *If ye love me, keep my commandments,* Mat. v. 3, 4, 5, 6, 7, 8, 9, 20, 21, 22, 24. Mat. vii. 1, 2, 3, etc.

Use 2. We have rich consolation from the article of Christ's dying; the sinner's debts are paid, his band, and the hand-writing of blood and eternal vengeance, is cancelled, and taken out of the way; the gates of the prison broken, and the *prisoners brought out by the blood of the everlasting covenant,* 1 Pet. ii. 24. *With his stripes we are healed,* Isa. liii. 5. *The chastisement of* *our peaces, or treaties of peace,* as the word bears, *were upon him, and with his stripes we are healed.* The word stripe in either languages,* is a mark of a wound, where blood and humours are neighboured together; it leads us to this, and that the only medicine of sick and dead sinners, was that which is sickness, pain, swellings from nails in hands and feet to Jesus Christ. Christ the physician's pain was our ease, his wounds the healing and covering of our wounds with his skin, and his death the life of sinners. To visit the sick, and help him at his bed-side with counsel and art, is favour; but it is physick of grace, not of nature, that the physician should be the sick man, the pained, the groaning and dying patient, and ly down in his bed, and make his life and blood a medicine to cure our diseases and wounds. In a law-challenge, the believer is so freed from eternal wrath, that if Satan and conscience say, *Thou art a sinner, and under the curse of the law;* he can say, It is true, I am a sinner, but I was hanged on a tree and died, and was made a curse in my head and law-surety Christ, and his payment and suffering is my payment and suffering.

Use 4. Sin is a sad debt; the law is a severe craver. 1. It is pastime to a fool to sin: it is no pastime nor sport to Christ to satisfy for sin. 2. There is as much justice and vengeance in the gospel, as in the law; the gospel-suffering for our sin, was as salt and sour to Christ, as the law-vengeance would have been to us: the Lord never minded that any should bear sin either by acting or suffering, gratis, and at an easy rate. 3. Will ye not read bloody justice pursuing sin on the blue stripes and scarlet wounds, on innocent Jesus's back

*[Heb. habburah] a blue swelling of a wound, or hole or a confluence of hamours and blood associated, Psal. xxxviii. 6. [Heb. habar] sociatus, junctus, fuit, [Gr. Molops] a wound from the rising of the skin, and causing a greatness and mark appear to the eye, that it may be known there is a wound.

back and sides, his head and hands and feet? Will ye, young men, Eccles. xi. 9. laugh and sin, and must Christ weep, and shout and cry for pain, when he suffers for sin? sinners, ye have merry days in your lusts: O but it was a doleful and wearisome time to Christ to pay for sin! the drunkard sings and drinks; when Christ answers his bill, he sighs. Solomon, Eccles. ii. *in the days of his vanity, sought to give himself to wine,* v. 3. *to lay hold on folly;* v. 10. *and whatever his eyes desired, he with-held not from them, he kept no joy from his heart.* But Christ had a sad night in the garden; O but he had a heavy soul, when, with tears and strong cries, he prayed; when justice squeezeth a sweat of blood out of Christ's body, and he looks like sorrow and sadness itself, dying, and bleeding, and crying, *My God, my God, why hast thou forsaken me?* Never mother's son, after this, make a sport of sin, or sin with good will and delight.

What death, [Gr. poio thanàto] what quality or kind of death, he was to die.

The quality and kind of Christ's death is most remarkable; for three characters were printed and engraven on the death of the cross which Christ died.

1. *Pain.* 2. *Reproach and shame.* 3. *The curse of God and man.*

The pain in Christ's death comes under a twofold consideration, 1. Naturally, 2. Legally: the nature of the death was painful, for death of itself is painful; the man pays that debt with ease, and nature smiling and sporting. Die who will, it will cost you of your flesh: when Asa dies, he cries, Ah, my feet! when David dies, he complains, O my cold body! the Shunamite's child, Ah, my pained head; Uzziah, Oh, my leprous skin! Do not pamper nor idolize your body; if wicked men have not one band or cord in their death, but steal down to the grave in a moment beside death's knowledge, yet they pay dear for it, Job xxiv. 20. *The worms shall feed sweetly on them;* life is a great pearl. But there be three things besides, that made the death of Christ painful,

1. *Vio-*

1. *Violence.* 2. *Slowness of dying.* 3. *Many degrees of life taken from him.*

Violence, it is to die of any disease or of pain. 1. But when five or six deaths do all start equally at one land-port, and at one race, and strive which of them shall dispatch the poor man soonest, the pain is the more. Ye know the complaint of our blessed Saviour, Psal. xxii. 16. *They pierced my hands and my feet;* and John xix. 34. *One of the soldiers with a spear pierced his side, and forthwith came there out blood and water.* Here, by scripture, be five deaths, that invade a living man, death on every hand, and death on every leg, and death on his side, tho' this last came a little too late, the soldiers had no law to pierce his side; but to make sure work he should be dead, by a sort of chance to men, which yet sweetly was subservient to the decree of God and the prophecies; Christ was thus served. 2. Now, a violent death it must be, when strong and great nails did pierce the most nervous parts of his body, his hands and his feet; one iron-wedge thrust in at his left-pape, to pierce his heart, or to pierce through the temples of the head, would quickly have dispatched him. 2. As for the slowness of his death, four leisurely and slow violent deaths, to cause him bleed to death, were hard. The word saith, the blood is the life of the living creature; then look how long his blood was coming out, his life was dropping out as long. They say, the death of the cross will keep a man alive with his life in on the cross, above three or four hours, the man dying, and yet cannot die; these languishing deaths procuring a cruel favour, such as death's slow pace, and yet quick torment, are images of hell, *where men seek death, but cannot find it,* because death fleeth from them.

2. The lentness of death is much, when death is divided into four quarters; death at every hand, and at every foot, makes the pain the greater: when the weight and trunk of Christ's living body lifted up from the earth, hangeth upon four paining and tormenting pillars, the Lord's pierced hands and feet; as if

death

death had delighted to hold Christ long at sea, and denied him the last sad service. 3. And Christ had been before dying a terrible death in the garden, when he had been seethed and boiled in a sweat of blood; and two circumstances evidence that the two thieves' death was nothing in slowness of torments comparable to Christ's death, 1. The sad and direful prefaces and preparatories to Christ's death; as he was in the night before in a soul-death in the garden, and in a sweat of blood, there trickled out of his body down upon the ground [Gr. hosei thrómboi háimatos] as it were drops, great hail-stones of blood frozen or hardened together, as Stephanus thinks, through extreme terror; he was so scourged against all law, and crowned with thorns. 2. And so was he weakned in body, as he was not able to bear his own cross; it was his own complaint, Psal. xxii. 17. *I may tell all my bones.* Whatever the story of passion say, how Christ could have been so lean in twenty and four hours; it is evident, he complains his *strength was dried up like a potsherd,* and that death was more painful to Christ than to these that died the same death; yea, Christ began to die the night before: he was then under violent death of soul and body above the hours that he was on the cross. When others are long tormented with pain, that pain is rather the fore-runner of death, than death; for death stays but a moment in doing that sad service in bringing the soul out: but death all this time twenty-four hours, was acting upon Christ, both the second death, the Lord's anger and curse being on him; and then bodily pain, with the curse of the law, all this time wrought upon him. Some say, gall and vinegar were given to men to be crucified, to make them less sensible of that extreme pain. And consider his death legally, may we not say, as Christ in bearing the pains of the second death did suffer that which all the elect should have sustained in their souls for ever, so Christ did bear many millions of bodily deaths? It may be a question, if Christ's suffering for Peter be Christ's

suffer-

suffering for David; for sure Peter's sins and David's sins together, are more than David's sins alone; and if on Christ the Lord *laid the iniquity of us all,* Isa. liii. 6. it must be a greater punishment, than if the Lord had laid the iniquity of some few, one or two, upon Christ: say, that the elect were three millions of redeemed ones, as we cannot determine the number, sure this must be a sadder death, than if Christ had died but for ten men: it is true, it was an infinite pain in regard of the one infinite person that did bear our iniquities, yea, and so subjective it was an infinite love with which, in election and free redemption, Christ followed all the elect of God withal but terminative, as his love is bounded on sundry persons, Paul speaks of it as if there had been not one man loved but himself, Gal. ii. 20. *Christ loved me, and gave himself for me.* Tho' the Lord Jesus passed in one bill, the election and redemption of all the family of the first-born, yet every soul has a *white stone, and a new name, that no other elect man knows, but he himself;* as every flower, every rose, every meadow, and several garden, has its several rays, beams and comfort, and vigor of heat from the sun, yet all these rays and beams are but one in the sun's body; so, tho' Christ died but one death for all the elect, yet in the height of pain it was many deaths to him.

3. Again, consider how much of life Christ had, the removing of it by violence must be so much the more painful: life natural had in Christ a sweet and peaceable dwelling, the possession of life was with excellent delights, like a tree growing on the bank of a sweet river of oil, wine and honey; it was planted beside the glorious Godhead personally, and had sweet company, and that made it pleasant: the more beautiful, pleasant, and green the *flower of Jesse* was, the more violence and pain it was to hew down this delicious tree of life, and to cut him *out of the land of the living;* it had not been so much to cut down a thistle or a thorn-tree, or to take away the life of a common man, whose life is not privileged with grace, and the grace of a personal
union

CHRIST DYING AND DRAWING SINNERS TO HIMSELF.

union with God; yea, the destroying of the life of an angel, could never have been such violence. And then 'tis considerable, that Christ was not suffered to go to the grave without blood, and that his skin and winding-sheet were bespotted with blood. Christ paid not this sum quickly, as many die: 'tis true, there was more will and love infinitely in his blood, than violence and pain, every stream of blood flowing in a channel of love; and it is also sure, the soul and the Godhead were not separated, but the precious life of Christ was expelled, and that by a bloody death, out of a sweet paradise; and death was a rough, sad and thorny journey to Christ: weapons of iron on hands and feet came against the Lord, to fetch the soul out of the body.

2. *Shame.*

The second character engraven on Christ's death was shame and reproach; in which consider,

1. *How shame could be on Christ dying.* 2. *What shame was on him.* 3. *How it stood with his honour as King.*

1. *Shame,* is taken either fundamentally in the cause, or formally; sin, and sin acted by men against the law of God, is the only foundation of shame: when the people fell in idolatry, Exod. xxxii. 25. *Aaron made the people naked to their shame;* so, when Tamar dissuades her brother from incest, 2 Sam. xiii. 12. she saith, *And I, whither shall I cause my shame to go? And as for thee, thou shalt be as one of the fools of Israel.* Shame and sin are of one blood; for sinning is a shameful reproaching of the creature: and thus, Christ was no more capable of shame, nor of sin; *for he had done no violence, neither was there any guile in his mouth.* Christ-man came out of the womb clothed with a precious white robe of innocency and abundance of grace; he never contracted one black spot on that fair robe of the highest image of God, from the womb to the grave; and so there was no shame, but fundamentally glory in Christ all his life. But there is shame formally in sin, and that, 1. Which we call thinking of shame, or being ashamed actively: 2. In bearing of shame

pas-

passively. In the former consideration; because sin is a shameful thing in itself, Jer. xi. 13. *Ye set up altars to that shameful thing, even altars to burn incense to Baal:* there is an internal blushing and shame rising from sin, when the sinner, if the conscience thro' a habit of sin be not turned brazen and hard, thinks ill of sin, and esteems itself base in doing ill; Rom. vi. 21. *What fruit had ye then of these things, whereof ye are now ashamed?* Adam and Eve were not ashamed before they sinned: now, Christ-man had this ingenuity, which heathens called half a virtue, *viz.* Shamefastness, or a power to think ill of sin: Christ of himself (though he could not sin, as Adam had a power, before the fall, to pity and commiserate the sick and miserable, though there was no formal object for that power afore men sinned) could think ill of sin; Christ (I say) thought ill of sin, and esteemed the creature base in sinning. Heathens said, *virtue was of a red blushing colour;* and the scripture condemns the shamelessness of sinners, that are not abased themselves for sin, and cannot be ashamed: so the Lord burdens his people with this, Jer. iii. 3. *And thou hadst a whore's forehead, thou refusedst to be ashamed,* Heb. *to blush,* Isa. ii. 9. *The shew of their countenance* (that cannot blush at sin) *doth witness against them, and they declare their sin as Sodom, they hide it not.* Zeph. iii. 5. *But the unjust knoweth no shame.* In this, Christ our Lord, (to come to the second point) being our surety, though he could not be ashamed of any sin he did himself, for that he never sinned, yet being made sin for us, he did bear the shame of our sin. And so Christ was not free of shame passively, as it is a punishment of sin; for it is a penal evil of the creature. Dan. xii. 2. *Many that sleep in the dust shall awake, some to shame and everlasting contempt.* Ezek. xxxii. 4. *Elam and all her multitude are slain----------they have borne their shame, with them that go down to the pit.* That which is penal in shame, the Lord Jesus did bear; he saith of himself, Isaiah l. 6. *I gave my back to the smiters, and cheeks to them that plucked off the hair, I hid not my face from shame*

and

CHRIST DYING AND DRAWING SINNERS TO HIMSELF.

and spitting. Heb. xii. 2. *He endured the cross, despising the shame.* In these respects he did bear our shame; 1. That he being the Lord *of glory, and thought it no robbery to be equal with the Father, he abased himself to come so low as to be a man, and the lowest of men, a servant,* Phil. ii. 6, 7, 8. Matth. xx. 28. and Isa. lxix. 7. *Thus saith the Lord the Redeemer of Israel, and his holy One, to him whom man despiseth,* Hebr. *to one despised in soul, a contemned soul, abhorred by the nation, to a servant of lords.* 2. All the tokens of reproach and shame were on his suffering: As, 1. In gestures, the putting a crown of thorns on his head, and a reed for a sceptre in his hand, to scorn his kingly power, saluting him with mocking and bowing the knee to him. 2. In words, saying, *Hail King of the Jews:* a scorning his prophetical dignity, in blind-folding him, and covering his face, and saying *prophesy who is he that smote thee?* And, to deride his priesthood, they put a robe on him; and when he is on the cross, and offering himself as our priest, in a sacrifice to God, *all that passed by wagged their head, and shot out the lip, saying, He trusted in God, let God save him:* then the spitting on his face, in the law was great shame, Deut. xxv. 9. the wife of the brother that would not build his brother's house, *did spit on his face;* so Job complains, Chap. xxx. 10. that the children of fools and base men abhorred him, *and spared not to spit on his face.* O but there is now much glory and beauty of glory on that face! 'Tis more glorious than the sun. 3. His death had a special note of shame, the death of a robber and an ill-doer; so it is called Christ's reproach, Heb. xiii. 13. *Let us go forth therefore unto him, with the camp, bearing his reproach,* or bearing his cross, which was a reproachful thing; for it is a clear allusion to the manner of Christ's going out of the city of Jerusalem to mount Calvary bearing his own cross; it was a reproachful thing to see the *Lord of glory* bear shame on his back, and to behold Jesus going through the city, out of the ports of Jerusalem, with a shameful cross between his shoulders, and all the

chil-

children and boys and base ones of the city wondering at him, and crying, Hue after him. O wo to Jerusalem, when they shut Christ out at their ports, and will lodge him no longer; and wo to them that put that shame on him, as to lay the reproachful and cursed cross on his back, and no man would bear it for him: and the suffering of Christ, Heb. xi. 26. is called the reproach and *the shame of Christ,* Psal. xxii. 7. *But I am a worm* [Heb. velo-ish] *no man of note, the reproach, the manifest or published shame or reproach of Adam,* of frail men, the contempt of the people, the publick disgrace or neglect of the people. Now the third particular is, How could it consist with the glory of Christ as King, to be shamed? It is, I must confess, a strange expression, the Son of God shamed; yet 'tis scripture expression, Heb. xii. 2. Isai. l. 7. But such a shame as they could put on Christ, may well stand with the personal union.

For, 1. Shame, as arising from the ill conscience of sin, they could not put on Christ. Jer. ii. 26. *As the thief is ashamed when he is found, so is the house of Israel ashamed:* they could not catch Christ in any sin; and so, though they shamed him, he was not shamed, nor could he hide his face for confusion.

2. Shame is a breaking of the hope and confidence of those who look for great things, 2 Chron. xxxii. 21. *The Lord sent an angel, which cut off all the mighty men of valour, and the leaders and captains in the camp of the king of Assria: so he returned with shame of face to his own land.* And Isa. xxx. *Ye trust* (saith the Lord) *in the shadow of Egypt,* ver. 3. *Therefore shall the strength of Pharaoh be your shame.* Ver. 5. *They are all ashamed of a people that could not profit them, nor be a help nor profit, but a shame and also a reproach:* Now, thus the confidence that Christ had in God could not be broken; God could not fail Christ; his hope was ever green, before the sun: he said it, and it was true, Isa. l. 7. (Christ's faith and boldness in his Father was as hard as flint) *For the Lord God will help me, therefore shall I not be confounded; therefore have*

I set my face as a flint, and I know that I shall not be ashamed.

3. But it is clear, in pulling off his garments and scourging him, so they shamed him, as Jer. xiii. 26. *Therefore will I discover thy skirts on thy face, that thy shame may appear:* they brought Jesus bound, as if he had been a common thief, to Pilate, Mat. xxvi. 2. and in regard of this Isaiah prophesied, liii. 3. *He was despised and rejected of men* (the text will bear) Christ was no body----------*and we hid as it were our faces from him;* they put so much disgrace and shame on blessed Jesus, he was so basely handled, that we blushed and were ashamed to look upon him; all his friends thought shame of him. 1. But this was but the lying estimation of unbelieving men, who could not see his glory; but the repenting thief, when they render him most shameful and abased, by faith saw him a King who had the keys of paradise at his girdle, when he prayed, *Lord, remember me when thou comest to thy kingdom:* and he was most un-king like at that time; and he had as much shame on him, as he was able to bear; he was branded as the greatest thief of the three, dying a thief's death, going out at the ports of life, bleeding, pained, cursed, shamed, forsaken, despised, mocked; all his glory was now under the ashes, and covered with shame. The sun seemed to be ashamed to see the Creator of the sun in so painful and so shameful a condition, and therefore the sun runs away and hides itself, and is not able to behold the Lord of glory hanged on a tree; the rocks and mountains, the stones and fair temple, as if they would burst for sorrow, and cannot endure so base a condition as the Creator was in now. And, as if death and the graves were grieved, and malecontent to serve the justice of God, for the sin of man, they will lodge their prisoners the dead no longer; but the graves are opened. 2. Shame is but an opinion, and men can bestow their opinion amiss, and so did the world on Christ; there was glory and fulness, yea, infinite glory in Christ, but they saw it not; few see the worth, fewer can weigh the weight of Christ's ex-

cel-

cellency. Men's glory is but [Gr. doxè] a mere opinion, and often but a lie: and it took nothing of real glory from Christ, whatever they esteemed him; say that the sense of a man would judge the sun no better than a two-penny candle, this takes nothing from the excellency of the sun. 2. The sun is the sun, when it hides its beams and rays of light and heat; Christ was the Lord of glory, when he drew in all his majesty, and caused the rays of glory and honour retire and hide themselves under all the shame, baseness and disgrace that men could lay upon him. A voluntary condescension of Christ was all here.

3. *A curse.*

The third character engraven on Christ's death, is the curse of God; in which consider, 1. *What a curse was on Christ dying.* 2. *How he was a curse, and the causes of it.*

To curse, in both languages, is to pray evil, to devote to destruction either in word or deed. Now the curse that Christ was made, 1. Was the Lord's pronouncing him a curse: 2. The setting of him apart, as appointed for wrath and judgment: 3. The dishonour done to him, the nothinging or despising of Christ, was a part of his curse. Now in the curse of these three, we know, Deut. xxi. 23. the Lord pronounceth him *accursed that hangeth on a tree:* Paul, in Gal. iii. 10, 12. applies it to Christ; it was a ceremonial curse, I grant, Deut. xxi. but had a special relation to Christ, who was under a real and moral curse; for such a curse is upon the sinner for idolatry, and the highest breaches of the moral law, Deut. xxvii. as to set light by father and mother, to *remove the neighbour's land-mark,* and by fraud or rapine, to take his lands from him: such a curse was laid on Christ, an higher curse than to be hanged on a tree; to be hanged was a note of a temporal curse, but except the man died in sin, no mark of the eternal displeasure of God, but as typical and relative to Christ, for whose sake only this curse was put on the death of the cross: it was in equivalency an eternal vengeance, and that wrath which all the elect were for

ever

ever to suffer in hell; the apostle saith, Gal. iii. 10, 11, 12, 13. Such a curse, as is due *to those that abide not in all that is written in the law of God to do it,* was upon Christ. Now, this was a real and moral curse; because, *first,* due to the Gentiles, who were not obliged to the law of ceremonies; and was, *secondly,* due to thousands that died not on the tree.

2. Christ was devoted and set apart, in the eternal counsel of God, for suffering the punishment of sin; when God first purposed (if there be order of first and second in the eternal decrees of God) the Lord devoted and set apart this Lamb, *before the foundation of the world was laid,* to be a bloody sacrifice for sin; he was separated from the flock to be killed, and for our sakes he devoted, vowed and sanctified himself for that work: Christ was of all mankind separated to be an atonement and an expiation for sin; he was dieted for the race, to run through death and hell; he was fitted to suffer; no man, so furnished to undergo the wrath of God, as he.

3. As to be accursed, comes under the third notion, to wit, to be dishonoured; so was Christ under a curse, Psal. xxii. 7. *No man,* Isa. liii. 3. *The last of men; the contempt and the refuse of men,* Acts iv. 11. *the stone rejected by you builders* (saith Peter) [Gr. *ho lithos ho excuthenetheis*] that nothinged stone, not so much esteemed as an arrant murderer Barabbas: and this death of the cross, now especially in the christian world, is become most base; as the *burial of an ass,* Jer. xxii. was a sign of God's displeasure, so is hanging, nations having (not without God's providence) casten their consent together, that it should be the death of the poor and basest of men: so Peter, as if it had been only of men's chusing, Acts v. 30. *The God of our fathers raised up Jesus, whom ye slew and hanged on a tree;* and Acts ii. 23. *whom by wicked hands ye have crucified and slain.* Hanging on a tree, is more than slaying: to kill a man, is all ye can do; but to put a man to a base death, that is cursed both of God and man, is far worse, 'tis more than the worst: and that a king lineally de-

scended

scended of kings, and of the blood royal, the kingly tribe of Judah, the man on earth that only by birth and law had title to the crown of Judea, should be put to so base a death, is the worse that wicked men or devils can do.

I may add yet a fourth consideration, Gen. iii. 17. All the creatures are put under the curse of man's sins: Christ died such a death, as took the creatures off the curse; and Col. i. 20. Christ, having made peace through the blood of his cross, reconciled all things to himself, whether *they be things on earth, or things in heaven.* 2. Now, how Christ could be a curse, is harder: there is a thing intrinsically and fundamentally cursed, and there is a thing extrinsically and effectively cursed; none but he that sinneth, is intrinsically and fundamentally cursed; for in this regard 'tis a personal evil. Christ was not intrinsically abominable, hateful, and an execrable thing to God.

Object. "But if Christ suffered all that we were to suffer for our sins, then as God must in justice abhor and hate with a hatred of abomination the sinner, and the sinner is such an one as God must let out his displeasure against him, so God must hate and abhor his person; therefore God's displeasure not only pursued Christ by way of punishment, that extrinsically he was cursed, but also the Lord in justice behoved to hate and abhor the person of the Son of God with the hatred of abomination, that he intrinsically should be a curse, as well as the sinner, in whose person he stands."

Answ. Christ the surety behoved to suffer all and every punishment due to the elect, either in the same kind and coin, as death, or in the equivalency and in as good: for there were some punishments that may be well changed the one in the other; as death natural, or by violence, was changed in the death of the cross: we have no ground to think, if Christ had never come to die for us, that the death of all mankind must have been the death of the cross: so God's hating and abominating the sinner, must be and was changed in

God's

God's forsaking of Christ, when he complained, *My God, my God, etc.* in regard this was all as penal and sad to Christ, as the other, to wit, to be abominated and hated in our persons as accused of God, not to say that it was not congruous to the condition of him who is the Son of the eternal God by nature, and by an unspeakable generation, to be in his person abominated and abhorred of God, as a man intrinsically cursed, as the sinner who sinneth in person is: and not to add also (which may be said) the kind of punishment; this, not this, is arbitrary to the law-giver: now, the apostle saith not Christ was cursed, but, Gal. iii. 10. [Gr. genomenos huper hemôn katára] *he was made a curse for us,* extrinsically a curse, as 2 Cor. v. 21. *God made him sin for us,* that is, what was a penal in the curse and sin, and whatever was congruous and suitable to his holy person, that the Lord Jesus came under: sure, as Christ took on him our nature, so he changed persons and names with us legally; he was made the sinner, and the sinner made the son: there was reciprocation of imputation here; Christ was you legally and by law, and ye are sons in him. The law was a bloody bond, and our names and souls were inked with the blood of the eternal curse; *but blot out* (saith Christ) *my brethrens' names out of the blood bond, and write in my name, for blood and the curse of God;* and there was a white gospel-bond drawn up, and the elect's names therein. Then the two writs run thus in the new covenant; Christ was made a curse, and liable to pay all our debts and law-penalties to the blood and death; and the poor sinner eternally blessed in Jesus Christ, even to perfect imputed righteousness and everlasting life. Christ changed your bleeding even to the second death, and made it blessings for evermore to new and everlasting life.

Use 1. If Christ died such a violent and painful death; then death, violent or natural, is not much up or down.

(1.) Sweet Jesus had it to his choice, he would choose the sourest of deaths, to go to the grave in blood;

Christ's winding-sheet was blooded; a good prince, a ransomer of the house of God, Josiah, died in blood: many of the worthiest that died in faith, died not in their beds, were (Heb. xi. 35, 36, 37.) *tortured, had trial of bonds and imprisonment, they were stoned, they were sawn asunder, were tempted, were slain with the sword.* The first witness in the christian church after the Lord's ascension, *Stephen, a man full of the Holy Ghost and of faith,* was stoned to death, Psal. lxxix. 2. *The bodies of thy servants have they given to be meat to the fowls of the heaven, the flesh of thy saints to the beasts of the earth:* many thousand martyrs have been burnt quick, extremely tormented with new-devised most exquisite torments, as to be roasted on a brander, to be devoured with lions and wild beasts.

2. Violence more or less is an accident of death, as it is the same hand folded in, or the fingers stretched out; violent death is but a death on horseback, and with wings, or a stroke with the fist, as the other death is a blow with the palms of the hand; natural death is death going on foot, and creeping with a slower pace; violent death unites all its forces at once, and takes the city by storm, and comes with sourer and blacker visage; death natural divides itself in many several bits of deaths; old age being a long spun-out death, and nature seems to render the city more willingly, and death comes with a whiter and milder visage; the one has a salter bite, and teeth of steel and iron; the other has softer fingers, and takes asunder the boards of the clay tabernacle more leisurely, softly, tenderly and with less din, as not willing that death should appear death, but a sleep: the violent death is as when apples green and raw are plucked off the tree, or when flowers in the bud, and young, are plucked up by the roots; the other way of dying is, as when apples are ripened and are filled with well-boil'd summer-sap, and fall off the tree of their own accord in the eater's mouth; or when flowers wither on the stalk: some dying full of the days, have, like banqueters, a surfeit of time; others are suddenly plucked away when they are green; but which

of

of the ways you die, not to die in the Lord is terrible, ye may know ye shall die by the fields ye grow on while ye live. A believer on Christ, breathes in Christ, speaks, walks, prays, believes, eateth, drinketh, sickens, dies in Christ; Christ is the soil he is planted in, he groweth on the banks of the paradise of God; when he falleth, he cannot fall wrong. Some are trees growing on the banks of the river of fire and brimstone; when God hews down the tree, and death fells them, the tree can fall no otherwise than in hell. O how sweet to be in Christ, and to grow as a tree planted on the banks of the river of life! when such die, they fall in Christ's lap and in his bosom, be the death violent or natural; 'tis all one whether a strong gale and a rough storm shore the child of God on the new Jerusalem's dry land, or if a small calm blast even with rowing of oars bring the passenger to heaven, if once he be in that goodly land.

2. To die in faith, (*The righteous has hope in his death*) is the essential qualification to be most regarded, that is the all and sum of well-dying; make sure work of heaven, and let the way or manner, violent or natural, be as God will, 'tis amongst the indifferents of death; saints have died either way. To die in Christ, in the hope of the resurrection, is the fair and good death. To die in sin, Job viii. 21. that is the ill death, and the black death.

3. To die ripened for eternity, is all and sum; 'tis said of some, *they died full of days.*

Object. How is a man full and ripe for death?

Answ. In these respects, 1. When the man is mortified to time, and is satisfied with days, he desires no more life, he lies at the water-side, near-by death, waiting for wind and tide, like a passenger who would fain be over the water; so dying Jacob, in the midst of his testament, Gen. xlix. 18. *Lord, I have waited for thy salvation; Lord,* when shall I have fair passage? Job saith, chap. xiv. 14. *All the time I am on the sentinel, or the time of my warfare, I will wait till my last change come.* So Paul saith, Phil. i. 23. *Having a*

desire

desire to be dissolved, and to be with Christ, which is far better; the man desires not to stay here any longer.

2. He would go to sea; when all his land-business is ended, the courts are closed, and if the sun be low and near his setting, lo the way ends with the day; see the lodging hard at hand, 2 Tim. iv. 7. *I have finished my course, I have kept the faith.* 8. *Henceforth is laid up for me a crown of righteousness:* sweet Jesus, ere he died, said, *It is finished,* all is done; he is on the scaf-fold, and nods on his executioner, Death, Friend, come do your office, I pray you see your task be ended.

3. The man seeth the crown; he is come to the stone-wall or the hedge of paradise, and seeth the apples of life hanging on the tree, and hears the musick of heaven: Stephen, Acts vii. 50. *I saw heaven opened.*

4. He goes not away pulled by the hair, but willingly, gladly, Heb. xi. 8, 15. They desire a better country. Job v. 26. *Like a shock of corn in his season:* it would be the loss of the corn to be longer out of the barn; death shall not come while it be welcome. Job vii. 3. As the hired servant panteth for the shadow, so he for death. All these four were in Jesus Christ.

Had Christ so much pain in his death, that his death and the cross were all one, so as he had five deaths on him at once, four on his body, death on every hand, death on every foot, and a death on his soul, ten thousand millions of pounds weightier and sadder? Then let us correct all our errors and misjudgings touching the cross.

Error 1. We love to go to paradise through a paradise of roses, and a land-way to heaven, and a dry fair white death; we would have Christ and the cross changed, which saith, *Whoever would follow Christ, let him take up his cross* [Gr. kath' he meran] *daily, and follow him,* Luke vi. 23.

2. We forget that heaven is fenced with a huge great wood of thorns; we must crowd through, though our skin be scratched even to blood and death. Life eternal is like a fair, pleasant, rich and glorious city in the midst of a waste wilderness; and there lies round about this city, at all the corners of it, a wood of briers and

thorns,

thorns, scorpions serpents and lions abounding in it, and the wood is ten thousand miles of bounds on all hands, of a journey of threescore years at some parts; there is no high road-way in the wood, no back entry about; wise professors seek a way about the cross; God has given wings to none to fly over the wood: or 'tis like a fair king's palace in an island of the sea; 'tis a most pleasant isle for all kind of delights, but there is no way to it by dry-land. Would ye have valley-ground, summer-meadows, fields and gardens of flowers and roses all your way? and how is it that the Lord will not give peace to his church? nay, but there is not a way to heaven on this side of the cross, or on that side of the cross, but directly, straight through we must go; when the apostles went through the churches *confirming the brethren,* Acts xiv. 22. they preached that the cross was gospel; and [Gr. dia pollôn thlipseon deî hemas] *through the midst of affliction,* or under flailing and threshing we must go; there is not a way about to shift the cross, but we must *enter into the kingdom of God,* this very way, and no other.

3. The blood was not dried off Christ's hands and feet, and his winding-sheet, till he was in the flower of the higher palace of his father's kingdom, and within the walls; and so his church must not think hard of it, if she go not a dry death to heaven.

Error 2. We tacitly condemn the wisdom of God in our murmuring under the cross; cannot Christ lead his people to heaven a better way than through the swords, spears and teeth of malignants? and must new armies of Irish murderers land on us again? These would be considered: 1. Paul encouraging the Thessalonians, saith, 2 Thess. iii. 3. *No man should be moved by these afflictions:* why, *for yourselves know we are appointed thereunto from eternity.* The wise Lord did brew a cup of bloody sufferings for his church, and did mould and shape every saint's cross in length and breadth for him; our afflictions are not of yesterday's date and standing: before the Lord set up the world, as it now is, he had all the wheels, pins, wedges, works, and every material

al by him, in his eternal mind; all your tears, your blood, all the ounces and pounds of gall and wormwood ye now drink, they were an eternal design and plot of God's wise decree before the world was, they were the lot God did appoint for your back, they are no sourer, no heavier this day, than they were in the Lord's purpose before time; your grave, O saints, is no deeper than of old the Lord digged it, your wound no nearer the bone than mercy made it; your death is no blacker, no more thorny and devouring than Christ's soft hands framed it; ere God gave you flesh and skin and heart in your blood, Christ's doom and the church's doom of the black cross was written in heaven: so Christ smiles and drinks with this word, John xviii. 11. *Shall I not drink the cup that my Father hath given me?* 2. Rom. viii. Predestination is the first act of free-grace, and ver. 29. in that act a communion with Christ in his cross is passed; this we consider not: will ye not think good to set your shoulders and bones under the same burden that was on Christ's back? we fear the cross less at our heels and behind our back than when it is in our bosom. The Lord Jesus speaks of his suffering often afore-hand, and it is wisdom to make it less, by antidated patience and submission, before we suffer; it were good, would we give our thoughts, and lend some words to death, as Christ here doth ere it come: opinion, which is the pencil that draws the face, arms and legs of death and sufferings, might honey our gall; if a martyr judge a prison a palace, and his iron chains golden bracelets, sure his bonds are as good as liberty; if a saint count death Christ's master-usher to make way to him for heaven, then death cannot be a mill to grind the man's life to powder: faith can oil and sugar our worm-wood; and if Christ come with the cross, it has no strength; the believer has two skins on his face against the spittings of storm and hail-stones; Christ can make a saint sing in hell, as impatient unbelief could cause a man sigh and weep in heaven. 3. We forget that the church is the *vineyard of the Lord of hosts,* and that the owner of the farm

must

must hire Satan and wicked men to be his vine-dressers and reapers; but the crop is the Lord's, not theirs; they are plowers, but they neither know the soil, nor the husbandman, Psal. cxxix. 2.

Error 3. When we see we must suffer, we tacitly are offended that Christ will not give us the first vote in our own jury, and that he would not seek our own advice in this kind of cross, not this. Except to one man, David, God never referred the choice of a cross, but then grace made the choice. Sure Scotland would have chosen famine or pestilence, rather than the sword of a barbarous unnatural enemy; but it must not be referred to the wisdom of the sick, what should be his physick: we often say, any cross but this; especially if there be any letter of reproach on the cross, a shameful death or distraction of mind; but the Lord seeth nothing out of heaven or hell so good for you as that; that, and no other. 2. We would have the pound-weights of affliction weighed in our balance: oh this is too heavy; hence David's and Job's over complaining, *Oh my calamity is heavier than the sand of the sea,* Job vi. 3. and, *Am I a sea or a whale that thou settest a watch over me?* Chapter vii. 12. Should God deal with a man as with a fish or a beast? 3. We desire to be creators of such and such circumstances of our own grief: so we storm often at the circumstances, as at the very poison of the cross; as if God had, through forgetfulness, and a slip of wisdom, left that circumstance out of his decree, as the painter that draws the whole body exactly, but forgetteth to draw one of the five fingers; and in the mean while, that circumstance, which we wrestle most against in our thoughts, was specially intended of God: how often doth this fire our thoughts, and burn them up with fretting? *Had I done this, I might have eschewed this heaviest and sadded calamity:* had I gone to sea when the wind and sailors called me, but the fourth part of an hour sooner I had not been in dry land, where I am now butchered to death, so, had I but spoken a word, I might have saved all this loss and labour; and not this man come in with an ill counsel and one unhappy word, many hundred thousands had not been killed in battle. And Martha, John xi. 21. is upon this distemper, for she saith to Jesus, *Lord, if thou hadst been here, my brother had not died:* she would say, it was an ill hap, Christ was unluckily in another place when *my brother died;* but the wise decree of God had carved these circumstances so, that Christ's absence was specially decreed in that affliction, v. 15. *Jesus said plainly, Lazarus is dead, and I am glad for your sakes, that I was not there (to the intent that ye may believe,)* etc. Look up in the affliction to the saddest and blackest circumstance in the cross: infinite wisdom was not sleeping, but from eternity, with understanding and counsel, the Lord decreed and framed that saddest circumstance, even that Shimei a subject should curse David his prince; and that he should charge him with blood against Saul, of which he was most free, and at that time, and no other time, when he was fleeing for his life from his son Absalom; but all the sad circumstances were moulded and framed on the wheels of the decree of him who deviseth all, shapes our woes, *according to the counsel of his will.* We would have our Lord to remove the gall, the worm-wood, and the fire-edge out of our cross, and we lust for some more honey and sugar of consolation to be mixed with it. It were good if we could, by grace, desire three ills to be removed from our cross: 1. That of its nature it be not sinful, such as hardness of heart; we may in our election and choice, pray that it be not both a sinful plague of God on the soul, and a judgment to us: 2. We may pray, that the affliction may be circumstanced, and honeyed with the consolations of Christ, and with faith and patience, and a spiritual use of the affliction: 3. We may pray, it may not be a burden above our back, and such as we are not able to bear; and this we may as lawfully choose and pray, as say, *Lord, lead us not into temptation.*

Use 3. Was there shame and reproach on Christ's cross? Fy on all the glory of the world; let us not think, 1. Too much of this piece airy, windy, vain o-

pinion

pinion of men's esteem, and their applause; 'tis but a short-living, hungry hosanna, when your name is carried through a spot or bit of this clay-stage, for a day or two; they'll wonder at your but nine nights. Christ's *fame spread abroad through all the country,* and now he is shamed and a reproached man; now the whole people cry out, *Away with him, away with him, crucify him.* The ground of man's glory is *his goodliness or graciousness,* his [Heb. Hesed] all his endowments and brave parts, and all this glory, Isa. xl. 6. *is as the flower of the field:* his glory has a month, and lives the poor twelfth part of a year; and Herod is gone to the worms, and his silks rotten and gone; and Shebna is tossed like a ball in a large place, and must hear this, Isa. xxii. 18. *Thou shalt die* (in a strange land) *and there thy chariots of thy glory shall be the shame of thy Lord's house.* 'Tis an earthly thing, Phil. iii. 19. *Whose glory is their shame, who mind earthly things.* Hos. iv. 7. *I'll change their glory into shame;* and when Ephraim glories in children, God sews wings to that glory, and it flies away, Hos. ix. 11. *As for Ephraim, their glory shall fly away as a bird.* The ten tribes boasted of their strength and multitude, but the Lord saith, Isa. xvii. 4. *The glory of Jacob shall be made thin.* 2. God in a special manner sets himself in person against this glory; Isa. xxiii. 9. *The Lord of hosts has purposed to stain the pride of all glory, and to bring into contempt all the honourable of the earth.* Isa. x. 12. *I'll punish the glory of the high looks of the king of Assyria.* Hab. ii. 16. The Lord lays a right curse on Caldee's glory; *The cup of the Lord's right-hand shall be turned into thee, and shameful spuing shall be thy glory.* 3. 'Tis the sweet fruit of Christ's death and abasement, that we learn to lay down our credit under the Lord's feet, Phil. ii. *Let this same mind be in you, that was in Christ Jesus:* O that must be a high and an aspiring mind! for he was the high and lofty One; no, he teaches all his to be abased, v. 6. *Who being in the form of God, thought it no robbery to be equal with God,* v. 7. *but he emptied himself;* he was full of majesty and glory,

but

but he made himself of no reputation, and an empty thing, *and took upon him the form of a servant, and was made in the likeness of men---and humbled himself:* ah! let never man go with high sails, nor count much of world's glory, after Jesus Christ: ah! our reputation and name is as tender to us as paper, as our skin; a scratch in it, or a rub, is a provocation cannot be expiated; as if we minded in the airy cloud of men's fame, to fly up to heaven, and frothy fame were as good to lay hold on Christ as fervent faith: breach of our privileges of state is more now than blasphemy against God.

Use 4. Now, if Christ was made a curse for us, that we might be delivered from the curse, we are comforted in Christ's being made a curse for us, in regard of, 1. *Extreme love.* 2. *Perfection of blessedness.*

For this act of love, we are assured he that will be made the curse of God for us, will be any thing. Four great steps of love were here, every one of them greater than another. 1. *To be a man.* 2. *To be a dying man.* 3. *To be as a sinning man.* 4. *To be a cursed man.*

Consider these four as they grow out of the root of love. A spirit sinless and holy is a happy thing; the Son of God, being God, is a Spirit, and so in another condition than man, he was above bones and clay, and the motion of hot air going in and out at the nostrils; 'tis a sort of cumber to carry about a piece of dust of more than a hundred and fifty bits of clay, organs, five senses, two hands, two legs, head, tongue, lips, throat, shoulders, breast, back, so many fingers, toes, liths, joints, veins, muscles, then belly, stomach, heart, liver, bowels, and a number of cumbersome vessels; let them be a hundred and fifty fragments of warm, red and bloody clay, they require more than an hundred and fifty servants of clay, of meat, raiment, medicine, to serve them; and the more needy a creature is, the more miserable. A spirit is above all these, and needs not senses, nor servants to serve the senses and life; O but Christ was happy

from

from eternity! And consider what a low loup of love was this; *The word made flesh, God manifested in the flesh,* is the greatest mystery of love in the world: here God an infinite spirit made man, has need of two eyes of clay, two ears, two legs, two hands; he must come under the necessities of all these hundred and fifty organs. Can ye tell what secrets of love are here? God looks out at two clay-windows, the two eyes of a man; God walks with the two clay-legs of a man, *He dwelt amongst us* (saith John i. 14.) *he pitched his clay-tent with us, full of grace and glory;* grace and glory dwelling in clay, is one of the deep wonders of the world.

But, 2. We would accept to be men; but if it were referred to our choice, we must die in pain, and be tumbled in a cold hole of clay in the earth, and see the sun no more, it may be, we would take it to our advisement, ere we choosed life: Christ knew on such terms, if he should be made a creature of clay, and if the high and lofty God should be clothed with such rags, a coat of clay, so far below his beauty, he must die; yet he would be a man, a dying man; and we know what sad and sour accidents were in his death.

But, 3. Ye will kill an honest-hearted and ingenuous innocent man, ere ye move him to take with a fault, when he has done no fault: Job was called an hypocrite by his friends, but he would never take with it, *he would maintain his own righteousness, till he died;* the martyrs, ere they would take sin on them by acting it, and deny Jesus Christ, they would rather choose the gallows, torture, the teeth of lions, burning quick, or any thing: but Christ Jesus takes it patiently to stand as the thief, the bloody man, the false man, and as all the wicked men of the world: he could not act sin; but he said, *Father, make me the sinner;* I neither stole, but let my face be blacked with theft; I never shed innocent blood, but let the stain and blot of the murderer be upon me; I never lied, but let me be as a liar, and stand so before justice; and *God made him sin,* 2 Cor. v. 21. When a man willingly goeth to prison for a broken man, 'tis a real acknowledgment that he takes on him the broken man's debts; 'tis as good as if he had said, *Crave me for him:* a moral blot to be put on an honest, holy, harmless man is a high measure of self-denial and love; Christ said, *Here am I, crave me, Lord.*

But this is nothing, Christ was a man; 2. A dying man; 3. Made as a sinner, and as a wicked and unhonest man; but God blessed him, he was made a blessing of God, and that is comfort enough: no, it was not so; God made him a curse, an execrable thing; all the broad *curses written in the book of the law,* came on him. See Christ made clay, dying clay, as sinning clay, cursed clay: what would ye have more? Christ is as if his Father abhorred him, and would not once give him one cast of his eye.

2. All perfection of blessedness comes to us by this, that *Christ was made a curse for us,* Gal. iii. 14. *That the blessing of Abraham might come on the Gentiles through Jesus Christ, that we might receive the promise of the Spirit through faith:* this is the true freedom from the law, to be freed from the curse thereof, in believing Christ was made a curse for you; according to that, Rom. vi. 14. *For sin shall not have dominion over you, for ye are not under the law, but under grace;* which doctrine is clear, Rom. vii. where expresly we are said to be freed from the dominion of the law, as the wife is freed from the law of subjection to her husband, if the husband be dead: which is a comparison, and holdeth not in all, but only in so far as the two husbands, the law and Christ, stand in opposition the one to the other: now, the opposition is, that the law has dominion to justify the legal observers of it, and guide the wise to life eternal; but the conditions are hard, and *now because of the flesh impossible.* Christ again, the better husband, leadeth his bride to heaven in sweeter terms, *by believing in him that justifieth the ungodly,* who has satisfied for our breach of the law.

3. The

3. The law hath dominion over the wife that is in subjection to it, to condemn her, if she break to this spiritual husband, in thought, word, or deed: but the two husbands both agree in this, that both command holy walking; as the apostle excellently sheweth, 1 Cor. ix. 20. *To them that are under the law, I am as under the law, that I might gain them that are under law:* Verse 21. *To them that are without law, as without law (being not without law to God, but under the law to Christ) that I might gain them that are without law:* hence we teach, that the believer, married to the second and better husband Christ, is not freed from the rule and directing power of the law to lead us in the ways of sanctification and holiness; but we are freed from the dominion of the law, that it cannot justify us, nor condemn us, because in Christ we are justified by his imputed righteousness laid hold on by faith, and saved freely in him by his blood. Hence give me leave to vindicate our doctrine in this, from the wicked aspersions cast on it by Antinomians, especially Mr. Towne.

Mr. Towne's assertion of grace against Doctor Taylor, page 3.

"When 'tis said, We are not under the law, but under grace, Rom. vi. by the word (law) I understand the moral law or decalogue, with all its authority, dominion, offices and effects; and by grace is understood the gospel of Christ. If ye were (saith he) under the power and teaching of the law, 'tis true sin would then lord it over you, in that the law is the strength of sin, 1 Cor. xv. But ye are translated into another kingdom, where the enemy ye so fear, is spoiled of all its armour, and power whereon it dependeth; and your king, you now live under, doth freely communicate abundant and effectual grace of justification and sanctification, so to fortify you, that ye shall be more than conquerors; therefore fear not, only be strong in the faith thereof."

Answ. 1. Not to mind Mr. Towne that elsewhere he meaneth by the law, that we are not under, not the mo-

ral law only, but the ceremonial also; if we be freed from all authority of the law, then hath the sixth command no authority from God to teach that murdering of our brother is a sin, that idolatry is contrary to the second command; then all acts of holiness and worship performed by the believer, must be will-service and will-worship: for if the law do not teach and direct us what is holy walking, what sin; the gospel, by the Antinomian way, doth not teach any such thing in the letter; then it is all unwritten will-walking, that a believer doth; this is licence, not holiness, we are called unto.

2. Then is it not the law's office to reveal sin to us? Paul saith contrary, Rom. iii. 20. *For by the law is the knowledge of sin.* Rom. vii. 7. *I had not known lust, except the law had said, Thou shalt not covet.* Free a believer from all *the offices of the law,* then the believer, when he lies and whores, and murders, is not obliged to know or open his eyes, and see from the light of the law that these be sins; for Mr. Towne looseth him from *all the offices of the law:* Paul misjudged himself, when in his believing condition, he saith, Rom. vii. 14, 15. *For we know that the law is spiritual, but I am carnal, sold under sin.*

3. From the law's teaching of believers, to infer that the law lordeth it over a believer, is a great fallacy.

4. If the enemy sin be spoiled of all power, even of indwelling and lusting against the Spirit, then the believer cannot fail against a law; then he may say, he has no sin, which John saith is a lie.

5. If Christ *communicate abundant effectual grace of sanctification,* then is sanctification perfect; but the scripture saith the contrary, *In many things we offend all;* and we are not perfect in this life, *nor are we more than conquerors* in every act of sanctification. Nor is that Paul's meaning, Rom. viii. that we are never foiled, and that lusts in some particular acts have not the better of us too often, but that finally, in the strength of Christ, the saints are so far forth *more than conquerors,* that nothing

thing can work the apostasy and separation of the *saints from the love of God in Christ.*

Mr. Towne's assertion of grace, pag. 4, 5.

"Mark three grounds of mistakes: 1. That justification and sanctification are separable, if not in the person, yet in regard of time and word of ministration, as if the gospel revealed justification; the law were now become an effectual instrument of sanctification: 2. That to ease men of the law's yoke, is to suffer them to range after the course of the world, and their own fleshly lusts; not considering that the righteousness of faith unites them to Christ their Lord, Head and Governour, that they may be led by his free Spirit, and swayed by the sceptre of his kingdom: 3. That all zealous and strict conformity to the law of works, tho' but in the letter, is right sanctification."

Answ. 1. Not nay of these are owned by Protestant divines; they are Mr. Towne's forged calumnies. To the first, I cannot see that sanctification is any thing at all by Antinomian grounds but meer justification; and that he is an Antinomian saint, that believeth Christ satisfied, and performed the law for him, but no letter of law or gospel layeth any obligation on him to walk in holiness. But the gospel only revealeth ingrafting of the branch in Christ the vine-tree and stock of life and the bringing forth fruits, by the faith of Christ, to be the only true sanctification; but if the apples be not of the right seed, and conform to the directing rule of all righteousness, the law of God, they are but wild grapes. We *never made the law the effectual instrument of sanctification;* a help it is, being preached with the gospel; but neither is the gospel of itself the effectual instrument of sanctification, except the Spirit of grace accompany it, nor the law of it self.

2. The second is a calumny also: but we would desire to know how Antinomians can free themselves of it; for the righteousness of faith doth not so unite believers to Christ as to their governour, so as Christ governeth them by the Spirit and the word, *for the letter of the whole*

whole word, both law and gospel (say (a) they) *holdeth forth nothing but a covenant of works; to search the scripture,* (b) *either law or gospel, is not a sure way of searching and finding of Christ;* and Mr. Towne passeth in silence all guidance of the saints, by commandments of either law or gospel, and tells us of *a leading by a free Spirit only.* So that by Antinomians, we are no more under the gospel as a directing and commanding rule, than we are under the law. What hindereth then but Antinomian justification bids us live as we list? We think the gospel commandeth every duty and forbiddeth every sin, as the law doth, under damnation; what is sin to the one, is to the other. But the gospel forbiddeth nothing to a justified believer under the pain of damnation, more than to Jesus Christ. 2. A dead letter forbiddeth no sin, commandeth no duty; but the gospel of itself, without the Spirit, is a dead letter, as well as the law; the major is the Antinomian doctrine, the assumption is undeniable.

3. Pharisaical conformity to the law we disclaim; but if any could be strictly and perfectly conform to the law of works, as Christ was, we should think such a man perfectly sanctified; but, through the wickedness of the flesh, that is unpossible. I know not what Mr. Towne means by a *conformity to the law, though but in the letter;* if he means that the literal meaning and sense of the law requireth no spiritual, inward, and compleatly perfect obedience, he is no good doctor of the law; and if it be not such an obedience, it is not zealous and strict obedience. But it is ordinary to Antinomians now to term these whom the prelatical party of late called Puritans and strict Precisians, because they strove to walk closely with God, *Pharisees and out-side professors,* who think to be justified and saved by their own righteousness; so far are they at odds with sanctification. If, by conformity to the law in the letter, Mr. Towne means external obedience, without faith in Jesus Christ, or union with him; he knows Protestant divines acknowledge no sound sanctification, but that

which

(a) Rise, Reign, Error 9.   (b) Error 39.

CHRIST DYING AND DRAWING SINNERS TO HIMSELF.

which is the natural issue and fruit of justification, and flows from *faith which purifieth the heart;* and such strict conformity to the law as floweth from saving faith, we hold to be true sanctification, though all enemies to holy walking cry out against it, such as mockers of all religion, the Prelatical and Antinomian party, who mock strict walking, and long prayer, and humble confession of sins, and smiting of conscience for sin.

Towne, page 5.

"Blind and sinister suspicion, and causeless fear, inclined doctor Taylor to this exposition, to say, our apostle looseth no christian from obedience and rule of the law, but he dares not trust a believer to walk without his keeper; as if he judged no otherwise of him than of a malefactor of Newgate, who would run away, rob, kill, play his former pranks, if the jailor or his man be not with him, when he is abroad."

Answ. 1. There is a twofold keeping in of sinners, one merely legal, such as that of wicked men, Psal. xxxii. 9. *Who are like the horse or mule, and have no understanding, whose mouth must be held in with bit and bridle lest they come near unto you;* the law hath not power over wicked men ever with terrors of hell and the curse of God, because often they be given up to a hard heart (and what cared Pharaoh, who was under the law, for this keeper?) and to a reprobate mind, and to any that commit *sin with greediness, having the conscience burnt with a hot iron, and being past feeling,* Rom. i. 28, 29. Eph. iv. 17, 18, 19. 1 Tim. iv. 2. The law is no keeper; they care no more for Mr. Towne's goal, than a lion doth for the *crying of a shepherd; he will not abase himself for it:* all the restraint that law lays on a natural man, is when the conscience is wakened, or some great plague is on Pharaoh, then he dare not keep the people captive. But Antinomians have a good opinion of slaves of Satan, who judge them to be civil and externally honest devils, and make limbs of hell of a good sweet calm nature, who stand naturally in awe of God's law; but, Rom. iii. 9, 10, 11. among the whole tribe and race of mankind, Jews and Gentiles, see what they care for the Antinomian goaler, the law; they believe not one word of the law, saith ver. 11. *There is none that understandeth, there is none that seeketh God,* ver. 12. *They are all gone out of the way* (where is the keeper, now, and his sword, and spear?) *they are altogether become unprofitable, there is none that doth good, no not one,* ver. 13. *There throat is an open grave, with their tongues they have used deceit, the poison of asps is under their lips,* etc. The law layeth not naturally a bridle on the outer man; but observe that the conscience be restrained and awed by the law, and under any natural remorse for sin committed or to be committed, is a sinful bondage that Christ must deliver us from. 1. Then, stupefaction and deadness of conscience not to care for the law of God, more than a prisoner who has broken goal, and now is in the hedges and high-ways robbing and murdering, cares for his old keeper, is to Antinomians mortification, and a crucifying of old Adam. 2. Job's not daring to lift his arm against the fatherless, chap. xxxi. must be the power of old Adam in him; David's bones broken for his adultery and murder, must be the power of old lusts in him. 3. Then the less tenderness of conscience and fear for sin as sin, the more mortification of lust. 4. Grace as grace, stupifieth and deadneth conscience; so Antinomians must teach.

    2. Men naturally do more good for the praise of men, and are more afraid to do ill, for the ax and the gibbet of the magistrate, than for any fear of hell or judgment of the law of God. Towne cannot speak of this keeper; there is a second restraint that the law mixt with the love of Christ layeth on the godly and believer, and he has need of this keeper; so Joseph saith, Gen. xlii. 18. *This do and live, for I fear God:* there was a keeper over Job, that *he durst not lift up his*

hand

CHRIST DYING AND DRAWING SINNERS TO HIMSELF.

hand against the fatherless, chap. xxxi. why ver. 23. *For destruction from God was a terror to me, and by reason of his highness I could not endure:* And this keeper in the conscience, *smites David's heart, when he renteth but the lap of Saul's garment,* and keeps him that he dare not kill him. This was not legal bondage; for Christ commanded (Mat. x. 28, 29. Luke xii. 5.) us to fear him *that can cast both soul body in hell,* rather ere we deny him before men *who can but kill the body;* and, 1 Pet. ii. 17. Col. iii. 22. Acts ix. 31. Acts xiii. 16. it is commanded to us. I grant, the object of this fear is not so much hell, as the offending of God, but it is commanded in the law of God: but Mr. Towne will have the believer so free, so perfect, as the law needeth not to teach and direct him in one step; he doth all without a keeper, or one letter of a command, by the free impulsion of a spirit separated from scripture: that is right down, a believer is neither under law nor gospel, but a spirit separated from the gospel and all letter of it, and from the law, guides him.

Towne, Pag. 5, 6

"But I muse why you omit to show what it is to be under grace, which is the member opposite to being under the law. Paul treateth of sanctification, and yet maketh this contrariety of being under the law, and under grace: the law must be taken comprehensively, with all his offices and authority; and that the reason is firm, that sin shall not have dominion over him who liveth under the grace of the gospel, because it hath a sanctifying virtue and power in it to subdue sin."

Answ. Dr. Taylor did not omit to expound what it is *to be under grace,* if you had not omitted to read his words, he is clear to any unpartial reader: but let your exposition stand; sin shall have no dominion over you, for ye are not under the law, as teaching, directing, regulating believers in the way of righteousness, but under grace, that is, under the gospel, which giveth power to subdue sin, without any ruling, teaching or directing power of the law: but what is the power of

subduing

subduing sin, to Antinomians, I pray you? Not sanctification, as in words they say; but justification, that is a power to believe Christ by doing and suffering has fulfilled and obeyed the law for you, but ye are under no command to walk according to the rule of righteousness in the law; so that to be under the law, is just contrary to personal and real sanctification and walking in love and evangelick duties, even as to *be under the law,* and to *be under grace,* are opposed by the apostle: then, as we are obliged, not to be under the law, but under grace, so are we obliged to no personal sanctification or holy walking, but to objective and imputative sanctification only, that is, only to believe in Christ as made our righteousness and sanctification. Now, as we are not obliged to be inherently righteous, so are we not obliged to be inherently and personally sanctified and holy, for that is to be under the law, as the rule of righteousness: now we are freed from the law as our rule of righteousness, and from the law *with all its offices and authority,* saith Mr. Towne; and to remain under the law as a rule of righteousness, and to walk holily, as being obliged from the conscience of any command either of law or gospel, is legal bondage, from which Christ has set us free; as to be circumcised is a part of the law-yoke, so they teach; then to be inherently holy is unlawful to Antinomians.

Mr. Towne, Page 6.

"Yet I wish that I be not mistaken, for I never deny the law to be an eternal and inviolable rule of righteousness: but yet affirm, that 'tis the grace of the gospel which effectually and truly conformeth us thereunto."

Answ. 1. I wish Mr. Towne do mistake; for he that teacheth that believers are freed from the law, as a rule teaching and directing, and from the law with all its offices and authority; he denieth the law to believers to be an eternal and inviolable rule of righteousness, or then he must speak contradictions, to wit, that the believer is not under the law as a rule of righte-

ousness

eousness; for so (saith Towne) *he should not be under grace, which is contrary to the apostle,* Rom. vi. 14. and yet he is under the law as an eternal and inviolable rule of righteousness. For I ask, To whom is the law an eternal and inviolable rule of justice? to the believer or no? If to the believer, then he must be under it; but Antinomians say, that is Pharisaical and Popish; that is, to put Christ's freeman (saith Towne) *under his old keeper the law, as if he were a malefactor.* If the law be no eternal and inviolable rule of righteousness, why doth Mr. Towne say so.

2. That rule to the which the grace of the gospel doth conform us, that rule we must be under; but Mr.Towne saith, *The grace of the gospel truly conformeth us to the eternal and inviolable rule of righteousness;* ergo, etc.

3. An inviolable rule of justice cannot be violated and contraveened by these to whom it is a rule without sin, else 'tis not an inviolable rule: then if believers cannot violate the law, and murder, and commit adultery, but they must sin by violating the rule; then, as believers are obliged not to murder, nor to commit adultery, so must they be under the inviolable rule of righteousness; contrary to which Antinomians teach. All that Mr. Towne can say against us in this argument, is a calumny, that we make the law, not the gospel, to give power to subdue sin; but the truth is, neither law nor gospel giveth grace, but the God of grace hath promised in the gospel, grace, and a new heart and a new spirit to the elect: and grace goeth not along with the gospel, as a favour of equal extension with the preached gospel; but millions hear the gospel, who remain void of grace, and have no right to any promise of grace. The law leaveth not off to be the rule of righteousness, though it cannot effectually make its disciples holy and conform to the rule; no more than the gospel should not be the law and rule of faith, because without the influence of the Spirit of grace it can make no disciples conform to Jesus Christ and his image; for, many elect, for a long time, hear the gospel,

and

and have no grace to obey, while the time of conversion come; and many are more blinded and hardned, that the gospel is preached to them; and it were better they had never heard *nor known the way of truth.*
Towne, page 6, 7.

'Rom. vii. 6. The meaning is, Through faith is bred assured confidence, lively hope, pure love toward God, invocation of his name, without all wavering, or doubting or questioning his good-will, audience and acceptance, which could never be attained by all the zeal and conscience towards God, according to the law of works.------And the knowledge of the glory of God, is given according to a covenant of meer grace, without addition or mixture of works-----and the opposition is plain to be not so much between the gross hypocrite (who is only brought to outward subjection and correspondency to the law) as between him that in good earnest and in down-uprightness of heart, giveth over himself wholly to the law of God, Rom. x. 2. (as the wife to the husband and guide of her youth) to be ordered in all things, inwardly and outwardly, after the mind of God therein according to his legal conscience, which is never pacified with works; and the man who knoweth and worshippeth God alone, according to the gospel of grace.'

Answ. This is a close perverting of the word of truth. 1. The Antinomian. Faith may here be smelled, that by faith is *bred assured confidence, without all wavering, fear or doubting,* etc. Then, whoever once doubt or waver, are yet under the law of works; a doctrine of despair to broken reeds, who are not under the law, but married to a new husband Christ, and yet cry, *Lord, I believe, help my unbelief: why fear ye, O ye of little faith?* Is there not doubting here, and a broken faith, which Christ softly bindeth up.

2. The covenant of grace and gospel commandeth faith, and also good works as witnesses of our faith; but Towne will have good works, in any notion of an evangelick command, to stand at defiance with a covenant of mere grace, when grace is the fountain and

cause

cause to our walking in Christ, 2 Cor. i. 10. *By the grace of God, we had our conversation in the world; in simplicity and godly sincerity.* 1 Cor. xv. 10. *I laboured more abundantly than they all, yet not I, but the grace of God, that is in me.* 'Tis true, holy walking by the grace of God, and Christ's righteousness, put together in justification, is a wicked mixture, which we detest.

3. The opposition, Rom. vii. is between any unconverted man under the law, be he hypocrite, or a civil devil, or be he any other man, on the one part; and a believer married to Christ, and dead to the law, on the other; for that which is common, not to gross hypocrites only, but to all natural men out of Christ, is ascribed to the man that is under the law, by the apostle; as, (1.) He is under the law's dominion and condemnation, v. 1. The law has power over him, as the living husband over the wife, v. 2. (3.) The poor man cannot look to Jesus, to another lover and husband; the law as a hard husband leads him, and cries, *Obey perfectly, or be eternally damned.* (4.) He is a man in the flesh, in whose members concupiscence and lust rageth; as a young vigorous mother bringeth forth children, lusts of the flesh to death, as married to hell the second death, v. 5. (5.) He serves *God according to the oldness of the letter,* that is, carnally, hypocritically, like an out-side of a rotten Pharisee, and not according to the *newness of the Spirit,* that is, in a spiritual manner.

Yet Mr. Towne extols him, 'As one that in good earnest and downrightness of heart, yieldeth and giveth over himself to the law of God (as the wife to the husband) to be instructed and ordered in all things, inwardly, and outwardly, after the mind of God.' But no unconverted man can be said so to do, except Antinomians be gross Pelagians. But, I think, Antinomians, with Mr. Crispe, think the person under the law in all this chapter to be the believer, personating or acting the person of a scrupulous believer, under a temptation of doubting: but clear it is, Paul speaks of a man under the law, in the flesh; and in opposition to him, of one under grace; of one married to the law, and of

one

one married to Christ; in the first part of the chapter, of one in the flesh, and so unrenewed, v. 5. *For when we were in the flesh,* etc. and of one that is dead to the law, married to Christ, and serves the Lord spiritually. And 'tis clear, that the apostle counteth it a part of deliverance from the law, and a fruit of our marriage to God, that, (v. 4.) *we bring forth fruits to God,* and walk holily. (2.) That the motions of sins bring forth wicked works, as children to the second death, v. 5. (3.) That we serve the Lord (v. 6.) in newness of Spirit, and walk in Christ.

Now, Mr. Towne, as setting himself to contradict Paul, saith, page 6. *This is an addition and mixture of works and faith,* and cannot stand with a covenant of mere grace.
      Towne, p. 8.
'How can Christ redeem us from the law, being under the law for us, except believers be redeemed from the law, in that same very sense and extent that Christ was under it, as a Mediator? But was not Christ under the rule and obedience also, as well as under the reign to death, seeing he came to do the will of his Father, and fulfil all righteousness, Mat. iii. 15.

Answ. 1. We cannot every way be said to be *redeemed from the law, in that same sense that Christ was under it:* for Christ was under the law of ceremonies, to free the Jews from observing that law; I hope we Gentiles are not that way freed from the law of ceremonies; for that law did never oblige the Gentiles, except the Gentiles had adjoined themselves, in some profession, to the then visible church.

2. If Christ was under the law as the rule, to free us from the law as the rule; then, Why did Christ command us to imitate him in doing his Father's will, and submitting to that same rule that he submitted to? as is clear, Mat. xi. 29. *Learn of me that am meek.* John xv. 10. *If ye keep my commandments, ye shall abide in my love; even as I have kept my Father's commandments, and abide in his love.* John xiv. 15. *If ye love me, keep my commandments.* John xiii. 15. *For I have*
          given

given you example, that ye should do as I have done unto you. Eph. v. 1, 2. Rev. iii. 21. Heb. xii. 1. 1 Pet. ii. 21, 22. John xv. 23. But Antinomians (a) say, That these that be in Christ, are not under the law, or commands of the word (even of the letter of the gospel) as the rule of life; and that christians are not bound to conform themselves, in their life, to the directions of the word; contrary to Psal. cxix. 9. Isa. viii. 20. and contrary to all the gospel-exhortations given in the New Testament by Christ and his apostles. And they say, (b) that *the example of Christ's life* (even in subjecting himself to the law as a rule of righteousness) *is not a pattern, according to which we are to act and live:* in a word they will have the Spirit separated from the word, and from the example of Christ, and all the cloud of witnesses to be no rule to us; to which I oppose that one precious word of the beloved disciple, 1 John ii. 26. *He that saith he abideth in him, ought so to walk, even as he hath walked.* But observe, 1. All means that do not efficaciously bow the will to obedience to God, and convert the soul, are rejected by them, as not obliging the conscience; such as are the law, the letter of the gospel, all the promises, exhortations and precepts of the gospel, the example of the Lord, who commandeth us, 1 Pet. i. *to be holy as he is holy;* the example of Christ, of all the prophets, apostles, martyrs and saints, because all these are some other thing than grace, and may prove ineffectual: hence,

 1. The gospel, as contradistinguished from the law, is not the gospel written or preached; but the grace that resideth nowhere but in God, and in Jesus Christ, is the gospel; so say they, (c) 'The faith that justifieth us is in Jesus Christ, and never had any actual being out of Christ. 2. There is no habitual grace inherent in believers; all such must be a created thing, grace is an uncreated favour only in God:' for all that

which

 (a) Rise, Reign, Er. 4, 5. (b) Er. 6. (c) Rise and Reign, Er. 26.

which is called habitual grace in us, is ineffectual to act graciously, and cannot produce supernatural acts, except the Holy Ghost act and move it; hence they say, (d) 'That the new creature or the man, (or the new heart, or new spirit, the circumcised, the opened heart, the law in the inward parts, the one heart, the renewed mind, the inner man, the law of the mind, Christ dwelling in the heart by faith) mentioned in the gospel, is not meant of grace, but of Christ; and therefore (e) we must not pray for gifts and graces, but only for Christ: and (f) so a man may have all graces and poverty of spirit, and yet want Christ.'

2. We are patients in justification, sanctification, believing in Christ; and we are blocks all the way to heaven; mind, will, affection, memory, love, desire, joy, fear, and all in us, act nothing in supernatural acts; there is not such a thing as grace in any of the saints, but grace is nothing but Christ without us, drawing us as blocks, as dead stones, in the way to heaven, having no activity but to sin, (g) even after we believe in Christ; and (h) Christ works in the regenerate as in dead men.

3. Omissions of duties commanded in the gospel are no sins; for none are, (i) 'To be exhorted to believe, but such whom we know to be the elect of God, or to have his Spirit in them effectually; and (k) a man may not be exhorted to any duty, because he hath no power to do it.' Then law, gospel, exhortations, commands, promises, threatnings, are to no purpose; these that want grace to obey, are not liable to obey, nor guilty, nor under wrath, because they believe not in the Son of God; and these that are under grace, are under obligation to no commands at all; and farewell all scripture

from

(d) Rise, Reign, Er. 7. Cornwall's Conference of Mr. John Cotton, q. 2, arg. 6. p. 16, 17. (e) Rise, Reign, Er. 23, p. 5. (f) Er. 25. (g) Er. 36. p. 7. (h) Er. 14. p. 3. (i) Er. 22. p. 5. (k) Er. 59. p. 11.

from henceforth. Yea, Mr. Towne is frequent in this, *We are not under the law, as our rule;* Why? *Because* (saith he) *it cannot effectually work obedience in us:* but so all the word of God, the gospel without the Spirit, must be no rule of obedience at all, because the scripture, the gospel, and all the promises without the Spirit, are just alike and uneffectual to work us to obedience.

But not one word of Old or New Testament frees us from the law as our rule of righteousness; and all the scriptures that speak of our freedom from the law, do directly speak of our freedom from the curse and condemnation of it, because we cannot be justified thereby; as Gal. iii. 10. *For as many as are of the works of the law, are under the curse: for it is written, Cursed is every one that continueth not in all things that are written in the book of the law to do them:* this must be to do them in a legal way, 1. He must do them all, in thought, inclinations, motions of the heart, and all the strength of the soul, in all his actions, in all his words, and in a spiritual manner, as the law charges, otherwise he is cursed; then all mankind, both such as are in Christ or out of Christ, are cursed. Now, if the simple doing of the things of the law, as 'tis a rule of our life, did involve us in a curse; then to honour father and mother, which Paul certainly commandeth as a gospel-duty, Eph. vi. 1, 2. and the loving of our brother, to which John, 1st epistle, chapters ii. iii. iv. v. exhorteth us unto, should involve us in a curse; which is absurd.

2. He must continue to the end in doing all the law; if ever he fail, he is under a curse: now, thus it is clear, Paul saith we are freed in Christ from a necessity of justification by the works of the law; for Paul addeth in the next words, v. 11. *But that no man is justified by the law in the sight of God, is evident; for the just shall live by faith.* If the living by faith did exclude works, and keeping of the law in any respect at all, as the keeping of the law is a witness of the life of faith; then to do the things of the law, as 'tis

an

an eternal rule of righteousness, should also involve us in the curse, and argue that we seek to be justified by the law, and so that we are fallen from Christ; even as to be circumcised, doth involve a man to be a debtor to the whole law, and argueth a falling from Christ, and the grace of the gospel. For Antinomians contend, that we are the same way freed from the moral law, as it is a rule of righteousness, that we are freed from the ceremonial law; but we are freed, under the pain of a curse, and of falling from Christ and the grace of the gospel, from the literal observing of circumcision, Acts xv. And Gal. v. 1, 2, 3, 4. as the ceremonial law is a rule of righteousness. And if any should pretend the impulsion and leading of the Spirit, not any letter of the law, and thereupon be circumcised, and should renounce the law of ceremonies, as a rule of righteous walking, as Antinomians profess, they obey father and mother, and love their brother, and abstain from idolatry, not because the law is their rule, or the letter of the law swayeth their conscience, but because the Spirit of Christ leadeth them; If (I say) any upon this spirit would be circumcised, and eat the passover, and sacrifice lambs and blood to God now; this spirit is no gospel-spirit, but the spirit of Satan leading such from Christ; if then we are not to obey the moral law, as a rule of life and righteousness, but are freed from it, the same way that we are freed from the ceremonial law; then to love God and our brethren, in any notion, should be sin; as to be circumcised, in any notion, is to fall from Christ, Acts xv. Gal. v.

Mr. Towne has a strange evasion for this, pag. 138.

'The Spirit is free, why will ye controul and rule it by the law? Whereas the nature of the Spirit is freely to conform the heart and life to the outward rule of the law, without the help of the law, as a crooked thing is made straight according to the line and square, and not by them; and thus, while a believer serveth in newness of the spirit, the Spirit freely and cheerfully moving him, and inclining him to keep the law, which is merely passive, herein they do wickedly, who hence take liberty to sin.'

Answ. 1. To do the will of God, merely as commanded

CHRIST DYING AND DRAWING SINNERS TO HIMSELF.

manded from the power of an outward commandment or precept in the word, is but legal, and brings forth but mixt obedience, or finer hypocrisy (saith (a) Saltmarsh) and Mr. Towne saith, That it is to controul the free Spirit, and to rule it by a law; and Famulists of New England (as the old Libertines) say, "All (b) verbal covenants, or covenants expressed in words, are covenants of works, and such as strike men off from Christ; and (c) the whole letter of the scripture holdeth forth a covenant of works; and (d) 'tis dangerous to close with Christ in a promise of the gospel, because the promise is an external created letter, and the Spirit is all." This is to make a battle and contrariety between the word of God and the gospel, as written or preached, and the Spirit; whereas, 1. That which the scripture saith, the Spirit of God saith: the command and gospel-promise is the sense and mind of the Holy Spirit; for that the scripture is quickened by the Spirit, 2 Tim. iii. 16. and the *word is the seed of God, and of the new birth,* 1 Pet. i. 23. *and mighty in operation, and powerful, and sharper than a two-edged sword,* Heb. viii. 12. Nor is it possible that any can believe the report of the gospel, because it is the gospel report, but the arm of the Lord, and the power of God in the gospel, must be revealed to them, Isa. liii. 1. 1 John xii. 37, 38, 39. For John saith, the not receiving the report of the gospel is judicial blindness, and unbelief. When Joseph dare not oppress his brethren, and Job dare not lift up his arm against the fatherless, because the sixth command saith, *Thou shalt not murder;* this is but finer hypocrisy in Joseph and Job, and a controuling of the free Spirit. Better believer David, Psal. cxix. 6. *Then shall I not be ashamed, when I have a respect to all thy commandments.* No doubt the Lord concurred freely with Adam in the act of obeying God in abstaining from the fruit of the forbidden tree; if therefore Adam should obey God, out of conscience to God's command

(Eat

(a) Saltmarsh Flowings of Free-grace, last part, c. 40. p. 178. (b) Rise, Reign, 74. (c) Er. 9. (d) Er. 62.

(Eat not) he should either controul the free Lord in his working, which none in conscience can say; or then Adam must have been loosed from obedience to that command, *If ye eat, ye shall die;* as we are now loosed from the law and the second death, though we break the law, according to the Antinomian way. Yea, 'tis unconceivable how these that are under grace, do obey the gospel enjoining faith, because the Lord Jesus commanded them; but they must sin in so doing, because they controul *the free Spirit of God,* in not obeying for the free impulsion of the Spirit, but for the literal command of God; for sure, to controul the free Spirit, is sin; and to obey for the letter of the command, to Antinomians, is to controul the free Spirit. But 'tis blasphemy to say, that there is a contrariety between the letter of the Lord's command, either in law or gospel, and the free impulsion of the Spirit working in us by grace to will and do, and obey the command: for to obey the voice of the Lord in his prophets and apostles, and to obey the Lord himself, are all one in the word; but this is the error of old Anabaptists and Enthusiasts; to reject the word and all teaching by men and the word, and to lean to the only immediate inspirations and free motions of the Holy Ghost; and to do or obey, for any other teaching is the way of the legal and law-men, led by the letter, not by the Spirit. If any obey or do God's will, out of by-respects, or for fear of punishment or hope of reward, they do not God's will, nor obey they from the power of an outward command, nor do they controul the free Spirit, because the very letter and outward commandment enjoineth inward, spiritual sincere obedience, far from hypocrisy, and forbiddeth, in the sense of the letter of it, all servile respects, and service of God for hire. Antinomians believe, That the law, as the law, doth command men to obey for fear of hell, as a servant for beating obeyeth his master; or that it commandeth perfect obedience for hire of life eternal; I doubt not to say, this is not far from blasphemy; for the law is *spiritual, and holy, and good, and most just: 'tis a clean and undefiled law,* Psal. cxix. and Rom. vii. is the express

image of the *good, acceptable, and perfect will of God* Rom. xii. 2. Then the law, as the law, can command no finer hypocrisy, no servile, no mercenary obedience for hire; for the law cannot command sin. 'Tis true, Luther saith, that the *law compelleth men to obey God;* but he speaketh of the accidental operation and fruit of the law, because of our sinful disposition, and of the condemning law, as it works on our corruption; the holy law commandeth no man to obey God wickedly.

2. The letter of the gospel carrieth to us, and holdeth forth free-grace, openeth the bowels and heart of Christ, calleth *on the weary and loaden, to come to Christ:* speaketh heaven, glory, and the promise in the womb of it: though it *be but the foolishness of preaching of men, yet 'tis the power of God to salvation;* and there is such a majesty, so much of heaven, in the womb and bowels of the word, that as I never read or heard the like of it, so I shall hate that religion that joins with Popery, to call it ink-divinity, and a letter, and a legal servile thing; so did the Libertines in Calvin's time.

3. All tendeth to this, that we *despise prophesying,* neglect the word, commands, promises, covenant of grace, and all these inferior means, and so praying, experience, conference, hearing, reading, sacraments, because without the Spirit these are lifeless and dead; for (saith Towne) *the means are passive,* shall be all so many restraints laid on the free Spirit of God. But so we should not fail nor traffick, we should not plow nor care; we should not watch the city, nor build houses, because all these are fruitless without the influence of a blessing from heaven. If their meaning be, that we are not to trust or rest on the means, the word, promises, covenant of grace, but to seek Christ himself in all these, 'tis good; but then to seek Christ in his own way, is not to controul his Spirit, as Mr. Towne fancieth.

Now, what Towne doth mean in saying, that the *Spirit freely comformeth the heart and life to the outward rule of the law, without the help of the law,* is hard to conjecture: for if the meaning be, that the Spirit needeth the help of the law to make us know our sins, to hum-

ble

ble us, and chase us to him *who is the end of the law;* then surely the Spirit by the help of the law worketh these in us, as God maketh corns to grow by husbandry, rain, good soil, and by nature his hand-maid; no man can say God works here without the help of the law. If the meaning be, that the law of itself cannot convert a man to God, Antinomians father most falsely such a dream on us; nay, the gospel of itself cannot effectuate this without the Spirit: but if the Spirit conform us to the outward rule of the law, then must the law be yet a rule of our obedience: how are we then freed from the law as a rule of our obedience, if the Spirit led us back to this rule?

And Rom. iii. Rom. vii. Gal. iii. & 2 Cor. iii. where the apostle speaketh of our freedom from the law, he ever speaketh of our freedom from the law as it condemneth, as it worketh wrath, as it involveth us in a curse, as it can justify us, or give life; never as it doth regulate, direct, teach, and lead us in the way of righteousness.

Mr. Towne, Pag. 9.

"What freeth a believer from the curse, but because he is a new creature in Christ, and is made personally, perfectly and everlastingly righteous? And the principal debt is obedience, the failing wherein bindeth over to the curse and death."

Answ. That new creature is sanctification, not justification, 2 Cor. v. 17. *If any man be in Christ,* that is, if he be justified, *he is a new creature,* that is, he is sanctified; else, by the Antinomian gloss, the meaning must be *(If any man be justified in Christ, he is justified in Christ)* Paul speaketh not such nonsense.

2. It is true, we owe active obedience to the law as a debt, but that is the debt of absolutely perfect obedience; how shall it follow that Christ has loosed us from all debt of active obedience, because he has loosed us from all necessity of perfect active obedience under the pain of damnation? But the law, as in the hand of *Jesus the Mediator,* or the law as spiritualized and lustred with gospel-law and free-grace, and drawn down to a covenant of free-grace, requireth not exact perfect

obedience

CHRIST DYING AND DRAWING SINNERS TO HIMSELF. 721

obedience under pain of losing salvation; yea, it requireth obedience as the poor man is able to give it, by the grace of God, that the man enter in the possession of life eternal; but that he may have ransom-right by merit and conquest to heaven, or to free justification in Christ, the law cannot crave either legal or evangelick obedience: this then is no more a good consequence, than to say, Christ has by his death freed us from death and suffering as they are cursed by the law, and satisfactory to justice, therefore Christ hath freed us from death and sufferings in any respect.

Yea, Paul showeth what law it is that we are freed from, Rom. viii. 2. It is the law condemning and killing, called the law of sin and death; and he saith expressly Christ died for this end, ver. 4. *That the righteousness of the law might be fulfilled in us, who walk not after the flesh, but after the Spirit.* Hence I argue, these that ought to fulfil the righteousness of the law, by walking after the Spirit, *and mortifying the deeds of the flesh,* are not freed from the law as a rule of righteousness, but are obliged, by virtue of command, to this rule: for Paul proveth that there is a commanding power enjoining righteous walking, above us, even when we are led by the Spirit; 1. Because we are obliged to mind the things of the Spirit, not of the flesh, ver. 5. 2. *To be spiritually minded is life,* as to *be carnally minded is death eternal,* ver. 6. 3. *We are to be subject to the law;* then we must be spiritually, not carnally minded: for the carnal mind cannot come under such subjection, ver. 7. 4. We are to please God in our walking; then we cannot walk in the flesh, ver. 8. 5. *Because we are dead to sin,* v. 9, 10. *We are not debtors,* nor owe we to the flesh any service, v. 19. But sure, by a commandment, we owe service to Christ. Again, the apostle, Gal. v. treating of that common place of Christian liberty, especially moveth the Antinomian doubt, and saith, ver. 13. Christian liberty is not licentiousness, nor an occasion to the flesh; and commandeth, that *we serve one another in love,* ver. 13. Now, here was a fit place, if Paul had been an Antinomian, to say, but ye are freed

from

from the law as a rule of righteousness; and if I command you to love one another, I bring you back to bondage again, I clap you up in goal again, and deliver you to your old keeper: No, saith he; but, 1. This *is liberty, to serve one another in love:* and 'tis an evangelick fulfilling of the law; *For all the law* (saith he, ver. 14) *is fulfilled in this one word, Thou shalt love thy neighbour as thyself;* and ver. 16. There is an express command, *walk in the Spirit:* and ver. 18. It might be said then, we may live as we list, we are free from all lords; 'tis true (saith the apostle, ver. 18.) ye are not under the law to condemn you, but yet ye are not lawless, ye must be led by the Spirit. And ver. 19. Fly the works of the flesh, ver. 19. such as adultery, fornication, etc. Now, the law expressly forbiddeth the works of the flesh. And Rom. vii. the very Antinomian doctrine is obviated; for, ver. 6. *But now we are delivered from the law.* O then, might some say, then we are freemen: he answers, not so; we are delivered from the law, that we should serve God in a spiritual manner. But again, ver. 7. Paul proponeth the special objection of the carnal Libertine, If we be freed from the law, *what shall we say then? Is the law sin?* This doubt ariseth both from ver. 5. and ver. 6. Ver. 5. he said, *The motions of sin that were by the law, did work in our members sinful motions;* he infers then, It may appear to some that the law is a factor and agent for sin; *Is the law sin?* by way of solicitation, ver. 6. *We are not under the law:* then it would appear that the removed law is not a dispensation to sin, and so the law is sin; if we be freed from it, we may sin. Paul saith, The law is not so removed and dead, but there is a good and holy use of the law; it remaineth as a rule of righteousness, touching what we should fly, and what we should follow: thus the law is neither a factor for sin, nor a dispensation to sin, because it discovereth and forbiddeth sin; for (saith he) *I had not known lust to be sin, but by the law:* and this the Antinomian now moveth, we are freed from the law, being once justified; whatever we do, it is not against a

law

law nor a rule, for we are under the law as a rule; and what we do, tho' to our sense and feeling it be adultery and a debt against the seventh command, yet truly in the sight of God, it is no more sin, than any thing Christ doth, is sin; we are as clean of it, ere we commit it, as Christ or the glorified spirits in heaven: and therefore the law gives us a dispensation to do these things, being justified, which the unjustified cannot do, but they must, in doing it, sin, because the unjustified man is under the law as a rule of justice, which we are not under; and so we have a dispensation and an antidated one to sin, beforehand; but because we are under no rule of righteousness, it is to us no sin. Take two servants, the master commandeth one of them, *Eat all fruit of the garden;* but I forbid you, the fellow-servant, under a pain, eat not of this tree in the east-end of the garden; to the other he giveth no such charge or command: the former servant, eating of the tree in the east, transgresseth not his master's command, because he is under no law forbidding; the other, eating of that same tree, is a transgressor, because he is under a forbidding command: so here, if the justified be not under the ten commandments as a rule of life, though they swerve from all the ten, yet they sin not; for Saltmarsh saith, *Where there is no law, there is no sin.*

Mr. Towne saith, "Although the Spirit bring forth in the saints the fruits of holiness according to the law, Gal. v. 22. Eph. v. 9. Yet without Christ we can do nothing, unless as the impor branch, we suck and derive life and sap from him, which is the spirit of faith. What if it be affirmed, even in true sanctification, the law of works is a mere passive thing, as the king's high-way, which a christian freely walketh in? You have not a face to deny it, Psal. cxix. 31."

Answ. If the Spirit of grace bring forth in the saints fruits of holiness according to the law, then is the law to the saints a rule of their walking, which the Antinomians deny: 'tis true, it may be, the law to the Holy

Spirit

Spirit in his person acting immediately in the saints, is passive, for the law cannot work on the Holy Spirit; but that the saints are mere patients and blocks in all their holy walking, is gross Libertinism, and maketh God the author of sin, as before is said: and this way also the saints are freed from the gospel, and the command of faith, and all the promises, no less than from the law; because neither law nor gospel can be a rule to the person of the Holy Ghost, in his immediate actions; the Spirit is free in his operations, and subjecteth both law and gospel to his gracious breathings, but is subject to none.

2. Mr Towne and Antinomians would lay upon Protestant divines, that they teach the saints may walk in holiness without the grace of Christ, because they will have the saints under the law ruling and directing, and this law-ruling of itself giveth no grace to obey? But this is a calumnious consequence; the promises of the gospel in the letter giveth no grace to obey; the Spirit bloweth when and where he listeth, and giveth grace freely to the gospel preached: yet we teach not that any can believe and obey the gospel without the grace of Christ.

3. The law is so passive of itself to Christ, to Adam in the state of innocency, in this sense, that the law, as the law, commandeth obedience to both, but containeth not any legal promise of giving grace to obey to either Adam or Christ; as the gospel containeth a promise of bestowing grace to believe, in all the elect. Now, if this be the cause why the justified are freed from the law as a rule of righteousness, because there is no legal promise made to them by which they are enabled to keep the law; then was Christ Jesus and Adam in his innocency freed from the law as a rule of righteousness which is most absurd; for the law, as the law, commanded Christ to fulfil all righteousness, Mat. iii. 15. but so did it Adam: but show a legal promise made to Christ, by the law, that he should have grace to obey the law; indeed the Lord promised him the Spirit above measure, but this was no law promise: so God

created

created Adam according to his own image, with perfect concreated strength and power to keep the law; but the law, as the law, made no promise to Adam, that he should be kept in obedience. But if this be called action or activity in the law, to rule, guide, direct and command obedience as a rule, then the law is nowise passive; 'tis more than the king's high-way: no way crieth to the conscience of the traveller, this is the way; no king's way showeth the traveller his error, as the law in its directing, ruling and teaching power, breaketh in upon the conscience, and declareth to the justified man the way he should walk in, and convinceth him of his unrighteousness, and daily faults.

Towne, page 10.

"The law wrappeth every man in sin, for the least transgression; so that while a man remaineth a sinner, he necessarily abideth under this fearful curse."

Answ. Still Antinomians bewray their engine. If we say, even being justified we have no sin, we lie; and who can say, *I have cleansed my heart, I am pure from sin, and there is not a just man on earth that sinneth not:* 1 John i. 10. Prov. xx. 9. Eccles. vii. 20. Then there cannot be a man on earth, but he is under the curse of God. But Antinomians say, and that truly, that the justified persons are freed from the curse; then they have no sin, nay, they cannot sin, by their arguing, for they will have the curse essentially and unseparably to follow sin: which is most false: sin dwelleth in all the justified so long as they are here, but they are here delivered from the curse.

Our deliverance from misery and the bondage of the law is twofold, as our misery is twofold. 1. There is a guilt of sin, or our obligation to eternal wrath, and all the punishments of sin, according to the order of justice by the law of God; the other misery is the blot of internal guilt of sin, by which sin dwelleth in us by nature, as a king and lord-tyrant, awing us by the law of sin.

In regard of the former, Christ is our Saviour, *merito* by the merit of his death; in regard of the latter, Christ

is

is our Saviour, *efficacia,* by giving us the Holy Ghost and faith to lay hold on righteousness in Christ, and grace to walk holily before him.

In regard of the former, we are freely and perfectly justified and pardoned at once from all sins, in our person and state; through the sense of this, and in regard of deliverance from temporal judgments and doubtings, and fears of eternal wrath, every day while we seek daily bread, we desire that our sins may be forgiven: nor is this prayer a temporary pattern that perished with Christ, as some perversely say; for Peter, after the Lord's ascension, saith to Simon Magus, Acts viii. 22. *Pray God, if perhaps the thought of thine heart may be forgiven thee.*

In regard of the latter, we are sanctified by degrees, never perfectly in this life; the dominion of sin is removed in sanctification, as the damnation thereof in justification; only sin dwelleth in us, while we are here.

In regard of the former misery, faith in Christ is the only means and way to get out of our bondage and misery; in regard of the latter, repentance and the whole trace of our new obedience are the means to escape out of this misery. Nor do we make acts of sanctification compartners and joint causes or conditions in the work of justification; for this is from Christ alone, solely, immediately as by looking on the brazen serpent only, the stung Israelites were cured: nor doth weeping or acts of obedience move the Lord to wash, justify and pardon our sins, but repentance and new obedience are means tending to our escaping out of the latter bondage; as the rising of the sun is a way to the full noon-light day, tho' we can attain to no meridian nor full noon-day of sanctification while the body of sin keepeth lodging in us, in this life. But the law of works is not so enwrapt and entwined together (as Mr. Towne dreameth) that if a man lay hands on any, even the least link, he inevitably pulleth the whole chain on himself; as he that is circumcised, Gal. v. *made himself debtor to the whole law:* for circumcision, not only in the matter of justification, but also of sanctification, is now unlawful. So to repent, and love the brethren, to obey our parents, as looking thereby for remission of sins, should be unlawful and a falling from Christ; but in the matter of sanctification, and of testifying our thankfulness to Christ for the work of our redemption, and as the way to the possession of the kingdom, they are not unlawful, but commanded as necessary duties, *by which an entrance is ministred to us into the heavenly kingdom.*

Yea, our holy walking, since it is no merit, but a fruit of grace, and a condition required in such as are saved, and have opportunity to honour Christ that way, taketh not away the freedom of grace; for where the scripture saith, *We are saved by grace without works,* as Tit. iii. Eph. ii. Salvation is spoken of there in regard of the title, right, *jus* or claim the saints have to heaven, excluding all merits of works; our obedience is not full, compleat and perfect; only they are counted so, and accepted in Christ, Phil. iv. 18. Heb. xiii. 15, 16. Col. iii. 17.

Mr. Towne answereth with other Antinomians; "The just and wise God, who accepteth every thing by due weight and measure, as it is found to be, he doth not, nay cannot account that which is but inchoate and partial for full and compleat obedience; nor can it stand with justice to accept any thing which is not first perfect, seeing that perfection and absoluteness is the ground of acceptance, both of our persons and performances; ye must make both the tree and the fruit perfectly good before God.

"2. What God (saith he) hath manifested to be detestable and accursed, that he cannot accept: but he that manifested by scripture, that whatever is not absolutely perfect, is detestable and accursed, Gal. iii. 10. Hab. i. 13. Rom. i. 18. The proposition is grounded on the immutableness of God's nature, who cannot deny himself, Jam. i. 17. and his exact justice, who will not suffer the loss of the least title of his righteousness, Mat. v. 18. God is no respecter of persons, his law inviolable, and can suffer no abatement."

Answ.

Answ. God in justification accounts us righteous in Christ, and positively guiltless, as freed from obligation to eternal wrath, and clothed with Christ's righteousness; but he accounts not us non-sinners and free from indwelling sin, that should be an unjust account, for we are not so; but God accounteth our works perfect only negatively, that is, such they are before God, as he will not enter in judgment with us for them, but graciously pardoneth the sins of these works; but God doth not account these works positively worthy of life eternal, even in Christ, as he accounteth our persons, far less doth he judge them meritorious: hence there is a twofold acceptation; one of good-will to our persons in Christ, that is, that good-will of free election, by which he *rendreth us accepted in his Beloved:* there is another acceptance of complacency, according to which God is said to love and reward our good works, even to *a cup of cold water,* John xiv. 21, 23. Mat. x. 42. 2 Thes. i. 7. Heb. vi. 10. and that of free grace, they are called perfect, as perfection is opposed to hypocritical; but not perfect simply, Phil. iii. 12. but the acceptance of our works in Christ is an acceptance inferior to the acceptance of our persons in justification: hence God *takes pleasure in those that fear him,* because they fear him, not as tho' his love *quoad effectum,* in itself had a cause in the creature, or can wax or increase, or can admit of a change, but because he bestoweth the fruits of his love out of free-grace and a gracious promise to our sincere walking; and this is rather the fruit of his love, *amor quoad effectum,* than God's love itself. All this proceedeth from a gross mistake of the nature of justification.

I answer, 2. to that, "That which is inchoate, sinfully defective, and incompleat, that the righteous and unchangeable God cannot account perfect and compleat, or that which is sinfully defective, or that which is sinful, God cannot account not sinful:" It is true, it were an erroneous and unjust account; now the proposition is true, but the assumption most false: the good works of the regenerate and justified are sinful; but

God's

God's accounting of them perfect, putteth no contradiction on them to account them not sinful: God accounts not David's adultery to be an act of chastity; this is the Papist's argument against the imputed righteousness of Christ, which Antinomians, being utterly ignorant of the nature of justification, bring against us. The other part of the distinction is, that which is sinful and defective in itself, and inherently, or really and physically, That God cannot account perfect; that is, God cannot account it and the doer, legally free from obligation to eternal wrath, for the satisfaction of another, the surety of sinners, who has paid and suffered for it: that is most false, and should destroy the Protestant justification. When we say, God accounteth the good works of believers good and perfect, so as the imperfection and sin of them is removed; we mean not, by removing of the sin of these works, the total annihilation of sin, in its essence, root and branch; it dwelleth in us in its compleat essence while we are here, Rom. vii. 17, 23. Prov. xx. 9. 1 John i. 8, 10. only the dominion by sanctification is abated, and the guilt and obligation to eternal wrath is removed in justification: and this argument may well be retorted; *Whoever is a sinner, the righteous and immutable God, whose judgment is according to verity, and cannot suffer the loss of the least title of his righteousness,* Mat. v. 18. *cannot esteem him just and perfectly righteous:* but all men, even the regenerate, are sinners. No answer, no distinction can be accommodated to this argument, which may not be applied to their argument; for God is no less just, righteous, immutable, true, no respecter of persons, and his law inviolable in his accounting of persons right and perfect, than in accounting of works righteous and perfect. Now, that the fruits and the tree are both good and simply perfect, and all the works of the justified perfect in Christ, is a point of new divinity, very contrary, first to scripture, which saith, James iii. 2. *In many things we offend all.* 1 John i. 8. *If we say we have no sin, we deceive ourselves.* Verse 10. *If we say we have not sinned, we make him a liar, and his*

word

word is not in us. Antinomians say, John speaking of a mixt multitude, is to be meant to speak of the unregenerate mixed with the justified.

Answ. 1. John takes in himself. 2. He speaketh of such as confess their sins and are pardoned, ver. 9 (2.) of such as have an advocate in heaven, if they sin, chap. ii. 1. and these are the justified and regenerate; and Prov. xx. 9. *Who can say, I have made my heart clean, I am pure from my sin?* he speaks not there of a mixed multitude, but sendeth a law-defiance to all mankind, justified, or not justified; yea, Eccles. vii. 20. *There is not a just man on earth, that doth good, and sinneth not;* these words are so wisely framed, that they exclude not the justified in Christ, who undoubtedly do good, but they do not so good (saith Solomon) but they sin; so Paul complaineth of sin dwelling in him, Rom. vii. (2.) Sin original after justification, to Antinomians must be no sin, as to Papists 'tis no sin after baptism: (3.) If our works be perfect in the sight of God, then we may be justified by our works; for Antinomians say, If Christ esteem our works perfect, he may account us righteous for them, and we may be said to be justified both by works and by grace, because 'tis free grace that the Lord accounts our works righteous. (4.) We constantly deny, that Christ by his death hath given to our works a power of meriting heaven; but if God in Christ, count them simply perfect, there is no reason to deny this, because our works are simply perfect by Antinomians' ways; this is more Pharisaical than Popish justification.

oooOOOOooo FINIS oooOOOOooo

www.ingramcontent.com/pod-product-compliance
Lightning Source LLC
Chambersburg PA
CBHW030124240426
43672CB00005B/14